The Joan Palevsky Imprint in Classical Literature

In honor of beloved Virgil—

"O degli altri poeti onore e lume . . ."

—Dante, *Inferno*

The publisher gratefully acknowledges
the generous contribution to this book provided
by the Jane K. Sather Professorship
in Classical Literature Fund.

SATHER CLASSICAL LECTURES

Volume Sixty-Seven

Homer the Preclassic

Homer the Preclassic

Homer the Preclassic

Gregory Nagy

UNIVERSITY OF CALIFORNIA PRESS

Berkeley   Los Angeles   London

University of California Press, one of the most distinguished university presses in the United States, enriches lives around the world by advancing scholarship in the humanities, social sciences, and natural sciences. Its activities are supported by the UC Press Foundation and by philanthropic contributions from individuals and institutions. For more information, visit www.ucpress.edu.

University of California Press
Berkeley and Los Angeles, California

University of California Press, Ltd.
London, England

First paperback printing 2017

Library of Congress Cataloging-in-Publication Data

Nagy, Gregory.
   Homer the preclassic / Gregory Nagy.
     p. cm. — (Sather classical lectures ; v. 67)
   Includes bibliographical references and index.
   ISBN 978-0-520-25692-7 (cloth : alk. paper)
   ISBN 978-0-520-29487-5 (pbk.: alk. paper)
   1. Homer—Criticism and interpretation.   2. Epic poetry, Greek—History and criticism.   3. Oral tradition—Greece—History—To 1500.
I. Title.
PA4037.N344   2011
883'.01—dc22   2010048822

Manufactured in the United States of America

21 20   19   18   17
10 9   8   7   6   5   4   3   2   1

CONTENTS

ILLUSTRATIONS

MAPS

FIGURES

ABBREVIATIONS

ATL   B. D. Meritt, H. T. Wade-Gery, and M. F. McGregor, eds., *The Athenian Tribute Lists*, 4 vols. (Cambridge, Mass., 1939–53).

BA   *The Best of the Achaeans: Concepts of the Hero in Archaic Greek Poetry* (Nagy 1979)

BA²   *The Best of the Achaeans*, 2nd ed. (Nagy 1999)

CEG   *Carmina epigraphica Graeca saeculorum viii–v a.Chr.n.* (P. A. Hansen 1983)

DELG   *Dictionnaire étymologique de la langue grecque* (Chantraine 2009)

DK   *Die Fragmente der Vorsokratiker*, 6th ed. (Diels and Kranz 1951–52)

EH   "The Epic Hero" (Nagy 2005a)

FGH   *Die Fragmente der griechischen Historiker* (Jacoby 1923–)

GM   *Greek Mythology and Poetics* (Nagy 1990b)

HC   *Homer the Classic* (Nagy 2008a/2009a)

HPC   *Homer the Preclassic* (Nagy 2009b)

HQ   *Homeric Questions* (Nagy 1996b)

HR   *Homeric Responses* (Nagy 2003a)

HTL   *Homer's Text and Language* (Nagy 2004a)

IG   Deutsche Akademie der Wissenschaften, *Inscriptiones Graecae* (Berlin, 1873–)

LP   "The Library of Pergamon as a Classical Model" (Nagy 1998)

LSJ   *A Greek-English Lexicon*, 9th ed. (Liddell, Scott, and Jones 1940)

PH   *Pindar's Homer: The Lyric Possession of an Epic Past* (Nagy 1990a)

PMG   *Poetae Melici Graeci* (Page 1962)

PP   *Poetry as Performance: Homer and Beyond* (Nagy 1996a)

PR   *Plato's Rhapsody and Homer's Music: The Poetics of the Panathenaic Festival in Classical Athens* (Nagy 2002)

PREFACE

There are two different publication dates for this book: 2009 for the published version that was "born digital" on the website of the Center for Hellenic Studies, and 2010 for the published version as printed by the University of California Press. (The online version contains updated annotations stemming from 2010 and thereafter. These annotations track relevant new debates or discoveries. At II§7 of the online version, for example, corresponding to p. 134 of the printed version, there is an annotation referring to a new debate on the historical value of myths about the so-called "Aeolian Migration.")

There are many people I want to thank for helping me—so many that I am unable to list them all by name. In general, I express my appreciation to the academic community of the Department of Classics at the University of California in Berkeley, who hosted me as the Sather Professor when I gave my six Sather Classical Lectures in the spring semester of 2002. In particular, I thank Elizabeth Baughan, John Ferrari, Andrew Garrett, Crawford Greenewalt, Mark Griffith, Erich Gruen, Alexander Herda, Robert Knapp, Leslie Kurke, Patricia Larash, Anthony Long, Donald Mastronarde, Stephen Miller, Charles Murgia, Ellen Oliensis, Paul Psoinos, Alain Renoir, Laura Steele, Andrew Stewart. I take this opportunity to thank also all my other colleagues and friends. Seven names stand out: Christopher Dadian, Soo-Young Kim, Leonard Muellner, Anita Nikkanen, Jill Curry Robbins, Noel Spencer, and Aliya Williams. My debt to these seven is beyond measure.

Finally, I thank Paul Psoinos for his peerless copy editing, Yue Joy Deng and Jeffrey P. Emanuel for their accurate proofreading, and Valerie Woelfel for her perceptive line drawings.

Introduction

This book, *Homer the Preclassic*, which is based on the Sather Classical Lectures of spring 2002, covers the preclassical era of Homeric reception. It is complemented by a twin book, *Homer the Classic* (Nagy 2009), which covers the classical era. Between the two of them, *Homer the Classic* and *Homer the Preclassic* cover six ages of Homeric reception. Here are the six ages, arranged in a sequence going backward in time:

Homer the Classic in the Age of Virgil

Homer the Classic in the Age of Callimachus

Homer the Classic in the Age of Plato

Homer the Classic in the Age of Pheidias

A Preclassical Homer from the Dark Age

A Preclassical Homer from the Bronze Age.

The first four entries in this list correspond to the titles of the four chapters in *Homer the Classic*. The last two entries correspond to the titles I give to the two parts of this twin book, *Homer the Preclassic*.

The idea of viewing Homer through several different time frames is consistent with my overall approach to Homer, which goes beyond current debates concerning Homeric orality or literacy.[1] These debates presuppose some alternative ideas that I do not share. In terms of such ideas, Homer was not really classical or

---

1. *HR* 1–3. For a survey of the relevant debates, see de Vet 2005; at her p. 268n37, she could have made fuller reference to the important work of de Lamberterie 1997/2001.

even preclassical: he was primordial.[2] Such a primordial Homer, whether or not his name was Homer, was some kind of primitive; if he was a genius, he was a primitive genius.

By contrast, the Homer of *Homer the Classic* and *Homer the Preclassic* is more than just a hypothetical person. He is a historical concept. As a concept, Homer is a metonym for the text and the language attributed to Homer in historical times. By *metonym* I mean an expression of meaning by way of connecting something to something else, to be contrasted with *metaphor,* which I define for the moment as an expression of meaning by way of substituting something for something else.[3]

2. For an overall critique of such ideas, see Graziosi 2002:90–93.
3. *HTL* xi.

A Preclassical Homer from the Dark Age

THINKING MY WAY BACKWARD from the classical period of the fifth century B.C.E., I confront a preclassical period that I divide into two ages, the Dark Age and the Bronze Age. I start here in Part I with the Dark Age. Then, in Part II, I will proceed to the Bronze Age.

The term *Dark Age* refers to discontinuities, real or perceived, after the time of the Bronze Age, which comes to an end sometime around the eleventh century B.C.E. There is much speculation about the nature of such discontinuities and about their causes. Such speculation, however, is not relevant to what I am about to do, which is, to offer a working redefinition of a Dark Age viewed exclusively in terms of the study of Homer. Here in Part I, the Dark Age is the Dark Age of Homer.

For those who specialize in Homer, there is a chronological chasm separating the era of historical events in the classical period of the fifth and the fourth century B.C.E. from the prehistoric era of events like the Capture of Troy, which is the single most important point of reference for Homeric narrative—and which coincides roughly with the end of the Bronze Age as archaeologists define it. We are left in the dark, as it were, about Homer for a vast stretch of time. We experience a strong sense of discontinuity with a past not recorded in writing. Denied access to any Homeric texts that could date back to the life and times of Homer, we feel cut off from this Homer. We cannot even have any direct way of knowing when the Homeric *Iliad* and *Odyssey* were first written down.[1]

---

1. HTL 3–24. The question of dating the earliest phases of written texts recording what we know as the Homeric *Iliad* and *Odyssey* cannot be answered by way of comparing the surviving evidence about epigrams, attested already in the earliest phases of ancient Greek alphabetic literacy. The genre of the

From the standpoint of surviving written evidence, if we work our way forward in time from the Bronze Age, all we can say is that the Dark Age of Homer stays dark until we reach the beginnings of a span of time marked by the fifth century B.C.E. So my working definition of the Dark Age of Homer is: a length of time extending from the end of the Bronze Age all the way to the fifth century B.C.E.—that is, all the way to the beginnings of recorded history, as represented by Herodotus and Thucydides. The perspectives of these two historians, I will argue, provide a glimpse into such a Dark Age of Homer—to the extent that both Herodotus and Thucydides searched for realities that predated their own times. In the course of their search, as we will see, both these early historians relied in significant ways on the authority of what we know as Homer.

The Dark Age of Homer, then, is delimited on both sides by objective dating criteria. On the far side, the eleventh century B.C.E. marks the end of the Bronze Age as defined by the evidence of archaeology. On the near side, the fifth century B.C.E. marks the beginnings of direct reportage about history and prehistory.

Here in Part I of *Homer the Preclassic*, I propose to build a model that accounts for the continuity of Homeric poetry during the Dark Age—despite the discontinuities posited by some historians. As I will argue, this continuity depends on the oral traditions that culminated in the Homeric *Iliad* and *Odyssey* as performed at the festival of the Panathenaia in Athens in the classical period, during the fifth century B.C.E.[2] (Here and hereafter, I use the term *Panathenaia* primarily with reference to the quadrennial or Great Panathenaia, as distinct from the annual or Lesser Panathenaia.)[3]

Already at the beginning of my inquiry into the Dark Age of Homer, the question arises: What could be the antecedent of such a classical Homer as performed in the fifth century? For an answer, I concentrate on the era of the Peisistratidai, a dynasty of *turannoi* 'tyrants' who ruled Athens from 546 to 510 B.C.E. As we will see, a direct antecedent of the classical Homer was the preclassical Homer of this era.

In the twin book *Homer the Classic*, I link the reception of Homer during the fifth century B.C.E. with the politics of what we call today the Athenian empire,

---

epigram—that is, a form of poetry meant to be recorded in inscriptions—had an existence separate from all other early poetic genres, including the epics ascribed to Homer: unlike other poetic genres, the genre of the epigram required the technology of writing. It is essential to add that this technology was required not for the sake of composition but rather for the sake of recording and thereby memorializing the composition. On the conceptual separation of mentally composing an epigram and physically inscribing it, see *HQ* 14, 35–36, with more on various controversies surrounding this question. I will return to this topic below in chapter 2, in the section entitled "Homer the Epigrammatist."

2. In other studies as well, I have concentrated on the central role of Athens in the transmission of the Homeric *Iliad* and *Odyssey*. See especially *PR* 9–35. For still other such studies, I single out Cook 1995.

3. On the history of the annual and the quadrennial Panathenaia, see Shear 2001.

which was establishing control over Greek cities formerly dominated by the Persian empire. Here in *Homer the Preclassic* I link the reception of Homer with earlier phases of Athenian imperialism, in the era of the Peisistratidai.

What was evolving already in this earlier era can be described as an earlier form of the Athenian empire, even though it cannot compare in scale with the imperial might of the Athenian democratic regime in the fifth century. As we will see, a predemocratic Athenian empire was actively being shaped by the Peisistratidai. As we will also see, the Homer we know from the democratic era was in turn shaped by the imperial interests of Athens in the predemocratic era of these Peisistratidai.

One sign of such imperial interests was the Athenian initiative of occupying territories contiguous to Troy, formerly occupied by Aeolic-speaking Greeks. I will save for Part II my investigation of this initiative, which is relevant to the oldest recoverable phases of content in Homeric poetry.

Another sign of such imperial interests in the era of the Peisistratidai was the Athenian initiative of appropriating the island of Delos, an age-old religious and political center of Ionic-speaking Greeks. This Athenian initiative, as we will see, was most relevant to shaping the preclassical Homer in the era of the Peisistratidai.

It is well known that the city of Athens dominated the island of Delos to make a show of Athenian imperial power in the era of the democracy in the fifth century B.C.E. What is far less well known is that Athens was already dominating Delos in the era of the Peisistratidai, and that these earlier phases of domination already show clear indications of Athenian imperial power.[4] Among these indications, as I will argue, was the idea of Homer as an Ionian who speaks for all Ionians.

4. On Delos and the Peisistratidai, I find the discussion of Aloni 1989:43–44 most helpful.

1

Homer and the Athenian Empire

THE ATHENIAN EMPIRE

I offer here an overview of what we know about the Athenian empire in the era of the democracy in the fifth century B.C.E. The basic facts can be found in the history of Thucydides, who highlights what gradually happened to Athens as a world power in the period extending from the end of the Persian War, with the establishment of the Delian League in 478 B.C.E., to the outbreak of the Peloponnesian War in the year 431: what had started as a *xummakhia* 'alliance' of the city of Athens with various other cities evolved into an *arkhē* 'rule' by Athens over these cities (Thucydides 1.67.4, 1.75.1, etc.).[1] This 'rule' is the essence of the Athenian empire.

Of special interest is the *arkhē* 'rule' by Athens over the Ionian cities of Asia Minor and its outlying islands, as distinct from the non-Ionian cities drawn into the political sphere of the evolving empire.[2] The Ionian connections with Athens—as distinct from Dorian or Aeolian connections—were particularly compelling, since the Delian League was conceived as an alliance of Ionians who shared in a common Ionian kinship (Thucydides 1.95.1; Aristotle *Constitution of the Athenians* 23.4).[3] I add this apt formulation: "The reference to Ionian kinship [in Thucydides 1.95.1] is a brief allusion to a major element in fifth-century Athenian propaganda, the projection of Athens as mother-city of the whole empire, irrespective of the colo-

---

1. Meiggs 1972:376.
2. Meiggs 1972:294.
3. See also the discussion by Meiggs 1972:295, with specific reference to the *horoi* 'boundary stones' of Samos.

nial realities."[4] To put it another way: "the concept of *xungeneia* ['kinship'] was stretched until it had become almost a metaphor for a relationship of obedience and control."[5]

ATHENS AS HOMER'S IMPERIAL METROPOLIS

The imperial sense of the noun *arkhē* 'rule' and of the corresponding verb *arkhein* is actually attested in a context that is relevant to Homer. We find it in the dialogue of Plato called the *Ion*, named after the *rhapsōidos* 'rhapsode' called Ion who hails from the Ionian city of Ephesus and whose name actually means, appropriately enough, 'the Ionian' (*Iōn*).[6] In the dramatic time of the dialogue, this rhapsode is about to perform the poetry of Homer in competition with other rhapsodes, and the occasion is the festival of the Panathenaia in Athens (*Ion* 530b). We are about to see the rhapsode's use of the verb *arkhein* in a most revealing context. When Plato's Socrates questions Ion's expertise in the craft of a *stratēgos* 'general'—a craft supposedly derived from Homer's own expertise in matters of war—Ion pointedly retorts that his home city of Ephesus has no generals of its own, since it is 'ruled' (*arkhetai*, from *arkhein*) by Athens (*Ion* 541b–c). As we are about to see, the ties that bind the cities of Athens and Ephesus together correspond to the ties between a mother city—a metropolis—and a daughter city.

In responding to the point made by Ion, Socrates says that Athenians do in fact occasionally choose generals who are non-Athenians (Plato *Ion* 541d).[7] In the same breath Socrates adds that the people of Ephesus are not even really non-Athenians, since Ephesus, as an Ionian city, is after all a daughter city of Athens, which claims to be the metropolis (*mētropolis*) or 'mother city' of all Ionians (*Ion* 541c–d). As Socrates puts it: 'After all, you Ephesians were Athenians in ancient times, weren't you?' (*Ion* 541d τί δέ; οὐκ Ἀθηναῖοι μέν ἐστε οἱ Ἐφέσιοι τὸ ἀρχαῖον;).

This idea, that Ephesus is a daughter city of Athens, is not an ad hoc invention by Socrates or by Plato. In the late fifth century, the historical period that corresponds to the dramatic date of Plato's *Ion*, the idea that Athens was the metropolis or 'mother city' of all Ionian cities was generally accepted by the Greek-speaking world, whether they were allies or enemies of Athens. This idea, as mythologized in the *Ion* of Euripides (1575–88) and as historicized in both Herodotus (1.147.2)

4. Hornblower 1996:73.
5. Hornblower 1996:73.
6. For more on Ion of Ephesus as a generic 'Ionian', see Porter 2001:281n93, with reference to Callimachus *Iambi* 13.30–32; see also the remarks of Hunter 1997:46–47.
7. See Moore 1974:433–38 on the services performed for Athens by Herakleides of Klazomenai as *stratēgos* 'general'. He is mentioned in Plato *Ion* 541c–d.

and Thucydides (1.2.6, with qualifications), was generally linked to the political reality of the Athenian empire.[8]

Of particular relevance to the status of Ion as a rhapsodic performer of Homeric poetry at the Panathenaia is the fact that Ionian cities were actually obliged to participate in the quadrennial celebration of the Great Panathenaia in Athens (as distinct from the annual celebration of the Lesser Panathenaia): for example, they had to send official delegates to attend this festival, and such attendance was considered "an extension of a general tradition linking colony to mother-city."[9]

Here I return to the remark made by Plato's Socrates when Ion the rhapsode points to the status of his native city of Ephesus as a tributary of Athens. As we have seen, Socrates follows up by remarking that Ephesus is after all a daughter city of Athens. In other words, Ion of Ephesus is a virtual Athenian, since Ion's identity as an Ionian is not only dominated by the Athenians: it is actually determined by them.

What I have said so far about Plato's *Ion* is taken from the twin book, *Homer the Classic*, where I argue that the picturing of Ion as a virtual Athenian is linked to his role as a professional rhapsode who performs Homer at the Panathenaia. And there are further arguments to be added here about something that Plato has elided in his *Ion*. It has to do with the craft of the rhapsode who performs at the festival of the Panathenaia in Athens. The fact is, this craft is politically as well as culturally important. More than that, this craft is all-important for Athens, since Ion specializes in performing Homeric poetry, which is the premier form of poetry as performed at the premier festival of the Athenians, the Panathenaia. Ion may seem unimportant as an Ionian, but he becomes all-important as a virtual Athenian in the act of performing Homer for a receptive audience of some twenty thousand celebrants attending the festival of the Panathenaia in Athens (Plato *Ion* 535d).[10] On the occasion of this festival, Athenians are notionally hosting the Ionians of the Delian League in an era marked by the rule of Athens over all Ionians. On this festive occasion, all Ionians are virtual Athenians, assembling in their mother city to

---

8. On the *Ion* of Euripides, see especially Barron 1964:48. See also his pp. 39–40, where he argues that the Eponymoi to whom the inscriptions on the *horoi* of Samos refer are the four sons of Ion, heroes of the four Ionian civic lineages or *phulai*. Barron (p. 45) concludes that "the headquarters of the cults of Ion and the Ionic Eponymoi must have been at Athens." We must note, however, that the four old *phulai* of Athens were replaced by ten new *phulai* instituted after the reform of Kleisthenes in 508/7 B.C.E. A primary source of reportage about this reform is Herodotus 5.66.2.

9. Meiggs 1972:294–95. See also his p. 294, with reference to lines 11–13 of *IG* I² 45 (Meiggs and Lewis 1988 no. 49), where the wording of the inscription specifies that the people of Brea, as a daughter city of Athens, must send a cow along with a panoply to the Great Panathenaia and a phallus to the Dionysia. See also Barron 1964:47. On the "international atmosphere" of the Great Panathenaia, see Shear 2001:121.

10. *PR* 28.

hear the epics of Homer. On this occasion, Ion the Ionian is re-enacting Homer himself by way of performing Homer.

So the identity of Ion as rhapsode was defined by the *Panathenaic Homer,* that is, by Homer as performed at the Panathenaia. Even the identity of Athens as an imperial power was defined by this Panathenaic Homer. The Athenian standard for performing Homer at the Panathenaia was a self-expression of the Athenian empire. The Panathenaic Homer was an imperial Homer.

What I am calling an *Athenian standard* was simultaneously an Ionian standard. In other words, the Panathenaic Homer was simultaneously an Ionian Homer. That is because the Athenian empire was at least notionally an Ionian empire. The Delian League, as an earlier form of the Athenian empire, was a clear and most forceful expression of Ionian identity. Moreover, the Ionian identity of the Athenian empire could be maintained and even reaffirmed most consistently by invoking the idea that Athens is the metropolis or 'mother city' of all Ionian cities. As we see in Plato's *Ion,* this idea explains how a rhapsode like Ion could be pictured as performing for all Ionians by virtue of performing Homer at the festival of the Panathenaia.

With the passage of time, however, the Ionian identity of the Athenian empire became blurred as it outgrew its identification with the Delian League. Symptomatic is the fact that the treasury of the Delian League was ultimately transferred from Delos to Athens, sometime around the middle of the fifth century B.C.E. (Plutarch *Aristeides* 25.2–3).[11] With the blurring of the Ionian identity of the empire, we can expect a concomitant blurring of Homer's own Ionian identity as the model for epic performance at the Panathenaia in the era of the democracy in Athens.

HOMER THE IONIAN

For a clearer picture of Homer's Ionian identity, we need to shift our perspective farther back in time—back to the era of the tyrants in Athens. In this earlier era, the festival of the Panathenaia in Athens was not the only notional setting for the performance of Homer before a festive assembly of all Ionians. There was another festival that served as such a setting: the Delia, celebrated on the sacred island of Delos.

As we are about to see, Peisistratos as tyrant of Athens took the initiative of appropriating this festival of the Delia. Then, not many years thereafter, a similar initiative was taken by Polycrates, tyrant of Samos, in the context of his overall plan to build a maritime empire of Ionian islanders. Still later, the festival reverted to Athens under the rule of the sons of Peisistratos.[12] For Athens in the earlier as well

---

11. Thucydides does not mention this transfer at 1.92.2, where we might have expected such a mention, nor anywhere else in his history: see Hornblower 1991:146.

12. For a sketch of the relative chronology, involving Naxos as well as Samos and Athens, see Aloni 1989:46–47, 54–55, 62–63, 122–23.

as later phases of what became the Athenian empire, the initiative of appropriating Delos and the Panionian festival of the Delia was linked to the initiative of appropriating Homer. This Homer was an Ionian Homer, who ultimately evolved into the Homer of the Athenian festival of the Panathenaia, the Panathenaic Homer.

This Ionian Homer is still clearly visible in the *Homeric Hymn to Apollo*—as quoted by Thucydides in a celebrated passage concerning the identity of Homer. I begin by quoting this passage in its entirety. As we are about to see, Thucydides actually makes two quotations from the *Homeric Hymn to Apollo*, the text of which turns out to be in some ways different from the text of the *Hymn* that survives in the medieval manuscript tradition. In my requotations of the two quotations made by Thucydides, I will add in each instance the text of the medieval transmission, noting in my footnotes the various textual differences between the Thucydidean quotation and the medieval transmission of the *Hymn*. As I indicate in these footnotes, most if not all of these textual differences can be shown to be authentic formulaic variations. Here, then, is the text in its entirety:[13]

[3.104.2] ἀπέχει δὲ ἡ Ῥήνεια τῆς Δήλου οὕτως ὀλίγον ὥστε Πολυκράτης ὁ Σαμίων τύραννος ἰσχύσας τινὰ χρόνον ναυτικῷ καὶ τῶν τε ἄλλων νήσων ἄρξας καὶ τὴν Ῥήνειαν ἑλὼν ἀνέθηκε τῷ Ἀπόλλωνι τῷ Δηλίῳ ἁλύσει δήσας πρὸς τὴν Δῆλον. καὶ τὴν πεντετηρίδα τότε πρῶτον μετὰ τὴν κάθαρσιν ἐποίησαν οἱ Ἀθηναῖοι τὰ Δήλια. [3] ἦν δέ ποτε καὶ τὸ πάλαι μεγάλη ξύνοδος ἐς τὴν Δῆλον τῶν Ἰώνων τε καὶ περικτιόνων **νησιωτῶν·** ξύν τε γὰρ γυναιξὶ καὶ παισὶν ἐθεώρουν, ὥσπερ νῦν ἐς τὰ Ἐφέσια Ἴωνες, καὶ **ἀγὼν** ἐποιεῖτο αὐτόθι καὶ **γυμνικὸς** καὶ **μουσικός,** χορούς τε ἀνῆγον αἱ πόλεις. [4] δηλοῖ δὲ μάλιστα Ὅμηρος ὅτι τοιαῦτα ἦν ἐν τοῖς **ἔπεσι** τοῖσδε, ἅ ἐστιν ἐκ **προοιμίου** Ἀπόλλωνος·

> ἀλλ' ὅτε Δήλῳ, Φοῖβε, μάλιστά γε θυμὸν ἐτέρφθης,
> ἔνθα τοι ἑλκεχίτωνες Ἰάονες ἠγερέθονται
> σὺν σφοῖσιν τεκέεσσι γυναιξί τε σὴν ἐς ἀγυιάν·[14]
> ἔνθα σε πυγμαχίη τε καὶ ὀρχηστυῖ[15] καὶ ἀοιδῇ
> μνησάμενοι τέρπουσιν, ὅταν καθέσωσιν[16] **ἀγῶνα.**   150

[Beginning of a point of insertion: The preceding verses, as quoted by Thucydides, correspond to the following verses as transmitted by the medieval manuscript traditions of the *Homeric Hymn* (3) *to Apollo* 146–50.]

> ἀλλὰ σὺ Δήλῳ, Φοῖβε, μάλιστ' ἐπιτέρπεαι ἦτορ,
> ἔνθα τοι ἑλκεχίτωνες Ἰάονες ἠγερέθονται

---

13. An earlier form of my commentary on the *Homeric Hymn* (3) *to Apollo* appeared in Nagy 2009e.

14. Compare *Iliad* IV 162, σὺν σφῇσιν κεφαλῇσι γυναιξί τε καὶ τεκέεσσιν; also *Odyssey* viii 525, ἄστεϊ καὶ τεκέεσσιν ἀμύνων νηλεὲς ἦμαρ.

15. Compare *Odyssey* viii 253, ναυτιλίῃ καὶ ποσσὶ καὶ ὀρχηστυῖ καὶ ἀοιδῇ; also *Odyssey* xvii 605–6, πλεῖον δαιτυμόνων· οἱ δ' ὀρχηστυῖ καὶ ἀοιδῇ | τέρποντ'.

16. On this variant καθέσωσιν, see Martin 2000b:421n61.

αὐτοῖς σὺν παίδεσσι καὶ αἰδοίης ἀλόχοισιν.
οἱ δέ σε πυγμαχίη τε καὶ ὀρχηθμῷ[17] καὶ ἀοιδῇ
μνησάμενοι τέρπουσιν, ὅταν στήσωνται **ἀγῶνα**.   150

[End of point of insertion. Now, to resume what Thucydides is saying . . .]

[3.104.5] ὅτι δὲ καὶ **μουσικῆς** ἀγὼν ἦν καὶ **ἀγωνιούμενοι** ἐφοίτων ἐν τοῖσδε αὖ δηλοῖ,
ἅ ἐστιν ἐκ τοῦ αὐτοῦ **προοιμίου·** τὸν γὰρ Δηλιακὸν χορὸν τῶν γυναικῶν **ὑμνήσας**
ἐτελεύτα τοῦ ἐπαίνου ἐς τάδε τὰ ἔπη, ἐν οἷς καὶ ἑαυτοῦ ἐπεμνήσθη·

ἀλλ᾽ ἄγεθ᾽, ἱλήκοι μὲν Ἀπόλλων Ἀρτέμιδι ξύν,   165
χαίρετε δ᾽ ὑμεῖς πᾶσαι. ἐμεῖο δὲ καὶ μετόπισθε
μνήσασθ᾽, ὁππότε κέν τις ἐπιχθονίων ἀνθρώπων
ἐνθάδ᾽ ἀνείρηται **ταλαπείριος ἄλλος** ἐπελθών·
ὢ κοῦραι, τίς δ᾽ ὔμμιν ἀνὴρ ἥδιστος ἀοιδῶν
ἐνθάδε πωλεῖται, καὶ **τέῳ τέρπεσθε** μάλιστα;   170
ὑμεῖς δ᾽ εὖ μάλα πᾶσαι **ὑποκρίνασθαι** ἀφήμως·[18]
τυφλὸς ἀνήρ, οἰκεῖ δὲ Χίῳ ἔνι παιπαλοέσσῃ.

[Beginning of another point of insertion: The preceding verses, as quoted by Thucydides, correspond to the following verses as transmitted by the medieval manuscript traditions of the *Homeric Hymn* (3) *to Apollo* 165–72.]

ἀλλ᾽ ἄγεθ᾽, ἱλήκοι μὲν Ἀπόλλων Ἀρτέμιδι ξύν,   165
χαίρετε δ᾽ ὑμεῖς πᾶσαι· ἐμεῖο δὲ καὶ μετόπισθε
μνήσασθ᾽, ὁππότε κέν τις ἐπιχθονίων ἀνθρώπων
ἐνθάδ᾽ ἀνείρηται **ξεῖνος ταλαπείριος** ἐλθών·
ὢ κοῦραι, τίς δ᾽ ὔμμιν ἀνὴρ ἥδιστος ἀοιδῶν
ἐνθάδε πωλεῖται, καὶ **τέῳ τέρπεσθε** μάλιστα;   170
ὑμεῖς δ᾽ εὖ μάλα πᾶσαι **ὑποκρίνασθαι** ἀφ᾽ ἡμέων[19]
τυφλὸς ἀνήρ, οἰκεῖ δὲ Χίῳ ἔνι παιπαλοέσσῃ.

[End of point of insertion. Now, to resume what Thucydides is saying . . .]

[3.104.6] τοσαῦτα μὲν Ὅμηρος ἐτεκμηρίωσεν ὅτι ἦν καὶ τὸ πάλαι μεγάλη ξύνοδος καὶ
ἑορτὴ ἐν τῇ Δήλῳ· ὕστερον δὲ τοὺς μὲν χοροὺς οἱ **νησιῶται καὶ οἱ Ἀθηναῖοι** μεθ᾽ ἱερῶν

17. Compare *Odyssey* viii 261–64:
κῆρυξ δ᾽ ἐγγύθεν ἦλθε φέρων φόρμιγγα λίγειαν
Δημοδόκῳ· ὁ δ᾽ ἔπειτα κί᾽ ἐς μέσον· ἀμφὶ δὲ κοῦροι
πρωθῆβαι ἵσταντο, δαήμονες ὀρχηθμοῖο,
πέπληγον δὲ χορὸν θεῖον ποσίν.

18. This variant reading ἀφήμως, as preserved here in the quotation by Thucydides, is to be contrasted with the variant reading ἀφ᾽ ἡμέων found in the medieval manuscript tradition of the *Homeric Hymn* (3) *to Apollo.* See the next note.

19. This variant reading ἀφ᾽ ἡμέων in the medieval manuscript tradition of the *Homeric Hymn* (3) *to Apollo* is to be contrasted with the variant reading ἀφήμως in the quotation by Thucydides. See the previous note.

ἔπεμπον, τὰ δὲ περὶ τοὺς **ἀγῶνας** καὶ τὰ πλεῖστα κατελύθη ὑπὸ ξυμφορῶν, ὡς εἰκός, πρὶν δὴ οἱ Ἀθηναῖοι τότε τὸν **ἀγῶνα** ἐποίησαν καὶ ἱπποδρομίας, ὃ πρότερον οὐκ ἦν.

[3.104.2 ('The island of)] Rheneia is so close to Delos that Polycrates, tyrant of the people of [the island-state of] Samos, who had supreme naval power for a period of time and who had imperial rule [*arkhein*] over the islands, including Rheneia, dedicated Rheneia, having captured it, to the Delian Apollo by binding it to Delos with a chain. After the purification [*katharsis*], the Athenians at that point made for the first time the quadrennial festival known as the Delia. [3] And, even in the remote past, there had been at Delos a great coming together of Ionians and neighboring **islanders** [*nēsiōtai*], and they were celebrating [ἐθεώρουν, 'were making *theōria*'] along with their wives and children, just as the Ionians in our own times come together [at Ephesus] for [the festival of] the **Ephesia**; and a **competition** [*agōn*] was held there [in Delos], both in **athletics** and in *mousikē* [*tekhnē*],[20] and the cities brought choral ensembles. [4] Homer makes it most clear that such was the case in the following **verses** [*epos*, plural], which come from a *prooimion*[21] of Apollo:

> But when in Delos, Phoebus, more than anywhere else, you delight
>   [*terpesthai*] in your heart [*thumos*],
> there the Ionians, with khitons trailing, gather
> with their children and their wives, along the causeway [*aguia*],[22]
> and there with boxing and dancing and song
> they have you in mind and delight [*terpein*] you, whenever they set up
>   a **competition** [*agōn*].   150

[Beginning of a point of insertion: The preceding verses, as quoted by Thucydides, correspond to the following verses as transmitted by the medieval manuscript traditions of the *Homeric Hymn* (3) *to Apollo* 146–50.]

> But you in Delos, Phoebus, more than anywhere else delight [*terpesthai*]
>   in your heart,
> where the Ionians, with khitons trailing, gather
> with their children and their circumspect wives.
> And they with boxing and dancing and song
> have you in mind and delight you, whenever they set up a **competition**
>   [*agōn*].   150

20. Comparable to the *agōn* 'competition' mentioned here by Thucydides (3.104.3) is the *agōn* 'competition' in *mousikē* 'craft of the Muses' at the Panathenaia, where the word *mousikē* includes the *tekhnē* 'craft' of rhapsodes. Supporting evidence comes from Aristotle *Constitution of the Athenians* (60.1), Plutarch *Pericles* (13.9–11), Plato *Ion* (530a), Isocrates *Panegyricus* (4.159), and other sources. See *PR* 36–53; also Shear 2001:350. As my argumentation proceeds, we will see that the medium for performing the *Homeric Hymn to Apollo* was a rhapsodic medium.

21. Here and hereafter, I leave this word *prooimion* untranslated. It can be used with reference to the beginning of a *humnos* or 'hymn', as in the case of the Homeric *Hymns*. I analyze the technical meaning of this word ('prooemium') and its etymology ('initial threading') in *HC* 2§92.

22. On this *aguia* as the *via sacra* of Delos, see Aloni 1989:117–18.

[End of point of insertion. Now, to resume what Thucydides is saying . . .]

[3.104.5] That there was also a competition [*agōn*] in *mousikē* [*tekhnē*],[23] in which the Ionians went to engage in competition [*agōnizesthai*], again is made clear by him [Homer] in the following verses, taken from the same *prooimion*. After making the subject of his *humnos* the Delian *khoros* of women, he was drawing toward the completion [*telos*] of his song of praise, drawing toward these verses [*epos,* plural], in which he also makes mention of himself—

> But come now, may Apollo be gracious, along with Artemis;   165
> and you all also, hail [*khairete*] and take pleasure, all of you [Maidens
>   of Delos]. Keep me, even in the future,
> in your mind, whenever someone, out of the whole mass of earth-
>   bound humanity,
> comes here [to Delos], **after arduous wandering, someone else,**[24]
>   and asks this question:
> "O Maidens, who is for you the most pleasurable of singers
> that wanders here? **In whom** do you take the most **delight** [*terpesthai*]?" 170
> Then you, all of you [Maidens of Delos], must very properly **respond**
>   [*hupokrinasthai*], without naming names:[25]
> "It is a blind man, and he dwells in Chios, a rugged land."

[Beginning of another point of insertion: The preceding verses, as quoted by Thucydides, correspond to the following verses as transmitted by the medieval manuscript traditions of the *Homeric Hymn* (3) *to Apollo* 165–72.]

> But come now, may Apollo be gracious, along with Artemis;   165
> and you all also, hail [*khairete*] and take pleasure, all of you [Maidens
>   of Delos]. Keep me, even in the future,
> in your mind, whenever someone, out of the whole mass of earth-
>   bound humanity,

23. The word *agōn* 'competition' as used here by Thucydides (3.104.5) needs to be correlated with his use of the same word earlier on in the passage that I am quoting here (3.104.3).

24. This version, as quoted by Thucydides, at first seems to foreclose the option of imagining the same singer returning again and again to Delos. That option is left open in the alternative version that we find in the medieval manuscript tradition: see below. As I argue in *HC* 2§39, both versions actually keep the option open for imagining the same singer returning eternally to Delos. On the formulaic integrity of both versions, see Aloni 1989:111–12.

25. See the note above on the variant ἀφήμως, as attested in this quotation by Thucydides (3.104.5). In *HC* 2§27n25, I make an argument for interpreting ἀφήμως to mean 'without naming names'. The adjective ἄφημος was understood to be a synonym of ἀπευθής (as we see in the scholia to Aratus 1.270.2 [ed. J. Martin 1974]). This word ἀπευθής is used in the sense 'without information', as in *Odyssey* iii 88 and 184. When the Delian Maidens are asked to respond to the question 'Who is the singer?', they respond without naming names: that is, without giving information about the singer's name. See also De Martino 1982:92–94.

arrives here [to Delos], **after arduous wandering, as a guest entitled
to the rules of hosting**,[26] and asks this question:
"O Maidens, who is for you the most pleasurable of singers
that wanders here? **In whom** do you take the most **delight?**"   170
Then you, all of you [Maidens of Delos], must very properly **respond**
    [*hupokrinasthai*] about me:[27]
"It is a blind man, and he dwells in Chios, a rugged land."

[End of point of insertion. Now, to resume what Thucydides is saying . . .]

[3.104.6] So much for the evidence given by Homer concerning the fact that there
was even in the remote past a great coming together and **festival** [*heortē*] at Delos;
later on, the **islanders** [*nēsiōtai*] **and the Athenians** continued to send choral ensembles, along with sacrificial offerings, but various misfortunes evidently caused the
discontinuation of the things concerning the **competitions** [*agōnes*] and most other
things—that is, up to the time in question [the time of the purification], when the
Athenians set up the **competition** [*agōn*], including chariot races [*hippodromiai*],[28]
which had not taken place before then.

                                                                    Thucydides 3.104.2–6

The organizing ('making': ἐποίησαν)—or reorganizing—of the festival of the
Delia by the Athenians, as described here by Thucydides, took place in the winter
of 426 B.C.E.[29] Even from the understated account of Thucydides, it is clear that
the occasion must have been a monumental spectacle: "The surprising space given
to the Delos episode was perhaps the most [Thucydides] would allow himself by

26. This version, as we find it in the medieval manuscript tradition, leaves open the option of imagining the same singer returning again and again, in an eternal loop, to the seasonally recurring festival
of the Delia.

27. As I already noted, the variant ἀφ' ἡμέων, which I translate here as 'about me', is attested in the
medieval manuscript tradition, whereas the variant ἀφήμως, which I interpret to mean 'without naming names', is attested in the quotation by Thucydides. I think that both ἀφ' ἡμέων and ἀφήμως can be
explained as authentic formulaic variants. My translation 'about me' for ἀφ' ἡμέων is merely a cover for
the deeper meaning of this expression, which could be rendered as 'representing me', as when a group
represents a lead speaker in contexts of group performance. See *HC* 2§§27–40, where I argue that the
Homeric Hymn to Apollo represents Homer in the act of interacting with the local chorus of the Delian
Maidens. He acts as a poet-director for the Maidens as he cues them to perform their response to the
perennial question: Who is the best poet of them all? The *Hymn* gives a riddling response, making a
representation of Homer by Homer about Homer, as performed for Homer by the Delian Maidens. That
is the force of the expression ἀφ' ἡμέων at verse 171 of the *Hymn*: the Maidens are cued 'by me' to respond dialogically to a question 'about me'. Relevant is the formulation of Bakker 2002:21 about the preverb *apo*: "In the case of verbs denoting speech, the addition of *apo*- turns the sensibility to context into
an immediately dialogic sense: *apo-logeomai* 'speak in return', 'defend oneself against', *apo-krinomai* 'reason in return', 'answer.'"

28. See Rhodes 1994:260.

29. Hornblower 1991:527; Rhodes 1994:258–59.

way of recognition that it was a spectacular moment in the lives of all eye-witnesses."[30] The magnificence of this occasion is directly pertinent to the politics and poetics of the Delian League in the earlier phase of the Peloponnesian War.[31]

The Athenocentrism inherent in the reorganization of the festival of the Delia at Delos is made explicit in the myth that connects Theseus, as culture hero of Athens, with the Delia: he is described as the founder of an *agōn* 'competition' there (Plutarch *Theseus* 21.3).[32] Though the Athenocentrism is left implicit in the account of Thucydides, the underlying idea is unmistakable: "Thucydides claims, as Athenian propaganda must have done at the time, that the Athenians were not creating something new but reviving an ancient Ionian festival, and the emphatic way in which he does this, and cites 'Homer' in support, suggests that he is rebutting the alternative view."[33] The "alternative" view was of course represented by Sparta and its primarily Dorian allies in the Peloponnesian League, who were openly hostile to the Delian League—that is, to Athens and its primarily Ionian allies.

The Ionian orientation of the festival of the Delia, as opposed to the Dorian orientation of other major festivals, was a central motive in the Athenocentric reorganization of this festival by Athens in 426 B.C.E. Here is an apt formulation by a modern commentator on Thucydides: "The opportunity was taken to assert Athenian interest in Apollo, who at Delphi seemed now almost exclusively Peloponnesian and Dorian, and to start another international [interpolis] festival, the other four [the festivals of the Olympia, Pythia, Isthmia, and Nemea] being, as it happened, in Peloponnesian hands."[34] Another commentator adds: "The Delian activity of 426, in its imperial aspect, [can be explained] as evidence of an Athenian desire to reaffirm the 'Ionianism' of the Delian league in a period when Olympia, with its strongly Dorian associations, had recently been the venue for a meeting [at Olympia] which had been markedly hostile to Athens."[35]

The setting of the festival of the Delia as reorganized in 426 is parallel to the setting of the *Homeric Hymn to Apollo* itself. In terms of the *Hymn*, as quoted and in-

30. Hornblower 1991:523.

31. On the Delian League as an alliance of Ionians, the formulation of Aristotle *Constitution of the Athenians* 23.4 is decisive; see also Thucydides 1.95.1. For more on the politics and poetics of the Delian League, as reflected in compositions intended for choral performances at the festival of the Delia, see the survey by Kowalzig 2007 ch. 2.

32. Hornblower 1991:523; Rhodes 1994:258.

33. Rhodes 1994:259.

34. Gomme 1956:414. See also Hornblower 1991:521.

35. Hornblower 1991:521. The meeting in question, which takes place in Olympia, is recounted by Thucydides 3.9–14 (the speakers are the Mytilenaeans). As I will argue later, the *Homeric Hymn* (3) *to Apollo* as we have it is a combination of a *Hymn to Delian Apollo* and a *Hymn to Delphian Apollo*. The Delphian aspect of the *Hymn* would be compatible with the cultural outlook of Sparta. This aspect, however, is eclipsed by the Ionian outlook of the *Hymn* as a whole.

terpreted by Thucydides, the speaker in this setting is the speaker of the *Hymn*, Homer. And Thucydides recognizes the speaker of the *Hymn* as Homer himself (3.104.4, 5, 6). The ancient historian thinks he is quoting the words of Homer as he quotes from the *Hymn* the verses we recognize from the medieval manuscript transmission of Homer (Thucydides 3.104.4 and 5: *Hymn to Apollo* 146–50 and 165–72). This thinking of Thucydides is a most valuable piece of evidence about ancient ideas of Homer. It goes to the root, as we will see, of the conventional Athenian idea of Homer.[36]

HOMER AND THE PANIONIAN FESTIVALS
OF DELOS AND BEYOND

In the verses of the *Homeric Hymn to Apollo* quoted by Thucydides (146–50), the speaker pictures Delos as a festive center where representatives of all Ionian cities converge in a grand assembly to validate their common origin by celebrating a Panionian festival. In commenting on the *Homeric Hymn to Apollo*, Thucydides says that this supposedly Homeric description of the festival indicates a prototype of the Delia, to be contrasted with the contemporary version that was organized ('made') by the Athenians to be celebrated on a quadrennial basis:

καὶ τὴν πεντετηρίδα τότε πρῶτον μετὰ τὴν κάθαρσιν ἐποίησαν οἱ Ἀθηναῖοι τὰ Δήλια.

After the purification [*katharsis*], the Athenians at that point made for the first time the quadrennial festival known as the **Delia**.

Thucydides 3.104.2

As we will see, the wording *prōton* 'for the first time' here refers to the first time that this festival was celebrated on a quadrennial basis, not to the first time that this festival was ever celebrated. The *katharsis* of the island of Delos signals the Athenian inauguration of this festival at Delos in its quadrennial form. This particular inauguration, to repeat, can be dated to the winter of 426 B.C.E. But Thucydides says that there had been also an earlier Athenian *katharsis* of Delos, and that it took place at the initiative of the tyrant Peisistratos of Athens (3.104.1). This earlier *katharsis* signals an earlier Athenian inauguration of the same festival of the Delia at Delos. Besides Thucydides, Herodotus too (1.64.2) refers to this earlier *katharsis*, and he specifies that it was initiated by Peisistratos.[37]

By now Thucydides has given two distinct chronological landmarks for two distinct phases in the history of the Panionian festival known as the Delia. The earlier Athenian organization of that festival in the sixth century, in the era of the Peisi-

---

36. See also Graziosi 2002:222–26, who adduces Choricius *Laudatio Marciani* 2.3.
37. See again Hornblower 1991:527.

stratidai, is viewed as a precedent for its later Athenian organization in the fifth century, in the era of the democracy. The earlier Athenian organization, which is connected with the initiative of the tyrant Peisistratos, indicates that the city of Athens "had 'ruled the waves' in the sixth century as well as the fifth."[38] In terms of what Thucydides is saying, there was already a prototype of the Athenian empire in the era of the Peisistratidai in the sixth century B.C.E., preceding the Athenian empire that we see in the era of the democracy in the fifth century B.C.E. I infer that there was also already a version of the *Homeric Hymn to Apollo* in that earlier era.

As we will see, the figure of Homer in the *Homeric Hymn to Apollo* is a construct that fits the era of the Athenian regime of the Peisistratidai—and of the non-Athenian regime of the tyrant Polycrates of Samos. In the case of Polycrates, we can even posit an occasion for his commissioning the performance of the *Homeric Hymn to Apollo* as we have it. The occasion is signaled in the passage I quoted earlier from Thucydides: it was the time when Polycrates had chained the island of Rheneia to the island of Delos. On that occasion, according to later sources, Polycrates organized an event that resembled a combination of two festivals, the Delia and the Pythia, for an ad hoc celebration on the island of Delos.[39] The *Homeric Hymn to Apollo*, with its combination of hymnic praise for both the Delian and the Pythian aspects of the god Apollo, fits the occasion. Such an occasion has been dated: it happened around 522 B.C.E.[40] Soon after the occasion, Polycrates was overthrown and killed by the Persians. Peisistratos had died earlier, in 528/7. On the occasion of the celebration organized by Polycrates, as we will see later, the performer of the *Homeric Hymn to Apollo* was a rhapsode by the name of Kynaithos.

THE PERFORMANCE OF EPIC AT THE PANATHENAIA IN THE ERA OF THE PEISISTRATIDAI: THE LATER YEARS

As we consider what happened after the death of Polycrates, the focus of attention shifts from the festival of the Delia in Delos to the festival of the Panathenaia in Athens. For a starting point I choose the historical moment in time when control of the Delia was lost by Polycrates of Samos and regained by the Peisistratidai of

38. Hornblower 1991:520, who also comments at p. 519 on the "vigorous Aegean foreign policy" of the Peisistratidai. See in general his pp. 519–20 for comments on the survival of various ideologies from the era of the Peisistratidai to the era of the democracy, such as various Panhellenic features of the Eleusinian Mysteries.

39. Zenobius of Athos 1.62; *Suda* s.v. *tauta kai Puthia kai Dēlia*; for a fuller collection of sources, see Aloni 1989:35n2, 83n1.

40. Burkert 1979:59–60; Janko 1982:112–13. West 1999:369–70n17 argues for 523, but his dating criteria depend on whether or not we posit a perfect match between the datable events narrated by Herodotus and Thucydides.

Athens. This would have happened, as we just saw, soon after the premier performance of what we know as the *Homeric Hymn to Apollo* in Delos. There is general agreement that this particular performance at Delos preceded the celebration at Athens of the quadrennial Panathenaia by Hipparkhos son of Peisistratos in the summer of 522.[41] So we are looking at a historical moment in time that took place during the later years of the rule of the Peisistratidai in Athens. (As I noted earlier, Peisistratos had died already by 528/7.) As I will now argue, the epic poetry performed at the festival of the quadrennial Panathenaia at this historical moment in the year 522 was a prototype of what eventually evolved into the Panathenaic Homer. By the time of Thucydides in the late fifth century, more than a hundred years later, this Panathenaic Homer had evolved into a form that resembles most closely what we still recognize today as the Homeric *Iliad* and *Odyssey*. And for Thucydides as an Athenian, the speaking *I* who narrates the Homeric *Iliad* and *Odyssey* as performed at the festival of the Panathenaia is the same person as the speaking *I* of Homer in the *Homeric Hymn to Apollo*.

Essential for my argument is a basic historical fact about the performance of Homeric poetry at the quadrennial Great Panathenaia within a span of time extending from the era of Hipparkhos son of Peisistratos in the late sixth century B.C.E. all the way to the era of Lycurgus of Athens in the late fourth: throughout this span of time, the performers of Homeric poetry at the Panathenaia were rhapsodes who simultaneously competed as well as collaborated with each other in their Homeric performances. This fact is made evident by what is said in a set of three passages that I will now proceed to analyze.

The first of the three passages comes from a work attributed to Plato and named after Hipparkhos son of Peisistratos. The words I am quoting are spoken by Plato's Socrates, who is just on the verge of naming Hipparkhos as an Athenian of the past who deserves the admiration of Athenians in the present:

... Ἱππάρχῳ, ὃς ἄλλα τε πολλὰ καὶ καλὰ ἔργα σοφίας ἀπεδέξατο, καὶ τὰ Ὁμήρου ἔπη πρῶτος ἐκόμισεν εἰς τὴν γῆν ταύτην, καὶ ἠνάγκασε τοὺς **ῥαψῳδοὺς** Παναθηναίοις ἐξ **ὑπολήψεως ἐφεξῆς** αὐτὰ διιέναι, ὥσπερ νῦν ἔτι οἴδε ποιοῦσιν.

[I am referring to] Hipparkhos, who accomplished many beautiful things in demonstration of his expertise [*sophia*], especially by being the first to bring over [*komizein*] to this land [Athens] the verses [*epos*, plural] of Homer, and he required the **rhapsodes** [*rhapsōidoi*] at the Panathenaia to go through [*diienai*] these verses **in sequence** [*ephexēs*], **by relay** [*ex hupolēpseōs*], just as they [the rhapsodes] do even nowadays.[42]

"Plato" *Hipparkhos* 228b–c

---

41. Burkert 1979:60; West 1999:382.
42. There is an indirect reference to this passage in Aelian *Varia Historia* 8.2.

This story amounts to an aetiology. (By *aetiology*, I mean a myth that motivates an institutional reality, especially a ritual.)[43] As I have argued in earlier work, the institutional reality described here in the Platonic *Hipparkhos*, where rhapsodes compete with one another as they perform by relay and in sequence the epics of Homer at the festival of the Panathenaia, is a ritual in and of itself.[44] Moreover, the principle of equity that is built into this ritual event of rhapsodic competition corresponds to the need for equity in the ritual events of athletic competition. As Richard Martin observes: "The superb management of athletic games to assure equity could easily have been extended by the promoters of the Panathenaic games in this way."[45] To emphasize the ritualistic nature of this regulation of rhapsodic competitions, I refer to it as the *Panathenaic Regulation* instead of using the less expressive term *Panathenaic Rule*.[46] And the very idea of a Panathenaic Regulation, where rhapsodes collaborate as well as compete in the process of performing, by relay, successive parts of integral compositions like the Homeric *Iliad* and *Odyssey*, can be used to explain the unity of these epics as they evolved over time.[47] This evolution can best be understood in the light of Douglas Frame's argument that the Homeric performance units stemming from this Panathenaic Regulation stem ultimately from earlier Homeric performance units that evolved at the festival of the Panionia as celebrated in the late eighth and early seventh centuries B.C.E. at the Panionion of the Ionian Dodecapolis in Asia Minor: according to Frame's explanation, the Panionian versions of the *Iliad* and the *Odyssey* were divided into six rhapsodic performance units each, adding up to twelve rhapsodic performance units representing each one of the twelve cities of the Ionian Dodecapolis; each one of these twelve rhapsodic performance units corresponds to four *rhapsōidiai* or 'books' of the Homeric *Iliad* and *Odyssey* as we know them ('books' 1–4, 5–8, 9–12, 13–16, 17–20, 21–24).[48]

Hipparkhos left his mark in defining the festival of the Panathenaia in Athens not only because he was the one who was credited with instituting the Panathenaic Regulation. He actually died at the Panathenaia. He was assassinated on the festive quadrennial occasion of the Great Panathenaia held in the year 514 B.C.E., and his spectacular death is vividly memorialized by both Thucydides (1.20.2, 6.54–59) and Herodotus (5.55–61). Despite the assassination, however, the older brother of Hipparkhos, Hippias, maintained his family's political control of Athens. In the year

43. *BA* 16§2n2 (= p. 279).
44. *PR* 42–47. For a comparative perspective on the concept of competition-in-collaboration, see *PP* 18.
45. Martin 2000b:422.
46. *PR* 36–69.
47. *PR* 42–47; *HC* 2§§297, 304, 325; 3§§4, 6, 33.
48. Frame 2009 ch. 11.

510, Hippias was finally overthrown, and this date marks the end of the *turannis* 'tyranny' of the Peisistratidai, which then gave way to the *dēmokratia* 'democracy' initiated in 508 by Kleisthenes, head of the rival lineage of the Alkmaionidai.

The new regime of the Athenian democracy highlighted not Hipparkhos but the earlier figure of Solon as the culture hero of the Panathenaic Regulation. In the second of the three passages I am currently examining, the achievement of Solon is described as follows:

τά τε Ὁμήρου ἐξ ὑποβολῆς γέγραφε ῥαψῳδεῖσθαι, οἷον ὅπου ὁ πρῶτος ἔληξεν, ἐκεῖθεν ἄρχεσθαι τὸν ἐχόμενον.

He [Solon, as lawgiver of the Athenians] has written a law that the words of Homer are to be **performed rhapsodically** [*rhapsōidein*], by **relay** [*hupobolē*], so that wherever the first person **left off** [*lēgein*], from that point the next person should **start** [*arkhesthai*].

Dieuchidas of Megara *FGH* 485 F 6, via Diogenes Laertius 1.57

As we see from this second passage, the regime of the Athenian democracy gave credit to Solon and not to the Peisistratidai for the establishment of the Panathenaic Regulation, since Solon was now imagined as the culture hero of a primal democracy that had preceded the *turannis* 'tyranny' of the Peisistratidai in Athens.[49] The democratic aetiology of the new regime displaced the predemocratic aetiology of the old regime. From the standpoint of the old regime, as we saw in the first passage, the originator of the Panathenaic Regulation was Hipparkhos of the Peisistratidai, not the earlier figure of Solon.

The predemocratic version of the aetiology of the Panathenaic Regulation, featuring Hipparkhos, makes more sense than the democratic version featuring Solon. As we are about to see, the predemocratic version is consistent with a whole nexus of additional information concerning the early phases of the Panathenaia. This is not to say, however, that Hipparkhos himself should be credited with instituting rhapsodic contests at the Panathenaia. It is only to say that he instituted a reform of these rhapsodic contests by introducing the Panathenaic Regulation.[50]

I now turn to a third passage about the Panathenaic Regulation. The speaker in this passage avoids any direct attribution of the Panathenaic Regulation to Solon, despite the fact that he speaks in terms that presuppose the prevailing ideologies of the Athenian democracy; instead, he attributes the Regulation to the initiative of unnamed ancestors of the Athenians of his day.[51] Here is the passage, taken from a speech delivered by the Athenian statesman Lycurgus in 330 B.C.E.:[52]

49. I should add that Solon was a culture hero for the Peisistratidai as well. There is a useful discussion by Aloni 1989:43–45, 122n2.
50. Shear 2001:366.
51. *PR* 14.
52. Further discussion of this passage in *PH* 1§10n20 (= pp. 21–22), *PR* 10–12. See also Shear 2001:367.

βούλομαι δ᾽ ὑμῖν καὶ τὸν Ὅμηρον παρασχέσθαι **ἐπαινῶν**. οὕτω γὰρ ὑπέλαβον ὑμῶν οἱ πατέρες σπουδαῖον εἶναι ποιητήν, ὥστε νόμον ἔθεντο καθ᾽ ἑκάστην πενταετηρίδα τῶν Παναθηναίων μόνου τῶν ἄλλων ποιητῶν **ῥαψῳδεῖσθαι** τὰ ἔπη, ἐπίδειξιν ποιούμενοι πρὸς τοὺς Ἕλληνας ὅτι τὰ κάλλιστα τῶν ἔργων προῃροῦντο.

I wish to adduce[53] for you Homer, **quoting [*epaineîn*]** him,[54] since the reception[55] that he had from your [Athenian] ancestors made him so important a poet that there was a law enacted by them that requires, every fourth year of the Panathenaia,[56] the **rhapsodic performing [*rhapsōideîn*]** of his verses—his alone and no other poet's. In this way they [your (Athenian) ancestors] made a demonstration [*epideixis*],[57] intended for all Hellenes to see,[58] that they made a conscious choice of the most noble of accomplishments.[59]

Lycurgus *Against Leokrates* 102

53. The orator Lycurgus, in 'adducing' the various classical authors whom he quotes, is doing so in his role as a statesman.

54. To make his arguments here in *Against Leokrates* 102, the orator is about to adduce a quotation from Homer, the equivalent of what we know as *Iliad* XV verses 494–99. On my reasons for translating *epaineîn* as 'quote', see *PR* 27–28. Adducing a Homeric quotation is presented here as if it were a matter of adducing Homer himself. In the same speech, at an earlier point, Lycurgus (*Against Leokrates* 100) had quoted 55 verses from Euripides' *Erekhtheus* (F 50 ed. Austin). At a later point (*Against Leokrates* 107), he quotes 32 verses from Tyrtaeus (F 10 ed. West), whom he identifies as an Athenian. (So also does Plato in *Laws* 1.629a.) On the politics and poetics of the Athenian appropriation of Tyrtaeus *and* of his poetry, see *GM* 272–73. I suggest that the Ionism of poetic diction in the poetry of Tyrtaeus can be explained along the lines of an evolutionary model of rhapsodic transmission: see *PH* 2§3 (= pp. 52–53) and 14§41 (= pp. 433–34), and *HQ* 111; see also *PH* 1§13n27 (= p. 23) on Lycurgus *Against Leokrates* 106–7, where the orator mentions a customary law at Sparta concerning the performance of the poetry of Tyrtaeus. For more on *epaineîn*, see now Elmer (forthcoming).

55. I deliberately translate *hupolambanein* as 'receive' (that is, 'reception') here in terms of *reception theory*. In terms of rhapsodic vocabulary, as we saw above in "Plato" *Hipparkhos* 228b–c, *hupolēpsis* is not just 'reception' but also 'continuation' in the sense *reception by way of relay*. Further analysis in *PR* 11n8.

56. In the original Greek, the counting is inclusive: every 'fifth' year.

57. Comparable is the context of *epideigma* 'display, demonstration' in "Plato" *Hipparkhos* 228d, as discussed in *PH* 6§30 (= pp. 160–61); see also *PH* 8§4 (= pp. 217–18) on *apodeixis* 'presentation, demonstration'. The basic idea behind what is being 'demonstrated' is *a model for performance*. The motivation as described here corresponds closely to the motivation of Hipparkhos as described in the first of the three passages that I have been analyzing.

58. By implication, the Panhellenic impulse of the 'ancestors' of the Athenians in making Homer a classic is mirrored by the impulse of Lycurgus, statesman that he is, to quote extensively from such classics as Homer, Tyrtaeus, and Euripides. See also "Plutarch" *Lives of the Ten Orators* 841f on the initiatives taken by Lycurgus to produce a State Script of the dramas of Aeschylus, Sophocles, and Euripides (commentary in *PP* 174–75, 189n6, 204).

59. I infer that the *erga* 'accomplishments' include poetic accomplishments: on the mentality of seeing a reciprocity between noble deeds and poetry that becomes a noble deed itself in celebrating noble deeds, see *PH* 2§35n95 (= p. 70), 8§5 (= pp. 218–19).

This third passage makes it explicit that the *epē* 'verses' (*epos,* plural) performed at the Panathenaia belonged to Homer only, to the exclusion of other poets. As we are about to see, the poets to be excluded were other authors, as it were, of epic. These authors, from the standpoint of the Athenian democracy in the fourth century B.C.E., were understood to be the poets of the epic Cycle and, secondarily, the poets Hesiod and Orpheus. I will have more to say about these poets at a later point in my argumentation; for now, however, I concentrate on the idea that they are seen as poets of epic, not of other forms of poetry.

The *epē* 'verses' (*epos,* plural) to which the Athenian orator is referring in this third passage are the dactylic hexameters performed by competing *rhapsōidoi* 'rhapsodes', not the lyric meters performed by competing *kitharōidoi* 'citharodes' and *aulōidoi* 'aulodes'. At the Panathenaia, there were separate competitions of *rhapsōidoi* 'rhapsodes', of *kitharōidoi* 'citharodes' (*kithara* singers), of *aulōidoi* 'aulodes' (*aulos* singers), of *kitharistai* 'citharists' (*kithara* players), and of *aulētai* 'auletes' (*aulos* players), as we learn from an Athenian inscription dated at around 380 B.C.E. (*IG* II² 2311) that records Panathenaic prizes.[60] We learn about these categories of competition also from Plato's *Laws* (6.764d–e), where we read of rhapsodes, citharodes, and auletes—and where the wording makes it clear that the point of reference is the Panathenaia.[61] I mention these other categories of competing performers because the festival of the Panathenaia featured citharodic and aulodic competitions in lyric as well as rhapsodic competitions in epic.[62] In the passage I have just quoted from Lycurgus, the use of the word *rhapsōidein* 'rhapsodically perform' makes it clear that the poets who are being excluded from the Panathenaia are not the lyric poets, whose compositions are performed by citharodes and aulodes. In other words, Lycurgus is referring here not to lyric poets like Anacreon and Simonides. Rather, he is referring to epic poets other than the Homer he knows. It is these other epic poets who are being excluded from the Panathenaia. Lycurgus here is referring exclusively to rhapsodic competitions in epic, not to citharodic or aulodic competitions in lyric. When Lycurgus refers to 'Homer' in this passage, he means the author of the *Iliad* and the *Odyssey*.[63]

My argument, based on the actual wording of Lycurgus in *Against Leokrates* (102), is that the *Iliad* and *Odyssey* were reperformed as a continuous narration at the quadrennial festival of the Great Panathenaia. This argument is supported by the testimony of Dionysius of Argos (*FGH* 308 F 2): from the surviving reportage

60. Further discussion in PR 38–39, 42n16, 51. The portion of the inscription that deals with rhapsodes is lost, but it is generally accepted that rhapsodic competitions were mentioned in this missing portion.

61. *PR* 38, 40, 42.

62. *HC* 3§§27–33.

63. *HC* 3§33.

about what Dionysius said, we can see that he must have focused on the continuity that was evident in these two epics.[64] It remains to be seen, however, whether such continuous narration was only notional in any given historical phase of the Great Panathenaia.[65]

A moment ago, I used the names Anacreon and Simonides as examples of poets whose lyric compositions could be performed competitively at the Panathenaia. I mentioned their names for a specific reason. In the first of the three passages I quoted about the Panathenaic Regulation, we saw an association of Hipparkhos with Homer at the Panathenaia. Here I quote that passage again, but this time I extend the quotation to include what the speaker says about a parallel association of the same Hipparkhos with these two lyric poets, Anacreon and Simonides:

> . . . Ἱππάρχῳ, ὃς ἄλλα τε πολλὰ καὶ καλὰ ἔργα **σοφίας** ἀπεδέξατο, καὶ τὰ Ὁμήρου ἔπη πρῶτος **ἐκόμισεν** εἰς τὴν γῆν ταύτην, καὶ ἠνάγκασε τοὺς ῥαψῳδοὺς Παναθηναίοις ἐξ ὑπολήψεως ἐφεξῆς αὐτὰ διιέναι, ὥσπερ νῦν ἔτι [228c] οἵδε ποιοῦσιν, καὶ ἐπ' Ἀνα- **κρέοντα τὸν Τήιον** πεντηκόντορον στείλας **ἐκόμισεν** εἰς τὴν πόλιν, **Σιμωνίδην** δὲ **τὸν Κεῖον** ἀεὶ περὶ αὐτὸν εἶχεν, μεγάλοις μισθοῖς καὶ δώροις πείθων· ταῦτα δ' ἐποίει βουλόμενος παιδεύειν τοὺς πολίτας, ἵν' ὡς βελτίστων ὄντων αὐτῶν ἄρχοι, οὐκ οἰόμενος δεῖν οὐδενὶ **σοφίας** φθονεῖν, ἅτε ὢν καλός τε κἀγαθός.

> [I am referring to] Hipparkhos, who accomplished many beautiful things in demonstration of his **expertise** [*sophia*], especially by being the first to **bring over** [*komizein*] to this land [Athens] the verses of Homer, and he forced the rhapsodes [*rhapsōidoi*] at the Panathenaia to go through [*diienai*] these verses in sequence, by relay [*ex hupolēpseōs*], just as [228c] they [the rhapsodes] do even nowadays. And he sent out a state ship to **bring over** [*komizein*] **Anacreon of Teos** to the city [Athens]. He also always kept in his company **Simonides of Keos**, persuading him by way of huge fees and gifts. And he did all this because he wanted to educate the citizens, so that he might govern the best of all possible citizens. He thought, noble as he was, that he was obliged not to be stinting in the sharing of his **expertise** [*sophia*] with anyone.

> "Plato" *Hipparkhos* 228b–c

I highlight the two instances of the word *sophia* 'expertise' in this extended passage. The use of this word here is strikingly archaic: it expresses the idea that Hipparkhos demonstrates his expertise in poetry by virtue of sponsoring poets like Homer, Anacreon, and Simonides (the latter is coupled with Anacreon: *Hipparkhos* 228c), who are described as the ultimate standards for measuring expertise in poetry.[66] In the overall logic of the narrative, Hipparkhos makes this kind of gesture because he wants to demonstrate to the citizens of Athens that he is not 'stinting with his *sophia*' (228c σοφίας φθονεῖν), since he provides them with the poetry and

---

64. *PP* 68; *PR* 10–12, 47.
65. Burgess 2004.
66. *HQ* 80n49.

songmaking of Homer, Anacreon, and Simonides; by implication, his *sophia* is the key to the performances of these three poets in Athens.[67]

In the case of Homeric poetry, as we see from the larger context of this extended passage taken from the Platonic *Hipparkhos*, the tyrant is being credited not only with the regulation of Homeric performances at the Panathenaia but also with the more basic initiative of actually introducing the epic performances of Homer at this festival. Moreover, the wording makes it clear that this initiative is thought to be a parallel to the tyrant's initiative of introducing the performances of lyric compositions by contemporary poets like Anacreon and Simonides, ostensibly at the same festival. The use of the word *komizein* (228b), in expressing the idea that Hipparkhos 'brought over' to Athens the *epē* 'verses' (*epos,* plural) of Homer, is parallel to the use of the same word *komizein* (228c) in expressing the idea that Hipparkhos also 'brought over' to Athens the poet Anacreon—on a state ship, from the island of Samos.[68]

What is implied by the second of these two initiatives of Hipparkhos is that the tyrant undertook a veritable rescue operation in transporting to Athens the lyric poet Anacreon from Samos. In Samos, Anacreon had been a court poet of the Panionian maritime empire of Polycrates of Samos. To make this point, I turn to the story told by Herodotus about the final days of Polycrates, culminating in the gruesome execution of the tyrant by agents of the Persian empire (3.125.2–3). Right before the bitter end, we get a glimpse of happier times: Polycrates is pictured as reclining on a sympotic couch and enjoying the company of that ultimate luminary of Ionian lyric poetry, Anacreon of Teos (3.121.1).[69] My point is, the Ionian lyric tradition represented by Anacreon had to be rescued from the Persians once the old Panionian maritime empire of Polycrates of Samos had collapsed, soon to be replaced by the new Panionianism of the Peisistratidai of Athens. Once the rescue operation had succeeded, it could now be Hipparkhos, not Polycrates, who got to enjoy the sympotic company of lyric celebrities like Anacreon.

In the logic of this narrative, Hipparkhos did something far more than simply invite lyric poets for ad hoc occasions of performance at, say, symposia: rather, he institutionalized their performances. Once his initiative succeeded, the Ionian lyric compositions of poets like Anacreon of Teos could be performed in citharodic or aulodic competitions at the Panathenaia in Athens, along with the Dorian lyric compositions of poets like Simonides of Keos.[70]

67. *PH* 6§§30–31 (= pp. 160–62).

68. *HQ* 81n50.

69. In Pausanias 1.2.3, the consorting of Anacreon with Polycrates is drawn into a parallel with the consorting of poets with kings in general.

70. Nagy 2007b:235–36, 243–46, 252; see also *HQ* 81n50. For more on Simonides as a protégé of the Peisistratidai, see Graziosi 2002:225–26.

We have just seen one of the two Panathenaic initiatives of Hipparkhos as narrated in the Platonic *Hipparkhos*. Now I turn to the other initiative. The narrative implies that Hipparkhos the tyrant undertook another rescue operation by virtue of transporting to Athens the epic poetry of Homer. In this case, as we are about to see, it is implied that Hipparkhos transported not the poet Homer but Homer's notional descendants, called the *Homēridai*; further, by contrast with the case of Anacreon, Hipparkhos brought the *Homēridai* over to Athens not from the island of Samos but from the island of Chios.

At a later point in my argumentation, I will analyze the extant information we have about the *Homēridai* of Chios. As we will see, these *Homēridai* are the topic of a highly compressed but illuminating discussion in the scholia for Pindar's *Nemean* 2. Moreover, they are well known to classical authors, who speak about them in passing as a matter of common knowledge. Two important examples, as we will also see, are the casual references made by Isocrates (*Helen* 65) and by Plato (*Ion* 530d, *Republic* 10.599e).

For the moment, I will leave the topic of the *Homēridai* of Chios, but not before I offer an outline of what I hope to reconstruct in the course of my upcoming analysis:

1. There must have been some kind of traditional story about the initiative of the Peisistratidai in importing the *Homēridai* from Chios to Athens.
2. This story was designed to explain the function of the *Homēridai* as regulators of rhapsodic competitions in performing epic at the festival of the Panathenaia. By implication, the *Homēridai* brought with them to Athens the Panathenaic Regulation. In other words, the Panathenaic Regulation was basically an Ionian tradition imported by way of Chios to Athens in the era of the Peisistratidai.[71]

---

71. About this Ionian tradition, stemming ultimately from the festival of the Panionia as celebrated in the late eighth and early seventh centuries at the Panionion of the Ionian Dodecapolis in Asia Minor, I rely on the findings of Frame 2009 ch. 11.

2

Homer Outside His Poetry

HOMER IN THE *LIFE OF HOMER* TRADITIONS

So far, we have been considering the concept of Homer as defined by the *Homeric Hymn to Apollo* and by the epics attributed to Homer. Now we will see that there is further definition to be found outside this poetry, in a body of narratives known as the *Lives of Homer*. In what follows, I offer an analysis of the evidence provided by these *Lives*.[1] Two *Lives* stand out in my analysis. One of them is *Vita 1*, sometimes

---

1. I offer the following system for referring to these *Lives* (with page numbers as printed by Allen 1912):

Vita 1: *Vita Herodotea*, pp. 192–218
Vita 2: *Certamen*, pp. 225–38
Vita 3a: Plutarchean *vita*, pp. 238–44
Vita 3b: Plutarchean *vita*, pp. 244–45
Vita 4: *Vita quarta*, pp. 245–46
Vita 5: *Vita quinta*, pp. 247–50
Vita 6: *Vita sexta* (the "Roman *Vita*"), pp. 250–53
Vita 7: *Vita septima*, by way of Eustathius, pp. 253–54
Vita 8: *Vita* by way of Tzetzes, pp. 254–55
Vita 9: *Vita* by way of Eustathius (on *Iliad* IV 17), p. 255
Vita 10: *Vita* by way of the *Suda*, pp. 256–68
Vita 11: *Vita* by way of Proclus, pp. 99–102.

Also relevant is a detail in *Michigan Papyrus* 2754, originally published in Winter 1925, which supplements what we read in the *Certamen* about a universalized reception for Homer. See also Vogt 1959, who confirms Winter's reading of *Homēros* in line 17 of the *Michigan Papyrus*. Albert Henrichs (2002.05.07) kindly informs me that this reading was reconfirmed in September 1983 by Ludwig Koenen, who re-examined the papyrus for him. For further confirmation, see now Colbeaux 2005:77. There

known as the *Herodotean Life*, and the other is *Vita* 2, the *Contest of Homer and Hesiod*, which is sometimes called the *Certamen* for short.[2]

The evidence of these *Life of Homer* traditions reveals traces of earlier as well as later concepts of Homer. While the later concepts correspond closely to the Panathenaic Homer of the *Iliad* and *Odyssey*, the earlier concepts predate this Homer of the Athenians. In effect, the *Lives of Homer* can be read as sources of information about the reception of both the earlier Homer and the later Panathenaic Homer. The information is varied and layered, requiring a combination of synchronic and diachronic analysis.[3] In the end, such a combined analysis yields a prehistory and history of Homeric reception from the Dark Age onward.

The *Life of Homer* traditions represent the reception of Homeric poetry by narrating a series of events featuring purportedly live performances by Homer himself. In the narratives of the *Lives*, Homeric composition is consistently being situated in contexts of Homeric performance. In effect, the *Lives* explore the shaping power of positive and even negative responses by the audiences of Homeric poetry in ad hoc situations of performance. To put it another way, the narrative strategy of the *Lives* is a staging of Homer's reception.

My describing the *Life of Homer* traditions as a *staging* converges with my aim to show that the narratives of these *Lives* are myths, not historical facts, about Homer. To say that we are dealing with myths, however, is not at all to say that there is no history to be learned from the *Lives*. Even though the various Homers of the various *Lives* are evidently mythical constructs, the actual constructing of myths about Homer can be seen as historical fact.[4] These myths about Homer in the *Lives* can be analyzed as evidence for the various different ways in which Homeric poetry was appropriated by various different cultural and political centers throughout the ancient Greek-speaking world. And these myths, in all their varieties, have basically one thing in common: Homeric poetry is pictured as a medium of performance, featuring Homer himself as the master performer.

---

is now also another system for numbering the *Lives*, introduced by West 2003a. Wherever I cite his work, I will produce his numbering as well as the numbering that follows the system of Allen 1912. There is a new edition of *Vita* 1 and *Vita* 2 by Colbeaux (2005).

2. There was evidently an intermediate phase that preceded the final phase of the text that has come down to us as the *Certamen*. The intermediate phase draws extensively from a lost work, the *Mouseion* of Alcidamas, who flourished in the first half of the fourth century B.C.E. For background on the problems of sorting out the compositional layers of the *Certamen* and the *Mouseion*, see O'Sullivan 1992 and Debiasi 2001. For a sketch, see West 2003a:298.

3. For my use of the words *synchronic* and *diachronic*, see *HR* 1, with reference to Saussure 1916:117.

4. I can make this point about *Lives of Poets* traditions in general: see *BA*² preface §7n (= p. ix) for further citations. For typological parallels in Iranian traditions, see Davidson 2001a.

THE MAKING OF HOMERIC VERSE
IN THE *LIFE OF HOMER* TRADITIONS

For analyzing diachronically as well as synchronically the reception of Homer as reflected in the *Life of Homer* traditions, I have built a model for the periodization of such reception. This model is meant to account for the accretive layering of narrative traditions contained within the final textual versions of these *Lives*. I posit three periods of ongoing reception, and I frame these periods in terms of a time line that tracks the city-state of Athens as a dominant political and cultural force in the history of Homeric reception. I call these three periods *pre-Athenocentric, Athenocentric,* and *post-Athenocentric.*

As we will see, the post-Athenocentric period of Homeric reception is characterized by the use of *graphein* 'write' in referring to Homer as an author. From the standpoint of this period, the performance of Homeric poetry at the Panathenaia in Athens and at other festivals in other cities is no longer perceived as a factor in defining Homer as the author of this poetry. The use of *graphein* in the post-Athenocentric period needs to be distinguished from what we find in the Athenocentric and pre-Athenocentric periods, when Homer is said to *poieîn* 'make' whatever he composes, not to *graphein* 'write' it.

The post-Athenocentric period is exemplified by such relatively late sources as Plutarch and Pausanias, in whose writings Homer is already seen as an author who 'writes', *graphei*, whatever he composes.[5] The Athenocentric period, by contrast, is reflected in the usage of Aristotle and Plato, in whose writings we still see Homer as an artisan who 'makes', *poieî*, and who is not pictured as one who writes.[6]

I translate *poieîn* as 'make' in order to underline the fact that the direct object of

---

5. See, for example, Plutarch *On Affection for Offspring* 496d, *Table Talk* 668d; Pausanias 3.24.11, 8.29.2.

6. For examples of expressions involving 'Homer' as the subject and *poieîn* as the verb of that subject, see Aristotle *On the Soul* 404a, *Nicomachean Ethics* 3.1116a and 7.1145a, *On the Generation of Animals* 785a, *Poetics* 1448a, *Politics* 3.1278a and 8.1338a, *Rhetoric* 1.1370b. Note especially the wording in Aristotle *History of Animals* 513b, καὶ Ὅμηρος ἐν τοῖς ἔπεσιν εἴρηκε **ποιήσας**, and 575b, διὸ καὶ Ὅμηρόν φασι **πεποιηκέναι** τινὲς ὀρθῶς **ποιήσαντα**. See also Plato *Phaedo* 94d, *Hippias Minor* 371a, *Republic* 2.378d. Note especially the wording in Plato *Ion* 531c–d: . . . καὶ περὶ τῶν οὐρανίων παθημάτων καὶ περὶ τῶν ἐν Ἅιδου, καὶ γενέσεις καὶ θεῶν καὶ ἡρώων; οὐ ταῦτά ἐστι περὶ ὧν Ὅμηρος τὴν **ποίησιν πεποίηκεν**; (I note with special interest the usage, here and elsewhere, of *poiēsis* as the inner object of *poieîn*.) Of related interest is the use of *ho poiētēs* 'the Poet' to refer by default to Homer: the many examples include Plato *Republic* 3.392e (ὁ ποιητής φησι) and Aristotle *On the Cosmos* 400a (ὥσπερ ἔφη καὶ ὁ ποιητής). Note also such periphrastic expressions as we find in Plato *Hippias Minor* 364e: ὅτι **πεποιηκὼς** εἴη ὁ **ποιητής**. For an early example of *poieîn* with Homer as subject, see Herodotus 2.53.2: οὗτοι δέ εἰσι οἱ **ποιήσαντες** θεογονίην Ἕλλησι καὶ τοῖσι θεοῖσι τὰς ἐπωνυμίας δόντες καὶ τιμάς τε καὶ τέχνας διελόντες καὶ εἴδεα αὐτῶν σημήναντες. Homer shares the role of subject here with Hesiod.

this verb is not restricted to any particular product to be made by the subject—if the subject of the verb refers to an artisan. In other words, *poieîn* can convey the producing of any artifact as the product of any artisan. It is not restricted to the concept of the song or poem as artifact or of the songmaker or poet as artisan. To cite an early example: in *Iliad* VII (222), the artisan Tukhios *epoiēsen* 'made' the shield of Ajax. By contrast with the verb *poieîn*, the derivative nouns *poiētēs* 'songmaker, poet' and *poiēsis* 'songmaking, poetry' are restricted, already in the earliest attestations, to the production of songs or poems. I note the exclusion of artifacts other than songs or poems or of artisans other than songmakers or poets. The noun *poiēma* 'song, poem, poetic creation' has likewise been restricted, though not completely; in the usage of Herodotus, for example, *poiēma* still designates artifacts that are not songs or poems (1.25.1, 2.135.3, 4.5.3, 7.85.1). As for the compound-noun formant *-poios*, it is not at all restricted to song or to poetry.[7] (For example, *agalmatopoios* is 'statue maker', as in Herodotus 2.46.2.)

In what follows, I will track usages of *poieîn* 'make' and *graphein* 'write' with reference to Homer in two *Lives of Homer*, *Vita* 1 (the *Herodotean Life*) and *Vita* 2 (*Contest of Homer and Hesiod*). I will also track the connected usages of three nouns derived from *poieîn*: namely *poiētēs*, *poiēsis*, *poiēma*. In what I reconstruct as the Athenocentric and the pre-Athenocentric periods of Homeric reception as narrated in the *Lives*, we will see Homer pictured as an author but not as a writer. More precisely, Homer is an artisan who makes songs or poems that become activated in performance. To the extent that these songs or poems are attributed to him, Homer is an author, but the authorization of this author, as we will see, depends on the performance, not on the written text, of his songs or poems.[8] Moreover, as we will also see, the performer must be Homer himself.

In making this point, I am offering an adjustment to the theory that Homer is pictured as an *absent author* in the *Lives of Homer*.[9] According to this theory, stories about Homer as an author who 'makes' poems—as expressed by the verb *poieîn*—can be viewed as evidence for such an absent author: just as an artisan who *epoiēse* 'made' a vase (as signaled by countless vase inscriptions reading *epoiēse* plus the name of the maker of the vase) potentially becomes the absent author of the vase, so also Homer becomes the absent author of the songs or poems that he 'made'.[10] This theory needs to be adjusted in the light of stories picturing Homer in contexts of performance. In such contexts, as we see in the *Lives*, the performance of the com-

---

7. For an overall survey of such usages, see Ford 2002:132–39.

8. On Homer as author, see *PH* 12§69 (= pp. 373–74); also *PP* 62–63, 70–74, 80–81, 86, 150, 220.

9. For an analysis of this theory, I cite the admirable book of Graziosi 2002. In view of my discussions of Homeric authorship, as cited immediately above, I hope it is clear that I am not ignoring the concept of Homer as author.

10. Graziosi 2002:42.

position requires the real or notional presence of Homer for the purpose of making the performance authoritative. In the narrative logic of the *Lives*, Homer cannot afford to be an absent author. As we will see, Homer is an author only to the extent that his real or notional presence authorizes the occasion of performance. In the narrative logic of the *Lives*, Homer embodies the ongoing fusion of the composer with the performer. In other words, we see here a poetics of presence, not a poetics of absence.

In the case of other *Life of Poets* traditions, we see analogous patterns of narration. For example, we read in Herodotus (1.23) that Arion 'makes' (*poieîn*) dithyrambs, which are actualized when he 'teaches' (*didaskein*) them in Corinth; similarly in Herodotus (6.21.2), Phrynichus 'makes' (*poieîn*) the drama called *The Capture of Miletus*, which is actualized when he 'teaches' it in Athens.[11]

I need to add that oral composition can be metaphorized as written composition in the post-Athenocentric period, and, at least to that extent, we may think of Homer as a writer. Nevertheless, as we are about to observe, the *Lives* simply do not metaphorize performance as an act of performing written texts.

My point remains that the *Lives* require the real or notional presence of Homer for authorizing the performance of Homer. This narrative requirement holds up even in relatively late contexts—in what I reconstruct as the post-Athenocentric period of Homeric reception as narrated in the *Lives*. Even in such late contexts, where the poems attributed to Homer are described as his writings, the narrative still requires the notional performance of these poems, and the model performer must still be Homer himself.

Later on, when we look at post-Athenocentric contexts where the poems of Homer are pictured as texts written by Homer the writer, we will see that even in these contexts the poems must still be authorized by Homer the performer. Accordingly, although I concentrate on the reception of Homeric poetry as actual performance in the Athenocentric and pre-Athenocentric periods, the reception of Homeric poetry as notional performance in the post-Athenocentric period is also relevant.

What follows is an inventory of nineteen passages in the *Lives of Homer* where the words *poieîn* 'make' or *graphein* 'write' refer to the 'making' of Homeric song or poetry by Homer himself. All passages are taken from *Vita* 1 and *Vita* 2, and I list the passages in their order of occurrence within each of these two narratives.[12]

---

11. For more on the hermeneutics of 'teaching' (*didaskein*) as the authorization of a composition in performance, see *PH* 12§61n168 (= p. 371). A related example is Herodotus 4.35.3, where Olen 'makes' (*poieîn*) a *humnos* that is 'learned' (*manthanein*) by 'islanders and Ionians'; Olen also 'made' other *humnoi* that are 'sung' (*āidein*) at Delos. (The narrative implies that Olen came to Delos for the performance.) For a slightly different interpretation of the Herodotean passages I have just cited, see Graziosi 2002:43.

12. There is an abbreviated version of this inventory in Nagy 2004e.

ἐδείκνυον δὲ οἱ Νεοτειχεῖς μέχρις ἐπ᾽ ἐμοῦ τὸν χῶρον ἐν ᾧ κατίζων τῶν ἐπέων τὴν ἐπίδειξιν ἐποιέετο, καὶ κάρτα ἐσέβοντο τὸν τόπον.

Even as recently as my own time, the people of Neon Teikhos used to show off the place where he [Homer] used to sit and make [*poieîn*] performance [*epideixis*] of his verses [*epos,* plural]. They venerated greatly this site.[17]

Vita 1.119–22

At Neon Teikhos, then, Homer formally performs his compositions by 'making' (*poieîn*) what is called his *epideixis* 'performance'. Here we see that the act of performance itself, even as a process, is something that can be 'made'. It is not just the composition that is being 'made'. In the narrative logic of *Vita* 1, the 'making' of Homeric verse is a combination of two processes, composition and performance.

Even the 'making' of Homeric epigrams is a matter of performance:

ποιεῖ καὶ τὸ ἐπίγραμμα τόδε, τὸ ἔτι καὶ νῦν ἐπὶ τῆς στήλης τοῦ μνήματος τοῦ Γορδίεω ἐπιγέγραπται.

He [Homer] made [*poieîn*] also this epigram [*epigramma*], which even to this day is found inscribed [*epigraphesthai*] on the stele of the memorial of the man from Gordion [King Midas].

Vita 1.133–34

We see Homer here in the act of 'making' an epigram, to be inscribed on the tomb of King Midas of Phrygia. This report about the Midas Epigram of Homer is explicitly said to originate from a tradition native to the Aeolian city of Cyme (*Vita* 1.131).[18] In the *Contest of Homer and Hesiod* as well (*Vita* 2.261–64), we will see another reference to Homer's 'making' the poem that becomes the Midas Epigram.[19] Later on, we will examine the performative aspects of both these references concerning Homer's making of epigrams. For now, however, I will simply follow the thread of the story in *Vita* 1, continuing where we left off. In the next passage to be examined, Homer is still residing in the Aeolian city of Cyme:

17. The theme of venerating a place that had made direct contact with Homer himself is characteristic of hero cult. On Homer as cult hero, see *BA* 17§9n3 (= p. 297), citing Brelich 1958:320–21; see also *PP* 113n34, with references to sites named after Homer in Chios, Smyrna, and Delos. Strabo 14.1.37 C646 emphasizes the special claim of Smyrna on Homer; he notes that the Smyrnaeans in his time have a *bibliothēkē* and a quadrangular stoa called the *Homēreion*, containing a *neōs* 'shrine' of Homer and a *xoanon* 'wooden statue' of him.

18. The special significance of Cymaean traditions will be explored further below.

19. According to the story of Homer's Midas Epigram as told in *Vita* 1 (131–40), Homer is commissioned to compose the epigram while he is a resident of Cyme. According to *Vita* 2 (261–64), on the other hand, the commissioning happens sometime after the Contest of Homer and Hesiod in Chalkis. I will have more to say later about the sequence of events in Homer's life as retold in *Vita* 1.

the narrative accepts this version of Homer's blinding, as opposed to a version claimed by the people of Ithaca, who say that Homer was blinded on their island (1.84–87). Only after Homer comes back to Smyrna, already blind after his illness in Colophon, does he formally embark on a career of 'songmaking' or 'creating poetry', *poiēsis* (1.92–94): ἐκ δὲ τῆς Κολοφῶνος τυφλὸς ἐὼν ἀπικνέεται εἰς τὴν Σμύρναν καὶ οὕτως ἐπεχείρει τῇ ποιήσει 'leaving Colophon, he arrives in Smyrna, now blind, and that is the way things are as he now tries his hand at the making of poetry [*poiēsis*]'.

By implication, the narrative of *Vita* 1 views Homer's mnemonic sequencing of memorabilia during his journey in the realms of Ithaca and beyond as a process distinct from the process of actually composing a narrative based on these memorabilia. In terms of the narrator's inference, there is a distinction between the process of composing and a previous process of remembering things to be put into a composition that has yet to happen. In effect, the narrative here is postponing the actual process of Homeric composition for later occasions, for later moments in the life of Homer. In terms of the narrator's inference, the occasion of writing is not being linked directly with the occasions of Homeric composition, which are still just waiting to be narrated in *Vita* 1. Throughout the narrative of *Vita* 1, in fact, the act of composing is nowhere linked directly with the act of writing.

By contrast, as we are about to see in all the other relevant passages taken from *Vita* 1, the act of composition is everywhere linked with the act of performance. Nowhere in *Vita* 1 do we ever see Homer in the act of writing down what he is actually composing.

The next example shows Homer as a poet who makes *humnoi*, which I translate for the moment as 'hymns':

... τοὺς ὕμνους τοὺς ἐς θεοὺς πεποιημένους αὐτῷ ...

... the hymns [*humnoi*] to the gods that had been made [*poieîn*] by him [Homer] ...[15]

Vita 1.113–14

This reference concerns Homer's 'making' (*poieîn*) of *humnoi* in an Aeolian city by the name of Neon Teikhos. In the same city, Homer also performs an epic about the deeds of Amphiaraos in the war against Thebes (1.113).[16] The narrative continues with an explicit reference to Homer's performances of his compositions:

15. The word *humnoi* here in *Vita* 1.113–14 may refer to *Homeric Hymns* such as we know them, which may be followed by performances of epics or of other forms of poetry, even of song. In other words, I think that we need not assume performances of a series of *Homeric Hymns*.

16. It can be argued that this epic performance is part of what we know as the *Thebaid* or *Seven against Thebes*: Colbeaux 2005:254.

ερόντων ἐν τῇ Κύμῃ ὁ Μελησιγένης τὰ ἔπεα τὰ
. ἐν τοῖς λόγοις ἔτερπε τοὺς ἀκούοντας· καὶ αὐτοῦ
δὲ ὅτι **ἀποδέκονται** αὐτοῦ τὴν **ποίησιν** οἱ Κυμαῖοι
οντας, ...

the meeting places [*leskhai*] of the elders in Cyme
rses [*epos*, plural] **made** [*poieîn*] by him. With his
ences [*akouontes*]. And they became his **admirers**
the people of Cyme **accepted** [*apodekhesthai*] his
ng [*helkein*] his audiences into a **state of familiar-**

Vita 1.141–46

me precious indications of performer-audience
me, Homer is said to have 'performed' (*epideik-*
verses or *epē* (*epos*, plural) that he had 'made'
(*akouontes*) him perform, 'accepted' (*apodekhe-*
'acceptance' or reception by the audience is cor-
(*sunētheia*) to the songmaking; this familiarization
er's drawing power or attraction.[21] The reception
hat his audiences in Cyme became overall *thau-*
ater point, we will examine further this particu-
ception.

hich I will have more to say later, Homer moves
overished and dependent on the subsidy of pa-
man called Thestorides, who turns out to be a rise profession is initially described as the teach-
s (195), makes Homer an offer: Homer will be
the condition that he agrees to two things de-
torides will be allowed to possess written copies
that Homer has 'made' (*poieîn*) and is 'making'
gree to 'attribute' (*anapherein*) these verses to
art of the narrative:

ῶν ἐπέων **ἀναγράψασθαι** καὶ ἄλλα **ποιῶν** πρὸς

mer is called *Melēsigenēs*. I save for later my analysis of the
from *Melēsigenēs* to *Homēros*.
nherent in the word *apodekhesthai* 'accept', see *PH* 8§4 (= pp.
t *sunēthia* in the sense 'habituation to anomalies'.
to what I published in Nagy 2004e on the story of Thestorides
see Cassio 2003, whose interpretations differ from mine.

... [and if Homer would allow] a **writing up** [*ana-graphesthai*] of the verses [*epos*, plural] of his that he had **made** [*poieîn*] and of other verses that he was about to **make** [*poieîn*] and attribute them to him ['Thestorides] always ...

Vita 1.198–200

In the logic of the wording in this passage, Homer's own act of composing—past, present, and future—does not depend on someone else's act of writing down his compositions.

Having accepted the deal offered by Thestorides, Homer stays in Phocaea and 'makes' the *Little Iliad* and the *Phokais*, while Thestorides has it all written down:

διατρίβων δὲ παρὰ τῷ Θεστορίδῃ **ποιεῖ** Ἰλιάδα τὴν ἐλάσσω, ἧς ἡ ἀρχή

Ἴλιον ἀείδω καὶ Δαρδανίην εὔπωλον,
ἧς πέρι πολλὰ πάθον Δαναοί, θεράποντες Ἄρηος·

καὶ τὴν καλουμένην Φωκαΐδα, ἥν φασιν οἱ Φωκαεῖς Ὅμηρον παρ' αὐτοῖσι **ποιῆσαι**. ἐπεὶ δὲ τήν τε Φωκαΐδα καὶ τἆλλα πάντα παρὰ τοῦ Ὁμήρου ὁ Θεστορίδης **ἐγράψατο**, διενοήθη ἐκ τῆς Φωκαίης ἀπαλλάσσεσθαι, τὴν **ποίησιν** θέλων τοῦ Ὁμήρου ἐξιδιώσασθαι

Spending his time in the house of Thestorides, he [Homer] **made** [*poieîn*] the *Little Iliad* [literally, the '*Smaller Iliad*'], which begins this way:

I sing Troy and the land of the Dardanoi, famed for horses.
Many things for the sake of this land did the Danaoi suffer, those attendants [*therapōn*, plural] of Ares.[23]

He [Homer] also made the so-called *Phokais*, which the people of Phocaea say Homer had **made** [*poieîn*] in their city. And when Thestorides had the *Phokais* and all his [Homer's] other things **written down** [*graphesthai*] from Homer, he ['Thestorides] made plans to depart from Phocaea, wishing to appropriate the **songmaking** [*poiēsis*] of Homer.

Vita 1.202–10

I note that the narrative treats the act of Homer's 'making' (*poieîn*) and Thestorides' 'writing down' (*graphesthai*) as separate events. Then, as we saw in the passage just quoted, Thestorides sails away from Phocaea. The narrative makes explicit the motive for this action: Thestorides intends to appropriate the poetry of Homer by performing it somewhere else, in the absence of Homer. But Homer refuses to let himself become an *absent author,* as we are about to see.

In the narrative that ensues (*Vita* 1.210 and following), Thestorides sails from Phocaea to the island of Chios, where he goes about performing (*epideiknunai* 1.215, 222) the verses or *epē* (*epos*, plural) of Homer as if they were his own. Meanwhile,

23. The generic warrior, by virtue of being the *therapōn* 'attendant' of Ares, is also his 'ritual substitute': see *BA* 2§8 (= p. 32), 17§§3–6 (= pp. 291–95).

ἐπ' ἐμοῦ τὸν χῶρον ἐν ᾧ κατίζων τῶν ἐπέων τὴν
] οντο τὸν τόπον.

the people of Neon Teikhos used to show off the
and **make** [*poieîn*] performance [*epideixis*] of his
ed greatly this site.[17]

Vita 1.119–22

formally performs his compositions by 'making'
is 'performance'. Here we see that the act of per-
is something that can be 'made'. It is not just the
In the narrative logic of *Vita* 1, the 'making' of
of two processes, composition and performance.
epigrams is a matter of performance:

τι καὶ νῦν ἐπὶ τῆς στήλης τοῦ μνήματος τοῦ Γορδίεω

his **epigram** [*epigramma*], which even to this day is
] on the stele of the memorial of the man from Gor-

Vita 1.133–34

ct of 'making' an epigram, to be inscribed on the
This report about the Midas Epigram of Homer is
a tradition native to the Aeolian city of Cyme (*Vita*
er and Hesiod as well (*Vita* 2.261–64), we will see
aking' the poem that becomes the Midas Epigram.[19]
erformative aspects of both these references con-
grams. For now, however, I will simply follow the
ntinuing where we left off. In the next passage to be
g in the Aeolian city of Cyme:

ce that had made direct contact with Homer himself is charac-
hero, see *BA* 17§9n3 (= p. 297), citing Brelich 1958:320–21; see
named after Homer in Chios, Smyrna, and Delos. Strabo 14.1.37
myrna on Homer; he notes that the Smyrnaeans in his time have
called the *Homēreion*, containing a *neōs* 'shrine' of Homer and a

naean traditions will be explored further below.
er's Midas Epigram as told in *Vita* 1 (131–40), Homer is com-
ile he is a resident of Cyme. According to *Vita* 2 (261–64), on the
ns sometime after the Contest of Homer and Hesiod in Chalkis.
sequence of events in Homer's life as retold in *Vita* 1.

back in Phocaea, Homer finds out about this misappropriation and angrily resolves to make every effort to travel to Chios in order to set things straight (1.224–25). He lives through many adventures while trying to make his way to Chios (1.225–75). After finally arriving on the island (1.275–76), Homer 'makes' (*poieîn*) new poems there (1.335). Thestorides hears about the presence of the composer and, to avoid being exposed as a pseudo-Homer—that is, as an unauthorized performer who claims the compositions of Homer—he abruptly leaves Chios (1.336–38). Throughout this narrative, the scripted performances of Thestorides are being contrasted with the unscripted compositions of Homer. Also, Thestorides is described as a teacher of *grammata* 'letters' (1.185, 223), whereas Homer becomes, once he is finally established in the city of Chios, a teacher of *epē* 'verses' (*epos*, plural; 1.341).

This distinction between a teacher of *epē* 'verses' (*epos*, plural) and a teacher of *grammata* 'letters' seems to elevate Homer from his former status as teacher of *grammata* in Smyrna—a status he inherits from Phemios in *Vita* 1.50–52, as we saw previously. This is not to say, however, that the word *grammata* implies, in and of itself, a distinction between *written* and *oral*. As we also saw previously (1.37–38), even the undifferentiated usage of *grammata* includes the performing arts, *mousikē*. In *Vita* 2 as well, we will see that Homer himself is again described as a teacher of *grammata* (2.16).

In this whole story of Homer in Phocaea, it is essential to note that the scripted performances of Thestorides are all unauthorized by Homer, and only the unscripted performances of the genuine composer are authorized.[24]

At this point the narrative lists the poetic activities of Homer while he is living in the countryside of the island of Chios:

καὶ τοὺς Κέρκωπας καὶ Βατραχομυομαχίαν καὶ Ψαρομαχίην καὶ Ἑπταπακτικὴν καὶ Ἐπικιχλίδας καὶ τἄλλα πάντα ὅσα παίγνιά ἐστιν Ὁμήρου ἐνταῦθα **ἐποίησε** παρὰ τῷ Χίῳ ἐν Βολισσῷ.

And he [Homer] **made** [*poieîn*] there, in the house of the man from Chios, at Bolissos [on the island of Chios], the following: *Kerkopes*, the *Battle of Frogs and Mice*, the *Psaromakhia*, *Heptapaktikē*, the *Epikikhlides*, and all the other playful verses of Homer.

Vita 1.332–35

I draw attention to some details in the context of this passage: Homer is now on the island Chios in the house of someone called 'the man from Chios', and he is 'making' (*poieîn*) these playful poems in the countryside, before he moves to the city of Chios. The rustic compositions listed in this passage are the poems that initially establish Homer's reputation on the island, and it is the news of these rustic poems that force Thestorides to flee from the city of Chios and from the island altogether (1.336–38).

24. More below on Thestorides as the purported author of the *Little Iliad*.

After his stay in the countryside of Chios, Homer moves to the city of Chios and becomes established there. His reception is conveyed by way of an expression we have already seen in an analogous context: Homer's audiences throughout Chios become overall *thaumastai* 'admirers' of his (*Vita* 1.342). Later on, I will have more to say about this way of referring to Homeric reception.

While he stays in the city of Chios, Homer is composing the *Odyssey*:

... ποιήσας Ὀδυσσέα ὡς ἐς Τροίην ἔπλεε Μέντορι ἐπιτρέψαι τὸν οἶκον ὡς ἐόντι Ἰθακησίων ἀρίστῳ καὶ δικαιοτάτῳ ...

... [Homer,] having **made** [*poiein*][25] it happen that Odysseus, at the time when he was sailing off to Troy, placed Mentor in charge of his household, since he [Mentor] was the best and most righteous man among the people of Ithaca ...

Vita 1.350–52

In this description of Homer composing the *Odyssey* in Chios (*Vita* 1.347), the poet is described as 'making' (*poiein*) special things take place inside the epic plot of the *Odyssey*. For example, Homer 'fits' (*en-harmozein*) into his 'songmaking' (*poiēsis*, Vita 1.349) the name of his own friend Mentor, and thus he 'makes' (*poiein*) it happen that Odysseus places Mentor in charge of the hero's household (1.350–352).

Still in the city of Chios, Homer is described as composing the 'big' *Iliad*:

ἐμποιεῖ ἐς τὴν **ποίησιν**, ἐς μὲν Ἰλιάδα τὴν μεγάλην Ἐρεχθέα μεγαλύνων ἐν νεῶν καταλόγῳ τὰ ἔπεα τάδε

δῆμον Ἐρεχθῆος μεγαλήτορος, ὅν ποτ' Ἀθήνη
θρέψε Διὸς θυγάτηρ, τέκε δὲ ζείδωρος ἄρουρα. [*Iliad* II 547–48]

καὶ τὸν στρατηγὸν αὐτῶν Μενεσθέα **αἰνέσας** ...

He [Homer] **made** [-**poiein** of en-**poiein**] the following verses [*epos*, plural][26] **fit in-side** [*en*- of en-**poiein**] his **songmaking** [*poiēsis*]. Inside the big *Iliad*, glorifying Erekhtheus in the Catalogue of Ships, he made these verses [*epos*, plural]:

the district [*dēmos*] of Erekhtheus, the one with the great heart; him did
    Athena once upon a time
nurture, she who is the daughter of Zeus, but the life-giving earth gave birth
    to him. [*Iliad* II 547–48]

---

25. I draw attention to a detail in the syntax of *Vita* 1.350–52: the verb *poiein* here takes an accusative-plus-infinitive construction, meaning 'make it happen that'. This kind of usage, where Homer 'makes' (*poiein*) it happen that characters should do or be what he wants them to do or be in the plot of the narrative, is attested also in Plato (*Theaetetus* 149a, etc.).

26. The 'following verses' include passages from both the *Iliad* and the *Odyssey*. The extract I am quoting here gives only the verses quoted from the *Iliad*.

He [Homer] also **praised** [*aineîn*] their [the Athenians'] general, Menestheus.[27]

Vita 1.379–84

In this passage describing Homer as composing the 'big' *Iliad*, he is 'making' (*poieîn*) special things take place inside the epic plot of the *Iliad*. Specifically, Homer 'makes' the *epē* 'verses' (*epos*, plural) about Erekhtheus and Athens take place inside the *Iliad*; also he 'makes' verses about the leader of the Athenians, Menestheus, thereby glorifying or 'praising' him as well.[28]

At this point, the narrative surveys the achievements of Homer so far:

Ἀπὸ δὲ τῆς **ποιήσεως** ταύτης εὐδοκιμεῖ Ὅμηρος περί τε τὴν Ἰωνίην καὶ ἐς τὴν Ἑλλάδα ἤδη περὶ αὐτοῦ λόγος ἀνεφέρετο· κατοικέων δὲ ἐν τῇ Χίῳ καὶ εὐδοκιμέων περὶ τὴν **ποίησιν**, ἀπικνεομένων πολλῶν πρὸς αὐτόν, συνεβούλευον οἱ ἐντυγχάνοντες αὐτῷ ἐς τὴν Ἑλλάδα ἀπικέσθαι.

From this **songmaking** [*poiēsis*] Homer achieved genuine fame around Ionia, and there was already talk about him that was making its way into Hellas. While he kept on maintaining his home in Chios and having genuine fame for his **songmaking** [*poiēsis*], many people came to visit [*aphikneîsthai*] him.[29] Upon encountering him, people kept on advising him to visit Hellas.

Vita 1.372–76

As a consequence of Homer's *poiēsis* 'songmaking'—and here *poiēsis* refers cumulatively to all the instances of Homer's 'making' (*poieîn*) of verses just narrated—Homer's fame in Ionia has already become widespread. At this point in the narrative, Homer is still in Chios. Only now does the narrative finally introduce the theme of Homer's traveling to the mainland of Hellas. And yet, though Homer is described as by now eager to make a tour of all Hellas (*Vita* 1.376–77), he implicitly stays in Chios for a longer period as he continues to make verses that center on the glorification of Athens (1.378–99). The word that refers to Homer's 'making' of verses continues to be *poieîn*:

27. After quoting these *epē* 'verses' (*epos*, plural) from the *Iliad*, the narrative goes on to quote *epē* 'verses' that Homer *en-poieî* 'makes inside' the *Odyssey*, which I do not include here in this extract.

28. On *aineîn/epaineîn* 'praise' as a rhapsodic equivalent of 'perform', see PR 27–28; also pp. 11, 33, 44. The actual 'praise' of Homer is both subjective (Homer as *laudator*) and objective (Homer as *laudandus*). On the objective praise of Homer, see especially *Vita* 2.205–6, where all the Hellenes 'praise' (*epaineîn*) Homer for his performance.

29. Here and elsewhere, the idea of 'come to visit' (*aphikneîsthai*) implies the idea of 'come as an audience'. See also *Vita* 1.55–57: καὶ αὐτοῦ θωυμασταὶ καθειστήκεισαν οἵ τε ἐγχώριοι καὶ τῶν ξένων οἱ ἐσαπικνεόμενοι 'they became his **admirers** [*thaumastai*]—both the local people [the people of Smyrna] and people from other cities who came visiting'. I will have more to say later about the idea of *thaumastai* 'admirers' of Homer.

ἐς δὲ τὴν Ὀδυσσείην τάδε **ἐποίησεν** . . .

inside the *Odyssey* he **made** [*poieîn*] these verses . . .

Vita 1.394

. . . **ἐμποιήσας** δὲ ἐς τὴν **ποίησιν** ταῦτα . . .

. . . having **made** [*poieîn*] these verses take place inside [*en-* of *en-poieîn*][30] his **song-making** [*poiēsis*] . . .

Vita 1.399

With the telling of these two further contexts, Homer has at long last finished his glorification of Athens by way of 'making' (*poieîn*) verses. He can now finally leave Chios and set sail to tour the rest of Hellas (*Vita* 1.400), and he arrives at the island of Samos as a transitional stopover (1.401).[31]

Up to now, the narrative of *Vita* 1 has maintained the status of Chios as a definitive setting for Homer's glorification of Athens. As I will show later on, this association of Chios and Athens in *Vita* 1 reflects, however indirectly, the worldview of the Athenian empire.

Now I turn to the last remaining example of *poieîn* in *Vita* 1:

Ὅτι δὲ ἦν Αἰολεὺς Ὅμηρος καὶ οὔτε Ἴων οὔτε Δωριεύς, τοῖς τε εἰρημένοις δεδήλωταί μοι καὶ δὴ καὶ τοῖσδε τεκμαίρεσθαι παρέχει. ἄνδρα **ποιητὴν** τηλικοῦτον εἰκός ἐστι τῶν νομίμων τῶν παρὰ τοῖς ἀνθρώποις **ποιοῦντα** ἐς τὴν **ποίησιν** ἤτοι τὰ κάλλιστα ἐξευρόντα **ποιέειν** ἢ τὰ ἑωυτοῦ, πάτρια ἐόντα.

That Homer was an Aeolian and not an Ionian nor a Dorian is demonstrated by what has been said so far, and it can be proved even more decisively by way of the following: it is likely that a **songmaker** [*poiētēs*] who is of such ancient pedigree, and who draws upon ancestral customs prevalent among humans, would be **making** [*poieîn*] things take place inside his **songmaking** [*poiēsis*] that were either the most beautiful things he could ever **make** [*poieîn*] with his poetic invention or his very own things as he inherited them from his ancestors.

Vita 1.517–22

In the previous contexts of *poieîn* that we have examined up to this point, we have seen various aetiologies explaining various aspects of the Homeric tradition. Now, in this last example taken from *Vita* 1, we see an aetiology that is meant to explain the whole tradition. I draw attention to the fact that this aetiology specifies an Aeolic rather than Ionic genealogy for Homer. As we will see later on, this specification reflects the pre-Athenocentric outlook of *Vita* 1.

---

30. Previously, we saw an example of *epē* 'verses' (*epos*, plural) that Homer *en-poieî* 'makes inside' the *Iliad*.

31. I find it significant that the narrative places Samos as the point of transition for Homer's journey to areas of Homeric reception that extend beyond Asia Minor. See further below.

Having now finished with *Vita* 1 (the *Herodotean* Life), I turn to *Vita* 2 (the *Certamen*). I start with this overall description of Homer's activities in Asia Minor:

ποιήσαντα γὰρ τὸν Μαργίτην Ὅμηρον περιέρχεσθαι κατὰ πόλιν ῥαψῳδοῦντα.

Having made [*poieîn*] the *Margites*, Homer went wandering around [*perierkhesthai*] from city to city, performing in the manner of *rhapsodes* [*rhapsōidên*].[32]

Vita 2.55–56

The narrative here picks up where a previous phase of the narrative in *Vita* 2 (15–17) had left off. There, in the previous phase, it is said that Homer started his career of 'poetry' (*poiēsis*, 2.17) in Colophon (2.15), having 'made' (*poieîn*, 2.17) the *Margites*; here, in the present phase, it is said that Homer, having 'made' (*poieîn*, 2.55) the *Margites* in Colophon, now goes wandering around other cities, performing poetry wherever he goes (2.55–56). The wording is compressed and elliptic: it is not specified what poem Homer performs in what city. I render the expression Ὅμηρον περιέρχεσθαι κατὰ πόλιν (2.55–56) not as 'Homer went wandering all around the city' (of Colophon) but as 'Homer went wandering around from city to city', having left the city of Colophon, where he had 'made' the *Margites*. I will justify this interpretation as my argumentation proceeds.

In its elliptic reference to Homer's poetic tour of multiple cities starting with Colophon in Asia Minor, the narrative of *Vita* 2 abruptly switches to the mainland of Hellas, to which I will refer, in a shorthand, as the Helladic mainland. Suddenly we find Homer at Aulis, in Boeotia (2.54–55). Aulis is said to be the setting for a competition between Homer and Hesiod (2.54–55); later on, the setting is said to be Chalkis, in Euboea (2.68).

The act of Homeric composition, as signaled by the word *poieîn* 'make' (*Vita* 2.55) in the elliptic passage that refers, as I argue, to Homer's poetic tour of multiple cities starting with Colophon in Asia Minor, is syntactically correlated with the act of Homeric performance, as signaled by the word *rhapsōidên* 'perform in the manner of rhapsodes' (2.56) in the same passage. There are multiple performances to follow in multiple cities on the Helladic mainland. The same word *rhapsōidên* recurs in a later part of the narrative, where Homer is shown performing his *poiēmata* 'poetic creations' in Corinth (2.286).

In terms of the overall narrative structure of *Vita* 2, the critical moment in Homer's biography is his contest or *Certamen* with Hesiod. After he is defeated by Hesiod (2.254–55), Homer goes on with his life as a wandering performer: περιερχόμενος ἔλεγε τὰ ποιήματα 'as he went wandering around [*perierkhesthai*], he was telling his poetic creations [*poiēmata*]' (2.255). The wording here is parallel to the

---

32. On Homer as the author of the mock epic *Margites*, the prime testimony is that of Aristotle *Poetics* 1448b30.

wording in the previous part of the narrative, as I quoted it earlier: ποιήσαντα γὰρ τὸν Μαργίτην Ὅμηρον περιέρχεσθαι κατὰ πόλιν ῥαψῳδοῦντα 'having made [*poieîn*] the *Margites*, Homer went wandering around [*perierkhesthai*] from city to city, performing in the manner of rhapsodes [*rhapsōideîn*]' (2.55–56). Of special relevance is Plato's passing reference to the myth of the *Certamen*: both Homer and Hesiod are pictured as 'performing in the manner of rhapsodes' (*rhapsōideîn*) as they 'go wandering around' (*perierkhesthai*) from city to city (Plato *Republic* 10.600d–e ῥαψῳδεῖν . . . περιιόντας).

Previously, we saw that Homer's wanderings had taken him from Colophon to a variety of other stops. The first stop to be mentioned is Aulis, in Boeotia. Although the text of *Vita* 2 names Aulis as the setting for Homer's contest with Hesiod at the start of *Vita* 2 (54–56), the setting shifts at a later part of the narrative to Chalkis, in Euboea (2.68). Whether or not we are dealing here with a conflation of two distinct versions is immaterial. After the contest with Hesiod, the next stop for Homer seems to be Thebes, in Boeotia. At least, the narrative of *Vita* 2 implies that Homer goes to Thebes at this point: after the *Margites* in Colophon, the next Homeric composition to be mentioned by name in the narrative is the *Thebaid* (2.255–57), followed by the *Epigonoi* (2.258–60). Since Aulis is described as belonging to Boeotia (2.54–55), this description may be the sign of a narrative connection with Boeotian Thebes.

The next Homeric composition to be mentioned is the Midas Epigram. Homer is commissioned by the sons of Midas to compose an epigram for the dead king of Phrygia (2.260–70). I draw attention to the wording:

οἱ Μίδου τοῦ βασιλέως παῖδες Ξάνθος καὶ Γόργος παρακαλοῦσιν αὐτὸν **ἐπίγραμμα ποιῆσαι** ἐπὶ τοῦ τάφου τοῦ πατρὸς αὐτῶν, ἐφ' οὗ ἦν παρθένος χαλκῆ τὸν Μίδου θάνατον οἰκτιζομένη. καὶ **ποιεῖ** οὕτως . . .

The sons of King Midas, Xanthos and Gorgos, invited him [Homer] to **make** [*poieîn*] an **epigram** [*epigramma*] on the tomb of their father, on top of which was a bronze maiden lamenting the death of Midas. And he [Homer] **made** [*poieîn*] it [the epigram] thus . . .

Vita 2.261–64

In *Vita* 2, this epigram is connected with another epigram, which in turn connects the *Life of Homer* to the cultural and political interests of the city-state of Athens. The point of entry for this connection is Apollo's Delphi:

λαβὼν δὲ παρ' αὐτῶν φιάλην ἀργυρᾶν ἀνατίθησιν ἐν Δελφοῖς τῷ Ἀπόλλωνι, ἐπιγράψας . . .

Φοῖβε ἄναξ δῶρόν τοι Ὅμηρος καλὸν ἔδωκα
σῇσιν ἐπιφροσύναις· σὺ δέ μοι κλέος αἰὲν ὀπάζοις.

Receiving from them [the sons of Midas] a silver *phialē*, he [Homer] dedicated it in Delphi to Apollo, **writing an epigram** [*epigraphein*] on it . . .

> Lord Phoebus! I, Homer, have given you a beautiful gift,
> with the help of your impulses of wisdom [*epiphrosunai*].[33] And may you
> grant [*opazein*][34] me fame [*kleos*] forever.

> *Vita* 2.271–74

Homer's visit to Delphi is handled differently at an earlier point in the text of *Vita* 2: there it is implied that Homer goes to Delphi sometime before his contest with Hesiod at Aulis, in Boeotia (2.56–58). But here, in the part of *Vita* 2 I just quoted, Homer goes to Delphi sometime after his contest with Hesiod at Chalkis, in Euboea. After Chalkis, the first place Homer visits seems to be Thebes, as we have already seen (2.255–99); then, after Thebes, he composes the Midas Epigram in honor of the late king of Phrygia (2.260–71); then, after being rewarded with a silver *phialē* that he won as compensation for the Midas Epigram, he goes to Delphi, where he dedicates the silver *phialē* to Apollo after composing the Delphi Epigram that he inscribes on the *phialē* (2.271–74).[35]

Homer's production of this epigram in Apollo's Delphi marks the narrative point of transition to his authorization as the master poet of the Homeric *Iliad* and *Odyssey*:

μετὰ δὲ ταῦτα **ποιεῖ** τὴν Ὀδύσσειαν ἔπη μ,β′, **πεποιηκὼς** ἤδη τὴν Ἰλιάδα ἐπῶν μ,εφ′.

After this [after making the Delphi Epigram] he [Homer] **made [*poieîn*]** the *Odyssey*, 12,000 verses, having already **made [*poieîn*]** the *Iliad*, consisting of 15,500 verses.

> *Vita* 2.275

In the sequence of the last three events we have just seen, the logic of the narrative is clarified. One event is Homer's 'making' of the Midas Epigram, where the act of poetic creation is made explicit by way of the verb *poieîn*. The second event is Homer's 'making' of the Delphi Epigram, where the act of poetic creation is not made explicit. And the third event is Homer's 'making' of the *Iliad* and *Odyssey* combined, where the act of poetic creation is once again made explicit by way of the verb *poieîn*.

The reference to Homer's 'making' of the *Iliad* and *Odyssey* combined is essentially a reference to the Panathenaic Homer—that is, to the Homer of the Athenians. As I have argued, the performance of this combination of epics was perceived as a distinctly Athenian institution. So it is significant that the narrative mentions the *Iliad* and *Odyssey* at precisely the moment when Homer comes to Athens. In other words, the narrative waits till the point where Homer comes to Athens before it shows him in the act of composing something that corresponds to Homer as he is actually known in Athens. And the signature, as it were, for this point in

33. In *Odyssey* v 437 there is a comparable context of *epiphrosunē* in the sense of an 'impulse of wisdom' that is given to a mortal by a helping divinity.

34. The usage here of *opazein* 'grant' is comparable to what we see in the coda of a hymnic *prooimion*, as in *Homeric Hymn* (31) *to Helios* 17. More on this later.

35. According to *Vita* 3a.61–62, by contrast, Homer goes from Delphi to Thebes.

the narration is Homer's Delphi Epigram, which is Homer's point of departure as he heads for Athens. As we have seen, Homer personally dedicates this epigram to Apollo at Delphi, and it is this action in the narrative sequence that leads to his coming 'from there' to Athens (*Vita* 2.276–77 παραγενόμενον δὲ ἐκεῖθεν εἰς Ἀθήνας).

Unfortunately for us, the narrative of *Vita* 2 fails to give any further details about the circumstances of Homer's 'making' of the *Iliad* and *Odyssey*. (There is only one exception, which concerns something that seems obvious in terms of the internal logic of the overall narrative: it is said explicitly that the *Iliad* was 'made' before the *Odyssey*—though the narrative fails once again to give any further details.) But at least the narrative succeeds in being consequential about one single overriding idea: that Homer's arrival in Athens must be preceded by Homer's 'making' of the *Iliad* and *Odyssey* combined.

By now I have examined every example of *poieîn* 'make' with reference to the life of Homer as narrated in *Vita* 2—except for the very last example. Before I turn to that example, I need to summarize the overall narrative sequence of *Vita* 2:

A. Homer starts his career of poetry in Colophon (2.15), having 'made' (*poieîn*) the *Margites* (2.17).

B. Having 'made' (*poieîn*) the *Margites* in Colophon, he now goes wandering around other cities, performing poetry wherever he goes (2.55–56).

C1. He goes to Aulis, in Boeotia (2.54–55). At Aulis he competes with Hesiod (2.54–55).

C2. Alternatively, he goes to Chalkis, in Euboea (2.68), where he competes with Hesiod and is defeated by him (2.68–211).

D. He now goes wandering around other cities, performing poetry wherever he goes (2.255).

E. He performs the epic called the *Thebaid* (2.255–57) and the epic called the *Epigonoi* (2.258–60). The venue seems to be Thebes.

F. He 'makes' (*poieîn*) the Midas Epigram (2.260–70). The venue seems to be Phrygia, though the narrative does not specify that Homer actually went there.

G. He goes to Delphi, taking with him the *phialē* he had received as compensation for 'making' the Midas Epigram, and he dedicates it, having composed his Delphi Epigram to be inscribed on it (2.270–74).

H. He 'makes' (*poieîn*) the *Odyssey*, having already 'made' (*poieîn*) the *Iliad* (2.275–76).

I. He goes from Delphi ('from there') to Athens, where he performs a riddle as he enters the building of the city council or *bouleutērion* (2.276–85).[36]

---

36. I note that Homer's songmaking here is described as 'improvisation' (σχεδιάσαι, *Vita* 2.279). We may compare the setting of Homer's performing his riddle in Athens, the *bouleutērion*, with the setting

J. He goes to Corinth, where he 'performs in the mode of a rhapsode' (*rhapsōideîn*) his 'poetic creations' (*poiēmata*) (2.286–87 ἐκεῖθεν δὲ παραγενόμενος εἰς Κόρινθον ἐρραψῴδει τὰ ποιήματα).

K. He goes to Argos (2.287–315), where he 'speaks' (*legein*)[37] verses that are taken from the *Iliad* (2.288 καὶ λέγει ἐκ τῆς Ἰλιάδος τὰ ἔπη τάδε).

L. After staying a while in Argos, he sails over to Delos (2.315–22), where he 'speaks' (*legein*)[38] the *Homeric Hymn to Apollo* (2.317 λέγει ὕμνον εἰς Ἀπόλλωνα).

M. After being celebrated in Delos with special honors that compensate him for his songmaking, Homer goes to the island of Ios, where he fails to understand a riddle and dies in a fit of depression (2.322–38)—but not before he 'makes' (*poieîn*) an epigram for his own tomb. In the passage that tells about Homer's composition of this epigram, we see the last attestation of *poieîn* 'make' with reference to the life of Homer as narrated in *Vita 2*:

... ποιεῖ τὸ τοῦ τάφου αὐτοῦ ἐπίγραμμα.

... he [Homer] **made** [*poieîn*] his own tomb's **epigram** [*epigramma*].

Vita 2.333

With this passage, we come to the end of my inventory of nineteen passages showing forms of either *poieîn* 'make' or *graphein* 'write' with reference to the making of poetry by Homer. I conclude that the word *poieîn* 'make' is the standard term for referring to Homeric composition in both the pre-Athenocentric and the Athenocentric phase of the *Lives of Homer*. What Homer 'makes' in these *Lives* is not limited, however, to epic. As we saw in both *Vita 1* (133–34) and *Vita 2* (261–64), Homer also *poieî* 'makes' what is known as the Midas Epigram. These two references, then, show most clearly that 'writing', *graphein*, is not a prerequisite for the composing of an epigram by Homer. In both references, the 'writing down' of the epigram is not being connected directly with the actual composition of the epigram. From the standpoint of the pre-Athenocentric and the Athenocentric periods of Homeric reception, then, the physical process of inscribing the epigram is viewed as independent of the mental process of Homer's 'making' (*poieîn*) the poem.[39]

---

of Homer's performing his corresponding riddle in Samos, the *phrētrē* (*Vita 1.421*). As we will see later, the *phrētrē* is the place where the *phrētores* of Samos hold their meetings.

37. I note the use of *legein* here in the sense 'perform poetry'.

38. Again I note the use of *legein* here in the sense 'perform poetry'.

39. On the conceptual separation of mentally composing an epigram and physically inscribing it, I refer again to my remarks at the beginning of Part I.

HOMER THE EPIGRAMMATIST

I draw attention to the highlighting of Apollo at two opposite ends of the narrative sequence in the narrative of *Vita* 2. At both ends, the highlighting is achieved by way of a Homeric epigram. At one end, Homer leaves his signature, as it were, in Apollo's Delphi as the author of the Delphi Epigram (2.271–74). It is at this point that the narrative makes its transition to Homer's composition of the *Iliad* and *Odyssey* in their entirety (2.275). Then, toward the other end of the narrative, Homer leaves his signature in Apollo's Delos as the author of the *Homeric Hymn to Apollo* (2.315–22). And then, at the very end, he leaves his last signature on the Ionian island of Ios, in his capacity as the author of his own Homer Epigram (2.333). In what follows, I have more to say about this Homer Epigram.

In the *Lives of Homer*, we find two passages where it is said explicitly that Homer composed an epigram for his own tomb on the island of Ios, and that the epigram was inscribed on the tomb only after he died (*Vitae* 2.333 and 5.48–49). And the wording of the epigram of Homer for his own tomb, as given in *Vita* 1 (515–16) and *Vita* 2 (337–38; also at *Vitae* 3a.73–74, 4.24–25, 5.51–52, 6.63–64, 10.54–55 and 220–21), is also attested in the *Greek Anthology* (7.3).

Similarly, the epigram of Homer for the tomb of Midas, as given in *Vita* 1 (135–40) and *Vita* 2 (265–70), is also attested in the *Greek Anthology* (7.153).[40] In this case, however, the attribution to Homer is merely a variant: as the title of the epigram in the *Greek Anthology* (7.153) makes clear, the composition is attributed either to Homer or to Kleoboulos of Lindos. Among the sources that attribute the authorship of the epigram to Kleoboulos rather than Homer is Simonides (*PMG* 581; Diogenes Laertius 1.89). Such alternative attributions reflect an outlook that tends to restrict Homer to the authorship of epics, excluding epigrams. As my argumentation progresses, I will have more to say about such a pattern of restriction, which becomes intensified with the passage of time.

HOMER'S RECEPTION IN PERFORMANCE

As we have seen so far in the *Life of Homer* traditions, the Poet's compositions come to life in performance, not in writing. The story of Homeric reception is the story of the ways in which Homer's audiences respond to his performances. For a premier example, I return to the description of Homer's reception at Cyme: καὶ αὐτοῦ θωυμασταὶ καθεἰστήκεσαν 'they [the people of Cyme] became his admirers [*thaumastai*]' (*Vita* 1.143–44). The wording here needs to be compared with the wording that describes Homer's earlier reception in the city of Smyrna: καὶ αὐτοῦ θωυμασταὶ καθεἱστήκεισαν οἵ τε ἐγχώριοι καὶ τῶν ξένων οἱ ἐσαπικνεόμενοι 'they became his

---

40. See also the other sources as listed by Allen 1912:198 at lines 135–40.

admirers [*thaumastai*]—both the local people [the people of Smyrna] and people
from other cities who came visiting' (1.55–57). In the second case, Homer's reception by the local population is viewed in tandem with his reception by audiences
from out of town. (The narrative then goes on to explain that Smyrna, as a busy sea-
port, attracted all kinds of visitors.) In the city of Cyme, the context of performance
is ἐν ταῖς λέσχαις τῶν γερόντων 'at gatherings of elders' (1.142). What Homer does
not receive in the city-state of Cyme is formal subsidy from the state (the expression
for such state subsidy is δημοσίῃ τρέφειν 1.47).[41] As for Smyrna, the contexts of performance are explicitly informal: οἱ οὖν ξένοι, ὁκότε παύσοιντο τῶν ἔργων, ἀπεσχό-
λαζον παρὰ τῷ Μελησιγένει ἐγκαθίζοντες 'visitors from out of town, whenever they
were done with work, would spend their free time sitting [and listening] at the place
of *Melēsigenēs* [Homer]' (1.59–60).[42] In Neon Teikhos, Homer performs an epic about
the deeds of Amphiaraos in the war against Thebes (1.113) and 'the hymns [*humnoi*] to the gods that he [Homer] had composed [*poieîn*]' (1.113–14); following up
on these performances, he displays his poetic learning by responding to anything
his audiences wanted to say, thus earning their admiration: καὶ περὶ τῶν λεγομένων
ὑπὸ τῶν παρεόντων ἐς τὸ μέσον γνώμας ἀποφαινόμενος θαύματος ἄξιος ἐφαίνετο
εἶναι τοῖς ἀκούουσι 'by commenting in public concerning what was said by those
attending his performances, he appeared to his listeners as someone most worthy of
admiration [*thauma*]' (1.114–16).[43] On the island of Chios, before he enters the city
of Chios, Homer as performer is 'held in admiration [*thauma*]' by the rustic herdsman Glaukos: ἐν θωύματι εἶχεν αὐτόν (1.309–10).[44] In the city of Chios, once he is
established as a teacher of *epē* 'verses' (*epos*, plural), Homer's reception is described
this way: καὶ πολλοὶ θαυμασταὶ αὐτοῦ καθεστήκεσαν 'and many became his admirers [*thaumastai*]' (1.342–43). In Samos, Homer's reception gets the same sort of
description: in the building of the Samian *phrētrē* 'confraternity' where Homer performs his poetry, his listeners 'gave him honor [*timē*] and were in admiration
[*thauma*] of him' (1.431 αὐτὸν ἐτίμων καὶ ἐν θωύματι εἶχον).

41. On the correlation of this detail concerning Homer's lack of complete success in Cyme with the
receding importance of Cyme as a city noted for the reception of Homeric poetry, see above.

42. On the name *Melēsigenēs*, I will have more to say later. Formally, as we have already seen, Homer
in Smyrna does not even embark on a songmaking career until a later time, marked at *Vita* 1.93–94.

43. Homer here is performing what amounts to dialogic commentaries on his performances. For
more on dialogic commentaries, see *HC* ch. 4, where I examine the performances of figures like Hippias
of Elis and Ion of Ephesus.

44. Later on in the narrative (*Vita* 1.312), the herdsman Glaukos as solo audience of Homer is described this way: ἔκπληκτος ἦν ὁ Γλαῦκος ἀκούων 'and, hearing him, he was bedazzled [verb *ek-plēg-*]'.
On *ekplēxis* 'bedazzlement' as the audience's response to Homeric performance, see especially Plato *Ion*
535b, with reference to the effects of the rhapsode's re-enacting scenes of terror, as when Odysseus stands
at the threshold, ready to shoot the suitors, or when Achilles lunges at Hector; also scenes of pity, concerning Andromache, Hecuba, and Priam. See also O'Sullivan 1992:74.

In *Vita* 2, we see references to successful Homeric performance as a way of imagining an absolutized Panhellenic reception: the 'Hellenes' as Homer's audience universally 'admire' (*thaumazein*) him and 'praise' (*epaineîn*) him for his ability to fit his verses into context while he is performing in competition with Hesiod (2.205–6 θαυμάσαντες δὲ καὶ ἐν τούτῳ τὸν Ὅμηρον οἱ Ἕλληνες ἐπῄνουν). Both poets, Homer and Hesiod, competed 'admirably [*thaumastōs*]' (2.70–71 ἀμφοτέρων δὲ τῶν ποιητῶν θαυμαστῶς ἀγωνισαμένων). At a later point, we hear that the 'golden verses' of Homer are approved by all Hellenes: ῥηθέντων δὲ τούτων τῶν ἐπῶν, οὕτω σφοδρῶς φασι θαυμασθῆναι τοὺς στίχους ὑπὸ τῶν Ἑλλήνων ὥστε χρυσοῦς αὐτοὺς προσαγορευθῆναι 'when these verses [*epos,* plural] were spoken [*rēthēnai,* aorist for *legesthai*],[45] it is said that the lines were so intensely admired [*thaumazesthai*] by the Hellenes that they were called golden' (2.90–92).[46]

What immediately follows this detail in *Vita* 2 is a most striking parenthetical remark, which turns out to be central to the preoccupation of all these narratives with the audiences' admiration of Homer-in-performance: καὶ ἔτι καὶ νῦν ἐν ταῖς κοιναῖς θυσίαις πρὸ τῶν δείπνων καὶ σπονδῶν προκατεύχεσθαι πάντας 'and even to this day, everyone makes a preliminary prayer, before feasting and libation, at sacrifices [*thusiai*] that are common [*koinai*] to all' (2.92–94). As I will argue later, these prayers are being made to Homer himself as a cult hero.

I conclude this brief survey of Homeric reception as reported in the *Life of Homer* traditions by signaling the centrality of the word *thusia* 'sacrifice' in the parenthetical remark I just quoted. This word means not only 'sacrifice' but also, metonymically, 'festival'. The use of *thusia* in the sense 'festival' is prominently attested in Plato's *Timaeus* (26e), where the word actually refers to a Panhellenic festival: in this case, the referent is none other than the premier festival of Athens, the Panathenaia.[47] It was on this occasion, at the Feast of the Panathenaia, that the Homeric *Iliad* and *Odyssey* were formally performed in Athens.[48] The use of this word *thusia* in referring to the festival of the Panathenaia will be central to the rest of my overall argumentation.[49]

---

45. Again I note the use of *legein* here in the sense 'perform poetry'.

46. See also θαυμασθῆν[αι] at line 30 of the third-century (B.C.E.) Flinders Petrie Papyrus (Allen 1912:225).

47. *PR* 83. See also *HC* ch. 3.

48. *PR* 9–22. See also *HC* ch. 2 and ch. 3.

49. Relevant is the use of *thuein* 'sacrifice' with reference to the festival of the Heraia at Argos in Herodotus 1.31.5 (*heortē* at 1.31.2, *panēguris* at 1.31.3); also the use of *thusia* 'sacrifice' with reference to the festival sacred to Adrastos at Sikyon in Herodotus 5.67.4 (in collocation with *heortē*).

HOMER AS A MODEL PERFORMER
AT PANHELLENIC FESTIVALS

In the passage I just quoted from *Vita* 2 (92–94), we saw a reference to a custom of praying to Homer in the context of *thusiai* 'sacrifices' that are *koinai* 'common' to all Hellenes. In such a context, the word *thusia* conveys not only the notion of sacrifice but also the notion of a Panhellenic festival that frames a sacrifice. As I will now argue, the figure of Homer in the *Life of Homer* traditions is a personal representative of sacrifices that are *koinai* 'common' to all Hellenes in the context of Panhellenic festivals. A premier example is the use of the word *koinos* 'common' with reference to Homer himself in the context of his performance of the *Homeric Hymn to Apollo* at the Panhellenic festival of the Delia on the island of Delos:

ἐνδιατρίψας δὲ τῇ πόλει χρόνον τινὰ διέπλευσεν εἰς Δῆλον εἰς τὴν **πανήγυριν**. καὶ σταθεὶς ἐπὶ τὸν κεράτινον βωμὸν λέγει **ὕμνον** εἰς Ἀπόλλωνα οὗ ἡ ἀρχή

μνήσομαι οὐδὲ λάθωμαι Ἀπόλλωνος ἑκάτοιο.

ῥηθέντος δὲ τοῦ ὕμνου οἱ μὲν Ἴωνες **πολίτην** αὐτὸν **κοινὸν** ἐποιήσαντο, Δήλιοι δὲ γράψαντες τὰ ἔπη εἰς λεύκωμα ἀνέθηκαν ἐν τῷ τῆς Ἀρτέμιδος ἱερῷ. τῆς δὲ **πανηγύρεως** λυθείσης ὁ ποιητὴς εἰς Ἴον ἔπλευσε πρὸς Κρεώφυλον

After he [Homer] stayed a while in the city [of Argos], he sailed over to Delos to the **festival [*panēguris*]** there. And, standing on the Altar of Horn he speaks the *humnos* to Apollo, the beginning of which is

> I will keep in mind and not leave out of mind Apollo, who makes things work from afar.

Then, after the *humnos* was spoken, the Ionians made him [Homer] their **common citizen [*koinos politēs*]**. And the people of Delos, writing down his verses [*epos*, plural] on a white tablet [*leukōma*; in Latin, *album*], dedicated them in the sacred space of Artemis. Then, after the **festival [*panēguris*]** was declared to be finished, the Poet [*poiētēs*] sailed to Ios to meet Kreophylos.[50]

Vita 2.315–22

Just as the word *koinai* 'common' is appropriate for describing *thusiai* 'sacrifices' at Panhellenic festivals, *koinos* 'common' is appropriate for describing the role of Homer himself in the context of performing at such festivals.

As I note in the twin book *Homer the Classic*, the use of *koinos* 'common' in the passage I just quoted reflects the Athenocentric appropriation of Homer as a spokesman for the Delian League.[51] The idea is that all the Ionians who are assembled at the festival of the Delia on the island of Delos respond to Homer's perfor-

---

50. The identity of this Kreophylos will be explained later.
51. *HC* ch. 4 section 3.

mance of the *Homeric Hymn to Apollo* by acclaiming him as a *politēs* 'citizen' of all their cities—that is, as a citizen who is *koinos* 'common' to all Ionians in all their cities.

Such a universalizing appropriation of Homer can be seen elsewhere as well in the *Life of Homer* traditions. In the following passage, for example, the poetry of Homer is described as the *koinon* 'common good' of all Hellenes:

ταύτη[ν] οὖν αὐτῷ τῆς παιδιᾶς χάριν ἀ|ποδίδω[μεν ἀγ]ῶνος αὐτοῦ καὶ τὴν ἄλλη[ν] ποί|ησιν δι᾽ ἀγ[χιστ]είας μνήμης τοῖς βουλομέ|νοις φιλοκαλεῖν τῶν Ἑλλήνων εἰς τὸ **κοινὸν** | παραδῶμεν.

So let us pay him [Homer] back for the favor [*kharis*] of the amusement of the *Contest* [*of Homer and Hesiod*] itself, and, as for the rest of his *poiēsis* [the rest of Homer's songmaking besides what is quoted in the *Contest of Homer and Hesiod*], let us hand it down, through our shared inheritance of memory, to those who wish to take part in love of the beautiful, for the **common** [*koinon*] good of the Hellenes.

Michigan Papyrus 2754 lines 19–23

We see in this passage what amounts to an aetiology of Homer himself as the model performer of poetry at Panhellenic festivals. As such, he serves the *koinon* 'common good' of all Hellenes. Similarly, as we saw in the previous passage, Homer is the *koinos politēs*, a member of society who is 'common' to all societies that take part in a given Panhellenic festival.

A moment ago, I applied the word *aetiology* to these two contexts where Homer is being described as the one single thing held in common by all Hellenes attending Panhellenic festivals. (I have in mind the working definition that I used earlier: an aetiology is a myth that motivates an institutional reality, especially a ritual.) Two primary examples of ritual are relevant, sacrifice and festival, both of which I view here exclusively within the context of ancient Greek traditions. Both concepts, sacrifice and festival, can be expressed by way of a single Greek word, *thusia*, which as we saw means not only 'sacrifice' but also, metonymically, 'festival'. Two other Greek words of immediate relevance are *panēguris* and *heortē*, both meaning the 'festival' that serves as the setting for the *thusia* as 'sacrifice'. The ritual dimension of these words *thusia* 'sacrifice' or 'festival', *heortē* 'festival', and *panēguris* 'festival' brings to life the ritual dimension of Homeric performances. If I am right in arguing that the *Life of Homer* traditions once served as aetiologies for the performances of Homer, it follows that the *Lives* themselves, as aetiologies, bring to life the ritual dimension of these performances.

A myth like the story about Homer in Delos, as narrated in *Vita 2*, is not only an aetiology of the festival of the Delia. My point is, this myth is also an aetiology of the reception of Homer himself as the model performer at that festival. As we will see, the myth about Homer in Delos motivates the institutional reality of Homeric reception, just as surely as it motivates the institutional reality of the festival that defines Homer. As we will also see, this formulation can be expanded even further: in a larger sense, even the overall narratives of the *Lives of Homer* are aetiologies of Homeric reception. So, when I say that the figure of Homer in the *Lives of Homer* is a personal representative of sacrifices that are *koinai* 'common' to all Hellenes in the context of Panhellenic festivals, I am really saying that these *Lives* are aetiologies of Homer as the model performer of poetry at these festivals. In this connection, I note with interest that the birth of Homer himself is pictured as taking place on the occasion of a *heortē* 'festival' (*Vita* 1.28). Homer was born for performance at the festival.[52]

Here I return to the parenthetical remark that gave rise to this ongoing survey of references to Homer as the model performer at Panhellenic festivals:

καὶ ἔτι καὶ νῦν ἐν ταῖς **κοιναῖς θυσίαις** πρὸ τῶν δείπνων καὶ σπονδῶν προκατεύχεσθαι πάντας.

And even to this day, everyone makes a preliminary prayer [to Homer], before feasting and libation, at **sacrifices** [*thusiai*] that are **common** [*koinai*] to all.

Vita 2.92–94

An essential question remains. Why would all Hellenes make a preliminary prayer to Homer in the context of *thusiai* 'festivals' described as *koinai* 'common' to all? The answer emerges from further details that we find in the narrative of *Vita* 2. It turns out that Homer is honored as a cult hero by way of individual aetiologies motivating the reception of his performances in individual cities. A key is the noun *timē* (or the verb *timân*), meaning 'honor', which can be used in the sacral sense of 'honor by way of cult'.[53] In the *Contest of Homer and Hesiod* tradition, Homer is acknowledged as worthy of hero cult in all Hellenic societies:

καὶ ζῶν | καὶ θανὼν **τετίμηται** παρὰ πᾶσιν ἀνθρώ|ποις.

Living or dead, he [Homer] is **honored** [*timân*] among all men.

Michigan Papyrus 2754 lines 17–19

References in the *Lives of Homer* to the various local traditions of various cities bear out this universalizing statement about Homer as the individual cult hero of individual cities. A case in point is the city of Corinth: Homer is 'honored' (*timân*) by the people of Corinth in return for his performing in their city (2.287 τιμηθεὶς δὲ μεγάλως). Another case in point is the city of the island-state of Samos. *Vita* 1 tells about the reception of Homer by a civic confraternity known as the *phrētores*

---

52. The idea of a festival is implicit, I think, in the figure of Homer's mother, Kretheis, who is described in *Vita* 1.39–41 as an accomplished woolworker. As we will see later, woolworking is central to a climactic moment at a festival like the Panathenaia, where a woven woolen robe is presented to Athena as the goddess who presides at the festival.

53. *BA* 7§1n2 (= p. 118).

of Samos: καὶ αὐτὸν ἐτίμων καὶ ἐν θωύματι εἶχον 'they [the *phrētores*] honored [*timân*] him and held him in admiration [*thauma*]' (1.431). In this context, Homer is performing for the *phrētores*, and it is specified that he is attending a festival: the *phrētores* in Samos had invited him to participate in the celebration of a *heortē* 'festival' (1.407–8 συνεορτάσοντα). It is further specified that the *heortē* is the Apatouria (1.401–2 ἔτυχον δὲ οἱ ἐκεῖσε τὸν τότε καιρὸν ἄγοντες ἑορτὴν Ἀπατούρια).

The festival of the Apatouria seems to be a traditional setting for the performance of epic poetry in Ionian cities, including Athens. There is an incidental reference to such a setting in Plato's *Timaeus* (21a–b), where we find the figure of Critias reminiscing about his childhood and recalling an occasion when he and his little friends were 'playing rhapsode' (21b ἆθλα γὰρ ἡμῖν οἱ πατέρες ἔθεσαν ῥαψῳδίας). It happened on the day of Koureotis, during the festival of the Apatouria, and it was also on this occasion that the supposedly original telling of the mock epic of Athens and Atlantis took place (21a–b). As I have argued elsewhere, the object of this childish game of playing rhapsode at the Apatouria was to win celebrity status as the star rhapsode of the Panathenaia.[54]

Returning to my list of examples showing Homer as cult hero, I turn to the last two examples. They are the city-state of Argos and the island-state of Chios. After hearing the performances of Homer, the people of Argos 'honor' (*timân*) him for glorifying them with his verses in their city, and they participate in two sets of seasonally recurring *thusiai* 'sacrifices', one of which takes place in Argos and the other in Chios:

αὐτὸν μὲν πολυτελέσι δωρεαῖς **ἐτίμησαν**, εἰκόνα δὲ χαλκῆν ἀναστήσαντες ἐψηφίσαντο θυσίαν ἐπιτελεῖν Ὁμήρῳ καθ' ἡμέραν καὶ κατὰ μῆνα καὶ κατ' ἐνιαυτὸν ‹καὶ› ἄλλην θυσίαν πενταετηρίδα εἰς Χίον ἀποστέλλειν. ἐπιγράφουσι δὲ ἐπὶ τῆς εἰκόνος αὐτοῦ. . . .

They [the people of Argos] **honored** [*timân*] him [Homer] with costly gifts and, setting up a bronze statue to him, they decreed that **sacrifice** [*thusia*] should be offered to Homer on the right day and in the right month, every year, and that another ***thusia*** should be delegated to Chios every four years. This is the epigram they inscribed on his statue [quotation follows]. . . .

Vita 2.303–8

In this local Argive context, we see the usage of the word *thusia* in two senses. First, the people of Argos participate in a *thusia* 'sacrifice' to Homer as cult hero of performance; this sacrifice takes place in Argos on a seasonally recurring basis. Second, the people of Argos participate in a *thusia* 'sacrifice' to Homer that takes place in Chios on a seasonally recurring basis. This other sacrifice takes place on the occasion of a quadrennial festival in Chios, which is designated metonymically by the same word, *thusia*. The participants in this quadrennial festival, highlighted by a

54. PR 53–56 (especially p. 56).

sacrifice made to Homer, are evidently not only the people of Chios but also other people sent as delegates from their own cities. By implication, this quadrennial festival in honor of Homer in Chios is the setting for performances of Homeric poetry. I see here a prototype for the quadrennial festival of the Great Panathenaia in Athens, which is the premier setting for performances of Homeric poetry from the standpoint of the Athenian empire. I repeat what I have been saying from the start: *thusia* is the word of choice for designating the festival of the Panathenaia (Plato *Timaeus* 26e).

THE *HOMERIC HYMN TO APOLLO* AS AN AETIOLOGY
OF HOMERIC PERFORMANCE AT THE DELIA

The cursory reference to Chios as the setting for a quadrennial *thusia* 'festival' honoring Homer in the narrative of *Vita* 2 (307–8) is pertinent to a pointed reference to Chios in the *Homeric Hymn to Apollo*:

πρὸς δὲ τόδε μέγα **θαῦμα**, ὅου κλέος οὔποτ' ὀλεῖται,
κοῦραι Δηλιάδες Ἑκατηβελέταο θεράπναι·
αἵ τ' ἐπεὶ ἂρ πρῶτον μὲν Ἀπόλλων' **ὑμνήσωσιν**,
αὖτις δ' αὖ Λητώ τε καὶ Ἄρτεμιν ἰοχέαιραν,
μνησάμεναι ἀνδρῶν τε παλαιῶν ἠδὲ γυναικῶν   160
ὕμνον ἀείδουσιν, θέλγουσι δὲ φῦλ' ἀνθρώπων.
πάντων δ' ἀνθρώπων φωνὰς καὶ κρεμβαλιαστὺν
μιμεῖσθ' ἴσασιν· φαίη δέ κεν αὐτὸς ἕκαστος
φθέγγεσθ'· οὕτω σφιν καλὴ συνάρηρεν ἀοιδή.
ἀλλ' ἄγεθ' ἱλήκοι μὲν Ἀπόλλων Ἀρτέμιδι ξύν,   165
χαίρετε δ' ὑμεῖς πᾶσαι· ἐμεῖο δὲ καὶ μετόπισθε
μνήσασθ', ὁππότε κέν τις ἐπιχθονίων ἀνθρώπων
ἐνθάδ' ἀνείρηται ξεῖνος ταλαπείριος ἐλθών·
ὦ κοῦραι, τίς δ' ὕμμιν ἀνὴρ ἥδιστος ἀοιδῶν
ἐνθάδε πωλεῖται, καὶ τέῳ **τέρπεσθε** μάλιστα;   170
ὑμεῖς δ' εὖ μάλα πᾶσαι **ὑποκρίνασθαι** ἀφ' ἡμέων.[55]
τυφλὸς ἀνήρ, οἰκεῖ δὲ Χίῳ ἔνι παιπαλοέσσῃ,
τοῦ πᾶσαι μετόπισθεν ἀριστεύουσιν ἀοιδαί.
ἡμεῖς δ' ὑμέτερον κλέος οἴσομεν ὅσσον ἐπ' αἶαν
ἀνθρώπων στρεφόμεσθα πόλεις εὖ ναιεταώσας·   175
οἱ δ' ἐπὶ δὴ πείσονται, ἐπεὶ καὶ ἐτήτυμόν ἐστιν.
αὐτὰρ ἐγὼν **οὐ λήξω** ἑκηβόλον Ἀπόλλωνα
ὑμνέων ἀργυρότοξον ὃν ἠύκομος τέκε Λητώ.

---

55. Besides the variant ἀφ' ἡμέων 'about me' as attested in the manuscript tradition of the *Homeric Hymn* (3) *to Apollo*, we have already also considered the variant ἀφήμως as attested in the quotation by Thucydides.

And on top of that, there is this great thing of **wonder** [*thauma*],[56]
   the fame [*kleos*] of which will never perish:
the Delian Maidens, attendants [*therapnai*] of the one who shoots
   from afar.
So when they make Apollo their ***humnos*** first and foremost,[57]
followed in turn by Leto and Artemis, shooter of arrows,
they keep in mind men of the past and women too,[58]   160
as they sing the ***humnos***, and they enchant all different kinds of humanity.
All humans' voices and rhythms
they know how to **re-enact** [*mimeîsthai*]. And each single person would say
   that his own voice
was their voice. That is how their beautiful song has each of its parts fitting
   in place.
But come now, may Apollo be gracious, along with Artemis;   165
and you all also, **hail** [*khairete*] and take pleasure, all of you [Maidens
   of Delos]. Keep me, even in the future,
in your mind, whenever someone, out of the whole mass of earthbound
   humanity,
arrives here [to Delos], after arduous wandering, as a guest entitled
   to the rules of hosting, and asks this question:
"O Maidens, who is for you the most pleasurable of singers
that wanders here? In whom do you take the most **delight** [*terpesthai*]?"   170
Then you, all of you [Maidens of Delos], must very properly **respond**
   [*hupokrinesthai*][59] about me:[60]
"It is a blind man, and he dwells [*oikeîn*][61] in Chios, a rugged land,
and all his songs will in the future prevail as the very best."
And I[62] in turn will carry your fame [*kleos*] as far over the earth

---

56. In the *Lives of Homer*, as we have seen, *thauma* 'wonder' marks the universal response to Homer's poetry.

57. On the occasion of singing a *humnos*, the god who is being sung in the *humnos*—who is the subject of the *humnos*—is metonymically equated with the *humnos* itself: by metonymy, the god *is* the song.

58. The syntax of this verse re-enacts the meaning of the Homeric name *Melēsigenēs*, which as we see figures prominently in the *Life of Homer* narratives.

59. The 'responsion' conveyed by this verb *hupokrinesthai* is performative, not just interpersonal.

60. See the note on the Greek text of line 171.

61. In everyday contexts, of course, *oikeîn* means 'dwell [in a house]'. On the other hand, this same verb *oikeîn* is used in sacral contexts of hero cults to designate the 'dwelling' of a hero's talismanic body inside the sacred ground where he or she is worshipped: documentation in *PH* 9§27n99 (= p. 269). Here in the *Homeric Hymn* (3) *to Apollo* 172, the implication of *oikeîn* is that the body of Homer—regardless of where he was reputed to have died—found its final resting place on the island of Chios, where a hero cult was established in his honor: see *BA* 17§9n3 (= p. 297) and *PP* 113n34, following Brelich 1958:320–21. From the standpoint of *Life of Homer* traditions, such a claim anchors Homer as the ancestor of the *Homēridai* of Chios, who are thus legitimated as the true 'descendants of Homer'.

62. Literally, 'we'.

as I wander, throughout the cities of men, with their fair populations.   175
And they will all believe—I now see—[63]since it is genuine [*etētumon*].
As for me, I will not **leave off** [*lēgein*][64] making far-shooting Apollo
my *humnos*,[65] the one with the silver quiver, who was borne by Leto
  of the fair tresses.

Homeric Hymn (3) *to Apollo* 156–78

The *Homeric Hymn to Apollo* is saying here many of the same things said by the
Life of Homer traditions. One thing stands out. The speaker of the *Hymn* says explicitly that his home is the island of Chios (171–73). This detail turns out to be a
most explicit signature. For Ionians in general, the Chiote signature is a sign that
the speaker is an Ionian singer from Chios. For the people of Chios in particular,
the speaker is Homer, the ancestor of the *Homēridai* of Chios. As for the Athenians, the same signature is a sign of their ownership of Homer. In what follows, I
will argue that the *Homēridai* of Chios authorize the performances of the Homeric
Iliad and *Odyssey* at the Panathenaia in Athens. So when Thucydides recognizes
the speaker of the *Hymn* as Homer (3.104.4, 5, 6), he is thinking like an Athenian.

In the *Life of Homer* traditions, as we saw, the figure of Homer is pictured as a
singer who wanders from city to city, performing his songs at festivals celebrated
in the cities he visits. Festivals provide an occasion for the itinerant Homer to engage in performance, and the story of Homer's mythical performance at a given
festival can become an aetiology that explains the reality of seasonally recurring
Homeric performances at that given festival. The performance of Homer at Delos, as
narrated in *Vita* 2 (313–21), is a premier example of such an aetiology. The *Homeric
Hymn to Apollo*, in and of itself, is another premier example of such an aetiology.
We can see that it contains in its own right a compressed *Life of Homer* story, spoken by the figure of Homer himself as he performs at a festival sacred to Apollo,
primary god of Delos. This compressed *Life of Homer* story is dramatized by the
Homeric Hymn to Apollo, where the figure of Homer quotes the Delian Maidens in
the act of prophesying his ultimate career as a singer whose songs will prevail
throughout the Hellenic world.

Just as the *Lives of Homer* function as aetiologies of Homer, we see that the *Ho-*

---

63. The particle δή here has an "evidentiary" force, indicating that the speaker has just *seen* something:
in other words, that the speaker has achieved an insight just a moment ago ('Aha, now I see that . . . ').
See Bakker 1997:74–80 and 2005:146.

64. As I noted earlier, the verb *lēgein* 'leave off' conveys a mentality of *relay performance*: one performer 'leaves off' in order for the next performer, waiting for his turn, to 'take up' (*hupolambanein*)
where his predecessor 'left off'. If a performer says that he will *not* 'leave off', this means that there is no
chance for the successor to 'take up' the continuity.

65. On the occasion of singing a *humnos*, the god who is being sung in the *humnos*—who is the
subject of the *humnos*—is metonymically equated with the *humnos* itself: by metonymy, the god *is* the
song. We can see the same phenomenon at verse 158, earlier on in this same passage.

meric Hymn to Apollo is an aetiology in its own right. It is an aetiology not only for the festival of the Delia but also for Homer as the spokesman for that festival. By *Homer* here I mean not only the notional speaker of the *Homeric Hymn to Apollo* but also the notional ancestor of the *Homēridai* of Chios, who are destined to become the authorizers of Homeric performance at the festival of the Panathenaia in Athens.

3

Homer and His Genealogy

THE *HOMĒRIDAI* OF CHIOS

I return to the cursory reference to Chios as the setting for a quadrennial *thusia* 'festival' honoring Homer in the narrative of *Vita* 2 (307–8). As we saw, this reference is pertinent to the context of a *Homeric Hymn to Apollo* to be performed at Delos. In other words, it is pertinent to the festival of the Delia. It is also pertinent to the indirect reference made by the narrative of *Vita* 1 to the quadrennial *thusia* 'festival' of the Panathenaia in Athens. As we have already seen, Homer is pictured as composing both the *Iliad* and the *Odyssey* in the city of Chios (*Vita* 1.346–99). The only two epics performed at the festival of the Panathenaia are the only two epics composed by Homer in the city of Chios and, in the course of composing these two epics, he keeps augmenting his composition by adding verses that center on the glorification of Athens (1.378–98). Only after he finishes his glorification of Athens does Homer finish composing the *Iliad* and *Odyssey*: only then does he take leave of Chios and set sail to tour the rest of Hellas (1.400), arriving at Samos as his first port of call (1.401). Samos is merely a transitional stopover before Homer's arrival in Hellas: in this context, his intended point of arrival in Hellas is explicitly the city of Athens (1.483–84). At a later point in my argumentation, I will return to the detail about Samos, which is typical of a recurrent theme in the *Lives of Homer*—that is, the role of Samos as a transition to Athens. For now, I simply highlight the fact that the destination of Homer in this story is Athens. And the intended Homeric trajectory, starting from Chios and ending in Athens, is an indirect recognition of a fundamentally Athenocentric theme. As we are about to see, this theme is tied to a lineage of epic performers who trace themselves back to Homer. As we are told by the narrative of *Vita* 2, it is in Chios that Homer fathers this lineage of epic performers. They are known as the *Homēridai*:

Χῖοι δὲ πάλιν τεκμήρια φέρουσιν **ἴδιον** εἶναι **πολίτην** λέγοντες καὶ **περισῴζεσθαί** τινας ἐκ τοῦ **γένους** αὐτοῦ παρ᾽ αὑτοῖς Ὁμηρίδας καλουμένους

The people of Chios, on the other hand [in rivalry with other claims on Homer made by other cities], adduce proof for their claim that Homer is their very **own fellow citizen** [*politēs*], saying that there exist **surviving** members of a **lineage** [*genos*] who originate from him [Homer] called the *Homēridai*.

Vita 2.13–15

This reference in *Vita* 2 makes it explicit that the tracing of the *Homēridai* back to Homer is a Chiote tradition—and that this tradition aetiologizes the Chiotes' claim to the poet Homer by way of the *Homēridai*. There is also another such reference in Strabo (14.1.35 C645). Moreover, as we learn from Harpocration (s.v. *Homēridai*), both Hellanicus of Lesbos (*FGH* 4 F 20) and Acusilaus of Argos (*FGH* 2 F 2) say that the *Homēridai* were a *genos* 'lineage' in Chios that was named after Homer himself: Ὁμηρίδαι· γένος ἐν Χίῳ, ὅπερ Ἀκουσίλαος ἐν γ΄, Ἑλλάνικος ἐν τῇ Ἀτλαντιάδι ἀπὸ τοῦ ποιητοῦ φησιν ὠνομάσθαι 'the *Homēridai*: a lineage [*genos*] in Chios; Acusilaus in Book 3 and Hellanicus in the *Atlantias* say that it was named after Homer'.[1]

The idea that the *Homēridai* were a Chiote lineage descended from Homer was not just a Chiote tradition. It also became an Athenian tradition. Here I find it essential to quote again the passage concerning the initiative of Hipparkhos the son of Peisistratos in introducing the performance of Homer at the Panathenaia:

... Ἱππάρχῳ, ὃς ἄλλα τε πολλὰ καὶ καλὰ ἔργα σοφίας ἀπεδέξατο, καὶ τὰ Ὁμήρου ἔπη πρῶτος **ἐκόμισεν** εἰς τὴν γῆν ταύτην, καὶ ἠνάγκασε τοὺς ῥαψῳδοὺς Παναθηναίοις ἐξ

---

1. On the *Homēridai* as transmitters of Homeric poetry, see *PP* 62–63, 188n4. West (1999) argues that the name of Homer, *Homēros*, is merely a back-formation derived from *Homēridai*, and that Homer is a "fictitious person" (p. 372). West (p. 374n31) cites four of my books in order to make the point that I too regard *Homēros* as a fiction—or, rather, as "a mythical, prototypical author"—and then he adds: "It is not clear to me whether [Nagy] regards the Homeridai as prior." Here is my clarification: in matters of symbolic filiation, it is not a question of chronological priority. Rather, it is a question of logical priority—in the logic, that is, of the myth. For example, the *Asklēpiadai* of Cos trace themselves back to *Asklēpios*, counting nineteen generations from Asklepios to Hippocrates (Soranus *Vita Hippocratis* 1). The ancestor is a matter of myth, but the filiation is a matter of history. For the name *Asklēpiadai* to be functional in its historical context, the myth of *Asklepios* as the prototypical healer must be a foregone conclusion. West (p. 374) actually discusses this example of Asklepios and the *Asklēpiadai*. This example, however, can be used as a counterargument to his argument about Homer and the *Homēridai*. For the name *Homēridai* to be functional in the historical context of the Panathenaia, the myth of *Homēros* 'Homer' as a proto-author must be a logical prerequisite. In terms of Homeric reception, Homer is no fiction, even if he is indeed a myth. In different historical contexts, on the other hand, the name *Homēridai* could have been aetiologized by way of different myths. More about this subject as my argumentation proceeds.

ὑπολήψεως ἐφεξῆς αὐτὰ διιέναι, ὥσπερ νῦν ἔτι οἵδε ποιοῦσιν, καὶ ἐπ᾽ Ἀνακρέοντα τὸν Τήιον πεντηκόντορον στείλας ἐκόμισεν εἰς τὴν πόλιν, Σιμωνίδην δὲ τὸν Κεῖον ἀεὶ περὶ αὐτὸν εἶχεν, μεγάλοις μισθοῖς καὶ δώροις πείθων· ταῦτα δ᾽ ἐποίει βουλόμενος παιδεύειν τοὺς πολίτας, ἵν᾽ ὡς βελτίστων ὄντων αὐτῶν ἄρχοι, οὐκ οἰόμενος δεῖν οὐδενὶ σοφίας φθονεῖν, ἅτε ὢν καλός τε κἀγαθός.

[I am referring to] Hipparkhos, who accomplished many beautiful things in demon-stration of his expertise [*sophia*], especially by being the first to **bring over** [*komizein*] to this land [Athens] the verses [*epos*, plural] of Homer, and he required the rhap-sodes [*rhapsōidoi*] at the Panathenaia to go through [*diienai*] these verses in sequence [*ephexēs*], by relay [*ex hupolēpseōs*], just as they [the rhapsodes] do even nowadays. And he sent out a state ship to **bring over** [*komizein*] **Anacreon of Teos** to the city [Athens]. He also always kept in his company **Simonides of Keos**, persuading him by way of huge fees and gifts. And he did all this because he wanted to educate the citi-zens, so that he might govern the best of all possible citizens. He thought, noble as he was, that he was obliged not to be stinting in the sharing of his expertise [*sophia*] with anyone.

"Plato" *Hipparkhos* 228b–c

As I argued in chapter 1, the use of the word *komizein* 'bring over' with reference to the initiative of rescuing the lyric poetry of Anacreon by bringing it over from Samos and by introducing the performance of such poetry at the Panathenaia is parallel to the use of the same word with reference to the initiative of ostensibly res-cuing the epic poetry of Homer by bringing it over from Chios. In the latter case, it is made explicit that Hipparkhos introduced the performance of Homer's epic compositions at the Panathenaia. What is only implicit, however, is the idea that Homer's poetry was brought over from Chios in particular, whereas it is made ex-plicit that Anacreon and his poetry were brought over from Samos. In what fol-lows, I will show that Chios was in fact the provenience of the Homeric tradition of performance that the Peisistratidai 'brought over' to Athens, and that the medi-ators were in fact the *Homēridai* of Chios.[2] I will also show that the story about the initiative of the Peisistratidai amounts to an aetiology explaining the function of the *Homēridai* as the authorizers of Homer in Athens—and as the Ionian origina-tors of the institution that I defined in chapter 1 as the *Panathenaic Regulation*.

Most relevant is a passing reference in Plato, where we learn that the garland of gold that Ion of Ephesus expects to win in competition for first prize in rhapsodic performance of Homer at the feast of the Panathenaia is to be awarded by the *Homēridai* (*Ion* 530d). As I argue in the companion volume *Homer the Classic*, this reference to the *Homēridai* shows that the Athenians in the late fifth century rec-

2. See also Graziosi 2002:225–26, noting that Simonides, who like Anacreon was brought to Athens by the Peisistratidai ("Plato" *Hipparkhos* 228b–c), refers to Homer as 'the man from Chios' in one of his songs (Simonides F 19.1–2, ed. West).

ognized the *Homēridai* of Chios as the official regulators of rhapsodic competitions in performing the Homeric *Iliad* and *Odyssey* at the Panathenaia in Athens.[3] The fact that Ion is pictured as already wearing a golden garland when he performs at the Panathenaia implies that he is a tenured Panathenaic rhapsode.

From what we have seen so far, I am ready to draw the conclusion that the references in the *Lives of Homer* (notably in *Vita* 1) to Athens as the ultimate destination for Homer's would-be performance of his *Iliad* and *Odyssey* are linked to the presence of the *Homēridai* at the rhapsodes' actual performances of the Homeric *Iliad* and *Odyssey* at the Panathenaia in Athens. And this recurrent presence of the *Homēridai* at the Panathenaia compensates for the primal absence of Homer from this festival. The presence is a matter of ritual, while the absence is a matter of myth.

In earlier work, I have argued that these *Homēridai* were actually a source for the *Life of Homer* narrative traditions.[4] Direct evidence comes from what the *Homēridai* themselves are reported as saying—or not saying—about Homer. A shining example of what they do say comes from an Athenian witness, reporting a myth about Homer's experience of an epiphany by Helen:

λέγουσιν δέ τινες καὶ τῶν Ὁμηριδῶν ὡς ἐπιστᾶσα τῆς νυκτὸς Ὁμήρῳ προσέταξεν ποιεῖν περὶ τῶν στρατευσαμένων ἐπὶ Τροίαν, βουλομένη τὸν ἐκείνων θάνατον ζηλωτότερον ἢ τὸν βίον τὸν τῶν ἄλλων καταστῆσαι

Some people—including especially the *Homēridai*—say that she [Helen] appeared to Homer at night and ordered him to make poetry [*poieîn*] about the men who went to fight at Troy, wishing to make their death more enviable than the life of all others.

Isocrates (10) *Helen* 65

This report is most valuable for showing that the stories we see retold in *Lives of Homer* like *Vita* 2 are not at all unknown to Athenians. The familiarity that is presupposed in the reference made by Isocrates makes it clear that the repertoire of the *Homēridai* is not just a Chiote repertoire. It is for the Athenians an Athenian repertoire.[5]

Here I add a report about what the *Homēridai* say—or do not dare say—about themselves:

εἰ δὲ καὶ ἤρισεν Ὅμηρος Ἡσιόδῳ τῷ Ἀσκραίῳ καὶ ἡττήθη, ὅπερ ὄκνος τοῖς Ὁμηρίδαις καὶ λέγειν, ζητητέον ἐν τοῖς εἰς τοῦτο γράψασιν

---

3. *HC* ch. 3§36. This is not to say that Homer was "invented" in Athens, which is what West 1999 argues; I agree with the counterargument of Graziosi 2002:76.

4. *PP* 179–80n97. See also Graziosi 2002:50 and (already) Allen 1912:186–87.

5. In *Nemean* 2.8, Pindar associates the *Homēridai* not with Chios per se but more directly with Athens. It is no accident that this epinician song of Pindar's was commissioned by an Athenian family.

Whether Homer had a contest with Hesiod of Ascra and was defeated by him—**a sub-ject that is taboo for the *Homēridai* even to put into words**—has to be researched by consulting those who have written about this subject.

> Eustathius *Commentary* 1.6.28–30 on *Iliad* (introduction)

We see here that the repertoire of the *Homēridai* is restricted to Homer, to the ex-clusion of Hesiod. I will have more to say below in Part II about this exclusionary Homeric repertoire.

The presence of the *Homēridai* in the Athenocentric narrative of *Vita* 2 is par-allel to another detail in the same narrative: as we have already seen, Homer actu-ally performs in Athens (2.276–85). By contrast, as we saw in the non-Athenocen-tric narrative of *Vita* 1, Homer never gets to perform in Athens. This significant absence of Homer from Athens in *Vita* 1 is parallel to another significant absence in this non-Athenocentric narrative. That is, the *Homēridai* seem to be missing from the narrative of *Vita* 1. But they are not really missing. They are intentionally elided.

According to *Vita* 1, as we saw previously, the ultimate epic repertoire of the Pana-thenaia was made not in Athens but in Chios. Homer himself is pictured as com-posing both the *Iliad* and the *Odyssey* in the city of Chios. As we also saw in *Vita* 1, Homer dies before he ever reaches Athens. Nevertheless, despite the fact that the narrative of *Vita* 1 thus elides Athens as a venue for Homer's performance, it rec-ognizes the importance of Athens as a referent for Homer's composition. As we also saw previously, *Vita* 1 highlights the explicit references that Homer is making to Athens when he composes the *Iliad* and *Odyssey* in Chios. Thus *Vita* 1 recognizes the role of Chios as a definitive source for the glorification of Athens by Homer. *Vita* 1 also recognizes the Athenian appropriation of a Chiote version of Homer, since it makes a de-facto equation between the ultimate Panathenaic version of Homer and the Chiote version—that is, the version of the *Iliad* and *Odyssey* that Homer himself supposedly composed in the city of Chios.

Although the non-Athenocentric narrative of *Vita* 1 accepts the concept of Homer as the composer of the Panathenaic *Iliad* and *Odyssey*, it elides the concept of the *Homēridai* as authorized performers of what their Chiote ancestor had no-tionally composed on their island. The elision is expressed by way of a contradic-tion. Homer has no sons according to this non-Athenocentric narrative: he fathers only two daughters in Chios, one of whom dies unmarried, while the other is mar-ried off by her father to a man from Chios (*Vita* 1.343–45).[6] I see here a non-Atheno-

---

6. West 2003a:303 points out that the detail about the unmarried and married daughters of Homer, as told in *Vita* 1, shows another contradiction. This detail is at odds with a detail told in another story, according to which the poet Stasinus received the *Cypria* as a dowry in return for marrying the daugh-ter of Homer (*Vita* 10.36). West (p. 309) argues that this story is already attested in Pindar, and it "pre-supposes a dispute over which poet was the author of that epic."

centric or even anti-Athenocentric contradiction, consistent with the overall outlook of *Vita* 1, which stands in sharp contrast with the Athenocentrism of *Vita* 2.
To disconnect the *Homēridai* of the Panathenaia in Athens from *Homēros* in Chios
is to disconnect Homer himself from Athens by delegitimizing his would-be descendants.[7] I conclude by adding yet another version of Homer's lineage: according to a tradition reported in the *Suda* (*Vita* 10.34–36), Homer fathers two sons
and one daughter in Chios. Either of these two sons may have been claimed by the
Homēridai of Chios as a link to Homer.

There is also another contradiction in the non-Athenocentric narrative of *Vita* 1.
It involves the sequencing of the last two major Ionian cities that it mentions, the
island-states of Chios and Samos. As we have already seen, *Vita* 1 pictures Homer
as 'making' the *Iliad* and the *Odyssey* in the city of Chios (1.346–99). Also, Homer
plans to launch his songmaking tour of all Hellas from Chios (1.374–77). As for
Samos, this Ionian island-state becomes a transitional stopover before Homer's
intended arrival in Hellas: in this context, his intended point of arrival in Hellas
is specified as the city of Athens (1.483–84). Thus Homer's presence in Chios and
Samos prefigures his presence in Athens. After Homer's extended tour of composing and performing during his transitional stopover in Samos (1.399–484), he leaves
the island and arrives at another transitional stopover, the island of Ios (1.484–85),
which turns out to be his terminal stop, since this is the place where he dies, am-
bushed by a riddle (1.485–516). So here is the contradiction: according to *Vita* 1,
Homer's personal appearance in Athens never happens. What had started off as an
Athenocentric accretion fails to materialize, and the narrative ends by maintaining
what seems to be a non-Athenocentric outlook. Such a non-Athenocentric ending
may reflect a pre-Athenocentric version of the *Life of Homer* featuring Samos as the
highlight of Homer's poetic tour. Such a version would best suit the poetics and
politics of the tyrant Polycrates of Samos.

From the viewpoint of *Vita* 1, Athens cannot be the venue for any performance
by Homer. This idea is evidently parallel to another idea, that Homer fathered no
sons in Chios. These ideas, I argue, add up to an ideology that contradicts the ideology of the Athenians, who considered their city to be the legitimate venue for
the performance of Homer by the legitimate descendants of Homer, the *Homēridai*
of Chios.

I argue, then, on the basis of both the negative evidence of *Vita* 1 and the positive
evidence of *Vita* 2, that Chios was a vital link for the Panathenaic Homer and that
Athens had appropriated an official Chiote version of the Homeric *Iliad* and *Odyssey*

---

7. Claiming that the *Homēridai* of Chios had no ancestor called *Homēros*, West 1999:372 mentions
only the testimony about the daughters of Homer in the *Herodotean Life of Homer* (*Vita* 1.343–45), without mentioning the testimony about the *Homēridai* as 'descendants of Homer' in the *Certamen* (*Vita*
2.13–15), which I quoted earlier.

for performance at the festival of the Panathenaia in Athens. I started this section by focusing on a quadrennial festival at Chios, which the natives of this island-state evidently linked with Homer. Now I have come full circle at the end of this section by focusing on a parallel: the quadrennial festival of the Panathenaia at Athens is evidently linked with Homer as the notional ancestor of the *Homēridai* of Chios.

A POST-ATHENOCENTRIC VIEW OF THE *HOMĒRIDAI*

From an Athenocentric point of view, as we have seen, the speaker of the *Homeric Hymn to Apollo* is Homer himself, implicitly the ancestor of the *Homēridai* of Chios. From a post-Athenocentric point of view, by contrast, the man from Chios who speaks in the *Hymn* is not Homer but someone called Kynaithos, who must be later than Homer and who may not even be descended from Homer:

Ὁμηρίδας ἔλεγον τὸ μὲν ἀρχαῖον τοὺς ἀπὸ τοῦ Ὁμήρου γένους, οἳ καὶ τὴν **ποίησιν** αὐτοῦ **ἐκ διαδοχῆς** ᾖδον· μετὰ δὲ ταῦτα καὶ οἱ **ραψῳδοὶ** οὐκέτι τὸ γένος εἰς Ὅμηρον ἀνάγοντες. ἐπιφανεῖς δὲ ἐγένοντο οἱ περὶ Κύναιθον, οὕς φασι πολλὰ τῶν ἐπῶν **ποιήσαντας ἐμβαλεῖν** εἰς τὴν Ὁμήρου **ποίησιν.** ἦν δὲ ὁ Κύναιθος τὸ γένος Χῖος, ὃς καὶ τῶν **ἐπιγραφομένων** Ὁμήρου **ποιημάτων** τὸν εἰς Ἀπόλλωνα γεγραφὼς ὕμνον ἀνατέθεικεν αὐτῷ. οὗτος οὖν ὁ Κύναιθος πρῶτος ἐν Συρακούσαις ἐραψῴδησε τὰ Ὁμήρου ἔπη κατὰ τὴν ξθ΄ Ὀλυμπιάδα, ὡς Ἱππόστρατός φησιν.

Homēridai was the name given in ancient times to those who were descended from the lineage of Homer and who also sang his **poetry** [*poiēsis*] in succession [*ek diadokhēs*]. In later times, [it was the name given also to] **rhapsodes** [*rhapsōidoi*], who could no longer trace their lineage back to Homer. Of these, Kynaithos and his association became very prominent. It is said that they are the ones who **made** [*poieîn*] many of the verses [*epos*, plural] of Homer and **inserted** [*en-ballein*] them into his [Homer's] **poetry** [*poiēsis*]. Kynaithos was a Chiote by lineage, and, of the **poetic creations** [*poiēmata*] of Homer that are **ascribed** to him [*epigraphein*] as his [Homer's], it was he [Kynaithos] who **wrote** [*graphein*] the *humnos* to Apollo and attributed it to him [Homer].[8] And this Kynaithos was the first to **perform rhapsodically** [*rhapsōideîn*] in Syracuse the verses [*epos*, plural] of Homer, in the 69th Olympiad [504/1 B.C.E.], as Hippostratus says [*FGH* 568 F 5].

Scholia for Pindar *Nemean* 2.1c lines 1–10

The ultimate source for most of what is being said here in this compressed and elliptic account is Aristarchus of Samothrace, head of the Library of Alexandria in the second century B.C.E.[9] The account does not specify whether Kynaithos is re-

8. Martin 2000b:419n58 suggests that the phrasing here could mean instead: 'and dedicated it to him [Apollo]'. See also Collins 2004:184.

9. See *HTL* 28–29n14, where I argue that Aristarchus is the basic source for the statement up to the portion mentioning the testimony of Hippostratus concerning the date of a rhapsodic performance by Kynaithos in Syracuse.

ally one of the *Homēridai* of Chios who claim descent from Homer—or whether he is simply a rhapsode who impersonates Homer. But the fact that he is from Chios suggests that he is in fact one of the *Homēridai*. In any case, the account specifies that Kynaithos and his associates belong to a category of poets who are more recent than Homer: that is, post-Homeric. The poet of the *Homeric Hymn to Apollo*, according to this account, is the newer poet Kynaithos, not the older poet Homer.

The methodology of Aristarchus in identifying what he considered to be non-Homeric elements in the Homeric text is reflected in his usage of the term *neōteroi* 'newer' as a designation of poets who supposedly came after Homer; similarly, he used the term *neōterikos* 'neoteric' as an adjective describing features that distinguish these 'newer' poets from the genuine Homer.[10] For Aristarchus, non-Homeric meant post-Homeric. From here on, I will use the term *neoteric* in this sense, without prejudging whether the neoteric poets were really 'newer' than Homer. In the commentaries or *hupomnēmata* of Aristarchus as paraphrased in the Homeric scholia, we find that Hesiod and the poets of the epic Cycle were treated as such *neōteroi* or 'newer' poets.[11]

In the passage I just quoted from the scholia for Pindar, the supposedly newer poet Kynaithos and his associates are being accused of 'interpolating' (*en-ballein*) additional verses to augment the verses of Homer—and of ascribing to Homer various other compositions. Supposedly, these newer poets illegitimately interpolated additional verses to augment the original verses of Homer.

Such a point of view is evidently post-Athenocentric, in sharp contrast to the Athenocentric point of view we saw in the testimony of Thucydides himself. According to Thucydides, the author of the *Homeric Hymn to Apollo* is none other than Homer. We saw corroborating testimony in the Athenocentric narrative of *Vita* 2 in the *Life of Homer* tradition, where the *Hymn to Apollo* is likewise attributed to the authorship of Homer. Further, as we saw in both the Athenocentric narrative of *Vita* 2 and the pre-Athenocentric narrative of *Vita* 1, Homer is the poet of not only *humnoi* but also epigrams, such as the Midas Epigram. Even further, as we saw in the pre-Athenocentric narrative of *Vita* 1, Homer himself engages in the activity of 'interpolation' (*en-poieîn*) when he adds verses glorifying Athens while composing the *Iliad* and *Odyssey* in Chios. At a later point, I will reinterpret the concept of 'interpolation' (*en-poieîn, en-ballein*) from the standpoint of the pre-Athenocentric period in the *Life of Homer* traditions.[12]

10. The term *neōteroi* reflects the usage of Aristarchus himself, not only of the Aristarcheans who came after him and whose testimony is transmitted in the scholia. See Severyns 1928:33–34n4.

11. On Hesiod as *neōteros* according to the Aristarcheans, see Severyns 1928:39, 89; on the poets of the Cycle as *neōteroi*, see especially Severyns p. 63, who argues that Aristarchus considered the Cycle to be a major component of this neoteric category.

12. See also *HTL* 29n14, with reference to the meaning of *en-ballein* 'interpolate' in the scholia for Pindar *Nemean* 2.1c.

Whether or not Kynaithos is to be considered a legitimate member of the lineage of the *Homēridai* of Chios, the wording of this passage taken from the scholia for Pindar contains a precious detail about the *Homēridai* themselves: they are described as an association of performers, and they not only claim to be descended from Homer but also 'sing his poetry in succession' (οἳ καὶ τὴν ποίησιν αὐτοῦ ἐκ διαδοχῆς ᾖδον).

More needs to be said about the expression *ek diadokhēs*, which is conventionally translated as 'in succession'.[13] This translation leaves it open whether the 'succession' is from ancestor to descendant or from one participant to another while taking turns. We see an example of the first sense in the scholia for Pindar's *Olympian* 6 (158a), where Hieron is said to have inherited a priesthood *ek diadokhēs* 'in succession' from one of his ancestors. We see an example of the second sense in the scholia for Pindar's *Pythian* 12 (25; ed. Semitelos), where the three Graiai are said to share one eye and one tooth, using them *ek diadokhēs* 'in relay'—that is, by taking turns. There is another example in Aristotle's *Physics* (5.227a28–29): καὶ οἷον ἡ λαμπὰς ‹ἡ› ἐκ διαδοχῆς φορὰ ἐχομένη, συνεχὴς δ' οὔ 'and just as the torch race by relay [*ek diadokhēs*] is locomotion that is consecutive but not continuous'. (The metonymic meaning of *lampas* 'torch' as 'torch race' is attested also in the Aristotelian *Constitution of the Athenians* [57.1.8].) Moreover, the expression *ek diadokhēs* can mean 'taking turns' in contexts where it is used together with *allēlois* 'with each other'. A case in point is a passage from Aristotle (F 347.15 ed. Rose, via Aelian *Varia Historia* 1.15) where he describes how a mother bird and a father bird warm the eggs in their nest by taking turns (*ek diadokhēs*) with each other (*allēlois*). In another passage from Aristotle (F 433.9 ed. Rose, via Harpocration s.v. *prutaneis*), we read that the ten *phulai* of Athens each preside over the *Boulē* by taking turns (*ek diadokhēs*) with each other (*allēlais*). In the scholia A for *Iliad* XVIII (506d), *ek diadokhēs* refers to the scene on the Shield of Achilles where the elders take turns in rendering judgment regarding the litigation. In the scholia D for *Iliad* I (604), *ek diadokhēs* refers to the relay singing of the Muses: καὶ αὗται Ἀπόλλωνος κιθαρίζοντος ἐκ διαδοχῆς παρὰ μέρος ᾖδον 'and they, while Apollo was playing the kithara, were singing in relay [*para meros*], by taking turns [*ek diadokhēs*]'.

So also in the scholia for Pindar's *Nemean* 2 (1c), I conclude that *ek diadokhēs* refers to the relay singing of the *Homēridai*: οἳ καὶ τὴν ποίησιν αὐτοῦ ἐκ διαδοχῆς ᾖδον 'and they [the *Homēridai*] also sang his [Homer's] poetry [*poiēsis*] by taking turns [*ek diadokhēs*]'.[14] Still, the synchronic succession of relay singing may be a ritualized way of representing the diachronic succession of singing Homer's songs from one generation to the next. In order to represent this diachronic succession of generations, there has to be a synchronic grouping of these generations as a corpora-

---

13. So West 1999:368.
14. See also Collins 2004:183n9.

tion of practitioners. That corporation is named as the *Homēridai*, the 'descendants of Homer'. In the act of performance, the descendants are all synchronized as one corporation who incorporate the ancestor by taking turns in re-enacting him. The same can be said about, say, the mother bird and the father bird that feed their young in relay: that principle of relay is the model for the idea that each new generation has to follow the practice of the previous generation in feeding the young. Or again, the principle of the relay in the Athenian torch race is a ritualized way of expressing the continuity of the tradition of torch racing in and of itself. We may compare the idea of the *Asklēpiadai*, notional descendants of the prototypical physician *Asklēpios*, who are figured as a corporation of physicians who practice medicine by continuing the practice of their ancestor. So also the *Homēridai*, notional descendants of *Homēros*, are figured as a corporation of singers who continue the practice of singing Homer. For them to sing in relay is a synchronic ritualization of the diachronic continuity.

In the scholia for Pindar's *Nemean* 2 (1c), the idea that members of this corporation of the *Homēridai* sing the poetry of Homer in relay, taking turns, is then followed up by the idea of generational succession. But the legitimacy of this succession is questioned. From an Aristarchean perspective, the successors of Homer are not genuinely doing what their predecessor had done, and so they are not genuine. So they are illegitimate. This supposedly illegitimate corporation, described as οἱ περὶ Κύναιθον 'Kynaithos and his association', engage in various poetic activities like 'interpolating' (*en-ballein*) additional verses to augment the supposedly genuine verses of Homer or 'ascribing' (*epi-graphein*) to Homer a *humnos* that they composed on their own. Even though the statement as recorded in the scholia for Pindar rejects the poetic activities of 'Kynaithos and his associates' as illegitimate, typical of those who are more recent than the genuine Homer, it nevertheless sets up a parallel between them and the *Homēridai*—as associations of performers. By implication, just as the *Homēridai* sing Homer as a group, taking turns, so too 'Kynaithos and his associates' sing Homer as a group, taking turns. Whatever it is that 'Kynaithos and his associates' may do, the statement is explicit about what is done by the *Homēridai*: they sing the poetry of Homer 'by taking turns' (*ek diadokhēs*).

So we see here in the scholia for Pindar *Nemean* 2 (1c) a precious attestation of a poetic practice that can be understood as the basis of the Panathenaic Regulation, which requires that rhapsodes take turns in performing Homer at the festival of the Panathenaia in Athens. What makes this attestation all the more precious is that the *Homēridai* themselves—not just rhapsodes—are being described here as the models of such a poetic practice.[15]

From what we have seen so far, the linking of Homer and the *Homēridai* of Chios

---

15. The very concept of *Homēros*, as a notional prototype of the *Homēridai*, is glossed at verse 164 of the *Homeric Hymn* (3) *to Apollo*. See *HC* 2§§43–45.

with the Panathenaia dates back at least as far as the later years of the Peisistratidai. In those later years, as we saw already in chapter 1, the Panathenaic Regulation started to take shape. Ultimately, this Regulation led to the restricting of the epic repertoire of the Panathenaia to the Homeric *Iliad* and *Odyssey*, performed by rhapsodes who took turns in narrating the entire sequence of these two epics. This is not to say, however, that the epic repertoire of rhapsodes performing at the Panathenaia was restricted to the Homeric *Iliad* and *Odyssey* already in the earlier years of the Peisistratidai. Such a restriction, as I will argue, was starting to take hold only in the later years. Nor is it to say that the principle of rhapsodic relay that we see at work in the Panathenaic Regulation originated at the Panathenaia. This principle, as mediated by the *Homēridai* of Chios, was already operational in the late eighth and early seventh centuries B.C.E. at the festival of the Panionia held at the Panionion of the Ionian Dodecapolis in Asia Minor.[16] I will have more to say later about the evolution of Homeric poetry at the Panionia, but for now I continue to focus on its evolution at the Panathenaia. And my point remains that the Panathenaic Homer started taking shape only in the later years of the Peisistratidai, with the introduction of the Panathenaic Regulation by way of the *Homēridai*.

THE PERFORMANCE OF EPIC AT THE PANATHENAIA IN THE ERA OF THE PEISISTRATIDAI: THE EARLIER YEARS

In the earlier years of the era when the Peisistratidai ruled Athens, by contrast with the later years, the epic repertoire at the Panathenaia was not yet centered on the Homeric *Iliad* and *Odyssey*: it still included epic traditions we can describe as Cyclic, Hesiodic, and Orphic. In what follows, I will briefly consider each of these three epic traditions.

I start with the Cyclic traditions, giving here a general summary based on arguments I developed in earlier work.[17] For a lengthy period of time in the evolution of the Panathenaia, the epic Cycle was not distinguished from the Homeric tradition of epic performance. During this time, the epics of the Cycle were not anti-Homeric or even non-Homeric: they were simply Homeric. Homer was considered to be the poet of an epic Cycle that included what we know as the *Iliad* and *Odyssey*. Only gradually did the Homeric *Iliad* and *Odyssey* become differentiated from the epic Cycle. In the course of this differentiation, the *Iliad* and *Odyssey* became the

---

16. Frame 2009 ch. 11. Also, I agree with Frame's argument (pp. 583–84) that the Homeric *Iliad* and *Odyssey*, as epic traditions, "reached Athens almost immediately after they took root on Chios, and that even earlier they may have begun to be known in Athens directly from the Panionia." In terms of this argument, Hipparkhos can be credited only with the actual authorization of the *Homēridai* as regulators of epic performances by rhapsodes at the Panathenaia in Athens.

17. *PH* 2§§37–53 (= pp. 70–81).

only epics that were truly Homeric, while the Cycle became non-Homeric. The epics of the Cycle were then reassigned to poets other than Homer. For example, the *Aithiopis* and the *Iliou Persis* were reassigned to Arctinus of Miletus (Proclus summary p. 105.21–22 and p. 107.16–17 ed. Allen). Similarly, the *Little Iliad* was reassigned to Lesches of Lesbos (p. 106.19–20: his native city is specified as Mytilene). In earlier times, by contrast, the entire epic Cycle had been assigned to Homer.[18]

At the festival of the Panathenaia in Athens, as we saw in chapter 1, it was only in the late sixth century B.C.E. that Homer was starting to become differentiated as the author of two epics, the *Iliad* and the *Odyssey*. And, as I will argue in the Epilegomena, it was in this period that the epics of the epic Cycle were reassigned to such figures as Arctinus of Miletus and Lesches of Lesbos. At the festival of the Panionia at the Panionion of the Ionian Dodecapolis in Asia Minor, on the other hand, I will argue that such a differentiation was taking place far earlier, as early as the late eighth and early seventh century B.C.E.[19] I add here that we have just seen a comparable differentiation involving the *Homeric Hymn to Apollo*: the authorship of this *Hymn* was at some point reassigned from Homer to a newer poet, Kynaithos of Chios. In this case we can be more precise about the relative date of the reassignment. It must have happened sometime after the era of Thucydides, since the historian still identifies the speaker of the *Hymn to Apollo* as Homer.

I now turn to the second of the three epic traditions current in the earlier years of the Peisistratidai: that is, the Hesiodic tradition. Whereas the epic Cycle became distinct from the epic of Homer only gradually in the Athenian performance traditions of the late sixth and early fifth century, the epic of Hesiod was already distinct by the sixth century. Moreover, the Hesiodic tradition was not only distinct from the Homeric tradition: it could directly compete with it. In *Vita* 2—that is, in *The Contest of Homer and Hesiod*—we have already seen two versions of a myth that aetiologizes this competitive relationship between the Homeric and the Hesiodic traditions. According to one version, as we saw, Homer and Hesiod had a contest at Chalkis, in Euboea (2.68); according to another version, their contest took place at Aulis (2.54–55), situated on the mainland in Boeotia, across the strait from Euboea. There are also traces of a third version, according to which the Contest of Homer and Hesiod took place at Delos:

Φιλόχορος δὲ ἀπὸ τοῦ συντιθέναι καὶ ῥάπτειν τὴν ᾠδὴν οὕτω φησὶν αὐτοὺς προσ-
κεκλῆσθαι. δηλοῖ δὲ ὁ Ἡσίοδος λέγων·

ἐν Δήλῳ τότε πρῶτον ἐγὼ καὶ Ὅμηρος ἀοιδοὶ
μέλπομεν, ἐν νεαροῖς ὕμνοις ῥάψαντες ἀοιδήν,
Φοῖβον Ἀπόλλωνα χρυσάορον, ὃν τέκε Λητώ. [Hesiod F 357]

18. *HQ* 38, 89–91; relevant comments by Burgess 2001:15 and 200n44.
19. This relative chronology, as we will see in the Epilegomena, follows the argumentation of Frame 2009 (especially ch. 11).

ῥαψῳδῆσαι δέ φησι πρῶτον τὸν Ἡσίοδον Νικοκλῆς. Μέναιχμος δὲ ἱστορεῖ τοὺς
ῥαψῳδοὺς στιχῳδοὺς καλεῖσθαι διὰ τὸ τοὺς στίχους ῥάβδους λέγεσθαι ὑπό τινων.
ἄλλως. Ὁμηρίδαι πρότερον μὲν οἱ Ὁμήρου παῖδες, ὕστερον δὲ οἱ περὶ Κύναιθον
ῥαβδῳδοί· οὗτοι γὰρ τὴν Ὁμήρου ποίησιν σκεδασθεῖσαν ἐμνημόνευον καὶ ἀπήγ-
γελλον· ἐλυμήναντο δὲ αὐτῇ πάνυ. αἰεὶ οὖν τὴν ἀρχὴν ὡς ἐπὶ τὸ πλεῖστον ἐκ Διὸς
ἐποιοῦντο προοιμιαζόμενοι, ἐνίοτε δὲ καὶ Μουσῶν.

Philochorus [FGH 328 F 212] says that they [rhapsōidoi] were called that on the basis of the idea of composing—that is, stitching together [rhaptein]—the song. Proof
for this comes from Hesiod, who says:

> In Delos, back then at the very beginning, I and Homer, singers [aoidoi],
> sang-and-danced [melpein],[20] **stitching together [rhaptein]**[21] a song in new
> **humnoi**,
> making Phoebus Apollo the subject of our song,[22] the one with the golden
> weapon, the one born of Leto. [Hesiod F 357]

Nicocles [FGH 376 F 8] says that Hesiod was the first to **perform rhapsodically** [rhap-
sōideîn]. The investigations of Menaechmus indicate that **rhapsodes** [rhapsōidoi] were
called **verse singers** [stikhōidoi] because verses [stikhoi] were called staffs [rhabdoi] by
some people. Here is another version: the Homēridai were in former times the descendants of Homer, but then, in later times, they were a group comprised of Kynaithos
and his associates, who were called "rhabdōidoi" ["staff singers"]. For these [Kynaithos
and his associates] are the ones who used to bring back to memory and to perform
the poetry [poiēsis] of Homer, which had been scattered. But they mistreated [lumai-
nesthai] it [the poetry]. And they [the Homēridai] always started with a prooimion,
making mostly Zeus their point of departure and occasionally the Muses.

Scholia for Pindar Nemean 2.1d lines 14–29

In the case of the passage we have just seen illustrating the idea of a competition
between Homer and Hesiod, we can see that this competition can be staged on
Homer's terms, as it were. This passage shows that Kynaithos and his associates
claimed to be the performers of genuinely Homeric poetry. Evidently, this group
of performers made an additional claim: that they were genuinely descended from
Homer. That is, Kynaithos and his associates were would-be Homēridai.

In line with the argument I made in the case of the previous passage I quoted

20. The verb melpein/melpesthai and the noun molpē convey the combination of singing and dancing: PH 12§29n62 (= p. 350) and n64 (= p. 351).

21. The verb rhaptein 'stitch together' here is an explicit reference to the performances of rhapsodes,
since the word rhapsōidos means, etymologically, 'he who stitches together [rhaptein] songs [aoidai]'.
See PP 61–69; also Schmitt 1967:300–301 (with a definitive discussion of the morphology of rhapsōidós),
Durante 1976:177–79, BA 17§10n5 (= p. 298), and PH 1§21 (= p. 28). On the accent of rhapsōidós, see
Durante p. 177.

22. When I use the expression subject of song here, I mean the subject matter of the humnos, not
the grammatical subject. In the grammar of a humnos 'hymn' as a song, the divinity who figures as the
subject of the song is in fact the grammatical object of the verb of singing the song.

from the scholia for Pindar, I argue once again that the unnamed source who reports what I just summarized in this passage is Aristarchus. Once again, our unnamed source is critical of the claims of Kynaithos and his associates. He refuses to acknowledge that Homeric poetry was successfully 'brought back to memory' and 'performed' by these would-be descendants of Homer. Instead, he claims that Kynaithos and his group 'mistreated' the body of Homeric poetry. And, as we saw in the earlier passage that I quoted from the scholia for Pindar, this alleged mistreatment involved the adding of verses that were not genuinely Homeric.

To test the supposition that Kynaithos added verses to Homer's own verses, let us consider the structure of the *Homeric Hymn* (3) *to Apollo* as we have it. This *Hymn* appears, at least on the surface, to be a combination of two originally separate *Hymns,* and so it seems reasonable to understand the Pindaric scholia to mean that Kynaithos did add verses to an earlier *Hymn* composed by Homer. In terms of such an understanding, the verses supposedly added by Kynaithos could be described as Hesiodic rather than Homeric. Here is why. These verses constitute the part of the *Homeric Hymn to Apollo* that celebrates the god Apollo as he was worshipped at Delphi. In other words, the referent of these verses was the Pythian Apollo, not the Delian Apollo, who was worshipped at Delos. And as Richard Martin has shown, the verses of the *Homeric Hymn to Apollo* celebrating the Pythian Apollo are distinctly Hesiodic in style, whereas the verses celebrating the Delian Apollo are distinctly Homeric.[23] By the term *Hesiodic* he means the style that is characteristic of the *Theogony* and *Works and Days*; by *Homeric* he means the style that is characteristic of the *Iliad* and *Odyssey*.

If it is true that Kynaithos performed the *Homeric Hymn to Apollo* at the festival of the Delia at Delos in, say, 522 B.C.E., it follows that this would-be descendant of Homer conflated a *Homeric Hymn to Apollo* with a rival Hesiodic *Hymn,* treating the Hesiodic version as an aspect of an overall Homeric tradition that recognized the myth of the Contest of Homer and Hesiod, actually dramatizing that myth in the form of a juxtaposition of Homeric and Hesiodic versions of hymns to Apollo.[24] This juxtaposition of two distinct styles in performing a *Hymn to Apollo* anticipates a rivalry between two distinct kinds of epic performance that could potentially follow such a *Hymn.*

As we saw earlier, the initiator of this juxtaposition of Homeric and Hesiodic traditions in a single performance at the festival of the Delia in 522 B.C.E. or thereabouts was the tyrant Polycrates of Samos. His appropriation of the Homeric and the Hesiodic traditions by way of juxtaposing them can be viewed as a sure indication that these two traditions were already distinct from each other at this time. And this particular time coincides with the later years of the Peisistratidai of Athens.

23. Martin 2000b.
24. Martin 2000b.

I conclude, then, on the basis of the overall picture that emerges from the surviving glimpses of stories about the Contest of Homer and Hesiod, that the distinctions between Homer and Hesiod that we see being highlighted in these stories can be traced back to the earlier years of the Peisistratidai.

I now turn to the third of the three epic traditions current in the earlier years of the Peisistratidai: that is, the Orphic tradition. Like the epics ascribed to Hesiod, the epics ascribed to Orpheus were already distinct from the Homeric tradition at that time. The most striking evidence involves, once again, Polycrates of Samos, the most powerful rival of the Peisistratidai in the earlier years of their tyranny in Athens. Just as Kynaithos, under the patronage of Polycrates, appropriated the verses of Homer and Hesiod, so also Pythagoras, under the same patronage, appropriated the verses of Orpheus. I quote this summary of the relevant testimonia: "Pythagoras, who began his career in Polycrates' Samos, started (or was among the first to adopt) the practice of composing poems under the name of Orpheus."[25] I show here an example of such testimonia:

Ἴων δὲ ὁ Χῖος ἐν τοῖς Τριαγμοῖς φησιν αὐτὸν ἔνια ποιήσαντα ἀνενεγκεῖν εἰς Ὀρφέα.

Ion of Chios in his *Triagmoi* [*FGH* 392 F 25a = DK B 2] says that he [Pythagoras] made some poetry that he attributed to Orpheus.

Diogenes Laertius 8.8

I interpret this opaque statement to mean that Pythagoras performed in the persona of Orpheus verses attributed to Orpheus. The attribution to Orpheus and the self-identification with Orpheus are simultaneous in the moment of performance.[26] Similarly, Kynaithos identifies with Hesiod when he performs the verses sacred to the Pythian Apollo, just as he identifies with Homer when he performs the verses sacred to the Delian Apollo.[27] In this connection, I note with interest a tradition about the self-presentation of Pythagoras: he customarily wore a golden garland, a white robe, and trousers (Aelian *Varia Historia* 12.32).[28] I will postpone till the Epilegomena a discussion of the detail about the trousers, which conjures up the Thracian associations of Orpheus. For now I concentrate on the detail about the golden garland. In Plato's *Ion*, the rhapsode Ion boasts that he will win as first prize a golden garland awarded by the *Homēridai* when he performs Homer in the rhapsodic competition at the Panathenaia (*Ion* 530d); there are also two other contexts where the rhapsode's golden garland is mentioned (535d, 541c), and, in one of these, Ion is pictured as already wearing it while performing Homer at the Panathenaia (535d).

25. West 1999:373, with further reference to West 1983:7–20, 108–11. See now Riedweg 2002, especially p. 101.
26. Martin 2001.
27. Martin 2000b.
28. Riedweg 2002:14.

THE HOMERS OF THUCYDIDES AND HERODOTUS

The Panathenaic Homer of the Peisistratidai that I have been reconstructing here is noticeably different from the figure I reconstruct in the twin book *Homer the Classic*, namely the Panathenaic Homer of the democracy in Athens during the second half of the fifth century.[29] The figure we now see emerging is an earlier form of Homer, more congenial to what I am calling the *Dark Age*. This earlier Homer was thought to have performed not only the *Iliad* and *Odyssey*. As we saw from Thucydides, this Homer performed also the *Homeric Hymn to Apollo*. We saw that in *Vita* 2 as well. As for the Homer of *Vita* 1, this figure is even more noticeably different from the Panathenaic Homer of the democracy in Athens during the second half of the fifth century. The Homer of *Vita* 1 is an even earlier form of Homer, who composed not only the *Homeric Hymns* but even the epics of the epic Cycle—or at least some of those epics. As I will now argue, the Homer of *Vita* 1 matches roughly the Homer of Herodotus, while the Homer of *Vita* 2 matches the Homer of Thucydides.

I start with Thucydides. What this historian ordinarily means by *Homer* is the Panathenaic Homer: that is, the poet of the *Iliad* and *Odyssey*. As we know from all his references to Homer above and beyond his references to the *Homeric Hymn to Apollo,* the only epics that Thucydides attributed to Homer were the *Iliad* and the *Odyssey*, the two epics traditionally performed at the Panathenaia in his time. To this extent, the Homer of Thucydides in the second half of the fifth century B.C.E. was roughly the equivalent of the Homer of Plato and Aristotle in the fourth century. And yet, exceptionally, Thucydides also attributes to Homer what we call the "Homeric" *Hymn* (3) *to Apollo*. How are we to account for this exception?

In general, Thucydides would have been speaking as an Athenian when he spoke of Homer. His experience, like that of any other Athenian in his time, would have been based on actually hearing the Homeric *Iliad* and *Odyssey* being performed at the seasonally recurring festival of the Panathenaia. Speaking as an Athenian, he would have expected his addressees to know what he knew was said by Homer. In fact, whenever Thucydides uses Homer as evidence, he does so with an attitude that reveals an expectation of full familiarity.[30] But his use of the *Homeric Hymn to Apollo* stands in sharp contrast. In this case he quotes extensively from Homer, whereas his quotations and citations are minimal in other cases. According to a noted modern commentator on Thucydides, these extensive quotations show that Thucydides did not expect his addressees to know the words spoken by Homer in this *Hymn*.[31]

29. *HC* 3§33.

30. Hornblower 1991:17, especially with reference to Thucydides 1.3.3.

31. Hornblower 1991:523. At *PP* 81n64, I had gone so far as to suggest that Thucydides may have heard this *Hymn to Apollo* performed at the Panathenaia. I would now say it differently. It is more likely, I now think, that such a performance would have been a special event at one particular celebration of

In quoting from the *Homeric Hymn to Apollo,* Thucydides is taking the stance of an impartial antiquarian conducting an objective study that goes far beyond the common knowledge of his fellow Athenians.

The situation is different in the case of Herodotus. When he speaks of Homer, he does not speak as an Athenian, and the Homer he cites is not simply presumed to be the Panathenaic Homer. In other words, the Homer he cites is not necessarily restricted to the figure known only as the poet of the *Iliad* and *Odyssey.* In one context, for example, Herodotus attributes to Homer an epic about the sons of the Seven against Thebes called the *Epigonoi* (4.32), though he goes on to express some doubt about the attribution (4.32–33).[32]

In another context, Herodotus makes a point of distinguishing Homer from what he describes as the poet of the *Cypria,* and, in making this distinction, he actually quotes a passage from the Homeric *Iliad* to prove his point:

Δοκέει δέ μοι καὶ Ὅμηρος τὸν λόγον τοῦτον πυθέσθαι· ἀλλ᾽, οὐ γὰρ ὁμοίως ἐς τὴν ἐποποιίην εὐπρεπὴς ἦν τῷ ἑτέρῳ τῷ περ ἐχρήσατο, [ἐς ὃ] μετῆκε αὐτόν, δηλώσας ὡς καὶ τοῦτον ἐπίσταιτο τὸν λόγον. Δῆλον δέ, κατά περ ἐποίησε ἐν Ἰλιάδι (καὶ οὐδαμῇ ἄλλη ἀνεπόδισε ἑωυτόν) πλάνην τὴν Ἀλεξάνδρου, ὡς ἀπηνείχθη ἄγων Ἑλένην τῇ τε δὴ ἄλλῃ πλαζόμενος καὶ ὡς ἐς Σιδῶνα τῆς Φοινίκης ἀπίκετο. Ἐπιμέμνηται δὲ αὐτοῦ ἐν Διομήδεος Ἀριστηίῃ· λέγει δὲ τὰ ἔπεα ὧδε·

ἔνθ᾽ ἔσαν οἱ **πέπλοι παμποίκιλοι,** ἔργα γυναικῶν
Σιδονίων, τὰς αὐτὸς Ἀλέξανδρος θεοειδὴς
ἤγαγε **Σιδονίηθεν,** ἐπιπλὼς εὐρέα πόντον,
τὴν ὁδὸν ἣν Ἑλένην περ ἀνήγαγεν εὐπατέρειαν. [*Iliad* VI 289–92]

Ἐπιμέμνηται δὲ καὶ ἐν Ὀδυσσείῃ ἐν τοῖσδε τοῖσι ἔπεσι·

τοῖα Διὸς θυγάτηρ ἔχε φάρμακα μητιόεντα,
ἐσθλά, τά οἱ Πολύδαμνα πόρεν Θῶνος παράκοιτις
Αἰγυπτίη, τῇ πλεῖστα φέρει ζείδωρος ἄρουρα
φάρμακα, πολλὰ μὲν ἐσθλὰ μεμιγμένα, πολλὰ δὲ λυγρά. [*Odyssey* iv 227–30]

Καὶ τάδε ἕτερα πρὸς Τηλέμαχον Μενέλεως λέγει·

---

the Panathenaia, connected with the celebration of the Delia in 426. On the occasion of most celebrations of the Panathenaia in the fifth century B.C.E., I think that only the *Iliad* and the *Odyssey* were performed. Like the rest of hexameter poetry, the *Hymn to Apollo* would have become too outmoded in content to be performed regularly at the Panathenaia in the late fifth century B.C.E. As we are about to see from the upcoming analysis of its content, the *Homeric Hymn* (3) *to Apollo* as we have it is far more suitable for performance at the Panathenaia in the late sixth century.

32. In Herodotus 5.67.1, the reference to rhapsodic contests in performing *Homēreia epea* at a festival in Sikyon during the tyranny of Kleisthenes does not specify the content of this 'Homeric epic' except to say that the themes of this epic highlight Argos and the Argives. These themes are of course appropriate not only to the *Iliad* but also to the *Thebais* and the *Epigonoi*: further analysis in *PH* 1§10n22 (= p. 22).

Αἰγύπτῳ μ' ἔτι δεῦρο θεοὶ μεμαῶτα νέεσθαι
ἔσχον, ἐπεὶ οὔ σφιν ἔρεξα τεληέσσας ἑκατόμβας. [*Odyssey* iv 351–52]

Ἐν τούτοισι τοῖσι ἔπεσι δηλοῖ ὅτι ἠπίστατο τὴν ἐς Αἴγυπτον Ἀλεξάνδρου **πλάνην**·
ὁμουρέει γὰρ ἡ Συρίη Αἰγύπτῳ, οἱ δὲ Φοίνικες, τῶν ἐστι ἡ **Σιδών**, ἐν τῇ Συρίῃ οἰκέουσι.
    Κατὰ ταῦτα δὲ τὰ ἔπεα καὶ τόδε [τὸ χωρίον] οὐκ ἥκιστα ἀλλὰ μάλιστα δηλοῖ ὅτι
οὐκ Ὁμήρου τὰ Κύπρια ἔπεά ἐστι ἀλλ' ἄλλου τινός· ἐν μὲν γὰρ τοῖσι Κυπρίοισι εἴρηται
ὡς τριταῖος ἐκ Σπάρτης Ἀλέξανδρος ἀπίκετο ἐς τὸ Ἴλιον ἄγων Ἑλένην, εὐαέϊ τε
πνεύματι χρησάμενος καὶ θαλάσσῃ λείῃ· ἐν δὲ Ἰλιάδι λέγει ὡς ἐπλάζετο ἄγων αὐτήν.
Ὅμηρος μέν νυν καὶ τὰ Κύπρια ἔπεα χαιρέτω.

I think that Homer was aware of this story [the story of Helen in Egypt]. But, because
it [this story] was not as appropriate for epic composition as was the other one [the
other story] that he used, he omitted it, though he made it clear that he was aware of
this story [the story of Helen in Egypt] as well. It is clear on the basis of the way he
composed in the *Iliad* (and nowhere else has he [Homer] retraced his steps to this)
the detour of Alexandros [Paris]—how he [Paris], as he was bringing Helen, was blown
off course and was detoured in various places,[33] and then how he reached Sidon in
Phoenicia. He [Homer] mentions the story [of Helen in Egypt] in the part about the
greatest deeds of Diomedes. And the epic words he says are as follows:

> There they were, the *peploi*, completely **pattern-woven** [*poikiloi*], the work
>   of women
> from **Sidon**, whom Alexandros [Paris] himself, the godlike,   290
> had brought home [to Troy] from the land of **Sidon**, sailing over the vast sea,
> on the very same journey as the one he took when he brought back home [to
>   Troy] also Helen, the one who is descended from the most noble father.
> [*Iliad* VI 289–92]

He mentions it [the story of Helen in Egypt] in the *Odyssey* also, in these epic words:

> Such magical things she had, the daughter of Zeus,
> things of good outcome, which to her did Polydamna give, wife of Thon.
> She was Egyptian. For her, many were the things produced by the life-giving
>   earth,
> magical things—many good mixtures and many baneful ones. [*Odyssey* iv 227–30]

And these other things are said to Telemakhos by Menelaos:

> I was eager to return here, but the gods still held me in Egypt,
> Since I had not sacrificed entire hecatombs to them. [*Odyssey* iv 351–52][34]

33. For a parallel to the syntax of τῇ τε δὴ ἄλλη πλαζόμενος καὶ . . . , see Herodotus 3.61.3.
34. I question the judgment of modern editors who bracket sections 4 and 5 of Herodotus 2.116.
Granted, the topic in these sections is the detour of Menelaos and Helen in Egypt after the war at Troy, not
the detour of Paris and Helen before the war. But these passages are relevant to what Herodotus says thereafter (2.118–19) about Helen in Egypt after the war. Herodotus is making the point that there are other Homeric stories about Helen in Egypt, whereas there are no other Homeric stories about Helen in Phoenicia.

In these epic verses the Poet makes clear that he knew of the **detour** of Alexandros [Paris] to Egypt; for Syria borders on Egypt, and the Phoenicians whose territory is **Sidon** dwell in Syria.

In terms of these epic verses, this shows most clearly that the epic of the *Cypria* is not by Homer but by someone else. For in the *Cypria* it is said that on the third day after setting sail from Sparta Alexandros [Paris] arrived in Troy bringing Helen, having made good use of a favorable wind and smooth seas. In the *Iliad*, on the other hand, he [Homer] says that he [Paris] was detoured as he was bringing her [Helen]. So much for Homer and the epic of the *Cypria*.

Herodotus 2.116.1–117.1

I offer a paraphrase of the arguments made here by Herodotus:

In a non-Homeric version of an epic called the *Cypria* (a version known to Herodotus but not to us), it is said that Paris and Helen sailed to Troy without making any detour. There is an alternative version in the Homeric *Iliad*, and Herodotus quotes the relevant verses. In this version, it is said that Paris and Helen did make a detour: they went to Phoenicia before they went to Troy. On the basis of an Egyptian story about Paris and Helen, Herodotus goes on to argue that they went to Egypt as well as Phoenicia, and that Homer knew it. After all, Egypt is next to Phoenicia. But the problem is, Homer later elided the story of Helen in Egypt as inappropriate. So the *Iliad* tells the story about Helen in Troy, not the story about Helen in Egypt. And the *Odyssey* follows the *Iliad* in accepting the story of Helen in Troy. Both epics, however, show traces of the story of Helen in Egypt, though the traces in the *Iliad* are only indirect.

Next, I offer a critical analysis of this paraphrase:

Herodotus considers the stories about detours in Egypt and Phoenicia within the larger context of stories about Helen in Egypt. Upon retelling an Egyptian version of a story about a detour of Paris and Helen in Egypt after he abducted her from Sparta (2.112–15), Herodotus says that Homer must have known that story (2.116.1). Then, in order to show that this is so, Herodotus offers proof (2.116–17), quoting a passage from the *Iliad* (VI 289–92) and two passages from the *Odyssey* (iv 227–30, 351–52). The passage from the *Iliad* concerns the detour of Paris and Helen before the war at Troy, while the two passages from the *Odyssey* concern the detour of Menelaos and Helen after the war.[35] The first passage is meant as indirect proof that the story of Helen in Egypt was recognized by Homer in the *Iliad,* while the other two passages are meant as direct proof that the story of Helen in Egypt was recognized by Homer in the *Odyssey.* The passages from the *Odyssey* are relevant to what Herodotus goes on to argue about the story of Helen in Egypt: he finds that this story is more believable than the story of Helen in Troy (2.118–19). In the Egyptian version, Paris is forced to leave Helen behind in Egypt after the two of

35. See again the previous note.

them are detoured there (2.115.5). That is where Menelaos finds her after the war. According to this Egyptian version, then, Helen never went to Troy. For Herodotus, this version makes more sense than the Homeric version that dominates the *Iliad* and *Odyssey*.

I conclude by considering again the fact that Herodotus distinguishes Homer as the poet of the *Iliad* from the poet of the *Cypria*. This fact shows that the historian is familiar with the Panathenaic Homer. That is, he thinks of Homer as the poet of the two epics performed at the Panathenaia, the *Iliad* and the *Odyssey*. Nevertheless, Herodotus does not presuppose that everyone thinks this way. That is why he makes a point of establishing the distinction in the first place. Herodotus speaks of the poet of the *Cypria* as someone who may be considered to be Homer by others, though he knows better.

4

———

Homer in the Homeric *Odyssey*

THE FESTIVE POETICS OF AN
ONGOING *HUMNOS* IN *ODYSSEY* VIII

When Thucydides quotes Homer, he imagines the Poet in the act of personally performing at the festival of the Delia in Delos. This historian's view, as we have seen, is Athenocentric. To be contrasted is the view of Aristarchus, which is post-Athenocentric. For Aristarchus, the poet of the *Homeric Hymn to Apollo* is a neoteric rhapsode, Kynaithos of Chios. For Thucydides, the performer of the *Homeric Hymn to Apollo* is Homer himself, and the Poet's *Hymn to Apollo* is a *prooimion* to whatever epic Homer will perform. Theoretically, the *Hymn to Apollo* may be a *prooimion* to the Homeric *Iliad* or *Odyssey*. Or at least the *Hymn* may be a *humnos* that connects with an epic performed by Homer at the Delia on Delos. Such an epic could be seen as a prototype of the epic performed by rhapsodes at the festival of the Panathenaia in Athens. And, as Douglas Frame has shown, such a prototype would most closely resemble versions of the Homeric *Iliad* and *Odyssey* as already performed by the *Homēridai* at the festival of the Panionia at the Panionion of the Ionian Dodecapolis in Asia Minor during the late eighth and early seventh centuries B.C.E.[1] We will take a closer look at the Panionia at a later point, but for now I concentrate on the basic idea of performing Homeric poetry at a festival. This idea brings me to the first and the third songs of Demodokos in *Odyssey* viii, which represent an earlier form of epic as performed at a festival. As we will see, this earlier form of epic is defined by the concept of *humnos* in the context of a festival. As we will also see,

---

1. Frame 2009 ch. 11.

this earlier form represents the morphology of the epic Cycle, as opposed to the later form of the Homeric *Iliad* and *Odyssey*.

As I argue in the twin book *Homer the Classic*, the ending of the epic of the first song of Demodokos is continually deferred, and this deferral is marked by the expression *aps arkhesthai* 'start again and again' at verse 90 of *Odyssey* viii.[2] Each time the singer restarts his song, Odysseus starts weeping, and his continuously restarted outpouring of tears is expressed by the wording *aps . . . goân* 'lament again and again' (92). Only Alkinoos, king of the Phaeacians, notices the unexpected reaction of Odysseus to the epic performance in the first song of Demodokos (viii 93–95). The king's own reaction is to defer even further any kind of epic ending. Postponing any more restartings of the ongoing epic performance by Demodokos, Alkinoos announces that the time for eating and drinking and 'the *phorminx*'—a metonymy for the singing of Demodokos, who accompanies himself on the stringed instrument called the *phorminx*—is to be stopped for the moment (98–99). As we are about to see, the singing of Demodokos will be restarted in a festive context that resembles the festive context of the Delia as dramatized in the *Homeric Hymn to Apollo*.

Before any further singing by Demodokos can take place, the time has come for sporting events: that is, athletic contests to be held in the public gathering space of the Phaeacians (viii 100–101). The king refers to boxing, wrestling, jumping, and footracing (103). The first athletic event turns out to be the footrace (120–25), followed by wrestling (126–27), jumping (128), discus throwing (129), and, finally, boxing (130). There is a striking parallel to be found in a passage we have already examined here. That passage comes from the *Homeric Hymn* (3) *to Apollo* (146–55), describing a festival of all Ionians gathered on the island of Delos. For the moment I focus on one detail in that passage: the occasion of that Delian festival is described as an *agōn* 'competition' (149). The competitive events at that festival include athletics—boxing is the example that is highlighted—as well as dancing and singing (149). So also in *Odyssey* viii, as we are about to see, the overall occasion is described as an *agōn* in athletics, dancing, and singing. In analyzing the context of this festive occasion, I hope to show its relevance to the poetry performed by Demodokos in *Odyssey* viii.

In the competitive atmosphere of the athletic contests of *Odyssey* viii, Odysseus is provoked into participating in the competition. Responding to the challenge, he wins easily in a discus throw (186). Then he goes on to challenge the Phaeacians to compete with him in boxing, wrestling, or footracing (206)—or in archery (215–28), or in throwing the javelin (229). Only in footracing does he choose not to compete (230–33). The competitive rhetoric of Odysseus, highlighting his strengths and weaknesses as an athlete, mirrors his strengths and weaknesses as the central hero of the Homeric *Odyssey*. His rhetoric about his prowess in archery is particularly

2. *HC* ch. 2.

telling, since it anticipates what will happen in the overall epic plot of the *Odyssey*: essential for the hero's victory over the suitors is his bow. But there is more to it. The competitive rhetoric in *Odyssey* viii extends from athletic to poetic competition, and the context of these two modes of competition turns out to be the same occasion. That occasion is the *dais* 'feast':

δαιτί τε τέρπηται καὶ ἀοιδῆς ὕμνον ἀκούων

. . . so that he [Odysseus] might take delight [*terpesthai*] in the feast [*dais*] and in listening to the ***humnos*** of the song.

Odyssey viii 429

The word *dais* here, basically meaning 'feast', refers short-range to an occasion of communal dining (*dorpon* 'dinner', viii 395), which will take place after sunset (417). The intended guest of honor at this feast is Odysseus. This occasion of communal dining leads into the third song of Demodokos (484–85). So much for the short-range reference. I will argue, however, that there is also a long-range reference: the word *dais* here refers metonymically to a stylized festival that has been ongoing ever since an earlier occasion of communal dining, which actually led into the first song of Demodokos (71–72).

To make this argument about the word *dais* 'feast', I start by comparing the metonymic use of the word *thusia* 'sacrifice' in the sense of 'festival'. I return here to a classic example: that is, the use of *thusia* 'sacrifice' in Plato's *Timaeus* (26e) with reference to the entire complex of events taking place at the festival of the Panathenaia in Athens.[3] As we can see from this and other examples of the word, *thusia* refers not only to the sacrifice and sacrificial cooking of the sacrificial animal, or to the distribution of the cooked meat and the consequent eating and drinking: it refers also to the whole complex of competitive events that take place at any given festival, including not only athletics but also performances of poetry, song, and dance.[4]

The divinity who presides over such a festive occasion is not only the prime recipient of the *thusia* 'sacrifice': in the context of the overall festival, that divinity becomes also the subject of that festival—that is, the subject of the *humnos* that inaugurates that festival. A classic example is the use of the word *humnos* in Plato's *Timaeus* with reference to the goddess Athena as the subject of the *humnos* and, by extension, as the subject of the overall festival of the Panathenaia in Athens:

Ἄκουε δή, ὦ Σώκρατες, λόγου μάλα μὲν ἀτόπου, παντάπασί γε μὴν ἀληθοῦς, ὡς ὁ τῶν ἑπτὰ σοφώτατος Σόλων ποτ᾽ ἔφη. ἦν μὲν οὖν οἰκεῖος καὶ σφόδρα φίλος ἡμῖν Δρωπίδου τοῦ προπάππου, καθάπερ λέγει πολλαχοῦ καὶ αὐτὸς ἐν τῇ ποιήσει· πρὸς

3. *PR* 53, 83.
4. *PR* ch. 2.

δὲ Κριτίαν τὸν ἡμέτερον πάππον εἶπεν, ὡς ἀπεμνημόνευεν αὖ πρὸς ἡμᾶς ὁ γέρων, ὅτι μεγάλα καὶ θαυμαστὰ τῆσδ' εἴη παλαιὰ ἔργα τῆς πόλεως ὑπὸ χρόνου καὶ φθορᾶς ἀνθρώπων ἠφανισμένα, πάντων δὲ ἓν μέγιστον, οὗ νῦν ἐπιμνησθεῖσιν πρέπον ἂν ἡμῖν εἴη σοί τε ἀποδοῦναι **χάριν** καὶ τὴν θεὸν ἅμα ἐν τῇ **πανηγύρει** δικαίως τε καὶ ἀληθῶς οἷόνπερ **ὑμνοῦντας** ἐγκωμιάζειν.

[Critias is speaking.] Listen, then, Socrates, to a story that is very unusual but alto-gether true—as the wisest of the Seven Wise Men, Solon, once told it. He was a rela-tive and good friend of Dropides, my great-grandfather—as he himself says several times in his poetry. And he [Dropides] told Critias, my grandfather. As the old man recalled to us from memory, there were ancient deeds, great and wondrous, that orig-inated from this city [Athens] and that have disappeared through the passage of time and through the ruination that befalls humanity. He went on to say that of all these deeds, there was one in particular that was the greatest, which it would be fitting for us now to bring to mind, reciprocating you [Socrates] with its **pleasurable beauty** [*kharis*] while at the same time rightly and truthfully **celebrating** [*enkōmiazein*] the goddess on this the occasion of her **festival** [*panēguris*], just as if we were making her the subject of a *humnos*.

Plato Timaeus 20d–21a

In this passage, the immediate occasion of the dialogue that we know as the *Timaeus* is equated with the ultimate occasion of the festival celebrating the gene-sis of the goddess who presides over the city of Athens. Further, the discourse ex-tending from what is said by Timaeus to what is said by Critias is equated with a *humnos* to be sung in worship of this goddess.[5] Even further, Plato uses the tech-nical language of rhapsodes in conveying the continuities and discontinuities of the discourse extending from the *Timaeus* as text to the *Critias* as text.[6]

In this passage, the figurative *humnos* mentioned by the speaker starts with a simulated hymnic *prooimion*, which is designed to introduce the narration of a sim-ulated epic: that is, the story about the destruction of Atlantis. The *pleasure* of the impending story's *beauty,* as conveyed by the word *kharis*, is being offered by the speaker, Critias, to Socrates as the immediate recipient. But the actual context of *kharis* in this passage makes it clear that the ultimate recipient of such a pleasura-ble offering is the goddess Athena. The speaker here is engaging in a parody of a *Hymn to Athena*, and the joke is that Socrates has momentarily replaced Athena as the primary recipient of what is called *kharis*, which refers here to the beautiful and pleasurable offering of a stylized *humnos*. This offering corresponds to the hymnic salutation *khaire* 'hail and take pleasure' in the context of a hymnic *prooimion*. In the same breath, the speaker goes on to acknowledge the goddess Athena as the ul-

---

5. On the interruption of the discourse after it extends from the *Timaeus* to the *Critias* of Plato, see *PR* 65–69.

6. *PR* 66, 68–69.

timate subject of a *humnos* to be performed on the occasion of her feast: that is, at the festival of the Panathenaia in Athens. The *humnos* that is notionally inaugurated by this mock hymnic *prooimion* can then proceed to the narration of the story about the destruction of Atlantis, a mock epic that rivals the epic traditions about the destruction of Troy.[7]

By contrast, a *humnos* inaugurated by a real *prooimion* can lead into real epic—or into some other such undertaking of epic proportions. It is no accident that the wording of Plato's mock *prooimion* mirrors closely the wording of real *prooimia*, such as the prose *prooimion* we find at the beginning of the *History* of Herodotus:

Ἡροδότου Ἁλικαρνησσέος ἱστορίης ἀπόδεξις ἥδε, ὡς μήτε τὰ γενόμενα ἐξ ἀνθρώπων τῷ χρόνῳ ἐξίτηλα γένηται, μήτε ἔργα μεγάλα τε καὶ θωμαστά, τὰ μὲν Ἕλλησι, τὰ δὲ βαρβάροισι ἀποδεχθέντα, ἀκλέα γένηται, τά τε ἄλλα καὶ δι’ ἣν αἰτίην ἐπολέμησαν ἀλλήλοισι.

This is the public presentation of the inquiry of Herodotus of Halicarnassus, with the purpose of bringing it about that whatever results from human affairs may not, with the passage of time, become evanescent, and that great and wondrous deeds—some of them publicly performed by Hellenes, others by barbarians—may not become things without fame [*kleos*]; in particular,[8] [this presentation concerns] what cause made them wage war against each other.

Herodotus 0.0 (*prooemium*)

The precision of Plato's wording in the mock *prooimion* we find in the *Timaeus* (21a) is evidenced by the expression τὴν θεὸν ... ἐν τῇ πανηγύρει δικαίως τε καὶ ἀληθῶς ... ὑμνοῦντας ἐγκωμιάζειν 'rightly and truthfully celebrating [*enkōmiazein*] the goddess on this the occasion of her festival [*panēguris*], . . . making her the subject of a *humnos*'. I highlight the use of the verb *enkōmiazein* 'celebrate' with the accusative case of the divinity who presides over the festival and who is the subject of the *humnos* that inaugurates the festival. We may compare the parallel use of the verb *kōmazein* 'celebrate' in Pindar's imitation of the *prooimion* of Zeus as performed by the *Homēridai*:

τόν, ὦ πολῖ|ται, **κωμάξατε** Τιμοδήμῳ σὺν εὐκλέϊ νόστῳ·| ἁδυμελεῖ δ’ **ἐξάρχετε φωνᾷ**.

Him [Zeus, presiding over the festival of the Nemea] you, O citizens of the city, must **celebrate** [*kōmazein*] for the sake of Timodemos, at the moment of his homecoming marked by genuine fame [*kleos*], and, in sweet-sounding song, you must **lead off** [*exarkhein*] with your **voice**.

Pindar *Nemean* 2.23–25

---

7. PR 65–69, 84–86.

8. The construction here is analogous to Plato's rhetorical device of saying, in effect, "one [superlative] example out of many potential examples."

As I show in the twin book *Homer the Classic*, the act of *kōmazein* 'celebrating' here is compared explicitly to the performing of the *prooimion* of Zeus:[9]

Ὅθεν περ καὶ Ὁμηρίδαι | ῥαπτῶν ἐπέων τὰ πόλλ᾿ ἀοιδοί | ἄρχονται, Διὸς ἐκ προοιμίου.

[Starting] from the point where [*hothen*] the *Homēridai*, singers, most of the time [*ta polla*] begin [*arkhesthai*] their stitched-together words, from the *prooimion* of Zeus ...

Pindar *Nemean* 2.1–3

Just as Athena presides over the festival of the Panathenaia, so also Zeus presides over the festival of the Nemea. Just as Athena is pictured as a hymnic subject, so also is Zeus. Moreover, as I will argue later, Zeus is a transcendent hymnic subject: he can preside over a *humnos* even if that *humnos* is being performed at a festival sacred to another god. This way, as I will also argue later, Zeus gets to preside over a *humnos* that leads to a transcendent form of epic as its hymnic consequent, and that epic form is the poetic legacy inherited by the 'descendants of Homer', the *Homēridai*.[10]

This formal relationship between the concept of *humnos* and the concept of epic as a hymnic consequent is most relevant to Plato's reference in the *Timaeus* (21a) to a *humnos* sung for the goddess Athena in the context of her own festival, the Panathenaia. As I argue in *Homer the Classic*, the central narrative of such a *humnos* sung for Athena at the Panathenaia is the story of her birth and her joint victory with Zeus and the other Olympians over the Giants in the Gigantomachy, which is imagined as taking place on the day of her birth.[11] As I also argue, the narrative of the Gigantomachy was woven into the woolen robe or Peplos of Athena, which was presented to the goddess at the climactic conclusion of the Panathenaic Procession, which was in turn the climactic conclusion of the entire festival of the Panathenaia. There is a mythological parallelism between the *humnos* as a notionally prototypical song and the Peplos of Athena as a notionally prototypical fabric. Not only was the narrative of the Gigantomachy woven into the Peplos of Athena: it was also sculpted into the east metopes of the Parthenon. And the narrative of the birth of Athena was sculpted into the east pediment looming above the east metopes. So the sculptural narrative of the Parthenon starts with the birth of Athena on the east pediment and, moving farther down, proceeds to the victory of Athena and her fellow Olympians over the Giants. Then, from this starting point on the east face of the temple, the sculptural narrative of the Parthenon moves counterclockwise to

---

9. *HC* 2§72.

10. On epic as a *hymnic consequent*, see *HC* 2§§97, 109, 113–14, 116.

11. *HC* 1§131. Here I disagree with the objections of those who think that the birthday of Athena cannot be simultaneous with the day of her own victory over the Giants in the larger context of the Gigantomachy. These objections do not take into account the Athenian agenda inherent in the myth of Athena's birth, fully armed, from the head of Zeus.

the north face. A narrative of the Trojan War was sculpted into the north metopes. I have just reached here a point I anticipate in the twin book *Homer the Classic*. There I argue that the sculptural narrative of the east pediment and of the east metopes is a virtual *Hymn to Athena* while the sculptural narrative of the north metopes is a virtual epic of the Trojan War. The two narratives approximate respectively a most grand *prooimion* and a most grand epic, where *prooimion* and epic connect with each other into one single, continuous, notionally seamless *humnos*.[12]

Having reviewed what can be gathered about the conceptual world of the word *humnos* in combination with the word *thusia* in the sense of 'festival', I now apply this comparative evidence to my argument about the combination of this same word *humnos* with the word *dais* 'feast' at *Odyssey* viii 429. In terms of this argument, to repeat, *dais* here refers to a stylized festival.

In fact, a festival has been in progress ever since verse 38 of *Odyssey* viii, where Alkinoos orders the holding of a *dais* 'feast' as the occasion for hosting Odysseus as a guest of honor. This hosting, as the king announces at verse 42, is a sequence of events leading up to a future point in the ongoing narrative—a point where the proper arrangements will finally be in place for sending the guest back to his homeland (28–33). From the very start, the singer Demodokos is to attend the feast, singing for the assembled audience (43–45). The stylized festival officially begins when the king himself slaughters the sacrificial animals (59–60), whose meat is then cooked and made ready for the 'feasting', which is called a *dais* already at verse 61 of *Odyssey* viii.

The sequence of festive events now proceeds to the actual feasting on food and drink (71); after the eating and drinking are over (72), the next event is the performance of the first song of Demodokos (73–82).[13] Then Alkinoos postpones further performance (98–99), as I have already noted, and the audience proceeds from the closed space of eating and drinking to the open space of athletic competitions (100–101). Odysseus engages in these competitions with a winning throw of the discus (186–200), and he reinforces his stylized athletic victory by boasting of his overall athletic superiority (201–33).

Alkinoos responds to the hero's victory and the ensuing boast by conceding that the Phaeacians cannot compete with Odysseus in conventional athletic events like boxing or wrestling (viii 246). When it comes to athletic prowess, the king chooses to boast only about the Phaeacians' swiftness in running and sailing (247). We see here the embedding of a narrative link between anterior and posterior details in

---

12. *HC* 4§246.

13. It is made explicit at *Odyssey* viii 72 that the first performance of Demodokos follows the feasting. I note with interest that the setting for the epic action described in the first performance is a *dais* 'feast', and that this *dais* is further described as a 'feast of the gods' at *Odyssey* viii 76: *theōn en daiti thaleiēi*. The same epithet *thaleiēi* is also used to describe the ongoing *dais* of *Odyssey* viii at 99. This epithet is of special interest in light of the meaning of the noun *thaliai* in the plural, 'festivities' (as in xi 603).

the narration. Earlier, Odysseus had conceded that he cannot run competitively, and that his running skills have been blighted by too much sailing (230–33). The Phaeacian king's boast that links prowess in running with prowess in sailing is readily accepted by Odysseus, since he knows he will have to rely on the prowess of the Phaeacians in sailing if he is ever to succeed in his own quest for a homecoming.

Next, the rhetoric of competition shifts from athletics to poetry, song, and dance. What is most dear to the Phaeacians, Alkinoos goes on to say, is the following sequence of delights, headed by the festive notion of the *dais*:

αἰεὶ δ᾽ ἡμῖν **δαίς** τε φίλη **κίθαρίς** τε **χοροί** τε
εἵματά τ᾽ ἐξημοιβὰ λοετρά τε θερμὰ καὶ εὐναί.

Dear to us always is **feasting** [*dais*], also the *kitharis,* and occasions of **singing and dancing** [*khoroi*],
also the changing of costumes from one occasion to the next, also warm baths, and lying around in bed.

Odyssey viii 248–49

At this point, we see the embedding of another narrative link between anterior and posterior details in the narration. The theme of swift-footedness makes it possible for the narrative to shift from the subtheme of nimble footracing to the subtheme of nimble footwork in dance: that is, in the song-and-dance ensemble of the *khoros*:

"ἀλλ᾽ ἄγε, Φαιήκων **βητάρμονες** ὅσσοι ἄριστοι,   250
παίσατε, ὥς χ᾽ ὁ ξεῖνος ἐνίσπῃ οἶσι φίλοισιν,
οἴκαδε νοστήσας, ὅσσον περιγινόμεθ᾽ ἄλλων
ναυτιλίῃ καὶ ποσσὶ καὶ **ὀρχηστυῖ** καὶ **ἀοιδῇ.**
Δημοδόκῳ δέ τις αἶψα κιὼν **φόρμιγγα** λίγειαν
οἰσέτω, ἥ που κεῖται ἐν ἡμετέροισι δόμοισιν."   255
ὣς ἔφατ᾽ Ἀλκίνοος θεοείκελος, ὦρτο δὲ κῆρυξ
οἴσων **φόρμιγγα** γλαφυρὴν δόμου ἐκ βασιλῆος.
αἰσυμνῆται δὲ κριτοὶ ἐννέα πάντες ἀνέσταν,
δήμιοι, οἳ κατ᾽ **ἀγῶνα** ἐῢ πρήσσεσκον ἕκαστα,
λείηναν δὲ **χορόν,** καλὸν δ᾽ εὔρυναν **ἀγῶνα.**   260
κῆρυξ δ᾽ ἐγγύθεν ἦλθε φέρων **φόρμιγγα** λίγειαν
Δημοδόκῳ· ὁ δ᾽ ἔπειτα κί᾽ **ἐς μέσον·** ἀμφὶ δὲ κοῦροι
πρωθῆβαι ἵσταντο, δαήμονες **ὀρχηθμοῖο,**
πέπληγον δὲ **χορὸν** θεῖον ποσίν. αὐτὰρ Ὀδυσσεὺς
μαρμαρυγὰς θηεῖτο ποδῶν, θαύμαζε δὲ θυμῷ.   265
αὐτὰρ ὁ **φορμίζων** ἀνεβάλλετο καλὸν ἀείδειν
ἀμφ᾽ Ἄρεος **φιλότητος**[14] ἐϋστεφάνου τ᾽ Ἀφροδίτης,

---

14. There is a variant reading attested: φιλότητα in the accusative, instead of φιλότητος in the genitive.

ὡς τὰ πρῶτ' ἐμίγησαν ἐν Ἡφαίστοιο δόμοισι
λάθρῃ·

[Alkinoos is speaking.] "Let's get started. I want the best of the Phaeacian
   acrobatic dancers [*bētarmones*]   250
to **perform their sportive dance** [*paizein*],[15] so that the stranger, our guest,
   will be able to tell his near-and-dear ones,
when he gets home, how much better we [Phaeacians] are than anyone else
in sailing and in footwork, in **dance** and **song.**
One of you go and get for Demodokos the clear-sounding *phorminx,*
bringing it to him. It is in the palace somewhere."   255
Thus spoke Alkinoos, the one who looks like the gods, and the herald [*kērux*]
   got up,
ready to bring the well-carved *phorminx* from the palace of the king.
And the organizers [*aisumnētai*], the nine selectmen, all got up
—they belonged to the district [*dēmos*]—and they started arranging
   everything according to the rules of the **competition** [*agōn*].
They made smooth the place of the **singing and dancing** [*khoros*], and they
   made a wide space of **competition** [*agōn*].   260
The **herald** [*kērux*] came near, bringing the clear-sounding *phorminx*
for Demodokos. He [Demodokos] moved **to the center** of the space. At his
   right and at his left were boys [*kouroi*]
in the first stage of adolescence [*prōthēboi*], standing there, **well versed in
   dancing** [*orkhēthmos*].
They pounded out with their feet a **dance** [*khoros*], a thing of wonder, and
   Odysseus
was observing the sparkling footwork. He was amazed in his heart [*thumos*].   265
And he [Demodokos], **playing on the phorminx** [*phormizein*], **started**
   [*anaballesthai*] singing beautifully
about [*amphi*] the **bonding** [*philotēs*] of Ares and of Aphrodite, the one
   with the **beautiful garlands** [*stephanoi*],
about how they, at the very beginning,[16] mated with each other in the palace
   of Hephaistos,
in secret.

                                               Odyssey viii 250–69

The dancing of the dashing young Phaeacians is in concert with the singing of
the second song by Demodokos, whom we find once again singing to the accompaniment of the *phorminx* he is playing. The subject of his song is the primal *philotēs*
or sexual 'bonding' between Ares and Aphrodite. The song begins at verse 266 and

15. On *paizein* as 'perform a sportive dance', see especially *Odyssey* xxiii 147. See also the Hesiodic
Shield 277.
16. The syntax of the indirect question here, appropriate to the introduction of the main subject of
the performance, includes the concept of *ta prōta* 'in the beginning'—which has cosmogonic implications.

ends a hundred verses later, at verse 366. Morphologically, this song is a hymnic *prooimion* in and of itself. Marking the song as a hymnic *prooimion* is the technical term *anaballesthai* 'start up' at verse 266.[17] Another hymnic marker is the use of the preposition *amphi* at verse 267 to set the hymnic subject of the *prooimion*. Grammatically, this hymnic subject is the object of the preposition.[18] To repeat, this hymnic subject of the song is the *philotēs* or sexual 'bonding' between Ares and Aphrodite. Underneath the lighthearted surface of merry ribaldry is a serious and hymnic personification of *philotēs* as a mystical and even divine agency. The hymnic syntax of *amphi* conveys the idea that *Philotēs* 'Bonding' is a divinity in her own right, transcending the forces represented by the literally bonded Aphrodite and Ares as divine lovers.[19] There are indications of such a theme in a fragment of a *humnos* by Empedocles (DK B 35): the mysticism of *Philotēs* 'Bonding' as personified in this *humnos* is reminiscent of what we know as Orphic traditions.[20]

As part of the ongoing *humnos* of *Odyssey* viii and beyond, the second song of Demodokos is morphologically different from the first and the third songs. The difference is evident already in the wording at verse 267, signaling the beginning of the second song. As we have just seen, this second song requires a new hymnic *prooimion*, which tells the initializing story of Ares and Aphrodite. I am using the term *initializing* here to convey a spatial as well as temporal dimension, matching the spatial dimension of *prooimion* in its etymological sense, 'initial threading [*oimē*]'.[21] This term *initializing* is also relevant to the context of *anaballesthai* 'start up' at verse 266.[22]

It has generally been thought that the second song of Demodokos represents a poetic form that is somehow newer than the epic of Homeric poetry. As Walter Burkert has observed, however, the "divine burlesque" that characterizes this narrative sequence is in fact not innovative but archaizing, and there are numerous parallels to be found in the myths and rituals of Near Eastern civilizations; this observation

17. In *GM* 54, I translate the adverb *amboladēn* in the *Homeric Hymn* (4) *to Hermes* 426 as 'playing a prelude', as if this term referred primarily to the playing of a musical instrument. An alternative interpretation is 'singing a *prooimion*', as argued by Pagliaro 1953:41–62.

18. Technically, the object of the preposition *amphi* can be in either the genitive or the accusative case. Earlier, I noted the attestation of both the genitive and the accusative in the textual transmission of this verse. For more on *amphi* as the introductory element of a *prooimion*, see *PH* 12§41n101 (= p. 358).

19. Relevant is the etymology of the name *Arēs*: see Sinos 1980:33–34.

20. Already in ancient scholarship, as Burkert 1960:133n6 points out, there were attempts to link the concept of *Philotēs* in Empedocles DK B 35 with the hymnic reference to the sexual bonding or *philotēs* between Ares and Aphrodite in *Odyssey* viii 267 (Heraclitus *Homeric Questions* 69; scholia for *Odyssey* viii 267; Eustathius 1.298.34 at *Odyssey* viii 267).

21. *HC* 2§92.

22. Again I compare *Homeric Hymn* (4) *to Hermes* 426, where I interpret *amboladēn* as 'singing a *prooimion*'.

applies also to the "divine burlesque" that characterizes some of the narrative se-
quences in the *Iliad*—especially in Rhapsodies I, XIV, XX, and XXI—and in the
Homeric Hymns.[23] So it is unjustified to view the second song of Demodokos as an
innovative interpolation within the epic narrative of the *Odyssey.*[24] Such a view was
current already in the world of ancient scholarship: we are told in the scholia for
the *Birds* of Aristophanes (at verse 778) that editors of Homer athetized the verses
about the love affair of Ares and Aphrodite.

I argue that the second song of Demodokos is an older form of poetry embedded within a newer form of poetry as represented by the *Odyssey*: this older form
is analogous to what we know as the *Homeric Hymns*. As I argue in *Homer the Classic*, the morphology of the *Homeric Hymns* is actually older, not newer, than the
morphology of the Homeric *Iliad* and *Odyssey*: the *Homeric Hymns* have hymnic
prooimia, and they allow for metabasis to follow. (By *metabasis* I mean a moving
ahead and shifting forward to the performance that follows.)[25] By contrast, as we
will see, the Homeric *Iliad* and *Odyssey* have no hymnic *prooimia* and allow for no
metabasis.

There is a further complication: as I am about to argue, the first and the third
songs of Demodokos are morphologically older, as epics, than the epic performed
by Odysseus in *Odyssey* ix, x, xi, and xii. The first and the third songs are typical
of the epic Cycle, whereas the song of Odysseus is typical of—and coextensive with—
the epic that we identify as the Homeric *Odyssey*. In terms of this argument, then,
there are actually two levels of embedding in *Odyssey* viii:

1. The older form of the epic Cycle, as represented by the first and the third songs
   of Demodokos, is embedded within the newer form of the Homeric *Odyssey*.
2. The even older form of the *Homeric Hymn,* as represented by the second song of
   Demodokos, is embedded within the relatively newer form of the epic Cycle, as
   represented by the continuation of the first song of Demodokos by way of his
   third song.

Unlike the first and the third songs of Demodokos, which make Odysseus dis-
solve into tears, the second song makes him happy, and the word that describes
the hero's feelings is *terpesthai* 'take delight' (viii 368). Later on, Alkinoos will use the
same word in collocation with the word *humnos* (429). The delight of Odysseus, as
signaled at this point in the narrative (viii 368), is not only a reaction to the exte-
rior form of this *prooimion* that tells the story of Ares and Aphrodite. It is also an
exteriorization of the interior meaning of the embedded story.

23. Burkert 1960:132.

24. For citations of works that adhere to this view, see Burkert 1960:132n3.

25. *HC* 2§§97–117, with details about metabasis as a shift from the hymnic *prooimion* into the main
part of the performance.

The initializing story of the second song of Demodokos turns out to be pertinent to the ongoing epic story of Odysseus. But this pertinence, as we are about to see, is different from the pertinence of the first and the third songs. Highlighted in the second song is the revenge of the god Hephaistos, who is playing the role of the outraged husband. Hephaistos is angry at the dashing young Ares for seducing Aphrodite, the wife of Hephaistos (276). This theme of the anger of Hephaistos is pertinent to the story of Odysseus, which is still in the making: at the end of the *Odyssey*, Odysseus will have his own revenge as the outraged husband who is angry at the dashing young suitors for trying to seduce his own wife, Penelope. We can see in the ensuing victory of Hephaistos over Ares a narrative link between the inner and the outer stories: just as Hephaistos flaunts his slowness of foot when he boasts that he has bested Ares, described as the swiftest of all the gods in his footwork (329–31), so also Odysseus flaunts his own slowness of foot when he competes with the Phaeacians, attributing such slowness to the "sea legs" of sailors who have done too much sailing (230–33). Conversely, Alkinoos flaunts the fleet-footedness of the dashing young Phaeacians in both footracing and dancing, linking this skill with their skill in sailing (247).

Implicitly, the Phaeacians' skill in dancing is being applied in the choral performance of the second song of Demodokos. The Phaeacian dancers are dancing the parts. That is, they are implicitly dancing the parts of such characters as the swift Ares and the slow Hephaistos while the singer is explicitly singing the same parts in concert. (This is not to rule out any accessory choral singing on the part of the dancers.) Moreover, the Phaeacians' fleet-footedness in footracing and dancing matches the fleet-footedness associated with the god Ares himself, who is traditionally pictured as a nimble runner and dancer.[26]

The dancers' displays of fleet-footedness in dancing the part of Ares may have been highlighted further by displays of mock slow-footedness in dancing the part of Hephaistos. Pointedly, the slow-footed Odysseus does not participate in the dancing, just as he did not participate in any footracing. He does not have to dance now, but he will sing later. And, just as he does not have to dance now, he will not have to sail later: when the time comes, the Phaeacians will do the sailing for him, just as they are doing the dancing for him right now—both the fast dancing of Ares and the slow dancing of Hephaistos.[27] In sum, the content of the second song of Demodokos points to the epic future of Odysseus, whereas the content of the first and the third songs, the story of Troy, points to his epic past.

The second song of Demodokos, as a hymnic *prooimion*, is followed not by epic

---

26. On the traditional themes of picturing the god Ares as 'swift of foot'—in dancing as well as in running—see *BA* 20§§10–16 (= pp. 327–35).

27. As O. M. Davidson points out to me, the non-dancing of Odysseus would make him not a very good match for the eligible princess of the Phaeacians, Nausikaa.

singing but by further choral dancing and perhaps singing (viii 370–80). The setting is described as an *agōn* 'competition' (380). The same word *agōn* occurs at an earlier point as well, where it refers to the setting for the actual singing of Demodokos when he performs his second song (259, 260). Still earlier, *agōn* refers to the athletic competition (200, 238).

Responding to the second song, Odysseus expresses his appreciation (viii 381–84), and his gesture leads to a series of friendly exchanges climaxing in the giving of gifts to the still-unnamed guest (summarized at 428). It is at this climactic point of the festive continuum that Alkinoos arranges for an evening of eating, drinking, and singing to continue the ongoing festivities, expressing his wish that Odysseus should 'take delight'—*terpesthai*—in the *dais* 'feast' as he listens to the *humnos* (429).

The three attestations of the word *agōn* in *Odyssey* viii (259, 260, 380) are indicative of the festivities that have been ongoing ever since the ritual start marked by animal sacrifice (59–61), which inaugurates the *dais* 'feast' (61). There is a striking parallel to be found in the *Homeric Hymn* (3) *to Apollo*: as I noted earlier, the word *agōn* 'competition' is used there with reference to a recurrent festival of Apollo on the island of Delos (150). At that event, Ionians from all over the Greek-speaking world gather to compete not only in athletics—boxing is the example that is highlighted—but also in dancing and singing (149). From the standpoint of the *Hymn*, Homer himself is competing at that *agōn*, performing an ongoing *humnos* (178). So also in *Odyssey* viii, Demodokos is competing at an *agōn*, performing his own ongoing *humnos* (429). But who exactly is competing with Demodokos?

The setting of this festive *agōn* of *Odyssey* viii will in fact extend into *Odyssey* ix, x, xi, and xii, where the hero of the *Odyssey* gets a chance to perform his own epic, which is his own odyssey. Starting his performance in *Odyssey* ix, Odysseus describes the ideal occasion for a performing *aoidos* 'singer' (ix 3–4), and that occasion is a feast (5–12). There is no *telos* 'outcome', the hero says, that brings more *kharis*—more pleasurable beauty—than the singing of an *aoidos* amidst the *daitumones* (7), that is, amidst the participants in a feast:

ἦ τοι μὲν τόδε **καλὸν** ἀκουέμεν ἐστὶν **ἀοιδοῦ**
τοιοῦδ', οἷος ὅδ' ἐστί, θεοῖσ' ἐναλίγκιος **αὐδήν**.
οὐ γὰρ ἐγώ γέ τί φημι **τέλος χαριέστερον** εἶναι   5
ἢ ὅτ' **ἐϋφροσύνη** μὲν ἔχῃ κάτα **δῆμον** ἅπαντα,
δαιτυμόνες δ' ἀνὰ δώματ' ἀκουάζωνται **ἀοιδοῦ**
ἥμενοι ἐξείης, παρὰ δὲ πλήθωσι τράπεζαι
σίτου καὶ κρειῶν, μέθυ δ' ἐκ κρητῆρος ἀφύσσων
οἰνοχόος φορέῃσι καὶ ἐγχείῃ δεπάεσσι·   10
τοῦτό τί μοι **κάλλιστον** ἐνὶ φρεσὶν εἴδεται εἶναι.

This is indeed a **beautiful** thing, to listen to a **singer** [*aoidos*]
such as this one [Demodokos], the kind of singer that he is, comparable
to the gods in **the way he speaks** [*audē*],

for I declare, there is no **outcome** [*telos*] that has **more pleasurable beauty**
 [*kharis*]   5
than the moment when the **spirit of festivity** [*euphrosunē*][28] prevails
 throughout the whole **community** [*dēmos*]
and the **people at the feast** [*daitumones*], throughout the halls, are listening
 to the **singer** [*aoidos*]
as they sit there—you can see one after the other—and they are sitting
 at tables that are filled
with grain and meat, while wine from the mixing bowl is drawn
by the one who pours the wine and takes it around, pouring it into their cups.   10
This kind of thing, as I see it in my way of thinking, is the **most beautiful** thing
 in the whole world.

Odyssey ix 3–11

The performance of Odysseus in this setting will last for well over two thousand
Homeric verses still to come, from here all the way to verse 23 of *Odyssey* xiii, where
we find that the *dais* 'feast' has just been restarted yet again by Alkinoos—this time,
in the morning—to inaugurate the preparations for finally sending Odysseus back
to his homeland. This morning *dais* is a continuation of the previous day's *dais*,
which had started in the daytime, when the first and the second songs of Demodokos
were performed, and which had extended into an evening of eating, drinking, and
singing. That phase of the feasting was the occasion for the third song of Demodokos, followed by the monumental odyssey of Odysseus. The restarting of the
dais in the morning (23) is marked by another sacrifice: this time, Alkinoos slaughters a sacrificial ox (24), and this time the divine recipient of the sacrifice is mentioned by name: he is Zeus himself (25).

The ensuing description of this restarted *dais* in *Odyssey* xiii is a case of ring composition. In Homeric narration, which is a linear movement forward in the dimension of time, from one point to the next, the narrative device of ring composition exemplifies a complementary circular movement backward in the dimension
of space: there is a cycling back from one given point in the space of narration to
an anterior point, picking up from there details that recycle forward into the ongoing narration, thereby augmenting it. In the present case, the narration about the
restarted *dais* in *Odyssey* xiii picks up and then augments the earlier narration about
the ongoing *dais* in *Odyssey* viii. At verse 429 of *Odyssey* viii, we saw the programmatic use of the word *terpesthai* 'take delight' in describing the expected reaction
of the audience as it listens to the ongoing *humnos* at the ongoing *dais*. This theme
is now picked up and augmented in *Odyssey* xiii: once the *dais* is restarted (23), the
whole community proceeds to feast at the *dais* (26), and once again they all 'take
delight', as expressed once again by way of the word *terpesthai* (27). Once again there

---

28. On the programmatic implications of *euphrosunē* 'mirth' as the atmosphere, as it were, of the
poetic occasion, see *BA* 5§39 (= p. 91), 12§15 (= p. 235); and *PH* 6§92 (= p. 198), following Bundy 1986:2.

is singing and dancing (the word *melpesthai*, again in verse 27, can refer to both singing and dancing) led off by an *aoidos* 'singer', and once again this singer is Demodokos (27–28).[29] So the entertainment of the ongoing *humnos* at the ongoing *dais* of verse 429 in *Odyssey* viii extends all the way from one day to the next. The singer who sang at the *dais* that had started on the previous day at verse 61 of *Odyssey* viii is now singing once again at the *dais* that got restarted on the next day at verse 23 of *Odyssey* xiii. To repeat, just as the audience 'took delight'—*terpesthai*—when Demodokos sang at the *dais* in verse 91 of *Odyssey* viii, they are still taking delight when he sings at the *dais* in verse 27 of *Odyssey* xiii.

Intervening within the vast time span of the ongoing *humnos* in the *Odyssey* is the performance of the singer who sings his own odyssey, Odysseus himself. The extended performance of Odysseus, intervening between the end of the third song performed by Demodokos in *Odyssey* viii and the beginning of a new round of that singer's singing in *Odyssey* xiii, is implicitly competitive, as we saw from the use of the word *agōn* 'competition' as a marker of the festive occasion of *Odyssey* viii (259, 260, 380). As we also saw, this occasion is not just festive: in terms of its morphology, it is a real 'festival' in the technical sense of what is called in classical sources a *thusia*, and this festival has been ongoing ever since its inauguration by animal sacrifice (59–61), which inaugurates the *dais* 'feast' (61). On the basis of all this contextual evidence, then, I conclude that the occasion for the ongoing *humnos* consisting of competing performances by Demodokos and Odysseus is an ongoing festival.

A POETIC CRISIS AT A FESTIVAL

The ongoing *humnos* mentioned at verse 429 of *Odyssey* viii, which I have interpreted as a festive program of successive performances by Demodokos, reaches a critical moment at verse 492. Here the yet-unnamed Odysseus challenges the singer to perform a metabasis—that is, a shifting forward in the subject of the song:

αὐτὰρ ἐπεὶ πόσιος καὶ ἐδητύος ἐξ ἔρον ἕντο,   485
δὴ τότε Δημόδοκον προσέφη πολύμητις Ὀδυσσεύς·
"Δημόδοκ', ἔξοχα δή σε βροτῶν αἰνίζομ' ἁπάντων·
ἢ σέ γε Μοῦσ' ἐδίδαξε, Διὸς πάϊς, ἢ σέ γ' Ἀπόλλων·
λίην γὰρ **κατὰ κόσμον** Ἀχαιῶν οἶτον ἀείδεις,
ὅσσ' ἔρξαν τ' ἔπαθόν τε καὶ ὅσσ' ἐμόγησαν Ἀχαιοί,   490

---

29. The reading that is rejected by Aristarchus for *Iliad* XVIII 604, τερπόμενοι· μετὰ δέ σφιν ἐμέλπετο θεῖος ἀοιδός, can be independently authenticated on the basis of the parallel wording and context of the reading we see here in *Odyssey* xiii 27, τερπόμενοι· μετὰ δέ σφιν ἐμέλπετο θεῖος ἀοιδός, which is the reading transmitted in the medieval manuscript tradition. See HC 2§74. Toward the end of Part II, I will analyze the variant reading accepted by Aristarchus for XVIII 604.

ὥς τέ που ἢ αὐτὸς παρεὼν ἢ ἄλλου ἀκούσας.
ἀλλ᾽ ἄγε δὴ **μετάβηθι** καὶ **ἵππου κόσμον** ἄεισον
δουρατέου, τὸν Ἐπειὸς ἐποίησεν σὺν Ἀθήνῃ,
ὅν ποτ᾽ ἐς ἀκρόπολιν δόλον ἤγαγε δῖος Ὀδυσσεὺς
ἀνδρῶν ἐμπλήσας, οἳ Ἴλιον ἐξαλάπαξαν.   495
αἴ κεν δή μοι ταῦτα **κατὰ μοῖραν καταλέξῃς**,
αὐτίκα καὶ πᾶσιν μυθήσομαι ἀνθρώποισιν,
ὡς ἄρα τοι **πρόφρων θεὸς ὤπασε** θέσπιν ἀοιδήν."

When they had satisfied their desire for drinking and eating,   485
then Odysseus, the one with many a stratagem, addressed Demodokos:
"Demodokos, I admire and pointedly praise you, more than any other
  human.
Either the Muse, child of Zeus, taught you, or Apollo.
All too well, **in accord with its *kosmos*,** do you sing the fate of the Achaeans
—all the things the Achaeans did and all the things that were done to them,
  and they suffered for it—   490
you sing it as if you yourself had been present or had heard it from
  someone else.
But come now, move ahead and **shift forward [*metabainein*]** and sing
  the **kosmos** of the **horse**,
the **wooden horse** that **Epeios** made with the help of Athena,
the one that Odysseus, the radiant one, took to the acropolis as a stratagem,
having filled it in with men, who ransacked Ilion.   495
If you can **tell** me these things **in due order [*katalegein*], in accord with proper
  apportioning [*moira*],**
then right away I will say the authoritative word [*muthos*] to all mortals:
I will say, and I see it as I say it, that the **god [*theos*], favorably disposed** toward
  you, **granted [*opazein*]** you a divinely sounding song."

Odyssey viii 485–98

The reference to metabasis at verse 492 signals a poetic crisis in the ongoing *hum-nos* of Demodokos, a critical moment centering on a shift of subject. The most re-cent subject, which had been marked by a new *prooimion* in the second song of De-modokos, is about to be left behind. As we saw, the subject of the second song reveals a shift from the subject of the first song, which was an epic about the Trojan War. But now there is a call for yet another shift, moving beyond the subject of the sec-ond song as formalized in that song's *prooimion*. This new shift—this metabasis, as formulated by Odysseus—will lead back to the subject of the first song, which was an epic about the Trojan War.

As I argue in *Homer the Classic*, Demodokos responds to the poetic challenge of Odysseus, and his hymnic metabasis shifts the ongoing *humnos* forward to a point where the epic that had once been stopped by Alkinoos (viii 98–99) can at long last continue.[30] The program of the festival, its ongoing *humnos*, can now move forward again. But the epic consequent of the third song of Demodokos does not start where the epic of the first song had left off. As I explain in *Homer the Classic*, the objective of the metabasis is to move ahead, shift forward, to a new starting point, and this new starting point of the third song of Demodokos is to be situated farther ahead than the previous stopping point of the first song.

When Odysseus calls for a metabasis or 'shifting forward' to take place in the third song of Demodokos, the point of reference for this shifting forward is not the second song but the first. Why does Odysseus skip over the second song altogether? The answer, I submit, has to do with the differences in form between the second song on one hand and, on the other, the first and the third songs combined. At the critical moment when Odysseus issues his poetic challenge to Demodokos, the ongoing *humnos* has come to a crossroads: either it will continue in the ways of a poetic form exemplified for us by the *Homeric Hymns*, or it will recycle back to the poetic form that has been on hold ever since Alkinoos the king stopped the first song of Demodokos (viii 98–99): that form is exemplified for us by the epic Cycle.[31]

A moment ago, I described the second song of Demodokos as a form exemplified by the *Homeric Hymns*. Such a description needs to be qualified: it is anachronistic to apply the term *Homeric* to a *humnos* that is followed by athletic dancing rather than epic as its hymnic consequent. The form of the second song is not so much Homeric as it is *pre-Homeric*—in the sense that it looks older than the prevailing form of the *Iliad* and *Odyssey* as we know them.

As for my describing the first and the third songs of Demodokos as a form exemplified by the epic Cycle, I have given my overall reasons for this description in *Homer the Classic*.[32] Here I simply review one Cyclic feature in particular: that is, the metabasis from the first to the third song. This metabasis moves forward the point of restarting the epic narration. In other words, metabasis moves forward the recycling of the epic. This device of metabasis is not only typical of the general epic form that we know as the Cycle: it is also antithetical to the specific epic form that we know as Homeric poetry, which was regulated by the principle of the *Panathenaic Regulation*.[33] This rule, as we have seen ever since chapter 1, requires each successive performer of Homeric poetry at the Panathenaia to continue the epic performance at exactly the point where the anterior performance left off.

It would be anachronistic, however, to describe the first and the third songs of Demodokos as pre-Homeric on the grounds that they do not conform to the Pana-

---

30. *HC* 2§§303–5.
31. *HC* 2§307.
32. *HC* 2§§307–11.
33. *HC* 2§§297, 304.

thenaic Regulation and are therefore Cyclic in form. As I have argued all along, the concept of the epic Cycle was in earlier times not at all incompatible with the concept of Homer.

I repeat here the essentials of my ongoing argumentation. The epic Cycle was in earlier times considered to be part of the Homeric tradition. In these earlier times, the epic Cycle was not anti-Homeric or even non-Homeric: it was Homeric. In these earlier times, further, Homer was the poet of an epic Cycle that included the earlier forms of what we know as the *Iliad* and *Odyssey*. Only in later times were the Homeric *Iliad* and *Odyssey* differentiated from the epic Cycle, which thus became non-Homeric. What intervenes between the earlier and later times, at least in the history of Athens, is the Panathenaic Regulation. In terms of this regulation, the Panathenaic Homer of the *Iliad* and *Odyssey* is *regular* epic, whereas the Cycle is *preregular* epic. This is not to say, however, that the Panathenaic Homer was the very first form of such regular epic: the Panathenaic Regulation must have stemmed ultimately from a Panionian Regulation, as I infer from the argumentation of Douglas Frame concerning the evolution of a Homeric performance tradition consisting of twenty-four rhapsodies each for the *Iliad* and *Odyssey* in the late eighth and early seventh centuries, at the festival of the Panionia held at the Panionion of the Ionian Dodecapolis in Asia Minor.[34]

AN *AGŌN* BETWEEN DEMODOKOS AND ODYSSEUS

In the sustaining context of the ongoing festival in *Odyssey* viii, the stage is set for an implicit *agōn* 'competition' between Demodokos and Odysseus as *aoidoi* 'singers'. As we have just seen, the metabasis signaled at verse 492 of *Odyssey* viii indicates that the poetry of Demodokos is about to start—or, better, restart—the general epic form of what we know as the Cycle. Following up on the performance of Demodokos, as we are about to see, Odysseus proceeds by performing the special epic form that we know as Homeric poetry. To formulate this implicit competition in terms of the Dark Age, what we are about to see is a competition between *preregular* and *regular* epic.

Once the third song of Demodokos gets under way, we notice that its effect is linked with the effect of the first song. First I review the wording of the first song:

κῆρυξ δ᾽ ἐγγύθεν ἦλθεν ἄγων ἐρίηρον ἀοιδόν,
τὸν περὶ Μοῦσ᾽ ἐφίλησε, δίδου δ᾽ ἀγαθόν τε κακόν τε·
ὀφθαλμῶν μὲν ἄμερσε, δίδου δ᾽ ἡδεῖαν ἀοιδήν.
τῷ δ᾽ ἄρα Ποντόνοος θῆκε θρόνον ἀργυρόηλον   65
μέσσῳ δαιτυμόνων, πρὸς κίονα μακρὸν ἐρείσας·
κὰδ δ᾽ ἐκ πασσαλόφι κρέμασεν φόρμιγγα λίγειαν

34. Frame 2009 ch. 11.

αὐτοῦ ὑπὲρ κεφαλῆς καὶ ἐπέφραδε χερσὶν ἑλέσθαι
κῆρυξ· πὰρ δ᾽ ἐτίθει κάνεον καλήν τε τράπεζαν,
πὰρ δὲ δέπας οἴνοιο, πιεῖν ὅτε θυμὸς ἀνώγοι.   70
οἱ δ᾽ ἐπ᾽ ὀνείαθ᾽ ἑτοῖμα προκείμενα χεῖρας ἴαλλον.
αὐτὰρ ἐπεὶ πόσιος καὶ ἐδητύος ἐξ ἔρον ἕντο,
Μοῦσ᾽ ἄρ᾽ ἀοιδὸν ἀνῆκεν ἀειδέμεναι κλέα ἀνδρῶν,
οἴμης, τῆς τότ᾽ ἄρα κλέος οὐρανὸν εὐρὺν ἵκανε,
νεῖκος Ὀδυσσῆος καὶ Πηλεΐδεω Ἀχιλῆος,   75
ὥς ποτε δηρίσαντο θεῶν ἐν δαιτὶ θαλείῃ
ἐκπάγλοισ᾽ ἐπέεσσιν, ἄναξ δ᾽ ἀνδρῶν Ἀγαμέμνων
χαῖρε νόῳ, ὅ τ᾽ ἄριστοι Ἀχαιῶν δηριόωντο.
ὣς γάρ οἱ χρείων μυθήσατο Φοῖβος Ἀπόλλων
Πυθοῖ ἐν ἠγαθέῃ, ὅθ᾽ ὑπέρβη λάϊνον οὐδὸν   80
χρησόμενος. τότε γάρ ῥα κυλίνδετο **πήματος ἀρχὴ**
Τρωσί τε καὶ Δαναοῖσι **Διὸς μεγάλου διὰ βουλάς.**
ταῦτ᾽ ἄρ᾽ ἀοιδὸς ἄειδε περικλυτός· αὐτὰρ Ὀδυσσεὺς
πορφύρεον μέγα φᾶρος ἑλὼν χερσὶ στιβαρῇσι
κὰκ κεφαλῆς εἴρυσσε, κάλυψε δὲ καλὰ πρόσωπα·   85
αἴδετο γὰρ Φαίηκας ὑπ᾽ ὀφρύσι **δάκρυα** λείβων.
ἦ τοι ὅτε **λήξειεν** ἀείδων θεῖος **ἀοιδός**,
δάκρυ᾽ ὀμορξάμενος κεφαλῆς ἄπο φᾶρος ἕλεσκε
καὶ δέπας ἀμφικύπελλον ἑλὼν σπείσασκε θεοῖσιν·
αὐτὰρ ὅτ᾽ ἂψ **ἄρχοιτο** καὶ ὀτρύνειαν ἀείδειν   90
Φαιήκων οἱ ἄριστοι, ἐπεὶ τέρποντ᾽ ἐπέεσσιν,
ἂψ Ὀδυσεὺς κατὰ κρᾶτα καλυψάμενος **γοάασκεν**.
ἔνθ᾽ ἄλλους μὲν πάντας ἐλάνθανε **δάκρυα** λείβων,
Ἀλκίνοος δέ μιν οἶος ἐπεφράσατ᾽ ἠδ᾽ **ἐνόησεν**.

The herald came near, bringing with him a **singer** [*aoidos*], very trusted,
whom the Muse loved exceedingly. She gave him both a good thing
    and a bad thing.
For she took away from him his eyes but gave him the sweetness of song
    [*aoidē*].
For him did Pontonoos place a chair, silver-studded,   65
right in the midst of the people who were feasting, propping the chair
    against a tall column,
and the herald took from a peg the clear-sounding *phorminx* that was
    hanging there
above his head, and he presented it to him so he could take it in his hands.
The herald did this. And next to him he put a beautiful basket and a table.
He put next to him also a cup of wine to drink from whenever he felt
    in his heart the need to do so.   70
And, with hands reaching out swiftly, they made for the good things that
    were prepared and waiting.
When they had satisfied their desire for drinking and eating,

the Muse impelled the singer to sing the glories [*klea*] of men,
starting from a **thread** [*oimē*] that had at that time a fame [*kleos*] reaching
    all the way up to the vast sky.
It was the quarrel of Odysseus and Achilles son of Peleus,   75
how they fought once upon a time at a sumptuous feast [*dais*] of the gods
with terrible words, and the king of men, Agamemnon,
was happy in his mind [*noos*] at the fact that the best of the Achaeans were
    fighting.
**For this is the way he was told it would happen by Phoebus Apollo, uttering
    an oracle,**
in holy Delphi, when he crossed the stone threshold,   80
to consult the oracle. And that was when the **beginning** [*arkhē*] of **pain** [*pēma*]
    started rolling down [*kulindesthai*]
upon Trojans and Danaans—**all on account of the plans of great Zeus.**
So these were the things that the singer [*aoidos*], well known for his glory,
    sang. But Odysseus,
taking his great purple cloak in his strong hands,
pulled it over his head and covered his beautiful looks.   85
For he felt ashamed in front of the Phaeacians, as he was pouring out **tears**
    [*dakrua*] from beneath his eyebrows.
Whenever the godlike **singer** [*aoidos*] **would leave off** [*lēgein*] singing,
he [Odysseus] would wipe away his **tears** [*dakrua*] and take off from his head
    the cloak
and, taking hold of a cup that had two handles, he would pour libations
    to the gods.
But whenever he [the singer] **started** [*arkhesthai*] **again** [*aps*] as he was urged
    to sing on   90
by the best of the Phaeacians—for they were delighted by his words—
Odysseus would start **weeping** [*goân*] **all over again** [*aps*], covering his head
    with the cloak.
So there he was, escaping the notice of all while he kept pouring out his **tears**
    [*dakrua*].
But Alkinoos was the only one of all of them who was aware, and he **took note**
    [*noeîn*].

Odyssey viii 62–94

    The first song of Demodokos, as I noted previously, keeps on restarting, and,
each time it restarts, Odysseus sheds tears: the continuously restarted outpouring
of tears is expressed by the wording *aps . . . goân* 'lament again and again' at verse
92, which parallels the wording that expresses the continuous restarting of the first
song of Demodokos, *aps arkhesthai* 'start again and again' at verse 90. Then, in the
third song, a connection is established with the first song, as if the third directly
followed the first. By way of this connection, the third song will now appear to be

a new restarting of the first, which was continually being restarted until Alkinoos stopped it (98–99). Here I review the wording of the third song:

ὡς φάθ᾽, ὁ δ᾽ ὁρμηθεὶς θεοῦ ἤρχετο, φαῖνε δ᾽ ἀοιδήν,
ἔνθεν ἑλών, ὡς οἱ μὲν ἐϋσσέλμων ἐπὶ νηῶν   500
βάντες ἀπέπλειον, πῦρ ἐν κλισίῃσι βαλόντες,
Ἀργεῖοι, τοὶ δ᾽ ἤδη ἀγακλυτὸν ἀμφ᾽ Ὀδυσῆα
εἴατ᾽ ἐνὶ Τρώων ἀγορῇ κεκαλυμμένοι ἵππῳ·
αὐτοὶ γάρ μιν Τρῶες ἐς ἀκρόπολιν ἐρύσαντο.
ὡς ὁ μὲν ἑστήκει, τοὶ δ᾽ ἄκριτα πόλλ᾽ ἀγόρευον   505
ἥμενοι ἀμφ᾽ αὐτόν· τρίχα δέ σφισιν ἥνδανε βουλή,
ἠὲ διατμῆξαι κοῖλον δόρυ νηλέϊ χαλκῷ,
ἢ κατὰ πετράων βαλέειν ἐρύσαντας ἐπ᾽ ἄκρης,
ἢ ἐάαν μέγ᾽ ἄγαλμα θεῶν θελκτήριον εἶναι,
τῇ περ δὴ καὶ ἔπειτα τελευτήσεσθαι ἔμελλεν·   510
αἶσα γὰρ ἦν ἀπολέσθαι, ἐπὴν πόλις ἀμφικαλύψῃ
δουράτεον μέγαν ἵππον, ὅθ᾽ εἴατο πάντες ἄριστοι
Ἀργεῖοι Τρώεσσι φόνον καὶ κῆρα φέροντες.
ἤειδεν δ᾽ ὡς ἄστυ διέπραθον υἷες Ἀχαιῶν
ἱππόθεν ἐκχύμενοι, κοῖλον λόχον ἐκπρολιπόντες.   515
ἄλλον δ᾽ ἄλλῃ ἄειδε πόλιν κεραϊζέμεν αἰπήν,
αὐτὰρ Ὀδυσσῆα προτὶ δώματα Δηϊφόβοιο
βήμεναι, ἠΰτ᾽ Ἄρηα, σὺν ἀντιθέῳ Μενελάῳ.
κεῖθι δὴ αἰνότατον πόλεμον φάτο τολμήσαντα
νικῆσαι καὶ ἔπειτα διὰ μεγάθυμον Ἀθήνην.   520
ταῦτ᾽ ἄρ᾽ ἀοιδὸς ἄειδε περικλυτός· αὐτὰρ Ὀδυσσεὺς
τήκετο, δάκρυ δ᾽ ἔδευεν ὑπὸ βλεφάροισι παρειάς.
ὡς δὲ γυνὴ κλαίῃσι φίλον πόσιν ἀμφιπεσοῦσα,
ὅς τε ἑῆς πρόσθεν πόλιος λαῶν τε πέσῃσιν,
ἀστεῖ καὶ τεκέεσσιν ἀμύνων νηλεὲς ἦμαρ·   525
ἡ μὲν τὸν θνήσκοντα καὶ ἀσπαίροντα ἰδοῦσα
ἀμφ᾽ αὐτῷ χυμένη λίγα κωκύει· οἱ δέ τ᾽ ὄπισθε
κόπτοντες δούρεσσι μετάφρενον ἠδὲ καὶ ὤμους
εἴρερον εἰσανάγουσι, πόνον τ᾽ ἐχέμεν καὶ ὀϊζύν·
τῆς δ᾽ ἐλεεινοτάτῳ ἄχεϊ φθινύθουσι παρειαί·   530
ὡς Ὀδυσεὺς ἐλεεινὸν ὑπ᾽ ὀφρύσι δάκρυον εἶβεν.
ἔνθ᾽ ἄλλους μὲν πάντας ἐλάνθανε δάκρυα λείβων,
Ἀλκίνοος δέ μιν οἶος ἐπεφράσατ᾽ ἠδ᾽ **ἐνόησεν**

Thus he [Odysseus] spoke. And he [Demodokos], setting his point
    of departure [*hormētheis*], started [*arkhesthai*] from the god [*theos*].
    And he made visible the song,
taking it from the point where they [the Achaeans], boarding their ships
    with the strong benches,   500

sailed away, setting their tents on fire.

That is what some of the Argives [Achaeans] were doing. But others of them
    were in the company of Odysseus, the one with the great glory, and they
    were already

sitting hidden inside the Horse, which was now in the meeting place of the
    Trojans.

The Trojans themselves had pulled the Horse into the acropolis.

So there it was, standing there, while they [the Trojans] were saying many
    different things,   505

sitting around it. There were three different plans:

to cut open the hollow wood with pitiless bronze, or to throw it off the
    rocky heights after pulling it up to the peak [of the acropolis],

or to leave it, great artifact [*agalma*] that it was, as a charm [*thelktērion*]
    of the gods

—which, I now see it, was exactly the way it was sure to [*mellein*] reach
    an outcome [*teleutân*],   510

because it was fate [*aisa*] that the place would be destroyed, once the city
    had enfolded in itself

the great Wooden Horse, when all the best men were sitting inside it,

the Argives [Achaeans], that is, bringing slaughter and destruction upon
    the Trojans.

He sang how the sons of the Achaeans destroyed the city,

pouring out of the Horse, leaving behind the hollow place of ambush.   515

He sang how the steep citadel was destroyed by different men in different
    places.

—how Odysseus went to the palace of Deiphobos,

how he was looking like Ares, and godlike Menelaos went with him,

and how in that place, I now see it, he [Demodokos] said that he [Odysseus]
    dared to go through the worst part of the war,

and how he emerged victorious after that, with the help of Athena, the one
    with the mighty spirit.   520

Thus sang the singer [*aoidos*], the one whose glory is supreme. And
    Odysseus

dissolved [*tēkesthai*] into tears. He made wet his cheeks with the tears flowing
    from his eyelids,

just as a woman cries, falling down and embracing her dear husband,

who fell in front of the city and people he was defending,

trying to ward off the pitiless day of doom hanging over the city and
    its children.   525

She sees him dying, gasping for his last breath,

and she pours herself all over him as she wails with a piercing cry. But
    there are men behind her,

prodding her with their spears, hurting her back and shoulders,

and they bring for her a life of bondage, which will give her pain and sorrow.

Her cheeks are wasting away with a sorrow [*akhos*] that is most pitiful
[*eleeinon*].   530
So also did Odysseus pour out a piteous tear [*dakruon*] from beneath his brows;
   there he was, escaping the notice of all while he kept pouring out his tears [*dakrua*].
But Alkinoos was the only one of all of them who was aware, and he **took note**
   [*noeîn*].

Odyssey viii 499–533

The effect of the sorrowful themes in the first song is now being recycled in the
third song, by way of ring composition. When Odysseus hears the third song, he
literally 'dissolves' into tears (522 *tēkesthai*). The hero pours forth 'a tear' (522/531
dakru/dakruon) all over again. The wording ἐλεεινὸν . . . δάκρυον εἶβεν 'he poured
forth a piteous [*eleeinon*] tear' (531), with reference to the third song, recycles by
way of ring composition the earlier wording δάκρυα λείβων 'pouring forth tears',
with reference to the first song (86).

The restarting of the tears of Odysseus in response to the third song of Demodokos points back to the starting point of the first song, the beginning of the
epic, as retold in verses 73–83: that beginning is said to be the *pēmatos arkhē* 'beginning of the pain' at verse 81, and that primal pain is equated with the story of
the Trojan War. That 'beginning', which leads inexorably to the Trojan War, is
equated with what is prophesied by Apollo at verses 79–81—and with what is being planned by Zeus at verse 81. In the first song of Demodokos, the plot of the epic
is actually being equated with the prophecy of Apollo and the planning of Zeus.

I stress again that the pain felt by Odysseus during the first song of Demodokos
is actually restarted in the third song. Just as Odysseus weeps in response to the
first song, so also he weeps in response to the third. Correspondingly, the actual
story of the pain in the first song is restarted in the third. The restarted pain matches
perfectly the restarted story of the pain. Since the ultimate cause of the pain is identified as Zeus in the story of the first song (viii 82), the restarting of that pain in the
third song must be caused by Zeus as well.

We are now on the verge of seeing what is still missing in the wording of *Odyssey*
viii 499. There the god who figures as the hymnic subject of the epic about to be
performed is unnamed: he is simply the *theos* 'god'. We will know for sure when we
finally reach verse 25 of *Odyssey* xiii that the god who is the ultimate hymnic subject of the ongoing *humnos* is Zeus himself, who presides over the festival that has
been ongoing ever since verse 38 of *Odyssey* viii, where Alkinoos orders the holding of a *dais* 'feast' as the occasion for hosting Odysseus as a guest of honor.

In other words, given the coextensiveness of this ongoing *dais* with the ongoing
humnos that celebrates the *dais*, we now see that Zeus is the god who ultimately
presides over both the ongoing festival of the Phaeacians and the ongoing *humnos*
that gives meaning to that festival. To repeat the essence of my argument, Zeus is
the ultimate hymnic subject.

It remains to ask why Zeus was not explicitly named as the hymnic subject of the third song of Demodokos. The answer is to be found in the song performed after Demodokos finishes singing his third song at verse 521 of *Odyssey* viii and before he starts up his singing again at verse 27 of *Odyssey* xiii to mark the end of the stylized festival of the Phaeacians. That intervening song will be the epic performed by Odysseus himself. That epic will be his own odyssey, for which there is no overt hymnic subject to be found at the beginning of his performance in *Odyssey* ix. The epic of Odysseus is in this respect Homeric—if by *Homeric* we mean something that is typical of the *Iliad* and *Odyssey* as we know them. The epic of Odysseus is Homeric in another essential respect as well: unlike the epic of Demodokos, which relies on the narrative device of metabasis at the moment of restarting in the third song the performance that was started in the first song, the odyssey of the Homeric *Odyssey* avoids metabasis. In short, the *agōn* 'competition' between Demodokos and Odysseus at the ongoing feast of the Phaeacians—extending from verse 91 of *Odyssey* viii all the way to verse 27 of *Odyssey* xiii—is an *agōn* between non-Homeric and Homeric forms of poetry. Or, to restate the formulation in terms of the Dark Age, the competition reduces to a confrontation of preregular and regular forms of Homeric poetry.

The preregular story of Troy, in the process of being retold by Demodokos, leads up to the regular Homeric story of Odysseus, an odyssey in the making, which must make a break with the story of Troy if it is to succeed in moving on to the rest of the Homeric *Odyssey*—that is, to the story of the *nostos* 'homecoming' of the hero to Ithaca. The epic fame or *kleos* of Odysseus in the Homeric *Odyssey* depends on this *nostos*, not on the credit he is given for the destruction of Troy—a feat proclaimed already at the very beginning, in verse 2 of *Odyssey* i.[35] When Odysseus dissolves into tears as he listens to the preregular story of Troy, his own weeping interrupts that story. Nevertheless, as I show in *Homer the Classic*, the regular simile of the weeping woman continues the preregular story at exactly the point where the reporting of the story as retold by the regular master narrative had left off. That interruption makes it possible for the regular master narrative to move from the retrospective preregular story of Troy to the prospective regular Homeric story of Odysseus.[36]

35. *BA* 2§17 (= p. 40); *BA*² preface §§16–17 (= p. xii).
36. *HC* 2§§306–11.

5

Iliadic Multiformities

We have seen that the ongoing *humnos* of the stylized festival of the Phaeacians keeps getting stopped and restarted, and that in two cases the restarting activates a distinct hymnic *prooimion*. In the first case, the restarting leads to the second song of Demodokos, which activates a hymnic *prooimion* featuring the personified divine force of *Philotēs* 'Bonding' as its hymnic subject. In the other case, the restarting leads to the third song of Demodokos, which activates a hymnic *prooimion* featuring Zeus himself as its implied hymnic subject. It does not follow, however, that each restarting of epic requires a distinct hymnic *prooimion*. As I am about to argue, a hymnic *prooimion* is not obligatory for restarting or even starting a given epic—provided that Zeus happens to be the implied hymnic subject who authorizes that epic.

To make this argument, I start with the fact that Zeus is figured as the ultimate cause of the epic that is being narrated in the first song of Demodokos (viii 82) and that he must be the ultimate cause of the restarted epic in the third song as well—that is, according to the logic of the ring composition that links the first song with the third. According to the same logic, Zeus is not only the implied hymnic subject of the *prooimion* that restarts the epic performance (viii 499): he must be also the implied hymnic subject of the epic as it started in the first song, and this status is signaled by the narrator's declaration that the epic plot of the first song is equivalent to the Plan of Zeus (viii 82).

As we contemplate these links between the first and the third songs of Demodokos, we are left with the initial impression that the singer's second song is an intrusion into the ongoing epic about the destruction of Troy in *Odyssey* viii—an epic continuing from the first to the third song of Demodokos. The integration of this seemingly intrusive second song into the ongoing *humnos* requires both a distinct hymnic *prooimion* for the second song to start and yet another distinct hymnic *prooimion* for the third song to start—that is, to restart by way of metabasis—somewhere after the point where the first song left off. If it had not been for the second song, it seems as if the third song may not have needed a distinct hymnic *prooimion* of its own.

The third song of Demodokos needs Zeus as its hymnic subject in order to make it possible for the epic of the first song to resume successfully in the third. Otherwise, the seemingly intrusive second song threatens to divert the ongoing epic that is being maintained by the ongoing *humnos*. Within the framework of the *humnos*, Zeus as the supreme god ultimately reasserts control over the direction of the *humnos*. The diversion caused by the second song in the *humnos* is transcended by Zeus as the overriding hymnic subject of the overall *humnos*. In other words, the status of Zeus as the ultimate hymnic subject will override the status of any other god in the ongoing *humnos*, since Zeus is viewed as the ultimate cause of the ongoing epic that is being continued by the ongoing *humnos* linking the first and the third songs.

Zeus is not only the overriding hymnic subject of the ongoing *humnos* in *Odyssey* viii. He is also the overriding hymnic subject of all *humnoi* by virtue of his hierarchical supremacy over all gods celebrated by *humnoi*—a supremacy acknowledged either explicitly or implicitly in all *humnoi*. A most prominent example, as I show in *Homer the Classic*, is the virtual *Hymn to Zeus* represented by the Hesiodic *Theogony*; another prominent example is the ostentatiously hierarchical ordering built into the *Hymn to Zeus* by Callimachus.[1]

In the *Homeric Hymns*, on the other hand, the supremacy of Zeus as the hymnic subject is not obvious on the surface. The sequencing of the *Homeric Hymns* as they survive in the medieval manuscript tradition does not follow the strict hierarchical ordering we see in the sequencing of the *Hymns* composed by Callimachus. Such lack of hierarchy in the sequencing of attested *Homeric Hymns* may be an accident due to the vicissitudes of the medieval manuscript transmission. There may have been an earlier phase in the transmission of the *Homeric Hymns* where the sequencing was logically hierarchical. It may be relevant, as I argue in *Homer the Classic*, that the hierarchy of sequencing in the *Hymns* of Callimachus is based on Homeric models.[2] It may also be relevant that Pindar's imitation of a virtual *Homeric Hymn to Zeus* in his *Nemean* 2 makes it explicit, as we have seen, that Zeus is in fact the primary hymnic subject of the epics of Homer as performed by the heirs of Homer, the *Homēridai*.

1. *HC* 2§§8–21.
2. *HC* 2§§228–37.

Just now, I was careful to say that Zeus is the *primary* hymnic subject of the epics of Homer. In the precise wording of Pindar, Zeus is the god of the *prooimion* that is sung 'most of the time', *ta polla*, by the *Homēridai*:

Ὅθεν περ καὶ Ὁμηρίδαι | ῥαπτῶν ἐπέων τὰ πόλλ' ἀοιδοί | ἄρχονται, Διὸς ἐκ προοιμίου . . .

[Starting] from the point where [*hothen*] the *Homēridai*, singers, **most of the time** [*ta polla*] begin [*arkhesthai*] their stitched-together words, from the *prooimion* of Zeus . . .

Pindar *Nemean* 2.1–3

In this wording of Pindar, as I will now argue, we see a poetic formulation of a poetic principle: that is, the transcendence of Zeus as the ultimate hymnic subject.

To show the workings of this principle, I begin by considering passages where Zeus is not named as the god of a *prooimion* for a given epic. In such cases, the god who presides over the given festival that serves as the setting for the performance of that given epic will be named as the primary god of the *prooimion*. For example, in one of the *Homeric Hymns* we see an explicit reference to a festival that served as a setting for the performance of the *prooimion* addressing the god invoked in the *Hymn*. It happens in *Homeric Hymn* (6) *to Aphrodite* 19–20, which refers explicitly to the occasion of the festival where the performance of the *Hymn* is taking place: δὸς δ' ἐν ἀγῶνι | νίκην τῷδε φέρεσθαι, ἐμὴν δ' ἔντυνον ἀοιδήν 'I pray to you [Aphrodite] to grant that in the competition [*agōn*] that is at hand I may win victory. Arrange my song'.

Even in such *prooimia* performed at festivals that celebrate gods other than Zeus, Zeus figures as the supreme god who overrides in importance the god who is being celebrated at the given festival. In other words, the divinity who seems to be the primary subject of any *prooimion* is not the truly primary divinity—if Zeus is factored into the hymnic master plan. Any god of any *prooimion* can ultimately be replaced by Zeus, who is implicitly the true primary god of all *prooimia*. In the *Homeric Hymns*, we can see that gods who figure as the primary hymnic subjects of *prooimia* will nevertheless be described as secondary to Zeus. In the *Homeric Hymn* (32) *to Selene*, for example, where the *prooimion* addressed to the goddess leads overtly to an epic consequent (17–20), it is made explicit that Zeus is ultimately the primary god, both as the sexual partner of Selene herself (14–15) and as the father of the Muses, who are invoked here as his daughters (2) and, most important, who inspire the whole song in the first place (1–2).

Zeus is not the only god who transcends the occasionality of festivals by superseding the gods in whose honor the given festivals are being celebrated. Also transcendent are the Muses, whose poetic authority is derived from Zeus, as we saw in the example I just cited. And we have already seen an articulation of such transcendence in the scholia for Pindar's *Nemean* 2 (1d): αἰεὶ οὖν τὴν ἀρχὴν ὡς ἐπὶ τὸ πλεῖστον ἐκ Διὸς ἐποιοῦντο προοιμιαζόμενοι, ἐνίοτε δὲ καὶ Μουσῶν 'and they [the *Homēridai*] always started with a *prooimion*, making mostly Zeus their point of departure and occasionally the Muses.' Yet another such transcendent god is Apollo, the Muses' half-brother, who shares his poetic authority with these goddesses and who is also their choral leader. We have already seen an articulation of this relationship of the Muses with Apollo in Hesiodic poetry, which specifies that the authority of kings flows from Zeus, while the authority of poets flows from the authority of the Muses and of Apollo as their choral leader:

ἐκ γάρ τοι Μουσέων καὶ ἑκηβόλου Ἀπόλλωνος
ἄνδρες ἀοιδοὶ ἔασιν ἐπὶ χθόνα καὶ κιθαρισταί,
ἐκ δὲ Διὸς βασιλῆες· ὁ δ' ὄλβιος, ὅντινα Μοῦσαι
φίλωνται· γλυκερή οἱ ἀπὸ στόματος ῥέει αὐδή.

For the Muses and far-shooting Apollo are the sources
for the existence of singers [*aoidoi*] and players of the lyre [*kitharis*] on this earth.
And Zeus is the source for the existence of kings. Blessed [*olbios*] is he whom the Muses
love. And a sweet voice [*audē*] flows [*rheîn*] from his mouth.

Hesiod Theogony 94–97

We find a close parallel in one of the *Homeric Hymns:*

Μουσάων ἄρχωμαι Ἀπόλλωνός τε Διός τε·
ἐκ γὰρ Μουσάων καὶ ἑκηβόλου Ἀπόλλωνος
ἄνδρες ἀοιδοὶ ἔασιν ἐπὶ χθονὶ καὶ κιθαρισταί,
ἐκ δὲ Διὸς βασιλῆες· ὁ δ' ὄλβιος ὅν τινα Μοῦσαι
φίλωνται· γλυκερή οἱ ἀπὸ στόματος ῥέει αὐδή.   5
Χαίρετε τέκνα Διὸς καὶ ἐμὴν τιμήσατ' ἀοιδήν·
αὐτὰρ ἐγὼν ὑμέων τε καὶ ἄλλης μνήσομ' ἀοιδῆς.

Let me begin with the Muses, and Apollo, and Zeus.
For the Muses and far-shooting Apollo are the sources
for the existence of singers [*aoidoi*] and players of the lyre [*kitharis*]
   on this earth.
And Zeus is the source for the existence of kings. Blessed [*olbios*] is he
   whom the Muses
love. And a sweet voice [*audē*] flows [*rheîn*] from his mouth.   5
Hail and take pleasure [*khairete*], children of Zeus. Give honor [*timē*]
   to my song.
As for me, I will keep you in mind along with the rest of the song.

Homeric Hymn (25) to the Muses and Apollo

The correlation of Apollo and the Muses with Zeus as transcendent hymnic subjects is made explicit in *Odyssey* viii. As Odysseus says to Demodokos, in praising the accuracy of that singer's first song about the story of Troy, Demodokos must have been 'taught' by a Muse, described as the daughter of Zeus, or by his son Apollo:

ἤ σέ γε Μοῦσ' ἐδίδαξε, Διὸς πάϊς, ἤ σέ γ' Ἀπόλλων.

Either the Muse, child of Zeus, taught you, or Apollo.

Odyssey viii 488

If Demodokos sings his song successfully, Odysseus adds, it will be clear that 'the god' who presides over the singing was favorably disposed toward the singer:

αἴ κεν δή μοι ταῦτα **κατὰ μοῖραν καταλέξῃς,**
αὐτίκα καὶ πᾶσιν μυθήσομαι ἀνθρώποισιν,
ὡς ἄρα τοι **πρόφρων θεὸς ὤπασε θέσπιν ἀοιδήν.**

If you can **tell** me these things **in due order** [*katalegein*], **in accord with proper apportioning** [*moira*],
then right away I will say the authoritative word [*muthos*] to all mortals:
I will say, and I see it as I say it,[3] that the **god** [*theos*], **favorably disposed** toward you, **granted** [*opazein*] you a divinely sounding song.

Odyssey viii 496–98

I note that the name of the god is not given here: the wording refers simply to the *theos* 'god'. In the immediate context, *theos* here can be understood as either 'the Muse' or Apollo, as we see from what Odysseus has just said at verse 488, quoted immediately before this last quotation. The wording of verses 496–98 shows that the Muses and Apollo, like Zeus, can supersede other gods who could have presided over the third song of Demodokos. The hymnic *prooimion* that leads to the epic of the Wooden Horse is described here in words that correspond perfectly to the words of hymnic *prooimia* as we actually find them attested in the *Homeric Hymns*:

πρόφρονες ἀντ' ᾠδῆς βίοτον θυμῆρε' ὀπάζειν.
αὐτὰρ ἐγὼ καὶ σεῖο καὶ ἄλλης μνήσομ' ἀοιδῆς.

May you [Demeter and Persephone] be **favorably disposed** [*prophrones*], **granting** [*opazein*] me a livelihood that fits my heart's desire, in return for my song.
As for me, I will keep you in mind along with the rest of the song.

Homeric Hymn (2) to Demeter 494–95

Χαῖρε θεῶν μήτηρ, ἄλοχ' Οὐρανοῦ ἀστερόεντος,
πρόφρων δ' ἀντ' ᾠδῆς βίοτον θυμῆρε' ὄπαζε·
αὐτὰρ ἐγὼ καὶ σεῖο καὶ ἄλλης μνήσομ' ἀοιδῆς.

3. The particle ἄρα/ῥα/ἄρ 'so', 'then', has an "evidentiary" force, indicating that the speaker notionally sees what is simultaneously being spoken. See Bakker 2005:80, 84, 97–100, 104, 146, 172n33.

Hail and take pleasure [*khaire*], mother of the gods, wife of Ouranos of the stars.
Be **favorably disposed** [**prophrōn**], and **grant** [*opazein*] me a livelihood that fits my
    heart's desire, in return for my song.
As for me, I will keep you in mind along with the rest of the song.

Homeric Hymn (30) *to Gaia* 17–19

χαῖρε ἄναξ, **πρόφρων** δὲ βίον θυμήρε' **ὄπαζε**·
ἐκ σέο δ' ἀρξάμενος κλήσω μερόπων γένος ἀνδρῶν
ἡμιθέων ὧν ἔργα θεοὶ θνητοῖσιν ἔδειξαν.

Hail and take pleasure [*khaire*], lord, and be **favorably disposed** [*prophrōn*],
    granting [*opazein*] me a livelihood that suits my heart.
Taking my start from you I will give fame to the lineage [*genos*] of men,
heroes [*hēmitheoi*] that they are, whose deeds [*erga*] have been shown by gods
    to mortals.

Homeric Hymn (31) *to Helios* 17–19

χαῖρε ἄνασσα θεὰ λευκώλενε δῖα Σελήνη
πρόφρον εὔπλόκαμος· σέο δ' ἀρχόμενος κλέα φωτῶν
ᾄσομαι ἡμιθέων ὧν κλείους' ἔργματ' ἀοιδοὶ
Μουσάων θεράποντες ἀπὸ στομάτων ἐροέντων.

Hail and take pleasure [*khaire*], queen goddess, you with the white arms, shining
    Selene.
Be **favorably disposed** [**prophrōn**], you with the beautiful tresses [*plokamoi*].
    Taking my start from you I will perform the famous deeds [*kleos,* plural] of men,
singing of them, heroes [*hēmitheoi*] that they are, whose deeds [*ergmata*] singers
    celebrate with fame [*kleos*]—
attendants [*therapōn*, plural] of the Muses they are,[4] singing with voices evoking
    desire.

Homeric Hymn (32) *to Selene* 17–20

Technically, the unnamed *theos* 'god' at verse 498 of *Odyssey* viii could be any
one of these various gods presiding over various festivals. But the wording of the
immediate context makes it clear that the implied hymnic subject must be either
the Muse or Apollo. I repeat that wording:

αἴ κεν δή μοι ταῦτα **κατὰ μοῖραν καταλέξῃς**,
αὐτίκα καὶ πᾶσιν μυθήσομαι ἀνθρώποισιν,
ὡς ἄρα τοι **πρόφρων θεὸς ὤπασε** θέσπιν ἀοιδήν.

If you can **tell** me these things **in due order** [*katalegein*], in accord with **proper**
    apportioning [*moira*],
then right away I will say the authoritative word [*muthos*] to all mortals:

---

4. On the significance of the expression '*therapōn* of the Muses', see *BA* 17§6 (= p. 295).

I will say, and I see it as I say it, that the **god** [*theos*], **favorably disposed** toward
you, **granted** [*opazein*] you a divinely sounding song.

Odyssey viii 496–98

The ostentatiously nameless reference to 'the god' here is analogous to the nameless reference to 'the god' at the moment when Demodokos actually performs the
prooimion of his third song:

ὡς φάθ᾽, ὁ δ᾽ ὁρμηθεὶς θεοῦ ἤρχετο, φαῖνε δ᾽ ἀοιδήν,
ἔνθεν ἑλών, ὡς . . .

Thus he [Odysseus] spoke. And he [Demodokos], setting his **point of departure**
[*hormētheis*], **started** [*arkhesthai*] from the **god** [*theos*]. And he made visible
the song,
taking it from the point where . . .

Odyssey viii 499–500

As I have been arguing, we see from the short-term context that Demodokos
derives his poetic authority from 'the Muse' or from Apollo, and the implied hymnic subject seems to be one of these two gods. But we see from the long-term context, as signaled at verse 25 of *Odyssey* xiii, that the ultimate poetic authority for the
songs of Demodokos derives from Zeus himself. So the reference at verse 488 of
Odyssey viii to 'the Muse' and to Apollo as poetic authorities who figure as alternatives to each other serves to show that such gods are subordinated to the ultimate
poetic authority of Zeus. Once again, as we saw earlier in the case of the Hesiodic
Theogony (94–97) and the *Homeric Hymn* (25) *to the Muses and Apollo*, we see that
the Muses and Apollo can stand in for Zeus as hymnic subjects. Moreover, in the
case of *Odyssey* viii, it is made explicit that the Muses and Apollo can be invoked
as hymnic subjects of the *prooimion* that introduces the epic of the third song of
Demodokos.

OLDER AND NEWER VERSIONS OF THE *ILIAD*

The role of the Muses and Apollo as hymnic subjects who can be substituted for
Zeus as the ultimate hymnic subject of epic is particularly relevant to a precious
piece of surviving information about an older version of the *Iliad*—older, that is,
than the version known to us as the Homeric *Iliad*. According to this information,
there is an older form of the epic that starts with a hymnic *prooimion* proclaiming
the Muses and Apollo as the initial subject of the performance. As we examine the
actual wording of this information, we read about a copy of an *arkhaia Ilias* 'old
Iliad', acquired by Apellicon of Teos, which begins with this hymnic *prooimion*:[5]

5. Wilamowitz 1929. See LP (Nagy 1998) 215. See also West 2003a:454–55, "Life 10B."

ἡ δὲ δοκοῦσα ἀρχαία Ἰλιάς, ἡ λεγομένη Ἀπελλικῶντος [απελικωνος ms., corr. Nauck], προοίμιον ἔχει τάδε·

Μούσας ἀείδω καὶ Ἀπόλλωνα κλυτότοξον

ὡς καὶ Νικάνωρ μέμνηται καὶ Κράτης ἐν τοῖς διορθωτικοῖς.[6]

But what seems to be the **old Iliad** [*arkhaia Ilias*], the one that is called Apellicon's "Iliad," has this *prooimion*:

I sing the Muses and Apollo, famed for his bow and arrows.

This is the way Nicanor mentions it, and so too Crates in his *Diorthōtika*.

Vitae Homeri et Hesiodi ed. Wilamowitz p. 32.16–20

As we see from the information I just quoted, this verse in the *arkhaia Ilias* 'old *Iliad*' acquired by Apellicon was cited by Crates of Mallos, head of the Library of Pergamon in the second century B.C.E., and I infer that Apellicon acquired this text from that library.[7]

The same source gives further testimony about this *arkhaia Ilias* 'old *Iliad*': this text contained a three-verse alternative to the standard nine-verse beginning of the *Iliad* that we know from the medieval manuscript tradition of Homer. The three-verse alternative is cited with reference to the authority of the Peripatetic scholar Aristoxenus:[8]

Ἀριστόξενος δὲ ἐν αʹ Πραξιδαμαντείων φησὶ κατά τινας ἔχειν·

ἔσπετε νῦν μοι Μοῦσαι, Ὀλύμπια δώματ' ἔχουσαι,
ὅππως δὴ μῆνίς τε χόλος θ' ἕλε Πηλείωνα
Λητοῦς τ' ἀγλαὸν υἱόν· ὃ γὰρ βασλῆι χολωθείς ...

Aristoxenus, in Book 1 of his *Praxidamanteia* [F 91a ed. Wehrli], says that, according to some, it [the *arkhaia Ilias* 'old *Iliad*'] had:

So now tell me, Muses, who dwell in your Olympian abodes,
how it was—**I now see it**—that anger [*mēnis*] and rage [*kholos*] seized
    [Achilles] the son of Peleus,
and [Apollo] the radiant son of Leto. For he [Apollo], angry at the king
    [Agamemnon], ...

Vitae Homeri et Hesiodi ed. Wilamowitz p. 32.20–24

We see here an essential difference between the older *Iliad* as represented by the *arkhaia Ilias* and the newer *Iliad* as we know it. The beginning of the narrative of the older *Iliad*, as I have just quoted it, was preceded by the naming of the Muses

---

6. See Pfeiffer 1968:239n7 for the correction of a typographical error involving διορθωτικοῖς (which is the correct reading) in the book of Wilamowitz.

7. LP (Nagy 1998) 215, 222–23.

8. Wilamowitz 1929. See Muellner 1996:97, LP (Nagy 1998) 215n103. See also West 2003a:454–57, again in "Life 10B."

and Apollo as the hymnic subject, as we saw a few moments earlier in the last quotation but one. By contrast, the beginning of the newer *Iliad* is without such a naming of a hymnic subject:

Μῆνιν ἄειδε θεὰ Πηληϊάδεω Ἀχιλῆος
οὐλομένην, ἣ μυρί᾽ Ἀχαιοῖς ἄλγε᾽ ἔθηκε,
πολλὰς δ᾽ ἰφθίμους ψυχὰς Ἄϊδι προΐαψεν
ἡρώων, αὐτοὺς δὲ ἑλώρια τεῦχε κύνεσσιν
οἰωνοῖσί τε πᾶσι, Διὸς δ᾽ ἐτελείετο βουλή,　　　　　　5
ἐξ οὗ δὴ τὰ πρῶτα διαστήτην ἐρίσαντε
Ἀτρεΐδης τε ἄναξ ἀνδρῶν καὶ δῖος Ἀχιλλεύς.
Τίς τάρ σφωε θεῶν ἔριδι ξυνέηκε μάχεσθαι;
Λητοῦς καὶ Διὸς υἱός· ὃ γὰρ βασιλῆϊ χολωθεὶς . . .

The anger [*mēnis*], goddess, sing it, of Achilles son of Peleus—
disastrous anger that made countless sufferings [*algos,* plural] for the Achaeans,
and many steadfast lives it drove down to Hades,
heroes' lives, but their selves it made prizes for dogs
and for all birds, and the **Plan of Zeus was reaching its outcome** [*telos*]—　　5
sing starting from the point where the two—I **now** see it—first had a falling out,
　　engaging in **strife** [*eris*],
I mean, [Agamemnon] the son of Atreus, lord of men, and radiant Achilles.
So, which of the gods was it who impelled the two to fight with each other in strife
　　[*eris*]?
It was [Apollo] the son of Leto and of Zeus. For he [Apollo], infuriated at the king
　　[Agamemnon], . . .

Iliad I 1–9

There are other differences as well between the older and the newer *Iliad*. By contrast with the newer *Iliad* as we have just seen it quoted here, which features the Plan of Zeus at verse 5 as the ultimate driving force of the epic plot, the *arkhaia Ilias* 'old *Iliad*' is without a Plan of Zeus. Although both the older and the newer *Iliad* attribute the causality of events to Apollo—it all happened because the god was angry at King Agamemnon—the newer *Iliad* subsumes the divine agency of Apollo under the divine agency represented by the Plan of Zeus, whereas the older *Iliad* does not.

Here I turn to an argument that I make in *Homer the Classic* about Homer in the age of Callimachus. I say there that Callimachus leaves a Homeric signature by positioning his own *Hymn to Zeus* as *Hymn* 1 in his collection of *Hymns*—to be followed by his own *Hymn to Apollo* as *Hymn* 2.[9] Now I am arguing that the very idea of a *Hymn to Zeus* followed by a *Hymn to Apollo* signals two different ways of beginning a Homeric performance.

9. *HC* 2§§11–12.

We can expect that the differences between a *Hymn to Zeus* and a *Hymn to Apollo* will affect not only the form of Homeric performance as it starts but also the content of Homeric performance as it continues into the epic narrative after the hymnic start. To support this argument, I begin by taking a second look at the hymnic start of the *arkhaia Ilias* 'old *Iliad*':

Μούσας ἀείδω καὶ Ἀπόλλωνα κλυτότοξον.

I sing the Muses and Apollo, famed for his bow and arrows.

> *Vitae Homeri et Hesiodi* ed. Wilamowitz p. 32.19

An alternative hymnic start is actually attested in the corpus of *Homeric Hymns*:

Μουσάων ἄρχωμαι Ἀπόλλωνός τε Διός τε·
ἐκ γὰρ Μουσάων καὶ ἑκηβόλου Ἀπόλλωνος
ἄνδρες ἀοιδοὶ ἔασιν ἐπὶ χθονὶ καὶ κιθαρισταί,
ἐκ δὲ Διὸς βασιλῆες· ὁ δ' ὄλβιος ὅν τινα Μοῦσαι
φίλωνται· γλυκερή οἱ ἀπὸ στόματος ῥέει αὐδή.   5
Χαίρετε τέκνα Διὸς καὶ ἐμὴν τιμήσατ' ἀοιδήν·
αὐτὰρ ἐγὼν ὑμέων τε καὶ ἄλλης μνήσομ' ἀοιδῆς.

Let me begin with the Muses, and Apollo, and Zeus.
For the Muses and far-shooting Apollo are the sources
for the existence of singers [*aoidoi*] and players of the lyre [*kitharis*]
   on this earth.
And Zeus is the source for the existence of kings. Blessed [*olbios*] is he
   whom the Muses
love. And a sweet voice [*audē*] flows [*rheîn*] from his mouth.   5
Hail and take pleasure [*khairete*], children of Zeus. Give honor [*timē*]
   to my song.
As for me, I will keep you in mind along with the rest of the song.

> *Homeric Hymn* (25) *to the Muses and Apollo*

The hymnic start that I have just quoted could fit as the beginning of the *arkhaia Ilias* 'old *Iliad*' cited by Crates of Mallos, head of the Library of Pergamon. Also attested in the corpus of the *Homeric Hymns* is a hymnic start that could fit as the beginning of the newer *Iliad* as we have it:

Ζῆνα θεῶν τὸν ἄριστον ἀείσομαι ἠδὲ μέγιστον
εὐρύοπα κρείοντα **τελεσφόρον**, ὅς τε Θέμιστι
ἐγκλιδὸν ἑζομένῃ πυκινοὺς ὀάρους ὀαρίζει.
Ἵληθ' εὐρύοπα Κρονίδη κύδιστε μέγιστε.

I will sing Zeus as my subject, best of the gods, and most great,
   whose sound reaches far and wide, the ruler, the one who brings things to their
   outcome [*telos*], the one who has Themis

attentively seated at his side, and he keeps her company with regular frequency.
Be propitious, you whose sound reaches far and wide, son of Kronos, you who
are most resplendent and most great.

Homeric Hymn (23) to Zeus

The epithet of Zeus here at verse 2, *telesphoros* 'the one who brings things to
their outcome [*telos*]', would be a perfect hymnic motivation for the expression
Dios d' eteleieto boulē 'and the Plan of Zeus was reaching its outcome [*telos*]' at the
beginning of the newer *Iliad* as we have it:

Μῆνιν ἄειδε θεὰ Πηληϊάδεω Ἀχιλῆος
οὐλομένην, ἣ μυρί' Ἀχαιοῖς ἄλγε' ἔθηκε,
πολλὰς δ' ἰφθίμους ψυχὰς Ἄϊδι προΐαψεν
ἡρώων, αὐτοὺς δὲ ἑλώρια τεῦχε κύνεσσιν
οἰωνοῖσί τε πᾶσι, Διὸς δ' ἐτελείετο βουλή,   5
ἐξ οὗ δὴ τὰ πρῶτα διαστήτην ἐρίσαντε
Ἀτρεΐδης τε ἄναξ ἀνδρῶν καὶ δῖος Ἀχιλλεύς.
Τίς τάρ σφωε θεῶν ἔριδι ξυνέηκε μάχεσθαι;
Λητοῦς καὶ Διὸς υἱός· ὃ γὰρ βασιλῆϊ χολωθεὶς

The anger [*mēnis*], goddess, sing it, of Achilles son of Peleus—
disastrous anger that made countless sufferings [*algos,* plural] for the Achaeans,
and many steadfast lives it drove down to Hades,
heroes' lives, but their selves it made prizes for dogs
and for all birds, and the **Plan of Zeus was reaching its outcome [*telos*]**—   5
sing starting from the point where the two—I now see it—first had a falling out,
     engaging in **strife [eris]**,
I mean, [Agamemnon] the son of Atreus, lord of men, and radiant Achilles.
So, which of the gods was it who impelled the two to fight with each other in
     strife [eris]?
It was [Apollo] the son of Leto and of Zeus. For he [Apollo], infuriated
     at the king [Agamemnon], . . .

Iliad I 1–9

It is not only the newer *Iliad* that features the Plan of Zeus as the driving force
of its epic plot. We find the same theme in the epic Cycle, as we see from these verses
that survive from the text of the *Cypria*, the epic that narrates the beginning of the
Trojan War:

ἦν ὅτε μυρία φῦλα κατὰ χθόνα πλαζόμεν' αἰεὶ
‹ἀνθρώπων ἐπίεζε› βαρυστέρνου πλάτος αἴης,
Ζεὺς δὲ ἰδὼν ἐλέησε καὶ ἐν πυκιναῖς πραπίδεσσι
κουφίσαι ἀνθρώπων παμβώτορα σύνθετο γαῖαν,
ῥιπίσσας πολέμου μεγάλην ἔριν Ἰλιακοῖο,   5

ὄφρα κενώσειεν θανάτωι βάρος. οἱ δ᾽ ἐνὶ Τροίηι
ἥρωες κτείνοντο, Διὸς δ᾽ ἐτελείετο βουλή.

There was once a time when countless groupings of humans, wandering
   aimlessly without cease throughout the earth,
weighted down on the broad mass of Earth.
And Zeus, seeing all this, took pity on her, and in his compressed thoughts
he put together a plan to alleviate Earth, the one who nourishes all, of her
   burden of humans.
He fanned the **strife** [*eris*] of the Trojan War,   5
in order to make the burden [of overpopulation] disappear by way of death.
   And they, the ones in Troy,
those heroes were getting killed, and the **Plan of Zeus was reaching its outcome**
   [*telos*].

Cypria F 1.1–7 ed. Allen

So we see that a *prooimion* like the *Homeric Hymn* (23) *to Zeus* fits not only the
newer *Iliad* but also the *Cypria*, the first epic of the Cycle. Both these epics highlight the Plan of Zeus as a foundational theme. By contrast, a *prooimion* like the
Homeric Hymn (25) *to the Muses and Apollo* fits only the older *Iliad*, which does
not highlight such a theme.

To start an epic by naming Apollo as its hymnic subject is not only the mark of
an older *Iliad* in particular. It is also the mark of an older form of epic in general.
By contrast, the newer form of epic, as evidenced by the *Iliad* as we know it, has no
explicit hymnic subject. Zeus remains the implicit hymnic subject, however, through
the equation of the epic plot with the Plan of Zeus at verse 5 of *Iliad* I. As we just
saw in the *Homeric Hymn* (23) *to Zeus*, the status of Zeus as hymnic subject is correlated with such an equation of epic plot with the Plan of Zeus.

The newer *Iliad* as we know it not only signals Zeus as the implicit hymnic subject. It also signals Apollo as an alternative hymnic subject. While the epic plot is
said to be planned by Zeus, who is thus marked as the ultimate hymnic subject, the
agent of the epic plot is said to be Apollo. After equating the epic plot with the Plan
of Zeus at verse 5 of the *Iliad*, the epic narrator goes on to link the planning of Zeus
with the agency of Apollo, calling on 'the Muse' at verses 6–9 to sing of that agency:

Μῆνιν ἄειδε θεὰ Πηληϊάδεω Ἀχιλῆος
οὐλομένην, ἣ μυρί᾽ Ἀχαιοῖς ἄλγε᾽ ἔθηκε,
πολλὰς δ᾽ ἰφθίμους ψυχὰς Ἄϊδι προΐαψεν
ἡρώων, αὐτοὺς δὲ ἑλώρια τεῦχε κύνεσσιν
οἰωνοῖσί τε πᾶσι, **Διὸς δ᾽ ἐτελείετο βουλή**,   5
ἐξ οὗ **δὴ** τὰ πρῶτα διαστήτην **ἐρίσαντε**
Ἀτρεΐδης τε ἄναξ ἀνδρῶν καὶ δῖος Ἀχιλλεύς.
Τίς τάρ σφωε θεῶν ἔριδι ξυνέηκε μάχεσθαι;
Λητοῦς καὶ Διὸς υἱός· ὃ γὰρ βασιλῆϊ χολωθεὶς

The anger [*mēnis*], goddess, sing it, of Achilles son of Peleus—
disastrous anger that made countless sufferings for the Achaeans,
and many steadfast lives it drove down to Hades,
heroes' lives, but their selves it made prizes for dogs
and for all birds, and the **Plan of Zeus was reaching its outcome** [*telos*]—   5
sing, starting from the point where the two—**I now see it**—first had a falling
     out, engaging in **strife** [*eris*],
I mean, [Agamemnon] the son of Atreus, lord of men, and radiant Achilles.
So, which of the gods was it who impelled the two to fight with each other
     in strife [*eris*]?
It was [Apollo] the son of Leto and of Zeus. For he [Apollo], infuriated
     at the king [Agamemnon], . . .

Iliad I 1–9

Here I compare again the three-verse alternative to this nine-verse version:

Ἀριστόξενος δὲ ἐν α′ Πραξιδαμαντείων φησὶ κατά τινας ἔχειν·

ἔσπετε νῦν μοι Μοῦσαι, Ὀλύμπια δώματ' ἔχουσαι,
ὅππως **δὴ** μῆνίς τε χόλος θ' ἕλε Πηλείωνα
Λητοῦς τ' ἀγλαὸν υἱόν· ὃ γὰρ βασλῆι χολωθείς

Aristoxenus, in Book 1 of his *Praxidamanteia* [F 91a ed. Wehrli], says that, according
to some, it [the *arkhaia Ilias* 'old *Iliad*'] had:

So now tell me, Muses, who dwell in your Olympian abodes,
     how it was—**I now see it**—that anger [*mēnis*] and rage [*kholos*] seized
     [Achilles] the son of Peleus,
     and [Apollo] the radiant son of Leto. For he [Apollo], angry at the king
     [Agamemnon], . . .

Vitae Homeri et Hesiodi ed. Wilamowitz p. 32.20–24

As I said before, both the older and the newer *Iliad* attribute the events to the
agency of Apollo, but the newer *Iliad* subsumes that divine agency under the ultimate divine agency represented by the Plan of Zeus, while the older *Iliad* does not.
Moreover, the newer *Iliad* invokes a singular Muse, whereas the older *Iliad* invokes
an aggregate of Muses.

The same can be said about the first song of Demodokos. As in the newer *Iliad*,
the singer is inspired by a singular Muse, and the divine agency of Apollo is subsumed under the divine agency represented by the Plan of Zeus:

Μοῦσ' ἄρ' ἀοιδὸν ἀνῆκεν ἀειδέμεναι κλέα ἀνδρῶν,
οἴμης, τῆς τότ' ἄρα κλέος οὐρανὸν εὐρὺν ἵκανε,
νεῖκος Ὀδυσσῆος καὶ Πηλεΐδεω Ἀχιλῆος,   75
ὥς ποτε δηρίσαντο θεῶν ἐν δαιτὶ θαλείῃ
ἐκπάγλοισ' ἐπέεσσιν, ἄναξ δ' ἀνδρῶν Ἀγαμέμνων
χαῖρε νόῳ, ὅ τ' ἄριστοι Ἀχαιῶν δηριόωντο.

ὣς γάρ οἱ χρείων μυθήσατο Φοῖβος Ἀπόλλων
Πυθοῖ ἐν ἠγαθέῃ, ὅθ' ὑπέρβη λάϊνον οὐδὸν   80
χρησόμενος. τότε γάρ ῥα κυλίνδετο πήματος ἀρχὴ
Τρωσί τε καὶ Δαναοῖσι Διὸς μεγάλου διὰ βουλάς.

The Muse impelled the singer to sing the glories [*klea*] of men,
starting from a **thread** [*oimē*] that had at that time a fame [*kleos*] reaching
all the way up to the vast sky.
It was the quarrel of Odysseus and Achilles, son of Peleus,   75
how they fought once upon a time at a sumptuous feast [*dais*] of the gods
with terrible words, and the king of men, Agamemnon,
was happy in his mind [*noos*] at the fact that the best of the Achaeans were
fighting.
**For this is the way he was told it would happen by Phoebus Apollo, uttering
an oracle,**
in holy Delphi, when he crossed the stone threshold,   80
to consult the oracle. And that was when the **beginning** [*arkhē*] of **pain**
[*pēma*] started rolling down [*kulindesthai*]
upon Trojans and Danaans—**all on account of the plans of great Zeus.**

Odyssey viii 73–82

I emphasize again that the first song of Demodokos, like the newer *Iliad*, fea-tures Zeus as the implicit hymnic subject of its epic about the Trojan War—as sig-naled by a reference to the Plan of Zeus. In this respect, the first song of Demodokos is also like the epic Cycle, since the *Cypria* likewise features Zeus as the implicit hymnic subject of its epic about the Trojan War—as signaled again by a reference to the Plan of Zeus. On the basis of this likeness, I will hereafter use the term *Cyclic Iliad* in referring to the epic of the Trojan War as performed in the first song of Demodokos.

By contrast with both the Homeric *Iliad* and the Cyclic *Iliad* exemplified by the first song of Demodokos, the *arkhaia Ilias* 'old *Iliad*' exemplifies the relatively old-est form of epic—by virtue of starting with a *prooimion* naming Apollo as the ex-plicit hymnic subject of the epic. Such an epic is so old, in fact, that *Homeric* is too specific a term for describing it. The term *Hesiodic* can be applied to this form just as readily as *Homeric*. A case in point is the story that tells about a contest between Homer and Hesiod on the island of Delos. In this contest, both singers are per-forming a *Hymn to Apollo*:

Φιλόχορος δὲ ἀπὸ τοῦ συντιθέναι καὶ ῥάπτειν τὴν ᾠδὴν οὕτω φησὶν αὐτοὺς προσ-κεκλῆσθαι. δηλοῖ δὲ ὁ Ἡσίοδος λέγων·

ἐν Δήλῳ τότε πρῶτον ἐγὼ καὶ Ὅμηρος ἀοιδοὶ
μέλπομεν, ἐν νεαροῖς ὕμνοις ῥάψαντες ἀοιδήν,
Φοῖβον Ἀπόλλωνα χρυσάορον, ὃν τέκε Λητώ. [Hesiod F 357]

Philochorus [*FGH* 328 F 212] says that they [*rhapsōidoi*] were called that on the basis of the idea of composing—that is, stitching together [*rhaptein*]—the song. Proof for this comes from Hesiod, who says:

> In Delos, back then at the very beginning, I and Homer, singers [*aoidoi*],
> sang-and-danced [*melpein*],[10] **stitching together** [*rhaptein*] a song in new
> **humnoi**,
> making Phoebus Apollo the subject of our song, the one with the golden
> weapon, the one born of Leto. [Hesiod F 357]

Scholia for Pindar *Nemean* 2.1d

What kind of epic form, then, is represented by the *arkhaia Ilias* 'old *Iliad*'? Of the three non-Homeric forms of epic that we have been considering so far—that is, the Orphic, the Cyclic, and the Hesiodic forms—the last two can be ruled out: as far as we can tell from the *prooimion* of the *arkhaia Ilias* 'old *Iliad*', this epic was neither Cyclic nor Hesiodic in form. To start with the second of these two terms, we have just seen that *Hesiodic* is no more distinctive a term than *Homeric* with reference to the hymnic subject of Apollo. Moreover, we saw earlier that the *prooimia* of the *Theogony* and the *Works and Days* are variant *Hymns to Zeus*, not *Hymns to Apollo*. As for the term *Cyclic,* it is relevant to repeat that the epic Cycle is inaugurated in the *Cypria* by way of equating the epic plot of the whole Troy story with the planning of Zeus, not with the agency of Apollo. Moreover, even if we use the term *Cyclic* in a general sense to designate an epic form that is older than what we see in the Homeric *Iliad* and *Odyssey*, that sense is still inadequate for describing an epic form that is evidently even older than the Cycle.

By default, then, *Orphic* seems to be the most likely term for describing an epic form that is characterized by the naming of Apollo as the hymnic subject. In fact, the singing of epic in the style of Orpheus is traditionally connected with such a naming of Apollo. This connection is evident in the *Argonautica* of Apollonius of Rhodes. As I argue in *Homer the Classic*, this epic draws upon traditions that are evidently Orphic.[11] At the beginning of the *Argonautica*, we see the naming of the god Apollo as the hymnic subject of the epic, and the hero Orpheus himself is then named both as an epic subject and as a hymnic model for the epic singing:

Ἀρχόμενος σέο Φοῖβε παλαιγενέων κλέα φωτῶν   1
μνήσομαι οἳ . . .

. . .

Νῆα μὲν οὖν οἱ πρόσθεν ἔτι κλείουσιν ἀοιδοὶ   18
Ἄργον Ἀθηναίης καμέειν ὑποθημοσύνῃσι·
νῦν δ' ἂν ἐγὼ γενεήν τε καὶ οὔνομα μυθησαίμην   20

---

10. To repeat, the verb *melpein/melpesthai* and the noun *molpē* convey the combination of singing and dancing: *PH* 12§29n62 (= p. 350) and n64 (= p. 351).

11. *HC* 2§§167, 194, 216, 236.

ἡρώων, δολιχῆς τε πόρους ἁλός, ὅσσα τ᾽ ἔρεξαν
πλαζόμενοι· Μοῦσαι δ᾽ ὑποφήτορες εἶεν ἀοιδῆς.
Πρῶτά νυν Ὀρφῆος μνησώμεθα, τόν ῥά ποτ᾽ αὐτὴ
Καλλιόπη Θρήικι φατίζεται εὐνηθεῖσα
Οἰάγρῳ σκοπιῆς Πιμπληίδος ἄγχι τεκέσθαι.   25
αὐτὰρ τόνγ᾽ ἐνέπουσιν ἀτειρέας οὔρεσι πέτρας
θέλξαι ἀοιδάων ἐνοπῇ ποταμῶν τε ῥέεθρα·
φηγοὶ δ᾽ ἀγριάδες κείνης ἔτι σήματα μολπῆς
ἀκτῇ Θρηικίῃ Ζώνης ἔπι τηλεθόωσαι
ἑξείης στιχόωσιν ἐπήτριμοι, ἃς ὅγ᾽ ἐπιπρὸ   30
θελγομένας φόρμιγγι κατήγαγε Πιερίηθεν.
Ὀρφέα μὲν δὴ τοῖον ἑῶν ἐπαρωγὸν ἀέθλων
Αἰσονίδης Χείρωνος ἐφημοσύνῃσι πιθήσας
δέξατο, Πιερίῃ Βιστωνίδι κοιρανέοντα·

Beginning [*arkhesthai*] with you, **Phoebus [Apollo]**, I will **tell the glories [*klea*]
of men** born in ancient times,   1
having them in my mind [*mnēsasthai*], I mean the ones who . . . [here follows
a compressed narrative of the deeds of the Argonauts]

. . .

As for the ship [the *Argo*], the singers [*aoidoi*] of the past have maintained its fame
[*kleos*] up to now,   18
how it was made by Argos, with the help of Athena's instructions.
But now I would be ready to tell the story [*muthos*] of the lineage and names   20
of the heroes [the Argonauts], of their lengthy travels over the salt sea, and
of all the deeds they accomplished
in their wanderings. And may the Muses be the articulators [*hupophētores*][12]
of the song [*aoidē*].
First and foremost, let me **have in mind** [*mnēsasthai*] Orpheus. He it was
whom once upon a time she,
I mean Kalliope, who was bedded by the Thracian, as they say,
named Oiagros, bore in the region of the vista of Pimplēis.[13]   25
They say that he [Orpheus] had power over rugged mountain cliffs,
enchanting them with the sound of his singing. Power he had over the
streams of **rivers** as well.
Then there are those wild oak trees, signatures of that singing of his that
have lasted till now,
there at the Thracian headland, at Zōnē, still blooming,
standing there right next to each other, in a row, interwoven, and they were
the ones that, one after another,   30

---

12. See also *Iliad* XVI 235, where *hupophētai* refers to priests of oracular Zeus. As González 2000
argues, the Muses are mediators between Apollo and the poet.
    13. Here we see Orpheus linked with Kalliope as the Muse of kings.

he had enchanted with his *phorminx*, drawing them down from the heights
of Pieria.
Such was Orpheus, and he was received as a helper for the labors of Jason
the son of Aison, who trusted the instructions of Cheiron.
He [Jason] received him [Orpheus], that one who ruled over Bistonian Pieria.

Argonautica 1.1–2 and 18–34

AN INVENTORY OF EPIC FORMS

I offer here an inventory of epic forms that we have considered so far:

1. An epic that starts with a *prooimion* referring to Zeus as the transcendent hymnic subject. Such a *prooimion* is attested as the *Homeric Hymn* (23) *to Zeus*.
2. An epic that starts with a *prooimion* naming Apollo or the Muses (or both) as the hymnic subject—substituting for Zeus as the transcendent hymnic subject. Such a *prooimion* is attested in the *arkhaia Ilias* 'old *Iliad*' according to Nicanor and Crates.
3. An epic that starts with a *prooimion* that shows no explicit hymnic naming of Zeus as the transcendent hymnic subject and no explicit naming of Apollo or the Muses (or both) as the hymnic subject substituting for Zeus as the transcendent hymnic subject. Such a *prooimion* is attested at the beginnings of the Homeric *Iliad* and *Odyssey* as we know them. From here on, I will refer to an epic *prooimion* that has no naming of the hymnic subject as an **acephalic prooimion**.

To these three epic forms I now add a fourth: that is, an epic that starts with no explicit *prooimion*. Such is the case in the beginning of the *Little Iliad* as quoted in the *Herodotean Life of Homer*:

διατρίβων δὲ παρὰ τῷ Θεστορίδῃ **ποιεῖ** Ἰλιάδα τὴν ἐλάσσω, ἧς ἡ ἀρχή

Ἴλιον ἀείδω καὶ Δαρδανίην εὔπωλον,
ἧς πέρι πολλὰ πάθον Δαναοί, θεράποντες Ἄρηος·

Spending his time in the house of Thestorides, he [Homer] made [*poiein*] the *Little Iliad* [literally, the '*Smaller Iliad*'], which begins this way:

I sing Troy and the land of the Dardanoi, famed for horses.
Many things for the sake of this land did the Danaoi suffer, those attendants
[*therapōn*, plural] of Ares.

Vita 1.202–10

Even though there is no god invoked here as the hymnic subject, the actual syntax of this fourth kind of epic beginning is hymnic, as we see from the parallel syntax of *Homeric Hymns* 12.1, 18.1, and 27.1: in each of these verses, as in the verse that begins the *Little Iliad*, the verb *aeidō* 'I sing' is combined with the accusative of the hymnic subject (Hera in 12.1, Hermes in 18.1, Artemis in 27.1). The difference is, the hymnic subject in the first verse of the *Little Iliad* is not the sacredness of divinity per se but the sacred city of Troy itself.[14]

ACEPHALIC AND NONACEPHALIC *PROOIMIA*

The basic fact is that the Homeric *Iliad* and *Odyssey* have been transmitted with acephalic *prooimia* throughout the medieval manuscript tradition. The opposite situation evolved in the medieval manuscripts of the Hesiodic *Theogony* and *Works and Days*, which both survived with *prooimia* that contain a naming of the hymnic subject: they are the first 115 and the first ten verses of the respective poems in our modern edited texts.[15] We know that Crates, head of the Library of Pergamon, athetized both these sets of verses.[16] We also know that Aristarchus, head of the Library of Alexandria, athetized the first ten verses of the Hesiodic *Works and Days*.[17]

There are still other instructive examples of such critical decisions. It appears that both the Alexandrians and the Pergamenes had inherited a text of the Hesiodic *Theogony* that included the *Catalogue of Women*, and that "it was the Alexandrians, in all probability, who decided that the *Theogony* should end at line 1020, and the *Catalogue* begin there"; this decision prevailed into the medieval manuscript tradition.[18] Similarly, Apollonius of Rhodes decided that the *Works and Days* ended at verse 828, rejecting as spurious the verses that followed; this decision has prevailed, and in this case we have lost the rejected verses altogether.[19] Also, Aristophanes of Byzantium decided that the Homeric *Odyssey* ended at verse 296 of Rhapsody xxiii; this decision, as we know by hindsight, did not prevail.[20]

Such critical decisions concerning athetesis or omission can be traced back further, back to the age of Callimachus. The critics who edited the texts attributed to the likes of Homer and Hesiod during that age could not possibly have known that

---

14. I find it relevant that Troy is a *hieron ptoliethron* 'sacred city' in *Odyssey* i 2.

15. West 1966:150 and 1978:137. Pausanias 9.31.4 reports that he saw at Helicon an archaic text of the Hesiodic *Works and Days* engraved on a lead tablet. Since he also says that the Heliconians accept as authentically Hesiodic only the *Works and Days*—but without the *prooimion*—we may infer that the lead tablet featured no *prooimion*.

16. Pfeiffer 1968:241; Porter 1992:98; West 1966:50, 150, and 1978:65–66, 137. See also the *Life of Dionysius Periegetes* p. 72.59–60 ed. Kassel (1973).

17. Pfeiffer 1968:220. It looks as if the athetesis by Aristarchus was based partly on the fact that these verses were missing from a copy of the *Works and Days* found by Praxiphanes: see Pfeiffer p. 220n2.

18. West 1966:50.

19. West 1966:50 and 1978:64–65, 364.

20. West 1966:50. He infers that the 24-book division of the *Iliad* and *Odyssey* was already in place in the era of Aristophanes; at p. 50n3 he says about this division: "it may have been pre-Alexandrian." See now *PP* 182n107.

their editorial decisions would affect—in some cases irrevocably—the future history of these texts they were seeking to perfect. Even in cases of athetesis, let alone outright omission, their decisions have in some cases led to the permanent loss of significant portions of textual transmission in later times.

In the case of the Homeric *Iliad* and *Odyssey*, the medieval transmission of these epic texts featuring *prooimia* that are *acephalic*—that is, without the naming of a hymnic subject—evidently goes back to the age of Callimachus. In that age, as I argue in *Homer the Classic*, the old poetic form of the *prooimion* as represented by the *Homeric Hymns* was rethought as a new genre, separable from the old poetic form of the epic consequent.[21] The *Hymns* of Callimachus, which preclude an epic consequent, are the clearest examples of this new genre.

Given the separation of the *Homeric Hymns* from the Homeric *Iliad* and *Odyssey* as their epic consequent in the history of Homeric textual transmission starting with the age of Callimachus and thereafter, we today find it difficult to see by hindsight the prehistory of the links between *humnos* and epic consequent. As I have argued, some of this prehistory is still visible in the Homeric narrative of *Odyssey* viii.

As I have also argued, the attestation of a hymnic *prooimion* for an *arkhaia Ilias* 'old *Iliad*' shows an even older phase of this prehistory. By comparison, the acephalic *prooimion* of the Homeric *Iliad* represents a newer epic form.

VARIATIONS ON THE PLAN OF ZEUS

The Homeric *Iliad* has no explicit hymnic subject, no hymnic *prooimion*, but, nevertheless, Zeus is envisaged as the ultimate cause of the story of the Trojan War: the epic plot of that story is identified with the Plan of Zeus. To tell that story is tantamount to following through to the *telos* 'end'—that is, following through to the 'outcome' that the god had intended in the first place. That is the goal conveyed by the expression *Dios d' eteleieto boulē* 'and the Plan of Zeus was reaching its outcome [*telos*]' at verse 5 of *Iliad* I.

But the *telos* of the story that is the Homeric *Iliad* does not in the end reach all the way to the *telos* that Zeus ultimately intends, which is the destruction of Troy. The epic plot of the narrative in the *Iliad* as we have it does not reach that far. Thus the expression *Dios d' eteleieto boulē* 'and the Plan of Zeus was reaching its *telos*' at verse 5 of *Iliad* I presupposes a narrative framework that is far broader than the actual narrative that is getting under way in our *Iliad*. Zeus is in charge of that broader framework, but the epic plot of our *Iliad* cannot be explicitly equated with that framework.

By contrast with these limitations at the beginning of the Homeric *Iliad*, let us now reconsider the use of this same expression, *Dios d' eteleieto boulē* 'and the Plan

---

21. *HC* 2§§118–22. On epic as a *hymnic consequent*, I refer again to *HC* 2§§97, 109, 113–14, 116.

of Zeus was reaching its *telos*', in a fragment that evidently derives from somewhere near the beginning of the *Cypria*, which is the first in a sequence of epics constituting the epic Cycle. In this fragment, we read that the depopulation of Earth is caused by the Trojan War, which in turn is caused by the Plan of Zeus:

ἦν ὅτε μυρία φῦλα κατὰ χθόνα πλαζόμεν’ αἰεὶ
‹ἀνθρώπων ἐπίεζε› βαρυστέρνου πλάτος αἴης,
Ζεὺς δὲ ἰδὼν ἐλέησε καὶ ἐν πυκιναῖς πραπίδεσσι
κουφίσαι ἀνθρώπων παμβώτορα σύνθετο γαῖαν,
ῥιπίσσας πολέμου μεγάλην ἔριν Ἰλιακοῖο,   5
ὄφρα κενώσειεν θανάτωι βάρος. οἱ δ’ ἐνὶ Τροίηι
ἥρωες κτείνοντο, Διὸς δ’ ἐτελείετο βουλή.

There was once a time when countless groupings of humans, wandering
    aimlessly without cease throughout the earth,
weighted down on the broad mass of Earth.
And Zeus, seeing all this, took pity on her, and in his compressed thoughts
he put together a plan to alleviate Earth, the one who nourishes all, of her
    burden of humans.
He fanned the **strife** [*eris*] of the Trojan War,   5
in order to make the burden [of overpopulation] disappear by way of death.
    And they, the ones in Troy,
those heroes were getting killed, and the **Plan of Zeus was reaching its
    outcome** [*telos*].

Cypria F 1.1–7 ed. Allen

In the epic Cycle as it gets under way in the *Cypria*, the narration of the Trojan War is notionally being driven from beginning to end by the Plan of Zeus. This broader frame of narration is parallel to what we find in *Odyssey* viii—if we read the first and the third songs of Demodokos together as parts of a single narrative continuum. The beginning of the first song, which is an epic about the Trojan War, equates the whole plot of that epic with the Plan of Zeus, as we saw earlier when I quoted verse 82. Then, complementing the beginning of the first song, the end of the third song concludes by narrating the destruction of Troy. Meanwhile, already in the first song, the continuum is being maintained by way of restartings, as we saw from the wording *aps arkhesthai* 'start again and again' at verse 90, referring to the continuous restartings of the epic being performed by Demodokos. With each restarting of the first song, the epic continues where it last left off.

Whereas the first song of Demodokos keeps on continuing until it gets interrupted by Alkinoos, the third song seems to be heading toward a definitive conclusion. The third song, continuing the first song, starts at the point of metabasis that Odysseus had formulated for Demodokos. That starting point of narration, as formulated by Odysseus, leads Demodokos to follow through to the *telos* of the story of Troy: that is, all the way to the moment of Troy's destruction. As I argue in the twin book *Homer the Classic*, that story corresponds to the plot of the *Iliou Persis*, as summarized in the plot outline of Proclus.[22] In the epic Cycle, it is this particular epic that tells the story of the Wooden Horse and the ultimate destruction of Troy. Already in the *Cypria*, which is the first epic of the Cycle, the destruction of Troy is equated with the ending of the story. This ending is the ultimate *telos* or 'outcome' of the Plan of Zeus: again I recall the wording of the *Cypria*, where we read *Dios d' eteleieto boulē* 'and the Plan of Zeus was reaching its *telos*'. So the story of Troy's destruction will have a 'perfect' epic ending—that is, *telos*. The idea of such 'perfection', as we see from the wording of the *Cypria*, is equated with the idea of *telos*. This idea of epic *telos* is realized in the overall narrative of the epic Cycle.

In the *Iliad*, by contrast, this idea of epic *telos* can be realized only in the form of a prophecy. Here I turn to a most revealing passage, where we find Odysseus quoting the mantic words of Calchas, the seer, who is prophesying the end of the Trojan War, marked by the destruction of Troy:

τλῆτε φίλοι, καὶ μείνατ' ἐπὶ χρόνον ὄφρα δαῶμεν
ἢ ἐτεὸν Κάλχας μαντεύεται ἦε καὶ οὐκί.   300
εὖ γὰρ δὴ τόδε ἴδμεν ἐνὶ φρεσίν, ἐστὲ δὲ πάντες
μάρτυροι, οὓς μὴ κῆρες ἔβαν θανάτοιο φέρουσαι·
χθιζά τε καὶ πρωΐζ' ὅτ' ἐς Αὐλίδα νῆες Ἀχαιῶν
ἠγερέθοντο κακὰ Πριάμῳ καὶ Τρωσὶ φέρουσαι,
ἡμεῖς δ' ἀμφὶ περὶ κρήνην ἱεροὺς κατὰ βωμοὺς   305
ἔρδομεν ἀθανάτοισι τεληέσσας ἑκατόμβας
καλῇ ὑπὸ πλατανίστῳ ὅθεν ῥέεν ἀγλαὸν ὕδωρ·
ἔνθ' ἐφάνη μέγα σῆμα· δράκων ἐπὶ νῶτα δαφοινὸς
σμερδαλέος, τόν ῥ' αὐτὸς Ὀλύμπιος ἧκε φόως δέ,
βωμοῦ ὑπαΐξας πρός ῥα πλατάνιστον ὄρουσεν.   310
ἔνθα δ' ἔσαν στρουθοῖο νεοσσοί, νήπια τέκνα,
ὄζῳ ἐπ' ἀκροτάτῳ πετάλοις ὑποπεπτηῶτες
ὀκτώ, ἀτὰρ μήτηρ ἐνάτη ἦν ἣ τέκε τέκνα·
ἔνθ' ὅ γε τοὺς ἐλεεινὰ κατήσθιε τετριγῶτας·
μήτηρ δ' ἀμφεποτᾶτο ὀδυρομένη φίλα τέκνα·   315
τὴν δ' ἐλελιξάμενος πτέρυγος λάβεν ἀμφιαχυῖαν.
αὐτὰρ ἐπεὶ κατὰ τέκνα φάγε στρουθοῖο καὶ αὐτήν,
τὸν μὲν ἀρίζηλον θῆκεν θεὸς ὅς περ ἔφηνε·
λᾶαν γάρ μιν ἔθηκε Κρόνου πάϊς ἀγκυλομήτεω·
ἡμεῖς δ' ἑσταότες θαυμάζομεν οἷον ἐτύχθη.   320
ὡς οὖν δεινὰ πέλωρα θεῶν εἰσῆλθ' ἑκατόμβας,
Κάλχας δ' αὐτίκ' ἔπειτα θεοπροπέων ἀγόρευε·
τίπτ' ἄνεῳ ἐγένεσθε κάρη κομόωντες Ἀχαιοί;

22. *HC* 1§§119–22, 2§§281–350.

124

ἡμῖν μὲν τόδ᾽ ἔφηνε τέρας μέγα μητίετα Ζεὺς
ὄψιμον ὀψιτέλεστον, ὅου κλέος οὔ ποτ᾽ ὀλεῖται.   325
ὡς οὗτος κατὰ τέκνα φάγε στρουθοῖο καὶ αὐτὴν
ὀκτώ, ἀτὰρ μήτηρ ἐνάτη ἦν ἣ τέκε τέκνα,
ὣς ἡμεῖς τοσσαῦτ᾽ ἔτεα πτολεμίξομεν αὖθι,
τῷ δεκάτῳ δὲ πόλιν αἱρήσομεν εὐρυάγυιαν.
κεῖνος τὼς ἀγόρευε· τὰ δὴ νῦν πάντα τελεῖται.   330
ἀλλ᾽ ἄγε μίμνετε πάντες ἐϋκνήμιδες Ἀχαιοὶ
αὐτοῦ εἰς ὅ κεν ἄστυ μέγα Πριάμοιο ἕλωμεν.

Endure, my near and dear ones, and stay as long as it takes for us to find out
whether Calchas is prophesying something that is true or not.   300
For I know this well in my heart, and you all
are witnesses, those of you who have not been carried off by the demons
   of death.
It is as if it was yesterday or the day before, when the ships of the Achaeans
   at Aulis
were gathered, portending doom to Priam and the Trojans.
Standing around a spring, at a sacred altar,   305
we were sacrificing perfect [telēessai][23] hecatombs to the immortal ones
under a beautiful plane tree, in a place where sparkling water flowed.
Then there appeared [phainesthai] a great sign [sēma], a serpent [drakōn]
   with blood-red markings on its back.
Terrifying it was. **The Olympian** [Zeus] **himself had sent** it into the zone
   of light.
It darted out from underneath the altar, and it rushed toward the plane tree.   310
Over there were the nestlings of a sparrow, helpless young things.
In the highest branch amidst the leaves they were hiding in fear,
eight of them. The ninth was the mother that had hatched the young ones.
Then it devoured them, in a way that is pitiful [eleeina], while they were
   chirping.
And their mother was fluttering above, lamenting [oduresthai] for her dear
   little things.   315
Then it threw its coils around her, catching her by the wing as she was wailing
   over [amphiakhuia] them.
And when it devoured the young ones of the sparrow and the mother as well,
the same god that had made it visible [phainein] now made it most visible
   [arizēlos].
For the son of the crafty Kronos now made it into stone.
We just stood there, struck with awe [thauma] at what happened,   320
how such frightful portents invaded the hecatombs of the gods.
Then, right away, Calchas spoke, speaking the words of seers:

23. As we see from this context, the word *telos* can be used to express the idea of *perfection* in sacrifice.

"Why are you speechless, Achaeans with the elaborate hair?
Zeus, master of craft, made visible [*phainein*] this great portent [*teras*].
It is late in coming, late in reaching its **outcome** [*telos*], **and its fame** [*kleos*]
    will never perish.   325
Just as this thing devoured the young ones of the sparrow and the mother
    as well,
eight in number, while the mother made it nine, the one that hatched the
    young ones,
so also we will wage war for that many years in number,
and then, on the tenth year, we will capture the city with its broad streets."
Thus spoke that man. **And now I see that all these things are reaching their**
    outcome [*telos*].   330
So come now, all of you, hold your place, all you Achaeans with the fine shin
    guards,
stay here until we capture the great city of Priam.

Iliad II 299–332

THE SORROWS OF ANDROMACHE

In the *Odyssey*, this idea of epic *telos* as the 'outcome' of a story can be realized only in the form of a retrospective. Demodokos is challenged by Odysseus to narrate the epic of Troy's destruction (*Odyssey* viii 487–98), a virtual *Iliou Persis*, but Odysseus breaks down in tears during the narration of the story, and the hero's tears will interrupt the outcome of this story. The interruption takes the form of a simile that compares the weeping of the hero with the lament of an unnamed woman who has just been captured in war (viii 521–31). As I show in the twin book *Homer the Classic*, the simile of the unnamed lamenting woman is substituted for the *telos* or 'outcome' of the story that tells of the final tearful moments of Troy's destruction.[24] In the epic Cycle, as represented by the *Iliou Persis* attributed to Arctinus of Miletus, that unnamed lamenting woman would be Andromache.[25] In chapter 8, I will have more to say about the relevance of the unnamed lamenting woman in *Odyssey* viii (521–30) to the sorrows of Andromache as narrated in the *Iliou Persis*. For now, however, I concentrate on the relevance of this woman's tears to the sorrows of Odysseus. In the Homeric *Odyssey*, the tears of the captive woman lead to the tears of Odysseus, which in turn can now lead to the story of his own odyssey as a continuation of the tearful story that almost ended the narrative continuum at the feast of the Phaeacians. The story can now continue, shifting from an *Iliad* to an *Odyssey*.

When I say *Odyssey* here, I mean not the entire *Odyssey* as we know it but only the partial odyssey as told by Odysseus himself in Rhapsodies ix, x, xi, and xii of

---

24. *HC* 2§§334–44.
25. *HC* 2§344.

our *Odyssey*. Conversely, when I say *Iliad* here, I mean the entire 'song of Ilion' as sung by Demodokos, starting from the beginning of the Trojan War and extending all the way to the moment of Troy's destruction, which becomes the *telos* or 'outcome' of the singer's overall story. In other words, I do not mean the partial *Iliad* as we know it: rather, I mean the notionally complete *Iliad* of the epic Cycle, what I have been calling the *Cyclic Iliad*.

As I noted earlier, the continuum of song that starts with the singing of Demodokos in Rhapsody viii of the *Odyssey* and ends with the resumed singing of Demodokos in Rhapsody xiii is coextensive with the continuum of a festival that is being celebrated by the Phaeacians. Zeus presides over the ongoing festival, as we saw from the explicit naming of Zeus as the recipient of the animal sacrifice marking the closure of festivities at verse 23 of *Odyssey* xiii. Zeus is thus the ultimate hymnic subject of the ongoing *humnos*: that is, of all the singing—and dancing—that takes place during the festival. The transcendence of Zeus as the hymnic subject in this continuum of song is a sign of Homeric poetry. This sign is correlated with another sign, the Plan of Zeus, as announced at verse 82 of *Odyssey* viii, at the very start of the epic singing of Demodokos. In the logic of Homeric poetry, the Plan of Zeus is a unifying principle, showing that Zeus transcends all other gods as the hymnic subject of epic just as surely as Homeric poetry transcends all other epic.

Such a logic, as I just called it, is a unifying principle that transcends even Homeric poetry as we know it from reading the Homeric *Iliad* and *Odyssey*. We have seen from the explicit wording of the *Cypria* that the Plan of Zeus is also a unifying principle of the entire epic Cycle. Thus the Plan of Zeus, as a unifying principle, predates the differentiation of the Homeric *Iliad* and *Odyssey* from the epic Cycle. In other words, the epic Cycle was also Homeric—until the *Iliad* and *Odyssey* became differentiated as the sole representatives of Homeric poetry. This is not to say that the Cycle had a unified plot that rivaled the unity of the *Iliad* and *Odyssey*. It is just the opposite: the *Iliad* and *Odyssey* were differentiated from the epic Cycle precisely because their plots became more unified. A case in point is the avoidance of metabasis in the *Iliad* and *Odyssey*, to be contrasted with the active use of this device in the epic Cycle, as represented in the third song of Demodokos.

Conversely, I argue that the use of metabasis in the epic Cycle is a compensation for the lack of a unified plot. In terms of this argument, metabasis functions as an expression of notional unity in an epic plot that lacks real unity: the more this device is needed, the less unity there must have been to start with. A case in point is again the metabasis of the third song of Demodokos in *Odyssey* viii. The transition from the second to the third song, or even from the first to the third, would be arbitrary if it were not for the unified plot of the *Odyssey* as we have it.

Let us consider one last time the most general view of the Plan of Zeus as announced at the beginning of the *Cypria*, which is at the beginning of the epic Cycle. To be contrasted is the more special and therefore more Iliadic view of the Plan of

Zeus as announced at the beginning of the *Iliad* (I 5). In the twin book *Homer the Classic*, I consider another Iliadic passage where the god nods his head and thus signifies his Plan. This time, the Plan of Zeus is expressed not in terms of the overall plot, as in *Iliad* I, but in terms of one special theme that pervades the plot. That theme is a picture of Hector that is animated by the sorrows of Andromache. It is explicitly the Plan of Zeus that Hector will never return to Andromache (*Iliad* XVII 195–214).[26] This most special and therefore most Iliadic view of the Plan of Zeus is ultimately connected with the Plan of Zeus as announced at the very start of the epic singing of Demodokos (*Odyssey* viii 82).

26. *HC* 4§§259–70.

PART II

A Preclassical Homer from the Bronze Age

JUST AS I REDEFINED THE DARK AGE in Homeric terms as a transitional phase leading up to a notionally terminal phase of Homer the Classic, I now redefine the Bronze Age as the corresponding initial phase. In Homeric terms, this initial phase of Homer the Preclassic is marked by one central event, the Trojan War.

The Trojan War is a primary temporal frame of reference for the stories of the Homeric *Iliad* and *Odyssey*—stories that tell how women and men like Andromache and Hector and Achilles and Odysseus lived out their heroic destinies as planned for them by an epic plot controlled in sometimes unknown ways by the gods. The Trojan War is a war to end all heroic wars, marking the end of the age of heroes.[1]

The Trojan War is also a primary temporal frame of reference for the Bronze Age as determined by archaeologists, who appeal to objective dating criteria in making their determination. It marks the end of the Bronze Age as they know it. The centerpiece is the ancient city Troy, or Ilion, refounded as a New Ilion in the historical period. The old Ilion of the *Iliad* has been identified by some archaeologists as Troy VIIa (by others, as Troy VI), an earlier stratum of this New Ilion (which is Troy VIII).[2]

As in modern times, Troy was sought out in antiquity, most prominently by world rulers striving to link themselves with the heroes of the epic past. In 480 B.C.E., Xerxes the king of the Persians made sacrifice to Athena, surnamed *hē Ilias,* in New

1. Martin 1993.
2. Pfeiffer 1968:250–51, with special reference to the formulation of Carl Blegen concerning the identification of ancient Troy with the hill of Hisarlik, first excavated by Heinrich Schliemann (Blegen 1958).

Ilion.[3] He also made libations to the *hērōes* 'heroes' (Herodotus 7.43.2);[4] over a century later, Alexander the Great likewise sacrificed to Athena in New Ilion (Strabo 13.1.26 C593, Arrian *Anabasis* 1.11.7).

In ancient as well as modern times, then, the Trojan War was a decisive point of reference in situating whatever it is we call the Bronze Age. More than that, the Trojan War was in ancient times a decisive point of reference for situating and even defining whoever it is we call Homer.

3. On the historical and archaeological reality of the New Ilion, see the overview of Rose 2006.
4. On the political motives of Xerxes, see Haubold 2004.

6

Variations on a Theme of Homer

RIVAL DATINGS OF HOMER

In the *Life of Homer* traditions we find explicit references to the dating of Homer, linked directly to the dating of the Trojan War. In *Vita* 3a (25–44), which draws upon Book 3 of Aristotle's *Poetics* as its source (F 76 ed. Rose), it is said that Homer was conceived by his mother on the island of Ios at the time of the so-called Ionian Migration, led by one Nēleus, son of King Kodros of Athens (3a.25–27).[1] In *Vita* 3b (17–22), we are told that Aristarchus and his followers at the Library of Alexandria likewise assigned Homer's birth to the time of the Ionian Migration, which Aristarchus dated as happening sixty years after the Return of the Herakleidai, which in turn he dated as happening eighty years after the Capture of Troy. In the same source, *Vita* 3b (21–23), we are also told that Crates of Mallos and his followers at the Library of Pergamon dated Homer's birth as happening before the Return, only some eighty years after the Capture of Troy. Such variations in the dating of Homer turn out to be variations in the identity of Homer.

In these two different versions of the *Life of Homer*, the ultimate point of reference for dating the birth of Homer is the Return of the Herakleidai. The Return is also a point of reference for dating the Bronze Age in general. Following the ultimate "big bang" of the Trojan War toward the end of the Bronze Age, the Return is a second "big bang," signaling the cultural presence of Doric-speaking Greeks in

------

1. See Colbeaux 2005:226 on the research of Theagenes of Rhegium (DK B 2) concerning the *patris* 'fatherland' of Homer. West 2003a:309 notes in passing that Ios—not only Smyrna and Chios—figures as the home of Homer already in such sources as Simonides, Pindar, and Bacchylides.

the Helladic mainland and in outlying islands like Crete.[2] This second "big bang" is chronologically linked with a third "big bang," something generally known as the Ionian Migration, signaling the notional relocation of Ionic-speaking Greeks from the mainland of Hellas to the mainland of central Asia Minor and to outlying islands like Chios and Samos. The dating of the Ionian Migration is in turn traditionally linked with the dating of an alternative third "big bang," the Aeolian Migration, signaling the notional relocation of Aeolic-speaking Greeks from the mainland of Hellas to the mainland of northern Asia Minor and to the outlying island of Lesbos. According to Strabo (13.1.3 C582; cf. 14.1.3 C632), the Aeolian Migration happened four generations before the Ionian Migration. In Strabo and in the other sources, the Greek word typically translated as 'migration' is *apoikia*, which can also be understood as 'colonization'.

In these two different versions of the *Life of Homer*, the immediate point of reference for dating the birth of Homer is the *apoikia* 'colonization' initiated by the Ionians. In the version reported by Aristarchus, as we have just seen, Homer was born at the time of this *apoikia*. In the version reported by Crates, by contrast, Homer was born well before this time.

By implication, the version of Aristarchus pictures Homer as an Ionian. The same goes for other sources that date the birth of Homer after the Ionian *apoikia* 'colonization', notably Eratosthenes, who dates it one hundred years later (*Vita* 6.39–40), and Apollodorus, who dates it eighty years later (*Vita* 6.40). To be contrasted is the version of Crates, who dates the birth of Homer well before the Ionian *apoikia* 'colonization'. By implication, that version pictures Homer not as an Ionian but as an Aeolian.

The differences between the Ionian Homer of Aristarchus and the Aeolian Homer of Crates reflect salient differences in the *Life of Homer* traditions. Once again, I focus on the narratives of two *Lives* in particular, *Vita* 1 and *Vita* 2. From the analysis I presented in chapter 2, we saw that *Vita* 2 shows a distinctly Athenocentric outlook. That is, this narrative traces the unified cultural interests of the Athenian empire. By contrast, *Vita* 1 shows a pre-Athenocentric outlook. This narrative traces the diversified cultural interests of Aeolian and Ionian cities of Asia Minor and outlying islands. As we will now see, the pre-Athenocentric version of *Vita* 1 allows for an Aeolian Homer, while the Athenocentric version of *Vita* 2 requires an Ionian Homer.

A PRE-ATHENOCENTRIC *LIFE OF HOMER*

Vita 1 narrates the shaping of Homer's songmaking career in terms that predate the Athenocentric version of *Vita* 2. A case in point is the narratological sequencing of

2. How and Wells 1928: I, 123–24.

the cities that claim to have the closest ties to Homer. First in the narrative of *Vita* 1 is Cyme, explicitly described as an Aeolian city (*Vita* 1.3): it is mentioned in first place because it is recognized as the city of origin for Homer's genealogy—and the city where he was actually conceived (1.3–17). Second in the narrative of *Vita* 1 is Smyrna, described as an Aeolian daughter city of Cyme (1.18–19). Smyrna is recognized as the city where Homer was born (1.17–31). The same point is made by Strabo (14.1.37 C646), who emphasizes the special claim of Smyrna on Homer. The cities of Cyme and Smyrna were members of an ancient federation of twelve Aeolian cities on the mainland of Asia Minor; this federation was known as the Aeolian Dodecapolis. Herodotus (1.149.1) lists the twelve cities of this Aeolian Dodecapolis in the following sequence: Cyme, Lērisai, Neon Teikhos, Tēmnos, Killa, Notion, Aigiroessa, Pitanē, Aigaiai, Myrina, Gryneia, and Smyrna. I highlight the fact that the first and the last cities to be mentioned are Cyme and Smyrna.

Homer's songmaking career starts in Smyrna, upon his return from his journey to Ithaca: at the end of that journey (*Vita* 1.61–90), Homer is on his way back to Smyrna, but first he stops over at the Ionian city of Colophon, where he falls ill and becomes blind (1.90–92). Once Homer is back in Aeolian Smyrna, now a blind man, he embarks on a career of songmaking, *poiēsis* (1.92–94 ἐκ δὲ τῆς Κολοφῶνος τυφλὸς ἐὼν ἀπικνέεται εἰς τὴν Σμύρναν καὶ οὕτως ἐπεχείρει τῇ ποιήσει).

After an extended stay in Aeolian Smyrna, Homer sets out to Aeolian Cyme (*Vita* 1.95–96), but first he stops over at another Aeolian city, Neon Teikhos (1.96–97), which is explicitly described as a daughter city of Cyme (1.97–98). After a phase of composing and performing at Aeolian Neon Teikhos (1.97–122), Homer proceeds to another such phase of songmaking, at Cyme (1.123–89), and here he changes his name from *Melēsigenēs* to *Homēros* (1.162–66). At this point in the narrative, we see that two alternative names of Homer, *Melēsigenēs* and *Homēros*, are being explained in terms of a change from one name to another. In the myth as narrated in *Vita* 1, the change of Homer's name from *Melēsigenēs* to *Homēros* is signaled by Homer's leaving Smyrna, which later changed from an Aeolian to an Ionian city, and by his relocation to Cyme, which stayed an Aeolian city. As we will see later, the name *Homēros* was associated with the old Aeolian traditions of Cyme, and it is relevant to something that happened to *Melēsigenēs* when he was still in Smyrna.

For the Ionians, the name *Melēsigenēs* was traditionally connected with the name of the river *Melēs* in the environs of Smyrna, as we see in Strabo (12.3.27 C554). The river figures in a story about Homer's birth: Homer's mother gives birth to him on the banks of the *Melēs* (*Vitae* 1.28–29; 2.8–12; 3a.18–19, 35; 10.23–24); alternatively, *Melēs* is the river god who fathers Homer (*Vitae* 2.20–21, 27–28, 53, 75, 151; 3a.78; 3b.15; 4.2–3; 5.1; 6.29; 8.631; 10.1–2; 11 [Proclus summary p. 99 ed. Allen] line 16). In chapter 2, I have already drawn attention to a most relevant detail in *Vita* 1: the birth of Homer on the banks of the river *Melēs* happened on the occasion of a *heortē* 'festival' (1.28). In terms of the *Life of Homer* traditions, the meaning of this alternative name of Homer is validated by the narrative, which gives the name an aetiology. From the standpoint of historical linguistics, however, we can see that the name *Melēsigenēs* once had an earlier meaning: morphologically, it is to be interpreted as 'he who is concerned with genealogy [*genos*]'. That is, the component *genos* of *Melēsigenēs* refers to a form of poetry that centers on narrating origins.[3] The verb *melein*, as in *Melēsi-*, can designate the mental effort of a poet in concentrating on a given poetic subject.[4]

For the Aeolians, the association of the proper noun *Homēros* with the Aeolian city of Cyme was parallel to the association of the common noun *homēros*, which has the general meaning of 'hostage', with the special meaning of 'blind' in Cymaean— or, more generally, in 'Aeolic'—traditions. In the *Lives of Homer*, the primary mediator of Cymaean traditions is Ephorus of Cyme (*FGH* 70, *Vitae* 3a.8, 24; 3b.10– 11; 5.7; 6.11). According to *Vita* 1 (164–65), it is a Cymaean usage to call blind people *homēroi*. So the idea that Homer was recognized as a *homēros* in Cyme is directly connected with Homer's name. We may contrast the reportage of *Vita* 3a (23), where we read that the Cymaeans *and all the Ionians* exemplify this usage. The overall source here is named as Ephorus of Cyme (*Vita* 3a.8). I note with interest here the Ionian appropriation of a usage stemming from an Aeolian city, Cyme. Elsewhere, the usage of *homēroi* to designate blind people is described as Aeolic in general (*Vitae* 2.31, 4.6, 11.19). I will have more to say later on about the meaning 'blind' attributed to the word *homēros*. For now, I highlight simply the Aeolian and specifically Cymaean associations of this meaning.

After Homer's stay in Aeolian Cyme, the Aeolian phase of Homer's *Life* in *Vita* 1 comes to an end. Now starts an Ionian phase. From Aeolian Cyme Homer goes to Ionian Phocaea for another extended stay (*Vita* 1.190–224), after which he prepares to go to Ionian Chios (1.224–25). Before he reaches Chios, Homer has various other adventures, including a stopover at Ionian Erythrai (1.225–75). After his extended stay in Ionian Chios (1.346–98), he heads for Athens, making a transitional stopover at Ionian Samos (1.399–484).

From what we have seen so far, it is evident that the narrative of *Vita* 1 goes out of its way to stress that the origins of Homer are Aeolian, not Ionian. At the end of the narrative, Homer's Aeolian identity is made explicit:

Ὅτι δὲ ἦν Αἰολεὺς Ὅμηρος καὶ οὔτε Ἴων οὔτε Δωριεύς, τοῖς τε εἰρημένοις δεδήλωταί μοι καὶ δὴ καὶ τοῖσδε τεκμαίρεσθαι παρέχει. ἄνδρα **ποιητὴν** τηλικοῦτον εἰκός ἐστι τῶν νομίμων τῶν παρὰ τοῖς ἀνθρώποις **ποιοῦντα** ἐς τὴν **ποίησιν** ἤτοι τὰ κάλλιστα **ἐξευρόντα ποιέειν** ἢ τὰ ἑωυτοῦ, πάτρια ἐόντα.

---

3. West 2003a:310 translates *Melēsigenēs* as 'caring about his clan'. I propose, however, that the component *genos* implies not 'clan' but 'genealogy' in the sense of finding out about origins.

4. *PH* 12§22 (= pp. 347–48).

That Homer was an Aeolian and not an Ionian nor a Dorian is demonstrated by what has been said so far, and it can be proved even more decisively by way of the following: it is likely that a **songmaker** [*poiētēs*] who is of such ancient pedigree, and who draws upon ancestral customs prevalent among humans, would be **making** [*poieîn*] things take place inside his **songmaking** [*poiēsis*] that were either the most beautiful things he could ever **make** [*poieîn*] with his poetic invention or his very own things as he inherited them from his ancestors.

Vita 1.517–22

I draw attention to the fact that this aetiologizing statement specifies an Aeolian rather than Ionian genealogy for Homer. This Aeolian genealogy suits Homer's alternative name *Melēsigenēs* in its basic sense, 'he who is concerned with genealogy', as opposed to its reinterpreted sense, 'he who was born at [*or:* of] the river *Melēs*', which is linked to the later Ionian phase of the formerly Aeolian city of Smyrna. As for the name *Homēros*, it is connected to the earlier, Aeolian, phase of Smyrna. As we will see later, the change in name from *Melēsigenēs* to *Homēros* was correlated with something that happened to Homer while he was still in Aeolian Smyrna, and the consequences of what happened could be understood only in terms of his subsequent stay in Aeolian Cyme. After his stay in Cyme, Homer travels only in Ionian cities, but his name does not revert to *Melēsigenēs*: it stays *Homēros*, which suits Aeolian Cyme.[5]

By highlighting the Aeolian genealogy of Homer, *Vita* 1 disconnects him from the ideology of the "big bang" event of the Ionian Migration—that is, the *apoikia* 'colonization' notionally initiated by Athens as the metropolis or 'mother city' of the Ionian cities. There are many references to this Athenocentric ideology (Solon F 4a ed. West, via Aristotle *Constitution of the Athenians* 5.2; Herodotus 1.146.2; Thucydides 1.2.5–6; Euripides *Ion* 1575–88). Herodotus (1.147.2) gives a classic formulation: εἰσὶ δὲ πάντες Ἴωνες, ὅσοι ἀπ᾽ Ἀθηνέων γεγόνασι καὶ Ἀπατούρια ἄγουσι ὁρτήν 'Ionians are all those populations who originate from Athens and who celebrate the festival [*heortē*] of the Apatouria'. In this context the Apatouria, a festival sacred to Apollo, is viewed as a primarily Athenian institution. The ideology, as we can see from the wording of Herodotus, is indicative of an Athenocentric outlook.[6]

What Herodotus says about the festival of the Apatouria stands in sharp contrast with what is said in what is generally known as the pseudo-Herodotean narrative of

---

5. The locating of Aeolian Cyme as a point of transition from Aeolian to Ionian phases of Homer in *Vita* 1 may be relevant to a story we find embedded in the Hesiodic *Works and Days*: according to this story, the father of Hesiod emigrated from the mainland of Hellas to the city of Cyme on the mainland of Asia Minor—only to emigrate back to the mainland of Hellas. I propose that this story is an aetiology accounting for the fact that the diction of Hesiodic poetry is Ionic, not Aeolic.

6. Herodotus 1.147.2 adds that the Ionian cities of Ephesus and Colophon are exceptional in not celebrating the festival of Apatouria.

Vita 1. There we see a decidedly pre-Athenocentric outlook. By contrast with the formulation of Herodotus (1.147.2), for whom the *heortē* 'festival' of the Apatouria as celebrated in Ionian cities is proof that these cities were founded by Athens as their metropolis or 'mother city', the narrative of *Vita* 1 shows a most revealing set of details pointing to an alternative explanation of the relationship between the city-state of Athens and the Ionian city-states. One such detail emerges in the narrative of *Vita* 1 concerning Homer's stopover at the Ionian island-state of Samos: there he performs his poetry for a body of men called the *phrētores* (φρήτορες or, in Attic, φράτορες 1.404, 405, 408, 430), who are members of a civic confraternity or *phrētrē* (1.421 φρήτρη). This group had invited Homer to participate in celebrating a *heortē* 'festival' (1.407–8 συνεορτάσοντα), specified as the *heortē* of the Apatouria (1.401–2 ἔτυχον δὲ οἱ ἐκεῖσε τὸν τότε καιρὸν ἄγοντες ἑορτὴν Ἀπατούρια). The Samian political terms *phrētores* and *phrētrē*, mentioned in the context of the Apatouria of Samos, are evidently cognate with the Athenian political term *phratriai* 'phratries': it is relevant that the festival of the Apatouria in Athens was in fact the occasion when new members were enrolled into the *phratriai* 'phratries' (scholia for Aristophanes *Acharnians* 146). To say that these Athenian and Ionian forms are cognate with each other is not to say that the second set of forms is derived from the first. On the basis of what we have just seen, I infer just the opposite, that the two sets are in fact independent of each other. In other words, the Samian tradition of the *phrētrē* and *phrētores* is not derived from the Athenian tradition of *phratriai*. Rather, the two traditions are independent of each other, though they are cognate with each other. Later on, I will argue that the Samian setting of this detail in *Vita* 1 derives from the poetics and politics represented by Polycrates, tyrant of Samos.

A more direct example of a pre-Athenocentric outlook in the narrative of *Vita* 1 is its stance concerning the city of Smyrna: basically, *Vita* 1 ignores the historical fact that Aeolian Smyrna eventually became transformed into Ionian Smyrna. For background on this transformation, I turn to Herodotus, who gives us once again a classic formulation.

I summarize here the relevant account of Herodotus (1.149.1–151.2). On the mainland of Asia Minor, facing the outlying island of Lesbos, was a federation of twelve Aeolian cities—an Aeolian Dodecapolis—headed by the city of Cyme (1.149.1). The Aeolian cities on the mainland of Asia Minor in the region of Mount Ida were grouped separately from the Aeolian Dodecapolis (1.151.1). Herodotus does not list these cities by name. As for the island of Lesbos, it was politically organized as a federation of five Aeolian cities (1.151.2). Of the twelve Aeolian cities of the Aeolian Dodecapolis on the mainland of Asia Minor, one city was 'detached' (*paraluein*) by the Ionians; as we know from Herodotus, that city was Smyrna (1.149.1 μία γάρ σφεων παρελύθη Σμύρνη ὑπὸ Ἰώνων).

According to the foundational myth or aetiology that tells how Smyrna was transformed from an Aeolian into an Ionian city, the primal setting of this transformation was a festival (*heortē*) of Dionysus celebrated by the Aeolian people of Smyrna (Herodotus 1.150.1 τοὺς Σμυρναίους ὁρτὴν ἔξω τείχεος ποιευμένους Διονύσῳ): reportedly, some exiles from the Ionian city of Colophon, who had earlier been integrated into the Aeolian city of Smyrna, captured Smyrna while the Aeolians were celebrating their festival outside the city walls (again, 1.150.1). The stranded Aeolians of Smyrna were then absorbed by the remaining eleven Aeolian cities of the federation (1.150.2). According to Strabo (14.1.4 C633), Smyrna was eventually added to a rival federation of twelve Ionian cities, the Ionian Dodecapolis.[7] This is not to say that Smyrna actually became one of the twelve members of the Ionian Dodecapolis in the archaic period. Still, the wording of Herodotus indicates that Smyrna had requested membership in this Ionian federation:

> αἱ δὲ δυώδεκα πόλιες αὗται τῷ τε οὐνόματι ἠγάλλοντο καὶ ἱρὸν ἱδρύσαντο ἐπὶ σφέων αὐτέων, τῷ οὔνομα ἔθεντο **Πανιώνιον**, ἐβουλεύσαντο δὲ αὐτοῦ μεταδοῦναι μηδαμοῖσι ἄλλοισι Ἰώνων—οὐδ᾽ ἐδεήθησαν δὲ οὐδαμοὶ μετασχεῖν ὅτι μὴ Σμυρναῖοι.

> But these twelve cities took pride in the name ['Ionian'] and established a sacred space of their own, giving it the name **Panionion**, and they wished to give membership to no other Ionians [Ionian cities]—nor did any Ionians [any other Ionian city] request it, except for the Smyrnaeans.

> Herodotus 1.143.3

AN ATHENOCENTRIC *LIFE OF HOMER*

By contrast with the pre-Athenocentric outlook of the narrative in *Vita* 1, where Homer is born in the Aeolian city of Smyrna and must be an Aeolian, the Athenocentric outlook prevails in the narrative of *Vita* 2, *The Contest of Homer and Hesiod*: in this narrative, Homer must be an Ionian. In *Vita* 2, the various appropriations of Homer by various Aeolian and Ionian cities of Asia Minor and outlying islands become merged and unified into a singular appropriation of Homer by Athens as the metropolis or 'mother city' of the notional realm that is 'Ionia'. This Ionia is composed of all the Ionian cities of Asia Minor and the offshore Ionian island cities of Chios and Samos. In terms of the narrative of *Vita* 2, Homer must be coeval with the Ionian *apoikia* 'colonization' when the cities of this Ionia were being founded by Athens as their metropolis or 'mother city'.

The narrative of *Vita* 2 says that Homer was claimed as native son by many cities, and it specifies three, listing them in this order: Smyrna (2.9–12), Chios (2.13–15),[8]

---

7. Frame 2009 §4.7n19 dates the refounding of Smyrna somewhere between the late fourth and early third centuries B.C.E.

8. In this context, *Vita* 2 (14–15) refers to the *Homēridai* as *surviving* descendants of Homer in Chios. More later on the *Homēridai* as described in *Vita* 2.

and Colophon (2.15–17).[9] Retrospectively, all three cities are Ionian, since Smyrna switched its identity from an Aeolian to an Ionian city. This triad of cities represents the basic Athenocentric pattern. The same pattern is reflected in the poetry of Pindar (F 264 ed. Snell and Maehler), who reportedly refers to Homer as both Chiote and Smyrnaean (*Vita* 3b.7–8); in the words of Simonides (F 19 ed. West, via Stobaeus 4.34.28), Homer is a Chiote. (Cf. *Vita* 3b.8.)

From an Athenocentric standpoint, as represented by *Vita* 2, the recessive pre-Athenocentric traditions of an Aeolian Homer had to be covered over by the dominant Athenocentric traditions of the Ionian Homer. The Aeolian cities that had claimed contact with Homer had to be shaded over in order to achieve the proper highlighting for the rival Ionian cities. Only Smyrna, which had been transformed from an Aeolian into an Ionian city, could retain its pre-Athenocentric prestige as a Homeric city.[10] Other Aeolian cities, like Cyme, receded in importance.[11] From an Athenocentric point of view, the birth of Homer could be imagined as happening in Smyrna (*Vita* 3a.25–38), even if Homer was conceived on the island of Ios.[12] This Athenocentric version stands in sharp contrast with the pre-Athenocentric version of *Vita* 1, where Homer was born in Aeolian Smyrna (1.17–31) and conceived in Aeolian Cyme (1.3–17).

In the post-Athenocentric versions represented by the other *Lives* of Homer, by contrast, the prestige of Athens as the metropolis or 'mother city' of Ionia became devalued, whereas the older prestige of the various Aeolian and Ionian cities of Asia Minor and outlying islands could be revalidated. The rival versions of the various cities tend to be hierarchically arranged in the individual narratives of the post-Athenocentric *Lives*, though different *Lives* may privilege different versions at different points in their narratives. The post-Athenocentric *Lives* can bypass the Athenocentric period and revert to the pre-Athenocentric period, recapitulating many of

---

9. The main claim of Colophon for possession of Homer is the *Margites*, which is supposedly Homer's first composition (*Vita* 2.17).

10. The persona of Peisistratos, in an epigram (*Vita* 4.11–16 = *Vita* 5.29–34 = *Greek Anthology* 11.442), claims that the Athenians even founded Smyrna: εἴπερ Ἀθηναῖοι Σμύρναν ἐπῳκίσαμεν (*Vita* 4.16 = *Vita* 5.34). At a later point, I will argue that there are two phases involved in the Athenian imperial appropriation of Homer: an earlier phase, where Smyrna is the focus of Athenian claims, and a later phase, where Chios, as the home of the *Homēridai*, becomes the centerpiece of Homeric poetry.

11. I have already noted a case where the reporting of a Cymaean usage of *homēroi* as referring to blind people in *Vita* 1.164–65 is redefined in terms of a Cymaean *and* Ionic usage in *Vita* 3a.23. For another example of a recessive Cymaean tradition embedded within a predominantly Ionian context, see *Vita* 1.286–87. Also, the narrative of *Vita* 1 goes out of its way to emphasize the unimportance of Cyme in the shaping of Homer's repertoire: at the end of his visit to Cyme, Homer curses the Cymaeans, praying that their city should never produce an accomplished poet (*Vita* 1.190–92).

12. As we have seen, the story of Homer's conception in Ios was accepted by Aristotle (F 76 ed. Rose, via *Vitae* 3a.25–26, 3b.10, and 6.13–14). The same island of Ios, as we have also seen, is commonly figured as the place of Homer's death.

the rival versions stemming from the Aeolian and Ionian cities. The dominant phase, in all the attested *Lives* except *Vita* 1 and *Vita* 2, is the post-Athenocentric. Even in the post-Athenocentric *Lives*, however, as also in the Athenocentric *Life* of *Vita* 2, we find that the three Ionian cities of Smyrna, Chios, and Colophon—in that order—take pride of place in their claims on Homer.

AN AEOLIAN DATING OF HOMER

At the end of the narrative of *Vita* 1, the so-called pseudo-Herodotean *Life of Homer,* we find a relative chronology reaffirming the pre-Athenocentric idea that Homer was an Aeolian:

> One hundred thirty years after the Capture of Troy as narrated by the Homer of this *Life of Homer,* Aeolian cities were founded on the island of Lesbos [*Vita* 1.540–43], which had previously existed without any city [1.543 *apolis*].
>
> Twenty years after this settlement, Aeolian Cyme was founded [1.543–44].
>
> Eighteen years after this founding, Aeolian Smyrna was founded by Cyme, and at this moment Homer was born [1.545–47]; thus Homer was born 168 years after the Capture of Troy [1.552–53].
>
> Six hundred twenty-two years after the birth of Homer, Xerxes crossed the Hellespont from Asia Minor to Europe [1.547–50].

This pseudo-Herodotean chronology for dating the Capture of Troy in *Vita* 1 matches the chronology given by Herodotus himself, whose numbering of years converts to the date of 1270 B.C.E.[13] Likewise in *Vita* 1, the number of years converts to the date of 1270 B.C.E. So both *Vita* 1 and Herodotus are traditional, as it were, in their dating of the Capture of Troy. But the date given by Herodotus for Homer himself is by comparison idiosyncratic. Herodotus (2.53.1–3) says that Homer as well as Hesiod lived only around four hundred years before his own time. Such a calculation follows neither of the two traditional datings we have seen so far. At a later point, I will give further consideration to this idiosyncratic dating of Homer by Herodotus. For the moment, however, I simply review the two traditional Homeric datings we have seen so far, one of which is Athenocentric and the other non-Athenocentric. The Athenocentric dating of Homer, as I have already noted, is most prominently represented by Aristarchus in Alexandria, who followed Eratosthenes in calculating the Ionian Migration and the birth of Homer at 140 years after the Capture of Troy (*Vita* 3b.17–22). By contrast, the non-Athenocentric—and Aeolian—version is most prominently represented by Crates, head of the Library

---

13. Graziosi 2002:99.

in Pergamon, who dated Homer's birth as happening before the Return of the Herakleidai, only some eighty years after the Capture of Troy (*Vita* 3b.21–23).

HOMER THE AEOLIAN

In the pre-Athenocentric narrative of *Vita* 1, not only Cyme but even Smyrna is still Aeolian. That is, Smyrna has not yet turned Ionian. Thus the birthplace of Homer is an Aeolian city, and Homer is an Aeolian by birth. In the Athenocentric narrative of *Vita* 2, by contrast, Homer is born in Smyrna when it is already Ionian, and so Homer is an Ionian by birth. To put it another way, we see here the Homer of a diminished Aeolian Dodecapolis, who is becoming redefined as the Homer of an augmented Ionian Dodecapolis. At a later point, I will take a closer look at the concept of the Ionian Dodecapolis, a federation composed of twelve Ionian cities and complemented by additional Ionian cities like Smyrna. For now I focus on the rival federation of the Aeolian Dodecapolis and on the Aeolian island of Lesbos. Lesbos was politically organized as a federation of five cities, visualized by Strabo (13.2.1 C616) as a single unified state that claimed to be the metropolis or 'mother city' of the Aeolian cities on the Asiatic mainland. There is a comparable description in the pseudo-Herodotean *Vita* 1 of Homer: as we just saw, we read there that the cities on the island of Lesbos were the first Aeolian cities to be founded after the Capture of Troy. In that sense, Lesbos was the epicenter of the Aeolian Migration.

As we know from Thucydides, the federation of five cities on the island of Lesbos was dominated by one city in particular, Mytilene, as if all five cities had become united as one single unified city: the special political term for this union was *sunoikisis* (Thucydides 3.3.1). Accordingly, instead of specifying Mytilene or any of the other four cities that belonged to the federation of five cities in Lesbos (Mytilene, Methymna, Antissa, Eresos, Pyrrha), Thucydides generally refers to the whole island as if it were one single city-state, Lesbos, just as the island of Chios is conventionally equated with the city of Chios. In the work of Thucydides, we see the actual collocation of *Khioi* 'Chiotes' with *Lesbioi* 'Lesbians' (at 1.19 and 1.116.2, for example). A notable exception for Thucydides is the context at hand (3.1–3): here he focuses on one single Lesbian city, Methymna, which maintained its allegiance to Athens in the summer of 428 B.C.E. when the rest of the *sunoikisis* of Lesbos revolted from the Athenian empire. The exception proves the rule: the island of Lesbos was dominated by the city of Mytilene, best known to classicists as the poetic setting of Alcaeus and Sappho.

Already in the earliest historical times that we can reconstruct for this part of the Greek-speaking world, in the late seventh century B.C.E., the control exercised by the city of Mytilene over the island of Lesbos and its mainland territories in Asia Minor was threatened by the city of Athens. The threat was intensified in the sixth century, in the era of the tyrants of Athens, the Peisistratidai. As we saw in chapter

1, a predemocratic Athenian empire was already evolving and expanding in the era of these tyrants, and a prime objective of their expansionism was the domination of the Ionian cities situated on the islands to the east and, farther east, on the coastline of Asia Minor. As we are now about to see, another prime objective was the domination of Aeolian cities farther to the north, which had been dominated up to that time by the Aeolian city of Mytilene. As we saw in chapter 1, a vital aspect of Athenian imperial interests was the appropriation of Homer as a symbol of Ionian cultural identity. Now we are about to see another vital aspect: that is, the appropriation of Troy as a symbol of Aeolian cultural identity. As we will also see, the Athenians' appropriation of an Aeolian Troy resulted in their appropriation of an Aeolian Homer as well.

The territory of Troy in northern Asia Minor had been inhabited by Aeolians— and dominated by the Mytilenaeans—until the Athenians took the spectacular initiative of attempting to occupy this territory. Such attempts started toward the end of the seventh century B.C.E. The choicest part of this territory was the city of Sigeion and its environs. The city had been built near the northern end of the heights known as the Sigeion Ridge, which extends along the Aegean coastline of Asia Minor overlooking the entrance to the Hellespont. The Sigeion Ridge, some ten kilometers in length, extends from the promontory at the Bay of Beşike in the south all the way to the promontory of Sigeion (Kum Kale) in the north.[14] Modern historians describe Sigeion as the first overseas possession of Athens; a close second was the city of Elaious on the European side of the Hellespont, facing Sigeion on the Asiatic side.[15] As we are about to see, the initiative of possessing Sigeion transcended the objectives of wealth and power. There was also the objective of prestige—the prestige of poetry. At stake was the poetic territory that was Troy, and the ideology underlying the prestige of this Iliadic space turns out to be relevant to some of the oldest recoverable phases of content in Homeric poetry.

As I said a moment ago, the city of Sigeion had been controlled by the Aeolian city of Mytilene in Lesbos before it was captured from the Mytilenaeans by Athens. The capture must be seen against the backdrop of a protracted war between Mytilene and Athens over the possession of Sigeion, and the city seems to have changed hands more than once in the course of this war. The general outlines of the ongoing conflict emerge from the accounts of Herodotus (5.94–95), Strabo (13.1.38–39 C599–600), and Diogenes Laertius (1.74).[16]

In these accounts, the earlier years of the war between Mytilene and Athens over Sigeion are dominated by such celebrated protagonists as Alcaeus of Mytilene, Pittakos of Mytilene, Phrynon of Athens, and Periander of Corinth, who can all be

14. Cook 1984:167.
15. Cook 1973:178–88; Rose 2006:141; Erskine 2001:107–8; Hall 1997:42–44.
16. Aloni 2006:87–92. See also Antonelli 2000.

dated to the late seventh and early sixth century B.C.E. In the poetry of Alcaeus as read by Herodotus, Sigeion is pictured as already belonging to Athens: Herodotus notes that Alcaeus himself says in his own poetry that his armor was captured from him by the Athenians in a battle against the Mytilenaeans, and that it was displayed by the enemy inside the *Athēnaion* 'sacred space of Athena' in Sigeion (5.95.1 τὰ δέ οἱ ὅπλα ἴσχουσι Ἀθηναῖοι καί σφεα ἀνεκρέμασαν πρὸς τὸ Ἀθήναιον τὸ ἐν Σιγείῳ). Strabo quotes the words of Alcaeus telling about the captured armor, and these words actually give the name of Athena's sacred space as *Glaukōpion* (Alcaeus F 401B, via Strabo 13.1.37 C600). This same name, *Glaukōpion*, derived from the sacred epithet of Athena *glaukōpis* 'having the looks of the owl', is attested in Athens as well. There it applies to the sacred space of Athena Nike at the southwest corner of the acropolis (Callimachus F 238.11), and this space, like the *Glaukōpion* in Sigeion, can be dated as far back as 600 B.C.E.[17]

At some point during the ongoing war between Mytilene and Athens over Sigeion, this city and its environs must have reverted to Mytilene before reverting once again—and this time finally—to Athens. Herodotus specifies that Sigeion had to be recaptured from the Mytilenaeans by the Athenians under the leadership of Peisistratos, who installed his son Hegesistratos as the tyrant there (5.94.1). Herodotus goes out of his way to emphasize that this reversion of Sigeion from Mytilene to Athens in the era of Peisistratos was indeed final.

I leave it open whether the very first attempts to seize Sigeion from the Aeolians can be attributed to the Athenians specifically or, more generally, to the Ionians as represented especially by the city of Miletus, which claimed special ties to Athens as its notional mother city.[18] In any event, these early attempts in the seventh century B.C.E. could be viewed retrospectively as a purely Athenian initiative in the later era of the Peisistratidai.

It is in this context that we must view the retrospective statement made by Herodotus (5.95.2) about an earlier time when the city of Sigeion had been taken away from Mytilene and awarded to Athens as the result of an arbitration conducted by the tyrant Periander of Corinth. From the overall narrative of Herodotus (5.94–95), we can see what was really at stake in the arbitrated dispute between the two cities over the possession of Sigeion—a dispute that continued all the way to the time when Peisistratos finally succeeded in securing permanent Athenian control over the city. In the course of describing the rival claims and counterclaims in this continuing dispute between Mytilene and Athens, Herodotus makes it clear that these

---

17. Robertson 1996:70n55. Also Frame 2009 §3.74. See also Rose 2006:142–43 on the temple of Athena at Assos, which was similar in its Doric architecture to the temple of Athena at Sigeion.

18. On the special ties between Athens as mother city and Miletus as daughter city, I refer to the work of Frame 2009 ch. 10.

two cities equated the possession of the territory of Sigeion with the possession of the epic of the Trojan War. At stake was the poetic space of the Trojan War, to which Herodotus refers as *hē Ilias khōra*—simultaneously the territory of the epic of Troy (that is, of the *Iliad*) as well as the territory of the city of Troy (that is, of Ilion):

οἱ μὲν ἀπαιτέοντες τὴν **χώρην**, Ἀθηναῖοι δὲ οὔτε συγγινωσκόμενοι ἀποδεικνύντες τε λόγῳ οὐδὲν μᾶλλον Αἰολεῦσι μετεὸν τῆς Ἰλιάδος **χώρης** ἢ οὐ καὶ σφίσι καὶ τοῖσι ἄλλοισι, ὅσοι Ἑλλήνων συνεπρήξαντο Μενέλεῳ τὰς Ἑλένης ἁρπαγάς.

They [the Mytilenaeans] were demanding the return of the **territory** [*khōra*], but the Athenians rejected the demand, trying to demonstrate by way of what they said that the Aeolians were no more entitled to the **Iliadic territory** [*khōra*] than were they [the Athenians] and all the other Hellenes who had joined forces in avenging Menelaos for the abduction of Helen.

Herodotus 5.94.2

As the wording of Herodotus makes clear, the city of Mytilene in Lesbos claimed to be representing all Aeolic-speaking Hellenes in claiming possession of the Iliadic territory of Sigeion in the Troad. By contrast, the city of Athens claimed to be representing all Hellenes who took part in the Trojan War. That is why the interpolation, as it were, of Athens into the Trojan War is vital for the Athenians. We saw it also in *Vita* 1 (379–84), where Homer inserts the role of Athens into his *Iliad* while he is composing it in Chios, getting ready for his big tour of the Helladic mainland—a tour that is meant to start with Athens as the first stop. We see it also in the inscriptions commemorating the victory of the Athenians led by Kimon against the Persians at Eion in 475, in which the Athenian hero Menestheus was glorified.[19] (The relevant verses glorifying Menestheus are quoted by Aeschines 3.185.)

That the Aeolians equated Sigeion and its environs with Iliadic territory is also evident from information dating back to the earlier, Aeolian phase of Sigeion. As we read in Strabo (13.1.38 C599), the Mytilenaeans under the leadership of one Archeanax built the walls of the city of Sigeion from the stones of the ruined walls of the ancient city of Troy.

I highlight the importance of this piece of information, which is obscured by the overall argument that Strabo is trying to make. When Strabo (13.1.38 C599) reports that Aeolian Sigeion had been built from the stones of Troy, he thinks that this report actually validates his ongoing argument that the ancient city of Troy, or Ilion, was not the same thing as the new city of Ilion, the New Ilion.[20] In making this argument, Strabo says that he is following the antiquarian Demetrius of Scepsis, a *grammatikos* who lived in the era of Crates and Aristarchus: that is, in the second

---

19. Dué 2006:98–99; on the role of the Athenian hero Menestheus in the *Iliad*, see Dué pp. 92–95.
20. For a historical and archaeological overview of the New Ilion, see Rose 2006.

century B.C.E. Demetrius denied any continuity between the old Ilion and the city of New Ilion as it existed in his own day, and Strabo follows him in claiming that there was no trace left of the old Ilion. Supposedly, all the stones of the old Ilion were used up in the process of building the walls of other cities like Sigeion. At a later point, I will argue that the motives underlying this claim can be traced back to Athenian imperial ambitions.

7

Conflicting Claims on Homer

THE TOMB OF ACHILLES AND
THE TOPOGRAPHY OF THE TROAD

The Aeolians had their own motives for claiming the territory of Sigeion as their very own Iliadic space. The tomb of the hero Achilles was understood to be located in Aeolian territory, specifically in the environs of Sigeion. As we are about to see, the Aeolians connected this poetic territory, this Iliadic space, with epic references to the tomb of Achilles. And so too did the Athenians. Such conflicting claims on Iliadic space stemmed from conflicting claims on Homer himself.

In order to make this argument, I need to start by returning to two points I stressed earlier:

1. The city of Mytilene in Lesbos was supposedly representing all Aeolic-speaking Hellenes when it claimed the Iliadic territory of Aeolian Sigeion.
2. The motive of the Athenians in counterclaiming for themselves the territory of Sigeion was predicated on this previous claim of the Mytilenaeans.

So far, I have noted that the territory of Sigeion was understood to be the site of the tomb of Achilles. But there is more to it. Achilles was worshipped as a cult hero at this tomb. Both the tomb and the hero cult of Achilles in the vicinity of Sigeion in the Troad had been for the Aeolians a metonymy for the *Iliad*—that is, for their epic tradition about the Trojan War. The objective of the Athenians was to appropriate for themselves a comparable metonymy.

There is a plethora of external evidence about the status of Achilles as a cult hero.[1]

1. Shaw 2001 gives a survey.

Of particular interest is the fact that the attested hero cults of Achilles are pre-dominantly located at Aeolian sites.[2] One such site is the city of *Akhílleion*, located in territory that once belonged to the city of Sigeion in that other city's Aeolian phase of existence. This city of *Akhílleion*, some ten kilometers to the south of Sigeion, was built on the heights of the promontory at the Bay of Beşike, at the southern end of the Sigeion Ridge.[3] Nearby is a tumulus looking out over the sea. As we will see, it was claimed that this tumulus was the tomb of Achilles.

There was also a rival claim, however. It centered on a tumulus situated some ten kilometers to the north, on the slopes stretching from the heights of the promontory at the northern end of the Sigeion Ridge, in the immediate vicinity of the old city of Sigeion.[4] This tumulus, looking out over the sea of the Hellespont, was likewise claimed as the tomb of Achilles. As the discussion proceeds, we will have to confront this question: Which of these two rival tumuli matches the tomb of Achilles as described in the Homeric *Iliad*?[5]

As we learn from the stylized account of Philostratus in the *Heroikos* (52.3–54.1), the tomb of Achilles in the Troad was the site of seasonally recurring sacrifices offered to the hero. These sacrifices were performed by Aeolians. To be more specific, these Aeolians were Thessalians: that is, Aeolians originating from—and still living in—the territory on the Helladic mainland where the Iliadic hero Achilles himself was reputedly born and raised. So these Aeolians could claim a special connection to the territory on the Asiatic mainland where Achilles died and was buried. Such a claim is relevant to the imperial interests of Athens in the era of the Peisistratidai. We know that one of the sons of Peisistratos, Hegesistratos, was renamed *Thessalos* (in the Attic dialect, *Thettalos*) the 'Thessalian' (Aristotle *Constitution of the Athenians* 17.3–4), and we also know that this son was directly associated with Sigeion: after that city reverted to the Athenians, he was put in charge as tyrant of the city (Herodotus 5.94.1).[6] The Athenian tyrant's *ad hoc* name *Thessalos* evokes a

---

2. Shaw 2001:170.

3. Archaeologists have securely identified the site at Cape Burun as *Akhílleion*: see Burgess 2006:n56 and n58; 2009:122–23. Also Cook 1984:168. In the third century B.C.E., as Rose 2006:149 observes, the tumulus of Achilles at this site was enlarged.

4. Archaeologists have securely identified the site at Cape Yenişehir as Sigeion: see Burgess 2006; 2009:118–21. Also Cook 1973:178–86 and Aloni 1986:65n8.

5. For a summary of archaeological evidence about the tumuli in the Troad, see especially Burgess 2006. See also Cook 1973:185–86 and 1984:167–68; Aloni 1986:65n8; West 2002:208n8; Rose 1999:61–63, 2000:65–66, and 2006:140–41, 149.

6. In Aristotle *Constitution of the Athenians* 18.2, this son of Peisistratos is called *Thessalos* (*Thettalos*), but in 17.3–4 it is made explicit that his primary name was Hegesistratos and that *Thessalos* was his *parōnumion* 'side-name'. Herodotus (5.94.1) refers to him as Hegesistratos and says explicitly that he was an illegitimate son of Peisistratos, but Thucydides (1.20.2 and 6.55.1) calls him *Thessalos* and assumes that he was a legitimate son.

special Athenian connection with the Aeolians who inhabited Thessaly. Herodotus (5.63.3) highlights the ongoing alliance between the dynasts of Thessaly and the Peisistratidai of Athens.[7]

How, then, is such a Thessalian connection relevant to the imperial interests of the Athenians? These Aeolians on the Helladic mainland were the notional proto-types of the Aeolians on the island of Lesbos and, by extension, of the Aeolians on the Asiatic mainland. Thessaly was understood to be the point of origin for the Aeolian Migration—that is, for the colonization of the Aeolian cities on the island of Lesbos and, by extension, of the Aeolian cities on the Asiatic mainland. While the Athenians on the Helladic mainland figured themselves as the prototypes of the Ionians of Asia Minor and of its outlying islands, they figured the Thessalians as the prototypes of the Aeolians of Asia Minor and of its outlying islands, especially of Lesbos.

What I have just formulated can be reconciled with two references in the *Iliad* to a most singular event: the capture of all Lesbos by a single hero, Achilles of Thessaly (IX 128–31, 270–73).[8] I propose that the story of this capture was a charter myth that accounted for the early appropriation of Lesbos by the Thessalians and for a much later attempt at reappropriation in the specific context of their alliance with the Athenians. In terms of such a charter myth, as I will now argue, the tomb of Achilles could be located not only at the site of *Akhílleion,* as owned and operated by the Mytilenaeans of Lesbos, but also at the site of Sigeion, as owned and operated by the Athenians. As I will also argue, Homeric poetry was cited as testimony to validate either of these two rival sites.

Homeric poetry refers at least three times to the tomb of Achilles. There is a direct reference near the end of the *Odyssey*, when the ghost of Agamemnon in Hades speaks retrospectively about the funeral of Achilles. In that context, we find this description of the tomb of Achilles:[9]

ἀμφ' αὐτοῖσι δ' ἔπειτα μέγαν καὶ ἀμύμονα **τύμβον**
χεύαμεν Ἀργείων ἱερὸς στρατὸς αἰχμητάων
ἀκτῇ ἔπι προὐχούσῃ ἐπὶ πλατεῖ Ἑλλησπόντῳ,
ὥς κεν **τηλεφανὴς** ἐκ **ποντόφιν** ἀνδράσιν εἴη
τοῖσ', οἳ νῦν γεγάασι καὶ οἳ μετόπισθεν ἔσονται.

Next, over these [the bones of Achilles and Patroklos], a great and faultless **tomb** was built by us, the sacred band of Argive spearmen,

---

7. Shaw 2001:167n7.

8. I will have more to say later on about these two references.

9. *BA* 20§§20–28 (= pp. 338–46), cited by Shaw 2001:167. On prospective references in Homeric poetry, see Nagy 2001c.

on a promontory [*aktē*] jutting out over the vast Hellespont,[10]
so that it might be visible, shining forth from afar, for men at sea [*pontos*],[11]
both for those who live now[12] and for those who will live in the future.

Odyssey xxiv 80–84

There is also a second direct reference to this promontory. This time, it is in the *Iliad*. After the spirit of the dead Patroklos tells Achilles to build a tomb that will be shared by the two heroes after Achilles too is dead (*Iliad* XXIII 83–84, 91–92), a funeral pyre is prepared: men are sent out to the slopes of Mount Ida to chop down trees for timber to fuel the fires of cremation (110–24). Then the men bring the timber to the site where the tomb will be located:

κὰδ δ' ἄρ' ἐπ' ἀκτῆς βάλλον ἐπισχερώ, ἔνθ' ἄρ' Ἀχιλλεὺς
φράσσατο Πατρόκλῳ μέγα ἠρίον ἠδὲ οἷ αὐτῷ.

They [the Achaeans] placed them [the logs] in a row on the promontory [*aktē*] where Achilles
had marked out the place of a great tomb [*ērion*] for Patroklos and for his own self.

Iliad XXIII 125–26

After the body of Patroklos is cremated, Achilles says that the bones must be placed inside a golden urn and that a tomb must be built to house the urn. This tomb, made for the urn containing the bones of Patroklos as the other self of Achilles, will be incomplete until the bones of Achilles himself are placed inside the same urn, at which time the process of building the tomb will be completed:

τύμβον δ' οὐ μάλα πολλὸν ἐγὼ πονέεσθαι ἄνωγα,
ἀλλ' ἐπιεικέα τοῖον· ἔπειτα δὲ καὶ τὸν Ἀχαιοὶ
εὐρύν θ' ὑψηλόν τε τιθήμεναι, οἵ κεν ἐμεῖο
δεύτεροι ἐν νήεσσι πολυκλήϊσι λίπησθε.

I [Achilles] command that you [the Achaeans] make a tomb [*tumbos*], not very big, just big enough for now. Later, this same tomb you Achaeans
must make very wide and very high—those of you who, after me,
will be left behind, you with your ships that have many benches.

Iliad XXIII 245–48

The Achaeans who survive Achilles are pictured here as a seafaring people, and the hero's words prophesy that the tumulus built for his tomb will have a special

10. In the usage of the Homeric *Iliad*, as we will see, the name *Hellēspontos* refers not only to the strait of the Hellespont (or Dardanelles) but also to the Aegean Sea offshore from the Sigeion Ridge. See also Kraft, Kayan, and Oğuz 1982:37.
11. The light is pictured as visible 'from' the sea: that is, from the perspective of those who are at sea.
12. The time frame indicated as 'now' here is the era of the heroes who fought in the Trojan War.

meaning for them. That special meaning is made explicit in the passage I quoted earlier from the *Odyssey*, which likewise describes the tumulus built for the tomb of Achilles. This tumulus, situated on a promontory overlooking the Hellespont, is a sacred lighthouse flashing its *selas* 'gleam' of salvation for sailors.

There is another mention of this same image, again in the *Iliad*, and here we can see an additional reference, however indirect, to the tomb of Achilles. The narrative here visualizes the *selas* 'gleam' radiating from the bronze surface of the Shield of Achilles, and this gleam is compared to a light emanating from a distant watchfire burning at some solitary outpost situated on the coastal heights overlooking a stormy sea—a light flashing its gleam of salvation for sailors seeking to find their way:[13]

δύσετο δῶρα θεοῦ, τά οἱ Ἥφαιστος κάμε τεύχων.
κνημῖδας μὲν πρῶτα περὶ κνήμῃσιν ἔθηκε
καλὰς ἀργυρέοισιν ἐπισφυρίοις ἀραρυίας·   370
δεύτερον αὖ θώρηκα περὶ στήθεσσιν ἔδυνεν.
ἀμφὶ δ' ἄρ' ὤμοισιν βάλετο ξίφος ἀργυρόηλον
χάλκεον· αὐτὰρ ἔπειτα **σάκος** μέγα τε στιβαρόν τε
εἵλετο, τοῦ δ' ἀπάνευθε **σέλας** γένετ' ἠΰτε μήνης.
ὡς δ' ὅτ' ἄν ἐκ πόντοιο **σέλας** ναύτῃσι **φανήῃ**   375
καιομένοιο πυρός, τό τε καίεται ὑψόθ' **ὄρεσφι**
σταθμῷ ἐν οἰοπόλῳ· τοὺς δ' οὐκ ἐθέλοντας ἄελλαι
πόντον ἐπ' ἰχθυόεντα φίλων ἀπάνευθε φέρουσιν·
ὡς ἀπ' Ἀχιλλῆος **σάκεος σέλας** αἰθέρ' ἵκανε.

He [Achilles] put it [his armor] on, the gifts of the god, which
    Hephaistos had made for him with much labor.
First he put around his legs the shin guards,   370
beautiful ones, with silver fastenings at the ankles.
Next he put around his chest the breastplate,
and around his shoulders he slung the sword with the nails of silver,
a sword made of bronze. Next, the **Shield** [*sakos*], great and mighty,
he took, and from it there was a **gleam** [*selas*] from afar, as from
    the moon,
or as when, at sea,[14] a **gleam** [*selas*] to sailors **appears**   375
from a blazing fire, the kind that blazes **high in the mountains**
at a solitary[15] **station** [*stathmos*], as the sailors are carried unwilling
    by gusts of wind
over the fish-swarming **sea** [*pontos*], far away from their loved ones.

13. *BA* 20§§20-28 (= pp. 338-46), cited by Shaw 2001:167.

14. To repeat what I noted earlier, the light is pictured as visible 'from' the sea: that is, from the perspective of those who are at sea.

15. For parallel wording, see *Odyssey* xi 574: ἐν οἰοπόλοισιν ὄρεσσιν 'in the solitary heights of the mountains'.

So also did the gleam [*selas*] from the Shield [*sakos*] of Achilles reach
all the way up to the aether.

Iliad XIX 368–79

I draw attention to the word *stathmos* 'station', which refers here to the solitary
tumulus situated on the coastal heights. In another Homeric passage involving the
Shield of Achilles, we see a revealing attestation of this same word in collocation
with two related words:

ἐν δὲ νομὸν ποίησε περικλυτὸς ἀμφιγυήεις
ἐν καλῇ βήσσῃ μέγαν οἰῶν ἀργεννάων,
σταθμούς τε **κλισίας** τε κατηρεφέας ἰδὲ **σηκούς**.

Next, the one with the two great arms [Hephaistos], whose fame is supreme, made
  [an image of] a space for pasturing
in a beautiful mountainous place. It was a vast space, full of sheep with shining
  fleeces.
It [this space for pasturing][16] had ***stathmoi, klisiai*** with covering on top, and ***sēkoi***.

Iliad XVIII 587–89

These three words—*stathmos, klisia,* and *sēkos*—are applied here in the context
of describing a generic pastoral setting. When we compare the etymologies of these
three words with the contexts of their usage in other pastoral settings, we find that
their reconstructed meanings are interrelated: *stathmos*, derived from the root *sta-
meaning 'stand up', is the makeshift post of a herdsman's shelter or tent;[17] *klisia*, derived from the root *kli- meaning 'lie down' or 'lean', is the space in the shelter where
the herdsman reclines—or, alternatively, it is a 'lean-to' covering that affords a
makeshift shelter;[18] and *sēkos*, derived from the root *sak- meaning 'fill [an empty
space]', is the enclosure where the herdsman's herd is penned in.[19] By way of
metonymy, the *klisia* is not only an aspect of the shelter but also the entire shelter;
likewise, the *stathmos* is not only the post of the shelter but also the entire shelter
and everything contiguous with the shelter, including the *sēkos*.[20] In this sense, then,
the *stathmos* is the herdsman's 'station'.

---

16. This space for pasturing is also the space for picturing what is in the pasture.

17. I reconstruct such a basic meaning from the survey of facts presented in Chantraine *DELG* s.vv.
στάθμη and σταθμός.

18. This etymological interpretation, among others, is considered in *DELG* s.v. κλίνω.

19. This etymological interpretation, among others, is considered in *DELG* s.v. σηκός. In Hesychius
s.v., we read that σῆκα is what a shepherd shouts to his herd of sheep when he herds them back into
their penfold.

20. In the scholia T (hypothesis) at *Odyssey* iv 612, we find a list of words that ancient lexicogra-
phers connect with each other: μετασταθμήσω. τὸ γὰρ στῶ στήσω καὶ ἐπὶ σταθμοῦ λέγεται, ὅθεν γίνεται
καὶ ὁ σηκὸς στηκός τις ὢν καὶ δηλῶν σταθμόν τινα, ὅθεν καὶ ἡ ἀντισήκωσις ἀντιστάθμησίς τις οὖσα.

The pastoral word *sēkos* refers not only to the enclosure where a herd is penned in but also to the enclosure where a cult hero is buried and worshipped.[21] I will now argue that such sacral connotations are attached to the pastoral words *klisia* and *stathmos* as well. All three words connote traditional images typical of cult heroes.

In the *Iliad*, the word *klisia* refers to the abode that a hero like Achilles frequents in life: his *klisia* is his shelter, which marks the place where his ship is beached on the shores of the Hellespont during the Trojan War (VIII 224, XI 7, and so on). In later poetry we see a related use of *stathmos* (plural *stathma*) with reference to the places where the ships of Achaean heroes are beached on the shores of the Helles-pont ("Euripides" *Rhesus* 43); these places are also called *naustathma* 'ship stations' (*Rhesus* 136, 244, 448, 582, 591, 602, 673). Among these *stathma* 'stations' lining the coast of the Hellespont is the heroic space occupied by Achilles.

According to the *Iliad* (VIII 220–26 and XI 5–9), the ship of Achilles is beached farthest to the west on the coastline of the Hellespont, while the ship of Ajax is beached farthest to the east. I will explain presently how we know about the west-to-east alignment of this Iliadic visualization. For the moment, it is enough for me to highlight the simple fact that the station of Achilles on the coast of the Hellespont is marked by the space where his *klisia* 'shelter' stands at the beach (again, VIII 220–26 and XI 5–9). In the narrative topography of the *Iliad*, the hero's *stathmos* 'station' is imagined as the abode he frequents in the heroic time of the Trojan War. But it is also imagined as the abode that the hero frequents after death, in the future time of audiences listening to the story of the Trojan War. As I have argued, the *stathmos* of Achilles is pictured as his tomb, situated on the heights overlooking the space where his ship had once been beached. As we will see later, this solitary *stathmos* is pic-tured as a sacred space haunted by the spirit of the solitary hero after death.

In Strabo's description of the Troad, the word *naustathmon* 'ship station' is used with reference to a space in the immediate vicinity of Sigeion:

Μετὰ δὲ τὸ Ῥοίτειον ἔστι τὸ Σίγειον, **κατεσπασμένη** πόλις, καὶ τὸ **ναύσταθμον** καὶ ὁ Ἀχαιῶν λιμὴν καὶ τὸ Ἀχαϊκὸν στρατόπεδον καὶ ἡ στομαλίμνη καλουμένη καὶ αἱ τοῦ Σκαμάνδρου ἐκβολαί. συμπεσόντες γὰρ ὅ τε Σιμόεις καὶ ὁ Σκάμανδρος ἐν τῷ πεδίῳ πολλὴν καταφέροντες ἰλὺν προσχοῦσι τὴν παραλίαν καὶ τυφλὸν στόμα τε καὶ λιμνοθαλάττας καὶ ἕλη ποιοῦσι. κατὰ δὲ τὴν **Σιγειάδα ἄκραν** ἐστὶν ἐν τῇ Χερρονήσῳ τὸ **Πρωτεσιλάειον** καὶ ἡ Ἐλαιοῦσσα, περὶ ὧν εἰρήκαμεν ἐν τοῖς Θρακίοις. Ἔστι δὲ τὸ μῆκος τῆς παραλίας ταύτης ἀπὸ τοῦ Ῥοιτείου μέχρι **Σιγείου καὶ τοῦ Ἀχιλλέως μνήματος** εὐθυπλοούντων ἑξήκοντα σταδίων· ὑποπέπτωκε δὲ τῷ Ἰλίῳ πᾶσα, τῷ μὲν νῦν κατὰ τὸν **Ἀχαιῶν λιμένα** ὅσον δώδεκα σταδίους διέχουσα, τῷ δὲ προτέρῳ τριάκοντα ἄλλοις σταδίοις ἀνωτέρῳ κατὰ τὸ πρὸς τὴν Ἴδην μέρος. **τοῦ μὲν οὖν Ἀχιλλέως καὶ ἱερόν ἐστι καὶ μνῆμα πρὸς τῷ Σιγείῳ**, Πατρόκλου δὲ καὶ Ἀντιλόχου **μνήματα**, καὶ ἐναγίζουσιν οἱ Ἰλιεῖς πᾶσι καὶ τούτοις καὶ τῷ Αἴαντι.

---

21. There is a short survey of epigraphical and literary contexts in *DELG* s.v. σηκός.

After Rhoiteion is Sigeion, which is a **demolished** city, and there is also the **nau-stathmon** and the **harbor** [*limēn*] **of the Achaeans** and the Achaean camp [*stratopedon*] and the so-called mouth-of-the-marsh [*stomalimnē*] and the outlets [*ekbolai*] of the Scamander. For the rivers Simoeis and Scamander converge in the plain and bring together a great deal of alluvium there. They [the two rivers] silt up the coastline and make a blind mouth [*tuphlon stoma*], sea lagoons [*limnothalattai*], and marshes [*helē*]. And facing the **promontory** [*akrā*] **of Sigeion** on the Chersonesus is **the space of Protesilaos**[22] and Elaioussa [Elaious]. About these things I have already spoken in the section on Thrace. And the length of this coastline, if one sails in a straight line from Rhoiteion to **Sigeion and the tomb** [*mnēma*] **of Achilles**, is sixty stadia. And all of it [the coastline] is visible from on high in Ilion—I mean both the present-day Ilion, which is about twelve stadia away from the **harbor** [*limēn*] **of the Achaeans**, and the previous Ilion, which is thirty additional stadia farther uphill in the direction of Mount Ida.[23] **There is both a sacred precinct** [*hieron*] **and a tomb** [*mnēma*] **of Achilles in the vicinity of Sigeion**, and there are also **tombs** [*mnēmata*] of Patroklos and Antilokhos, and the people of Ilion make sacrifices [*enagizein*] to all these heroes as well as to Ajax.

Strabo 13.1.31–32 C595

On two separate occasions in this passage, Strabo's wording pairs the site of Sigeion, which he describes as a 'demolished city' (κατεσπασμένη πόλις), with the site of the *mnēma* 'tomb' of Achilles (13.1.31–32 C595). Why this city was no longer in existence in Strabo's time is a question I will address at a later point. For now I concentrate on the *mnēma* 'tomb' of Achilles, which Strabo locates in the immediate vicinity of this demolished city of Sigeion, and which he pairs with this city in measuring the distance of sixty stadia from the city of Rhoiteion farther to the east. This tomb of Achilles, located in the vicinity of Sigeion near the northern end of the Sigeion Ridge, cannot be the same thing as the tomb of Achilles located in *Akhílleion*, a site farther to the south on the Aegean coast, which was built on the heights of the promontory at the Bay of Beşike, near the southern end of the Sigeion Ridge. That *Akhílleion*, as I noted already, is some ten kilometers south of Sigeion. Strabo (13.1.39 C600) speaks of a *mnēma* 'tomb' of Achilles at this site as well.[24] I will have more to say later about that alternative tomb of Achilles.

In the passage of Strabo concerning the sights to see in the immediate vicinity

22. The tumulus containing the tomb of the hero Protesilaos, situated on the European side of the Hellespont, faces the tumulus containing the tomb of the hero Achilles on the Asiatic side. The word that refers to the tumulus of Protesilaos is *kolōnos* in Philostratus *Heroikos* 9.1. See Nagy 2001e:xxxiii–xxxiv n34, where I translate that word as 'landmark'. I will have more to say about *kolōnos* as the discussion proceeds.

23. Strabo subscribes to the idea of an old Ilion that is not where the New Ilion is located. This idea has been discredited in light of archaeological work at the New Ilion, which proves that this site can be identified with the old Ilion of the *Iliad* as we know it. For a historical and archaeological overview, see Rose 2006. I will have more to say later about the concept—and the reality—of the New Ilion.

24. See also Pliny the Elder *Natural History* 5.33.125.

of Sigeion, I highlight two other relevant points of interest besides the *mnēma* 'tomb' of Achilles. The first is something called the *naustathmon* 'ship station', and the second is 'the harbor [*limēn*] of the Achaeans' (ὁ Ἀχαιῶν λιμήν). Elsewhere in his work, Strabo mentions both these points of interest for a second time, and, this time around, he attempts to equate one with the other:

Καὶ μὴν τό γε **ναύσταθμον τὸ νῦν ἔτι λεγόμενον** πλησίον οὕτως ἐστὶ τῆς νῦν πόλεως, ὥστε θαυμάζειν εἰκότως ἄν τινα τῶν μὲν τῆς ἀπονοίας τῶν δὲ τοὐναντίον τῆς ἀψυχίας· ἀπονοίας μέν, εἰ τοσοῦτον χρόνον ἀτείχιστον αὐτὸ εἶχον, πλησίον οὔσης τῆς πόλεως καὶ τοσούτου πλήθους τοῦ τ᾽ ἐν αὐτῇ καὶ τοῦ ἐπικουρικοῦ· νεωστὶ γὰρ γεγονέναι φησὶ τὸ τεῖχος (ἢ οὐδ᾽ ἐγένετο, ὁ δὲ **πλάσας ποιητὴς ἠφάνισεν**, ὡς Ἀριστοτέλης φησίν)· ἀψυχίας δέ, εἰ γενομένου τοῦ τείχους ἐτειχομάχουν καὶ εἰσέπεσον εἰς αὐτὸ τὸ **ναύσταθμον** καὶ προσεμάχοντο ταῖς ναυσίν, ἀτείχιστον δὲ ἔχοντες οὐκ ἐθάρρουν προσιόντες πολιορκεῖν μικροῦ τοῦ διαστήματος ὄντος· **ἔστι γὰρ τὸ ναύσταθμον πρὸς Σιγείῳ**, πλησίον δὲ καὶ ὁ Σκάμανδρος ἐκδίδωσι διέχων τοῦ Ἰλίου σταδίους εἴκοσιν. εἰ δὲ **φήσει τις τὸν νῦν λεγόμενον Ἀχαιῶν λιμένα εἶναι τὸ ναύσταθμον**, ἐγγυτέρω τινὰ λέξει τόπον ὅσον δώδεκα σταδίους διεστῶτα τῆς πόλεως, ἐπὶ θαλάττῃ πεδίον νῦν προστιθείς,²⁵ διότι τοῦτο πᾶν πρόχωμα τῶν ποταμῶν ἐστι τὸ πρὸ τῆς πόλεως ἐπὶ θαλάττῃ πεδίον, ὥστε εἰ δωδεκαστάδιόν ἐστι νῦν τὸ μεταξύ, τότε καὶ τῷ ἡμίσει ἔλαττον ὑπῆρχε.

And here is another thing: the **naustathmon, as it is still called,** is so near the city as it exists today [the New Ilion] that one could reasonably wonder at the mindlessness of the people on one side [the Achaeans] and the cowardice of the people on the opposing side [the Trojans]. I say mindlessness if in fact they [the Achaeans] had that thing [the *naustathmon*] unwalled for such a long time while the city [the old Ilion] was so near and with such a large mass of population on the inside and of allied population on the outside. For the Poet [Homer] says that the wall [the Achaean Wall] had only recently come into existence. Or it never existed at all, **and the Poet made it up [*plattein*] and then made it disappear,** as Aristotle [F 162 ed. Rose] says.²⁶ And I say cowardice if in fact they [the Trojans] could do battle at the wall when the wall came into existence and could even penetrate it and reach the *naustathmon* itself, and yet, when it [the *naustathmon*] was still unwalled, they could not have the courage to besiege it, even though it was such a short distance away. **I say this because the naustathmon is in the vicinity of Sigeion** and, quite near it [Sigeion], the Scamander has its outlet—at a distance of twenty stadia from Ilion. **And if one were to say that the Harbor [*limēn*] of the Achaeans, as it is now called, is the same thing as the naustathmon,** one would be speaking of a place that is even closer, at a distance of twelve stadia from the city [Ilion], now adding in one's calculation a plain by the sea. I speak this way because this entire seaside plain in front of the city [Ilion] is an alluvial de-

25. Editors of Strabo, troubled by the manuscript reading ἐπὶ θαλάττῃ πεδίον νῦν προστιθείς, offer a variety of emendations. For me the reading makes sense as it is.

26. To paraphrase Aristotle (F 162 ed. Rose): Homeric poetry acknowledges the nonexistence of the Achaean Wall at the time of its own performance. See *BA* 9§§15–16 (= pp. 159–60), 20§22 (= p. 340).

posit of the rivers [Scamander and Simoeis]. So if the space in between [the space between the "harbor" and the city] is a distance of twelve stadia in the present, then it would have been only half that distance in the past.

Strabo 13.1.36 C598

As we see from this passage, Strabo knows not one but two traditions about the location of the *naustathmon*. According to one tradition, the place that is 'still' called the *naustathmon* is at a distance of twenty stadia from Ilion. Strabo adds that this place is quite near another place—where the river Scamander (its Turkish name today is Menderes) flowed into the sea in his time. But then he goes on to report an alternative tradition, according to which the *naustathmon* is the same thing as the 'harbor of the Achaeans', which he says is at a distance of twelve stadia from Ilion. In terms of the first of these two alternative traditions, the *naustathmon* is the equivalent of a modern harbor. (I say *modern* only in the sense that Strabo elsewhere actually uses the word *naustathmon* with reference to harbors as they existed in his own time: for example, at 4.1.9 C184, 4.1.10 C185, 4.5.2 C199, etc.). In the case of the second of these two traditions, however, Strabo equates the *naustathmon* not with a functional modern harbor but rather with an epic harbor—that is, with a harbor that had once existed in the epic past but exists no more. Strabo here is showing his awareness of epic connotations: the very term 'harbor of the Achaeans' refers to the time of the Trojan War. In a comparable context, Strabo describes Nauplía in the Argolid as the *naustathmon* 'ship station' of Argos—that is, as the city's ancient harbor (8.6.2 C368 τὸ τῶν Ἀργείων ναύσταθμον).[27]

What, then, is the 'harbor of the Achaeans'? And how are we to imagine the *naustathmon*? Was it where the "modern" harbor was located in Strabo's time, some twenty stadia away from the city of New Ilion, or was it where the harbor was supposed to be located in epic times—that is, some twelve stadia away? For answers, I turn to the evidence provided by modern geological studies of the Troad. As we see from this evidence, there existed in prehistoric times a Trojan Bay on the coastline of the Hellespont between the promontory of Sigeion to the west and the promontory of Rhoiteion to the east. Map 1 shows the relevant topography, as reconstructed by geologists on the basis of the existing geomorphology.[28]

27. Although Strabo in this context (8.6.2 C368–69) accepts the Argive aetiology of the name *Nauplia* as the 'sailing place' for the city, he rejects the part of the aetiology that claims *Nauplios* as the local hero, on the grounds that Nauplios is not mentioned in the Homeric *Iliad* or *Odyssey*. In this case and in many others, Strabo displays a stance of extreme antineoterism.

28. Kraft, Kayan, and Oğuz 1982:32: "Of the two schools of thought—that there was an embayment on the lower Scamander Plain three thousand and more years ago or that the lower Scamander Plain was then approximately in the same position as today—we find the latter to be untenable. It is now evident that there was a major marine embayment in the plains of the Scamander and [Simoeis] rivers during the past ten millennia." This point made by the geologists—that there was indeed a Deep Bay in the plain of Scamander—differs from what we read in Cook 1984, with whose judgments I will disagree

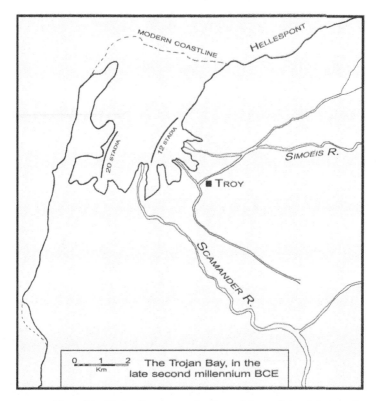

MAP 1. Map of the Trojan Bay area at the time of the traditional dating of the Trojan War, ca. 3250 B.P. Map by Jill Curry Robbins, based on Kayan 2003 fig. 7, Kraft 2003a fig. 5; Kraft 2003b fig. 5, with modifications based on personal communication from Peter Jablonka.

In the Bronze Age, as we see in map 1, the 'harbor of the Achaeans' was once a huge bay interrupting the coastline of the Hellespont. This bay had once been the harbor of the Trojans. In other words, Troy had once been a city with a great harbor positioned at the entrance to the Hellespont.[29] So the new geological evidence has rewritten the prehistory of the story told in our *Iliad*: we now see that the 'harbor of the Achaeans' had once been the harbor of the Trojans. But now, in the time

---

in the discussion that follows. In assessing the evidence about the Deep Bay in the Troad, I have benefited from a consultation with A. M. Snodgrass (2005.03.23).

29. Kraft, Kayan, and Oğuz 1982:35: "Surely a fortified city on a promontory overlooking a marine embayment controlling the Dardanelles must have had some ships. From the paleogeographic reconstructions here presented it would seem logical that any Bronze Age Trojan harbor or landing would have been located immediately west of the citadel or to the north."

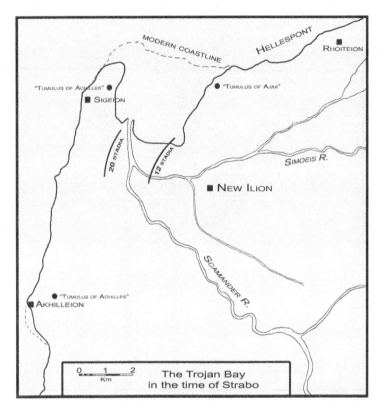

MAP 2. Map of the Trojan Bay area in Strabo's time, ca. 2000 B.P. Map by Jill Curry Robbins, based on Kayan 2003 fig. 7, Kraft 2003a fig. 5; Kraft 2003b fig. 4, with modifications based on personal communication from Peter Jablonka.

of the Trojan War, it was the Achaeans who stationed their ships there—at least according to the narrative of the *Iliad* as we know it. In a related context, Strabo speaks of the *naustathmon* as the northernmost point of the geographical area once controlled by Hector on the Trojan Plain (13.1.33 C596).

This Trojan Bay interrupting the coastline of the Hellespont was still in existence in the time of Strabo, though its dimensions were considerably reduced over the years by silting in the area where the river Scamander flowed into it.[30] Map 2 shows the relevant topography, as reconstructed by geologists on the basis of available geomorphological evidence, supplemented by relevant information from Strabo.

30. Herodotus (2.10.1) compares the silting at the delta of the Nile with the silting at the outlets of the Scamander (τὰ . . . περὶ Ἴλιον), the Caicus, the Cayster, and the Maeander (Cook 1984:166–67).

The reconstruction shown in map 2 highlights a difference between the two traditions reported in the last passage I quoted from Strabo. According to one tradition, as we saw, the *naustathmon* was the same thing as the 'harbor of the Achaeans', which Strabo says was located at a distance of twelve stadia from Ilion. Measuring that distance on the map, we see that the 'harbor of the Achaeans' would have to be located at some point near the center of the coastline as it curves around the bay.

Map 2, however, follows only the second of the two traditions reported by Strabo, according to which the *naustathmon* was not the same thing as the 'harbor of the Achaeans', which was located at a distance of twelve stadia from Ilion. Rather, the alternative *naustathmon* was located at a point farther to the west on the map. That point, according to the measurement of Strabo, was at a distance of twenty stadia from Ilion. Next to that point, as Strabo notes, was where the river Scamander flowed into the Trojan Bay in his day. Geologists have tracked through time the variations in the flow of the Scamander across the Trojan Plain, and their findings verify that the trajectory of the flow shifted farther and farther to the west with the passage of time.[31] The difference between the distances—twenty as opposed to twelve stadia separating ancient Troy from the outlet of the Scamander—reflects this westward shift in the path of the Scamander from earlier times to the later time of Strabo. Map 2 indicates this shift. To be contrasted is the opinion of Strabo about the location of the Scamander's outlet at the time of the Trojan War. To repeat, the geographer thinks that the outlet into the bay should be located at the predesignated point where the 'harbor of the Achaeans' was traditionally located, even though this outlet was not to be found at that predesignated point in his own time and had evidently shifted farther to the west along the coastline of the bay.

Like Strabo, Pliny the Elder recognized that the path of the river Scamander in the time of the *Iliad* had been different from the river's path in his own time (first century C.E.). He refers to the Iliadic course of the Scamander—also called Xanthos in the *Iliad*—as the *Palaeoscamander* as opposed to the *Scamander* of his day:[32]

> Scamander amnis navigabilis et in promuntorio quondam Sigeum oppidum. Dein portus Achaeorum, in quem influit Xanthus Simoenti iunctus stagnumque prius faciens, Palaeoscamander.
>
> The Scamander is a navigable river; and, at the promontory, there was once a city called Sigeion. The next thing to talk about is the harbor of the Achaeans, into which flows

---

31. Kraft, Kayan, and Oğuz 1982:37: "Certainly the shoreline of this time would have been complex, with marshes, muddy sands, many *asmaks*, and a possible birdsfoot delta of the Scamander River extending northwest toward the tip of the [Sigeion] Promontory." Herodotus (5.65.3) speaks of 'Sigeion-on-the-Scamander', using the preposition *epi* as 'on' (Cook 1984:166).

32. When Pliny speaks of the *Palaeoscamander*, he is thinking of the river's path in epic time, as distinct from the river's path in his own time.

the Xanthos—that is, the Palaeoscamander, which joins with the Simoeis before it forms a lagoon at the outlet.

Pliny the Elder Natural History 5.33

Why does Strabo say that the *naustathmon* in epic time must be located next to the outlet of the Scamander? It is because he thinks that the internal evidence of the *Iliad* requires such a location. As I will now argue, Strabo's opinion is actually borne out by that internal evidence. In making such an argument, I will examine the relevant references to the topography of the Troad in the *Iliad*. These references, as the work of Joseph Cuillandre has demonstrated, reveal a remarkable consistency and precision in visualizing that topography.[33] But there is more to it. It is not just a matter of consistency and precision. These references, I argue, are external indications of an internal reality, and that reality is the formulaic system of Homeric poetry—a system that organizes the external reality of what is pictured by that poetry.

The *Iliad* situates the *naustathmon,* imagined as the 'harbor of the Achaeans', in the Trojan Bay of the Hellespont. In the *Iliad,* we see an explicit reference to this bay: ἠϊόνος στόμα μακρόν 'the deep bay of the coast' (XIV 36).[34] According to the *Iliad,* the ships of the Achaeans are beached along the coastline of this bay, with their sterns pointing inward in the direction of the land and with their prows pointing outward in the direction of the water (I 409, XVIII 76; cf. XIV 32, XV 385).[35] So the *naustathmon* is not to be imagined as a harbor in the modern sense of the word: according to the *Iliad,* the ships of the Achaeans were neither anchored offshore in a harbor nor docked in a harbor.

As we see from the internal evidence of the Iliadic narrative, the beached ships of two heroes, Achilles and Ajax, are situated the farthest apart from each other: the ship of Achilles is at a point farthest to the west along the coastline of the bay, while the ship of Ajax is at a point farthest to the east. This relative positioning of the beached ships of Achilles and Ajax is determined by the Iliadic references to the beached ship of Odysseus, which is situated at a centerpoint of the bay's coastline extending from the ship of Achilles at one extreme in the west to the ship of Ajax at the other extreme in the east (VIII 220–26 and XI 5–9). Agamemnon is

---

33. Cuillandre 1944. For an alternative interpretation of the topography of the Troad as visualized in Homeric poetry, see Clay 2007. She makes this remark (p. 241) about the work of Cuillandre: "many of his assumptions can be shown to be wrong." She does not elaborate, however, on what these assumptions may be.

34. According to the scholia for *Iliad* XIV 36, Zenodotus, Aristophanes of Byzantium, and Aristarchus all agree in reporting the variant πολλόν 'vast' instead of μακρόν 'deep'. See Cuillandre 1944:18, who comments on the form στομαλίμνη as reported by Aristarchus in the context of *Iliad* VI 4. The idea of a Deep Bay was promoted in the ancient world by Demetrius of Scepsis and by a woman scholar, Hestiaia of Alexandria (probably Alexandria-in-the-Troad); see Cook 1984:165.

35. Cuillandre 1944:16.

shown standing on the ship of Odysseus, which is *en messatōi* 'in the middlemost space', when he projects his voice of authority and calls out to all the Achaeans stationed at their ships—from the ship of Achilles at one extreme all the way to the ship of Ajax at the other (VIII 220–26). Agamemnon's own ship, together with the ships of Diomedes and Nestor, is near the ship of Odysseus, and it is in this 'middlemost space' that the central station of the Achaeans is visualized by the narrative of the *Iliad* (XIV 27–36).[36]

It is this central station, this notional centerpoint, that Strabo identifies as the *naustathmon*, to be equated with the 'harbor of the Achaeans'. It is here, next to the beached ship of Odysseus, that the Achaeans of the *Iliad* hold their assemblies and perform their sacrifices (XI 807–8).[37] Such a centerpoint is not only topographical: it is also political—even sacral.

It is this central station that becomes the political stage of Agamemnon when he stands on the beached ship of Odysseus and projects his voice of authority to all the Achaeans stationed at their ships (VIII 220–26). And it is this central station that becomes the prime target of the Trojan hero Hector when he seeks to penetrate the defenses of the Achaeans. What stands in Hector's way is the Achaean Wall, with a central gate that leads to and from the central station, and it is through this gate that the forces of the Achaeans enter and exit the theater of war (VII 337–43); the *Iliad* even pictures the comings and goings of war chariots through this gate (VII 340).[38] And it is next to this gate that the sacred common tomb of the Achaean dead is located (VII 336–37). So we see here a sacred as well as strategic gateway to the *naustathmon*, which is both the topographical and the political centerpoint of the Achaeans.

I draw attention to the pointed sharing of this 'middlemost' space by two figures in particular, Agamemnon and Odysseus. As I noted, it is from the beached ship of Odysseus that Agamemnon projects his voice of authority. The sharing of the topographical centerpoint by these two heroes is homologous with their sharing of the political centerpoint, as far as the epic quarrels of Achilles are concerned: the quarrel between Achilles and Agamemnon in the *Iliad*, as I have argued at length elsewhere, is linked with the quarrel between Achilles and Odysseus in the "micro-Iliad" of *Odyssey* viii.[39] Stationed next to the political centerpoint, besides Odysseus, is the leader of the Athenians, Menestheus: he too, like Odysseus, is stationed next to the headquarters of Agamemnon (IV 327,[40] XII 331–77[41]).

---

36. Cuillandre 1944:18–19, 29, 34. Cf. Clay 2007:241.
37. Cuillandre 1944:18.
38. Cuillandre 1944:30n2. The concept of a *theater of war* is invoked by Clay 2007.
39. *BA* ch. 3 (= pp. 42–58).
40. Cuillandre 1944:77.
41. Cuillandre 1944:47.

In the course of the action narrated in the *Iliad,* Hector manages to penetrate the defenses of the Achaeans as he breaks through the gate of the Achaean Wall and heads for the all-important *naustathmon*. There he sets fire to the ship of Protesilaos (XV 704–6, XVI 122–24). Achilles sees from afar this critical moment when that ship catches fire (XVI 127).[42] He has been observing the battle scene, standing next to his own ship and in front of his *klisia* 'shelter' (XVI 255–56).[43] Hector's act of setting fire to the ship of Protesilaos is of deep symbolic value, since Protesilaos had been the first Achaean hero to land on the shores of the Troad—and the first to be killed by a pointedly unnamed Trojan warrior (*Iliad* II 699–792).[44] Accordingly, the ship of Protesilaos had been the first of all Achaean ships to be beached—and thus the nearest target for the threatening fire of Hector (XIII 681; XVI 286, 294–98).[45]

As we take a second look at map 2, the map of the Troad as described by Strabo, it is by now evident that the *naustathmon* must be located somewhere near the center of the coastline of the bay—immediately to the west of the Scamander's outlet as pictured on map 1. In terms of Strabo's reconstruction, to repeat, the Iliadic setting of the *naustathmon* is to be identified with the 'harbor of the Achaeans', which the geographer locates at a distance of twelve stadia from what we know as Troy. By contrast, Strabo's measurement of twenty stadia as the distance between this Troy and the actual outlet of the Scamander in his own time indicates how much farther to the west the pathway of the river had already veered.[46]

In order to define more precisely the location of the *naustathmon* in relation to the Scamander, I propose to combine the external evidence about the Trojan Bay with the internal evidence of the formulaic system that visualizes the Achaean ships stationed along the coastline of this bay. As we follow on map 2 the contour of this coastline, we see a U-shaped curve that starts at the station of Achilles in the northwest, near the promontory of Sigeion, and ends at the station of Ajax in the northeast, near the promontory of Rhoiteion. The section of the curve that extends from the northwest station of Achilles to the central station is much longer than the section that extends from the central station to the northeast station of Ajax. So the

42. The ship is half burned by the time Patroklos succeeds in putting out the fire (*Iliad* XVI 293–94).

43. Cuillandre 1944:59–60. In this context, he emphasizes the precision of the Iliadic visualization of what Achilles sees with his own eyes while observing the various battle scenes from the vantage point of his own ship. There is a remarkable example at *Iliad* XI (599–600), where a foregrounded figure blocks a backgrounded figure in the hero's line of vision: from the distant vantage point of his ship, Achilles sees the figure of Nestor driving a chariot, but his view of the chariot driver blocks his view of the chariot rider, the wounded Machaon, who happens to be standing to the right of Nestor. So Achilles is looking from the west toward the east as Nestor is driving his chariot in retreat from the south toward the north.

44. The symbolic value is further deepened if the original killer of Protesilaos is to be understood as Hector himself.

45. Cuillandre 1944:50.

46. Cuillandre 1944:65 notes the *glissement* of the Scamander toward the west over the course of time.

centerpoint is really off-center toward the east: it is situated much farther away from the station of Achilles and much closer to the station of Ajax, which is practically due north of the outlet of the Scamander.[47] Here is what the Homeric scholia say:

"ἐν δ' αὐτοῖς‹ι› πύλας ποιήσομεν": μία μὲν ἦν ἱππήλατος ἐπὶ τὸ ἀριστερὸν τοῦ ναυστάθμου πρὸς τὸ Ῥοίτειον, "νηῶν ἐπ' ἀριστερά, τῇ περ Ἀχαιοί | ‹ἐκ πεδίου› νίσοντο σὺν ἵπποισιν"· ἄλλας δὲ πυλίδας εἶχον πρὸς ἄλλας χρείας.

"We will make the gate there" [quotation from *Iliad* VII 339]: There was one chariot causeway to the left of the *naustathmon*, facing in the direction of Rhoiteion. "To the left of the ships, where the Achaeans used to return | from the battlefield with their chariot teams" [quotation from *Iliad* XII 118–19]. They had other smaller gates, used for other purposes.

Scholia T for *Iliad* VII 339b1 (exegetical scholia)

In the *Iliad,* the location of the Scamander's outlet corresponds to Strabo's locating of the *naustathmon* at a distance of twelve rather than twenty stadia from Troy. A case in point is a battle scene in *Iliad* XI, where the narrative concentrates on a north-to-south counterattack by the Achaean hero Ajax against the Trojans (489–97); meanwhile, the Trojan hero Hector is said to be ἐπ' ἀριστερά 'to the left' in the battle, positioned at the banks of the Scamander (498–99), where most of the fighting is concentrated (499–500). Standing on the stern of his beached ship, Achilles has been observing the ebb and flow of the battle (XI 400).[48] What he sees is the action to the right (that is, toward the west): at first the right wing of the Achaean forces is routed, but then Ajax comes to their aid and proceeds to counterattack, moving rapidly southward.[49] The narrative now highlights a detail about the action: Hector, who is at the far 'left' of the battlefield, does not notice the onslaught of Ajax, who is counterattacking at the other side of the battlefield (XI 497–99). That is, Ajax is counterattacking at the far right. At this point in our reading, we can catch a precious glimpse of the epic scene from a comment in the Homeric scholia for the relevant verse in *Iliad* XI (499). There we find this comment about the expression ἐπ' ἀριστερά 'to the left' in that verse: [ἐπ' ἀριστερά] σημείωσαι ὅτι ἀριστερὸς τοῦ ναυστάθμου ἐστὶν ὁ Σκάμανδρος 'note that the river Scamander is to the left of the ship station [*naustathmon*]'.[50] As we are about to see, the idea that the Scamander is 'to the left of the *naustathmon*' means that the Scamander is immediately to the east of the *naustathmon*. Or, to reverse the point of reference, the *naustathmon* is immediately to the west of the Scamander.

---

47. This positioning of the station of Ajax, as reconstructed on the basis of references to it in the *Iliad*, corresponds to the positioning in the *Ajax* of Sophocles, especially in verse 418; see Cuillandre 1944:24, 61.

48. Cuillandre 1944:96 notes the perpetual movement that characterizes this particular battle scene.

49. Cuillandre 1944:99–100 surveys the action.

50. Cuillandre 1944:65.

In this phase of the Trojan War, the fighting between the Achaeans and the Trojans on the Trojan Plain is consistently visualized as taking place to the right of the river Scamander—that is, to the west. This visualization reflects a reality built into the overall Iliadic narrative about the Trojan War. The narrative point of reference in the *Iliad* consistently follows the north-to-south perspective of the Achaeans.[51]

This epic visualization is compatible with the topographic reconstruction outlined by Strabo. In terms of this reconstruction, as we have seen, the *naustathmon* must be the same thing as the 'harbor of the Achaeans', and the outlet of the Scamander must be located next to the *naustathmon* in the epic time of the *Iliad,* not farther westward as in the actual time of Strabo. Moreover, the *naustathmon* must be located on the west side of the Scamander, as we see from the overall narrative logic of the *Iliad.*[52] So long as the anger of Achilles remains in force, the Trojans will remain in possession of the east side of the river while they continue to fight the Achaeans on the west side, as is the case in the battle scene in *Iliad* XI that we have just considered.[53] Only after Achilles rejoins his comrades-in-arms and returns to the battlefield will the Trojans be pushed back to the east side of the Scamander, which finally happens in *Iliad* XXI. There the raging Achilles pushes the Trojans back to the edge of the west bank of the Scamander (XXI 1); and there they perish, either at the hands of Achilles or by drowning (7–21)—unless they manage to escape by crossing over to the east bank of the river (2–4).[54]

Here I pause to offer a brief reassessment of the overall Iliadic visualization of the battles taking place on the Trojan Plain between the Achaeans and the Trojans. A primary Iliadic point of reference is the river Scamander, flowing south to north through the Trojan Plain.[55] In the narrative of the *Iliad,* most of the action takes place in the part of the plain that is situated to the west of the Scamander—so long as the anger of Achilles is in force. From the very start of our *Iliad,* the Trojan warriors are crossing at will from the east bank to the west bank of the Scamander, chariots and all; throughout the *Iliad,* they are fighting the Achaeans on the expansive west side of the Trojan Plain.[56] On this battleground, which is pointedly suitable for

51. Cuillandre 1944:41, 69.

52. Cuillandre 1944:63.

53. At this point, within the time frame of the narrative of *Iliad* XI, the position of Hector is at some distance to the east of the north-to-south advance of Ajax, who is at some distance to the west, and so the Trojan warrior has not yet caught sight of his Achaean adversary (XI 497–98). To say it from the Trojan point of view, the position of Ajax is at some distance to the west of Hector, who is standing at the east wing of the Trojan forces. And immediately farther east of where Hector stands is the river Scamander, flowing from south to north.

54. Cuillandre 1944:63, 74.

55. Cuillandre 1944:61 notes that the *Iliad* visualizes the south-to-north course of the Scamander as nearly perpendicular to the main ship station of the bay into which the river flows.

56. Cuillandre 1944:89 reconstructs the logistics. In the logic of the overall narrative of the *Iliad,* the Trojans must be guarding the points where the Scamander can be forded, since they shuttle back

chariot fighting, the Trojans are attacking from the south, while the Achaeans to the north are defending the Achaean Wall and the ships behind it. This battleground is delineated by the Scamander to the east, and the focal point of the battle is the central ship station of the Achaeans to the northeast, immediately to the east of which is the Scamander's outlet into the bay. This central station is defended by the left wing of the Achaean forces, on the east side, facing the attacks of the right wing of the Trojan forces led by Hector, on that east side. Because Hector is so consistently on the attack, he gravitates toward the east side of the battlefield, immediately to the south of the *naustathmon*. Facing north and flanked by the Scamander immediately to the east, he is positioned so far toward the east side of the battlefield that there are times when he fails to notice what is happening toward the west side of the battlefield, as we saw earlier in the battle scene of *Iliad* XI (497–99).[57]

Having rethought the topography of the Troad by way of combining the external evidence about what geologists call the "Deep Bay" with the internal evidence of the formulaic system that visualizes the Achaean ships stationed along the coastline of this bay, I am now ready to focus on a single most telling detail about the positioning of the ship of Achilles in relation to the positioning of his tomb.

The narrative of the *Iliad*, in picturing where the ship of Achilles is beached, situates this place on the west coastline of the Deep Bay, at a point that is closest to the tomb of Achilles. As we look once again at map 2, the map of the Troad as described by Strabo, we see that this tomb, situated on the heights of the promontory of Sigeion, must have had a commanding view of not one but two coastlines, one of which was the coastline of the bay to the east; the other, the coastline of the Aegean Sea to the west—that is, the coastline of the outer Hellespont. Up to now, I have been focusing on the coastline of the bay to the east, where the ship of Achilles is beached. Now I will concentrate on the coastline of the outer Hellespont to the west, where the tomb of Achilles looks out from the heights toward the sea.[58]

In a most memorable passage of the *Iliad* (XXIII 138–51), we can see the grieving figure of Achilles as he stands on the heights of the promontory and looks out

---

and forth between Troy on the east side of the river and the arena of battle on the plains of the west side. Even before we see any blood being spilled in our *Iliad*, the Trojans are already on the west side of the Scamander: see Cuillandre p. 75 for a topographical reconstruction of the initial scenes of Trojan-Achaean confrontation as visualized in the *Iliad*. Despite their freedom of movement in fording the Scamander, however, the Trojans continue to be stationed inside the walls of Troy. Much is made in the narrative about the first time they feel confident enough to camp outside the city walls (*Iliad* VIII 489–501). For more on the logistics of fording the Scamander, see Cuillandre 1944:74 on three verses in *Iliad* XXIV (349–51) concerning the moment when Priam crosses the river as he journeys from Troy to the station of Achilles.

57. For a parallel situation in a later battle scene, see XIII 674–75 and the commentary of Cuillandre 1944:48.

58. On the concept of the Hellespont as including the west coastline of the Troad, see Burgess 2006:n60.

toward the sea (143). Where he is standing, on the promontory (125 *aktē*), is the place he marks out for building the funeral pyre of Patroklos (125–26), which catches fire and burns only after the gods who control the winds that sweep over the seas of the Hellespont from the north (Boreas) and from the west (Zephyros) assent to the ignition (192–230).[59] This funeral pyre is at the same place where the tomb shared by Patroklos and Achilles will be built after Achilles himself is killed (126).[60] As Achilles looks out from these heights over the seas of the outer Hellespont, he is facing homeward, fixing his gaze in the direction of his native land of Thessaly and yearning for the river Sperkheios that flows through that distant land: it was to the waters of that river, which he will never live to see again, that he had hoped to sacrifice his long blond hair after he came of age to cut it.[61] Whenever Achilles looks west toward Thessaly, he could be standing at either of the two places where his tomb is located in the time of Strabo. The vantage point can be either Aeolian or Athenian.

How, then, are we to imagine this tomb of Achilles in the days when the city of Sigeion was still in its full glory? In the traditional way of visualizing places where heroes are buried, such a tomb would be a tumulus. Strabo's wording indicates the existence of a tumulus identified with the tomb of the hero Achilles situated on the slopes extending from the heights of the promontory of Sigeion. This tumulus is visualized as the counterpart of another tumulus: that is, the tomb of the hero Protesilaos. We have already seen Strabo's juxtaposition of the two tombs, one on the Asiatic side of the Hellespont and one on the European side, facing each other across the strait (Strabo 13.1.31 C595).[62] In the *Heroikos* of Philostratus (9.1), the word that refers to the tumulus of Protesilaos is *kolōnos*.[63] Comparable is the Homeric word *kolōnē* (*Iliad* II 811), referring to a prominent tumulus in the Trojan landscape where Hector marshals the military forces of the Trojans (811–15): it is described as a sacred place that is known to mortals as *Batieia* (813) and to immortals as the *sēma* 'tomb' of *Murinē* (814).

In the *Heroikos* of Philostratus, the same word *kolōnos* refers to the structure that the Achaeans built over the bodies of Achilles and Patroklos: it is envisioned as a tumulus situated on a headland overlooking the Hellespont—and matching the tumulus of Protesilaos on the other side of the strait:

---

59. Cuillandre 1944:19–20.

60. Cuillandre 1944:19.

61. Such an interpretation is supported by the scholia for *Iliad* XXIII (143). See Cuillandre 1944:19n3. Elsewhere in the *Iliad* (XXIV 12–13), Achilles is pictured standing on the beach facing west toward the Aegean seas of the Hellespont as its waters start reflecting the light of the rising sun. Regarding the marshy coastline to the west of the Sigeion Ridge, extending from the promontory of Sigeion to the promontory overlooking the Bay of Beşike, see Cuillandre 1944:22.

62. For a description of the tumulus of Protesilaos, see Leaf 1923:163.

63. See Nagy 2001e:xxxiii–xxxiv n34, where I translate *kolōnos* as 'landmark'.

τὸν μὲν δὴ **κολωνὸν**, ξένε, τοῦτον, ὃν ἐπὶ τοῦ μετώπου τῆς **ἀκτῆς** ὁρᾷς ἀνεστηκότα,
ἤγειραν οἱ Ἀχαιοὶ ξυνελθόντες, ὅτε τῷ Πατρόκλῳ ξυνεμίχθη ἐς τὸν τάφον, κάλλιστον
ἐντάφιον ἑαυτῷ τε κἀκείνῳ διδούς, ὅθεν ᾄδουσιν αὐτὸν οἱ τὰ φιλικὰ ἐπαινοῦντες.
ἐτάφη δὲ ἐκδηλότατα ἀνθρώπων πᾶσιν οἷς ἐπήνεγκεν αὐτῷ ἡ Ἑλλὰς οὐδὲ κομᾶν ἔτι
μετὰ τὸν Ἀχιλλέα καλὸν ἡγούμενοι χρυσόν τε καὶ ὅ τι ἕκαστος εἶχεν ἢ ἀπάγων ἐς
Τροίαν ἢ ἐκ δασμοῦ λαβών, νήσαντες ἐς τὴν πυρὰν ἀθρόα παραχρῆμά τε καὶ ὅτε ὁ
Νεοπτόλεμος ἐς Τροίαν ἦλθε, λαμπρῶν γὰρ δὴ ἔτυχε πάλιν παρά τε τοῦ παιδὸς παρά
τε τῶν Ἀχαιῶν ἀντιχαρίζεσθαι αὐτῷ πειρωμένων, οἵ γε καὶ τὸν ἀπὸ τῆς Τροίας
ποιούμενοι πλοῦν περιέπιπτον τῷ τάφῳ καὶ τὸν Ἀχιλλέα ᾤοντο περιβάλλειν.

This *kolōnos*, guest-stranger, which you see standing at the brow of the **promontory**
[*aktē*], was **built** [*ageirein* 'pile stones together'] by the Achaeans who came together
at the time when he [Achilles] was mixed together with Patroklos for their joint burial, having provided for himself [Achilles] and for that one [Patroklos] the most beautiful of funeral rites. And this is the origin of the custom of singing his name in praise
when people celebrate the bonds of love between friends. Of all mortals who ever existed, he [Achilles] was buried in the most spectacular way, what with all the gifts that
Greece bestowed upon him. No longer could the Greeks consider it a beautiful thing
to grow their hair long, once Achilles was gone.[64] Whatever gold or other possession
each of them had brought to Troy or had taken away from the division of spoils [spoils
taken at Troy] was now collected and piled up on top of the funeral pyre, right then
and there. The same thing happened also later when Neoptolemos came to Troy. He
[Achilles] received another round of glorious gifts from his son and from the Achaeans
who were trying to show their gratitude [*kharis*] to him. Even as they were getting
ready to sail away from Troy, they would keep throwing themselves on top of the place
of burial and believe that they were embracing Achilles.[65]

Philostratus *Heroikos* 51.12–13

Elsewhere in the *Heroikos*, in a passage describing an ancient yearly custom observed by Thessalians who sailed to Troy and performed sacrifice at the tomb of
Achilles, the word *kolōnos* refers, once again, to the tomb of Achilles, and in this
context it is used in collocation with another revealing word, *sēma* 'tomb' (53.11):

τὰ δὲ Θετταλικὰ **ἐναγίσματα** φοιτῶντα τῷ Ἀχιλλεῖ ἐκ Θετταλίας ἐχρήσθη Θετταλοῖς
ἐκ Δωδώνης· ἐκέλευσε γὰρ δὴ τὸ μαντεῖον Θετταλοὺς ἐς Τροίαν πλέοντας **θύειν** ὅσα
ἔτη τῷ Ἀχιλλεῖ καὶ σφάττειν τὰ μὲν ὡς θεῷ, τὰ δὲ ὡς ἐν μοίρᾳ τῶν κειμένων. καταρχὰς
μὲν δὴ τοιάδε ἐγίγνετο· ναῦς ἐκ Θετταλίας μέλανα ἱστία ἠρμένη ἐς Τροίαν ἔπλει
θεωροὺς μὲν δὶς ἑπτὰ ἀπάγουσα, ταύρους δὲ λευκόν τε καὶ μέλανα χειρόηθεις ἄμφω
καὶ ὕλην ἐκ Πηλίου, ὡς μηδὲν τῆς πόλεως δέοιντο καὶ πῦρ ἐκ Θετταλίας ἦγον καὶ
σπονδὰς καὶ ὕδωρ τοῦ Σπερχειοῦ ἀρυσάμενοι, ὅθεν καὶ **στεφάνους** ἀμαραντίνους ἐς
τὰ **κήδη** πρῶτοι Θετταλοὶ ἐνόμισαν, ἵνα, κἂν ἄνεμοι τὴν ναῦν ἀπολάβωσι, μὴ σαπροὺς

---

64. The wording connotes an aetiology, as if the death of Achilles were the single reason that explains why Achaeans no longer wear their hair long.

65. Translation adapted from Berenson and Aitken 2001:153.

ἐπιφέρωσι μηδ' ἐξώρους. νυκτὸς μὲν δὴ καθορμίζεσθαι ἔδει καὶ πρὶν ἅψασθαι τῆς γῆς ὕμνον ἀπὸ τῆς νεὼς ᾄδειν ἐς τὴν Θέτιν ὧδε ξυγκείμενον·

Θέτι κυανέα, Θέτι Πηλεία,
ἃ τὸν μέγαν τέκες υἱόν,
Ἀχιλλέα, τοῦ θνατὰ μὲν ὅσον
φύσις ἤνεγκεν,
Τροία λάχε, σᾶς δ' ὅσον ἀθανάτου
γενεᾶς παῖς ἔσπασε, πόντος ἔχει.
βαῖνε πρὸς αἰπὺν τόνδε **κολωνὸν**
μετ' Ἀχιλλέως ἔμπυρα . . .
βαῖν' ἀδάκρυτος μετὰ Θεσσαλίας,
Θέτι κυανέα, Θέτι Πηλεία.

προσελθόντων δὲ τῷ **σήματι** μετὰ τὸν **ὕμνον** ἀσπὶς μὲν ὥσπερ ἐν πολέμῳ ἐδουπεῖτο, δρόμοις δὲ ἐρρυθμισμένοις συνηλάλαζον ἀνακαλοῦντες τὸν Ἀχιλλέα, **στεφανώσαντες** δὲ τὴν κορυφὴν τοῦ **κολωνοῦ** καὶ βόθρους ἐπ' αὐτῇ ὀρύξαντες τὸν ταῦρον τὸν μέλανα ὡς τεθνεῶτι ἔσφαττον. ἐκάλουν δὲ καὶ τὸν Πάτροκλον ἐπὶ τὴν δαῖτα, ὡς καὶ τοῦτο ἐς **χάριν** τῷ Ἀχιλλεῖ πράττοντες, ἐντεμόντες δὲ καὶ **ἐναγίσαντες** κατέβαινον ἐπὶ τὴν ναῦν ἤδη καὶ **θύσαντες** ἐπὶ τοῦ αἰγιαλοῦ τὸν ἕτερον τῶν ταύρων Ἀχιλλεῖ πάλιν κανοῦ τε ἐναρξάμενοι καὶ σπλάγχνων ἐπ' ἐκείνῃ τῇ **θυσίᾳ** (**ἔθυον** γὰρ τὴν **θυσίαν** ταύτην ὡς θεῷ) περὶ ὄρθρον ἀπέπλεον ἀπάγοντες τὸ ἱερεῖον, ὡς μὴ ἐν τῇ πολεμίᾳ εὐωχοῖντο. ταῦτα, ξένε, τὰ οὕτω σεμνὰ καὶ ἀρχαῖα καταλυθῆναι μὲν ὑπὸ τῶν τυράννων φασίν, οἳ λέγονται μετὰ τοὺς Αἰακίδας ἄρξαι Θετταλῶν, ἀμεληθῆναι δὲ καὶ ὑπὸ τῆς Θετταλίας·

The Thessalian **sacrificial offerings** [*enagismata*] that came regularly to Achilles from Thessaly were decreed for the Thessalians by the oracle at Dodona. Evidently the oracle ordered the Thessalians to sail to Troy each year to **sacrifice** [*thuein*] to Achilles and to slaughter some sacrificial victims as to a god, while slaughtering other victims as for the dead. From the very beginnings, the following was the procedure: a ship sailed from Thessaly to Troy with black sails raised, bringing twice seven sacred ambassadors [*theōroi*], one white bull and one black bull, both tame to the touch, and wood from Mount Pelion, so that they would need nothing from the city [New Ilion].[66] They also brought fire from Thessaly as well as water drawn from the river Sperkheios for libations. As a consequence [of these practices], the Thessalians were the first to institute the custom of using unwilting **garlands** [*stephanoi*] for the **funerary rituals** [*kēdos,* plural: in honor of Achilles], in order that, even if the wind delayed the ship, they would not wear **garlands** [*stephanoi*] that were wilted or past their season [*hōra*].[67]

---

66. The ritually dramatized hostility between the Thessalians and the city of New Ilion may be a reflex of an old Thessalian connection with Sigeion as the rival city that represented the interests of Athens in the era of the Peisistratidai. As allies of Athens, the Thessalians would have been welcome as visitors to the sacred sites in the part of the Troad controlled by Sigeion in that era. In later times, however, the Thessalians would have become *personae non gratae* at the sacred sites taken over by New Ilion.

67. This detail in the ritual, where unwilting garlands are worn in honor of Achilles as cult hero, is I think related to the semantics of the epithet *aphthito-*, meaning literally 'unwilting', as applied to the

And evidently they found it necessary to put into the harbor at night and, before touching land, to sing from the ship a **hymn** [*humnos*] to Thetis, which is composed of these words:

> Thetis, sea-blue Thetis, consort of Peleus,
> you who bore the great son
> Achilles. The part of him that his mortal
> nature brought him
> was the share of Troy, but the part of him that from your immortal
> lineage was drawn by the child, the sea [*pontos*] has that part.
> Come, proceed to this steep **tumulus** [*kolōnos*]
> in the company of Achilles [to receive] the offerings placed over the fire.
> Come, proceed without tears in the company of Thessaly,
> you, sea-blue Thetis, you, consort of Peleus.

When they approached the **tomb** [*sēma*] after the **hymn** [*humnos*], a shield was banged upon as in battle, and together with rhythmic coordination they cried *alala!* while calling upon Achilles. When they had **garlanded** [*stephanoûn*] the summit of the **tumulus** [*kolōnos*] and dug sacrificial pits on it, they slaughtered the black bull as to one who is dead. They also called upon Patroklos to come to the feast, so as to **gratify** [make kharis for] Achilles. After they slit the victim's throat and **made** this sacrifice [*enagizein*], they evidently proceeded to go down to the ship, and, after **sacrificing** [*thuein*] the other bull on the beach again to Achilles and having begun the offering by taking from the basket and by partaking of the entrails for that **sacrifice** [*thusia*] (for they **sacrificed** [*thuein*] this **sacrifice** [*thusia*] as to a god), they sailed away toward dawn, taking the sacrificed animal so as not to feast in the enemy's country. These practices, guest-stranger, which are so holy and ancient, had been reportedly discontinued by the tyrants who are said to have ruled the Thessalians after the Aiakidai. And even the Thessalians neglected these practices.[68]

Philostratus Heroikos 53.8–14

In the passage I cited earlier from the *Heroikos* of Philostratus about the original epic act of building the *kolōnos* of Achilles, it is made clear that this act was imagined as a piling of stones, as we see from the use of the word *ageirein* (51.12).[69] The tumulus that is the *kolōnos* is mentally associated not only with the stones on its surface but also with the sacred corpse of the cult hero inside. For example, the *kolōnos* of Protesilaos, surrounded by elm trees, 'extends over' (*ep-ekhein*) the body of the cult hero (9.1). We see similar patterns of mental association in the *Oedipus at Colonus*

---

kleos or epic 'glory' of Achilles in *Iliad* IX 413. In *BA* 10§§1–5 (= pp. 174–77) and *PH* 7§6n23 (= p. 204), 8§11n42 (= p. 223), and 10§9n21 (= p. 278), I analyze further the semantics of *phthi*- 'wilt' in this and in other related poetic contexts.

68. Translation adapted from Berenson and Aitken 2001:157, 159. As we see from the overall context here, these practices were later reinstated.

69. Note the collocation *kolōnos lithōn* 'tumulus built of stones' in Herodotus 4.92.

of Sophocles: in that work the place name *Kolōnos* refers to a sacred grove (690, 889) where Oedipus' body is destined to receive an *oikos:* that is, an 'abode' befitting a cult hero (627).[70] There is a metonymy implicit in the name: the tumulus that is the *kolōnos* becomes, by extension, the name of the whole sacred grove—and, by further extension, the name of the whole deme of Attica in which the grove is situated.[71]

THE TOMB OF ACHILLES AS A LANDMARK
FOR THE FESTIVAL OF THE PANATHENAIA

The tumulus of the generic cult hero, as marked by the word *kolōnos*, is conventionally envisaged as shining white. For example, the place name Colonus, which is the metonym *Kolōnos*, is described with the epithet *argēs* 'shining white' in Sophocles *Oedipus at Colonus* (670). In Black Figure vase paintings, the tumulus of the generic cult hero is conventionally painted shining white, foregrounded against the red background of the fired clay. What this foregrounding represents is the white stucco that covers the tumulus of the cult hero.[72] There are a number of Black Figure paintings that show the tomb of Achilles this way, and I will concentrate here on two examples of such paintings. These paintings are found on vases to which I will refer simply as the Boston Hydria (fig. 1)[73] and the Münster Hydria (fig. 2).[74] Both are dated to the last two decades of the sixth century B.C.E. That date, as we will see, is most relevant to the content of the paintings. That date, moreover, matches roughly the date of the Polyxena Sarcophagus, which was excavated from such a tumulus, and which features a relief showing the sacrifice of Polyxena at the tumulus of Achilles.[75] This tumulus matches in appearance the tumulus of Achilles as represented on the Black Figure paintings.

---

70. On this context of *oikos*, see *PH* 9§27 (= pp. 268–69).

71. Nagy 2001e:xxxiv n34.

72. Stähler 1967:19, with citations.

73. The *editio princeps* is Vermeule 1965.

74. The *editio princeps* is Stähler 1967.

75. The *editio princeps* of the relief sculpture of the Polyxena Sarcophagus is Sevinç 1996; see also Rose 2006:143–46. In this sculpted ensemble, Polyxena is represented as near naked at the moment of her sacrificial slaughter, with her breasts exposed. I find it relevant to compare a detail in Euripides *Hecuba* (558): Polyxena tears the peplos that she is wearing at the moment of being slaughtered, thus exposing her breasts, and she is pictured at this moment as an *agalma* 'artifact' (561), as if she were a statue. Later on in the *Hecuba* (571–82), after Polyxena is slaughtered, a peplos is presented to her as a ritual offering. Similar to Polyxena, Iphigeneia in Aeschylus *Agamemnon* (208) is pictured as an *agalma* 'artifact' in the household of Agamemnon. When Iphigeneia is about to be sacrificed by her father in the *Agamemnon* (289), she is pictured as if she were in a painting. Perhaps this painting can be imagined as a painted relief sculpture. There is a similar painterly reference in the *Hecuba* (807), on which see Dué 2006:130. For more on the Polyxena Sarcophagus, see Dué pp. 125–26. On the picturing of Hecuba as a lamenting statue, see Dué p. 128n27.

FIGURE 1. *(top)* Attic black-figure hydria: Achilles dragging the body of Hector. Attributed to the Antiope Group. Museum of Fine Arts, Boston, 63.473. Drawing by Valerie Woelfel.
FIGURE 2. *(bottom)* Attic black-figure hydria: Achilles racing on foot around the tomb of Patroklos, whose *psukhē* (labeled as "ΦΣΥΧΕ") hovers over the tomb. Attributed to the Leagros Group. Münster, Wilhelms-Universität, 565. Drawing by Valerie Woelfel.

Both Black Figure paintings, as we see them on the Boston Hydria and the Münster Hydria, depict an athletic event known as the *apobatōn agōn*, which means 'contest of the *apobatai*' or 'apobatic contest'.[76] This event was part of the athletic program of the festival of the Panathenaia in Athens, and it featured a spectacular sudden-death moment of athletic bravura. We can imagine all eyes focused on the action that leads up to that moment when the competing athlete, riding on the platform of a four-horse chariot driven at full gallop by his charioteer, suddenly leaps to the ground from the speeding chariot. The term for such an athlete is *apobatēs*, meaning literally 'one who steps off'.[77] At the death-defying moment when he literally steps off the platform of the speeding chariot, the *apobatēs* is fully armed as a warrior. The various attested representations in vase paintings show the *apobatēs* armed with helmet, breastplate, shin guards, spear, sword, and shield.[78] Weighted down by all this armor, the *apobatēs* must hit the ground running as he lands on his feet in his high-speed leap from the platform of his chariot. If his run is not broken in a fall, he continues to run down the length of the racecourse in competition with the other running *apobatai,* who have made their own leaps from their own chariots.[79] In one of the two paintings that I will be considering, as well as in other paintings, the athletic event of this apobatic contest is correlated with an epic event that takes place in the Homeric *Iliad*. The hero Achilles, infuriated over Hector's killing of his dearest friend, Patroklos, tries to avenge this death by dragging behind his speeding chariot the corpse of Hector (XXII 395–405, XXIV 14–22).[80] In the painting on the Boston Hydria, we see Achilles at the precise moment when he cuts himself off from the act of dragging the corpse of Hector. This moment is synchronized with the precise moment when he leaps off, in the mode of an *apobatēs*,

---

76. Photius *Lexicon* α 2450; see also α 2449 and *Suda* α 3250. The paragraphs that follow are based on Nagy 2009d.

77. Dionysius of Halicarnassus *Roman Antiquities* 7.73.2–3; Harpocration s.v. In Eratosthenes *Katasterismoi* chapter 1, section 13, lines 19–22, we read that the figure of an *apobatēs* is a re-enactment of the prototypical chariot fighter (carrying a shield and wearing a three-plumed helmet) who rode next to Erikhthonios as chariot driver when Erikhthonios founded the festival of the Panathenaia in Athens. This prototypical *apobatēs* was traditionally imagined as the goddess Athena herself: for iconographic evidence, see Schultz 2007, especially p. 60; also Shear 2001:47–53. On the north side of the Parthenon Frieze (North XII), there is a depiction of an *apobatēs* who is being crowned with a garland: see Schultz p. 65.

78. Stähler 1967 gives a survey; also Schultz 2007. There is a vivid reference to the athletic event of the *apobatai* in a speech attributed to Demosthenes (61).

79. Dionysius of Halicarnassus *Roman Antiquities* 7.73.3. According to other sources, the *apobatēs* can leap on as well as off the platform of a racing chariot: see *Etymologicum magnum* p. 124 lines 31–34 ed. Kallierges and Photius *Lexicon* α 2450. Paintings of mythological scenes showing a warrior mounting his chariot may correspond to athletic scenes where the *apobatēs* mounts his chariot: see Vermeule 1965:44 on the Amphiaraos Krater.

80. Vermeule 1965 and Stähler 1967 survey a wide variety of relevant pictures besides the two that concern me primarily here, the pictures painted on the Boston Hydria and the Münster Hydria.

from the platform of the chariot that is dragging the corpse. The leap of Achilles here is the leap of the *apobatēs*. This moment, captured in the painting we see on the Boston Hydria, is what I will call the *apobatic moment*. I argue that this moment can be understood only in the context of the poetic as well as athletic program of the Panathenaia.

The first time that the *Iliad* pictures Achilles dragging the corpse of Hector, the event is witnessed by the dead hero's mother, father, and wife: Hecuba, Priam, and Andromache together lament the terror and the pity of it all (XXII 405–7, 408–29, 430–36, 437–515). As in the *Iliad*, the lamenting figures of Hecuba and Priam are pictured on one of the two Black Figure vases that presently concern me, the Boston Hydria (fig. 1). This vase, like the *Iliad*, pictures Achilles dragging the corpse of Hector—while the lamenting figures of Hecuba and Priam view this scene of terror and pity from a portico.

The next time the *Iliad* pictures Achilles dragging the corpse of Hector behind his chariot, we see this chariot being driven three times around the *sēma* 'tomb' of Patroklos (XXIV 14–18). At an earlier point in the narrative of the *Iliad*, this tomb is described as incomplete: it will not be complete until Achilles himself is buried there together with his friend Patroklos (XXIII 83–84, 91–92, 245–48).

As in the *Iliad*, this tomb of Patroklos is pictured on the Boston Hydria. The chariot of Achilles is shown furiously circling around the tomb, with the corpse of Hector in tow, and we see the hero at the very moment when he leaps off the speeding chariot, with his fierce gaze fixed on the portico where Priam and Hecuba lament the cruel fate of their son.

Every time we look through the painted window that frames this painted scene, we return to this same precise moment. As Emily Vermeule says: "The technique gives the impression that the myth is circling around in another world, outside the window frame through which the spectator views it, in endless motion which is somehow always arrested at the same place whenever we return to the window."[81] This moment is the critical moment of the *apobatēs*, the apobatic moment.

In the *Iliad*, a council of the gods is convened, and they express their collective moral disapproval of Achilles for his attempt to mutilate the corpse of Hector by dragging it behind his chariot (XXIV 22–76). Just before, we see that the god Apollo miraculously prevents the actual mutilation of the corpse (18–21). But now the council of the gods, headed by Zeus, decides to go one step further: the dragging of the corpse by Achilles must stop altogether. The divine course of action in stopping Achilles is explicitly said to be indirect: Iris as messenger of the gods is sent off to summon Thetis (74–75), who will be asked by Zeus to persuade her son to return the corpse of Hector to Priam (75–76); then Iris is sent off to Priam, who

81. Vermeule 1965:45.

will receive from the goddess a divine plan designed to make it possible for him to persuade Achilles to return the corpse of his son (143–58).

By contrast with the narration of the *Iliad*, the divine course of action narrated by the painting on the Boston Hydria is explicitly direct: the goddess sent from on high will personally stop the dragging of the corpse of Hector by Achilles. The painting shows the goddess in flight, just as she reaches the moment of her landing on earth: her feet, gracefully poised as if in a dance, are about to touch ground at the center of the picture, and her delicate hands make a gesture of lament evoking pity as she looks toward the lamenting Priam and Hecuba, whose own hands make a parallel gesture of lament evoking pity as they look toward Achilles. The fierce gaze of the furious hero is at this precise point redirected at Priam and Hecuba, who take their cue, as it were, from the gesture of lament shown by the goddess. The gaze of Achilles is thus directed away from the figure of Patroklos, who is shown hovering over a tomb that for now belongs only to him but will soon belong to Achilles as well. The charioteer of Achilles, oblivious to the intervention of the goddess, continues to drive the speeding chariot around the tomb, but, meanwhile, we find Achilles in the act of stepping off the platform. And he steps off at the precise moment when he redirects his fierce gaze from his own past and future agony to the present agony of Hector's lamenting father and mother. Here is the hero's apobatic moment.

The pity of Achilles for the parents of Hector in the painting of the Boston Hydria is achieved by way of a direct divine intervention that takes place while the dragging of the corpse is in progress. Once Achilles steps off his furiously speeding chariot, the fury that fueled that speed must be left behind as he hits the ground running and keeps on running until that fury is spent.

To be contrasted is the pity of Achilles for the father of Hector in the *Iliad* as we have it. This pity cannot be achieved by way of any direct divine intervention while the dragging of the corpse is in progress. In this case, the divine intervention is indirect: it is only after the gods guide Priam behind enemy lines to the tent of Achilles that the lamenting father succeeds in evoking the pity that the Iliadic hero will ultimately get to feel in *Iliad* XXIV.

The convergences between the painted and the poetic versions of the narrative far outweigh their divergences, and I infer that the internal logic of the Iliadic narrative that we see at work in the visual medium of the Boston Hydria is morphologically parallel to the internal logic of the Iliadic narrative that we see at work in the verbal medium of the Homeric *Iliad*.

It cannot be said, however, that the narrative of the painting must be derived from the *Iliad* as we know it. Such a further inference is unjustified. It cannot even be said that the narrative of the painting was derived from an *Iliad* that was different from the one we know. It would be simplistic to think that a narrative inherent in a painting that dates from the last two decades of the sixth century B.C.E. was derived from any text. The visual medium of heroic narrative by way of painting did not have to depend on the verbal medium of heroic narrative by way of poetry.[82]

On the other hand, it can be said that both the visual and the verbal media of heroic narrative were dependent on the basic principle of making contact with the traditional world of heroes—who were honored by way of ritual as well as myth. As I have argued extensively elsewhere, the rules of heroic narrative in the archaic period of Greek civilization were governed by the myths and rituals linked with the cult of heroes.[83] What applies to the medium of poetry applies equally to the medium of painting.

In the case of the Black Figure images we see on the Boston Hydria (fig. 1), the medium of the painting is evidently referring to a specific context—that is, to the festival of the Panathenaia in Athens sometime within the last two decades of the sixth century B.C.E., featuring the athletic event of the apobatic contest. The same can be said about the Black Figure painting we see on the Münster Hydria (fig. 2). In this second painting, Achilles is represented as engaging in a personalized apobatic race with himself. In the narrative of the Münster Hydria, Achilles is seen running alongside the speeding chariot. He has already leapt off its platform. Meanwhile, the *psukhē* of Patroklos—which can double for the *psukhē* of Achilles—is shown hovering over the hero's tomb or *sēma*, which occupies the dead center of the picture. This *psukhē* of Patroklos, labeled as ΦΣΥΧΕ in the painting, is running in the air—a miniature version of the running Achilles who is racing at ground zero in a re-enactment of the race being run by the other self who is running in the air.

In the Münster Hydria, as in the Boston Hydria, a goddess directly intervenes. The figure of this goddess, just barely visible on the fragmentary right side of the picture, is standing in the way of the onrushing chariot. Meanwhile, a council of the gods is in session on high—in a picture framed on the shoulder of the vase, situated above the main picture framed along the body of the vase.

It has been argued that the main picture on the Münster Hydria represents the notional beginnings of a hero cult shared by Achilles with his other self, Patroklos.[84] The two of them preside as cult heroes of the athletic event of the *apobatai* at the festival of the Panathenaia. The death of Patroklos, which is the prototype for the death of Achilles himself, is figured as the aetiology of this athletic event, which shows the ritual dimension of the cult hero as a complement to the mythical dimension that we see played out in narratives conveyed by painting as well as by poetry. The painting on the Münster Hydria shows Achilles as a prototypical participant in this hero cult by way of participating in this athletic event. Through his prototypical participation, Achilles shows the way for future athletes to participate

---

82. Lowenstam 1997.
83. *BA*² preface §3 (= p. vii) and *BA* introduction §§13–15 (= pp. 6–8).
84. Stähler 1967, especially p. 32.

in this athletic event of the *apobatai* at the seasonally recurring festival of the Panathenaia for all time to come.

A parallel argument can be made about the Funeral Games for Patroklos in *Iliad* XXIII.[85] Here too Achilles is shown as a prototypical participant in the hero cult of his other self, Patroklos. Here too he shows the way for future athletes to participate in his own hero cult by way of participating in the athletic events we see described in *Iliad* XXIII, especially in the chariot race. In this case, however, Achilles does not himself participate in the athletic events of the Funeral Games for Patroklos: rather, it is the other surviving Achaean heroes of the *Iliad* who serve as prototypical participants in the athletic events, while Achilles himself simply presides over these events as if he were already dead, having already achieved the status of the cult hero who will be buried in the tumulus to be shared with his other self, Patroklos.[86]

So we have seen that the Black Figure paintings on the Boston Hydria and on the Münster Hydria are both referring to a specific context: that is, to the festival of the Panathenaia in Athens sometime within the last two decades of the sixth century B.C.E., featuring the athletic event of the apobatic contest. But we must not forget that this festival also featured an all-important poetic event: competitive rhapsodic recitations of the Homeric *Iliad* and *Odyssey*. Just as the Black Figure paintings focus on one single moment in the athletic program of the Panathenaia, so also they are focusing on one single moment in the poetic program of the same festival. That moment is what I have been calling the apobatic moment. At the quadrennial Panathenaic festival held in the year 510 B.C.E. (and the same could be said about the earlier festivals of 514 B.C.E. and before, or about the later festivals of 506 B.C.E. and thereafter), the version of the *Iliad* performed in that era could have featured the same apobatic moment featured in the Black Figure paintings that art historians date back to the same era. It is the moment when the *apobatēs* steps off his chariot and runs the rest of the course on foot. The killer instinct of the fired-up athlete may now run itself out in the full course of the time it takes for him to run to the finish line.

This is also the apobatic moment when Achilles steps off his chariot and keeps on running until his fury finally runs out. Then he may finally engage with the feeling of pity—and re-engage with his own humanity.

Such a version of the *Iliad*, I argue, was current in the era when the Boston Hydria and the Münster Hydria were painted. It was in this era when the poetic program of the Panathenaia was being reformed by the tyrant Hipparkhos son of Peisistratos. As we have seen in chapter 1, this Athenian tyrant played a role in shaping the ultimate form of the Panathenaic Homer: that is, of the Homeric *Iliad* and

85. *GM* 88, 94, 217, 220.
86. *PH* 7§§10–19 (= pp. 207–14).

Odyssey as we know them. As we have also seen, Hipparkhos is credited with having established the Athenian institution that we know today as the Panathenaic Regulation, which concerns the performing of the Homeric *Iliad* and *Odyssey* at the festival of the Panathenaia. In terms of the Panathenaic Regulation, the Homeric *Iliad* and *Odyssey* became the standard epic repertoire of the quadrennial Panathenaic festival. In chapter 1, I quoted the passage in "Plato" *Hipparkhos* (228b–c) where we read what amounts to an aetiology of the Panathenaic Regulation. As I argued in that chapter, the custom of relay-performing the *Iliad* and *Odyssey* in sequence at the festival of the Panathenaia is a ritual in and of itself.[87]

Hipparkhos left his mark in defining the festival of the Panathenaia in Athens not only by way of instituting the Panathenaic Regulation. He actually died at the Panathenaia. As we noted earlier, he was assassinated on the festive quadrennial occasion of the Great Panathenaia held in the year 514 B.C.E., and his death is memorialized by both Thucydides (1.20.2 and 6.54–59) and Herodotus (5.55–61).

In short, the apobatic moment for Achilles as athlete goes back to this era, the late sixth century B.C.E., in the evolution of Homeric poetry as performed at the Panathenaia.

TWO TOMBS FOR ACHILLES

By now we have an answer to my question about the way the tomb of Achilles was imagined—back in the days when Sigeion was still in its full glory. I asked that question in the first place because the political situation had changed so drastically by the time of Strabo. The geographer goes out of his way, as we have seen, to describe the city of Sigeion as completely 'demolished' in his own time, and his wording makes clear that no stone was left in place (Strabo 13.1.31 C595 κατεσπασμένη πόλις). So, since Strabo pairs the city of Sigeion with the tomb of Achilles at Sigeion (13.1.31–32 C595), we may well ask about the status of this tomb in Strabo's time. As we are about to see, the rival tomb of Achilles that was situated farther south, at the southern end of the Sigeion Ridge, was still functional at this time. As for the tomb of Achilles that Strabo associates with the demolished city, which was situated at the northern end of the Sigeion Ridge, it too was still functional in Strabo's time. We are about to see how and why.

Here I must return for a moment to the early history of the struggle between Athens and Mytilene over the possession of Sigeion. By now we can see more clearly what was at stake in that struggle. To possess this city was not only to control access by sea to the Hellespont and beyond. It was also to control access by land to the epic space of the Trojan War, featuring as its premier Iliadic landmark the tomb of its premier Iliadic hero.

87. See also *PR* 10, 66.

The ongoing war between Mytilene and Athens over the sacred space of Achilles in particular and over the Iliadic territory of Sigeion in general was at one point settled by arbitration, and the arbitrator chosen by the two sides was Periander, tyrant of Corinth. Here I return to my analysis, in chapter 6, of what is said by Herodotus (5.94.2) about the claims and counterclaims of Mytilene and Athens: in the course of describing the arbitration between the warring cities, the historian says that the Mytilenaeans were at that time occupying a space called the 'city of Achilles', *polis Akhílleios* (or *Akhilléios* in the Ionic dialect used by Herodotus), whereas the Athenians occupied the city of Sigeion. The terms of arbitration set by Periander specified that the two parties were to keep the territories they occupied at the time of the arbitration, so that the Mytilenaeans got to keep the 'city of Achilles' while the Athenians got to keep Sigeion (Herodotus 5.95.2).

Here I draw attention to a most precious piece of information. It is provided by Timaeus of Tauromenium (fourth and the third centuries B.C.E.). According to this Timaeus (*FGH* 566 F 129), the tyrant Periander of Corinth used the stones of old Ilion in fortifying what was called the 'space of Achilles' (*Akhílleion*) as a counter-measure against the Athenians and as a help for the Mytilenaeans led by Pittakos. This testimony of Timaeus is reported by Strabo (13.1.39 C600) through the me-diation of Demetrius of Scepsis (F 27 ed. Gaede).

Strabo goes on to reject what Timaeus is claiming here; instead, he supports a claim made by Demetrius, who went out of his way to argue that this space known as *Akhílleion* was not fortified with the stones of the old Ilion. That negative claim is linked with another negative claim: Demetrius, followed by Strabo, rejects the idea that Periander, as the chosen arbitrator of the dispute between the Mytilenaeans and the Athenians, fought against the Athenians. But the reasoning here is flawed. Periander was not fighting against the Athenians: as an arbitrator, he simply made a ruling that went partly against the interests of the Athenians. His ruling stipu-lated that the Athenians could not have this space called *Akhílleion*. On the other hand, the ruling of Periander also went partly in favor of the Athenians, since it stipulated that they could keep the city of Sigeion.

Let us consider the reference that Strabo makes (13.1.39 C600) to the *mnēma* 'tomb' of Achilles on the heights of the promontory that forms the southern end of the Sigeion Ridge at what is called today the Bay of Beşike. As Strabo says, this *mnēma* 'tomb' was thought to be located inside the 'space of Achilles': that is, in-side what he calls the *Akhílleion*. In other words, the site of *Akhílleion* is visualized here as a settlement named after the sacral centerpoint of the hero's tomb. The name of the tomb is a metonym for the whole site. *Akhílleion* means, literally, 'space of Achilles', and its morphology is specifically Aeolic, stemming from the two-gender adjective *Akhílleios, Akhílleion*. Strabo adds pointedly that *Akhílleion*, which had once been a fortified Aeolian city, was in his own time merely 'a small settlement', *katoikia mikra* (again, 13.1.39 C600). By contrast, as we saw earlier, Herodotus refers to this same site as the 'city of Achilles', *Akhilléios polis* (5.94.2).[88]

At an earlier point in his survey of the Troad, Strabo refers to a *mnēma* 'tomb' of Achilles in a *hieron* 'sacred space' of Achilles that he locates πρὸς Σιγείῳ 'at Sigeion', adding that there are also *mnēmata* 'tombs' of Patroklos and Antilokhos in this vicinity, and that the people of New Ilion offer sacrifices to these three heroes as also to a fourth hero, Ajax (13.1.32 C596). The word used by Strabo in this context, *enagizein* 'offer sacrifice', indicates that the people of New Ilion worshipped Achilles, Patroklos, Antilokhos, and Ajax as cult heroes. The tomb of Achilles that Strabo locates 'at Sigeion', on the promontory to the northwest of the Trojan Bay of the Hellespont, is matched by the tomb of Ajax that Strabo locates at Rhoiteion, on the promontory to the northeast of this bay. Strabo (13.1.30 C595) describes Rhoiteion as a *polis* 'city' situated on the heights; overlooking (*epi*) its coastline (*ēiōn*) was the *mnēma* 'tomb' and the *hieron* 'sacred space' of Ajax, along with an *andrias* 'statue' of the hero.[89]

The tomb of Achilles that Strabo locates 'at Sigeion' (13.1.31–32 C595) is not to be confused with the tomb of Achilles that he locates at *Akhílleion* (13.1.39 C600). This other tomb is situated on the promontory of the Bay of Beşike, some ten kilometers farther south along the Sigeion Ridge. In what follows, I will at long last explore the reasons for the coexistence of two separate tombs of Achilles at a distance of ten kilometers from each other.

From what we have seen so far, I conclude that Strabo rejected the testimony of Timaeus concerning the fortification of *Akhílleion* because of a misinterpretation. Strabo—or his source, Demetrius—misinterpreted the motive of Periander in initiating the fortification. If I am right in understanding the arbitrator's motive as a sanctioning of the right of the Mytilenaeans to protect what they were allowed to retain after arbitration, then it follows that the fortifying of *Akhílleion* is parallel to the building of the walls of Sigeion—an earlier event also reported by Strabo.

In Strabo's report of this earlier event, we find another misinterpretation: he says that the stones of the old Ilion were used to build the walls of Sigeion because the old Ilion had been totally destroyed in the Trojan War and therefore rendered useless (13.1.38 C599). The underlying assumption is this: only the total destruction of Troy could justify the reusing of its stones for the purpose of building something new somewhere else. Strabo here is following the view of Demetrius of Scepsis (F 23 ed. Gaede), who maintained that the site of the old Ilion was not New Ilion, as claimed by that city's inhabitants, but a place known as ἡ τῶν Ἰλιέων κώμη 'the vil-

---

88. Cook 1984:168 comments on the site of *Akhílleion*, which features "plenty of Aeolic gray ware and other sherds dating from the sixth century or earlier down to middle Hellenistic."

89. For further references to the tumulus of Ajax in primary sources, see Leaf 1923:157–58.

lage [kōmē] of the people of Ilion [Ilieis]', which was located some thirty stadia away from New Ilion, in territory belonging to the city of Scepsis (13.1.35–36 C597–98; also 13.1.25 C593). As Strabo says explicitly, following Demetrius, there was no trace of any ancient city at this kōmē 'village'; on that basis, he claims that the stones used for the building of Sigeion must have been transported from there, so that no trace of the old Ilion was left behind (13.1.38 C599). In line with this reasoning, Strabo rejects the claim made by the inhabitants of New Ilion, who maintained that their city had not been completely destroyed by the Achaeans in the Trojan War and that it had never been left completely abandoned (13.1.40 C599). Strabo mentions this claim in the context of highlighting a counterclaim: if Troy had not been completely destroyed, there would have been no practical reason for the stones of this old city's walls to be transported to Sigeion for the added fortification of that city's walls.

I propose, however, that there are symbolic as well as practical reasons for the use of stones taken from the city walls of the old Ilion in order to fortify Sigeion and, later on, to fortify the Akhílleion: such a use establishes a symbolic connection between the old Ilion and the new Iliadic structures being built. Among these structures was the historical reality of New Ilion itself, an Aeolian city founded in the seventh (or possibly as early as the eighth) century B.C.E., which was built on the ruins of the old Ilion.[90] Archaeologists have successfully identified the old Ilion of the Iliad (whether it be Troy VI or Troy VIIa) as an earlier stratum of this New Ilion (Troy VIII), which was sought out in historical times by world rulers striving to link themselves with the heroes of the epic past. In 480 B.C.E., as we saw earlier, Xerxes made sacrifice to Athena, surnamed hē Ilias, in New Ilion; he also made libations to the 'heroes' (Herodotus 7.43.2); Alexander the Great likewise sacrificed to Athena in New Ilion (Strabo 13.1.26 C593; Arrian Anabasis 1.11.7).

The same kind of symbolism is inherent in the name of another Aeolian city on the Asiatic mainland, Neon Teikhos, which means 'New Wall'. In this case as well, the naming of the new structure is a functional metonym of the old Ilion.

Before the intrusion of the Athenians into the Troad, the Aeolian city of Sigeion had been marked by two Iliadic features: first, its city walls were built from the stones of the old Ilion; and second, it controlled what was considered to be the tomb of Achilles, located some ten kilometers farther south at the other end of the Sigeion Ridge. After the intrusion, the Aeolians lost the city of Sigeion but kept this tomb of Achilles, which they turned into a rival city fortified with walls built from the stones of the old Ilion. In the meantime, the Athenians must have adduced their own version of the tomb of Achilles—at Sigeion.

I propose that the Athenian version of the tomb of Achilles can be identified with

90. Seventh century: Blegen 1958:247–50. Eighth century: Cook 1973:101. See also Smith 1981:29n21. Smith p. 54 thinks that Troy was deserted between 1100 and 700 B.C.E.

one of two tumuli that are still visible to the northeast of the ancient site of Sigeion. Both these tumuli can be dated back to the early fifth century and, more likely, even farther back, to the sixth century.[91] The larger one of the two could have been adduced as the tomb that contained the bones of both Achilles and Patroklos as mentioned in the *Iliad* (XXIII 83–84, 91–92, 125–26, 245–48) and *Odyssey* (xxiv 76–77); and the smaller one, as the tomb that contained the bones of Antilokhos, which were kept separate from the bones of the other two heroes according to the *Odyssey* (xxiv 78–79).

This reconstruction matches, at least in part, the description of Strabo (13.1.32 C596): he refers to a *mnēma* 'tomb' of Achilles at a *hieron* 'sacred space' of Achilles that he locates πρὸς Σιγείῳ 'at Sigeion', but then he adds that there were also *mnēmata* 'tombs' of Patroklos and Antilokhos, and that the people of New Ilion offered sacrifices to these three heroes as also to a fourth hero, Ajax.

Strabo's mention of the tomb of Ajax in this same additional remark is most telling. Whereas the tomb of Achilles was located at the already extinct city of Sigeion on the promontory to the northwest of the Trojan Bay of the Hellespont, the matching tomb of Ajax was located near the still extant city of Rhoiteion, on the promontory to the northeast of this bay. As we have already seen, Strabo (13.1.30 C595) refers to a *mnēma* 'tomb' of Ajax at a *hieron* 'sacred space' of Ajax that he locates near the city of Rhoiteion.

A problem remains in the wording of Strabo (13.1.32 C596), which implies that there were separate tombs of Achilles and Patroklos at Sigeion.[92] To be contrasted is the Homeric version, according to which the bodies of Achilles and Patroklos shared a single tomb. I suggest that the problem is removed if we view such distinctions in terms of a postclassical antiquarian elaboration. By the time of Strabo, after all, it was the city of New Ilion that presided over the cult of heroes in the Troad, since the city of Sigeion itself had already been completely demolished, as the geographer himself notes explicitly in an earlier remark (13.1.31 C595). So the maintenance of the tombs no longer reflected the Athenian ideology of Sigeion.

From the standpoint of Athenian ideology, the tomb of Achilles had to be a tumulus in Sigeion, since the Athenians had lost through arbitration the environs of *Akhílleion*, which was the site of another tumulus identified with the tomb of Achilles. The tumulus at *Akhílleion*, belonging to the Aeolians, was evidently older and thus potentially more prestigious than the tumulus belonging to the Atheni-

91. Cook 1984:167 dates these tumuli to 480 B.C.E., "give or take fifty years" (with reference to Cook 1973:159–65). If we choose Cook's earlier option, his dating fits my argument. Cook's choice of the year 480 is linked with his conjecture that these tumuli were the tombs of the tyrant Hippias and his family.

92. There is a similar distinction in the report of Arrian *Anabasis* 1.12.1 concerning Alexander the Great and his veneration of the tombs of Achilles and Patroklos. Comments on this passage by Burgess 2006:n35 and n57, who mentions also the report of Plutarch *Alexander* 15.8–9 concerning honors paid by Alexander to Achilles.

ans. This older tumulus, known today as Beşik Tepe, can be dated as far back as the sixth or even the seventh century B.C.E.[93]

This is not to say, however, that we have to choose between one version or the other, as if the data of only one of the two versions could be valid. It is not simply a matter of conflicting data about what really happened in the Trojan War. Rather, it is a matter of conflicting data stemming from the traditions of conflicting groups that tell us more about their own conflicts than about what really happened in the Trojan War. So each of the two versions needs to be studied on its own terms. Arguing that there was only one tomb of Achilles seems to me as pointless as arguing that there was only one possible place for the Achaeans to land in the Troad. So it is not our place to choose which version was right. Rather, we need to find out what choices were made and by whom. And the choice made in the *Iliad* as we have it is the choice made by the Athenians. It is the Athenian version that prevails in this *Iliad*, not the Aeolian version. According to the Athenian version, the tomb of Achilles was located at the north end of the Ridge of Sigeion, whereas it was located at the south end according to the Aeolian version. Correspondingly, the Achaeans landed at the Trojan Bay on the Hellespont in the Athenian version, whereas they most probably landed at the Bay of Beşike in the Aeolian version.[94] So long as the Athenians dominated the Trojan landscape by way of their outpost at Sigeion, the Athenian version of the Iliadic tradition must have eclipsed the Aeolian version.

An Aeolian version about an Achaean landing at the Bay of Beşike would make for a different kind of *Iliad*. Some archaeologists prefer to envision such an *Iliad*, featuring the Bay of Beşike as the site for the beaching of the Achaean ships, but the *Iliad* we have simply cannot accommodate such a vision. Instead, our *Iliad* crowds all those ships into the Trojan Bay—that is, into the reduced space of what the bay had become by the first millennium B.C.E. The far more expansive space of the bay as it appeared in the second millennium B.C.E. had already long been forgotten. The crowding results in the stacking of beached ships along the south shore of the Trojan Bay, one horizontal row after the next.

This is not to say that there is no trace of an Aeolian *Iliad* in our *Iliad*. When Achilles stands at the tumulus of Patroklos and looks out homeward toward the west, he could be standing either at the northern or at the southern crest of the Sigeion Ridge. Moreover, even our *Iliad* shows glimpses of Trojan topography that require an Aeolian vantage point. A case in point is the scene in *Iliad* XIV (282–93) where Hera is about to mate with Zeus: as the scene opens, we see the god Hypnos accompanying the goddess Hera as she touches ground at Cape Lekton in the

---

93. Cook 1984:168.

94. Cook 1984:168, 170 argues for a landing at the Bay of Beşike. His argumentation unnecessarily assumes that there could have been only one version of the landing in the poetry of the *Iliad*.

Troad and proceeds up the slopes of Mount Ida to reach Zeus, who is seated on a peak called the *Gargaron akron*. The skyline envisaged here, as an archaeologist has noticed, matches what you would see from the vantage point of the city of Methymna on the northern shores of Aeolian Lesbos as you look across the strait to the mainland of the Troad:[95]

> [The *Gargaron akron* in *Iliad* XIV] must have been the massive peak (Koca Kaya) on which in due course the people of Methymna planted a city named Gargara. It is far from being the highest point of Ida (barely 2500 [feet] as against 5800 [feet] in the high Kaz Daği), and it would get no view of the Plain of Troy. But it is the dominant peak in the panorama across the strait from Lesbos, the whole stretch from Lekton to Gargara forming the skyline seen from Methymna.

The epic prestige of the older Aeolian vantage point is generally evident in the place names of the Troad. A case in point is the name of Sigeion itself. Even after the Athenians lost, through arbitration, the tumulus of Achilles at the south crest of the Sigeion Ridge, they managed to hold on to the name that refers metonymically to such a tumulus, which is the name of the city of Sigeion itself, *Sígeion*. The meaning of this name can be connected with the presence of the tomb of the hero Achilles in the environs of that city. Such a connection is confirmed by comparative evidence. In another part of the Greek-speaking world, at the city of Taras (the Latin Tarentum, modern Taranto) in Magna Graecia, there was a traditional explanation for the naming of the city after a sacred space of Achilles that was called *Sígeion* by 'the Trojans' who had once lived there:

> Ἐν Τάραντι ἐναγίζειν κατά τινας χρόνους φασὶν Ἀτρείδαις καὶ Τυδείδαις καὶ Αἰακίδαις καὶ Λαερτιάδαις, καὶ Ἀγαμεμνονίδαις δὲ χωρὶς θυσίαν ἐπιτελεῖν ἐν ἄλλῃ ἡμέρᾳ ἰδίᾳ, ἐν ᾗ νόμιμον εἶναι ταῖς γυναιξὶ μὴ γεύσασθαι τῶν ἐκείνοις θυομένων. ἔστι δὲ καὶ Ἀχιλλέως νεὼς παρ' αὐτοῖς. λέγεται δὲ μετὰ τὸ παραλαβεῖν τοὺς Ταραντίνους Ἡράκλειαν τὸν τόπον καλεῖσθαι ὃν νῦν κατοικοῦσιν, ἐν δὲ τοῖς ἄνω χρόνοις τῶν Ἰώνων κατεχόντων Πλεῖον· ἔτι δὲ ἐκείνων ἔμπροσθεν ὑπὸ τῶν Τρώων τῶν κατασχόντων αὐτὴν **Σίγειον** ὠνομάσθαι.

> They say that in Taras, at certain times of the year, they make sacrifice [*enagizein*] to the Atreidai, the Tydeidai, the Aiakidai, and the Laertiadai; also, that they conduct a sacrifice [*thusia*] separately to the Agamemnonidai on another day that is special to them. And on that day it is unlawful for women to taste of the meat that is sacrificed to those ones [the Agamemnonidai as cult heroes].[96] There is also in their territory a

---

95. Cook 1984:168. In this context, I am reminded of the evocative title of an article by West 2002, "The View from Lesbos." What I am arguing here is that the Homeric *Iliad* actually reflects "a view from Lesbos." The argument of West, however, differs from mine. For him, "the view from Lesbos" about Troy is strongly influenced by a preexisting Ionian tradition.

96. On the ritual significance of the distancing pronoun *ekeinos* 'that one' in referring to cult heroes, see Nagy 2001e:xxvii n20.

sacred space of Achilles. It is said that, after the people of Taras took over the place they still inhabit, it was called Herakleia, but that in previous times, when the Ionians were living there, it was called Pleion. And that, even before them, when the Trojans were occupying it, it was called *Sígeion*.

"Aristotle" *De mirabilibus auscultationibus* (*On Amazing Things Heard*) 840a6–15

The morphology of the place name *Sígeion* is parallel to that of *Akhílleion*, which as we saw is typical of the Aeolic dialect.[97] As for the root of this form *Sígeion*, it is cognate with the root of the adverb *sîga* 'silently' and of its derivatives, including the verb *sigân* 'be silent' and the adjective *sígēlos* 'silent'.[98] The name *Sígēlos* is even attested as the secret name of a cult hero. As we learn from a reference datable to the second or third century C.E. (Alciphron *Letters* 3.22.3), those who pass by the tomb of the cult hero *Sígēlos* must observe reverential silence.[99] In general, cult heroes attract a variety of epithets referring to the reverential silence required of those who are initiated into the mysteries of worshipping them.[100]

The observance of reverential silence in passing by the tomb of a cult hero is relevant to the naming of another Aeolian site, *Sigía*, which is directly comparable to the naming of the old Aeolian site *Sígeion*. Our information about *Sigía* comes from Strabo (13.1.46 C604). After finishing his brief survey of the territory of the *Akhílleion*, the geographer traces his way farther south along the Asiatic coastline. Next comes a territory called the *Akhaîion*.[101] Strabo describes this territory as the *peraia* of Tenedos. The word *peraia* conventionally refers to the part of a mainland that belongs to an outlying island. In this case, the outlying island is Aeolian Tenedos.[102] Strabo refers to the city of this island-state as a *polis Aiolis* 'Aeolian city'. A distinguishing feature of the Aeolian territory of the *Akhaîion* on the Asiatic mainland facing the island of Tenedos is a rocky height overlooking the sea. The name of the city founded on this height is *Khrúsa*. At this point, Strabo notes the intrusive presence of a new Hellenistic city, *Alexándreia Trōiás* or 'Alexandria-in-the-Troad', founded by Antigonus and refounded by Lysimachus (13.1.47 C604). The

---

97. Strabo uses the article *to* in combination with *Sígeion* (13.1.31 C595, 13.1.32 C596, 13.1.34 C597, 13.1.38 C599, 13.1.39 C600, 13.1.42 C602) as well as with *Akhílleion* (13.1.38 C600, 13.1.46 C604) and with *Rhoíteion* (13.1.31 C595, 13.1.34 C597, 13.1.42 C602).

98. On the derivation of *sigân* from the adverb *sîga*, see Chantraine *DELG* s.v. σῖγα.

99. Brelich 1958:157n229.

100. Brelich 1958:156–57.

101. Already at the first mention of *Akhaîion*, Strabo combines the name with the article *to* (13.1.32 C506; see also 13.1.46 C604, 13.1.47 C604).

102. In Pindar *Nemean* 11, we hear that the *laudandus* of the song, an aristocrat from Tenedos, is descended from ancestors who came from Amyklai with Orestes to settle Tenedos (line 34); these settlers of Tenedos are imagined as a bronze-clad horde of Aeolians (line 35).

geographer describes this new city as *sunekhēs* 'contiguous' with the ancient territory of the *Akhaîon*, and he says that the new city resulted from a merger of ancient cities that were *sunekheîs* 'contiguous' with the *Akhaîon*.[103] One of the cities he mentions here is *Kolōnai*. This name is the elliptic plural of the singular form *kolōnē*, which means 'tumulus'.[104] As we saw earlier, *kolōnē* in the *Iliad* refers to a prominent tumulus in the Trojan landscape (II 811), described as a sacred place that is known to immortals as the *sēma* 'tomb' of *Murinē* (II 814). As we also saw earlier, the related word *kolōnos* is attested in contexts where it refers to a tumulus fortified with stones that marks the place where a cult hero is buried. *Kolōnai* and the other old cities contiguous with the *Akhaîon* were later consolidated, Strabo says, into the new Hellenistic city of Alexandria-in-the-Troad. He adds that the name of the ancient site where the new consolidated city is located is *Sigía*. So the site of *Sigía* is associated with rocky heights overlooking the Hellespont and with tumuli marking the burial places of cult heroes. And this vision of tumuli is the essence of the meaning of the place name *Kolōnai*. What I have just said about the site of *Sigía* applies also to the site of *Sígeion*. Strabo actually uses the expression *Sigeiàs ákra*, the 'headland of Sigeion' as he proceeds to consider the heights where the *Akhílleion* is located (13.1.46 C604), and we have already considered in some detail the potential association of these heights with the tomb of Achilles.

I conclude, then, that both *Sígeion* and *Sigía* refer to heights imagined as markers of sacred places where tombs of heroes are located. As for the actual meaning of these Aeolic place names *Sígeion* and *Sigía*, both signal a sacred space of reverential silence. By metonymy, the naming of these heights *Sígeion* and *Sigía* is connected with the practice of observing reverential silence at the tombs of heroes.[105]

I close this section by noting some relevant details recorded roughly a half a millennium after Strabo. What we are about to see is a first-person account of a traveler heading from Alexandria-in-the-Troad, site of the ancient Sigia, to New Ilion,

103. For a historical overview of this merger of cities into a *koinon* including Alexandria-in-the-Troad, see Rose 2006:147–49, who highlights the significance of the sanctuary of Athena at New Ilion as a religious center of this *koinon*. In the era of this *koinon*, a Panathenaic festival was instituted in New Ilion, modeled on the original Panathenaic festival of Athens; the relevant evidence is surveyed by Rose, who concludes: "the Koinon chose the Panathenaic festival, based directly on the one in Athens. In addition to athletic and musical events, rhapsodes would have sung parts of the *Iliad* in the city's agora, which lay in front of the Troy VI fortification wall. That wall was no doubt presented as a remnant of Priam's citadel, and sections of it were repaired and exhibited to spectators near the Bouleuterion and on the road to the theater" (p. 148).

104. On the concept of an elliptic plural, and on examples of place names in the elliptic plural, see *HTL* 157–64.

105. From here on, I will write simply "Sigeion," "Sigia," and "Akhilleion."

site of ancient Troy, and from there to Akhilleion. The year is 354 C.E., and the traveler is Julian the Apostate:[106]

Πηγάσιον ἡμεῖς οὔποτ' ἂν προσήκαμεν ῥαδίως, εἰ μὴ σαφῶς ἐπεπείσμεθα ὅτι καὶ πρότερον, εἶναι δοκῶν τῶν Γαλιλαίων ἐπίσκοπος, ἠπίστατο σέβεσθαι καὶ τιμᾶν τοὺς θεούς· οὐκ ἀκοὴν ἐγώ σοι ταῦτα ἀπαγγέλλω τῶν πρὸς ἔχθραν καὶ φιλίαν τοιαῦτα λέγειν εἰωθότων, ἐπεὶ καὶ ἐμοὶ πάνυ διατεθρύλλητο τὰ τοιαῦτα περὶ αὐτοῦ καὶ μὰ τοὺς θεοὺς ᾤμην οὕτω χρῆναι μισεῖν αὐτὸν ὡς οὐδένα τῶν πονηροτάτων. Ἐπεὶ δὲ κληθεὶς εἰς τὸ στρατόπεδον ὑπὸ τοῦ μακαρίτου Κωνσταντίου ταύτην ἐπορευόμην τὴν ὁδόν, ἀπὸ τῆς Τρῳάδος ὄρθρου βαθέος διαναστάς, ἦλθον εἰς τὸ Ἴλιον περὶ πλήθουσαν ἀγοράν· ὁ δὲ ὑπήντησε καὶ βουλομένῳ τὴν πόλιν ἱστορεῖν (ἦν γάρ μοι τοῦτο πρόσχημα τοῦ φοιτᾶν εἰς τὰ ἱερὰ) περιηγητής τε ἐγένετο καὶ ἐξενάγησέ με πανταχοῦ. Ἄκουε τοίνυν ἔργα καὶ λόγους, ἀφ' ὧν ἄν τις εἰκάσειεν οὐκ ἀγνώμονα τὰ πρὸς τοὺς θεοὺς αὐτόν. Ἡρῷόν ἐστιν Ἕκτορος, ὅπου χαλκοῦς ἕστηκεν ἀνδριὰς ἐν ναΐσκῳ βραχεῖ. Τούτῳ τὸν μέγαν ἀντέστησαν Ἀχιλλέα κατὰ τὸ ὕπαιθρον· εἰ τὸν τόπον ἐθεάσω, γνωρίζεις δήπουθεν ὃ λέγω. Τὴν μὲν οὖν ἱστορίαν, δι' ἣν ὁ μέγας Ἀχιλλεὺς ἀντιτεταγμένος αὐτῷ πᾶν τὸ ὕπαιθρον κατείληφεν, ἔξεστί σοι τῶν περιηγητῶν ἀκούειν. Ἐγὼ δὲ καταλαβὼν ἐμπύρους ἔτι, μικροῦ δέω φάναι λαμπροὺς ἔτι τοὺς βωμοὺς καὶ λιπαρῶς ἀληλιμμένην τὴν τοῦ Ἕκτορος εἰκόνα, πρὸς Πηγάσιον ἀπιδών· "τί ταῦτα;" εἶπον, "Ἰλιεῖς **θύουσιν**;" ἀποπειρώμενος ἠρέμα ὡς ἔχει γνώμης. ὁ δέ· "καὶ τί τοῦτο ἄτοπον, ἄνδρα ἀγαθὸν ἑαυτῶν πολίτην, ὥσπερ ἡμεῖς," ἔφη, "τοὺς μάρτυρας, εἰ θεραπεύουσιν;"Ἡ μὲν οὖν εἰκὼν οὐχ ὑγιής, ἡ δὲ προαίρεσις ἐν ἐκείνοις ἐξεταζομένη τοῖς καιροῖς ἀστεία. Τί δὴ τὸ μετὰ τοῦτο; "Βαδίσωμεν," ἔφην, "ἐπὶ τὸ τῆς Ἰλιάδος Ἀθηνᾶς τέμενος." Ὁ δὲ καὶ μάλα προθύμως ἀπήγαγέ με καὶ **ἀνέῳξε τὸν νεών**, καὶ ὥσπερ μαρτυρόμενος ἐπέδειξέ μοι πάντα ἀκριβῶς σῶα τὰ ἀγάλματα, καὶ ἔπραξεν οὐθὲν ὧν εἰώθασιν οἱ δυσσεβεῖς ἐκεῖνοι πράττειν, ἐπὶ τοῦ μετώπου τοῦ δυσσεβοῦς τὸ ὑπόμνημα σκιογραφοῦντες, οὐδὲ ἐσύριττεν, ὥσπερ ἐκεῖνοι, αὐτὸς καθ' ἑαυτόν· ἡ γὰρ ἄκρα θεολογία παρ' αὐτοῖς ἐστι δύο ταῦτα, **συρίττειν** τε **πρὸς τοὺς δαίμονας** καὶ σκιογραφεῖν ἐπὶ τοῦ μετώπου τὸν σταυρόν. Δύο ταῦτα ἐπηγγειλάμην εἰπεῖν σοι· τρίτον δὲ ἐλθὼν ἐπὶ νοῦν οὐκ οἶμαι χρῆναι **σιωπᾶν**. Ἠκολούθησέ μοι καὶ πρὸς **τὸ Ἀχίλλειον** ὁ αὐτός, καὶ ὑπέδειξε τὸν **τάφον** σῶον· ἐπεπείσμην δὲ καὶ τοῦτον ὑπ' αὐτοῦ διεσκάφθαι· ὁ δὲ καὶ μάλα σεβόμενος αὐτῷ προσῄει. Ταῦτα εἶδον αὐτός· ἀκήκοα δὲ παρὰ τῶν νῦν ἐχθρῶς ἐχόντων πρὸς αὐτὸν ὅτι καὶ προσεύχοιτο λάθρᾳ καὶ προσκυνοίη τὸν Ἥλιον. Ἆρα οὐκ ἂν ἐδέξω με καὶ ἰδιώτην μαρτυροῦντα; Τῆς περὶ τοὺς θεοὺς διαθέσεως ἑκάστου τίνες ‹ἂν› εἶεν ἀξιοπιστότεροι μάρτυρες αὐτῶν τῶν θεῶν; Ἡμεῖς ἱερέα Πηγάσιον ἐποιοῦμεν ‹ἄν›, εἰ **συνεγνώκειμεν** αὐτῷ τι περὶ τοὺς θεοὺς δυσσεβές; Εἰ δὲ ἐν ἐκείνοις τοῖς χρόνοις, εἴτε δυναστείας ὀρεγόμενος, εἴθ', ὅπερ πρὸς ἡμᾶς ἔφη πολλάκις, ὑπὲρ τοῦ σῶσαι τῶν θεῶν τὰ ἕδη, τὰ ῥάκια ταῦτα περιαμπέσχετο καὶ τὴν ἀσέβειαν μέχρις ὀνόματος ὑπεκρίνατο (πέφηνε γὰρ οὐδὲν οὐδαμοῦ τῶν ἱερῶν ἠδικηκὼς πλὴν ὀλίγων παντάπασι λίθων ἐκ καταλύματος, ἵνα αὐτῷ σώζειν ἐξῇ τὰ λοιπά), τοῦτο ἐν λόγῳ ποιούμεθα, καὶ οὐκ αἰσχυνόμεθα ταὐτὰ περὶ αὐτὸν πράττοντες ὅσαπερ Ἀφόβιος ἐποίει καὶ οἱ Γαλιλαῖοι πάντες προσεύχονται πάσχοντα ἰδεῖν αὐτόν; Εἴ τί μοι

106. I follow the edition of Bidez 1924.

προσέχεις, οὐ τοῦτον μόνον, ἀλλὰ καὶ τοὺς ἄλλους, οἳ μετατέθεινται, τιμήσεις, ἵν' οἱ
μὲν ῥᾷον ὑπακούσωσιν ἡμῖν ἐπὶ τὰ καλὰ προκαλουμένοις, οἱ δ' ἧττον χαίρωσιν· εἰ δὲ
τοὺς αὐτομάτους ἰόντας ἀπελαύνοιμεν, οὐδεὶς ὑπακούσεται ῥᾳδίως παρακαλοῦσιν.

Pegasios is a man I would never easily have accepted into my company if it had not
been clearly proved to me that, even in the old days,[107] although he was a bishop of
the Galilaeans,[108] he understood how to worship and give honor [timē] to the gods.
These things that I am reporting to you are not hearsay coming from those who are
accustomed to say such things for negative or positive purposes, since I too had heard
such idle talk about him, and, I swear by the gods, I was ready to hate him more than
any other evildoer in the whole world. But when I was summoned to headquarters
by Constantius, of blessed memory,[109] and I was on my way to get there, and, having
stopped over at Alexandria-in-the-Troad[110] and proceeding from there at early dawn
toward Ilion, which I reached by midday when the marketplace was in full swing, he
[Pegasios] was there, waiting to greet me. And, when I expressed a desire to have a
close look at the city (that was my pretext for visiting the sacred places there), he became my guide and host, taking me all over the place. So now I want you to listen to
what I say about the things he did and said, from which one may infer that he was not
at all ignorant of the things that have to do with the gods. There is a hero precinct of
Hector, where a bronze statue is erected inside a small sacred building.[111] Facing this
statue they have set up the big statue of Achilles, which is standing outside in the open
space. If you have seen the place for yourself, you surely know what I am talking
about.[112] As for the story that tells why the big statue of Achilles that stands facing
him [Hector] happens to take up the entire open space, I will leave that for the guides[113]
to tell you.[114] Anyway, I found the altars still lit—I would say they were practically
still glowing—and the simulacrum of Hector was glistening, all daubed in olive oil.
Turning to Pegasios and looking him in the eye, I said: "So what is going on here: Are
the people of Ilion **making sacrifice** [*thuein*]?" I was trying to ease him into telling

107. Julian is referring back to a time when he was not yet emperor, and when the official imperial
religion had not yet reverted from Christianity to paganism.

108. Julian refers to the Christians derisively as 'Galilaeans'.

109. The date of the incident that is being narrated is 354 C.E. Toward the end of that year, Julian
was summoned to travel from Nicomedia, where he was staying at the time, to Milan, where Constantius II was staying (Bidez 1924:85n2). The present letter must have been written after 3 November 361,
which is when Constantius II died.

110. As we saw earlier, *Alexándreia Trōiás* was a Hellenistic city built on the site of ancient Sigia.

111. For a description of this statue of Hector, see Philostratus *Heroikos* 18.3–7.

112. The speaker is ostentatiously passing over in silence the details of what one can see. The rhetoric here simulates the sense of *muein*, which refers to visualization and verbalization in sacred contexts and to nonvisualization and nonverbalization in profane contexts. See *PH* 1§29 (= pp. 31–32), 2§30
(= pp. 66–67).

113. The term *peri(h)ēgētēs* designates a guide who is expert in sacral realia.

114. This time, the speaker is ostentatiously passing over in silence the details of what one can say.
See Zosimus 4.18.2 for a reference to the cults of Achilles as they existed in the fourth century C.E. (Bidez
1924:86n1).

me what he was really thinking. "And what is so strange about this," he said to me, "if they happen to venerate [*therapeuein*] a noble man who is their fellow citizen the same way we venerate the martyrs?" All right, so the image is not wholesome,[115] but the intention, if examined in terms of the circumstances that then prevailed, is quite sophisticated. "So now what comes next?"[116] "Let us go," I said, "to the precinct of Athena Ilias." With great eagerness he led me to the place and **opened the temple.**[117] Then, just as if he were bearing witness to his faith, he showed the statues, which were all perfectly intact, and he did not do any of the things that those impious ones[118] are accustomed to do, tracing on the forehead the sign of the Impious One.[119] Nor did he start hissing under his breath, the way those [impious ones] do. For the ultimate exaltation of theology for them [the Christians] adds up to these two things: **hissing at the** *daimones* and tracing the cross on the forehead. So these are the two things I said I would tell you. But a third thing occurs to me,[120] and now I think I must not **be silent** about it.[121] The same man [Pegasios] accompanied me to **the** *Akhilleion*, and he pointed out to me the **tomb** [of Achilles], which was intact. Previously, I had been led to believe that this tomb, as well as other sites, had been demolished by him. But he approached it [the tomb of Achilles] with the most worshipful reverence.[122] I saw these things with my own eyes,[123] and I have heard even from those who are now hostile toward him that he used to pray secretly to the god Helios and to worship him. Would you not accept me as a witness to what I saw, even if I were a private citizen? When it comes to each man's disposition concerning the gods, what witnesses would be more worthy to be believed than the gods themselves? Would I be making Pegasios a priest if I knew of any impious thought he might have with regard to the gods? And if in those old times—whether he was aspiring to high office or (and this is some-

---

115. The unwholesome *eikōn* 'image' that is produced here results from comparing Hector to a Christian martyr.

116. Here I follow the suggestion of G. W. Most in assigning this sentence to Pegasios and not to Julian as speaker. In any case, the syntax calls attention to the fact that a second experience is about to be narrated. As we will see, there will be three experiences in all.

117. By implication, the Christian bishop is unlocking the door to the temple of Athena Ilias at the site of old Ilion (within New Ilion) because there is at the time no pagan priest of Athena Ilias in charge of that temple (Bidez 1924:86n2).

118. That is, the Christians.

119. That is, Pegasios did not make the sign of the Cross, the sign of the crucified Christ, who is described here as the Impious One.

120. The speaker ostentatiously refers to this third experience as if he had just recalled it at this very moment. By implication, he should pass over the details in silence, but the spontaneous recall inspires him to break his silence. It is as if he would now reveal something that should not be revealed except in a sacred context.

121. There is a wordplay here, since the first detail to be mentioned after the noting of silence is the tomb of Achilles, which requires reverential silence on the part of those who approach it—as opposed to the hostile gesture of 'hissing at the *daimones*'.

122. Presumably, he approached the tomb of Achilles in reverential silence.

123. Once again, the rhetoric simulates the sense of *muein*, which refers to visualization and verbalization in sacred contexts and to nonvisualization and nonverbalization in profane contexts.

thing he has admitted to me many times already) it was for the sake of saving the abodes of the gods—he wore these rags[124] of his and acted out the role of impiety[125] (I say *acted out* because he has evidently harmed the sacred places nowhere—except for an altogether small number of stones that he took from a hostel,[126] and he did that in order to make it possible to save the rest of the stones), are we taking this into account, and are we not ashamed that we are doing all the same things to him that Aphobios used to do[127] and that all the Galilaeans wanted to see happening to him [Pegasios]? If you are going to pay any attention to me, you will honor not only this man [Pegasios] but also all the others who have converted, so that people may find it all the more easy to heed me as I call upon them to do the things that are good, while the other side may have all the less reason to be happy about anything. If I reject those who come to me of their own free will, then nobody will find it easy to heed my call.

Flavius Claudius Julianus Imperator (Julian the Apostate) Epistle 79

Toward the end of this epistle by Julian, we see a reference to the practice of reusing stones from pagan sanctuaries for the sake of building Christian edifices. Such reusing is reminiscent of the archaic Aeolian reuse of stones from the ruins of Troy for the building of new walls that reassert the continued presence of the old city.

RETHINKING THE TROJAN PAST

Keeping in mind this ancient Aeolian reuse, I return to the testimony of Strabo, who reports that the Mytilenaeans of Lesbos built the Aeolian city of Sigeion from the stones of the old Troy. As we saw, the geographer uses this precious testimony to make a point of his own. He says that the stones of the old site of Ilion were used for a new building project for a practical reason: because the old Ilion had been totally destroyed in the Trojan War and therefore rendered useless (13.1.38 C599). As I have been arguing, this point made by Strabo simply cannot be justified. That is because the motive of the Mytilenaeans and of the Aeolians whom they claim to represent was symbolic as well as practical.

The symbolism was connected with two basic historical facts that I have already noted. First, the Aeolians appropriated the ancient site of Troy when they gained control of the Troad. Second, the Mytilenaeans fortified the ancient site called Akhilleion, making it a new Aeolian countercity after they had lost through arbitration the old Aeolian city of Sigeion to the Athenians.

Strabo ignored the symbolic meaning of the stones used to build Sigeion and to

---

124. This is a derisive reference to the ecclesiastical robes worn by Christian bishops.

125. This is a derisive reference to the ecclesiastical duties performed by Christian bishops.

126. Such a *kataluma* 'hostel' was evidently an annex to a sanctuary, used for the lodging of those who came to visit the given sanctuary (Bidez 1924:87n2).

127. This reference to Aphobios has not been explained, so far as I know.

fortify Akhilleion because he ignored the Aeolian cultural agenda implicit in this meaning. The same can be said about his resistance to the idea that the city of New Ilion was a direct continuation of the old Ilion. In this regard, it is essential to keep in mind the fact that New Ilion, founded as an Aeolian city in the seventh (or even as early as the eighth) century B.C.E., retained a distinctly Aeolian and non-Athenian identity well into the fifth century—and, as we will see later, even into Strabo's time.

The Aeolian city of New Ilion and the Aeolian city of Akhilleion both affirmed an Aeolian identity by way of the same physical metonymy: both these cities, like the once Aeolian city of Sigeion, were physically connected to the old city of Ilion, since their new walls had been built with the stones of the old walls of Ilion.[128] By contrast with Akhilleion and New Ilion, the identity of the formerly Aeolian city of Sigeion was complicated by its Athenian redefinition after the city was repossessed once and for all by Peisistratos in the sixth century B.C.E. This Athenian redefinition of Sigeion was in turn complicated by the fact that the Persian empire became a major force in the politics of Greek cities in Asia Minor, Sigeion included, in the late sixth and early fifth centuries B.C.E. In the case of Sigeion, this city became a refuge for Hippias son of Peisistratos, after he was overthrown in 510 as tyrant of Athens and went over to the side of the Persians (Herodotus 5.94.1, Thucydides 6.59.4).

After 479, the Persian domination of the Troad gave way to Athenian domination. The next time we hear of Sigeion in the course of history, it figures as a satellite of the democratic Athenian empire. In the *Oresteia* trilogy of Aeschylus, presented in the year 458 B.C.E., the goddess Athena claims the territory of Sigeion as the political and poetic possession of Athens.[129] As the goddess makes her grand entrance in the third part of the trilogy, the *Eumenides*, she announces that she has just flown over to Athens from the territory of Sigeion, described metonymically as the banks of the river Scamander, where she has just finished claiming for herself—and thereby for her city—the territory of Sigeion. This territory, the goddess proclaims, had been assigned by the Achaeans to the Athenians as just reward for the participation of Athens in the Trojan War:

πρόσωθεν ἐξήκουσα κληδόνος βοὴν
ἀπὸ Σκαμάνδρου, γῆν καταφθατουμένη,
ἣν δῆτ᾽ Ἀχαιῶν ἄκτορές τε καὶ πρόμοι,
τῶν αἰχμαλώτων χρημάτων λάχος μέγα,
ἔνειμαν αὐτόπρεμνον ἐς τὸ πᾶν ἐμοί,
ἐξαίρετον δώρημα Θησέως τόκοις·

---

128. Leaf 1923:186: "The whole of the large stones from the N[orth] side of Hisarlik have been removed, and it is highly probable that, as Demetrios says, they were taken to build the more modern and flourishing coast towns in the neighbourhood."
129. Griffith 1995:98–99.

ἔνθεν διώκουσ' ἦλθον ἄτρυτον πόδα
πτερῶν ἄτερ ῥοιβδοῦσα κόλπον αἰγίδος.

From far away did I hear the shout of people calling for me,
all the way from Scamander, while I was taking possession of that territory,
which, as I found out, the leaders and chiefs of the Achaeans
had assigned to me as my great share of the spoils won by the spear in war.
They had assigned it [the territory of Sigeion] to me, root and branch and all,
  to be mine absolutely and for all time,
this exceptional gift bestowed upon the children of Theseus.
It is from there [that territory] I have come, pursuing my unweary step,
winging my way to the whirring sound made not by wings but by the folds
  of my aegis.

Aeschylus Eumenides 397–404

In an inscription dated to the middle of the fifth century B.C.E., we see the city
of Sigeion listed as a member of the Delian League (*IG* I³17), paying a thousand
drachmas yearly to the central treasury of the Athenians; by the year 418/7, we find
that the annual sum has been upgraded to a whole talent, which is some six times
the earlier amount (*ATL* I list 33).[130]

The city of Sigeion, claimed by the goddess Athena as her very own site in the
production of the *Oresteia* of Aeschylus in 458 B.C.E., must have been viewed as
an Asiatic replica of the ultimate site of Athena that was the city of Athens. And
while the formerly Aeolian city of Sigeion was being foregrounded as a new Athens
in Asia, the neighboring Aeolian cities of northern Asia Minor were being pushed
into the background, facing the threat of losing their Aeolian cultural identity. One
event stands out: in the summer of 427, the Athenians demolished the walls of Mytilene in Lesbos, confiscated the city's fleet of ships, and took possession of all the
cities on the Asiatic mainland that had formerly belonged to the Mytilenaeans
(Thucydides 3.50.1–3). Strabo takes note of these decisive events, inferring that the
site of New Ilion, the ancient Troy of the Aeolians, now belonged not to Mytilene
but to Athens (13.1.39 C600).

So the question arises, What did this ancient Troy of the Aeolians mean to the
Athenians? The answer is stark. For Athenians in the era of the democratic Athenian
empire, this ancient Troy simply did not exist. From the standpoint of Athenian
imperial propaganda, there could be no trace left of ancient Troy. The Athenians
owned Sigeion, with its own special links to the ancient Troy, and that was already
more than enough for them. As far as the Athenians were concerned, Sigeion was
all that was left of ancient Troy. After all, even the Aeolians had once claimed that
their former possession, the old Aeolian city of Sigeion, had been built from the

---

130. Meiggs and Lewis 1988:226.

stones of Troy. The big difference is, the Aeolians had made three further claims about New Ilion, as we know from Strabo (13.1.40 C599):

1. The old city of Ilion, with its own special temple of Athena, had not been completely demolished by the Achaeans in the Trojan War.
2. The old city of Ilion had not been completely abandoned and left uninhabited.
3. The walls of the new city of Ilion had been built from the stones of the old Ilion.

To be contrasted with these claims of the Aeolians is a counterclaim: that the old Ilion had in fact been totally demolished—and that the stones of its city walls had been completely used up in the fortifying of Sigeion. In terms of this counterclaim, there could be no trace left of the Troy of the Trojan War. This counterclaim, along with the claims of the Aeolians, is reported by Strabo (13.1.38 C599).

I propose that this counterclaim stems from the political interests of the Athenian empire. I also propose that the Athenian phase of Sigeion was meant to replace the New Ilion of the Aeolians. For the Aeolians, as also for the archaeologists of today, their New Ilion was the real Troy, rebuilt on the old site from the stones of the old Ilion. For the Athenians, however, the old Sigeion of the Aeolians was rethought as a would-be "New Ilion" built on a new site from the stones of the old site. As for the New Ilion of the Aeolians, it was no Ilion at all for the Athenians. That was the essence of the Athenian ideology.

A salient indication of such an Athenian ideology is the retrospective reference made by Herodotus (5.95.1) to 'the *Athēnaion* in Sigeion' (τὸ Ἀθήναιον τὸ ἐν Σιγείῳ) in his narration of the struggle between Athens and Mytilene over possession of 'the Iliadic territory', *hē Ilias khōra* (τῆς Ἰλιάδος χώρης). This *Athēnaion* or 'sacred space of Athena', located in Sigeion as it existed in its Athenian phase, must have been a rival to the sacred space of Athena located in the Aeolian New Ilion.[131] Both versions of that sacred space, the Aeolian one and the Athenian one, could be seen as re-enactments of the *neōs* 'temple' of Athena situated on the acropolis of Troy— as we see it pictured in *Iliad* VI (297).

In the years before 427—that is, before Athens succeeded in appropriating all the territories of the Troad that had once been dominated by Mytilene—the Athenians must have maintained a policy of claiming that Sigeion, with its temple of Athena, was a re-enactment of the old Ilion, and that the New Ilion of the Aeolians was a falsification. Such a policy is reflected in the words of Athena as I quoted them earlier from the *Oresteia* of Aeschylus. In the years after 427, however, when most of the Troad had come to be dominated by the Athenians, Athens was in the position to do something concrete about its claims against New Ilion. Strabo notes in

---

131. Robertson 1996 argues that the temple of Athena in Sigeion was matched by the temple of Athena Nike in Athens. He also argues that this Athenian temple can be dated back to around 600 B.C.E. See Frame 2009 §3.74.

passing that the territory of New Ilion was divided up between Sigeion to the west and Rhoiteion to the east for an unspecified period of time (13.1.42 C602). Such a period, I suggest, coincides with the years after 427.

But the Aeolian identity of New Ilion survived, endangered though it was during the period when Athenian domination extended to that part of the Troad.[132] The historian Hellanicus of Lesbos, whose publications can be dated as far back as 406 B.C.E. (scholia for Aristophanes *Frogs* 694), is on record as claiming in his *Trōïka* (*FGH* 4 F 25b) that New Ilion was in fact the same city as the old Ilion. Our source here is Strabo (13.1.42 C602), who adds that this claim of Hellanicus reflects the historian's partiality toward the people of the Aeolian New Ilion.[133] The birthplace of Hellanicus, Lesbos, indicates that his claim reflects his cultural identification with the Aeolians.

The Athenian domination of Aeolians in Asia Minor and in the outlying islands was not to last. Despite all the setbacks they suffered in the late fifth century at the hands of the Athenians, the Aeolians eventually recovered most of their cultural identity in the course of the next century. That is why the entire *paralia* 'coastline' of Asia Minor from Abydos in the far north all the way to Cyme in the far south could proudly be described as *Aiolis* 'Aeolian territory' by an Aeolian source from the second half of the fourth century B.C.E.: this source is Ephorus (*FGH* 70 F 163, by way of Strabo 13.1.39 C600), who was a native of the Aeolian city of Cyme. Strabo cites this testimony of Ephorus as an indication of the enduring power of Aeolian cultural identity— and, indirectly, of an ongoing Aeolian cultural resistance to Athenian domination.

In precisely this context, Strabo mentions a historical fact that turns out to be all-important for my argumentation: in the end, Sigeion was destroyed by the city of New Ilion, and this destruction had taken place long before Strabo's time. The geographer says that the city of Sigeion in his time was completely demolished (13.1.39 C600 κατεσπασμένη). We do not know the exact date or circumstances of this catastrophe that befell Sigeion in particular and Athenian prestige in general, but I estimate that it happened sometime in the second half of the fourth century. After the destruction did take place, New Ilion could once again become what the old Ilion had once been: that is, the dominant city of the Troad. Strabo goes out of his way to note the dominance of New Ilion in his own time (13.1.25 C593), when this Aeolian city controlled the Asiatic coastline of the Hellespont as far north as Dardanos (13.1.39 C600).

So, in the post-Athenocentric era of Strabo, a great city that had once stood out as the new Troy of Athens and the new Athens of Asia, Sigeion, no longer existed. It is implicit in Strabo's wording that Sigeion was no longer even a *katoikia* 'settle-

132. Leaf 1923:190 surveys the available evidence and concludes that the Athenians never even occupied the actual city of "Troy."

133. Pfeiffer 1968:250.

ment'; by contrast, the geographer makes it explicit that the old countercity of the Aeolians, Akhilleion, was at least still a *katoikia mikra* 'small settlement', featuring the *mnēma* 'tomb' of Achilles as its distinguishing landmark (13.1.39 C600). What now stood out in sharp contrast was New Ilion, which was by this time the premier city of the Troad, as Strabo attests (13.1.25 C593). Still, the geographer cannot resist making a disparaging remark about New Ilion: he says that it had in earlier times been a mere *katoikia* 'settlement', and that a simple *hieron* 'sacred space' of Athena had once been its only distinguishing landmark (13.1.42 C601).

The ultimate ascendancy of the city of New Ilion in the Troad was decisively ratified in the year 334 B.C.E., when Alexander the Great crossed the Hellespont from Europe into Asia Minor and defeated the forces of the Persian empire at the river Granicus in the Troad. The time had now come for New Ilion, instead of Sigeion, to be recognized once again as the site of the old Ilion. I say *once again* because, as I noted earlier, the Persians themselves had recognized New Ilion as the old Troy already at the time of the expedition of Xerxes in 480: according to Herodotus (7.43.2), the Persian king of kings made the grand gesture of sacrificing to Athena, surnamed *hē Ilias*, in New Ilion; he also offered libations to the 'heroes' there.[134] Later, in 334, after his victory over the Persians in the Troad, Alexander likewise sacrificed to Athena in New Ilion (Strabo 13.1.26 C593, Arrian *Anabasis* 1.11.7). Strabo says specifically that Alexander made sacrifice at the *hieron* 'sacred space' of Athena at New Ilion (13.1.26 C593). So Alexander ratified New Ilion as the genuine ancient Troy. Strabo also reports that Alexander the Great went on to transform the site from a *kōmē* 'village' into a *polis* 'city', and that the transformation was continued by Alexander's would-be successor Lysimachus (13.1.26 C593).[135] At this point, the geographer goes out of his way to add a disparaging remark: he notes that the *hieron* 'sacred space' of Athena at New Ilion had been *mikron kai euteles* 'small and of modest means' before the era of Alexander (again, 13.1.26 C593).

The good fortune of New Ilion did not stop with the beneficences of Alexander the Great and his successors. As Strabo notes, the ascendancy of this city in the era of Alexander was even further enhanced later on in the era of Roman domination at the special initiative of Julius Caesar, whose family claimed that their lineage could be traced all the way back to *Iulus*, the alternative name of Ascanius son of Aeneas (13.1.27 C594–95).[136]

I will have more to say later about this new imperial claim. But first, I return to the

---

134. See again Haubold 2004.

135. This passage of Strabo (13.1.26 C593), if I understand it correctly, goes on to mention the favor shown by Lysimachus not only to the city of New Ilion but also to the new city of Alexandria-in-the-Troad.

136. On the patronage bestowed on New Ilion by the successor to Julius Caesar, the emperor Augustus (and by his own successors), see Rose 2006:152–53; also Erskine 2001:245–53.

fact that Demetrius of Scepsis, followed by Strabo, rejected the idea that the Aeolian city of New Ilion was a continuation of the old Ilion, claiming that the old Ilion was totally destroyed and that this total destruction explains why the stones of the old Ilion had been reused by the Aeolians in fortifying the walls of the newer city of Sigeion (13.1.38 C599). I will now proceed to argue that this alternative line of thinking actually represents an alternative Athenian claim.

In his speech *Against Leokrates* (62), the Athenian statesman Lycurgus compares the total destruction of any city to the finality of death itself, and the prime example he cites is the destruction of Troy. Strabo (13.1.41 C601) cites this striking formulation by the Athenian Lycurgus as the basis for his own claim that the old Ilion was totally destroyed by the Achaeans and left *aoikēton* 'uninhabited'. To be contrasted is the claim made by the people of the city of New Ilion, as also reported by Strabo (13.1.40 C600): according to this claim, the old Ilion was not totally destroyed, and it was not left uninhabited. What we see here, in terms of my ongoing argument, is a traditional Aeolian claim promoting the cultural identity of the Aeolians, for whom the old Ilion extended directly into the city of New Ilion.

In saying that Troy no longer existed, the Athenian statesman Lycurgus was evidently tapping into the conventional thinking of Athenians at the time of his speech, which is dated to 330 B.C.E. Such thinking can also be dated farther back to a far earlier time. When the city of Sigeion was captured from the Aeolians by the Athenians in the late seventh century, the temple of Athena at Sigeion became a rival to the temple of Athena at New Ilion. We can reconstruct such an earlier time on the basis of a statement made by Strabo (13.1.42 C601), which can be divided into two parts. First, he concedes that the founding of New Ilion dates back to the days of the Lydian empire. So this part of his statement matches the modern archaeological dating of the site as far back as the seventh (or even eighth) century B.C.E. Second, after having conceded the early inhabitation of New Ilion, he goes on to insist that this site started not as a *polis* 'city' but merely as a *hieron* 'sacred space' of Athena, situated in the vicinity of what he describes as a mere *katoikia* 'settlement'. Such a dismissive description of the old site of Troy corresponds to what I reconstruct as an alternative Athenian ideology, which elides the New Ilion of the Aeolians while highlighting what had once been the New Ilion of the Athenians at Sigeion. As we have seen, that would-be "New Ilion" prominently featured a rival sacred space of Athena.

By contrast with such ideological agenda concerning Troy after the Trojan War, Strabo's own agenda can be viewed as scholarly rather than political. In denying the idea that the site of ancient Troy was the site of New Ilion, Strabo was following the learned theories of Demetrius of Scepsis, who likewise denied this idea. As we have already seen, Demetrius argued that the real site of ancient Troy was a place called ἡ τῶν Ἰλιέων κώμη 'the village [*kōmē*] of the people of Ilion [*Ilieis*]', located in the territory of Scepsis in the region of Mount Ida, at a distance of some thirty stadia from New Ilion (Strabo 13.1.35–36 C597–98; also 13.1.25 C593). Strabo says explicitly, following Demetrius, that there was no trace of any ancient city at this *kōmē* 'village'; on that basis, it is claimed that the stones used for the building of Sigeion must have been taken away from this village (13.1.38 C599).

Whereas this scholarly formulation about an alternative location for Troy stems from antiquarian theorizing, there were earlier versions of this formulation stemming from political ideology—in particular, from the ideology of the Ionians.

This ideology is evident in the Ionian epic tradition. The primary example is the Ionian epic of the *Iliou Persis*, attributed to Arctinus of Miletus. Here I offer a brief summary of the relevant parts of this epic:

> After Troy was completely destroyed by the Achaeans, a handful of prominent survivors sought to find alternative places to live. The most prominent of these survivors of Troy's total destruction was the hero Aeneas: he and his followers, interpreting the killing of Laocoön by two serpents as an omen of the total destruction of Troy, withdrew from that city before its destruction and moved back to his home in the highlands of Mount Ida.
>
> Proclus summary p. 107.24–26 ed. Allen

We also find a mention of this epic event in a fragment from the *Laocoön* of Sophocles (F 373, via Dionysius of Halicarnassus *Roman Antiquities* 1.48.2), where a messenger describes the withdrawal of Aeneas to an *apoikia* 'settlement', evidently situated in the region of Mount Ida.

This version of the Aeneas story matches not only the plot of the epic *Iliou Persis*. It matches also the local mythology of the city of Scepsis, located in the region of Mount Ida. As we learn from Strabo (13.1.53 C607), Demetrius of Scepsis claimed explicitly that the *basileion* 'royal palace' of Aeneas was in Scepsis.

The idea of a city founded by Aeneas in the region of Mount Ida reflects the political interests of Ionians in general, not only of Scepsis in particular. To make this point, I start by focusing on two details reported by Demetrius of Scepsis, by way of Strabo (13.1.52 C607):

1. The city of Scepsis, after being founded by Aeneas, was ruled jointly by Ascanius (*Askanios*) son of Aeneas and Scamandrius (*Skamandrios*) son of Hector.
2. The population of Scepsis was augmented at a later period by immigrants from the Ionian city of Miletus, whose presence led to a democratic form of government for the city.

Scepsis had a special meaning for Ionians not only because this city was supposedly the site of the palace of the hero Aeneas but also because the ancient site of Troy was supposedly located within its territory, in the highlands of Mount Ida. Here was the *kōmē* 'village' of the *Ilieis* 'people of Ilion', the site that Demetrius identified with the old Ilion (Strabo 13.1.35–36 C597–98; also 13.1.25 C593).

So the Trojan War, according to this Ionian version, supposedly happened in territory that Ionians claimed as their own. And the relocation of Aeneas to Scepsis after the Trojan War meant that this city could become the legitimate heir to the Trojan heritage—all within the framework of its own Ionian territory. In terms of this particular Ionian version of the Trojan War, everything happened within the Ionian territory of Scepsis.

In contrast with the version of the Trojan War that suited the interests of the Ionians, the Aeolians claimed that Troy was in fact not totally destroyed and that some of its population survived to rebuild the old city of Ilion as New Ilion. This rival version was actively promoted by the historian Hellanicus of Lesbos, whose publications can be dated as far back as 406 B.C.E. (scholia for Aristophanes *Frogs* 694). I have already noted the claim that he makes in his *Trōika* (*FGH* 4 F 25b), as reported by Strabo (13.1.42 C602), that the city of New Ilion was in fact the same place as the old Ilion; Strabo adds, as I have also noted, that this claim of Hellanicus—who was a native of Aeolian Lesbos—reflects the historian's partiality toward the people of the Aeolian city of New Ilion.

Modern archaeology has proved that the claim of the Aeolians as represented by Hellanicus of Lesbos was basically right and that the rival claim of the Ionians as later represented by Demetrius of Scepsis was wrong. There is in fact no historical or archaeological support for the claim that the old Ilion was located in the Ionian territory of Scepsis.[137]

Here I stop to review the mutually contradictory mythological claims that we have seen so far concerning what happened to Troy after the Trojan War:

1. The Athenians claimed that Troy was totally destroyed by the Achaeans and left uninhabited, as we see from a statement made by Lycurgus the Athenian (*Against Leokrates* 62). Strabo accepted this claim as true (13.1.41 C601), adducing the internal evidence of the *Iliad* as proof of the total destruction of old Ilion. As we will see later, what Strabo adduces as internal evidence is not compelling.
2. The people of the Ionian city of Scepsis claimed that Troy, supposedly located in their territory, was totally destroyed by the Achaeans and left uninhabited. But they also claimed that some survivors were relocated in Scepsis. Our source is Demetrius of Scepsis (F 23 ed. Gaede), by way of Strabo (13.1.35–36 C597–98; also 13.1.25 C593).
3. The people of the Aeolian city of New Ilion claimed that Troy was not totally destroyed and was not left uninhabited. The Aeolians converted the ruins of Troy into the city of New Ilion. Our source is Strabo (13.1.40 C600), evidently following Demetrius. Strabo (13.1.42 C602) cites an important textual source supporting this claim, the *Trōika* of Hellanicus of Lesbos (*FGH* 4 F 25b).

---

137. There is an engaging account by Pfeiffer 1968:250–51.

In terms of the third of these three claims, according to which Troy was not completely abandoned after its capture by the Achaeans, there was not only a surviving population that stayed in old Ilion but also a dynasty that ruled over such a population. There are traces of a traditional narrative about such a dynasty in the *Trōïka* of Hellanicus of Lesbos (*FGH* 4 F 31), as reported by Dionysius of Halicarnassus (*Roman Antiquities* 1.45.4–48.1): according to this narrative, Aeneas himself was at least indirectly involved in such a dynasty. Here is a summary of what Hellanicus says:

1. After Aeneas escaped the capture of Troy by retreating to the highlands of Mount Ida, he negotiated with the victorious Achaeans his relocation to the city of *Aíneia* on the Thermaic Gulf.[138]
2. Meanwhile, his son Ascanius was relocated as king of Daskylitis on the coast of the Sea of Marmara.
3. Eventually, Ascanius returned to the old Ilion, where he joined forces with Scamandrius (*Skamandrios*) son of Hector in refounding it as the New Ilion.[139]

In terms of this Aeolian version, the joint rule of the descendants of Aeneas and Hector over New Ilion was not to last, as we see from the following report in the Homeric scholia:[140]

οἱ δέ, ὅτι Αἰολεῖς ἐξέβαλον τοὺς ἀπογόνους Αἰνείου.

Other people say that the Aeolians expelled the descendants of Aeneas.

Scholia T for *Iliad* XX 307–8a1 (exegetical scholia)

What is being explained in the scholia here is a prophecy made by Poseidon concerning the descendants of Aeneas, the Aeneadae. In the *Iliad* as we have it, the god is prophesying that the Aeneadae will survive the Trojan War and will rule their subjects forever (XX 306–8), but the context makes it clear that this rule will never happen in the old city of Troy, which will have to be destroyed completely (XX 309–17). I will quote at a later point the actual wording that prophesies the eternal rule of the Aeneadae, which will be relevant to a later stage of my argumentation. For now, however, I simply emphasize one fact about this prophecy: it implies that the Aeneadae will have to be relocated from Troy. According to the scholia we are considering here, one school of thought explains this relocation in terms of a Roman version: the claim is that Homer knew about the prophecy of the Sibyl concerning

138. On this city of *Aíneia*, see Leaf 1923:277 and Erskine 2001:93–98.
139. I cannot agree with the reasoning of Smith 1981:28–29, who thinks that the Aeolians would not have claimed an affinity with such a pairing of Scamandrius and Ascanius. I will have more to say presently about the political agenda implicit in such a claim.
140. There have been attempts to emend the text of the scholia to say that the Aeolians did *not* expel the Aeneadae. For a summary, see Aloni 1986:22–23, 112–13. As is evident from my interpretation of the existing text, I see no compelling reason to accept such an emendation.

the future of Aeneas in Italy (οἱ μὲν διὰ Ῥωμαίους φασίν, ἅπερ εἰδέναι τὸν ποιητὴν ἐκ τῶν Σιβύλλης χρησμῶν). By contrast, according to the same scholia, another school of thought explains the relocation of the Aeneadae in terms of an alternative version claiming that this dynasty was expelled from old Ilion by 'the Aeolians' (οἱ δέ, ὅτι Αἰολεῖς ἐξέβαλον τοὺς ἀπογόνους Αἰνείου).

In terms of this alternative version, the relocation of the Aeneadae is not predicated on the total destruction of Troy. Whereas the descendants of Aeneas are expelled from Troy, the descendants of Hector remain in the city, which has become transformed into New Ilion. As we have seen, our source for the essentials of this story is the *Trōïka* of Hellanicus of Lesbos (*FGH* 4 F 31), by way of Dionysius of Halicarnassus (*Roman Antiquities* 1.45.4–48.1). And, as we have also seen, this source follows an explicitly Aeolian tradition. After the Trojan War, according to this version of the story, New Ilion was ruled jointly by Ascanius the son of Aeneas and Scamandrius the son of Hector and by their descendants. But then, as we can see from the scholia T for *Iliad* XX (307–8a1), New Ilion was at a later time ruled exclusively by the descendants of Hector—after the descendants of Aeneas were expelled by 'the Aeolians'.

To be contrasted with this Aeolian tradition about the New Ilion is the Ionian tradition about Scepsis. In this case, as we have seen, our source is Demetrius of Scepsis, by way of Strabo (13.1.52 C607). After the Trojan War, according to this version of the story, Scepsis was first ruled by Aeneas. Then it was ruled jointly by Ascanius the son of Aeneas and Scamandrius the son of Hector and by their descendants. But then it was ruled democratically by a coalition including immigrants from the Ionian city of Miletus.

According to the Aeolian tradition about New Ilion, we see that Scamandrius represents the Aeolians who dominate New Ilion, while Ascanius represents the Ionians who are eventually expelled from the city. According to the Ionian tradition about Scepsis, by contrast, Scamandrius represents the non-Ionians who rule jointly with the Ionians the relocated "New Ilion" that is Scepsis, and the dominantly Ionian character of this city is then reinforced by Ionians immigrating from Miletus, leader of the Ionian Dodecapolis.

Neither of these versions of the myths surrounding Scamandrius son of Hector is represented in the Homeric *Iliad*, according to which the Trojans of the future will be ruled exclusively by the descendants of Aeneas, not by any descendants of Hector. The wording comes from the god Poseidon himself, who prophesies as follows:

νῦν δὲ δὴ Αἰνείαο βίη Τρώεσσιν ἀνάξει
καὶ παίδων παῖδες, τοί κεν μετόπισθε γένωνται.[141]

141. According to the scholia A for *Iliad* XX 308, there was this variant in the City Editions: λίπωνται 'will survive' instead of γένωνται 'will be born'. On the City Editions, see the Prolegomena to *HC*.

But, now I know, the power of Aeneas[142] will rule over the Trojans,
and so too will his son, and his son's sons who will be born thereafter.[143]

Iliad XX 307–8

Strabo (13.1.53 C608) quotes these same Homeric verses and then proceeds to
quote a variant version:

νῦν δὲ δὴ Αἰνείαο γένος πάντεσσιν ἀνάξει[144]
καὶ παίδων παῖδες, τοί κεν μετόπισθε γένωνται.

But, now I know, the lineage of Aeneas will rule over all,
and so too will his son, and his son's sons, who will be born thereafter.

Iliad XX 307–8 (variant)

Depending on whether we follow the first or the second of the two versions as
reflected in these two textual variants, we can say that the population to be ruled
by the lineage of Aeneas will be either the Trojans or all humanity (*Iliad* XX 307).
Either way, the point that is being made in both versions is that the lineage of Aeneas will last forever (XX 307–8), whereas the lineage of Hector the son of Priam
will be extinct (XX 302–6). The same point is being made in a prophecy of the goddess Aphrodite in the *Homeric Hymn* (6) *to Aphrodite* (196–97).

The future Trojans who are destined to be ruled by the descendants of Aeneas—
and not by the descendants of Hector—could not be equated with the population
of the New Ilion dominated by the Aeolians, who as we have seen ultimately expelled the descendants of Aeneas from their city (scholia T for *Iliad* XX 307–8a1).
Nor could these future Trojans be equated with the population of the would-be "New
Ilion" that was Scepsis, who were ruled not exclusively by Ascanius the son of Aeneas but jointly by him and by Scamandrius the son of Hector and grandson of
Priam. Rather, as I will argue, these future Trojans were imagined as the population controlled by the would-be "New Ilion" that was Sigeion, and this population
was to be ruled exclusively by the descendants of Aeneas, not of Hector.

The conflicting Aeolian and Ionian myths about Troy after the Trojan War can
be correlated with an eventual differentiation of New Ilion and Scepsis as, respectively, Aeolian and Ionian cities. We know by hindsight that New Ilion was in fact a
predominantly Aeolian city, whereas Scepsis, once an Aeolian city, eventually shifted
toward an Ionian identity.[145] The earlier Aeolian identity of Scepsis matches the iden-

---

142. Literally, the subject is a metonym: 'the power of Aeneas' is 'powerful Aeneas'.

143. According to the variant I mentioned just above: 'who will survive thereafter'.

144. According to the scholia A and T for this line, the reading is Αἰνείω γενεὴ πάντεσσιν ἀνάξει.
I infer that this variant was reported by Aristonicus: as I argue in the Prolegomena to *Homer the Classic*,
this Alexandrian editor was based in Rome, not in Alexandria.

145. Leaf 1923:273 notes a shift from Aeolic to Ionic dialect in the language found on the coinage
of Scepsis around the fifth century B.C.E.

tification of the Aeolians with the descendants of Hector, who ruled the city jointly with the descendants of Aeneas (Strabo 13.1.52 C607). And, conversely, the later Ionian identity of Scepsis matches the identification of the Ionians with the descendants of Aeneas.

This is not to say that the Aeneadae were all along perceived as Ionians. Their Ionian identity was merely a function of the eventual Ionian identity of places where they were relocated after the Trojan War, such as Scepsis. That is why the identity of the Aeneadae is in fact Aeolian rather than Ionian if they are relocated to places that have an Aeolian identity. We see an example in a myth about Aeneas as retold by the mythographer Conon, who flourished in the first century B.C.E. and C.E. According to this source (Conon *FGH* 26 F 1.46), Aeneas founded a settlement in the region of Mount Ida but was later displaced from there by two surviving sons of Hector, namely by Oxynios and *Skamandros* (F 1.46.2);[146] Aeneas then migrated to the Thermaic Gulf (F.1.46.3), where he founded the city of *Aíneia*, also known as *Aînos* (F.1.46.4). The same name, *Aînos,* applies to a city on the banks of the river Ebros; that city, and *Aíneia* as well, were Aeolian settlements.[147]

Here I return to the two Iliadic versions of the prophecy made by the god Poseidon to Aeneas, as reflected in the two attested textual variants in the *Iliad* (XX 307–8). According to one version, as we saw, the lineage of Aeneas will rule all of humanity, not only the Trojans of the future. This version of the Aeneas story became suitable for appropriation by the lineage of Julius Caesar, who as we saw claimed to be descended from Aeneas. In terms of this version, the descendants of Aeneas would one day rule all humankind, in that the Roman imperial rule of Caesar and his successors was viewed to be universal. According to the other version, it was the Trojans themselves who would be ruled forever by the descendants of Aeneas. This other version, as I will argue, equated these notional Trojans with the population of the territories controlled by the "New Troy" of Sigeion.

These notional Trojans of the future were Ionians—as redefined by Athens. Or, to put it another way, they were non-Aeolians. That is because the *Iliad* pointedly avoids equating these notional Trojans with the Aeolians of New Ilion, who claimed to be the new Trojans inhabiting the city where the old Ilion had once stood. In terms of the prophecy uttered by Poseidon in the *Iliad* as we have it, the New Ilion of the Aeolians was the one place where the new Trojans would not and could not live, since the old Troy would be utterly destroyed and the new Trojans would have to be relocated to another city. Even in terms of the Aeolian version of the Trojan story, as we have seen, the descendants of Aeneas would ultimately be expelled from

146. The second of these two sons of Hector, *Skamandros,* seems to be the same figure as the Aeolian *Skamandrios:* that is, Scamandrius.

147. Aloni 1986:76, 102n37; Debiasi 2004:192–93. Such Aeolian links with Aeneas may help account for traces of Aeolic traditions in the wording of the prophecy about Aeneas in the *Homeric Hymn* (6) *to Aphrodite* (196–97). See Aloni pp. 78–82.

the new Troy known as New Ilion. And we know for a fact that New Ilion became a non-Ionian and notionally all-Aeolian site. In the *Iliad*, then, New Ilion is taken out of consideration as a place for the Aeneadae to rule forever.

Strabo (13.1.53 C608) surveys various alternative places linked with various alternative versions concerning the destiny of these Aeneadae, and these alternative places include the Latin territory linked with the Roman *Aeneid* tradition. Here I simply focus on the most immediate alternative, which corresponds to a version that suits the Ionians. Strabo (13.1.52 C607) mentions it at an earlier point, referring to the testimony of Demetrius of Scepsis as his authority. We have already examined this testimony of Demetrius, and I offer here only a brief restatement. For the Ionians, the place destined to be ruled by the descendants of Aeneas was a would-be "New Ilion" in the highlands of Mount Ida, the city of Scepsis. And the old site of the real Troy, the old Ilion, was supposedly located in territory controlled by the city of Scepsis. Like Scepsis, the old site was located in the highlands of Mount Ida. When this site was destroyed without a trace at the end of the Trojan War, the surviving Trojans supposedly moved to this city of Scepsis, and here it was that they were ruled by Ascanius the son of Aeneas, jointly with Scamandrius the son of Hector.

Strabo (13.1.52 C607) adds a revealing detail about the evolution of Scepsis: as time went by, according to Demetrius, the Ionian identity of Scepsis was enhanced by immigrants from the Ionian city of Miletus. I have already drawn attention to this link of Scepsis with Miletus, noting that it reinforces the compatibility of this version with the Ionian tradition. But now I add that it also highlights an emerging incompatibility with the Aeolian tradition.

I propose to review further the links between Scepsis and Miletus, but first I need to focus on the most salient example of ultimate incompatibility between the Ionian and the Aeolian versions of the actual location of ancient Troy. According to the Ionian version as restated by Demetrius and then by Strabo, the site of the old Ilion was the *kōmē* 'village' of the *Ilieis* 'people of Ilion' in the territory of Scepsis, some thirty stadia away from New Ilion (13.1.35–36 C597–98; also 13.1.25 C593). To repeat, it was this 'village of the people of Ilion' that had been the site of the old Ilion, Demetrius claims, despite his concession that he could see absolutely no trace of any epic ruins there.

The Trojan connections of Scepsis were not limited to this city's claim that 'the village of the people of Ilion', which was under its control, had once been the sacred ground of the real Troy of the Trojan War. The city also made direct claims to a hero who figures so prominently in the Trojan War, Aeneas. Not only was the city nominally ruled by the descendants of Aeneas. Scepsis also claimed to be the original site of the *basileion* 'royal palace' of Aeneas, as we have already seen from the testimony of Demetrius of Scepsis (by way of Strabo 13.1.53 C607). By implication, it was this palace that became the stronghold of the dynasty of Aeneas that survived the Trojan War.

The Aeneadae of the city of Scepsis represented the Ionians not only because Scepsis eventually became an Ionian city. More specifically, Scepsis was closely connected to the Ionian city of Miletus, which once dominated the federation of Ionian cities known as the Ionian Dodecapolis. So the connection here is not only Ionian in general but also Milesian in particular. As we have seen earlier, this Milesian connection is made explicit by Demetrius of Scepsis (by way of Strabo 13.1.52 C607), who reports that the Ionian identity of Scepsis was enhanced by immigrants from Miletus.

This Milesian connection of Scepsis is represented not only by the status of Aeneas as an adoptive dynastic hero of the city's predominantly Ionian population but also by his status as an epic hero who fought in the Trojan War. Here I return to the Ionian epic tradition about Aeneas that became part of the epic Cycle and was known as the *Iliou Persis*, an epic attributed to Arctinus of Miletus. As we have seen earlier, this Milesian epic narrates how Aeneas and his followers withdrew from Troy before its total destruction and moved back to his home in the highlands of Mount Ida (Proclus summary p. 107.24–26 ed. Allen).

There is a clear sign of this Ionian epic tradition in the Homeric narrative about the rescue of Aeneas by the god Poseidon in *Iliad* XX (290–352). This god, although he is generally pro-Achaean in the *Iliad*, has a special link to the figure of Aeneas. That is because Poseidon also has a special link to the Ionians belonging to the federation of the Ionian Dodecapolis headed by Miletus: as Poseidon *Helikōnios*, he was the chief god of the Panionion, the sacred site of the festival of the Panionia, which expressed the communality of the twelve cities of the Ionian Dodecapolis as headed by the city of Miletus (Pausanias 7.24.5, scholia **bT** for *Iliad* XX 404).

So far, in my survey of the Ionian and the Aeolian versions of the story of Troy's destruction, I have highlighted a point of mutual agreement. According to both the Ionian and the Aeolian versions, the new Trojan dynasty that succeeded the doomed old Trojan dynasty of Priam began with the joint rule of Ascanius the son of Aeneas and Scamandrius the son of Hector. We have seen that Demetrius of Scepsis follows the Ionian tradition about a new Troy under such a joint rule in Scepsis. And, earlier, we have seen that Hellanicus of Lesbos in his *Trōïka* (*FGH* 4 F 31) follows a corresponding Aeolian tradition about a new Troy under such a joint rule in New Ilion. Though the two traditions contradict each other about the place where the dynasty rules, they agree about the identities of the rulers.

In their mutual agreement, however, these two traditions are pointedly contradicted by a third tradition, which corresponds to what we find in the *Iliad* itself. To show this contradiction, I highlight a verse in the *Andromache* of Euripides (224), where Andromache speaks of the *nothoi* 'bastards' of Hector whom she nursed at her breast along with the legitimate son that the couple had together.[148] According to the scholia for this verse, Scamandrius was one of those bastards, and he is described as the son of Hector who survives the destruction of Troy and escapes to the highlands of Mount Ida (Σκαμάνδριος γὰρ ἀφικνεῖται εἰς τὰ ἐν Ἴδῃ).

By contrast, the son that Hector and Andromache had together does not escape. According to the Aeolian tradition as preserved in the epic named the *Little Iliad*, attributed to Lesches of Lesbos, this son of Hector is killed by the son of Achilles, Neoptolemos, after the capture of Troy (F 19.1–5); then Neoptolemos takes away as his Trojan war-prize not only Andromache (F 19.6–8) but even Aeneas himself (F 19.9–11).[149] There is another relevant detail in the Aeolian tradition: as we learn from Hellanicus of Lesbos (*FGH* 4 F 31), Scamandrius too is taken away by Neoptolemos as a war prize, but later he is released and allowed to go back to Ilion. In the exegetical scholia T for *Iliad* XXIV (735b) we read this revealing note about the son of Hector and Andromache: οἱ δὲ νεώτεροί φασιν αὐτὸν οἰκιστὴν ὕστερον γεγενῆσθαι Τροίας καὶ ἄλλων πόλεων 'according to the newer poets [*neōteroi*], he [Scamandrius] later became the founder of Troy and of other cities'. The term *neōteroi* 'newer poets' here fits poets of the epic Cycle like Lesches of Lesbos, poet of the *Little Iliad*.

What we have just seen in the Aeolian epic tradition as represented by Lesches of Lesbos can also be seen in the Ionian epic tradition as represented by Arctinus of Miletus. Likewise in this tradition, as we know from the epic of the *Iliou Persis* attributed to Arctinus of Miletus, the son that Hector and Andromache had together does not escape (F 2 ed. Allen, via scholia to Euripides *Andromache* 10). The same can be said about the Dorian tradition as represented by Stesichorus (*PMG* 202). In the case of the Ionian tradition of the Milesian *Iliou Persis*, we know of further details: the name of the doomed son is Astyanax, and his killer is not Neoptolemos but Odysseus (Proclus summary p. 108.8–9 ed. Allen).

To be contrasted with these Aeolian, Ionian, and Dorian versions is another version of the narrative, as preserved in the *Iliad*: here the death of the son that Hector and Andromache had together is explicitly prophesied by Andromache (*Iliad* XXIV 735), and here again the son's name is Astyanax (VI 403; XXII 500, 506). This time, however, the name Astyanax is said to be synonymous with Scamandrius (VI 402). This Iliadic version, by merging the identity of Scamandrius with that of Astyanax, eliminates the surviving son of Hector. Thus it contradicts the Aeolian tradition, which locates the new dynasty in New Ilion. And it also contradicts the Ionian tradition, even though that tradition locates the new dynasty not in New Il-

---

148. Andromache's reference here (Euripides *Andromache* 224) to her nursing the bastards of Hector when she was a queen is meant to contrast with the hostility of Hermione toward the bastard Molossos whom Andromache bore as a slave concubine of Neoptolemos: see Ebbott 2003:75–76.

149. There is a useful commentary in Aloni 1986:62–63.

ion but in Scepsis. In both cities, Scepsis as well as New Ilion, Scamandrius is part of the dynastic picture, sharing it with Ascanius.

Strabo (13.1.53 C608) notices the contradiction between what the *Iliad* says and what all the other versions say, including the preferred version of Demetrius. In the *Iliad*, it is prophesied that Aeneas and his descendants will rule over the Trojans. There is simply no room for Hector and his descendants—not for Astyanax, not even for Scamandrius. So Strabo is forced to contradict even Demetrius by admitting that the place where the Aeneadae will rule is not Scepsis—nor any of the other alternative places favored in other versions.

Strabo's logic here is on the mark. And we can take it further. The truth is, the place where the Aeneadae will rule must be the Troy of the *Iliad*, which is not necessarily the real Troy of Bronze Age archaeology.

From everything we have seen so far, this Troy of the *Iliad* is a fundamentally Athenian construct, and the visualization of this construct is based not on the New Ilion that was the old Ilion. Rather, it is based on the would-be New Ilion that was Sigeion.[150]

In the Iliadic version of the story of Troy's destruction, as we saw earlier, Aeneas survives that destruction, so that he and his descendants may rule the Trojans for the rest of time. From the standpoint of Athenian political interests, the prophesied rule of the Aeneadae over the new Trojans cannot be situated in the New Ilion of the Aeolians, which is a rival of Sigeion, the Iliadic city of the Athenians. And the Iliadic version of the overall Aeneas story affirms the Athenian interests by contradicting the Aeolian version, according to which the new Trojans will be ruled jointly by the descendants of Aeneas and the descendants of Hector—until the Aeolians finally succeed in excluding the Aeneadae altogether from New Ilion.

According to the Aeolian version as represented by Hellanicus of Lesbos, the new Trojans are destined to be ruled exclusively by the descendants of Hector in New Ilion. According to the Ionian version as represented by Demetrius of Scepsis, the new Trojans are destined to be ruled jointly by the descendants of Aeneas and the descendants of Hector in Scepsis. But according to the version preserved in the *Iliad*, the new Trojans are destined to be ruled exclusively by the descendants of Aeneas.

The Iliadic version of the Trojan War makes a clean break with both the Aeolian and the Ionian versions, in that the *Iliad* kills off Scamandrius by merging him with Astyanax, the child that Hector had with Andromache.[151] In this way, the *Iliad* affirms the Athenian version of the Trojan War. The Athenian reception of Homeric poetry was incompatible with the idea that the descendants of Hector

---

150. A similar point is made by Aloni 1986:94, though his line of argumentation differs from mine.

151. Smith 1981:57 thinks that the identification of Scamandrius with Astyanax is an Iliadic innovation.

would rule over New Ilion after the destruction of the old Ilion. Such an idea was evidently too close to the Aeolian reality of the New Ilion.

From the standpoint of the *Iliad*, as articulated in the prophecy of Poseidon concerning the future of Aeneas and his descendants, the future populations to be ruled by the Aeneadae would be imagined as Ionians—that is, Ionians as ultimately redefined by Athens. What is implied by the prophecy is an Ionian Aeneas who escapes the total destruction of Troy and relocates to territory controlled by Sigeion, a would-be new Troy for Athens in its imperial role as the notional mother city of all Ionians.

To be contrasted is the would-be Aeolian Aeneas whose new Troy would have been New Ilion—if only the Aeneadae had not been expelled from there in later times. Also to be contrasted is a more narrowly conceived Ionian Aeneas whose new Troy is Scepsis, where his descendants have to share the rule with the descendants of Hector. By the time of Strabo, this Ionian Aeneas of Scepsis eclipsed a more broadly conceived Ionian Aeneas associated with Sigeion and with Athens. That is because the city of Sigeion was already extinct by this time, as we saw earlier.

By contrast with the Iliadic version, which precludes any future for the Aeolian reality of a New Ilion ruled by the descendants of Hector, Athenian mythmaking could accommodate an attenuated version of that Aeolian reality, and such a version is in fact attested:

Στησίχορον μὲν γὰρ ἱστορεῖν ὅτι τεθνήκοι καὶ τὸν τὴν Πέρσιδα συντεταχότα κυκλικὸν ποιητὴν ὅτι καὶ ἀπὸ τοῦ τείχους ῥιφθείη· ᾧ ἠκολουθηκέναι Εὐριπίδην. εἰσί γε μὲν οἵ φασιν αὐτὸν καὶ πόλεις οἰκίσαι καὶ βασιλεῦσαι, ὧν τὰς δόξας Λυσίμαχος ἐν τῷ δευτέρῳ τῶν Νόστων ἀνέγραψεν· Διονύσιος δὲ ὁ Χαλκιδεὺς τὸν Ἀκάμαντα παρὰ Ἑλένου καὶ Ἀγχίσου φησὶ ‹διὰ› τὴν πρὸς Λαοδίκην οἰκειότητα Σκαμάνδριον τὸν Ἕκτορος εἰλη- φότα καὶ Ἀσκάνιον τὸν Αἰνείου ἐπιχειρῆσαι μὲν Ἴλιον καὶ Δάρδανον τειχίζειν, τῶν δὲ Ἀθηναίων αὐτὸ παραιτησαμένων, τηνικαῦτα τῆς ἐπιβολῆς ἀποστάντα τῆς Τρῳάδος Γέργιθα καὶ Περκώτην καὶ Κολωνὰς καὶ Χρύσην καὶ Ὀφρύνιον καὶ Σιδήνην καὶ Ἄστυρα καὶ Σκῆψιν καὶ Πολίχναν καὶ πρὸς τούτοις Δασκύλειον καὶ Ἰλίου κολώνην καὶ Ἀρίσβαν οἰκίσαντα ἀναγορεῦσαι οἰκιστὰς Σκαμάνδριον καὶ Ἀσκάνιον."

Stesichorus [*PMG* 202] attests that he [Astyanax] was killed, and the poet of the Cycle who composed the *Iliou Persis* [F 2 ed. Allen] attests that he [Astyanax] was thrown off the walls of Troy. And Euripides has followed this tradition. But there are those who say that he [the son of Hector] founded cities and ruled as king over them, and the opinions of these sources are written up by Lysimachus in the second book of his *Nostoi*: "Dionysius of Chalkis says that Akamas [of Athens], having taken (through his ties with Laodike) [1] Scamandrius the son of Hector and [2] Ascanius the son of Aeneas from [1] Helenos and from [2] Anchises, attempted to fortify with walls Ilion and Dardanos, but when the Athenians entreated him not to do so, then, having stopped his attempt at controlling the region of Troy, went on to found the cities of Gergis, Perkōtē, Kolōnai, Khrusē, Ophrynion, Sidēnē, Astyra, Scepsis, Polikhnē, and in addition to these, Daskyleion and Iliou Kolōnē and Arisba,[152] designating as founders of these cities Scamandrius and Ascanius."[153]

> Scholia for Euripides *Andromache* 10 (ed. Schwartz 1891),
> citing Lysimachus of Alexandria (ca. 200 B.C.E.: *FGH* 382 F 9),
> who quotes Dionysius of Chalkis (fourth century B.C.E.)

What we see here is a synthesis of Aeolian and Ionian versions—under the overriding control of an Athenian version. In the *Iliad* as we have it, by contrast, we see an unattenuated Athenocentric version that leaves no room for alternative Aeolian or Ionian versions. Strabo himself evidently took the position of agreeing with this unattenuated Athenocentric version of the *Iliad* as we have it, not with the attenuated Athenocentric version that leaves room for the rival Aeolian and Ionian versions. In taking this position, Strabo was not being pro-Athenocentric, nor was he being anti-Aeolian or anti-Ionian. Rather, he preferred the Iliadic version as we have it simply because he was trying to be antineoteric. In other words, he dismissed those aspects of Homeric poetry that Aristarchus and his followers would have labeled *neoteric*—that is, post-Homeric. As we saw earlier, the Aristarchean school labeled as *neoteric* anything they considered to be non-Homeric.[154] For Strabo, the total destruction of Troy is basically a Homeric theme, and any attenuation is neoteric: that is, post-Homeric.

Strabo (13.1.41 C601) cites Homeric passages that he interprets to mean that the destruction of Troy was total (*Iliad* VI 448, XII 15; *Odyssey* iii 130). In making his argument for the total destruction of Troy (1.2.4 C17, as well as 13.1.41 C601), he also cites other supposedly Homeric passages—passages not attested in the medieval manuscript tradition of the *Iliad* and *Odyssey*. There is an irony here, since these other passages cited by Strabo could be seen retrospectively as neoteric (that is, post-Homeric). Strabo has thus managed to produce otherwise unknown neoteric variants in his attempt to show that Homer is not neoteric.

Because he insists on the tradition that tells how Troy was totally destroyed, Strabo eliminates from consideration some important rival traditions. Chief among these are the traditions preserved and promoted by the inhabitants of New Ilion. A case in point is a complex of myths and rituals concerning the Locrian Maidens (13.1.41 C600). Strabo mentions only in passing this important complex of non-Ionian myths and rituals. Also mentioned only in passing is a most precious detail about the old statue of Athena in the temple of the goddess at New Ilion: this statue, as Strabo says in passing, is figured in a standing position (13.1.41

---

152. All the Aeolian cities listed here are in the general area of the Troad. So it is not that Akamas of Athens really stopped his attempt to control the Troad: in terms of the narrative, he simply stopped his attempt to fortify Ilion (that is, New Ilion) and Dardanos with new walls.

153. Helpful remarks in Aloni 1986:20.

154. See above, chapter 3, the section entitled "A Post-Athenocentric View of the *Homēridai*."

C601). By contrast, the statue of the goddess as represented in the *Iliad* is figured in a seated position (VI 303). Strabo makes a grand effort in arguing against those who make the claim that the wording of our *Iliad* can be understood to mean that the statue was really standing after all rather than sitting (again, 13.1.41 C601). Strabo's point is well taken, but his efforts would have been better spent if he had given his readers more details about other statues he mentions in passing—statues representing the goddess in a standing rather than seated position, as in Phocaea, Chios, and so on (once again, 13.1.41 C601). In any case, the overall evidence of archaic Greek traditions in the visual arts shows that the goddess could be represented in either a standing or a seated position. So the real question is not whether but why the statue of the goddess in the *Iliad* is represented in a seated position (VI 303).

My answer centers on the statue of Athena that had once been housed in the temple of the goddess in Sigeion. I propose that this statue represented Athena in a seated position and that the relevant passage as we see it in the *Iliad* refers to this seated statue in Sigeion, not to the standing statue in New Ilion. Earlier on, I argued that the city of Sigeion, claimed by the goddess Athena as her very own place in the production of the *Oresteia* of Aeschylus in 458 B.C.E., must have been viewed as an Asiatic replica of the ultimate place of Athena, the city of Athens. Now I am ready to argue that the very idea of an Asiatic Athens is matched by the idea of an Asiatic Athena Polias who resides in her temple at Sigeion—the same temple indicated by the references we saw in Alcaeus (F 401B, via Strabo 13.1.37 C600) and Herodotus (5.95.1). Such a statue of the goddess would have been a rival of the statue of Athena in her temple at New Ilion.

The closest thing to this reconstruction of an unattested archaic seated statue of Athena Polias in Sigeion is an attested seated Athena Polias in the Ionian city of Erythrai, which is described as follows:

ἔστι δὲ ἐν Ἐρυθραῖς καὶ Ἀθηνᾶς Πολιάδος ναὸς καὶ ἄγαλμα ξύλου μεγέθει μέγα καθήμενόν τε ἐπὶ θρόνου καὶ ἠλακάτην ἐν ἑκατέρᾳ τῶν χειρῶν ἔχει καὶ ἐπὶ τῆς κεφαλῆς πόλον· τοῦτο Ἐνδοίου τέχνην καὶ ἄλλοις ἐτεκμαιρόμεθα εἶναι καὶ ἐς τὴν ἐργασίαν ὁρῶντες ‹τοῦ› ἀγάλματος καὶ οὐχ ἥκιστα ἐπὶ ταῖς Χάρισί τε καὶ Ὥραις, αἳ πρὶν ἐσελθεῖν ἐστήκασιν ἐν ὑπαίθρῳ λίθου λευκοῦ.

There is also in Erythrai a temple [*nāós*] of Athena Polias and a huge wooden statue [*agalma*][155] of her sitting on a throne. She holds a distaff in each hand and wears a Vault of the Sky [*polos*] on her head. That this statue is the work [*tekhnē*] of Endoios we inferred by observing, among other things, the workmanship [*ergasia*] that went into the making of the statue [*agalma*] and especially on the basis of the white marble

---

155. The statue of Athena in her temple on the acropolis of Troy is called an *agalma* in Alcaeus (F 298.21).

representations of the Kharites and the Hōrai that stand in the open area before you go into the temple.

Pausanias 7.5.9

A statue of Athena residing in her temple at Sigeion need not be imagined as a masterpiece of Athenian or even Ionian art. It may have been a masterpiece of Aeolian art, since the city of Sigeion had once been Aeolian—just as New Ilion, site of the rival statue of the goddess, was still Aeolian. Nevertheless, the Athenians would have claimed such a statue residing in her temple at Sigeion as their very own Asiatic Athena Polias, just as they claimed the city of Sigeion as their very own Asiatic Athens. In 458 B.C.E., at the dramatic moment of the *Oresteia* when the goddess Athena herself is imagined as arriving from her city of Sigeion and speaking in her city of Athens, she refers to her sacred space in Sigeion as her new home (Aeschylus *Eumenides* 397–404). This moment predates by twenty years the installation of the definitive Athena Parthenos of Pheidias in her new temple on the acropolis of Athens in 438 B.C.E. Back in 458 B.C.E., an Athenian audience would be expected to picture the newly acquired Athena Polias residing in her temple in Sigeion in terms of the old Athena Polias residing in her temple on the acropolis in Athens. Pausanias describes the statue of Athena Polias in Athens (1.26.4), and he reports a myth that tells how this statue had fallen from the sky (1.26.6). (There is a comparable myth about the Palladium on the acropolis at Troy: it too had fallen from the sky ["Apollodorus" *Library* 3.12.3].) In brief, what we see being re-enacted by the verbal art of *Iliad* VI (303) is a new conceptualization of the old statue of Athena Polias.

Not only is Athena Polias at Athens matched by a Trojan Athena Polias at Sigeion. The attendant of Athena Polias at Athens, the Athenian hero called Erikhthonios, is matched by a Trojan hero called Erikhthonios. As we learn from *Iliad* XX (219, 230), the Trojan Erikhthonios was son of Dardanos and father of Tros, the ancestor of Aeneas. This match between the Athenian Erikhthonios and the Trojan Erikhthonios of the Dardanidai can be explained in terms of a differentiation of the Athenian figure of Erekhtheus into an earlier figure called Erikhthonios and a later figure called Erekhtheus in the official Athenian genealogy of kings. The sequencing of the Athenian Erikhthonios in this Athenian genealogy is synchronized with the sequencing of the Trojan Erikhthonios in the Trojan genealogy that culminates with Aeneas in the *Iliad*.[156] So the differentiation of the Athenian hero Erekhtheus into

---

156. See Heitsch 1965:128 on the synchronization of the Athenian Erikhthonios with the Trojan Erikhthonios. Also p. 124 on the appropriation of Erikhthonios around 610 B.C.E., when the Athenians appropriate Sigeion; also pp. 129–30 on the Athenian appropriation of Athena in the Troad, and on the relationship between this appropriation and the passage in *Iliad* VI referring to the Trojan women's offering of a peplos to Athena in her temple on the acropolis. In this context, Heitsch p. 129 also connects the reference in Aeschylus *Eumenides* 397–402 to Athena in the Troad.

an earlier Erikhthonios and a later Erekhtheus serves to connect the local Athenian hero with the epic Trojan hero Erikhthonios, ancestor of Aeneas. This way, the prestige of the Trojan genealogy of the Dardanidai, culminating in the dynastic figure of the epic hero Aeneas, is appropriated into the Athenian genealogy of kings. A signal of this Athenian appropriation in the *Iliad* is the pointed reference to four chariot horses owned by Anchises, father of Aeneas (V 271), complemented by two chariot horses owned by Aeneas himself (V 272).[157] As we learn from the Parian Marble (*FGH* 239, section 10), the Athenians claimed that Erikhthonios was the inventor of the four-horse chariot, on the occasion of the first chariot race held at the first Panathenaic festival in 1505/4 B.C.E.[158] So the Iliadic reference to the four-horse chariot team of Anchises is an implicit Athenian signature. To be contrasted are the two-horse chariot teams used by almost all warriors, including Aeneas himself (V 270–72), for fighting battles in the Trojan War. An exception is the four-horse chariot team used by Hector (VIII 185). He too, like Aeneas, is a descendant of the Dardanidai (XX 240).[159] So here again we see an implicit Athenian signature, since both Aeneas and Hector were appropriated by the Athenians in their version of the Trojan story.

In the course of time, something catastrophic happened to the Athenian frame of reference in the Troad: the total destruction of Sigeion. As we have seen, Strabo goes out of his way to describe the city of Sigeion as completely 'demolished' in his own time, and his wording makes clear that no stone was left in place (13.1.31 C595 κατεσπασμένη πόλις). Once this city was destroyed, the Athenian frame of reference was obliterated. Gone forever was the temple of Athena at Sigeion, a prime epic landmark for the Athenians. The Aeolian frame of reference could now be restored, and this restoration was furthered in the Roman era through the patronage accorded to New Ilion by Julius Caesar (13.1.27 C594–95). By favoring New Ilion, Caesar and his successors favored the Aeolian version of the Trojan story and obliterated the rival Athenian version. In this rival version, as we saw, Aeneas and his descendants were linked with Sigeion as a new Troy that was destined to rule the Ionian populations of the Troad. After the Roman intervention, however, Aeneas and his son Ascanius or *Iulus* were appropriated as founders of the new Troy that was Rome. Also, the Aeolian New Ilion was appropriated as the old Troy. Because of this second appropriation, Aeneas was eclipsed as a founder of Ionian cities like Scepsis: he was now primarily the founder of Rome, and the Ionian traditions about Aeneas and his descendants became marginalized and even trivialized. So, in the

157. The narrative introduces these two sets of chariot horses by saying that Anchises secretly bred six horses from the original chariot horses given by Zeus to Tros in compensation for the abduction of Ganymede (*Iliad* V 263–70); of these six, he kept four for himself and gave two to Aeneas (V 271–72).

158. According to the Parian Marble (*FGH* 239 section 23) Troy was captured in 1209/8 B.C.E.

159. Otherwise, Homeric references to four-horse chariot teams are confined to references to chariots used in chariot racing as distinct from warfare (*Iliad* XI 699–702, *Odyssey* xiii 81–83).

end, the Aeolian version of the Trojan story won out over the Ionian version as primarily defined by Athens.

The Roman appropriation of Troy and the Trojan story produced another result. Just as the Athenian version of the Trojan story lost out to the older Aeolian version because of the Romans, so also the Athenian version of Homer—the Homeric Koine—lost out to the Homerus Auctus, as edited in the Library of Pergamon and as appropriated in the epic poetry of Virgil. Below in the Epilegomena to this volume, I will explain the distinction I am making here between Athenian and Pergamene versions of Homer, as represented, respectively, by the Homeric Koine and the Homerus Auctus.

HOMER THE IONIAN REVISITED

In what we have just seen, I concentrated on a distant past dating back to a time when the Aeolians of Asia Minor were being pressured from the north by the Athenians and eventually lost to them the old Aeolian city of Sigeion, the site where Achilles, premier hero of the Aeolians, was believed to be buried in a tumulus situated nearby on the Sigeion Ridge. At an earlier stage of my argumentation, I had concentrated on another aspect of the distant past, when the Aeolians of Asia Minor were being pressured from the south by the Ionians and eventually lost to them the old Aeolian city of Smyrna, the site where Homer, premier poet of the Aeolians, was believed to have been born. In what follows, I return to the subject of this second loss suffered by the Aeolians of Asia Minor, which actually took place earlier than the loss of Sigeion. This earlier loss of Smyrna, like the later loss of Sigeion, had a permanent impact on the form and the content of Homeric poetry as we know it. Because of this loss, Homer became irrevocably Ionian.

After Aeolian Smyrna was captured by the Ionians and thus ceased to be a member of the federation known as the Aeolian Dodecapolis, Homer the Aeolian could become Homer the Ionian, just as Aeolian Smyrna became Ionian Smyrna. After the capture of Smyrna, as we saw earlier from what Herodotus says (1.150.2), the Aeolian population of the city was absorbed by the remaining eleven Aeolian cities of the old federation. Evidently, the capture of Smyrna was a collective defeat for the Aeolian Dodecapolis, with the subtraction of one city from their own existing twelve; and it was a collective victory for the rival federation of the Ionian Dodecapolis, though Smyrna was not added to the existing twelve cities as a thirteenth.[160]

---

160. There is a reference to the capture of 'Aeolian' Smyrna by Colophon in Mimnermus (F 9 ed. West), as quoted by Strabo (14.1.4 C633). On all matters related to the Ionization of Smyrna, I am indebted to the advice of Douglas Frame. For an essential discussion of the Ionian Dodecapolis and its role in the making of Homeric poetry in the late eighth and the early seventh century B.C.E., see Frame 2009 chs. 10 and 11.

According to Strabo (14.1.4 C633), Smyrna was eventually added to the federation of twelve Ionian cities, the Ionian Dodecapolis. As we will see, the idea that Smyrna actually became one of the twelve members of this Ionian confederation in the archaic period is anachronistic. Still, as I noted earlier, the wording of Herodotus indicates that Smyrna had requested membership in the Ionian Dodecapolis:

> αἱ δὲ δυώδεκα πόλιες αὗται τῷ τε οὐνόματι ἠγάλλοντο καὶ ἱρὸν ἱδρύσαντο ἐπὶ σφέων αὐτέων, τῷ οὔνομα ἔθεντο **Πανιώνιον**, ἐβουλεύσαντο δὲ αὐτοῦ μεταδοῦναι μηδαμοῖσι ἄλλοισι Ἰώνων—οὐδ᾽ ἐδεήθησαν δὲ οὐδαμοὶ μετασχεῖν ὅτι μὴ Σμυρναῖοι.

> But these twelve cities took pride in the name ['Ionian'] and established a sacred space of their own, giving it the name **Panionion**, and they wished to give membership to no other Ionians [Ionian cities]—nor did any Ionians [any other Ionian city] request it except for the Smyrnaeans.

> Herodotus 1.143.3

Smyrna had already turned Ionian by the time of the twenty-third Olympiad (Pausanias 5.8.7): that is, by the end of the eighth century. I quote this apt formulation: "[Smyrna], lying more than ten miles south of the [river] Hermus, and having Phocaea on the coast between it and Cyme, belonged naturally to the Ionian sphere."[161] The Ionization of Smyrna is evident in the *Homeric Hymn* (9) to Artemis, where the Ionian site of Klaros is ostentatiously linked with Smyrna and with the river Meles (connected in the local lore with Homer's alternative name *Melēsigenēs*) in a description of the territorial domain of the goddess (verses 3–6). Then, toward the end of the seventh century, Ionian Smyrna was destroyed by the Lydian empire, and this point in time can serve as a *terminus ante quem* for the description that we find in *Homeric Hymn* 9.[162] After this point, Smyrna ceased to exist, and it became known as one of the three proverbial extinct cities of archaic Greek poetry, along with Colophon and Magnesia-at-Sipylus.[163] According to Strabo (14.1.37 C646), Smyrna remained a noncity for hundreds of years, inhabited only 'in the mode of a *kōmē*' (κωμηδόν)—that is, in the mode of a 'village'—but then, toward the end of the fourth century B.C.E., the city was refounded by Antigonus and then once again refounded by Lysimachus.[164] So Smyrna was refounded at around the same time that New Ilion was refounded. As we saw earlier, Strabo (13.1.26 C593) reports that Alexander the Great transformed the site of New Ilion from a *kōmē* 'village' into a

---

161. How and Wells 1928: I, 124. On the dating of the loss of Smyrna by the Aeolians to the Ionians, see also Frame 2009:526n21.

162. Graziosi 2002:75.

163. See *PH* 9§§20–23 (= pp. 263–66) for an overview of passages referring to Smyrna, Colophon, and Magnesia-at-Sipylus as extinct cities.

164. In this passage of Strabo (14.1.37 C646), the notional refounding of Smyrna by Antigonus leads to another refounding by Lysimachus.

polis 'city' and that the transformation was continued by Alexander's would-be successor Lysimachus.[165] Like the New Ilion, which kept its previous Aeolian identity after its notional refounding, the new Smyrna kept its previous Ionian identity after its own refounding.

According to Strabo (14.1.4 C633), Smyrna was later added to the federation of twelve Ionian cities (that is, to the Ionian Dodecapolis), but he does not say whether the city's membership is to be dated after the refounding. Strabo does say, however, that the people of Smyrna had a special claim to Homer, and that they maintained a sacred precinct called the *Homēreion*, where the Poet was worshipped as a cult hero (14.1.37 C646).

As we see from this particular formulation by Strabo, the status of Smyrna as a member of the Ionian Dodecapolis after its refounding in the Hellenistic era was far less significant than its status as the primary claimant to the honor of being the birthplace of Homer. By this time, the membership of Smyrna in the Ionian Dodecapolis no longer had any significant effect on the identity of Homer. That is because the status of the Ionian Dodecapolis itself went into a drastic decline in the era that followed the destruction of Ionian Smyrna by the Lydian empire.

In the preceding era, however, the status of a city like Smyrna did in fact have a most significant effect on the identity of Homer. That is because the tradition of Homeric poetry was still in a formative phase at the time when Ionian Smyrna was destroyed by the Lydians and thus lost by the Ionians—and this time is not far removed from when Aeolian Sigeion was lost forever to the Athenians by the Aeolians.

This time marks a major difference in what subsequently happened to these two formerly Aeolian cities of Asia Minor. After the destruction of Smyrna by the Lydian empire toward the end of the seventh century B.C.E., that city ceased to exist for hundreds of years—to repeat Strabo's estimate of the chronology. Meanwhile, all during that period, the city of Sigeion continued to exist as an Athenocentric extension of Athens, an Asiatic Athens in the Troad, until it was finally obliterated around the same time when Smyrna was refounded as a city. For some three hundred years, then, the tradition of Homeric poetry was evolving in the context of an audience reception that recognized Sigeion as the definitive point of reference for visualizing the epic action in the Troad, and this particular point of reference was Athenocentric in its poetics as well as its politics. To put it another way, Sigeion was the Athenocentric lens through which the tradition of Homeric poetry continued to view the topography of the Troad for these three hundred years. Conversely, all during this period, nothing of Panhellenic importance was happening in Smyrna.

165. In this passage of Strabo (13.1.26 C593), the notional refounding of Ilion by Alexander leads to another refounding by Lysimachus; meanwhile, the founding of Antigonia by Antigonus leads to its refounding as Alexandria-in-the-Troad by Lysimachus. Strabo observes that Lysimachus made more of an effort in refounding Alexandria-in-the-Troad than he did in refounding the New Ilion.

By the time that Smyrna was refounded in the Hellenistic era by the dynasts I mentioned a moment ago, the tradition of Homeric poetry was no longer in a formative phase. And it no longer mattered whether Smyrna had once been Aeolian or Ionian.

The same can be said about the refounding of New Ilion by the same dynasts. By the Hellenistic era, to repeat, the tradition of Homeric poetry was no longer in a formative phase. So, by now, the question of whether or not New Ilion was really the same thing as the old Ilion was of little importance for the tradition of Homeric poetry. Also of little importance was the question of whether the tomb of Achilles was situated at the northern end of the Sigeion Ridge or at the southern end. Some three hundred years earlier, however, when the Athenians were struggling with the Aeolians over the territory of Sigeion, these same questions had been all-important. When the Aeolians succeeded in winning back through arbitration the tomb of Achilles at the south end of the Sigeion Ridge, the poetic as well as the political impact had been strong enough to force the Athenians to claim as a rival tomb of Achilles another tumulus situated at the north end of the Sigeion Ridge. It is this Athenocentric version of the tomb of Achilles that we see being pictured in the Homeric poetry of the *Iliad*, which as I have argued views the topography of the Troad through the Athenocentric lens of Sigeion. I should add that such an Athenocentric view is also an Ionian view: as we will see more clearly in what follows, Athenocentric trends in Homeric poetry were mostly a continuation of earlier Ionian trends emanating ultimately from Miletus.[166]

Some three hundred years later, in the Hellenistic era, when the Aeolian city of New Ilion finally succeeded in destroying the Athenocentric city of Sigeion, the Aeolians were left with the unwieldy double heritage of two tombs of Achilles, one at either end of the Sigeion Ridge. Our primary source, Strabo, does not say how or even whether the people of New Ilion ever solved the problem of explaining the coexistence of two rival tombs within what was now a unified political sphere, but such a problem would have been no novelty in this part of the Greek-speaking world, where rival cities were constantly making rival claims to the epic legacy of the Trojan War.

In the northern coastal territory of Asia Minor, as we have seen, the rival claims centered on the location of the tomb of Achilles as well as the location of Troy. As for the central coastal territory of Asia Minor, rival cities were making rival claims to the epic legacy of Homer himself. In this case, the rivalry centered on the question of locating the place where Homer was born, and among the cities claiming to be the birthplace of Homer, the city of Smyrna stood out.

The epic potential of Smyrna was not to last. During the centuries when it would have made all the difference in the world if Smyrna could assert its claim to be the birthplace of Homer, Smyrna did not exist. The obliteration of Smyrna, a city that

166. In making this point, I agree with the overall argumentation of Frame 2009.

had long ago swung into the orbit of the Ionians, was symptomatic of an overall decline in the wealth, power, and prestige of the federation of cities known as the Ionian Dodecapolis in the sixth century b.c.e. This decline can best be understood if
we view it against the backdrop of earlier times when this federation was still at the
height of its power. Back in those earlier times, as we are about to see, the federation
of the Ionian Dodecapolis was a prototype of the kind of economic, cultural, and political communality that Hellenes of later times associated with the Athenian empire.
And the spokesman for this communality was none other than Homer the Ionian.

I return here to the earlier years when Smyrna had just turned Ionian and had
thus become eligible for membership in the federation of the Ionian Dodecapolis.
Strabo (14.1.4 C633) focuses on this moment after listing the twelve cities that were
members of the original Ionian Dodecapolis, adding that Smyrna was ultimately
admitted. Strabo (14.1.3 C633) lists the twelve member cities of the original Ionian
Dodecapolis in the following order: Ephesus, Miletus, Myous, Lebedos, Colophon,
Priene, Teos, Erythrai, Phocaea, Klazomenai, Chios, Samos. He highlights two Ionian
cities in particular, Ephesus and Miletus, and I draw attention to his wording:

ἄρξαι δέ φησιν Ἄνδροκλον τῆς τῶν Ἰώνων ἀποικίας, ὕστερον τῆς Αἰολικῆς, υἱὸν
γνήσιον Κόδρου τοῦ Ἀθηνῶν βασιλέως, γενέσθαι δὲ τοῦτον Ἐφέσου κτίστην. διόπερ
τὸ βασίλειον τῶν Ἰώνων ἐκεῖ συστῆναί φασι, καὶ ἔτι νῦν οἱ ἐκ τοῦ γένους ὀνομάζονται
βασιλεῖς ἔχοντές τινας τιμάς, προεδρίαν τε ἐν ἀγῶσι καὶ πορφύραν ἐπίσημον τοῦ
βασιλικοῦ γένους, σκίπωνα ἀντὶ σκήπτρου, καὶ τὰ ἱερὰ τῆς Ἐλευσινίας Δήμητρος.

[Pherecydes (FGH 3 F 155)] says that the leader of the Ionian Migration [apoikia] was
Androklos, and that this migration was later than the Aeolian Migration. He goes on
to say that this Androklos was the legitimate son of Kodros, king of Athens, and that
this Androklos became the founder of Ephesus. That is why they say that the royal
palace [basileion] of the Ionians was established there [in Ephesus] and why even today those who are descended from the lineage [genos] of this man [Androklos] are
called kings [basileis] and have various privileges [timai]: the presidency at the contests [agōnes: contests of the festival of the Panionia]; a special kind of purple wear
that signifies royal lineage [genos]; a scepter, which they call not skēptron but skipōn;
and priestly control over the rites of Demeter Eleusinia.

Strabo 14.1.3 C632–33

καὶ Μίλητον δ᾽ ἔκτισεν Νηλεὺς ἐκ Πύλου τὸ γένος ὤν· οἵ τε Μεσσήνιοι καὶ οἱ Πύλιοι
συγγένειάν τινα προσποιοῦνται, καθ᾽ ἣν καὶ Μεσσήνιον τὸν Νέστορα οἱ νεώτεροί
φασι ποιηταί, καὶ τοῖς περὶ Μέλανθον τὸν Κόδρου πατέρα πολλοὺς καὶ τῶν Πυλίων
συνεξάραί φασιν εἰς τὰς Ἀθήνας· τοῦτον δὴ πάντα τὸν λαὸν μετὰ τῶν Ἰώνων κοινῇ
στεῖλαι τὴν ἀποικίαν· τοῦ δὲ Νηλέως ἐπὶ τῷ Ποσειδίῳ βωμὸς ἵδρυμα δείκνυται.

And Miletus was founded by Neleus, whose lineage [genos] was from Pylos. Both the
Messenians and the Pylians claim some kind of genealogical connection to him. In
line with this connection, the newer [neōteroi] poets call Nestor by way of the epithet

Messēnios 'Messenian'. They [the newer poets] say that many of the Pylians had gone to Athens to join the company of Melanthos, father of Kodros, and that this entire aggregate [*laos*] initiated the **colonization** [*apoikia*] **in common** [*koinēi*], along with the Ionians. There is also to be seen on the promontory called Poseidion an altar erected by Neleus.

Strabo 14.1.3 C633

I note here the association of the Ionian polis with the Ionian Migration or *apoikia*—that is, with the notionally original action that defined the Ionians of Asia Minor. And I note also the wording that refers to the Athenian participation in the Ionian Migration: in this context, the colonization by the Pylians, representatives of the heroic age, is described as an action taken *koinēi* 'in common', and the primary joiners in the common enterprise are the Athenians. Earlier on, I noted the implications of the adjective *koinos* 'common' in contexts having to do with the Athenian empire. Here too the expression *koinēi* 'in common' implies the makings of an imperial enterprise. And I note with interest the linking of this federation of the Ionian Dodecapolis not only with the Athenians, who represent here an early phase of a great empire, but also with the Pylians, who represent an even earlier great empire—what archaeologists describe as the Mycenaean empire of the Bronze Age.

Not only Strabo but also Herodotus alludes to these phases of empire. And he too refers to the federation of the Ionian Dodecapolis. In the version given by Herodotus, however, Miletus rather than Ephesus figures as the premier city in the Dodecapolis:

Μίλητος μὲν αὐτῶν πρώτη κεῖται πόλις πρὸς μεσαμβρίην, μετὰ δὲ Μυοῦς τε καὶ Πριήνη· αὗται μὲν ἐν τῇ Καρίῃ κατοίκηνται κατὰ ταὐτὰ διαλεγόμεναι σφίσι. Αἵδε δὲ ἐν τῇ Λυδίῃ· Ἔφεσος, Κολοφών, Λέβεδος, Τέως, Κλαζομεναί, Φώκαια· αὗται δὲ αἱ πόλιες τῇσι πρότερον λεχθείσῃσι ὁμολογέουσι κατὰ γλῶσσαν οὐδέν, σφίσι δὲ ὁμοφωνέουσι. Ἔτι δὲ τρεῖς ὑπόλοιποι Ἰάδες πόλιες, τῶν αἱ δύο μὲν νήσους οἴκηνται, Σάμον τε καὶ Χίον, ἡ δὲ μία ἐν τῇ ἠπείρῳ ἵδρυται, Ἐρυθραί· Χῖοι μέν νυν καὶ Ἐρυθραῖοι κατὰ τώυτὸ διαλέγονται, Σάμιοι δὲ ἐπ᾽ ἑωυτῶν μοῦνοι.

The first of them [the twelve cities] to be mentioned is Miletus, situated to the north. Next in order [moving from north to south] there are Myous and Priene. These cities are settlements situated in Carian territory, and they share the same dialect with each other. Next, the following cities are situated in Lydia: Ephesus, Colophon, Lebedos, Teos, Klazomenai, Phocaea. These cities are not at all consonant in dialect with the ones mentioned previously, but they are consonant with each other. Next there are three Ionian cities still to be mentioned. Of these three, two are settlements situated on islands, Samos and Chios. And one is a settlement situated on the mainland, Erythrai. The inhabitants of Chios and Erythrai have the same dialect, but the Samians have a dialect of their own.

Herodotus 1.142.3

Here I repeat the sequence of cities listed by Herodotus as members of this federation of the Ionian Dodecapolis: Miletus, Myous, Priene; Ephesus, Colophon, Lebedos, Teos, Klazomenai, Phocaea; Samos; Chios and Erythrai. The three semicolons that I just used in punctuating this sequence reflect the division of the twelve cities in this federation into four dialectal groups, as also indicated by Herodotus. I draw attention to two features of this division. First, there is the highlighting of Miletus, not Ephesus, at the head of the list. Second, there is the grouping of Samos, Chios, and Erythrai. Herodotus implies that the dialects of these three cities are more closely related to each other than to the dialects of the other nine cities, and then he goes on to say explicitly that the dialects of Chios and Erythrai are more closely related to each other than to the dialect of Samos, which is thus left to a category all by itself. This last grouping of three and subgrouping of two and one corresponds to the sequence of narration in *Vita* 1 of the *Life of Homer* tradition: in the course of the Poet's travels, he stops over at Ionian Erythrai on his way to Ionian Chios (1.225–75); after his extended stay in Ionian Chios (1.346–98), he stops over at Ionian Samos on his way to Athens (1.399–484).

8

Homeric Variations on a Theme of Empire

FOUR FESTIVALS AND FOUR MODELS OF EMPIRE

In the account of Herodotus, Miletus figures as the premier city in a federation of twelve cities that comprise the Ionian Dodecapolis. This privileging of Miletus reflects an early model of political dominance that shaped the later model that we know as the Athenian empire. To be contrasted is what we are told by Strabo: in his account, Ephesus figures as the premier city. Such privileging, as we are about to see, reflects an intermediate model. In the case of Miletus, its political dominance in the federation corresponded to its prominence at the festival of the Panionia; in the case of Ephesus, its prominence was manifested at the festival of the Ephesia. These two festivals, as we are about to see, represent two different models of empire, which I will compare with two further models of empire as represented by two other festivals, the Delia in Delos and the Panathenaia in Athens.

The festival of the Ephesia at Ephesus, as we saw in chapter 1, was a rival of the festival of the Delia at Delos. I quote again the relevant testimony of Thucydides:

ἀπέχει δὲ ἡ Ῥήνεια τῆς Δήλου οὕτως ὀλίγον ὥστε Πολυκράτης ὁ Σαμίων τύραννος ἰσχύσας τινὰ χρόνον ναυτικῷ καὶ τῶν τε ἄλλων νήσων ἄρξας καὶ τὴν Ῥήνειαν ἑλὼν ἀνέθηκε τῷ Ἀπόλλωνι τῷ Δηλίῳ ἁλύσει δήσας πρὸς τὴν Δῆλον. καὶ τὴν πεντετηρίδα τότε πρῶτον μετὰ τὴν κάθαρσιν ἐποίησαν οἱ Ἀθηναῖοι τὰ **Δήλια**. ἦν δέ ποτε καὶ τὸ πάλαι μεγάλη ξύνοδος ἐς τὴν Δῆλον τῶν Ἰώνων **τε καὶ περικτιόνων νησιωτῶν**· ξύν τε γὰρ γυναιξὶ καὶ παισὶν ἐθεώρουν, ὥσπερ νῦν ἐς τὰ **Ἐφέσια** Ἴωνες, καὶ **ἀγὼν** ἐποιεῖτο αὐτόθι καὶ **γυμνικὸς** καὶ **μουσικός**, χορούς τε ἀνῆγον αἱ πόλεις. δηλοῖ δὲ μάλιστα Ὅμηρος ὅτι τοιαῦτα ἦν ἐν τοῖς **ἔπεσι** τοῖσδε, ἅ ἐστιν ἐκ **προοιμίου** Ἀπόλλωνος.

[The island of] Rheneia is so close to Delos that Polycrates, tyrant of the people of [the island-state of] Samos, who had supreme naval power for a period of time and who had imperial rule [*arkhein*] over the islands, including Rheneia, dedicated Rheneia, having captured it, to the Delian Apollo by binding it to Delos with a chain. After the purification [*katharsis*], the Athenians at that point made for the first time the quadrennial festival known as the **Delia**. And even in the remote past there had been at Delos a great coming together of **Ionians and neighboring islanders** [*nēsiō-tai*], and they were celebrating [ἐθεώρουν 'were making *theōria*'] along with their wives and children, just as the Ionians in our own times come together [at Ephesus] for [the festival of] the **Ephesia**; and a **competition** [*agōn*] was held there [in Delos] both in athletics and in *mousikē* [*tekhnē*], and the cities brought choral ensembles. Homer makes it most clear that such was the case in the following **verses** [*epos*, plural], which come from a ***prooimion*** of Apollo. [Quotation follows.]

Thucydides 3.104.2–4

As we saw in chapter 1, the wording *prōton* 'for the first time' in this passage refers to the first time that the festival of the Delia was celebrated on a quadrennial basis, not to the first time that this festival was ever celebrated. The *katharsis* 'purification' of the island of Delos signals the Athenian inauguration of this festival at Delos in its quadrennial form. This particular inauguration, as we saw, can be dated to the winter of 426 B.C.E. But then Thucydides goes on to say that there had been also an earlier Athenian *katharsis* of Delos, and that it took place at the initiative of the tyrant Peisistratos of Athens (3.104.1). This earlier *katharsis* signals an earlier Athenian inauguration of the same festival of the Delia at Delos. Besides Thucydides, Herodotus too refers to this earlier *katharsis* 'purification', and he specifies that it was initiated by Peisistratos (1.64.2).[1]

Again as we saw in chapter 1, Thucydides thinks that the earlier Athenian organization of that festival in the sixth century, in the era of the tyrants, was a precedent for its later Athenian organization in the fifth century, in the new era of democracy. The earlier Athenian organization, which is connected with the initiative of the tyrant Peisistratos, is meant to suggest that the city of Athens "had 'ruled the waves' in the sixth century as well as the fifth."[2] Thucydides also thinks that there were earlier phases of the Delia, including the primal moment when Homer himself attended the festival and performed there. In this context, Thucydides compares the festival of the Delia as he knows it in his own time with the rival festival of the Ephesia:

1. See again Hornblower 1991:527. Athenian involvement in the Delia can be dated even farther back to the era of Solon: Aloni 1989:44–45.

2. Hornblower 1991:520. In the sixth century, however, the Persian empire still controlled most of the coast of Asia Minor; in that respect, then, there is a major difference with the fifth century, when that control was taken over by the Athenian empire. For more on the sixth century, see also Hornblower p. 519, who comments on the "vigorous Aegean foreign policy" of the Peisistratidai. I refer again to his pp. 519–20 for comments on the survival of various ideologies from the era of the Peisistratidai to the era of the democracy, such as various Panhellenic features of the Eleusinian Mysteries.

ἦν δέ ποτε καὶ τὸ πάλαι μεγάλη ξύνοδος ἐς τὴν Δῆλον τῶν Ἰώνων τε καὶ περικτιόνων νησιωτῶν· ξύν τε γὰρ γυναιξὶ καὶ παισὶν ἐθεώρουν, ὥσπερ νῦν ἐς τὰ Ἐφέσια Ἴωνες, καὶ ἀγὼν ἐποιεῖτο αὐτόθι καὶ γυμνικὸς καὶ μουσικός, χορούς τε ἀνῆγον αἱ πόλεις.

And even in the remote past there had been at Delos a great coming together of **Ionians and neighboring islanders** [*nēsiōtai*], and they were celebrating [ἐθεώρουν 'were making *theōria*'] along with their wives and children, just as the Ionians in our own times come together [at Ephesus] for [the festival of] the **Ephesia**; and a competition [*agōn*] was held there [in Delos] both in athletics and in *mousikē* [*tekhnē*], and the cities brought choral ensembles.

Thucydides 3.104.3–4

I note the wording used here by Thucydides in referring to the archetypal *agōn* . . . *gumnikos kai mousikos* 'competition in athletics and in *mousikē* [*tekhnē*]' (3.104.3–4). Using similar wording, he goes on to speak about an *agōn* 'competition' in *mousikē* (3.104.5 ὅτι δὲ καὶ μουσικῆς ἀγὼν ἦν) as he continues his historical reconstruction by quoting from the *Homeric Hymn to Apollo* (verses 165–72). The words he quotes are notionally spoken by Homer himself (3.104.4, 5, 6). So now we have been told not once but twice that there had been a prototypical era of celebrating the festival of the Delia in its prototypical form.

I note also the wording that Thucydides uses in referring to the celebrants of this prototypical festival: he speaks of 'Ionians and neighboring islanders [*nēsiōtai*]'. The significance of the distinction made here by Thucydides between 'Ionians' and 'islanders' is clarified by what he says after he quotes 'Homer' as the speaker of the *Homeric Hymn to Apollo* (verses 165–72):

τοσαῦτα μὲν Ὅμηρος ἐτεκμηρίωσεν ὅτι ἦν καὶ τὸ πάλαι μεγάλη ξύνοδος καὶ ἑορτὴ ἐν τῇ Δήλῳ· ὕστερον δὲ τοὺς μὲν χοροὺς οἱ νησιῶται καὶ οἱ Ἀθηναῖοι μεθ' ἱερῶν ἔπεμπον, τὰ δὲ περὶ τοὺς ἀγῶνας καὶ τὰ πλεῖστα κατελύθη ὑπὸ ξυμφορῶν, ὡς εἰκός, πρὶν δὴ οἱ Ἀθηναῖοι τότε τὸν ἀγῶνα ἐποίησαν καὶ ἱπποδρομίας, ὃ πρότερον οὐκ ἦν.

So much for the evidence given by Homer concerning the fact that there was even in the remote past a great coming together and **festival** [*heortē*] at Delos; later on, **the islanders** [*nēsiōtai*] **and the Athenians** continued to send choral ensembles, along with sacrificial offerings, but various misfortunes evidently caused the discontinuation of the things concerning the **competitions** [*agōnes*] and most other things—that is, up to the time in question [the time of the purification], when the Athenians set up the **competition** [*agōn*], including chariot races [*hippodromiai*],[3] which had not taken place before then.

Thucydides 3.104.6

When Thucydides says 'up to the time in question' here, he is not even distinguishing any more between the older reorganizing of the Delia in the era of Peisi-

3. See Rhodes 1994:260.

stratos and the newer reorganizing in the era of the early democracy. That is be-cause Thucydides is at this point more concerned about something that is clearly missing in his picture of the contemporary Delia—something he thinks was not missing in the idealized picture of the Delia that he reconstructs from the *Homeric Hymn to Apollo*. What, then, is this missing piece of the picture in the here and now of Thucydides?

The first time around, in the previous wording of Thucydides (3.104.3), we saw a reference to 'Ionians and neighboring islanders [*nēsiōtai*]'. The second time around, in his later wording (3.104.6), we see a reference to 'the islanders [*nēsiōtai*] and the Athenians'. What has been elided in the interim is the involvement of the nonislanders: that is, of the mainlanders—and when I say *mainlanders,* I mean the inhabitants of the Ionian cities situated on the mainland of Asia Minor. One of these cities is Ephesus, the site of the festival of the Ephesia—and the native city of Ion of Ephesus. Here I confront the problem of ascertaining the relevance of Ephesus, home of Ion the rhapsode, to the Ionian ideology of the Panathenaic Homer.[4]

In the sixth and fifth centuries B.C.E., the cities of mainland Ionia in Asia Minor, Ephesus included, had come under the political and cultural domination of the Ly-dian empire and, later, of the Persian empire (which overpowered the Lydian em-pire in 547 B.C.E.). So now we begin to see that these Ionian cities must have been cut off from the celebration of the Delia in the era of the tyrant Peisistratos in the sixth century and even in the earlier years of the democracy—that is, until the 460s B.C.E., when political control of coastal Asia Minor shifted from the Persian empire to the Athenian empire. In saying this I am following an incisive formulation that I found in a commentary on Thucydides: "The absence of the Ionians of Asia Minor (implied by *hoi nēsiōtai* ['the islanders']) was presumably due to the Lydian and Per-sian conquests, at least indirectly; hence Peisistratos had not been able to get them back."[5] Besides the historical figure of Peisistratos, tyrant of Athens, I am now ready to add to this formulation the historical figure of Polycrates, tyrant of Samos.

Like Peisistratos, Polycrates too had claimed Delos as a center for his own im-perial ambitions. The concept of *nēsiōtai* 'islanders' is in fact particularly relevant to the maritime empire of Polycrates, who is mentioned prominently by Thucydides in precisely this context:

ἀπέχει δὲ ἡ Ῥήνεια τῆς Δήλου οὕτως ὀλίγον ὥστε Πολυκράτης ὁ Σαμίων **τύραννος** ἰσχύσας τινὰ χρόνον ναυτικῷ καὶ **τῶν τε ἄλλων νήσων ἄρξας** καὶ τὴν Ῥήνειαν ἑλὼν ἀνέθηκε τῷ Ἀπόλλωνι τῷ Δηλίῳ ἁλύσει δήσας πρὸς τὴν Δῆλον.

[The island of] Rheneia is so close to Delos that Polycrates, **tyrant** of the people of [the island-state of] Samos, **who had supreme naval power for a period of time** and

---

4. This problem is raised in *HC* ch. 4.
5. Gomme 1956:415.

222 HOMERIC VARIATIONS ON A THEME OF EMPIRE

who had imperial rule [*arkhein*] over the islands, including Rheneia, dedicated
Rheneia, having captured it, to the Delian Apollo by binding it to Delos with a chain.

Thucydides 3.104.2

As we will now see, the figure of Homer in the *Homeric Hymn to Apollo* is a construct that fits the era of the Athenian regime of the Peisistratidai—and of the non-Athenian regime of the tyrant Polycrates of Samos. It is also a construct that fits the earliest recoverable era of the *Homēridai* of Chios, which coincides with the era of the Peisistratidai—and of Polycrates.

In the case of Polycrates, we can posit an actual occasion for his commissioning the performance of the *Homeric Hymn to Apollo* as we have it. The occasion is signaled in the passage I just quoted from Thucydides: it was the time when Polycrates had chained the island of Rheneia to the island of Delos. On that occasion, as we saw in chapter 1, Polycrates organized an event that resembled a combination of two festivals, the Delia and the Pythia, for an ad hoc celebration on the island of Delos.[6] The *Homeric Hymn to Apollo,* with its combination of hymnic praise for both the Delian and the Pythian aspects of the god Apollo, fits the occasion. Such an occasion has been dated: as we saw in chapter 1, it happened around 522 B.C.E.[7] Soon thereafter, Polycrates was overthrown and killed by agents of the Persian empire. Peisistratos had died in 528/7.

The rule of the tyrant Polycrates of Samos over the islands of the Aegean is a classic example of a maritime empire or *thalassocracy*:

Πολυκράτης γάρ ἐστι πρῶτος τῶν ἡμεῖς ἴδμεν Ἑλλήνων ὃς **θαλασσοκρατέειν** ἐπενοήθη, πάρεξ **Μίνω** τε τοῦ **Κνωσσίου** καὶ εἰ δή τις ἄλλος πρότερος τούτου **ἦρξε** τῆς θαλάσσης· τῆς δὲ ἀνθρωπηίης λεγομένης γενεῆς Πολυκράτης πρῶτος, ἐλπίδας πολλὰς ἔχων Ἰωνίης τε **καὶ νήσων ἄρξειν**.

Polycrates was the first of Hellenes I know of who conceived the idea of **thalassocracy**—except for **Minos** of **Knossos** and unless there was anyone earlier than Minos who **had imperial rule of** [*arkhein*] the sea. But Polycrates was the first among humans with a known lineage [who had such a rule]. He had high hopes of **having imperial rule of** [*arkhein*] **Ionia and the islands**.

Herodotus 3.122.2

καὶ Ἴωσιν ὕστερον πολὺ γίγνεται ναυτικὸν ἐπὶ Κύρου Περσῶν πρώτου βασιλεύοντος καὶ Καμβύσου τοῦ υἱέος αὐτοῦ, τῆς τε καθ᾽ ἑαυτοὺς θαλάσσης Κύρῳ πολεμοῦντες ἐκράτησάν τινα χρόνον. καὶ Πολυκράτης Σάμου τυραννῶν ἐπὶ Καμβύσου ναυτικῷ ἰσχύων ἄλλας τε τῶν νήσων ὑπηκόους ἐποιήσατο καὶ Ῥήνειαν ἑλὼν ἀνέθηκε τῷ Ἀπόλλωνι τῷ Δηλίῳ.

6. Zenobius of Athos 1.62; *Suda* s.v. *tauta kai Puthia kai Dēlia*.
7. Burkert 1979:59–60 and Janko 1982:112–13; West 1999:369–70n17 argues for 523 but concedes that the date of spring 522 is still possible.

Then, in the time of Cyrus the first king of the Persians and of his son Cambyses, the **Ionians** had an extensive naval power. Waging war with Cyrus, they seized possession of the sea around them and held on to it for some time. And Polycrates, who was tyrant of Samos in the time of Cambyses and who had supreme naval power, subjugated the islands, including Rheneia, and, having captured Rheneia, dedicated it to Delian Apollo.

Thucydides 1.13.6

The rule of Polycrates over his maritime empire of Ionians needs to be contrasted with the rule of the Persians over the Hellenic cities of Asia Minor in their mainland empire, within a time frame that covers roughly the second half of the sixth century B.C.E. and the first half of the fifth. Later on, I will have more to say about the maritime empire of the tyrant Polycrates. His empire is in some ways a precedent for the empire of the Athenians. As we will see, the proverbial Ring of Polycrates is a symbol of this imperial precedent. As we will also see, there is a related symbol to be found in a myth stemming ultimately from the Bronze Age. In this myth, Theseus of Athens dives into the sea to recover the royal imperial Ring of Minos, king of Knossos in Crete (Bacchylides Song 17).

At a later point, I will return to the myth of King Minos and his maritime empire or thalassocracy, which is for both Herodotus and Thucydides a Bronze Age precedent for the thalassocracy of the Athenian empire. It suffices here to confine myself to the relevant formulation I quoted earlier, concerning the reference made by Thucydides to the Ionian festival of the Delia at Delos: according to this formulation, the Ionians on the mainland of Asia Minor were distinct from the Ionians on the islands in the Aegean in that they could not participate in the Delia as once reorganized by Peisistratos—and, I must now add, as reorganized after Peisistratos by Polycrates of Samos.

Here I quote another incisive formulation—this one concerning the reorganization of the Delia by the Athenians almost a century later, in 426 B.C.E.: "The Athenians now restored everything, and enlarged the festival with chariot racing."[8] In terms of this formulation, Thucydides (3.104.2–3) is equating the reorganization or restoration of the Delia in the era of the democracy at Athens with a restored participation in the Delia by the Ionians of the cities on the mainland of Asia Minor. In terms of my reconstruction, the participation of the Ionian mainlanders in the Delia was an old tradition that predated the era of the Peisistratidai.

If the Ionian mainlanders did not participate in the festival of the Delia in the era of the Persian domination of Asia Minor, did they have access to an alternative festival? The answer is that there was in fact an alternative, and Thucydides knew it. It was the festival of the Ephesia in Ephesus, situated in the mainland of Asia Minor.[9] Here I quote again the precise wording of Thucydides about the Ephesia:

8. Gomme 1956:415. See also Plutarch *Nikias* 3.5–7 and the remarks of Gomme.
9. Frame 2009 §4.11 and endnote 4.2.

ἦν δέ ποτε καὶ τὸ πάλαι μεγάλη ξύνοδος ἐς τὴν Δῆλον τῶν Ἰώνων τε καὶ περικτιόνων νησιωτῶν· ξύν τε γὰρ γυναιξὶ καὶ παισὶν ἐθεώρουν, ὥσπερ νῦν ἐς τὰ Ἐφέσια Ἴωνες, καὶ ἀγὼν ἐποιεῖτο αὐτόθι καὶ γυμνικὸς καὶ μουσικός, χορούς τε ἀνῆγον αἱ πόλεις.

And even in the remote past there had been at Delos a great coming together of **Ionians and neighboring islanders**, and they were celebrating [ἐθεώρουν 'were making *theōria*'] along with their wives and children, just as the **Ionians** in our own times come together [at Ephesus] for [the festival of] the **Ephesia**; and a competition [*agōn*] was held there [in Delos] both in athletics and in *mousikē* [*tekhnē*], and the cities brought choral ensembles.

Thucydides 3.104.3–4

This time I am highlighting not only the first mention of the Ionians in this formulation of Thucydides but also the second. We see here that the Ionian mainlanders are still celebrating the Ephesia in the fifth century B.C.E., in the new era of Athenian democracy.[10]

In this light, I propose to reassess the politics and poetics of the Athenian empire, as an ideological construct, in terms of the earlier construct known as the Delian League. An essential piece of evidence is the parallelism that Thucydides sets up between the archetypal festival of the Delia at Delos, as extrapolated from the *Homeric Hymn to Apollo*, and the contemporaneous festival of the Ephesia at Ephesus, as extrapolated from the political realities of Thucydides' own day. It has been argued that "the Ephesia here mentioned by Th[ucydides] is none other than the Panionian festival or Panionia, the Festival of All the Ionians, which was celebrated in very early times, and again in the Roman imperial period, at a different site, one near Priene [on Cape Mycale]."[11] In terms of this argument, "the festival was originally celebrated at the [Panionion] on Cape Mycale, moved to Ephesus before the late fifth century, and moved back to the [Panionion] in 373."[12]

I propose an alternative formulation. To start, I stress the all-importance of the history of the Panionian festival of the Panionia, celebrated in a place known as the Panionion at Cape Mycale, near the city of Miletus, on the coast of Asia Minor. This festival of the Panionia defines the political dominance of Miletus as the premier city of the federation known as the Ionian Dodecapolis. An earlier phase of this festival of the Panionia was decisive in defining the cultural and political identity of

10. For more on the Ephesia, see Kowalzig 2007:103–4, 108–10.

11. Hornblower 1991:527, with further citations.

12. Rhodes 1994:259. In the fifth and fourth centuries B.C.E., as Hornblower 1991:522 observes, the shaping of the festival of the Ephesia at Ephesus was taking place in Asia Minor, which was under the overall political domination of the Persian empire: the Ephesia "continued to be celebrated on Persian soil throughout the fifth and fourth centuries." Still, Ephesus was notionally a member of the Delian League. To sum up the politics and poetics of Homer in Ephesus and in other Ionian cities of Asia Minor during the fifth and fourth centuries B.C.E., I offer this formulation: the imperial Homer straddled two empires, the Persian and the Athenian.

Ionians in Asia Minor and the Aegean islands. This earlier phase can be dated back to the eighth and the seventh centuries B.C.E., when this federation of the Ionian Dodecapolis was in its heyday. In the sixth century, however, this phase came to an end. Now both the Panionia and the Ionian Dodecapolis went into a precipitous decline inversely proportional to the rapid ascendancy of the Persian empire, which became the dominant power in all Asia Minor. The collapse of the Panionia in the early fifth century can be linked directly with the collapse of the political power once represented by the Ionian Dodecapolis in general and by the city of Miletus in particular. The decisive cause of the collapse was the defeat of the Ionian Revolt by the Persian empire in the 490s B.C.E.

Instead of saying that the festival of the Panionia was transformed into the Ephesia sometime after the failure of the Ionian Revolt, I propose this alternative formulation: the festival of the Panionia was discontinued by the Persians after the Ionian Revolt failed, whereas the festival of the Ephesia was allowed to continue. Later on, in 373 B.C.E., the festival of the Panionia was at long last restored in its ancestral setting, the Panionion at Cape Mycale.[13]

As the oldest and most prestigious of all Ionian festivals, the Feast of the Panionia must have figured most prominently in the evolution of the Homeric tradition. And as we have seen, there is a convincing argument to be made that a prototype of the Homeric *Iliad* and *Odyssey* was an epic tradition performed at the Panionia.[14] For the moment, however, I simply emphasize the priority of this festival of the Panionia in comparison with the other Ionian festivals we have been considering so far: that is, the Delia and the Ephesia.

Reconstructing forward in time as we track the history of the Panionia from the eighth century all the way to its discontinuation after the first decade of the fifth, we reach a moment in world history when a most decisive parting of ways takes place. After the defeat of the Ionian Revolt in the 490s, the festival of the Panionia was discontinued, and the pathway of Ionian identity reached a crossroads. Heading in one direction after the 490s was a festival like the Ephesia, celebrated by the Ionian mainlanders of Asia Minor and dominated by the mainland empire of the Persians until the 460s B.C.E., when political control of coastal Asia Minor shifted from the Persian empire to the Athenian. Heading in another direction was the festival of the Delia, celebrated by the Ionian islanders of the Aegean and dominated for a short time in the 520s by the island empire of the tyrant Polycrates of Samos. After Polycrates was overthrown and killed in 522 by agents of the Persian empire, control of the Delia reverted from the thalassocracy of Polycrates back to the evolving thalassocracy of Athens, initially in the era of the Peisistratidai and subsequently in the era of the new democracy.

13. Here I follow the reasoning of Frame 2009 endnote 4.2.
14. Again, I follow the reasoning of Frame 2009.

For a few decades after the 490s, when the Ionian cities of coastal Asia Minor were still being controlled by the Persian empire, the festivals of the Delia and the Ephesia could be seen as rival institutions. Representing the new Ionia of the Delian League was the festival of the Delia, evolving in the political sphere of the Athenian empire and connecting the Ionian islanders under the control of the Athenians. Representing the old Ionia, at least nominally, was the festival of the Ephesia, evolving in the political sphere of the Persian empire and connecting the Ionian mainlanders under the control of the Persians. Things changed in the 460s, as control over the Ionian cities of Asia Minor shifted from the Persian to the Athenian empire. Starting in the 460s, the prestige of both the Delia and the Ephesia could give way to the ultimate prestige of the Panathenaia in Athens. Just as the Delia and the Ephesia had eclipsed the Panionia, the Panathenaia could now eclipse these older festivals claiming Panionian status. The festival of the Panathenaia was evolving into the newest and the biggest of all Ionian festivals.

The separation of the mainland Ionians of Asia Minor from the island Ionians after the failure of the Ionian Revolt in the 490s is thought to have caused their cultural stagnation. Mainland Ionia during the period of the Persian domination—especially after the Ionian Revolt—has been described as an "intellectual backwater."[15] By comparison, the island Ionians evidently flourished. In fact, they were flourishing already in the sixth century under the regime of Polycrates and, later, under the new regime that replaced it, namely the Athenian empire of the sons of Peisistratos. After the fall of Polycrates, as I already noted a moment ago, the festival of the Delia had reverted to the control of the Peisistratidai. This festival, which had been of great importance in defining the cultural identity of the Ionians in the era of Polycrates, became even more important in the era of the sons of Peisistratos. In this new era, the Delia redefined Athens as the metropolis or 'mother city' of the Ionians. The performance of Homer at the Delia, as dramatized in the *Homeric Hymn to Apollo*, could now become an integral part of this redefinition. This Homer was of a new kind, representing the Athenian empire of the Peisistratidai.

This new sixth-century Homer in the era of the tyrants—and by *Homer* here I mean both the poet and the poetry—is an earlier form of the fifth-century Homer in the new era of democracy that followed. In other words, it is an earlier form of what I have been calling up to now the Panathenaic Homer, which is a form of the *Iliad* and *Odyssey* that resembles most closely what we still recognize today as the Homeric *Iliad* and *Odyssey*.

Identified as the poet who speaks at the festival of the Delia in the *Homeric Hymn to Apollo*, this new sixth-century Panathenaic Homer represents an epic tradition that tends to highlight the island Ionians and to shade over the mainland Ionians

---

15. Meiggs 1972:282.

of Asia Minor. This is not to say that the mainland Ionians of older times are not present in Homeric poetry. They are still very much there. But these older Ionians are shaded over, by way of epic distancing.

The epic distancing of the new Homer from the old Ionians of mainland Asia Minor is so effective that that these mainlanders are simply not featured in the Panathenaic Homer that we know as the *Iliad* and *Odyssey*. Moreover, the actual concept of Ionians occurs only once in the Panathenaic Homer, in *Iliad* XIII (685). Even in that unique context, the Ionians are deprived of any autonomous existence: they are closely bound to the Athenians, who are mentioned explicitly in that context (XIII 689).[16]

This epic distancing from the Ionians is to be expected in Homeric poetry, since the Trojan War is imagined as taking place well before the Ionian Migration. So it comes as no surprise that the names of the mainland cities of the Ionian Dodecapolis that once participated in the Feast of the Panionia are omitted in the Panathenaic *Iliad* and *Odyssey*. The only overt exception is a single mention of the most prominent of the twelve cities, Miletus. It happens in *Iliad* II, in the context of a catalogue of combatants who fight on the Trojan side in the Trojan War. Miletus is being featured on the wrong side, as it were. And, to accentuate the epic distancing, the population of Miletus is described here as non-Hellenic. In *Iliad* II (867), we hear that a hero called Nastes came to Troy as an ally of the Trojans, and he is described as the leader of the Carians, who are in turn described as *barbarophōnoi* 'non-Greek-speakers'. Immediately thereafter in *Iliad* II (868), the one city that is mentioned as inhabited by these Carians is Miletus; next (869), there is mention of one of the main landmarks of Miletus, Cape Mycale, with its 'steep headlands'. In sum, the Panathenaic Homer shades over not only the Ionians but also their cities in the Ionian Dodecapolis.[17]

There is comparatively less shading over when it comes to the island Ionians. The Panathenaic Homer makes incidental mention of the Ionian islands of Chios and Euboea in *Odyssey* iii (170–74) and of Euboea alone in vii (321). Also, there is a most conspicuous highlighting of the island of Delos in *Odyssey* vi (160).

Here I need to qualify a point made earlier, that the prestige of mainland Ionia was elided by the Persian empire during the sixth century and the first half of the fifth. Despite the historical reality of this elision, I will now argue that the cultural legacy of mainland Ionians was probably not quite as impoverished as we might

16. At *Iliad* XIII 700, there is also a mention of *Boiōtoi* 'Boeotians', which picks up the mention of *Boiōtoi* at XIII 685, where they are correlated with the Ionians. See Page 1959 on the *Boiōtoi* in the Catalogue of *Iliad* II and Giovannini 1969 on the Delphic orientation of the Catalogue.

17. As we have seen, the twelve cities of the Ionian Dodecapolis are listed by Herodotus (1.142.3); also the twelve cities of the Aeolian Dodecapolis (1.149.1).

imagine from descriptions of Ionia in the fifth century B.C.E. as an "intellectual back-water."[18] I return to the Ephesia as a case in point. In its heyday, as we will see, this festival was a rival of the Delia.

Between the 490s and the 460s, the festival of the Delia had served the purpose of providing an alternative to the festival of the Ephesia. After the 460s, especially in the 420s, it also served the purpose of providing an alternative to the festival of the Olympia: that is, to the Olympics. Conversely, the Ephesia had served its own purpose so long as Hellenes could view this festival as an alternative to the ideology of the Athenian empire—an alternative initiated by the Persian empire. But Ephesus and the rest of the Ionian cities of coastal Asia Minor swung over to the Athenian empire and away from the Persian empire in the 460s and thereafter, and thus the festival of the Delia was no longer necessitated as a counterweight to the Ephesia. Even more than before, cultural dominance could gravitate toward the Panathenaia, the prestige of which could by now occlude the prestige of any other Ionian festival. Just as the Delia would by now be viewed as less important than before, so too the Ephesia. For a figure like Ion, his status as a rhapsode from Ephesus would therefore be viewed as less important than his status as a rhapsode who performed at the Panathenaia of Athens.

A HOMERIC GLIMPSE OF AN IONIAN FESTIVAL

Here I take another look at the old Ionian festival of the Panionia, celebrated at a site that is notionally common to all Ionians, the Panionion of the Ionian Dodecapolis in Asia Minor:

> τὸ δὲ **Πανιώνιόν** ἐστι τῆς Μυκάλης χῶρος ἱρός, πρὸς ἄρκτον τετραμμένος, **κοινῇ** ἐξαραιρημένος ὑπὸ Ἰώνων **Ποσειδέωνι Ἑλικωνίῳ**· ἡ δὲ Μυκάλη ἐστὶ τῆς ἠπείρου ἄκρη πρὸς ζέφυρον ἄνεμον κατήκουσα Σάμῳ ‹καταντίον›, ἐς τὴν συλλεγόμενοι ἀπὸ τῶν πολίων Ἴωνες **ἄγεσκον ὁρτήν**, τῇ ἔθεντο οὔνομα **Πανιώνια**.

> The **Panionion** is a sacred space of Mycale, facing north, which was set aside for **Poseidon Helikōnios** by the Ionians, in a decision made **in common [koinēi]** by all of them; Mycale is a promontory of the mainland facing west toward Samos; it was here [in Mycale] that the Ionians gathered together from their respective cities and **celebrated** a festival [heortē] that they named the **Panionia**.

> Herodotus 1.148.1

I highlight the wording that refers to the primal decision that is notionally being made here by all the Ionians: the founding of the Panionia is said to be an action taken koinēi 'in common'. In chapter 7, we saw comparable wording in a context where Strabo (14.1.3 C633) refers to the founding of the Ionian Dodecapolis

18. Again, Meiggs 1972:282.

by the Ionians: there too the action is taken *koinēi* 'in common'. In that case, however, the action is said to be taken not only by the Ionians but also by the Athenians along with the Ionians. As I will argue, the wording in the text of Strabo marks the beginnings of the Athenian empire. As I will also argue, the linking of the Ionian Dodecapolis with the idea of this empire goes back to the Bronze Age.

Strabo gives a most vivid picture of the sight that travelers will see as they approach the promontory of Mycale by sea. It is a stunning view of the Panionion, site of the festival of the Panionia celebrated by the twelve cities of the Ionian Dodecapolis:

πρῶτον δ' ἐστὶν ἐν τῇ παραλίᾳ τὸ Πανιώνιον τρισὶ σταδίοις ὑπερκείμενον τῆς θαλάττης, ὅπου τὰ Πανιώνια, κοινὴ πανήγυρις τῶν Ἰώνων, συντελεῖται τῷ Ἑλικωνίῳ Ποσειδῶνι καὶ θυσία· ἱερῶνται δὲ Πριηνεῖς.

> First to be seen on the seacoast is the **Panionion**, situated three stadia above the sea, where the **Panionia**, a festival [*panēguris*] that is common [*koinē*] to the Ionians, is enacted for **Poseidon** *Helikōnios*, and sacrifice [*thusia*] is made to him; the people of Priene control the priestly duties [connected with the sacrifice].

> Strabo 14.1.20 C639

Earlier, Strabo (8.7.2 C384) says more explicitly that the Panionion, this notional center of the Ionian Dodecapolis, was actually located in the environs of Priene, and that this location near Priene is linked with the fact that the city controlled the priestly duties of performing the sacrifice (*thusia*) to Poseidon *Helikōnios* at the festival of the Panionia (τῆς Πανιωνικῆς θυσίας ἣν ἐν τῇ Πριηνέων χώρᾳ συντελοῦσιν Ἴωνες τῷ Ἑλικωνίῳ Ποσειδῶνι); Strabo goes on to say that the primacy of Priene as the place of sacrifice to Poseidon *Helikōnios*—and even as the agent of this sacrifice—was motivated by the fact that the people of Priene claimed as their place of origin the city of *Helikē* in the region of Achaea in the Peloponnese (8.7.2 C384 ἐπεὶ καὶ αὐτοὶ οἱ Πριηνεῖς ἐξ Ἑλίκης εἶναι λέγονται).

In the same context of considering the sacrificial duties of these priests of Priene, Strabo (8.7.2 C384) makes it explicit that the Ionians even in his own time worshipped Poseidon *Helikōnios* and celebrated (*thuein*) the festival of the Panionia at the Panionion (ὃν καὶ νῦν ἔτι τιμῶσιν Ἴωνες, καὶ θύουσιν ἐκεῖ τὰ Πανιώνια), and he proceeds to describe this festival as a *thusia* in the context of arguing that Homer actually mentions it in *Iliad* XX 404–5 (μέμνηται δ', ὡς ὑπονοοῦσί τινες, ταύτης τῆς θυσίας Ὅμηρος ὅταν φῇ . . . [the quotation from Homer follows]). I draw special attention to Strabo's metonymic use of *thusia* 'sacrifice' here to designate the whole festival of the Panionia. The geographer now proceeds to quote the verses of the *Iliad* (XX 404–5) that concern the sacrifice of a bellowing bull to Poseidon *Helikōnios* (ὡς ὅτε ταῦρος | ἤρυγεν ἑλκόμενος Ἑλικώνιον ἀμφὶ ἄνακτα). As he observes (again, 8.7.2 C384), the climax of the festival of the Panionia at the Panionion is the sacrifice of a bull to Poseidon *Helikōnios*—I note the word *thusia*, used here in the specific sense of 'sacrifice'—and special care must be taken by the sacrificers to induce the bull to bellow before it is sacrificed. Accordingly, Strabo continues, the reference in *Iliad* XX 404–5 to the sacrifice of a bellowing bull to Poseidon *Helikōnios* can be used to argue that the birth of Homer 'the Poet' par excellence is to be dated after the Ionian *apoikia* 'colonization', on the grounds that the poet actually mentions the Panionian sacrifice of the Ionians to Poseidon *Helikōnios* in the environs of Priene (τεκμαίρονταί τε νεώτερον εἶναι τῆς Ἰωνικῆς ἀποικίας τὸν ποιητήν, μεμνημένον γε τῆς Πανιωνικῆς θυσίας ἣν ἐν τῇ Πριηνέων χώρᾳ συντελοῦσιν Ἴωνες τῷ Ἑλικωνίῳ Ποσειδῶνι).

As we see from Strabo, then, this Homeric passage may well refer to the special way of sacrificing bulls at the festival of the Panionia at the Panionion in Priene. The testimony of Strabo is in fact corroborated by the Homeric scholia (bT for *Iliad* XX 404).[19]

Other than the mention of Poseidon *Helikōnios*, this passage in the *Iliad* contains no specific reference to Priene. In general, the Panathenaic Homer shades over its references to the Ionian Dodecapolis. But the references, as I noted earlier, are very much there.[20]

Strabo (8.7.2 C384) goes on to offer an alternative explanation: the description of the sacrifice of the bellowing bull in *Iliad* XX (404–5) stems from customs of worshipping Poseidon *Helikōnios* elsewhere—not in the environs of the Ionian Dodecapolis in Asia Minor but in the city of *Helikē* in the region of Achaea in the Peloponnese. (This city had been destroyed by a tsunami in 373 B.C.E.) As I have already noted, Strabo himself here recognizes *Helikē* as the place of origin for the people of Priene (8.7.2 C384 καὶ αὐτοὶ οἱ Πριηνεῖς ἐξ Ἑλίκης εἶναι λέγονται).

This alternative explanation offered by Strabo (8.7.2 C384) is a post-Athenocentric way of accounting for a pre-Athenocentric detail of Homeric poetry surviving from the Ionian traditions of the Panionia. Strabo's thinking here can be summarized this way: if this detail about the bellowing sacrificial bull in *Iliad* XX is Ionian by origin, then Homer must be dated after the Ionian *apoikia* 'colonization'. If Homer was to be dated before such an event, however, then the Poet supposedly saw this detail at a sacrifice that took place in a proto-Ionian setting: that is, in the Peloponnesus, which was the notional homeland of the Ionians in the era that preceded the Ionian Migration—an era that links Homer with the Bronze Age.

So even this rare glimpse of Homeric poetry as performed at the festival of the

---

19. As we see from the context of the Iliadic passage here, the mode of inflicting the mortal blow in sacrificing the bull highlights the vitality of the bull, who is "pumped up" with fear and rage. In the exegetical scholia **b**T for *Iliad* XX 406a (see also **b**T for 404b), the commentator takes great care in noting the explosion of arterial blood at the climactic moment when the sacrificial blow severs the carotid artery of the "pumped-up" animal. It appears that this mode of sacrificing the bull intensifies the rush of arterial blood spurting from the sacrificial blow.

20. A case in point is the Catalogue of Heroines in *Odyssey* xi, as studied by Frame 2009 ch. 7.

Panionia in the sacred space of the Panionion in Ionian Asia Minor is eclipsed by an ideology that rejects as post-Homeric anything that seems overtly Ionian in Homeric poetry. Such an ideology is basically Athenocentric in orientation. What results is that Ionian elements are removed from their setting in Asia Minor and relocated in a supposedly proto-Ionian setting in the Peloponnese. From there these proto-Ionian elements are then supposedly channeled to Asia Minor by way of Athens as the metropolis or 'mother city' of the Ionians. The Homer of the Panionia is thus eclipsed by the Homer of a rival festival, the Delia, which is the point of definition for the Athenian empire in its earlier phases. The Delia then gives way to yet another rival festival, the Panathenaia, which becomes the ultimate point of definition for the Athenian empire in its earlier phases.

The eclipsing of the Panionian Homer by the Panathenaic Homer is not unprecedented. Earlier, the Panionian Homer of the Ionian Dodecapolis had eclipsed what I call the Panaeolian Homer of the Aeolian Dodecapolis. The "big bang" in this case was the transformation of Aeolian Smyrna, native city of Homer, into Ionian Smyrna. The great significance attributed to this transformation is evident from all the concentrated attention devoted to it in the narratives I cited earlier from Herodotus (1.143.3, 149.1–151.2) and Strabo (14.1.4 C633).

As we trace the succession from a Panaeolian to a Panionian to a Panathenaic Homer, we can see signs of continuity in the ideology of the festivals held by the federations represented by these three different phases of Homer. This continuity has to do with the idea of commonality as expressed by the word *koinos* 'common, standard'. In the case of the Delian League, a conglomeration of Ionian cities headed by Athens as their notional metropolis or 'mother city', we saw that Homer himself is described as *koinos* in his dual role as premier performer at the festival of the Delia and as premier spokesman of the Delian League (*Vita* 2.319–20). In the case of the Ionian Dodecapolis, evidently headed by Miletus, we saw that Herodotus applies this same word *koinos* to the centralized sacred space called the Panionion, which served as the setting for the centralized festival of the Ionian Dodecapolis, the Panionia (1.148.1 τὸ δὲ Πανιώνιόν ἐστι τῆς Μυκάλης χῶρος ἱρός, πρὸς ἄρκτον τετραμμένος, κοινῇ ἐξαραιρημένος ὑπὸ Ἰώνων Ποσειδέωνι Ἑλικωνίῳ 'the Panionion is a sacred space of Mycale, facing north, that was set aside for Poseidon *Helikōnios* by the Ionians, in a decision made in common [*koinēi*] by all of them').[21] In the case of the Aeolian confederations, as we are about to see, there is indirect evidence in the relevant use of *xunos* 'common', synonym of the word *koinos* 'common' as used here by Herodotus.

21. Elsewhere too, Herodotus uses *koinos* 'common' in comparable contexts of commonality (as at 1.151.3, 166.1, 170.2; 2.178.2; and so on). And there are two instances where he uses the synonym *xunos* 'common' (4.12.3, 7.53.1).

Just as Homer figured as a spokesman for Ionian federations like the Ionian Do-decapolis, he could also speak for Aeolian federations. We have already considered one such federation, the Aeolian Dodecapolis as described by Herodotus (1.149.1). As we saw, this league of twelve Aeolian cities was once the major rival of the league of twelve Ionian cities in claiming the strongest of ties to Homer. In fact, one of these Aeolian cities, Smyrna, was recognized by most other cities as the most likely to deserve the honor of being the birthplace of Homer. Another rival in claiming the strongest of ties to Homer was a league of Aeolian cities headed by the city of Myti-lene on the island of Lesbos. This particular league, as we also saw earlier, once possessed the prime poetic real estate of the Homeric *Iliad*—ancient Troy and its environs in the Troad. As we are about to see, the identity of Homer as a spokesman for Aeolians was shaped primarily by the politics of this Aeolian league.

AN AEOLIC PHASE OF HOMER

The claims of the Aeolians on Homer can be correlated with an Aeolic phase in the prehistory of the language of Homeric poetry. This phase is evident in the linguistic evidence of the *Iliad* and *Odyssey*. I have assembled some of this evidence in previous work, and in what follows I offer a summary.[22]

On the basis of his research on the language of Homeric poetry, Milman Parry worked out a diachronic definition of this language.[23] It is a system composed of three dialectal phases, which can be described as Ionic, Aeolic, and Mycenaean.[24] I have listed these dialectal phases in chronological succession, moving backward in time to the oldest recoverable phase, Mycenaean. I use here the term *Mycenaean* instead of *Arcado-Cypriote* in the light of the decipherment of the Linear B tablets found at the palaces of Pylos and Knossos and elsewhere.[25] As this term *Mycenaean*

22. *PH* ch. 14 (= pp. 414–37).

23. Parry 1932. Summarized in Nagy 1972:59.

24. In the online version of Nagy 1972:59 (2008b), I offer an updating of my views, which I repeat here. I distance myself from speaking of successive dialectal "layers" in epic. In general, I am persuaded by the argumentation of Horrocks in criticizing various current "layer theories." (See especially Horrocks 1997:214.) Instead of speaking of earlier and later dialectal "layers" in Homeric poetry, I now prefer to speak of earlier and later dialectal "phases," since the term *phases* allows for an overlap and even a coexistence of relatively earlier and later dialectal forms at any given time in the evolution of epic. To the extent that the term *layer* may not allow for such overlap or coexistence, it now seems to me preferable not to use it. In general, my current thinking about the dialectal mix of epic is closest to that of Wachter 2000, especially p. 64n4. In the case of coexisting Aeolic and Ionic forms in epic, I should add, it is essential to distinguish between optional and obligatory Aeolic forms. Provided that we keep this distinction in mind, I can agree with Wachter's formulation concerning "optional" Aeolic forms such as αἰ vs. Ionic εἰ, ἔμμεν vs. Ionic εἶναι, and so on. Aeolic forms are obligatory where no corresponding Ionic forms fit the meter, but they are only optional where existing Ionic forms can be substituted.

25. Nagy 1972:58–70.

indicates, the earliest dialectal components of Homeric language can be reconstructed all the way back to the Bronze Age.

For the moment, I highlight the middle dialectal phase of the Homeric language, Aeolic. In the traditional phraseology of Homeric poetry, we see embedded a variety of forms that can be explained as Aeolic in provenience. In some cases, the forms can be further specified as stemming from the island of Lesbos.[26]

Going beyond this diachronic definition of the language of Homeric poetry, I now offer a redefinition that combines the diachronic perspective with the synchronic. The language of Homeric poetry is a system that integrates and thus preserves the following phases of dialects: dominant Ionic integrated with recessive Aeolic integrated with residual Mycenaean.[27] I emphasize the integration of dominant, recessive, and residual dialectal components because, following Parry, I view Homeric language synchronically as a working system, not as an inert layering of dialectal components matching the Ionic, Aeolic, and Mycenaean dialects.[28]

AN ATTIC PHASE OF HOMER

Besides Ionic and Aeolic and Mycenaean as, respectively, dominant and recessive and residual dialectal components of the language of Homeric poetry, there is also a fourth dialectal component. It is Attic, the dialect of the Athenians, which needs to be observed in the context of epic performances at the festival of the Panathenaia in Athens. Without the hindsight of history, Attic can be viewed as merely one of many dialects belonging to the general category of Ionic. When we add the hindsight of history, however, Attic can be viewed as something more than a subcategory of Ionic. Once Attic became the official language of the Athenian empire, it subsumed all the Ionic dialects spoken within the context of that empire. This new Attic, as an imperial language, had a lasting effect on the language of Homeric poetry. That is because this new language of Attic became the linguistic frame for the old language of Homer. In other words, the old language of Homer was now being spoken and heard primarily within the new Attic-speaking context of the Panathenaia in Athens.[29]

In the twin book *Homer the Classic*, I interpret the status of this new Attic as an imperial language to be contrasted with the status of old Attic as the local dialect of Athens. The new Attic is a regularized language, in that the idiosyncrasies of the old Attic dialect were leveled out by the generalities of the Ionic dialects taken all

26. Janko 1992:15–19, 303.

27. Nagy 1972:59; also pp. 25–26.

28. I speak of *inert layering* because, as I have just noted, I distance myself from the "layer" theories criticized by Horrocks 1997:214.

29. *HTL* 124. See also Cassio 2002:117, 126, 131.

together. This new Attic was a regularized Attic, as it were, and it became a frame dialect for all Ionic dialects. As a regularized dialect, this new Attic was an Ionic Koine. As the name *Koine* indicates, the new Attic was a federal language, even an imperial language.[30] It was the lingua franca of the Athenian empire. Such a regularized Attic, as I argue in *Homer the Classic*, was the essence of the Homeric Koine as defined by Aristarchus. And this Attic Koine was not only a federal language: it was also the linguistic basis of Homeric poetry. But the basis of that basis remained the Ionic dialect.

IONIC KOINE AND AEOLIC KOINE

Around 600 B.C.E., the language of the Homeric Koine would have been perceived simply as Ionic from the synchronic standpoint of native speakers of Ionic. It is only from the diachronic standpoint of historical linguistics that this language can be analyzed as a blending of the Ionic dialect with other dialects—a blending that takes place within the frame dialect of Attic. Around the same time, however, there were other forms of poetic language that competed with this dominantly Ionic Koine of Homer. A prime example is a dominantly Aeolic Koine of the island of Lesbos. This Koine is represented by the poetry of Sappho and Alcaeus, who flourished on the island of Lesbos around 600 B.C.E. I now offer a definition of this poetic language by combining the diachronic perspective with the synchronic. The poetic language of Sappho and Alcaeus is a system that integrates and thus preserves the following phases of dialects: dominant Aeolic integrated with recessive Ionic integrated with residual Mycenaean. As in the case of the language of Homeric poetry, I am following Parry in viewing the language of the poetry of Sappho and Alcaeus synchronically as a working system, not as an inert layering of dialectal components matching the Aeolic, Ionic, and Mycenaean dialects.[31]

The published work of Parry on the poetic language of Sappho and Alcaeus shows that he was looking for signs of oral traditions underlying not only the epic of Homeric poetry but also other ancient Greek genres, especially those genres that are classified under the general heading *lyric*.[32] Parry's research on the lyric traditions of Sappho and Alcaeus was cut short, however, by his premature death. In a book containing his collected papers, edited by his son Adam Parry (1971), Milman Parry's overall work is presented in a scholarly context that confines the question of oral traditions to Homer, virtually excluding the rest of archaic Greek poetry.[33] In the introduction that Adam Parry wrote for his father's book, we see that genres

---

30. *HC* ch. 4.
31. Nagy 1972:25–26, 59–60. Also *PH* 14§9 (= p. 418).
32. Parry 1932, reprinted in Nagy 2001h1:15–64. See also the introduction in Nagy 2001h1.
33. Parry 1971:ix–lxii.

other than epic are not actively considered. Moreover, we see a pronounced aversion to any engagement with the comparative evidence of oral poetics.[34] By contrast with the discontinuities inherent in this posthumous publication, the work of Albert Lord continued systematically the comparative methodology of Milman Parry, with applications to lyric as well as epic.[35] In terms of this methodology, to draw a line between Homer and the rest of ancient Greek poetry is to risk creating a false dichotomy. There is a similar risk in making rigid distinctions between "oral" and "written" in studying the earliest attested forms of Greek poetry in general.[36]

It is beyond the scope of my present inquiry to delve here into the poetic language of Sappho and Alcaeus. I already did that in previous work, where I assembled linguistic evidence to show that this poetic language, as it evolved on the island of Lesbos, is an independent witness to the continuity of poetry from the Bronze Age through the Dark Age.[37] Here I confine myself to concentrating on the Aeolian federation that was represented by this poetic language.

As we saw in chapter 6, the Aeolian cities of the island of Lesbos once belonged to a federation dominated by the city of Mytilene. As we also saw, this Aeolian city was engaged in an ongoing struggle with the nominally Ionian city of Athens over the possession of Sigeion and its environs in the Troad during the late seventh and early sixth centuries B.C.E. At stake was the possession of vitally important territory—important not only because of its strategic location on the Hellespont but also because of its prestige as a space made sacred by the heroes who fought in the Trojan War. The deeds of these heroes were memorialized by living poetic traditions that represented the conflicting claims of the rival federations headed by Athens and Mytilene. A primary focus of the conflict, as I have already emphasized, was the tumulus of Achilles.

The spiritual center, as it were, of this Aeolian federation was a *temenos* 'sacred precinct' mentioned in the poetry of Alcaeus (F 129.2, 130b.13). This precinct is described in the language of the poet as a grand federal sacred space common to the entire population of the island of Lesbos.[38] Louis Robert has succeeded in identifying the name of this precinct: it is *Messon*, mentioned in two inscriptions dated to the second century B.C.E., which Robert successfully connects with the present-day name *Mesa* (neuter plural).[39] The meaning of the name for this space, in both ancient and Modern Greek, is the 'Middleground', which corresponds to its central location on the island. It also corresponds to the description of this precinct, in the words of Alcaeus, as the *xunon* or 'common possession' of the people of Lesbos

---

34. See also Parry 1966, included in volume 2 of Nagy 2001h2.
35. Lord 1995:22–68.
36. Lord 1995:105–6.
37. Nagy 1974; *PH* appendix (= pp. 439–64).
38. Nagy 1993. In what follows, I repeat some of the argumentation that I published there.
39. Robert 1960. He also demonstrates the connectedness of Alcaeus F 129 with F 130.

(F 129.3).[40] This Aeolic word is the equivalent of Attic *koinon*, and the Attic form is actually attested in the epigraphical references to *Messon*.[41] In general, *koinon* is a word used for designating any possession that is communalized and standardized so as to belong to a federation.

Reinforcing the arguments of Robert, Marcel Detienne connects the name *Messon* in Lesbos with the political expression *es meson* 'aiming for the center', which conveys the agonistic convergence of divergent interests at the center of a symmetrically visualized civic space.[42] For comparison, he adduces the description given by Herodotus of a meeting of the general assembly of the federation of the Ionian Dodecapolis held at the Panionion (1.170.2): on this occasion, according to Herodotus, Thales of Miletus proposed the establishment of a single council that would represent all Ionian cities, to be located centrally in Teos as the *meson* 'middleground' of the Ionian world (1.170.3).[43]

As we have just seen, the combining of archaeological and epigraphical evidence makes it possible to locate the precinct mentioned in the poetry of Alcaeus.[44] Also relevant is the historical evidence, which sheds light on the political and religious reasons for the centralized location of this precinct on the island of Lesbos.[45] And here I will add the evidence provided by the poetry of Alcaeus as a traditional system of reference. His poetry helps explain why Alcaeus speaks of this precinct.

It has generally been assumed that the reference to the precinct of Messon in the poetry of Alcaeus is incidental—in other words, that Alcaeus refers to this precinct because he happens to be there as an exile from his native city of Mytilene. I have argued, however, that this setting of a centralized sacred space, figured as a no-man's-land in the wording of Alcaeus, is intrinsic to the message that is actually being delivered by the poetry.[46] Here I will focus on only one aspect of my argument: that this place, imagined as a politically neutral sacred space, was the

---

40. Nagy 1993:221, where I add that the use of the word *sunodoi* 'assemblies' in Alcaeus F 130b.15, in a fragmentary context, may be pertinent.

41. Robert 1960.

42. Detienne 1973:97. I add the qualification *agonistic* in light of the discussion of Loraux 1987:108–12.

43. Another example of such symmetrical visualization is the Spartan term for their civic space, *khoros*: see Pausanias (3.11.9), who adds that this space was the setting for the Spartan festival of the Gymnopaidiai. See *PH* 12§17 (= pp. 344–45), with further citations. The designation of this festive space as the *khoros* is relevant to a detail in the narrative of Herodotus (6.67.2) about an incident involving a king of Sparta who presided over the festival of the Gymnopaidiai after being deposed from his kingship by a rival king: the former king's official title as president of this festival was *arkhōn* 'leader', and Herodotus plays on the ominous political significance of the use of this word in the context of the explosive incident that he narrates. See *PH* 12§23n56 (= pp. 348–49).

44. Again, Robert 1960.

45. Again, Detienne 1973:97.

46. Nagy 1993.

setting for the seasonally recurring festival of the federation of Aeolian cities headed by Mytilene.

As we see from the wording of Alcaeus, there is a ritual event taking place in this precinct. I highlight the word *ololugē* (130b.20 [ὀ]λολύγας), designating the 'ululation' of the women of Lesbos; this ululation is described as *hierē* 'sacred' (ἴρα[ς]).[47] This ritual event has been identified with the native Lesbian tradition of a women's 'beauty contest' in the context of a festival—as mentioned, for example, by Theophrastus (F 112 ed. Wehrli, by way of Athenaeus 13.610a; cf. Hesychius s.v. Πυλαιίδες). We find further relevant details in the Homeric scholia, where we see that the name of this festival is the *Kallisteia*:

> Παρὰ Λεσβίοις ἀγὼν ἄγεται κάλλους γυναικῶν ἐν τῷ τῆς Ἥρας τεμένει, λεγόμενος Καλλιστεῖα. Ἡ δὲ Λέσβος νῆσός ἐστιν ἐν τῷ Αἰγαίῳ πελάγει, πόλεις ἔχουσα πέντε, Ἄντισσαν, Ἐρεσσόν, Μήθυμναν, Πύρραν, Μιτυλήνην [*sic*].

> Among the people of Lesbos there is a **contest** [*agōn*] in beauty held in the **sacred** **precinct** [*temenos*] of **Hera**, called the *Kallisteia*. Lesbos is an island in the Aegean Sea, and it has five cities: Antissa, Eressos, Methymna, Pyrrha, and Mytilene.

> Scholia D for *Iliad* IX 130

Besides the epithet *hierē* 'sacred' describing the ululation of the women of Lesbos at the event of this festival (Alcaeus F 130b.20 ἴρα[ς]), a second epithet is also applied: *eniausia* 'seasonally recurring' (130b.20 ἐνιαυσίας), indicating that the festival of the *Kallisteia* takes place on a seasonally recurring basis. The detail about a competition in beauty is reflected in the wording of the song of Alcaeus, where we read κριννόμεναι φύαν 'outstanding in beauty' (130b.17).[48] The event in question is more than a beauty contest, however; it is a choral event: that is, an event featuring competitions among *khoroi* 'choruses' composed of singing and dancing women and girls. The ritual act of ululation is typical of choral performances involving women and girls.[49] There is an important piece of supporting evidence in the *Greek Anthology* (9.189), where the same festival of the *Kallisteia*, which is said to be taking place in the *temenos* 'sacred precinct' of Hera, is described explicitly in choral terms of song and dance, with Sappho herself pictured as the leader of the *khoros* 'chorus'.[50]

As we see from the wording of Alcaeus in describing this precinct, it is sacred to Zeus (129.5), to Dionysus (129.8–9), and to the 'Aeolian goddess' (F 129.6 Αἰολήιαν . . . θέον). This goddess is evidently Hera.[51] This same precinct, I propose,

---

47. Gentili 1988:220, 306n30.

48. Page 1955:168n4.

49. Gentili 1988:220, 306n30.

50. Page 1955:168n4. On the validity of traditional representations of Sappho as a choral personality, see *PH* 12§60 (= p. 370).

51. On the equation of the 'Aeolian goddess' with Hera, I find the argumentation of Robert 1960 most persuasive.

is sacred to Alcaeus himself as a cult hero: in my previous work, I have argued that the self-dramatization of Alcaeus in this context (F 129 and 130) is a function of his status as a cult hero who is imagined here as speaking from the dead to future generations of women and girls who are singing and dancing in *khoroi* 'choruses' that compete in the sacred precinct at Messon in Lesbos.[52]

I will not go into further details here concerning my earlier research on the self-dramatization of Alcaeus at Messon. Instead, I return to the central argument of Robert, which converges with my own central argument. Basically, this sacred precinct at Messon in Lesbos was the festive setting for the choral performances of women and girls as pictured in the poetry of Sappho.

All this is not to say that the poetic medium of Sappho was choral. My point is simply that the poetry of Sappho is cognate with choral lyric poetry—not only in form but also in content.[53] Technically, Sappho's poetry can be described as *monodic*—provided we understand this term not as an antithesis but as a complement to the term *choral*:[54]

> I understand the monodic form [of Sappho] to be not antithetical to the choral but rather predicated on it. A figure like Sappho speaks as a choral personality, even though the elements of dancing and the very presence of the choral group are evidently missing from her compositions. Still, these compositions presuppose or represent an interaction offstage, as it were, with a choral aggregate.

HOMER THE AEOLIAN REVISITED

The language of Sappho and Alcaeus is cognate not only with the language of choral lyric poetry: it is cognate also with the poetic language of epic as represented by Homer.[55] Or, to say it more precisely, the Aeolic Koine as represented by the poetry of Sappho and Alcaeus is cognate with the Aeolic phase of Homeric poetry as we know it. This Aeolic phase of Homer is what I mean when I say *Homer the Aeolian*.

A prime example of the Aeolic Koine is Song 44 of Sappho, known as "The Wedding of Hector and Andromache" (F 44), which is replete with phraseology demonstrably cognate with the phraseology we find both in choral lyric poetry and in epic poetry as represented by Homer.[56]

I draw attention to two details in Sappho's "Wedding of Hector and Andromache." First, we see references to the choral performances of women and girls, including

---

52. Nagy 1993:223–25.

53. Nagy 1993:223n7.

54. *PH* 12§62 (= p. 371). As we can see from the work of Power 2010:261–63, some of Sappho's compositions are not only monodic but also citharodic.

55. *PH* 14§§6–9 (= pp. 416–18); *PH* appendix §§2–19, 27, 33–37 (= pp. 439–51, 455–56, 459–64).

56. *PH* appendix §37 (= p. 464), summarizing the essentials of what I present in Nagy 1974. As Power 2010:258–63 shows, Song 44 of Sappho reflects a citharodic medium of performance.

an explicit reference to choral ululation: γύναικες δ᾽ ἐλέλυσδον 'and the women cried out *elelu!*' (F 44.31). Second, we see references to masterpieces of pattern-weaving: κάμματα | πορφύρ[α] . . . ποίκιλ᾽ ἀθύρματα 'purple fabrics, . . . pattern-woven [*poikila*] delights' (F 44.8–10). In both cases, the wording of Sappho is cognate with the wording that describes in *Iliad* VI a ritual scene where the women of Troy present Athena with a choice 'robe' or *peplos*.[57] In the first case, I focus on the moment when the chief priestess of the Trojans places this peplos on the knees of the statue of the goddess (VI 302–3). At that moment, the women of Troy ululate as they extend their hands in a choreographed ritual gesture to Athena: αἳ δ᾽ ὀλολυγῇ πᾶσαι Ἀθήνῃ χεῖρας ἀνέσχον 'with a cry of *ololu!* all of them lifted up their hands to Athena' (VI 301). In the second case, I focus on the description of this choice peplos as a masterpiece of pattern-weaving: ὃς κάλλιστος ἔην ποικίλμασιν ἠδὲ μέγιστος 'the one [peplos] that was the most beautiful in pattern-weavings [*poikilmata*] and the biggest' (VI 294). The excellence of this pattern-woven fabric is highlighted by comparing it with all the other competing peploi that could have been chosen instead: ἔνθ᾽ ἔσάν οἱ πέπλοι παμποίκιλοι 'there [in the storechamber] it was that she kept her peploi, and they were completely pattern-woven [*pan-poikiloi*]' (VI 289). At a later point in my argumentation, I will return to these convergences of detail in *Iliad* VI and in Sappho's Song 44.

Going beyond the details, let us consider the overall scene depicted in Sappho's Song 44, "The Wedding of Hector and Andromache." The atmosphere of the song is festive on the surface but ominous underneath. At the happy moment of their wedding, both the bridegroom and the bride are already doomed, victims of the epic fate of Troy. We see a sign of this doom in the epithet applied to both Hector and Andromache at the end of Sappho's song, *theoeikeloi* 'equal to the gods' (F 44.34). The meaning of this epithet is generically appropriate to Hector and Andromache at the moment of their wedding, since bridegrooms and brides are conventionally identified with gods and goddesses within the ritual time frame of a wedding.[58] But the application of this epithet in the context of the overall scene is ominous underneath the surface. In the Homeric *Iliad*, which narrates the later misfortunes of both Hector and Andromache, the epithet *theoeikelos* 'equal to the gods' is applied only to Achilles (I 131, XIX 155).[59] In the *Iliad*, Achilles is the hero directly responsible for the death of Hector and for the sorrows of Andromache. Achilles is pictured as singing the *klea andrōn* 'glories of heroes' (IX 189) while accompanying himself on the lyre that had once belonged to Eëtion, father of Andromache (IX 186–89), whom Achilles had killed when he captured the Aeolian city of Thebe (VI 414–16). In effect, Achilles sings his *klea andrōn* 'glories of heroes' (IX 189) to the mournful tune of

57. From here on, I will write simply "peplos," except where I analyze the etymology of the word.
58. *PP* 84.
59. On the theme of Achilles as the "eternal bridegroom," see Dué 2006:82–83.

the sorrows of Andromache. The lyre here is a metonym for the transfer of these sorrows to Achilles. The irony we see here in the *Iliad* is comparable to what we see in Song 44 of Sappho, "The Wedding of Hector and Andromache." There too we find the same kind of irony, which depends on the poetic heritage that her lyric poetry has in common with the epic poetry of Homer.[60]

We can see a comparable irony in the scene depicted in *Iliad* VI, which is likewise festive on the surface but ominous underneath. The depiction of the offering of a peplos to the goddess Athena by the women of Troy evokes the joyous moment of the offering of the Panathenaic Peplos in Athens, but the ensuing narration of Troy's destruction dooms to failure a ritual act that could succeed only in Athens—at the festival of the Panathenaia. And the occasion of this festival in Athens is precisely the venue for the actual narration of Troy's destruction—a narration that takes place through the Panathenaic performance of the Homeric *Iliad* and *Odyssey*.

Just as the festive but ominous narration of the failed ritual of the peplos was performed on the occasion of a festival (that is, at the Panathenaia in Athens), I propose that the festive but ominous narration of the wedding of Hector and Andromache was traditionally performed on a comparable occasion. That occasion was the grand festival held seasonally at the sanctuary of Messon on the island of Lesbos, bringing together representatives of a grand federation of Aeolian cities headed by Mytilene, the city that rivaled Athens in the struggle for possession of the poetic real estate of the Troad in the late seventh and early sixth centuries B.C.E.

At such a federal festival, we may expect a variety of performances in both poetry and song. The poetry could be epic as well as lyric, and the singing of lyric could be nonchoral as well as choral. In the case of a composition like Sappho's "Wedding of Hector and Andromache," its stichic or line-by-line format indicates a form that is neither choral lyric nor even simply lyric but something closer to what we know as *epic*.[61] As I have argued in previous work, the meter and the phraseology of this particular composition are cognate with the meter and phraseology of epic as represented by the Homeric *Iliad* and *Odyssey*.[62] In other words, the lyric medium of Sappho is referring to a coexisting epic medium that is cognate with what we see in Homer. And this epic medium represents not the predominantly Ionic phase of Homer known to us from the *Iliad* and *Odyssey* but an Aeolic phase. I repeat: this Aeolic phase of Homer is what I mean when I say *Homer the Aeolian*.

---

60. Nagy 1974:118–39. It is relevant to note again the work of Power 2010:258–63, who shows that the form of this lyric poetry of Sappho reflects a citharodic medium of performance.

61. As Power 2010:257–73 shows, the medium for performing such a form of epic may be more citharodic than rhapsodic.

62. Nagy 1974:118–39.

A HOMERIC GLIMPSE OF AN AEOLIAN FESTIVAL

By arguing that the poetic form of Sappho's "Wedding of Hector and Andromache" is cognate with the poetic form of epics attributed to Homer, I am in effect saying that these two poetic forms stem, respectively, from Aeolic and Ionic poetic traditions that evolved independently of each other. In the course of history, however, these independent traditions became interdependent as a result of cultural contact. In previous work, I have argued that the dominantly Aeolic tradition as represented by the poetry of Sappho and Alcaeus shows signs of influence from a dominantly Ionic tradition as represented by Homeric poetry.[63] In this work I argue that the converse holds true as well: in other words, that the dominantly Ionic tradition as represented by Homeric poetry shows signs of influence from a dominantly Aeolic tradition that we find still attested in the poetry of Sappho and Alcaeus. We see a glimpse of this influence in the following three Homeric passages:

δώσω δ' ἑπτὰ γυναῖκας ἀμύμονα ἔργα ἰδυίας
Λεσβίδας, ἃς ὅτε Λέσβον ἐϋκτιμένην ἕλεν αὐτὸς
ἐξελόμην, αἳ κάλλει ἐνίκων φῦλα γυναικῶν.
τὰς μέν οἱ δώσω, μετὰ δ' ἔσσεται ἣν τότ' ἀπηύρων
κούρη Βρισῆος·

And I [Agamemnon] will give seven women, skilled in flawless handiwork [*erga*],
  women from Lesbos. These women, when Lesbos with all its beautiful settlements
    was captured by him [Achilles] all by himself,
  were chosen by me as my own share [of the war prizes], and in beauty they were
    winners over all other rival groups of women.
These are the women that I will give him. And there will be among them the
  woman whom I took away back then,
  the daughter of Briseus [Briseis].

Iliad IX 128–31

δώσει δ' ἑπτὰ γυναῖκας ἀμύμονα ἔργα ἰδυίας
Λεσβίδας, ἃς ὅτε Λέσβον ἐϋκτιμένην ἕλες αὐτὸς
ἐξέλεθ', αἳ τότε κάλλει ἐνίκων φῦλα γυναικῶν.
τὰς μέν τοι δώσει, μετὰ δ' ἔσσεται ἣν τότ' ἀπηύρα
κούρη Βρισῆος·

And he [Agamemnon] will give seven women, skilled in flawless handiwork [*erga*],
  women from Lesbos. These women, when Lesbos with all its beautiful settlements
    was captured by you [Achilles] all by yourself,
  were chosen by him as his own share [of the war prizes], and in beauty they were
    winners, back then, over all other rival groups of women.

63. Nagy 1974:137–39.

These are the women that he will give you. And there will be among them the
    woman whom he took away back then,
the daughter of Briseus [Briseis].

Iliad IX 270–73

ἐκ δ' ἄγον αἶψα γυναῖκας ἀμύμονα ἔργα ἰδυίας
ἕπτ', ἀτὰρ **ὀγδοάτην** Βρισηΐδα καλλιπάρῃον.

And they led forth right away the women, skilled in flawless handiwork,
seven of them, and the **eighth** was Briseis of the fair cheeks.

Iliad XIX 245–46

We see here three references to an ensemble of women who were captured by
Achilles when he captured their cities on the island of Lesbos. Foregrounded is Briseis, a woman who was one of these women captured by Achilles and who was then
awarded as a war prize to the hero by his fellow Achaeans. As for the other seven
women, they were awarded as war prizes to Agamemnon.[64]

In the Homeric scholia D (at *Iliad* IX 130), the first of these three references to
the women from Lesbos is linked with a historically attested custom that was native to Lesbos, a seasonally recurring beauty contest known as the *Kallisteia*. This
contest, as we saw earlier, was the defining event of a Panaeolian festival seasonally
celebrated at the federal sanctuary of Messon in Lesbos. According to the Homeric
scholia, the mention of the women of Lesbos in the *Iliad* is a poetic reference to this
festival. Such an interpretation, as I will now argue, is borne out by the internal evidence of the *Iliad*.

In examining this evidence, I start with the distancing word *tote* 'once upon a
time', pointedly referring to those glory days in the past when these Aeolian women
from Lesbos were prominent celebrities. Back then, according to the *Iliad*, these
women were superior κάλλει 'in beauty' to all other women from all other places
in the whole world. Foregrounded in this ensemble of beautiful Aeolian women is
Briseis herself, who is characterized in the *Iliad* as an Aeolian woman in her own
right. She too, like the other Aeolian women, was captured—and captivated—by
none other than Achilles.

As Casey Dué has demonstrated in her book about Briseis, this character is portrayed in the *Iliad* as distinctly Aeolian in her cultural formation.[65] Briseis is closely
linked with places controlled by the Aeolian federation of Lesbos in the sixth century B.C.E. According to one tradition, the native city of Briseis was the old settlement of Brisa on the island of Lesbos.[66] According to another tradition, Briseis was
the daughter of Brisēs, king of the city of Pedasos.[67] This city was located on the

64. Commentary on these passages in Aloni 1986:52.
65. Dué 2002.
66. Dué 2002:4n10.
67. Dué 2002:3n10.

mainland facing the island of Lesbos, and it was controlled by this island in the sixth century.[68] In the epic of the *Cypria*, Achilles captured Briseis when he captured the city of Pedasos (scholia T for *Iliad* XVI 57). In the epic of the *Iliad*, by contrast, Achilles captured Briseis when he captured the city of Lyrnessos (II 689–91). Like Pedasos, Lyrnessos was a city located on the mainland facing the island of Lesbos, and it too, like Pedasos, was controlled by Lesbos in the sixth century.[69]

I draw attention to an essential parallel to the capturing of Lyrnessos by Achilles in the *Iliad*: the capturing of the city of Thebe by the same hero (II 690–91). This parallelism between Lyrnessos and Thebe, as we are about to see, highlights a connection between Briseis and Andromache. Relevant is another captive woman, Chryseis, who was awarded as a prize to Agamemnon just as the captive woman Briseis was awarded as a prize to Achilles. Just as Briseis was from Brisa in Lesbos according to one tradition, so also Chryseis was from Chrysa or Chrysē on Lesbos.[70] And just as Briseis when she was married moved to Lyrnessos and was later captured by Achilles there (*Iliad* II 688–93), so also Chryseis when she was married moved to Thebe and was later captured by Achilles there (*Iliad* I 366–69).[71] Here is where we see the connection between Briseis and Andromache. A native of the city of Thebe is Andromache herself, but she moved to Troy when she was married to Hector. Unlike the fate of Chryseis, the fate of Andromache as a captive woman is thus postponed, since she was already married to Hector and living in Troy, not in Thebe, when Achilles captured Thebe.[72] If Andromache had not already moved to Troy, her fate would have matched the fate of Chryseis, who had moved to Thebe, or the fate of Briseis, who had moved to Lyrnessos. That is because Achilles captured both Thebe and Lyrnessos. And the fact is that Thebe, like Lyrnessos, was an Aeolian city. Like Lyrnessos, the Thebe of Andromache was yet another city located on the mainland facing the island of Lesbos, and it, too, like Lyrnessos, was controlled by Lesbos in the sixth century.[73] Like Chryseis and Briseis, then, Andromache is an Aeolian personality.

These three women are not simply Aeolian personalities. They are Aeolian choral personalities. This characterization is most evident in the case of Briseis, as we see from the words spoken by this character when she laments the death of Patroklos:

Βρισηῒς δ’ ἄρ’ ἔπειτ’ ἰκέλη χρυσέῃ Ἀφροδίτῃ
ὡς ἴδε Πάτροκλον δεδαϊγμένον ὀξέϊ χαλκῷ,
ἀμφ’ αὐτῷ χυμένη λίγ’ ἐκώκυε, χερσὶ δ’ ἄμυσσε

68. Dué 2002:24n15.
69. Dué 2002:24n15.
70. Dué 2002:59n32. On the archaeological excavations at Chrysa, see Özgünel 2003.
71. Dué 2002:51.
72. Dué 2002:12.
73. Dué 2002:24n15.

στήθεά τ᾽ ἠδ᾽ ἁπαλὴν δειρὴν ἰδὲ καλὰ πρόσωπα.   285
εἶπε δ᾽ ἄρα κλαίουσα γυνὴ **ἐϊκυῖα θεῇσι·**
Πάτροκλέ μοι δειλῇ πλεῖστον **κεχαρισμένε** θυμῷ
ζωὸν μέν σε ἔλειπον ἐγὼ κλισίηθεν ἰοῦσα,
νῦν δέ σε τεθνηῶτα κιχάνομαι ὄρχαμε λαῶν
ἂψ ἀνιοῦσ᾽· ὥς μοι δέχεται κακὸν ἐκ κακοῦ αἰεί.   290
ἄνδρα μὲν ᾧ ἔδοσάν με πατὴρ καὶ πότνια μήτηρ
εἶδον πρὸ πτόλιος **δεδαϊγμένον ὀξέϊ χαλκῷ,**
τρεῖς τε κασιγνήτους, τούς μοι μία γείνατο μήτηρ,
κηδείους, οἳ πάντες ὀλέθριον ἦμαρ ἐπέσπον.
οὐδὲ μὲν οὐδέ μ᾽ ἔασκες, ὅτ᾽ ἄνδρ᾽ ἐμὸν ὠκὺς Ἀχιλλεὺς   295
ἔκτεινεν, πέρσεν δὲ πόλιν θείοιο Μύνητος,
κλαίειν, ἀλλά μ᾽ ἔφασκες Ἀχιλλῆος θείοιο
κουριδίην ἄλοχον θήσειν, ἄξειν τ᾽ ἐνὶ νηυσὶν
ἐς Φθίην, δαίσειν δὲ γάμον μετὰ Μυρμιδόνεσσι.
τώ σ᾽ ἄμοτον κλαίω τεθνηότα μείλιχον αἰεί.   300
Ὣς ἔφατο κλαίουσ᾽, ἐπὶ δὲ στενάχοντο γυναῖκες
Πάτροκλον πρόφασιν, σφῶν δ᾽ αὐτῶν κήδε᾽ ἑκάστη.

But then Briseis, **looking like golden Aphrodite,**
saw Patroklos all **cut apart by the sharp bronze,** and when she saw him,
she **poured herself** [*kheîn*] **all over him** [in tears] **and wailed with a voice
   most shrill,** and with her hands she tore at
her breasts and her tender neck and her beautiful face.   285
And then she spoke, weeping, this woman who **looked like the goddesses:**
"O Patroklos, you have been most **gracious** [via participle of *kharizesthai*]
   to me in my terrible state and most **gratifying** [again, via participle of
   kharizesthai] to my heart.
You were alive when I last saw you on my way out from the shelter,
and now I come back to find you dead, you, the protector of your people;
that is what I come back to find. Oh, how I have one misfortune after the next
   to welcome me.   290
The man to whom I was given away by my father and by my mother the queen,
I saw that man lying there in front of the city, **all cut apart by the sharp bronze,**
and lying near him were my three brothers—all of us were born of one mother.
They are all a cause for my sorrow, since they have all met up with their time of
   destruction.
No, you did not let me—back when my husband was killed by swift Achilles,   295
killed by him, and when the city of my godlike Mynes [my husband] was
   destroyed by him
—you did not let me weep, back then, but you told me that godlike Achilles
would have me as a properly courted wife, that you would make that happen,
   and that you would take me on board the ships,
taking me all the way to Phthia, and that you would arrange for a wedding
   feast among the Myrmidons.

So now I cannot stop crying for you, now that you are dead, you who were
  always so sweet and gentle."   300
So she [Briseis] spoke, weeping, and the women mourned in response.
They mourned for Patroklos: that was their pretext, but they were all
  mourning, each and every one of them, for what they really cared for
  in their own sorrow.

Iliad XIX 282–302

As she performs her lament in this passage, Briseis comports herself as the
lead singer of a choral ensemble of women. The ensemble is shown in the act of
responding to her lament by continuing it. The continuation is an antiphonal performance, in the form of various different kinds of stylized weeping and gesturing, or even singing and dancing.[74] I use the term *antiphonal* to indicate that this
performance is an overt response to the initial lament of the lead singer[75]—a response conveyed by the preverb *epi-* 'in response': ἐπὶ δὲ στενάχοντο γυναῖκες 'and
the women mourned in response [*epi-*]'.[76]

In the logic of the ongoing narrative, this ensemble of women responding to the
lament of Briseis is the same as the ensemble of captive women from Lesbos mentioned in *Iliad* IX. In performing her lament in conjunction with the antiphonal
laments of these women, Briseis is linked with the predetermined choral role of these
women, who were 'once upon a time' celebrated as the most beautiful girls in the
whole world—back in those happier times before the Trojan War. In the lament of
Briseis, her identity merges with the identity of these captive women of Lesbos. Once
upon a time, they were the world's most marriageable girls, living the charmed life
of renowned choral celebrities and groomed to become the wives of their region's
most powerful rulers. Now they are miserable slaves, doomed to become the con-
cubines of their captors.

Despite their pitiful degradation in social status, these women of Lesbos retain
their aristocratic charisma. An outward sign is the highlighting of their *erga* 'handiwork' (IX 128, 270). The most prestigious form of such handiwork, as we will see
later, is these women's skill in pattern-weaving, a mark of excellence viewed as a
parallel to their universally acknowledged excellence in choral singing and dancing.

The aristocratic charisma of these women of Lesbos is foregrounded in the figure
of their lead singer, Briseis. As she begins to perform her lament, she is equated
with the goddess Aphrodite herself (XIX 282). We see later on in the *Iliad* an important parallel to this eroticized image of Briseis in the act of singing a lament. It

---

74. In traditional lament, the physiology of weeping and gesturing is integrated with the art of singing
and dancing. (I note the relevant remarks of Dué 2006:46.)

75. On antiphonal *tsakismata* in Modern Greek traditions of lamentation, see Dué 2006:159, with
citations.

76. Dué 2002:70–71, 81; and Dué 2006:43–44.

happens when Andromache sees the sight of Hector's corpse dragged by the chariot of Achilles. At that moment of overwhelming sorrow, the image of Andromache is simultaneously eroticized. While she is falling into a swoon (XXII 466–67), she tears off all the bindings that control and adorn her hair, the last and most important of which is her overall *krēdemnon* 'headdress' (XXII 468–70). Pointedly, this *krēdemnon* had been given by Aphrodite herself to Andromache on her wedding day (*Iliad* XXII 470–71). Such a personalized connection with the goddess marks the eroticism of the precise moment when Andromache's luxuriant hair comes undone with the loss of her headdress.[77]

This erotic moment is extended. Once Andromache revives from her swoon (XXII 473–76), her consciousness modulates instantaneously into a lament as sensual as it is sorrowful (XXII 477–514). This sensuality bears the mark of Aphrodite.

Here I adduce a passage from tragedy that echoes the sensuality of Andromache's lament in the *Iliad*. The passage is a set of verses introducing an aria of lamentation sung as a monody by the actor who plays the title role in the *Andromache* of Euripides. These verses touch on Andromache's mixed feelings of sorrow and sensuality:

ἡμεῖς δ' οἵσπερ ἐγκείμεσθ' ἀεὶ
θρήνοισι καὶ **γόοισι** καὶ δακρύμασιν
πρὸς αἰθέρ' ἐκτενοῦμεν· ἐμπέφυκε γὰρ
γυναιξὶ **τέρψις** τῶν παρεστώτων κακῶν
ἀνὰ στόμ' αἰεὶ καὶ διὰ γλώσσης ἔχειν.

But I, involved as I am all the time in **laments** [*thrēnoi*] and **wailings** [*gooi*] and outbursts of tears,
will make them reach far away, as far as the aether. For it is natural
for women, when misfortunes attend them, to take **pleasure** [*terpsis*]
in giving voice to it all, voicing it again and again, maintaining the voice from one mouth to the next, from one tongue to the next.

Euripides *Andromache* 91–95

In these verses, the actor who represents Andromache is speaking in a rhythm that we know as the iambic trimeter. In the verses that will follow, he will be singing in a rhythm that we know as elegiac, consisting of elegiac couplets (101–16). And the sung elegiac verses will show that the actor who sings them must be more than an actor: he is also a singing virtuoso. What the actor will sing is a monody, which is a solo song requiring special virtuosity in singing—the kind of virtuosity that transcends the singing skills of the chorus. It is the sung verses of this monody (101–16) that are being introduced by the spoken verses of the passage we are now considering (91–95). But the wording of these spoken verses anticipates not only the solo singing of Andromache. It anticipates also the antiphonal singing of a chorus

---

77. Detailed analysis by Dué 2006:4, 78, with citations.

of women who will continue to sing where the solo singing of Andromache leaves off. This chorus of women will share the sorrows of Andromache and will be 'maintaining the voice from one mouth to the next, from one tongue to the next' (95). This wording of Andromache, which merely imagines the antiphonal lament of a chorus of women, anticipates what will actually happen when the monody of Andromache leaves off: the solo lament performed by Andromache (101–16) will now be taken up by an antiphonal lament that is no longer imagined but actually performed (117–46). And the performers of this antiphonal lament are no longer an imaginary chorus but the tragic chorus that sings and dances in the *Andromache* of Euripides.

We find in the *Iliad* a striking parallel to this choral response sung and danced by an ensemble of women who share the sorrows of Andromache as she sings her solo lament. It happens at the closure of the lament performed by Andromache after she sees the corpse of her husband dragged behind the chariot of Achilles. After the quotation of her solo song of lament (*Iliad* XXII 477–514), what follows is a lamentation by Trojan women who continue where the soloist left off:

Ὣς ἔφατο κλαίουσ', ἐπὶ δὲ στενάχοντο γυναῖκες.

So she [Andromache] spoke, weeping, and the women mourned in response.

Iliad XXII 515

The solo song of lament performed by Andromache is matched by the antiphonal lamenting of the stylized chorus of Trojan women who respond to her.[78] The same can be said about the solo song of lament performed by Briseis, which is likewise matched by the antiphonal lamenting of a stylized chorus of women. These women, unlike the Trojan women who respond to Andromache, are already the captives of the Achaeans. The chorus of women who respond to Briseis are the women of Lesbos who had been captured by Achilles:

Ὣς ἔφατο κλαίουσ', ἐπὶ δὲ στενάχοντο γυναῖκες
Πάτροκλον **πρόφασιν**, σφῶν δ' αὐτῶν κήδε' ἑκάστη.

So she [Briseis] spoke, weeping, and the women mourned in response.
They mourned for Patroklos: that was their **pretext** [*prophasis*], but they were all mourning, each and every one of them, for what they really cared for in their own sorrow.

Iliad XIX 301–2

---

78. In the case of the final lament that we see in the *Iliad*, performed by Helen, the antiphonal response is performed not by a stylized chorus of women (as in VI 499, XIX 301, XXII 515, XXIV 746) but by the entire community or *dēmos* of the Trojans (XXIV 776). See Dué 2006:44. On the *khoros* 'chorus' as a stylization of the entire community, see *PH* 5§11 (= p. 142), 12§2 (= p. 339), 12§17 (= pp. 334–45), 12§29 (= pp. 350–51), 12§55 (= pp. 367–68), 12§75 (= pp. 377–78).

The narrative of the *Iliad* leaves unvoiced the antiphonal singing performed by the women of Lesbos in response to the lament of Briseis, but as we have just seen, the description makes clear nevertheless the nature of their performance. It is choral. This Iliadic reference to a choral performance by the women of Lesbos evokes those happier days when these women were singing—and dancing—as choral celebrities back home at their local festival. Those happy days of celebration are gone forever, and all they have left now is an occasion to lament their sorrowful fate, but their song of lament is still a choral song. In the *Iliad*, this theme extends from the women of Lesbos in particular to the women of Troy in general.[79]

The narrative of the *Iliad* actually comments on its omission of the choral wording voiced by the captive women of Lesbos. While they sing antiphonally a song of lament for Patroklos, these women are really lamenting their own misfortunes. The wording of the *Iliad* draws attention to the *prophasis* 'pretext' of the sorrow of the women of Lesbos over the death of Patroklos (XIX 302). That sorrow is for them secondary to their sorrow about their own fate. For the *Iliad*, however, the sorrow occasioned by the death of Patroklos must remain the primary epic concern, and so the choral lyric concerns of the captive women cannot be voiced by them.

But these choral lyric concerns are in fact voiced by Briseis, who has a share in these concerns by virtue of being the lead singer of the captive women of Lesbos. The poetics of *prophasis* 'pretext' apply not only to the captive women but also to their lead singer. Briseis too has her own choral lyric concerns, which transcend the epic concern of sorrow over the death of Patroklos. True, the wording of the lament voiced by Briseis expresses her sorrowful reaction at the sight of the corpse of Patroklos, 'cut apart by the sharp bronze' of Hector (*Iliad* XIX 283 δεδαϊγμένον ὀξέϊ χαλκῷ), but this image is prefigured by something that she saw at an earlier time in her life: it was the gruesome sight of the corpse of her own beloved husband 'cut apart by the sharp bronze' of Achilles (XIX 292 δεδαϊγμένον ὀξέϊ χαλκῷ).[80] And the sorrowful reaction of Briseis at this sight will later be matched by the sorrowful reaction of Andromache at the sight of the corpse of her own beloved Hector, who will also be killed by Achilles. There is even more to it. Retrospectively, the sorrowful reaction of Briseis is matched by the equally sorrowful reaction of the unnamed captive woman in the simile that interrupts the third song of Demodokos. Here I quote the verses that describe the sorrowful reaction of this captive woman at the sight of her dear husband's corpse:

ταῦτ᾽ ἄρ᾽ ἀοιδὸς ἄειδε περικλυτός· αὐτὰρ Ὀδυσσεὺς
τήκετο, δάκρυ δ᾽ ἔδευεν ὑπὸ βλεφάροισι παρειάς.

79. This theme is evident also in the tragedies of Euripides: see Dué 2006:12 on *Trojan Women* 582–86; also p. 141 on *Trojan Women* 474–97; also p. 15 on *Hecuba* 349–57.
80. Dué 2002:11.

the cities of Lesbos, especially with Mytilene, over the possession of a vital part of the Asiatic mainland: that is, the city of Sigeion and its environs in the Troad. As we saw earlier, the Athenian encroachment on the Troad did not necessarily undercut the identity of the Aeolian population who lived there, since Athens at the time of this conflict with the Aeolians in Asia Minor was an ally of the Aeolians in Europe: that is, with the Thessalians. And the Thessalians had their own claim on the Troad, as we know from a ritual described by Philostratus, which I quoted in chapter 7. In the era of the Peisistratidai and even earlier, the Athenians were allies of these European Aeolians of Thessaly and enemies of the Asiatic Aeolians of Lesbos, especially of the Mytilenaeans.

In the context of the conflict between the Athenians and the Aeolians of Lesbos over the Troad, the Athenians took the initiative of appropriating the poetic heritage of these Aeolians. Such appropriation took the form of actually displaying for public consumption the poetry of Lesbos at the festival of the Panathenaia in Athens. When the Homeric *Iliad* features Briseis singing her lament for Patroklos and, implicitly, for her husband, what is actually being heard by the audience at the Panathenaia in Athens is the lament of an Aeolian woman originating from the federation of Lesbos. So also when the Homeric *Iliad* features Andromache singing her lament for her husband, Hector, what is being heard by the Panathenaic audience is the lament of another Aeolian woman originating from the same federation.

The performance of such laments is adapted to the medium of the rhapsodes who perform Homeric poetry at the Panathenaia. So the laments of Briseis and of Andromache are performed as if they were monodic, not choral, though the Homeric narrative goes on to represent the performances of antiphonal responses by choral ensembles composed of women from Lesbos and from Troy, respectively. In both cases the prima donna of the choral ensemble is an Aeolian woman. So, by extension, the overall performance is imagined as an Aeolian choral lyric song. In other words, Homeric poetry represents Aeolian women in the act of performing choral lyric poetry.

At the Panathenaia in Athens, the performance of epic poetry by rhapsodes was not the only medium for representing Aeolian women in the act of performing choral lyric poetry. Another medium of representation was the performance of nonchoral lyric poetry. In this case, the performers were not rhapsodes. To make this point, I show a picture of Sappho and Alcaeus in a vase painting (fig. 3).

In figure 3 we see Sappho and Alcaeus pictured in the act of nonchoral lyric performance. The performers are to sing while accompanying themselves on stringed instruments. This picture was produced in Athens, sometime in the early fifth century B.C.E. Why, we may ask, were Sappho and Alcaeus appropriated in this way by the Athenian media of visual arts? To give the briefest possible answer: because the lyric poetry of Sappho and Alcaeus was likewise appropriated by the Athenian media of verbal arts. The songs that had once been the lyric repertoire of the Ae-

FIGURES 3A–B. Attic red-figure kalathoid vase: (a) obverse, Sappho (labeled as "ΣΑΦΟ") and Alcaeus (labeled as "ΑΛΚΑΙΟΣ"); (b) Dionysus and maenad. Attributed to the Brygos Painter. Munich, Antikensammlungen, 2416. Drawings by Valerie Woelfel.

olic Koine representing the federation of Lesbos were now part of the lyric reper-toire of *kitharōidoi* 'citharodes' who competed at the Panathenaia, matching the epic repertoire of *rhapsōidoi* 'rhapsodes' who competed at the same festival.[83] Just as the rhapsodic traditions of performing epic poetry at the Panathenaia in Athens were shaped prehistorically by this Aeolic Koine, so too were the citharodic traditions of performing lyric poetry.

From what we have seen so far, I conclude that poetry was a currency used by federations of cities as a self-expression of their federalism. The self-expression took the form of poetic performances at festivals celebrated in common by the cities be-longing to these federations, dominated by master cities like Mytilene on the island of Lesbos and Athens on the Helladic mainland. Another prominent example, as we saw in chapter 7, was Miletus on the Asiatic mainland. In the case of Mytilene, the federation of Aeolian cities it dominated was notionally a Panaeolian society. Similarly in the case of Miletus, the federation of Ionian cities it dominated was no-tionally a Panionian society. Much the same can be said in the case of Athens, though the composition of the federation it dominated was more complicated. Back when

83. On the transmission of the lyric poetry of Sappho and Alcaeus in the context of citharodic per-formances at the Panathenaia in Athens, see Nagy 2004b; also Nagy 2007b. For a thorough investiga-tion of the citharodic medium of performing monodic songs of Sappho and Alcaeus, see Power 2010.

the nexus of Ionian cities that eventually became the Delian League started to be dominated by Athens, this federation did not yet have the prestige of the Ionian Dodecapolis dominated by Miletus. Thus any claim to the effect that Athens was the leader of a Panionian society would have been weaker than the rival claim of Miletus. Later on, as the Delian League evolved into the Athenian empire, its claim to represent a Panionian society became so strong as to eclipse all other rival claims. But by then the Athenian empire had outgrown the necessity for claiming to represent such a Panionian society, since it could now claim to represent something much broader—something that was notionally all-encompassing. That something was a notionally Panhellenic society.

9

Further Variations on a Theme of Homer

HOMER THE FEDERAL HOSTAGE

The time has come to ask this fundamental question about the festive poetics of federal politics. How could Homeric poetry express the idea of a federal society? Or, to put it another way, how could a poetic figure like Homer serve as a spokesman for such a society? The answer, I propose, has to do with the meaning of the name *Homēros* 'Homer'.[1]

I start by reviewing what we know so far about this name. As I argued in chapter 3, the name of Homer and the meaning of his name are linked to the *Homēridai* of Chios, who were notional descendants of Homer and who re-enacted the performances of their ancestor at Panionian festivals, originally at the Panionia held at the Panionion of the Ionian Dodecapolis in Asia Minor.[2] Eventually, in the context of the Panionian festival of the Delia, they became virtual spokesmen for the Delian League. Then, as the federation of the Delian League evolved into the all-encompassing federation of the Athenian empire, the re-enactment of Homer by the *Homēridai* at the festival of the Delia in Delos was replaced by his re-enactment at the festival of the Panathenaia in Athens. So the city of Athens claimed not only Homer but also the *Homēridai* in extending the epic repertoire of the Delia to the Panathenaia.[3]

The Athenian connection of the *Homēridai* helps explain why the narrative of a decidedly non-Athenocentric *Life of Homer* like *Vita* 1 denies the idea that Homer

---

1. In what follows, I repeat many of the arguments I presented in Nagy 2006a.
2. On the *Homēridai* and the Panionia, see again Frame 2009 ch. 11.
3. Relevant is the reference to the *Homēridai* in Plato *Ion* 530d, as analyzed above in chapter 3.

54

had any sons. This way, as we saw in chapter 3, the narrative also denies the idea that Homer of Chios was linked to the *Homēridai* who performed at the Panathenaia and who claimed to hail from Chios. Evidently, the concept of *Homēridai,* even as a name, had something to do with the idea of an Athenian federation—an idea that is generally avoided in *Vita* 1.

In fact, the general idea of a federation is implicit in the meaning of the name from which *Homēridai* is derived, *Homēros*. This name is derived from the noun *homēros,* which has the primary meaning of 'hostage'. Before we consider this meaning of *homēros* as a common noun, however, we need to take one more look at the meaning of *Homēros* as a proper noun: that is, as the name of the master poet we know as Homer. The meaning of this name is recapitulated in the interaction between Homer and the Delian Maidens, those singing local Muses of the festival of the Delia in the *Homeric Hymn to Apollo:*[4]

οὕτω σφιν καλὴ συνάρηρεν ἀοιδή

That is how their beautiful song has each of its parts **fitting together** [*sun-arariskein*] in place.

Homeric Hymn (3) *to Apollo* 164

This description recapitulates the meaning of *Homēros* (Ὅμηρος) as a *nomen loquens.* Etymologically, the form is a compound **hom-āros* meaning 'he who fits [*or:* 'joins'] together', composed of the prefix *homo-* 'together' and the root of the verb *arariskein* (ἀρ-αρ-ίσκειν) 'fit, join'.[5] So *Homēros* is 'he who fits [the song] together'.[6] Relevant is the idea of the epic Cycle or *kuklos* in its earlier sense of referring to all poetry composed by Homer.[7] This meaning of *kuklos* as the sum total of Homeric poetry goes back to a metaphorical use of *kuklos* in the sense 'chariot wheel' (*Iliad* XXIII 340; plural, *kukla,* at V 722). The metaphor of comparing a well-composed song to a well-crafted chariot wheel is explicitly articulated in the poetic traditions of Indo-European languages (as in *Rig-Veda* 1.130.6); more generally in the Greek poetic traditions, there is a metaphor comparing the craft of the *tektōn* 'joiner, master carpenter' to the art of the poet (as in Pindar *Pythian* 3.112–14).[8] So the etymology of *Homēros,* in the sense 'fitting together', is an aspect of this metaphor: a master poet 'fits together' pieces of poetry that are made ready to be parts of an integrated whole, just as a master carpenter or joiner 'fits together' or 'joins' pieces of wood that are made ready to be parts of a chariot wheel.[9] And as we will now see,

---

4. On the Delian Maidens as the local Muses of Delos, see *HC* 2§§26–40.

5. Chantraine *DELG* s.v. ἀραρίσκω.

6. *BA* 17§§9–13 (= pp. 296–300).

7. For more on this earlier sense of *kuklos* with reference to all poetry composed by Homer, see Pfeiffer 1968:73 and *HQ* 38.

8. *BA* 17§§10–13 (= pp. 297–300), interpreting the evidence assembled by Schmitt 1967:296–98.

9. *PP* 74–75.

this etymology of Homer's name is compatible in meaning with the etymology of the noun *homēros* (ὄμηρος) in the sense 'hostage', which derives from the same compound **hom-āros* meaning 'he who fits [*or*: 'joins'] together'.[10]

A hostage is the visible sign of a pact or agreement between two parties: that is, of a 'joining together' or 'bonding'. Such a meaning evidently derives from metaphors of social bonding inherent in derivatives of *arariskein* (ἀρ-αρ-ίσκειν) 'fit, join': an ideal case in point is *arthmos* (ἀρθμός) 'bond, league, friendship' and related forms.[11] The etymology of the noun *homēros* (ὄμηρος) in the sense of 'hostage' is in turn compatible in meaning with the etymology of the verb *homērein* or *homēreuein* (ὁμηρεῖν, ὁμηρεύειν) in the sense of 'joining' the company of someone or 'accompanying' someone.

The meanings of *Homēros, homēros, homērein,* and *homēreuein* (Ὅμηρος, ὄμηρος, ὁμηρεῖν, and ὁμηρεύειν) are linked in the *Life of Homer* traditions, and the linkage is centered on the idea of Homer as a culture hero.[12] In the *Homeric Hymn to Apollo*, we saw the poetic idea of *Homēros* (Ὅμηρος) as a singer who 'fits together' the songs he makes at the festival of the Delia, in interaction with the local Muses of Delos, the Delian Maidens. In the *Life of Homer* traditions, we can see the political as well as poetic idea of *Homēros* (Ὅμηρος) as a culture hero who 'fits together' the societies he visits. Here I will focus on contexts where Homer is pictured as a 'hostage'—that is, *homēros* (ὄμηρος)—and as one who 'joins' the company of others: that is, *homērein* or *homēreuein* (ὁμηρεῖν, ὁμηρεύειν). In these contexts, as we are about to see, these words are conventionally associated with the theme of Homer's blindness.

In the *Life of Homer* traditions, the poet is conventionally pictured as blind, and his blindness is caused by some misfortune that happens to him in the course of his life. Different narratives feature different misfortunes. In some versions, he is blinded by some illness (*Vita* 1.84–87, 90–92); in other versions, his blinding is a divine punishment for some mistake, such as his defaming of Helen (*Vita* 6.51–57) or his conjuring a direct vision of Achilles entering battle in his second set of ar-

---

10. Some of the argumentation that follows is anticipated in Nagy 2006a.

11. *PP* 74–75n45, with reference to Chantraine *DELG* s.v. ἀραρίσκω (and with a discussion of an alternative explanation offered by Bader 1989:269n114). As I noted already in 1979 (*BA* 17§9n2 [= pp. 296–97]), I agree with Durante 1976:194–97 about the morphology of the reconstructed compound **hom-āros,* and although my interpretation of the semantics of this compound (*BA* 17§§10–13 [= pp. 297–300]) is different, I agree with his interpretation of attested Greek forms like ὁμαρο- in the sense 'festive assembly' or 'festival'; such meanings are cognate, I think, with the metaphorical sense 'joining' or 'bonding'. See also Debiasi 2001, especially pp. 12–16 with reference to the name Ὁμήριος (attested in fifth-century epigraphical evidence from Styra in Euboea: *IG* 9, 56.135).

12. On the idea of Homer as a culture hero—and cult hero—see again *BA* 17§9n3 (= p. 297), following Brelich 1958:320–21, and *PP* 113n34.

13. By implication, it is specifically the gleam from the second Shield of Achilles that blinds Homer. See Graziosi 2002:159, with reference to the blinding gleam of the hero's Shield in *Iliad* XIX 12–15. I

mor, the gleam of which is blinding to those who dare look at it (*Vita* 6.45–51).[13] For now, however, I bypass these versions by concentrating on the conventional association of Homer's blindness with the words *homēros* (ὅμηρος) and *homērein* or *homēreuein* (ὁμηρεῖν, ὁμηρεύειν).

In some versions of the *Life of Homer* traditions, as we have already seen in chapter 6, the naming of Homer as *Homēros* (Ὅμηρος) is explained on the grounds that the word *homēros* (ὅμηρος) means 'blind', not 'hostage'. I now propose to examine in detail the relevant passages. To begin, I need to stress that the explanation of *homēros* as 'blind' is problematic, since as we have seen the etymology of *homēros* points to the basic idea of bonding, not blinding. In some versions of the *Lives*, however, this meaning 'blind' is explicitly juxtaposed with the meaning 'hostage', presented as an alternative.

The equation of *homēros* with the meaning 'blind' is associated with 'the Aeolians'— that is, with speakers of the Aeolic dialect; more specifically, they are named as the people of Cyme,[14] Smyrna,[15] and Lesbos:[16]

φασὶ δ' αὐτὸν Μελησιγένη ἢ Μελησιάνακτα κεκλῆσθαι, **τυφλωθέντα δ' αὐτὸν** ὕστερον Ὅμηρον κληθῆναι· **οἱ γὰρ Αἰολεῖς τοὺς τυφλοὺς ὁμήρους καλοῦσιν.** πατρίδα δ' αὐτοῦ οἱ μὲν Σμύρναν, οἱ δὲ Χίον, οἱ δὲ Κολοφῶνα, οἱ δ' Ἀθήνας λέγουσιν.

They say that he was called *Melēsigenēs* or *Melēsianax*; but then, after he was **blinded** at a later point, that he was called *Homēros*. **For the Aeolians call blind people *homēroi*.** Some say his birthplace was **Smyrna**; others say it was Chios or Colophon or Athens.

Vita 4.4–9

τῶν βουλευτέων[17] ἕνα λέγεται ἐναντιωθῆναι τῇ χρήμῃ αὐτοῦ, ἄλλα τε πολλὰ λέγοντα καὶ ὡς εἰ τοὺς **ὁμήρους** δόξει τρέφειν αὐτοῖς ὅμιλον πολλόν τε καὶ ἀχρεῖον ἕξουσιν. ἐντεῦθεν δὲ καὶ τοὔνομα Ὅμηρος ἐπεκράτησε τῷ Μελησιγένει ἀπὸ τῆς συμφορῆς· **οἱ γὰρ Κυμαῖοι τοὺς τυφλοὺς ὁμήρους λέγουσιν·** ὥστε πρότερον ὀνομαζομένου αὐτοῦ Μελησιγένεος τοῦτο γενέσθαι τοὔνομα Ὅμηρος.

It is said that one of the members of the *boulē*[18] [in the city of Cyme] was opposed to his request [to give *Melēsigenēs* public subsidy], saying among other things that if they [the members of the *boulē*] decided to subsidize *homēroi*, they would have on their hands a multitude of good-for-nothing people. It was from that point onward that the

---

will have more to say in chapter 10 concerning the picture that is being projected, as it were, by the blinding gleam.

14. In the *Life of Homer* traditions, it is made clear that the city of Cyme was originally Aeolian.

15. In the *Life of Homer* traditions, it is also made clear that the city of Smyrna was originally Aeolian.

16. In the *Lives of Homer* and elsewhere, the word Λέσβιοι 'people of Lesbos', referring to inhabitants of the cities on the island of Lesbos, figures as a subcategory of Αἰολεῖς 'Aeolians'.

17. There is a variant reading here: βασιλέων.

18. In the variant reading: 'It is said that one of the kings . . . .'.

name of *Homēros* prevailed for *Melēsigenēs*, on the basis of the misfortune [of his being blind]. **For the people of Cyme call blind people *homēroi*.** That is how it happened that the man who was formerly named *Melēsigenēs* got this name *Homēros*.

Vita 1.160–66

καὶ πρῶτοί γε **Σμυρναῖοι** Μέλητος ὄντα τοῦ παρ' αὐτοῖς ποταμοῦ καὶ Κρηθηίδος νύμφης κεκλῆσθαί φασι πρότερον Μελησιγένη, ὕστερον μέντοι τυφλωθέντα Ὅμηρον μετονομασθῆναι **διὰ τὴν παρ' αὐτοῖς ἐπὶ τῶν τοιούτων συνήθη προσηγορίαν.**

And the **people of Smyrna** were the first to say that he [Homer] was earlier called *Melēsigenēs*, child of the river[-god] by that name [*Melēs*] in their territory and of the nymph *Krēthēis*; and that later, when he was blinded, he was renamed *Homēros* **in accordance with their customary local way of calling people like him.**

Vita 2.8–12

ἐκλήθη δ' Ὅμηρος διὰ τὸ πολέμου ἐνισταμένου **Σμυρναίοις** πρὸς **Κολοφωνίους** ὅμηρον δοθῆναι, ἢ τὸ βουλευομένων Σμυρναίων δαιμονίᾳ τινι ἐνεργείᾳ φθέγξασθαι καὶ συμβουλεῦσαι ἐκκλησιάζουσι περὶ τοῦ πολέμου.

And he was called *Homēros* for this reason: when a war broke out between the **people of Smyrna** and the **people of Colophon**, he was given as a **hostage [*homēros*]** [to the people of Colophon]. Or for this reason: when the people of Smyrna were deliberating, he voiced his words with a power that came from some unnamed divinity [*daimōn*], and he gave them counsel about the war as they met in public assembly.

Vita 10.25–28

οἱ μὲν οὖν Σμυρναῖον αὐτὸν ἀποφαινόμενοι Μαίονος μὲν πατρὸς λέγουσιν εἶναι, γεννηθῆναι δὲ ἐπὶ Μέλητος τοῦ ποταμοῦ, ὅθεν καὶ Μελησιγενῆ ὀνομασθῆναι· **δοθέντα δὲ Χίοις εἰς ὁμηρείαν Ὅμηρον κληθῆναι.** οἱ δὲ ἀπὸ τῆς τῶν ὀμμάτων πηρώσεως τούτου τυχεῖν αὐτόν φασι τοῦ ὀνόματος· **τοὺς γὰρ τυφλοὺς ὑπὸ Αἰολέων ὁμήρους καλεῖσθαι.**

Some say, claiming they have proof, that he was a Smyrnaean, and that his father was *Maiōn*. They go on to say that he was born on the banks of the river *Melēs*, after which he was named *Melēsigenēs*. They say further that **he was given to the people of Chios for service as a hostage [*homēreia*] and was thus called** *Homēros*. Others say that he happened to get this name because he was incapacitated in his eyesight. **For blind people are called *homēroi* by the Aeolians.**

Vita 11.14–20

ἐκαλεῖτο δ' ἐκ γενετῆς Μελησιγένης ἢ Μελησαγόρας, αὖθις δ' Ὅμηρος ἐλέχθη κατὰ τὴν Λεσβίων διάλεκτον, ἕνεκεν τῆς περὶ τοὺς ὀφθαλμοὺς συμφορᾶς, **οὗτοι γὰρ τοὺς τυφλοὺς ὁμήρους λέγουσιν,** ἢ διότι παῖς ὢν ὅμηρον ἐδόθη βασιλεῖ, ὅ ἐστιν ἐνέχυρον.

He was called *Melēsigenēs* or *Melēsagoras* from birth. Later, he was called *Homēros*, in accordance with the dialect of the **people of Lesbos**, because of the misfortune that happened concerning his eyes. **For these people [the Lesbians] call blind people** *homēroi*. Alternatively, [he was called *Homēros*] because, **when he was still a child, he was given as a hostage [*homēron*] to the king: that is, he was given as a guarantee.**[19]

Vita 6.41–45

ὀνομασθῆναι δὲ αὐτόν φασί τινες "Ομηρον διὰ τὸ τὸν πατέρα αὐτοῦ ὅμηρον δοθῆναι ὑπὸ Κυπρίων Πέρσαις, οἱ δὲ διὰ τὴν πήρωσιν τῶν ὀμμάτων· παρὰ γὰρ τοῖς Αἰολεῦσιν οὕτως οἱ πηροὶ καλοῦνται.

Some say that he was named *Homēros* because his father had been given as a **hostage [*homēros*]** by the **Cypriotes** to the **Persians.** Others say that it was because of the incapacitation of his eyesight. **For among the Aeolians that is how the incapacitated are called.**

Vita 2.29–32

μετωνομάσθη δ' Όμηρος ἐπειδὴ τὰς ὄψεις ἐπηρώθη· οὕτω δὲ ἐκάλουν οἵ τε Κυμαῖοι καὶ οἱ Ίωνες τοὺς τὰς ὄψεις πεπηρωμένους παρὰ τὸ δεῖσθαι τῶν ὁμηρευόντων, ὅ ἐστι τῶν ἡγουμένων. καὶ ταῦτα μὲν Έφορος.

He [*Melēsigenēs*] was renamed *Homēros* because he was incapacitated in his eyesight. **That is how the people of Cyme as well as the Ionians call those who are incapacitated in their eyesight,** since they [the blind] are in need of those who will *homēreuein* them: that is, those who will **lead** them around. So goes the report of Ephorus [*FGH* 70 F 1].

Vita 3a.20–24

I save for last the most striking example, which comes from Aristotle (F 76 ed. Rose), as mediated by *Vita* 3a. According to this source, Aristotle in Book 3 of his *Poetics* recounts a version of the *Life of Homer* according to which Homer is conceived on the island of Ios in the days of the Ionian *apoikia* 'migration' led by Neleus son of Kodros (*Vita* 3a.25–27). Homer's mother is a *korē* 'girl' who is a native of the island (3a.27 κόρην τινα τῶν ἐπιχωρίων); his father is an unnamed divinity or *daimōn* described as 'one who joins in the songs and dances [*khoroi*] of the Muses' (3a.28 τινος δαίμονος τῶν συγχορευτῶν ταῖς Μούσαις).[20] The pregnant girl flees to Aegina, where she is kidnapped by pirates who take her to the city of Smyrna, at that time occupied by the Lydians; there a man called *Maiōn*, who is described as a *philos* 'friend' of the king of the Lydians, takes a fancy to her (3a.32–33 εἰς Σμύρναν

19. Here *homēron* 'hostage' is neuter, in designating the bond that binds the hostage to the hostage-taker. The identity of the unnamed 'king' is unclear; I conjecture that the referent is the king of the Lydians, as mentioned in *Vita* 3a.32–33 (on which see below).

20. See also *Vita* 6.31–32, referring again to Aristotle (F 76 ed. Rose): Ἀριστοτέλης δὲ ἱστορεῖν φησιν . . . ἔκ τινος δαίμονος γεγενῆσθαι τὸν Όμηρον ταῖς Μούσαις συγχορεύσαντος 'Aristotle says that investigation can show [a version where] Homer was conceived by some divinity [*daimōn*] who joins in the songs and dances [*khoroi*] of the Muses'. I infer that the unnamed divinity is Apollo as *khorēgos* 'khoros leader' of the Muses. I have reservations about the translation of West 2003a:407: 'one of the sprites who dance with the Muses' (also p. 435: 'a sprite who danced with the Muses').

οὖσαν ὑπὸ Λυδοῖς τότε, τῷ βασιλεῖ τῶν Λυδῶν ὄντι φίλῳ τοὔνομα Μαίονι χαρίσασθαι). *Maiōn* marries the girl and adopts her son when he is born. Homer is still a child when he is orphaned by his mother and by his adoptive father. The city of Smyrna is then besieged by the Aeolians, and the leaders of the Lydians, trapped inside the city, make a proclamation asking for Aeolian 'volunteers' to join them in making an exit from the city. By implication, these 'volunteers' will be hostages that can serve as guarantees for the safe exit of the Lydians out of Smyrna as the Aeolians proceed to retake the city. Homer, as the adoptive son of a man described earlier as a 'friend' of the king of the Lydians, seems a prime candidate. Homer, in his childish naïveté, volunteers to 'join', *homēreîn* (ὁμηρεῖν):

> τῶν δὲ Λυδῶν καταπονουμένων ὑπὸ τῶν **Αἰολέων καὶ κρινάντων καταλιπεῖν τὴν Σμύρναν**, κηρυξάντων τῶν ἡγεμόνων τὸν βουλόμενον ἀκολουθεῖν ἐξιέναι τῆς πόλεως, ἔτι νήπιος ὢν Ὅμηρος ἔφη καὶ αὐτὸς **βούλεσθαι ὁμηρεῖν**· ὅθεν ἀντὶ Μελησιγένους Ὅμηρος προσηγορεύθη.

> As the Lydians were besieged by the **Aeolians** and decided to abandon Smyrna, their leaders sent out a proclamation saying that he who **volunteered** to **accompany** them should make an exit from the city [with them]. Homer, who was still a mere child, said that he too **volunteered** to join [*homēreîn*]. That is how he got to be called *Homēros* instead of *Melēsigenēs*.

> *Vita* 3a.39–44

Beyond this point, the narrative of *Vita* 3a does not say what happened to Homer while he was a hostage of the Lydians. But the language of the narrative up to this point leaves some indications: it euphemistically pictures the political hostage as a 'joiner', as if the bond between hostage and hostage-taker corresponded to an idealized bonding between 'guest' and 'host'. Homer himself is pictured as a 'hostage' by virtue of his 'joining' the Lydians as they make their exit from the besieged city of Smyrna.

Here it is relevant to highlight an observation made by Robert Dyer about the supposedly double meaning of *homēros* as either 'hostage' or 'blind' in Aeolic usage. As Dyer observes: "This ambiguity would be resolved if it [*homēros*] was applied there [in Aeolic contexts] to hostages returned to their homes after being blinded in retribution for a violation of the hostage agreement."[21] He cites, as an example of such a custom, a narrative about an event that takes place before the capture of the capital city of the Lydian empire, Sardis, by the Persian empire. (The date of this capture is 547 B.C.E.) The narrative concerns Croesus, king of the Lydians, and his son, who is evidently being held as a hostage by the Persians during the siege of Sardis:

> ... ὅπως τε πρὸ τῆς ἁλώσεως δίδοται ὁ παῖς Κροίσου ἐν ὁμήρου λόγῳ, δαιμονίου φαντάσματος ἀπατήσαντος Κροῖσον· ὅπως τε δολορραφοῦντος Κροίσου ὁ παῖς κατ᾽

---

21. Dyer 2006.

ὀφθαλμοὺς ἀναιρεῖται· καὶ ὅπως ἡ μήτηρ τὸ πάθος ἰδοῦσα ἑαυτὴν τοῦ τείχους ἀποκρημνίζει, καὶ θνήσκει.

And [Ctesias tells] how, before the capture [of Sardis], the son of Croesus is given up [to the Persians] **in the manner of a hostage [*homēros*]**, because the apparition of some unnamed divinity [*daimōn*] deceived Croesus. And [Ctesias tells] how, after Croesus devises a deceptive stratagem, his son **is killed before his eyes**. And [Ctesias tells] how the mother [of the victim], seeing what happened to him, throws herself to her death from the walls [of Sardis].

> Ctesias *FGH* IIIc 688 F 9 lines 40–43, via Photius *Bibliotheca* ed. Bekker 72.36b lines 2–6

Evidently, the father is figuratively blinded by the Persians in retribution for his violation of a hostage agreement. I stress that the blinding here is figurative: the father's vision is forever maimed by the sight of his son's violent death, inflicted as a punishment for a breach of contract committed not by the son but by the father himself. The mentality behind this kind of figurative blinding is evident in wording that describes a form of punishment where the figurative blinding is reinforced by physical blinding. I have found such wording in a description of the punishment inflicted on the captured renegade king Zedekiah, ruler of Jerusalem, by the overking Nebuchadnezzar, king of Babylon:

καὶ τοὺς υἱοὺς Σεδεκίου **ἔσφαξεν κατ᾽ ὀφθαλμοὺς αὐτοῦ**, καὶ τοὺς **ὀφθαλμοὺς** Σεδεκίου **ἐξετύφλωσεν** καὶ ἔδησεν αὐτὸν ἐν πέδαις καὶ ἤγαγεν αὐτὸν εἰς Βαβυλῶνα.

And he [Nebuchadnezzar, king of Babylon] **slaughtered** the sons of Zedekiah **before his eyes**, and then he **blinded the eyes** of Zedekiah and bound him in fetters and led him off to Babylon.

> Septuagint, *Kings* 4 (*Kings* 2, Masoretic text) chapter 25 section 7

Here I compare the wording in a later source, Georgius Cedrenus:

τὸν δὲ Σεδεκίαν χειρωσάμενος τὴν μὲν γυναῖκα καὶ τὰ τέκνα αὐτοῦ **κατ᾽ ὀφθαλμοὺς ἀνεῖλεν**, αὐτὸν δὲ **ἐκτυφλώσας** καὶ δεσμοῖς κρατήσας εἰς Βαβυλῶνα αἰχμάλωτον ἀνήγαγε.

He [the king of Babylon] seized Zedekiah and **killed** his wife and children **before his eyes**; then he **blinded** him, bound him in fetters, and led him off as a prisoner to Babylon.

> Georgius Cedrenus *Compendium historiarum*, vol. 1 p. 201 ed. Bekker

We see here the same wording applied to the punishment of Zedekiah as was applied to the punishment of Croesus: ὅπως τε δολορραφοῦντος Κροίσου ὁ παῖς κατ᾽ ὀφθαλμοὺς ἀναιρεῖται 'and [Ctesias tells] how, after Croesus devises a deceptive stratagem, his son **is killed before his eyes**'.

I return to the story about Homer in the Aeolian traditions native to Smyrna: as

I have reconstructed it, Homer was taken as a *homēros* 'hostage' by the Lydians evacuating the city when it was recaptured by the Aeolians. By implication, Homer was blinded by the Lydians while he was their hostage, presumably in retaliation for the hostile actions of the Aeolians who recaptured Smyrna. The Lydian mentality behind the blinding of hostages, as I have reconstructed it, is parallel to the Persian mentality behind the figurative blinding of Croesus in retaliation for his breaking of a hostage agreement.

Aside from such indirect analogies in the era that followed the Lydian empire, however, we may find more direct analogies in the era that preceded it, as represented by the Hittite empire. There is documentation, in this earlier era, of both relevant practices: the taking of hostages[22] and the blinding of those accused of breaking oaths.[23]

In sum, Homer in the *Life of Homer* traditions is a 'hostage' by virtue of his function as a bond, a tie that binds together the Hellenic cities situated in Asia Minor and in the major offshore islands. The cultural ties that unite these cities are expressed in his persona: he is a 'hostage' for them all. In the case of one city, Smyrna, Homer's ties are so close that his status as 'hostage' leads to his blinding: for this Aeolian city, the city of his birth, Homer is ready to give up his eyesight. For Aeolian Smyrna, Homer is not only a hostage: he is the blinded hostage *par excellence*. That is why Aeolian Smyrna marks the point where the name of Homer is changed from *Melēsigenēs* to *Homēros*.

The idea 'hostage' is reflected even in the name of the *Homēridai*. According to a myth preserved only in the antiquarian post-Athenocentric phase of the *Life of Homer* traditions, the *Homēridai* are named after *homēra* 'hostages' who had been taken and given in the context of a primordial battle of the sexes at the festival of Dionysus in Chios:

Σέλευκος δὲ ἐν βʹ Περὶ βίων ἁμαρτάνειν φησὶ Κράτητα νομίζοντα ἐν ταῖς ἱεροποιίαις Ὁμηρίδας ἀπογόνους εἶναι τοῦ ποιητοῦ· ὠνομάσθησαν γὰρ ἀπὸ τῶν ὁμήρων, ἐπεὶ αἱ γυναῖκές ποτε τῶν Χίων ἐν Διονυσίοις παραφρονήσασαι εἰς μάχην ἦλθον τοῖς ἀνδράσι, καὶ δόντες ἀλλήλοις ὅμηρα νυμφίους καὶ νύμφας ἐπαύσαντο, ὧν τοὺς ἀπογόνους Ὁμηρίδας λέγουσιν.

Seleucus in Book 2 of *Peri biōn* says that Crates[24] made a mistake in offering the opinion in his *Hieropoiiai* that the **Homēridai** were **descendants [apogonoi]** of the Poet. For they were named after the **hostages [homēra]** that were taken when, once upon a time, **during the festival of the Dionysia,** the wives of the Chiotes became deranged

---

22. Schuler 1965:113–14.

23. Oettinger 1976: I, 20, 25; III, 8. I am most grateful to Norbert Oettinger for his generous help (2003.11.09, 2003.11.10).

24. This Crates is perhaps the same Crates who was head of the Library of Pergamon.

and made war on their menfolk, and then they made peace with them after they ex-
changed bridegrooms and brides as **hostages** [*homēra*]. Their **descendants** [*apogonoi*]
are called *Homēridai*.

Seleucus, via Harpocration s.v. Homēridai

Whereas the pre-Athenocentric narrative of *Vita* 1 elides the *Homēridai* altogether, this alternative pre-Athenocentric narrative transmitted by Seleucus (first
century C.E.) recognizes the existence of a *genos* 'lineage' from Chios named the
Homēridai but elides their derivation from a notional ancestor called Homer. As
we have already seen, the etymological contradiction of deriving *Homēridai* either
from *Homēros* 'Homer' or from *homēra* 'hostages' can be resolved once we understand that the name of Homer, *Homēros*, is cognate with the word that means
'hostage', *homēros* or *homēron*. As we have also seen, a culture hero named *Homēros*
could be simultaneously a notional ancestor of a lineage called the *Homēridai* as
well as a notional *homēros* 'hostage'.

Still, this alternative myth leaves us with a problem that has not yet been addressed: the political contradiction between the Athenocentric and the pre-Athenocentric interpretations remains. The idea that the *Homēridai* are descendants of
hostages who figure in a myth that is native to Chios cannot be reconciled politically with the idea that they are descendants of a poet named *Homēros*. That is, the
two ideas cannot be reconciled so long as we think of this poet *Homēros* as the
Homer we see in *Vita* 1, in *Vita* 2, or in any of the *Lives of Homer*. The poet Homer
that we see in each of these *Lives* is claimed as native son by a multiplicity of rival
cities. He is a Panhellenic Homer who simply cannot be appropriated by any one
city. Even the pre-Athenocentric *Vita* 1 makes no claim that Homer is a native
Chiote. Only a local Chiote *Life of Homer* could make such a claim. And in fact we
do see in the *Lives* a variety of references to exactly that claim, that Homer is a native son of Chios (*Vitae* 3a.88, 3b.7–8, 4.7, 6.7–9, 9.7–9, 10.17, 11.12).[25] Nevertheless, each of these references acknowledges that such a claim stands in active competition with other claims of other cities that appropriate Homer as their own native
son. The general stance of the *Lives* is Panhellenic: the aim is to acknowledge a multiplicity of local claims and thereby to transcend them, even though there are distinct patterns of privileging some claims over others—privileging especially the
claims of Smyrna.

Just as different cities claim Homer as their native son in different stories, they
can also claim him as their very own hostage—whether he is given or taken as their

---

25. In some cases, the sources involve the poetry of Pindar (F 264 ed. Snell and Maehler; see *Vitae*
3b.7–8, 6.7–8, 9.7–9), Simonides (F 8; Homeric *Vita* 3b.8), and Theocritus (*Epigram* 27; Homeric *Vita*
6.8–9).

hostage. In three different stories, we have seen him taken as hostage by three different groups: the Lydians (*Vita* 3a.39–44), the people of Colophon (10.25–28), and the people of Chios (11.14–20). In each of these three stories, Homer serves as hostage on behalf of the people of Smyrna. So now once again we see Smyrna in the forefront of the cities that make claims on Homer. But there are also other groups besides the Lydians and the people of Smyrna, Chios, and Colophon that make claims on Homer as hostage. In another story, we have seen Homer's father serving as hostage on behalf of the people of Cyprus; in this case, the hostage-takers are the Persians (2.29–32). In yet another story, the hostage-taker is the Basileus 'King', who may be the king of the Lydians or, conceivably, the Great King of the Persians; in this case, the immediate context implies that the hostage-givers are the people of Lesbos (6.41–45).

As in the case of rival claims to Homer as the native son, these rival claims to Homer as the man who serves as a security linking adversarial communities are contained by the Panhellenism of the framing narratives. The general stance of the *Lives of Homer*, to repeat what I said earlier, is Panhellenic: the aim is to acknowledge a multiplicity of local claims and thereby to transcend them. In a Panhellenic sense, Homer becomes a hostage of all Hellenes. From the standpoint of the Athenian empire, Homer is its imperial hostage.

From an earlier point of view, however, Homer is the hostage not of an empire but of a federation that became a prototype for the Athenian empire: that is, the Delian League. As we saw in chapter 2, it is at the festival of the Delia at Delos, the central meeting place of the Delian League, that Homer achieves his poetic destiny as spokesman for the federation of all the Ionians who assemble at this Panionian festival (*Vita* 2.316, 321 *panēguris*). It is here that he achieves his political destiny as well: all the Ionians who are gathered at Delos and celebrating their festival receive Homer by making him their 'common citizen', their *koinos politēs* (2.319–20 οἱ μὲν Ἴωνες **πολίτην** αὐτὸν **κοινὸν** ἐποιήσαντο).[26] As we saw in chapter 7, the epithet *koinos* 'common, standard' refers to all that is held in common by members of a Panionian federation like the Delian League or, earlier, by the Ionian Dodecapolis. Homer is a federal hostage before he becomes an imperial hostage. His close ties to this federation of Ionians is underscored by a detail we find in the *Life of Homer* traditions: he dies on the Ionian island of Ios—next door, as it were, to the place where he became a federal hostage. His Ionian place for dying prevails as the only place reported in the *Lives of Homer* as Homer's place of death. Homer's place of birth is a variable, but his place of death is a constant, anchored in Ionia.

26. In *Vita* 2.13, the people of Chios claim that Homer is their own *politēs*. I agree with O'Sullivan 1992:102n234 that *politēs* means not 'native son' but merely 'citizen' in such contexts. A similar point is made by West 2003a:310n16.

HOMERIC VARIABILITY

As a perennial hostage to the politics of federation and empire, how could Homeric poetry survive? My answer is that this poetry negotiated its way to ultimate survival through its variability as a system, continually adjusting and readjusting itself to fit its multiple appropriations by competing powers. There are ample signs of this variability in the content of Homeric poetry wherever that poetry refers to itself—whether directly or indirectly. What we can see in these self-references is a poetic impulse, perpetuated through an ongoing system of oral poetry, to maintain a sense of currency.

The transition of Homeric poetry from an era of the tyrants to the succeeding era of democracy in Athens was a critical moment for the final shaping of this poetry. Before I attempt to confront this critical moment, I need to express my awareness of the difficulties of analyzing the final stage of such a lengthy process of shaping. I am also keenly aware of the difficulties of reconstructing the earlier stages. Symbolic of these difficulties is the darkness of the Dark Age of Homer.

Having noted these difficulties, I start the analysis by highlighting two basic facts. First, in the era of the Peisistratidai of Athens, Homeric poetry was under their control. Second, when the Peisistratidai were overthrown, the control of this poetry was transferred to the democracy. Such a transfer must have led to changes in the nature of this poetry. And, later on, there must have been further changes after Athens gained power over the Greek states that had once belonged to the Persian empire. So the task is to consider the nature of all these changes.

As I have argued elsewhere, there was considerable variation in the oral tradition that eventually became Homeric poetry as performed at the Panathenaia in Athens, and this variation offered choices among variants—choices that occasionally still survive in the Homeric textual tradition.[27] Each time a choice was made, there would be that much less variation and thus ever fewer choices left to be made in the ongoing evolution of this Panathenaic Homer. And it stands to reason that these choices that were being made best suited the cultural and political interests of the democratic era of Athens. Already in the earlier era of the Peisistratidai, however, the variations of Homeric poetry evolved in such a way as to suit Athenian interests. As we will see, the choices being made tended to suit Athenian interests already in the sixth century—that is, even before the formation of what we know as the Athenian empire of the fifth century.

In the Prolegomena to the twin book *Homer the Classic*, I speak of variants that we discover from the evidence of the surviving Homeric texts, in the form of manuscripts and marginalia and quotations and citations. But there is also internal ev-

---

27. *HTL* ch. 2, especially pp. 38–39.

idence, embedded in the textual tradition, showing variation in the act of composition. It is to this kind of evidence that I now turn.

THE PEPLOS OF ATHENA AND
THE POETICS OF SPLIT REFERENCING

What I just said about the Homeric tradition can also be said about oral traditions in general. The fact is, choices have to be made in the process of composition during performance. In order to see how such choices are actually made, we need to look at situations where the composition itself is referring to choices being made during performance. We can see such a reference in a passage I quote from *Iliad* V (734–35) in *Homer the Classic*.[28] The referent there is the Peplos of the goddess Athena. The wording of that passage was at one point in time understood to be an actual Homeric reference to the Panathenaic Peplos: that is, to the woolen fabric woven every four years for the festival of the Great Panathenaia.[29] This Homeric reference to the Peplos of Athena in *Iliad* V has its own Panathenaic subtext. I use the word *subtext* here metaphorically in referring to the Panathenaia, and I will use the word *text* metaphorically as well in referring to the narration of the Homeric *Iliad*. The *text* of the Iliadic narrative refers to the Peplos of Athena at the time of the Trojan War, whereas the *subtext* refers to the Peplos of Athena in the context of the seasonally recurring festival of the Panathenaia, which is the actual occasion for the Homeric narration. The reference, which happens in the context of actual performance at the Panathenaia, is split between text and subtext. We see here an example of a phenomenon that I propose to call *split referencing*.

To illustrate this concept of split referencing, I turn to a sequence of passages in *Iliad* VI. Once again, the referent is the Peplos of Athena. The narration focuses on a moment in the Trojan War when the women of Troy present a peplos to the goddess Athena inside her temple on the acropolis of Troy. In this case, the split referencing concerns, first, the ad hoc presentation of a peplos to Athena on the acropolis of Troy and, second, the seasonally recurring presentation of the Panathenaic Peplos to Athena on the acropolis of Athens. I now proceed to quote this sequence. It consists of three consecutive passages that state and restate, in increasing order of complexity, the ritual requirements of presenting the peplos to Athena:

πέπλον, ὅς οἱ δοκέει **χαριέστατος** ἠδὲ **μέγιστος**
εἶναι ἐνὶ μεγάρῳ καί οἱ πολὺ **φίλτατος** αὐτῇ,
θεῖναι Ἀθηναίης ἐπὶ γούνασιν ἠϋκόμοιο.

28. *HC* ch. 4.
29. Following the convention I started in *Homer the Classic*, I capitalize "Peplos" only when I refer to the Panathenaic Peplos.

The *peplos* that seems to her **to have the most pleasurable beauty** [*kharis*] and is
   the **biggest**
in the palace—the one that is by far the **most near and dear** [*philos*] to her—
she must take that one and lay it on the knees of Athena with the beautiful hair.

Iliad VI 90–93 (Helenos to Hector about what Hecuba should do)

πέπλον δ᾽, ὅς τίς τοι **χαριέστατος** ἠδὲ **μέγιστος**
ἔστιν ἐνὶ μεγάρῳ καί τοι πολὺ **φίλτατος** αὐτῇ,
τὸν θὲς Ἀθηναίης ἐπὶ γούνασιν ἠϋκόμοιο.

The *peplos,* whichever is for you **the one that has the most pleasurable beauty**
   [*kharis*] and is the **biggest**
in the palace—the one that is by far the **most near and dear** [*philos*] to you
   yourself—
take that one and lay it on the knees of Athena with the beautiful hair.

Iliad VI 271–73 (Hector to Hecuba about what she should do)

Ὣς ἔφαθ᾽, ἢ δὲ μολοῦσα ποτὶ μέγαρ᾽ ἀμφιπόλοισι
κέκλετο· ταὶ δ᾽ ἄρ᾽ ἀόλλισσαν κατὰ ἄστυ **γεραιάς.**
αὐτὴ δ᾽ ἐς θάλαμον κατεβήσετο κηώεντα,
ἔνθ᾽ ἔσάν οἱ **πέπλοι παμποίκιλοι**[30] ἔργα γυναικῶν
Σιδονίων, τὰς αὐτὸς Ἀλέξανδρος θεοειδὴς   290
ἤγαγε **Σιδονίηθεν** ἐπιπλὼς εὐρέα πόντον,
τὴν ὁδὸν ἣν Ἑλένην περ ἀνήγαγεν εὐπατέρειαν·
τῶν ἔν᾽ ἀειραμένη Ἑκάβη φέρε δῶρον Ἀθήνῃ,
ὃς **κάλλιστος** ἔην **ποικίλμασιν** ἠδὲ **μέγιστος,**
ἀστὴρ δ᾽ ὣς ἀπέλαμπεν· ἔκειτο δὲ νείατος ἄλλων.   295
βῆ δ᾽ ἰέναι, πολλαὶ δὲ μετεσσεύοντο **γεραιαί.**

So he [Hector] spoke, and she [Hecuba], going into the palace, summoned
   her handmaidens,
calling out to them. And they went around the city to assemble the **highborn
   women.**
Meanwhile she [Hecuba] descended into the fragrant storechamber.
There it was that she kept her **peploi,** and they were **completely pattern-woven**
   [*pan-poikiloi*],[31] the work of the women,[32]
* **women from Sidon,** whom Alexandros [Paris] himself, the godlike,   290

30. Besides the attestation of the variant παμποίκιλοι in the medieval manuscript tradition, the variant παμποίκιλα is also attested. Herodotus in his quotation of *Iliad* VI 289–92 gives παμποίκιλοι.

31. Besides the variant *pan-poikiloi* in the medieval manuscript tradition at *Iliad* VI 289, there is also *pan-poikila*. In the second form, the epithet describes the *erga* 'work' woven by the Phoenician women, where *erga* is in apposition with *peploi*; according to the Homeric Koine reading, *pan-poikiloi* describes directly the *peploi*. Herodotus gives this Homeric Koine reading.

32. Without verses 290–93, the peploi stored in Hecuba's storechamber would be the work of native Trojan women, not of imported Phoenician women. I think that such a compressed version with-

* had brought home with him from **Sidon**, sailing over the wide sea,
* **on that journey** when he brought also Helen, genuine daughter of the
     Father.[33]
Hecuba lifted out one and brought it as gift to Athena,
the one that was the **most beautiful** in **pattern-weavings** [*poikilmata*] and
     the **biggest**,[34]
and it shone like a **star**. It lay beneath the others.   295
She went on her way, and the many **highborn women** hastened to follow her.

> *Iliad* VI 286–96 (Hecuba goes ahead and does what she has to do)

In this sequence of three passages, we see three consecutive restatements of the same ritual act. I say three restatements instead of one statement and two restatements because none of the three passages is basic, from the standpoint of traditional formulaic diction. Not one of the three passages is formulaically predictable on the basis of the other two passages. To put it another way, the variation that we find in the three passages shows that none of the three forms is formally prior to the other two. What priorities we find are purely a function of the narration, not of any chronological order in the composition of the three passages. In terms of oral poetics, such variation is a display of virtuosity in the art of composition in performance.[35]

The third restatement, which is the longest and most complex, requires the greatest poetic virtuosity—and variability. Whereas the two previous restatements are prescriptive, performed by the characters in the narrative, the third is descriptive, performed by the master narrator. In the Homeric tradition, wording that requires the greatest poetic virtuosity is conventionally assigned to the master narrator as the ultimate virtuoso.[36] The focus of the narrative here is on the peplos to be presented to Athena, and the ritual reality of this peplos emerges from the variation in

---

out verses 290–93 must have once coexisted with the version expanded by these three verses. In both epic and dramatic traditions, the weaving skills of aristocratic Trojan women are accentuated.

33. I place asterisks before these three verses, highlighting that they are typical of the poetics of *enpoieîn*: that is, 'making (something) inside (something)'. As we saw in ch. 3, *Iliad* VI 289 and VI 290–92 (these three verses) are actually quoted by Herodotus (2.116.3), who claims that they are genuinely made by Homer himself. This claim is in line with his theory that the theme of a Phoenician detour is distinctly Homeric, as opposed to the theme of a direct voyage from Sparta to Troy. The concern of Herodotus over the authorship of these three verses implies that others may have argued that these verses were not composed by Homer. If we consider an alternative version without these three verses, then the peploi stored by Hecuba would have been woven by the 'highborn' women of Troy. See the previous note.

34. So now we see that the standards of *kallistos* 'most beautiful' and *megistos* 'biggest' are measured in terms of *poikilmata* 'pattern-weavings'.

35. Nagy 2004c.

36. On the concept of the Homeric master narrator as a character in his own performance, see *PP* 86, 220.

the three consecutive restatements that describe it. I note especially the metrical and formulaic variation necessitated by the shift in meaning from the first to the second restatement. In this one single shift, the ritual reality of the peplos is already being upgraded, right before our eyes, from seeming to being.

So we see choices being made each time the ritual is restated, and we see that each restatement entails further variability, focusing more and more on a master perspective. In the third passage, this variability is expressed by the words *pan-poikilos* and *poikilma*, both of which refer to the peplos that is being chosen for presentation to Athena (*Iliad* VI 289, 294). I will soon consider the meaning of these two words. For the moment, however, it will suffice to quote the climax of the narrative, which describes the actual presentation of the peplos to the goddess:

Αἳ δ' ὅτε **νηὸν** ἵκανον Ἀθήνης **ἐν πόλει ἄκρῃ**,
τῇσι θύρας ὤϊξε Θεανὼ καλλιπάρῃος
Κισσηῒς ἄλοχος Ἀντήνορος ἱπποδάμοιο·
τὴν γὰρ Τρῶες ἔθηκαν **Ἀθηναίης** ἱέρειαν.   300
αἳ δ' **ὀλολυγῇ** πᾶσαι Ἀθήνῃ χεῖρας ἀνέσχον·
ἣ δ' ἄρα **πέπλον** ἑλοῦσα Θεανὼ καλλιπάρῃος
θῆκεν Ἀθηναίης ἐπὶ γούνασιν ἠϋκόμοιο,
εὐχομένη δ' ἠρᾶτο Διὸς κούρῃ μεγάλοιο·
πότνι' Ἀθηναίη ἐρυσίπτολι δῖα θεάων   305
ἆξον δὴ ἔγχος Διομήδεος, ἠδὲ καὶ αὐτὸν
πρηνέα δὸς πεσέειν Σκαιῶν προπάροιθε πυλάων,
ὄφρά τοι αὐτίκα νῦν δυοκαίδεκα βοῦς ἐνὶ νηῷ
ἤνις ἠκέστας ἱερεύσομεν, αἴ κ' ἐλεήσῃς
ἄστύ τε καὶ Τρώων ἀλόχους καὶ νήπια τέκνα.   310

When these [women] had come to Athena's **temple at the top of the citadel**,
Theano of the fair cheeks opened the door for them,
daughter of Kisseus and wife of Antenor, breaker of horses,
she whom the Trojans had established to be priestess of **the Athenian
    goddess**.[37]   300
With a cry of **ololu!**[38] all lifted up their hands to Athena,
and Theano of the fair cheeks, taking up the **peplos**, laid it
along the knees of Athena the lovely-haired, and praying
she supplicated the daughter of powerful Zeus:
"O Lady Athena,[39] our city's defender, shining among goddesses: 305
break the spear of Diomedes, and grant that the man be
hurled on his face in front of the Scaean Gates; so may we

37. I draw attention to the use here of the adjective *Athēnaiē* instead of the substantive *Athēnē*.
38. Note the stylized movement accompanying the ritual cry or *ololugē*.
39. Once again, the adjective *Athēnaiē* is used here instead of the substantive *Athēnē*.

> instantly dedicate within your shrine twelve heifers,
> yearlings, never broken, if only you will have pity
> on the city of Troy, and the Trojan wives, and their innocent children." 310

Iliad VI 297–310

Looking back at the entire narrative sequence, I highlight two most salient visual details, namely the acropolis and the temple on the acropolis. These two details correspond to the two most visible details distinguishing the city of Athens from most other cities. I see at work here a split reference. The reference is split between Troy and Athens. The referent is both the prehistorical city of Troy and the historical city of Athens.

There are two other details that reinforce the split reference. One detail has to do with the use of the words *pan-poikilos* and *poikilma*. Both words refer to the peplos that is being chosen for presentation to Athena (*Iliad* VI 289, 294). The second detail has to do with the positioning of the statue of Athena at Troy: it is figured as sitting, not standing, since the worshippers are pictured as placing the peplos on the knees of the goddess (VI 303).

I take up the second detail first. As we saw in chapter 7 from a report by Strabo (13.1.41 C601), the statue of Athena in her old temple in Aeolian New Ilion was figured as standing, not sitting. So the reference in the *Iliad* to a seated statue of Athena at Troy blocks the visualization of the statue in Aeolian New Ilion. In effect, Homeric poetry negates a rival Aeolian version of Athena's statue. Relevant here is what I argued in chapter 7, that the statue of Athena in her old temple in Sigeion was similarly figured as sitting—not standing like the statue of Athena in her old temple in Aeolian New Ilion.[40] From an Athenocentric point of view, such a version would be viewed as a displacement of the Aeolian version and as a re-enactment of the Athenian version.

Next I take up the first detail, focusing on the words *pan-poikilos* and *poikilma*, which refer to the peplos that is being chosen for Athena (*Iliad* VI 289, 294). These words convey not only the general idea of *variation,* which is relevant to the variability of the wording that describes the ritual of presenting the peplos to Athena. More than that, they convey also the specific idea of pattern-weaving a picture into a fabric. Such a picture was pattern-woven into the Panathenaic Peplos of Athena. As I argue in the twin book *Homer the Classic*, the adjective *pan-poikilos* 'completely pattern-woven' is the epithet of the Panathenaic Peplos (scholia for Aristophanes *Birds* 827), and the noun *poikilma* designates the pattern-weaving

---

40. When divinities are imagined as receiving gifts, they are conventionally represented as sitting, not standing. I should add that the divine poses of standing and sitting have to do with the attitude of the divinity, not only with the physical reality of the image of the divinity, whether it be a statue, a painting, or a verbal description. On the poetics of describing the statue of Athena in Homeric and Virgilian epic, see Barchiesi 1998.

of the charter myth of the Gigantomachy into the Panathenaic Peplos (Plato *Euthyphro* 6b–c).[41]

In the narrative about the presentation of the peplos to Athena in *Iliad* VI, the peplos to be chosen is highlighted as the biggest of all the peploi (VI 90, 271, 294). It is the peplos that is most 'beautiful' or *kalon* (294), with the most 'pleasurable beauty' or *kharis* (90, 271). The size and the beauty of the fabric evoke a vision of the quadrennial Panathenaic Peplos, which is notionally the biggest and most beautiful of all imaginable peploi. As for the association of the word *kharis* 'pleasurable beauty' with the fabric, it is appropriate not only to the peplos that is being described but also to the medium that describes the peplos. That medium is Homeric poetry as performed at the quadrennial festival of the Panathenaia. The concept of *kharis* conveys the charisma of Homeric poetry as described by Homeric poetry. In terms of this description, the peplos of *Iliad* VI can be seen as a metaphor for epic as performed at the Panathenaia. This epic is notionally the biggest and the most beautiful of all epics. Like the peplos of *Iliad* VI, this epic as performed at the Panathenaia has more *kharis* than all other epics.

The *kharis* 'pleasurable beauty' of the peplos so elaborately described in *Iliad* VI is not only Panathenaic. It is also royal and even imperial in its grandeur. As we saw from the Homeric description, this peplos was woven by women whom Paris had brought over to Troy from Sidon in the course of his Phoenician detour (VI 289–292). This Phoenician connection is surely no accident. I propose that we see here an indirect reference to the provenience of the all-expensive and all-luxuriant purple that dyed the quadrennial Peplos of the Panathenaia. I will have more to say in the Epilegomena about the purple of the Peplos, which serves as a mark of grandeur suitable for kings and for their kingly empires. For now I simply maintain that the grandeur implied by this Phoenician connection suits also the description of the peplos described in *Iliad* VI. As we saw in chapter 3, Herodotus, (2.116.1–117.1) recognized this augmented description as truly Homeric in its grandeur, contrasting it with the unaugmented description that he knew from the epic *Cypria* of his day. The historian treats the unaugmented story of the direct voyage of Paris and Helen from Sparta to Troy as a foil for the augmented story of their Phoenician detour. The poet of the unaugmented story, as Herodotus sees it, is a foil for Homer as the rightful poet of the augmented story.

Here I stop to offer a summary of what we have seen so far in this Homeric narrative about the offering made by the women of Troy to Athena in her temple on her acropolis. The *text* of the narrative refers to the temple of Athena at Troy, while the *subtext* refers to the temple of Athena at Athens. On the basis of this narrative, I have developed the concept of *split referencing*, applying it to situations where the performer refers to the immediate world of performance at a given time and

41. *HC* ch. 4.

place as well as to the ulterior world of the composition as it exists ready-made for a variety of different times and places. In this sequence of passages describing the offering of a choice peplos to Athena, the implicit referent concerns Athens and Athenian interests, while the explicit referent concerns not only Athens but notionally all Hellenic city-states. The implicit referent is Athenian, while the explicit referent is Panhellenic. It is essential for me to add here that this argument for implicit Athenian reference does not preclude the existence of earlier stages of references that are pre-Athenian.

There remains the task of explaining *split referencing* in terms of oral traditions. I offer this formulation: variable features of an inaccessible referent are adjusted over time, through a lengthy process of ad hoc selection, to become features that fit an accessible referent. The repertoire of features, which are cognate with each other, evolves by way of an ongoing process that I will call a *selective adjustment of repertoire*. What results is that a reference to the inaccessible world in the story being told becomes a reference to the accessible world of the audience that hears the story as a story intended only for them to hear.

This is not to say that the ritual of the peplos in the narrative of *Iliad* VI was originally based on the ritual of the Peplos in the festival of the Panathenaia. It is only to say that a preexisting narrative tradition concerning ritual traditions of the peplos had been adjusted, over time, to fit the preexisting ritual tradition of the Panathenaic festival in Athens. And I stress that this festival was the actual occasion for the narrative as we have it in *Iliad* VI.

In terms of this narration, the ad hoc presentation of the peplos to Athena in Troy is a ritual failure; in terms of the festival of the Panathenaia, on the other hand, the seasonally recurring presentation of the peplos to Athena in Athens is notionally always a ritual success. In other words, the *text* is imperfect, but the *subtext* is notionally perfect. The perfect subtext is a mark of the Athenians, while the imperfect text is the mark of everyone else.

In the twin book *Homer the Classic*, I argue that the notional eternity of reweaving the Panathenaic Peplos on a seasonally recurring basis makes the rewoven Peplos the same thing, ritually speaking, as the Peplos that Athena had originally woven.[42] It is the standard of Athena that makes the ritual perfect. In this perfect ritual, there is a notional eternity not only in the giving but also in the receiving. Athena receives a newly rewoven Peplos on a seasonally recurring basis for all time to come. This standard of perfection for the ritual of the Panathenaia accentuates the imperfection of the ritual performed by the Trojan women, which is perforce a once-only event.

42. *HC* ch. 4.

10

Homer and the Poetics of Variation

We have seen how the technique of narrating the story about the presentation of a peplos to Athena in her temple at Troy corresponds to the technique of weaving the Panathenaic Peplos for presentation to Athena in her temple at Athens. And the occasion for presenting the woven Peplos, the festival of the Panathenaia, is also the occasion for presenting the narration of this story and all other Homeric stories. Narrating the story requires variation, just as weaving the Peplos requires variation. As I argue in *Homer the Classic*, the word that best captures the idea of variation in the weaving of the Peplos is the adjective *poikilos*, the general meaning of which is 'varied', and the specialized meaning of which is 'pattern-woven'.[1] This adjective, as I also argue in *Homer the Classic*, is closely related to the verb *poikillein*, which actually means 'pattern-weave'.[2] Now I turn to a most telling example of this adjective *poikilos*, appearing in a passage that shows a glimpse of Andromache weaving her web at a climactic moment in the plot of the *Iliad*. It is the moment just before she finds out that her husband, Hector, has died on the battlefield. This passage, as we will see, captures the essence of pattern-weaving as an overall metaphor for Homeric narrative:

Ὣς ἔφατο κλαίουσ᾽, ἄλοχος δ᾽ οὔ πώ τι πέπυστο
Ἕκτορος· οὐ γάρ οἵ τις ἐτήτυμος ἄγγελος ἐλθὼν
ἤγγειλ᾽ ὅττί ῥά οἱ πόσις ἔκτοθι μίμνε πυλάων,

1. *HC* ch. 4.
2. *HC* ch. 4.

ἀλλ' ἥ γ' ἱστὸν ὕφαινε μυχῷ δόμου ὑψηλοῖο
δίπλακα πορφυρέην,³ ἐν δὲ θρόνα ποικίλ' ἔπασσε.

So she [Hecuba] spoke, lamenting, but the wife [Andromache] had not yet heard,
Hector's wife: for no true messenger had come to her
and told her the news, how her husband was standing his ground outside the gates.
She [Andromache] **was weaving** [*huphainein*] a web in the inner room of the lofty
    palace,
a purple [*porphureē*]⁴ **fabric that folds in two** [*diplax*], **and she was inworking**
    [*en-passein*]⁵ **patterns of flowers** [*throna*] that were **varied** [*poikila*].

                                                                Iliad XXII 437–41

Archaeological research has shown that the artistic technique being represented
here is not *embroidery*, as is commonly assumed, but *pattern-weaving*.⁶ The narrative sequence woven into the web of Andromache is created by way of transverse
threading, described in our *Iliad* passage as either *porphureē* 'purple' or, according
to a variant reading also found in the medieval manuscript tradition, *marmareē*
'gleaming'. This variation, as we will see later, is essential for understanding the relevance of this passage to the festival of the Panathenaia.

The technique of weaving the fabric called *diplax* in this passage is analogous
to the technique of weaving a *peplos*. A case in point is the peplos presented by the
Trojan women to the statue of Athena in her temple on the acropolis of Troy. In
the description of this peplos, we have already seen a direct reference to the special technique of pattern-weaving in the original making of this peplos: the fabric
is the result of *poikilmata* (*Iliad* VI 294). This noun *poikilma* (plural *poikilmata*)
is derived from the verb *poikillein* 'pattern-weave'. I stress again that this noun refers
here to fabric that is "woven . . . rather than embroidered."⁷ Similarly, the story patterns narrating the Achaean and Trojan 'struggles' (*athloi*) that Helen 'sprinkles
into' (*en-passein*) her web in *Iliad* III (126) are "woven into the cloth and not embroidered on afterwards."⁸

The clearest example is the web of Andromache as described in the passage we
have just examined (*Iliad* XXII 441). The word *en-passein*, referring to the weaving of Andromache, means that she is 'inworking'—or, literally, 'sprinkling' various patterns into her web by way of pattern-weaving. These varied patterns are called
throna (XXII 441), which I have translated as 'patterns of flowers'. The word *throna*

3. There is a variant reading at verse 441 for πορφυρέην, which is μαρμαρέην.
4. There is a variant reading at verse 441 for *porphureē* 'purple', which is *marmareē* 'gleaming'.
5. Metaphorically, *en-passein* is to 'sprinkle': PR 93.
6. *PR* 93, citing Wace 1948, followed by Kirk 1985:280 and 1990:199.
7. Kirk 1990:199, relying especially on Wace 1948.
8. Kirk 1985:280, again relying on Wace 1948.

(singular *thronon*) can refer to floral patterns that are woven into the fabric.[9] Further, as we know from Theocritus (2.59) and other sources, *throna* are love charms.[10] Each flower in the sequence of flowers woven into the web is a love charm, an incantation that sings its own love song. Each flower is different from the next, and the sequence of flowers becomes a variety of love songs within one single sustained narrative, one single love story, which is the pattern-woven web in its entirety.[11]

The tradition of ancient Homeric commentary reports that *en-passein* is the native Cypriote term for what is called *poikillein* 'pattern-weave' in other parts of the Greek-speaking world. Here is the precise wording in the commentary on *en-passein* as pattern-weaving:

‹ἐν ... ἔπασσε›· ἡ δὲ ἐν πρὸς τὸ ἔπασσε. δηλοῖ δὲ κατὰ Κυπρίους τὸ ποικίλλειν, ἀφ' οὗ καὶ παστός.

"ἐν ... ἔπασσε": The ἐν goes with the ἔπασσε. In **Cypriote** usage, it evidently means *poikillein*. The word *pastos*[12] is derived from it.

Scholia **b** (BCD³) for *Iliad* XXII 441d1 (exegetical scholia)

‹ἔπασσε›· πάσσειν Κύπριοι τὸ ποικίλλειν, ἀφ' οὗ καὶ ὁ παστός.

"ἔπασσε": *passein* is the way Cypriotes say *poikillein*. The word *pastos* is derived from it.

Scholia A T for *Iliad* XXII 441d2

We also have comparative evidence for interpreting *poikillein* as referring to pattern-weaving. The verb *poikillein* itself, along with the adjective *poikilos*, meaning 'varied', is derived from the root **peik-*, also attested in Latin *pictura*. So *poikillein* means literally 'make (things) be *poikila*': that is, 'make (things) be varied'. These words *poikilos* and *poikillein* convey not only the general idea of variation. They convey also the specific idea of a picture, whether static or moving: in fact, they are cognate with the Latin word *pictura*. This word evokes for us the celebrated formulation *ut pictura poesis* 'like the painting is the poetry' in Horace's *Ars Poetica* (*Epistulae* 2.3.361).

9. See also Kirk 1985:280.

10. Petropoulos 1993.

11. To say that the sequence of flowers is ornamental (Lohmann 1988:59–60) is to undervalue the context: see Grethlein 2007. Moreover, I think that the patterns of pattern-weaving have an associative power that evokes not only the feelings of characters like Andromache (see also Lohmann p. 60, Segal 1971:40–41) but also the narrative that frames such personalized feelings.

12. As an adjective, *pastos* means 'sprinkled', and the derivation from *passein* 'sprinkle' is transparent. As a noun, masculine *pastos* (also feminine *pastas*) means 'bridal chamber' or 'bridal bed', as we see from the contexts surveyed by LSJ; such meanings may be metaphorical extensions of a specific meaning glossed as 'embroidered bed-curtain' in LSJ. (See Pollux 3.37, where *pastos* is explained as a bridal bed-curtain.) Once again, the translation 'pattern-woven' is preferable to 'embroidered'.

Relevant is a reference to weaving in Virgil's *Aeneid* (3.483), where the adjective *picturatae* is applied to the plural of the noun *vestis* 'fabric'. The weaver of the fabrics here is Andromache. This adjective *picturatae* is derived from the noun *pictura*, which refers not only to the process of painting but also to a kind of fabric work that highlights the virtuosity of patterning (as in Apuleius *Florida* 15: *tunicam picturis variegatam* 'a tunic variegated with patterned fabric work'). As I argue in the twin book *Homer the Classic*, Virgil's reference here to Andromache's woven fabrics actually evokes the Iliadic scene when she is pattern-weaving her web, right before the moment she finds out that her husband, Hector, has died on the battlefield.[13]

In this Iliadic scene, Andromache is narrating her own sorrows by way of pattern-weaving, as expressed by *en-passein*, synonym of *poikillein*, and this narration is being replayed by the subjectivized narration of Homeric poetry. In her apprehensiveness, anticipating the terrible and piteous news she is about to absorb about the fate of her husband, Hector, Andromache is passing the time by pattern-weaving a sequence of *throna*, 'flowers' that have the power of love charms. The sequence of *throna* tells its own story: it is a story of love, a love story in the making.

I note the relevance of the epithet of Aphrodite that appears as the first word in the first line of the first song in the ancient collection of songs attributed to Sappho: the goddess is invoked as *poikilothronos* (Sappho F 1.1). So Aphrodite is Our Lady of the varied pattern-woven floral love charms.[14] In chapter 8, we saw that Sappho likens herself to Aphrodite in this song by virtue of speaking with the voice of the goddess in a direct quotation (Sappho F 1.18–24). As we also saw there, Sappho is representing herself as a choral prima donna in assuming the role of Aphrodite, and this self-representation is parallel to the representations of Briseis and Andromache in the *Iliad*. The comparison with Aphrodite is linked in all three cases with the choral role of an Aeolian prima donna.

The sequence of *throna* that are pattern-woven by Andromache is telling its own love story, but this story is overtaken by the overall story of the *Iliad*. The retelling of this sequence by the *Iliad* is telling a story that is more than a love story: it is a story of terror and pity, a story of war, an Iliadic story in the making. The story is already in the making when Helen is seen for the first time in the *Iliad*. I quote the scene in *Iliad* III where we find Helen in the act of weaving her own web. She too is pattern-weaving, but the patterns she weaves into her fabric are not *throna*, love charms that thread a story of love. The varied patterns are instead *athloi* 'ordeals', a transverse threading of a story of war.[15] It is the story of the Trojan War:

13. *HC* ch. 1.
14. Details in *PR* 93; see also *PP* 101.
15. Clader 1976:7n8; see also Collins 1988:42–43.

τὴν δ' εὗρ' ἐν μεγάρῳ· ἣ δὲ μέγαν ἱστὸν ὕφαινε
δίπλακα πορφυρέην,[16] πολέας δ' ἐνέπασσεν ἀέθλους
Τρώων θ' ἱπποδάμων καὶ Ἀχαιῶν χαλκοχιτώνων,
οὕς ἕθεν εἵνεκ' ἔπασχον ὑπ' Ἄρηος παλαμάων·

She [Iris] found her [Helen] in the palace. She was **weaving** a great web,
a **purple** [*porphureē*][17] **fabric that folds in two** [*diplax*], and she was **inworking**
  [*en-passein*][18] many **ordeals** [*athloi*]
of Trojans, tamers of horses, and of Achaeans, wearers of bronze khitons,
—ordeals that they suffered at the hands of Ares all because of her.

Iliad III 125–28

As with the web of Andromache, the narrative sequence woven into the web of
Helen is created by way of transverse threading, described in our *Iliad* passage as
either *porphureē* 'purple' or, according to a variant reading also found in the medieval manuscript tradition, *marmareē* 'gleaming'. This variation, as we will see
presently, is essential for understanding the relevance of this passage to the festival
of the Panathenaia.

The pattern-weaving of Helen is parallel to the pattern-weaving of Andromache
and, by extension, to the Iliadic narrative about Andromache. A case in point is
the epithet *hippodamoi* 'horse tamers', applied to the Trojans in the narrative that
is pattern-woven by Helen (*Iliad* III 127). The plural form of this epithet *hippodamoi* 'horse tamers' is regularly applied in the *Iliad* to all the Trojans as an aggregate; the singular form of this same epithet *hippodamos* 'horse tamer' is applied in
the *Iliad* uniquely to Hector.[19] Moreover, this epithet happens to be the last word
of the *Iliad* as we know it, applied to Hector at the final moment of his funeral
(*Iliad* XXIV 804). So the sequence of Andromache's pattern-weaving in *Iliad* XXII,
continuing from the sequence of Helen's pattern-weaving in *Iliad* III, continues further into the sequence of Homeric narrative that completes the *Iliad*. In this way,
the overall narrative of the *Iliad* transforms the love story woven into the *diplax* of
Andromache. Her story of love modulates into the Iliadic story of war that Helen
was already pattern-weaving when we first laid eyes on her. This story of war told
by the pattern-weaving of Helen is linked to the overall story of war told by the narrative of the *Iliad* itself, which then overtakes the story of love told by the pattern-
weaving of Andromache. So the narrations woven into the *diplax* of Helen and into
the *diplax* of Andromache are both linked with the overall narration of the Homeric
Iliad.

16. There is a variant reading at verse 126 for πορφυρέην, which is μαρμαρέην.
17. There is a variant reading at verse 126 for *porphureē* 'purple', which is *marmareē* 'gleaming'.
18. To repeat, *en-passein* is to 'sprinkle': PR 93.
19. Sacks 1987.

PATTERN-WEAVING BACK INTO THE BRONZE AGE

The linking of the pattern-woven narrations of Helen and Andromache with the poetic narration of the *Iliad* is a matter of metonymy. As for the actual parallelism of this poetic narration with the craft of pattern-weaving, it is a matter of metaphor. In terms of the metaphor, the pattern-weaving of a fabric is the narrating of an epic. This metaphor is embedded in the narrative of Homeric poetry, and we see it at work in the Iliadic passages showing Andromache and Helen in the act of pattern-weaving at their looms. In these passages, the act of epic narration is figured metaphorically as an act of pattern-weaving. There is an analogous metaphor embedded in the etymology of *humnos*. As I argue in the twin book *Homer the Classic*, this noun *humnos* is derived from the verb root **huph-*, as in *huphainein* 'weave'.[20] This derivation is relevant to what I have argued in chapter 4 of the present book, that *humnos* is used in the Homeric *Odyssey* to refer to the continuum of epic narration. And now, in this part of the book, I am arguing that epic narration is visualized not only generally as the craft of weaving but also specifically as the specialized craft of pattern-weaving. Even more specifically, I am arguing that the epic narration of Homeric poetry is figured metaphorically as the specialized craft of pattern-weaving the Panathenaic Peplos of Athena. This craft, as I have reconstructed it so far, goes back to the sixth century B.C.E. As we are also about to see, it goes even farther back in time—all the way back into the Bronze Age.

In order to make a connection between the sixth century and the Bronze Age, I will start by taking a closer look at the word *diplax*, which as we have just seen refers to the web woven by Andromache as also to the web woven by Helen. The etymology of *diplax*, to be understood as a web 'folded in two', is related to the etymology of *peplos*, to be understood as a 'folding': in other words, something that is traditionally folded.[21] An important point of comparison for understanding the basic meaning of the noun *peplos*, derived from the root **pl-* 'fold', is the adjective *haploûs* 'simple', derived from a combination of the elements **sm-* 'one' and the same root **pl-* 'fold'. The meaning of Greek *haploûs* 'simple' is cognate with the meaning of Latin *simplex* 'simple', which is derived from the same combination of the elements **sm-* 'one' and the root **pl-* 'fold'. I propose that *sim-plex* is 'onefold' in the sense of having one fold—that is, unfolded, which is not the same thing as 'folded once' (which would be folded in two). Similarly, *du-plex* 'twofold' means folded as two—that is, folded in two, which is not the same thing as 'folded twice' (which would be folded in four). The same point applies to Greek *haploûs* 'simple'—that is, 'unfolded'—the meaning of which can be contrasted with the meaning of *diplax* 'fabric folded in two'. Here I

20. *HC* 2§91, where other possible etymologies are also explored.

21. Chantraine *DELG* s.v. πέπλος. As Susan Edmunds points out to me (2007.02.17), the tradition of folding may have to do with either how the woven work was worn or how it was stored when not worn.

FIGURE 4. Relief sculpture: presentation of the Peplos of Athena. Slab 5, East Frieze of the Parthenon, Athens. British Museum, Elgin Collection. Drawing by Valerie Woelfel.

find it relevant to evoke the image of the Peplos of the goddess Athena as represented in the sculpture of the Parthenon Frieze.[22] As we see from that image (fig. 4), the Peplos is being ritually folded at the moment of its presentation, and its selvedge (Greek *exastis*) is visible. On the basis of what we have seen, I offer this formula for explaining the etymology of *peplos* as 'a folding': when the peplos is folded in two, it is not fully on display; when it is unfolded as one, it is fully on display, opening up to show a single picture.[23] Similarly, the word *diplax* conveys the idea of a woven web that is ritually folded in two when it is not on display and then ritually unfolded as one when it is on display.[24]

I will now compare the two Homeric examples of *diplax* that we have seen so

22. I am mostly in agreement with the commentary of Shear 2001:752–53 with reference to the figures E34 and E35.

23. The size of the Peplos as represented on the Panathenaic Frieze depends on how many times the web is folded in two. I owe this observation to Susan Edmunds.

24. Oktor Skjærvø draws my attention to ancient Germanic traditions of weaving sumptuous wide-loom fabrics.

far with a particularly suggestive example of the same word in the *Argonautica* of Apollonius of Rhodes. As we will see, the usage of *diplax* by Apollonius provides a virtual commentary on the Homeric usages of both *peplos* and *diplax*, with specific reference to the Panathenaic Peplos of Athena.[25] More than that, this usage conveys a distinctly Panathenaic subtext. The *diplax* is described in these words:

αὐτὰρ ὅγ' ἀμφ' ὤμοισι, θεᾶς Ἰτωνίδος ἔργον,
δίπλακα πορφυρέην περονήσατο, τήν οἱ ὄπασσε
Παλλάς, ὅτε πρῶτον δρυόχους ἐπεβάλλετο νηὸς
Ἀργοῦς, καὶ κανόνεσσι δάε ζυγὰ μετρήσασθαι.

Then he [Jason] around his shoulders put the handiwork of the Itonian goddess [Athena],
a purple [*porphureē*] fabric that folds in two [*diplax*], pinning it. It was given to him by
Pallas [Athena] back when she began to set down the keel props of the ship
Argo and taught them how to measure out its beams by way of the carpenter's rule [*kanōn*].

Apollonius of Rhodes Argonautica 1.721–24

The mention of the word *diplax* here activates the metaphor of pattern-weaving as applied to the process of narrating in performance. It is significant that there is a narrative being woven into the *diplax* of Jason, as retold in the narrative of Apollonius in his *Argonautica* (1.725–67). It is also significant that Athena is identified as the weaver of this *diplax*, which she then gives to the hero Jason to wear. In a passage I cited earlier from the *Iliad*, Athena is identified as the weaver of the *peplos* that she herself wears (V 734–35). In the *Argonautica,* the fabric she weaves is her *ergon* 'handiwork' (1.721). This word indicates literally the labor of fabric work performed manually by the goddess herself. Athena's weaving technique matches that of professional male fabric workers. An explicit parallel is being drawn in this context between the pattern-weaving that the goddess herself performed in creating the *diplax* and the carpentry that she herself performed in creating the ship Argo. The context of the word *kanōn* in this passage of the *Argonautica* (1.724) allows for two different meanings to be activated at one and the same time: this word means not only 'carpenter's rule' but also 'weaver's heddle rod'.[26]

In this passage from the *Argonautica*, the epithet used by Apollonius in referring to the *diplax* made by Athena is *porphureē* 'purple' (1.722). Here I return to a textual variation that I highlighted earlier between *marmareē* 'gleaming' and *porphureē* 'purple' as the epithet referring to the *diplax* woven by Helen (*Iliad* III 126) as

---

25. On the poetry of Apollonius as a virtual interactive dictionary of Homer, see Rengakos 2001.

26. For *kanōn* as 'carpenter's rule', see Sophocles F 474.5 ed. Radt; as 'weaver's heddle rod', see *Iliad* XXIII 761, Callimachus F 66.4.

well as the *diplax* woven by Andromache (XXII 441). As we learn from the Homeric scholia (at III 126), the three major Alexandrian editors of Homer—Zenodotus, Aristophanes, Aristarchus—are all on record as preferring the variant reading *porphureē* 'purple', as opposed to a variant that we still see attested in the medieval manuscript tradition, *marmareē* 'gleaming'. Such an Alexandrian editorial preference, as I will argue, is all-important for a Hellenistic poet like Apollonius.

The Alexandrian editors of Homer, starting with Zenodotus in the age of Callimachus, interpreted in a special way the Homeric word *diplax* in the two Iliadic passages that we have been considering. In order to understand this interpretation, we must first take another look at the Peplos that was pattern-woven for presentation to Athena on the seasonally recurring occasion of the grand procession that took place at the Great Panathenaia. I draw attention to the dominant color of the Panathenaic Peplos, which is purple. This feature is prominently mentioned in descriptions that survive from the ancient world. I quote here a detailed example:[27]

> sed **magno intexens**, si fas est dicere, **peplo**,
> qualis Erechtheis olim portatur Athenis,
> debita cum castae solvuntur vota Minervae
> tardaque confecto redeunt **quinquennia** lustro,
> cum levis alterno Zephyrus concrebuit Euro   25
> et prono gravidum provexit pondere currum.
> felix illa dies, felix et dicitur annus,
> felices qui talem annum videre diemque.
> ergo **Palladiae texuntur in ordine pugnae**,
> **magna Giganteis ornantur pepla tropaeis**,   30
> **horrida sanguineo pinguntur proelia** cocco,
> additur **aurata** deiectus **cuspide** Typhon,
> qui prius Ossaeis consternens aethera saxis
> Emathio celsum duplicabat vertice Olympum.
> tale deae **velum** sollemni tempore portant,   35
> tali te vellem, iuvenum doctissime, ritu
> **purpureos** inter **soles** et **candida** lunae
> **sidera, caeruleis** orbem pulsantia **bigis**,
> naturae rerum magnis **intexere** chartis,
> aeterno ut sophiae coniunctum carmine nomen   40
> nostra tuum senibus loqueretur pagina saeclis.

But (I am) **weaving** (you) **into** [*in-texere*] the great—if it is sanctioned
to say it—**Peplos**,[28]

---

27. The dating of this description fits any of the following occasions for the celebration of the quadrennial or Great Panathenaia: 74/3, 70/69, 66/5, 62/1, 58/7, 54/3, 50/49. See Shear 2001:629.

28. In this particular poem, the *Ciris*, the reference to the Peplos of Athena as displayed at the festival of the Panathenaia in Athens may be influenced by references to the Peplos of Hera as displayed at

the kind of peplos that is carried in the city of Erekhtheus, in Athens, on the
   ancient occasion
when vows are kept by offering gifts that are owed to uncontaminated Minerva
   [Athena],
when the period of four years comes full circle as it slowly nears the oncoming
   fifth year [on the occasion of the quadrennial Panathenaia],
when the light Zephyrus wind accelerates in its rivalry with the alternating
   Eurus wind   25
and drives forward the Vehicle,[29] weighted down with its vast load.[30]
Blessèd is that day. That is what it is to be called. And blessèd is that year.
Blessèd as well are they who have seen such a year, such a day.
Thus does the **weaving [*texere*]** take place, the weaving that narrates in their
   proper **order [*ordo*] the battles of Pallas** [Athena],
and **the great folds of the Peplos**[31] are adorned **with signs that signal the
   moment when the Giants were turned back,**   30
and **terrifying battles** are **rendered in color [*pingere*]**, with the color of a dye[32]
   that is **blood-red,**
and added to that is the picturing of the Typhon repulsed by the **golden tip
   of the spear.**
He is the one who made the aether concrete[33] by using the rocks of Mount
   Ossa,
piling them on top of the peak of Emathia [Pelion] to double the height
   of Olympus
—such is the **Sail** [the **Peplos**][34] that they [the Athenians] carry for the
   goddess on that solemn occasion,   35
and it is by way of such a ritual that I would want (to weave) you (in), O most
   learned of young men: yes, exactly such a ritual,
so that you may be enveloped by the **purple flashes of the sun** and by the
   incandescent beams of the moon
—**beams** that pulsate against the orb of the world with the **galloping feet
   of the two blue horses drawing** the moon's **chariot.**

---

the festival of the Heraia in Argos. Such references to the Peplos of Hera were featured in a lost work of
the poet Calvus, the *Io*. See Lyne 1978:109–10.

   29. On the *currus* or 'Vehicle', see further in the paragraph that follows.

   30. This 'load' is the massive *velum* or 'Sail' that weights down the mast of the *currus* or 'Vehicle', on
which see further in the paragraph that follows.

   31. The plural *pepla* is a metonymy that stems from the basic meaning of *peplos* as 'fold'. The plural
conveys specific instances of the general visual impression created by the Peplos, which is the 'folding'
par excellence.

   32. The noun *coccum* means not just 'berry': it can also refer to any organism that stains like berries,
including the murex (Pliny the Elder *Natural History* 9.140). On *coccum* as 'dye', see Lyne 1978:114.

   33. The aether, which is conventionally imagined as a nonsolid space separating the celestial and
terrestrial realms, is here made solid by way of piling the rocks of the mountain.

   34. For more on the *velum* 'Sail' that is the Peplos, see further in the paragraph that follows.

Yes, I would want to **weave** (you) **in** [*in-texere*], into the great papyrus rolls
  of the Nature of the Universe,
so that a name conjoined with the ever recycling song of personified Wisdom   40
—your name—may be spoken by my page through the ages as they grow
  ancient.

Appendix Vergiliana, Ciris 21–41

In my working translation, I have used parentheses to indicate a syntactical link
that extends from verse 21 all the way to verse 36. Verse 21 signals that the cosmic
idea of the Gigantomachy, which weavers weave into the Peplos of Athena as featured at the festival of the quadrennial Panathenaia, will be 'woven' into the papyrus
rolls signaled at verse 36. The *currus* or 'vehicle' (verse 26) in this description of the
festival is the 'Vehicle' par excellence for the Athenians: it is the Athenian Ship of
State, which was paraded on wheels along the route of the Panathenaic Procession
on the occasion of the presentation of the Peplos to the goddess Athena as the ritual climax of the festival of the quadrennial Panathenaia. This Ship of State was
adorned with the pattern-woven Peplos of Athena, rigged to the mast of the Ship
as a ritually stylized Sail. The *velum* 'sail' in the description (verse 35) is the 'Sail'
par excellence: that is, the gigantic Peplos of Athena.[35]

The actual process of pattern-weaving the Panathenaic Peplos is expressed in this
passage by way of the Latin verb *pingere*, which means 'render in color' or 'paint'
(31). The root of this verb, from which the Latin noun *pictura* is derived, is cognate
with the root of the Greek verb *poikillein*, which as we have seen means 'pattern-
weave'.[36] The narrative thread or *fil conducteur* of the pattern-weaving is purple,
which is perceived as the color of blood (31 *sanguineo . . . cocco*). This color is associated with the theme of war (31 *horrida . . . proelia*) in the context of the narrative that is pattern-woven into the fabric—that is, the charter myth about the victory of Athena and the other Olympians over the Giants (30 *Giganteis . . . tropaeis*).
By metonymy, this dominant color of purple predominated in most ancient references to the overall color of the Panathenaic Peplos.[37]

I find it relevant that the primary opponent of Athena in the charter myth of the
Gigantomachy, as narrated on the occasion of the quadrennial Panathenaia, is *Porphuriōn*, king of the Giants (Pindar *Pythian* 8.12–13, Aristophanes *Birds* 1251, "Apollodorus" *Library* 1.6.1–2).[38] Thus the cosmic figure who shares with Athena a cen-

35. Barber 1991:361–65.

36. Barber 1991:359n2.

37. In another project, I will argue that there survives a reference to this color scheme in verses 61–
69 of Ovid *Metamorphoses* 6.1–145, retelling the myth of Arachne. The narrative woven by Athena centers on her victory over the Giants in the Gigantomachy (verses 70–82).

38. Whereas *Porphuriōn* is the primary opponent of Athena in the context of the Great Panathenaia,
her primary opponent in the context of the Lesser Panathenaia is *Astēr*. In *Odyssey* vii 58–62, by con-

tral place in the narrative of the Gigantomachy as pattern-woven into the Peplos of Athena on the occasion of the Great Panathenaia is the embodiment of purple.

So far, I have argued that the color of purple, as a dominant feature of the Panathenaic Peplos, is relevant to the choice of the epithet *porphureē* 'purple' in describing the *diplax* woven by Athena in the passage I quoted from the *Argonautica* (1.722). I have yet to argue that this choice is relevant to the variant reading *porphureē* 'purple' preferred by the Alexandrian editors over the variant reading *marmareē* 'gleaming' as the epithet of the *diplax* woven by Helen in the passage I quoted earlier from the *Iliad* (III 126). Before I can make such an argument, I must highlight the relevance of the variant reading *marmareē* 'gleaming'. As an epithet, *marmareē* refers to the luminosity of a color like purple, not to the color itself.[39] To restate in terms of contrasts in color, purple is perceived as red in some combinations and blue in others.[40] The semantics here are different from what we find in modern English, where the blue aspect of purple verges on violet whereas purple itself is the red aspect by default.

This variation between red and blue in the perception of purple is activated when purple is contrasted with another color, yellow.[41] As we can see from the cumulative evidence of references to the Panathenaic Peplos, this fabric is known for its yellow as well as purple coloring. Specifically, the yellow is associated with the color of saffron.

I take as my prime example a choral lyric passage from Euripides where captive Trojan women are imagining their future as slaves living in the foreign lands of their Hellenic captors. If they are to be taken to Athens, they imagine, their work there will be the weaving of the Peplos of Athena. Such an act of imagination is typical of the aristocratic ethos that characterizes Trojan captive women in both epic and

trast, we hear that the king of the Giants is Eurymedon, father of Periboia, who is mother of Nausithoos, ancestor of the Phaeacians.

39. Here I am guided by the general discussion of purple by Lepschy 1998, especially at p. 54. I have also been guided by the acute observations of Susan Edmunds (2007.02.27): "Luminosity in weaving is the illusion of light created by judicious placement of light, medium, and dark colors. Luster is another quality that thread can have (like fine silk, or wool prepared to preserve that quality in it). The luster in the thread will appear or not depending on how the fabric is woven (think of damask in white linen, for instance, where pattern is made by contrasting shinier weave with more matt weave)." She adds that the epithet *marmareē* "may describe one or another of these effects or, perhaps, the 'brilliance' of the overall effect of beautifully chosen colors and patterns."

40. A distinction between red and blue as two different kinds of purple dye for wool is evident in Akkadian (*argamannu* and *takiltu*) and Hebrew (*argaman* and *tekelet*): see Lepschy 1998:54.

41. Susan Edmunds (2007.02.27) notes: "The relative amounts of purple and yellow will affect color perception in the following ways: if they are complements (and this depends on which yellow and which purple), they will either intensify each other or cancel each other out (producing gray), depending on whether or not the eye blends them in seeing them (called 'optical mixing'): thus the effects will change with the distance of the viewer from the fabric."

tragedy.[42] Although their bad fortune has transformed them into slaves, they still think and behave like aristocrats.[43] These Trojan women, even though they will be slaves of the Hellenes, retain their aristocratic charisma by pathetically imagining themselves in the act of performing a task traditionally performed by the aristocratic women of Athens: that is, weaving the Peplos of Athena.[44] Here is their description of the Peplos and of the colors woven into it:

ἢ Παλλάδος ἐν πόλει | τὰς καλλιδίφρους Ἀθα|ναίας ἐν κροκέωι πέπλωι | ζεύξομαι
ἄρματι[45] πώ|λους ἐν δαιδαλέαισι ποι|κίλλουσ' ἀνθοκρόκοισι πή|ναις ἢ Τιτάνων
γενεάν,| τὰν Ζεὺς ἀμφιπύρωι κοιμί|ζει φλογμῶι Κρονίδας;

Or, in the city of Pallas [Athena], into [the texture of] the **saffron-colored peplos** of Athena, shall I yoke beautiful horses to her chariot [*harma*],[46] matching the beautiful chariot,[47] as I **pattern-weave [*poikillein*]** them [the horses and the chariot] with **threads colored by the blossoms of saffron**, or [as I pattern-weave] the generation of Titans[48] who were put to sleep by Zeus the son of Kronos with a lightning stroke that had fire flashing all around it?

Euripides Hecuba 466–74

In this pattern-woven picture of Athena riding on a chariot drawn by horses, the dominant color of the horses and the chariot is yellow. In the pattern-woven

---

42. I agree with the formulation of Dué 2006:114: "The sympathetic Trojans of Euripides are not a new phenomenon, but rather represent a continuity of treatment from the earliest Greek epic poetry onward."

43. Dué 2006:27, 109, following Rabinowitz 1998.

44. Relevant to this theme is the peplos presented to Athena by the Trojan women in *Iliad* VI.

45. I accept here the manuscript reading ἄρματι. See the next note.

46. The manuscript reading ἄρματι 'to her chariot [*harma*]' is supported by the information we find in the scholia that correspond to the end of Speech 1 (the *Panathenaic Oration*) of Aelius Aristides (1.404), where the orator sums up the accomplishment of having made the whole speech by comparing it to the Peplos woven for the Great Panathenaia (εἴργασται καὶ ἡμῖν ὁ λόγος ἀντὶ τοῦ πέπλου κόσμος, Παναθηναίων τῇ θεωρίᾳ 'I have made, in place of the Peplos, this speech of mine as an adornment for the spectacle of the Panathenaia'). Here is the relevant wording in the scholia commenting on the summation of Aristides: ἐν τοῖς Παναθηναίοις ὕφαινον αἱ παρθένοι Ἀθήνησι πέπλον, ἐν ᾧ ἅρμα ἦν ἐντετυπωμένον, καὶ ἃ κατὰ τῶν γιγάντων ἡ θεὸς ἔπραξεν 'at the Panathenaia, the maidens at Athens wove a Peplos in which was figured a chariot [*harma*] along with the deeds accomplished by the goddess [Athena] in the war against the Giants'.

47. I translate καλλιδίφρους, the epithet of the horses yoked to the chariot of Athena, as 'matching the beautiful chariot' in order to convey a link between this epithet and the noun ἄρματι. Editors have tried to emend the manuscript reading ἄρματι on the grounds that καλλιδίφρους means 'marked by a beautiful chariot', so that ἄρματι seems redundant. I propose, however, that the double use of 'chariot' can be explained as a verbal re-enactment of yoking the horses to the chariot. In the process, the beauty of the horses is linked to the beauty of the chariot—and vice versa. And the linking that is achieved through the artistic bravura of the poet matches the linking that is achieved through the artistic bravura of the pattern-weaver.

48. I interpret the reference here to Titans as a Panhellenic way of referring to the Athenian charter myth about the Giants who battle the gods for cosmic supremacy.

picture of the Giants in combat with the gods, by contrast, the dominant color is purple. And the interaction of these two colors produces a variation: the purple of the Peplos, as designated by the word *porphureē*, is red when it is foregrounded against the yellow. Conversely, if there is no such foregrounding, the purple defaults to blue. That happens when yellow is foregrounded against the purple as background. I should add that this foregrounded yellow would match the color of bronze—and of the gold that overlays the bronze—in a metalworked version of the pattern-woven narrative.[49]

What I just said about red as the foregrounded aspect of purple applies to the description of the narrative that is pattern-woven into the Panathenaic Peplos in the passage I quoted earlier from the *Ciris*. As we saw there, the dominant theme is red, matching the color of the blood shed by the Giants in their battle with the gods. So also in the narrative that is pattern-woven into the *diplax* made by Helen, the dominant theme is red, matching the color of the blood shed by Achaeans and Trojans alike—all for her sake. By implication, the same dominant theme prevails in the narrative that is pattern-woven into the *diplax* made by Andromache. In both cases, the variant epithet *marmareē* 'gleaming' describing the *diplax* refers to the luminosity of the purple, whereas the variant epithet *porphureē* 'purple' refers simply to the color.

Of the two alternatives *marmareē* 'gleaming' and *porphureē* 'purple' in the Iliadic passages we have considered, I propose that the Homeric Koine variant is *marmareē* 'gleaming', which is understandable as 'purple' to those who already know that the color of the fabric must be understood as purple. It goes without saying that all Athenians and their allies would know this fact about the fabric of the Panathenaic Peplos. To be contrasted is the variant preferred by the Alexandrian editors, *porphureē* 'purple', which actually specifies the local color. Such a specification would be understood by these editors as an additional detail that could otherwise be left unspecified. Whereas the variant *marmareē* 'gleaming' presumes an Athenocentric understanding that the color is purple and leaves this local color unspecified, the other variant specifies the color as an additional detail.

In his *Argonautica*, Apollonius of Rhodes pointedly chooses the variant *porphureē* 'purple' (1.722) in describing the *diplax* made by Athena for the hero Jason. From the standpoint of Apollonius, the choice of this epithet in his own poetry is a cross-reference to a choice made by the Alexandrian editors of Homer. As we will see later on, his choice is dictated by a logic that is typical of Hellenistic poetry. From the standpoint of Homeric poetry, by contrast, a choice between the variants *porphureē* 'purple' and *marmareē* 'gleaming' in the two Iliadic passages we have con-

---

49. In a comedy of Strattis, who flourished in the late fifth and the early fourth century B.C.E., we find that the threads for pattern-weaving the charter myth of the battle of the gods with the Giants into the Peplos have two colors: the Peplos is both κρόκινος 'saffron-colored' and ὑακίνθινος 'hyacinth-colored' (F 73 ed. Kassel-Austin, via scholia for Euripides *Hecuba* 468: ὅτι δὲ κρόκινός ἐστι καὶ ὑακίνθινος καὶ τοὺς Γίγαντας ἐμπεποίκιλται, δηλοῖ Στράττις).

sidered would have no effect on the point of reference—if that point of reference is the Panathenaic Peplos.

I am arguing that there is such a point of reference. There is a Panathenaic subtext in the Homeric references to the *diplax* woven by Helen and the *diplax* woven by Andromache. Once again, I use the word *subtext* here metaphorically in referring to the Panathenaia, and I will use the word *text* metaphorically as well in referring to the narration of the Homeric *Iliad*. The text of the Iliadic narrative refers to the weaving of themes that relate to the Trojan War, while the subtext refers to the narrating of these themes in the context of the seasonally recurring festival of the Panathenaia, which is the actual occasion for the Homeric narration. The reference, if it happens in the context of actual performance at the Panathenaia, is split between text and subtext. We see here once again an example of the phenomenon I call *split referencing*.

These two Iliadic passages involving the word *diplax* are linked with a third Iliadic passage. It involves the peplos presented by the Trojan women to Athena in *Iliad* VI. As we saw in chapter 9, where I analyzed this third passage, the peplos is described as the most excellent of an array of peploi that are all *pan-poikiloi* 'completely pattern-woven' (VI 289).[50] This epithet matches the epithet *poikila* 'varied' describing the floral patterns or *throna* woven into the *diplax* of Andromache (XXII 441). In the case of the *diplax*, I have already argued that its narrative is linked with the narrative of the *Iliad*. In the case of the peplos as well, I will now argue that its pattern-woven narrative is likewise linked with the narrative of the *Iliad*.

When Homeric poetry refers to the peplos presented by the Trojan women to Athena, it refers implicitly to the main theme woven into Panathenaic Peplos, the Gigantomachy. I focus on a striking detail in the description of the peplos destined for dedication to the cult statue of Athena in *Iliad* VI: that peplos is described as shining like an *astēr* 'star' (VI 295), just one verse after its description as the biggest and the most beautiful of all peploi by way of its *poikilmata* 'pattern-weavings' (294). We learn from Aristotle[51] that the notional origin of the annual or Lesser Panathenaia was motivated by a charter myth that told of the primal killing of a Giant named *Asterios* or *Astēr* by the goddess Athena.[52] The name, especially the variant of the name that we read in the second version, is striking: the Giant is simply 'Star'.[53] So also the Peplos dedicated to Athena at *Iliad* VI (295) shines like an *astēr* 'star'.

50. Earlier, I posited an alternative version where the weavers of these peploi are imagined as native Trojan women.

51. Aristotle F 637 (ed. Rose p. 395, via the scholia for Aristides p. 323 ed. Dindorf).

52. *Asterios* according to one set of scholia for Aristides (Aristotle F 637 ed. Rose p. 395.20). *Astēr* according to another set of scholia (Rose p. 395.5).

53. The wording of the second version is of interest: ἐπὶ Ἀστέρι τῷ γίγαντι ὑπὸ Ἀθηνᾶς ἀναιρεθέντι 'to commemorate *Astēr* the Giant, killed by Athena'. On the semantics of *epi* plus dative in contexts of aetiologizing various festivals, see *PH* 4§7 (= pp. 120–21); also 4§6n15 (= p. 119) and 5§12n38 (= p. 142).

There is some speculation that this Iliadic simile motivated the name of the Giant (*Astēr* or *Asterios*).[54] I argue instead that the simile and the name are both cognate with a traditional iconographic narratology of star patterns woven into the Peplos of Athena at the Panathenaia. These stars are telling their own story.[55]

Just as the cosmic figure who opposes Athena in the context of the Lesser Panathenaia is *Astēr*, the embodiment of a star, there is a corresponding cosmic figure who opposes her—as well as all the Olympian gods—in the context of the Great Panathenaia: he is *Porphuriōn*, king of the Giants (Pindar *Pythian* 8.12–13, Aristophanes *Birds* 1251, "Apollodorus" *Library* 1.6.1–2). As we saw earlier, this Giant is central to the charter myth of the Gigantomachy as narrated by rhapsodes for the occasion of the Great Panathenaia: as his name indicates, he is the embodiment of the color of purple woven into the Panathenaic Peplos. As we also saw earlier, this color is associated with the blood that is shed by the Giants in the narrative of the Gigantomachy and with the blood that is shed by Trojans and Achaeans alike in the story of the Trojan War as narrated by rhapsodes for the occasion of the Great Panathenaia.

So we have seen that various themes in the Gigantomachy converge, in the context of the Panathenaia, with the main theme of the epic performed at this festival: that is, the story of the Trojan War. Such a convergence can be explained in terms of the festival itself. It is on the occasion of this festival of the Panathenaia that the charter myth of the Gigantomachy is pattern-woven by weavers and the epic of the Trojan War is narrated by rhapsodes. At the Panathenaia, the charter myth of the Gigantomachy is a virtual *humnos* that presupposes as its hymnic consequent the epic of the Trojan War.[56]

By contrast with the narratives woven into the *diplax* of Helen and into the *diplax* of Andromache in Homeric poetry, the narrative that Athena pattern-weaves into the *diplax* featured in the *Argonautica* of Apollonius is Panathenaic without being overtly Homeric. Its Homeric signature is in the form of what is pattern-woven for the Panathenaia, not in the content of what is narrated at the Panathenaia in the era of the Athenian democracy. In the narrative of the *diplax* featured in the *Argonautica*, we see no direct reference to the Homeric narrative of the Trojan War, an event that stands out as the dominant theme of the epic poetry being performed at the Panathenaia in the democratic era. The poetic themes that Athena pattern-weaves into the *diplax* worn by Jason are non-Homeric or, better, pre-Homeric, since they narrate events that logically predate the Trojan War (*Argonautica* 1.730–67). These events would suit the poetic repertoire of rhapsodes who performed at the Panathenaia in the predemocratic era of the Peisistratidai.

So, any direct reference to Homeric themes would be inconceivable in the *Arg-*

---

54. Scheid and Svenbro 1994:28n48.
55. *PR* 93–94.
56. On epic as a *hymnic consequent*, see *HC* 2§§97, 109, 113–14, 116.

onautica. Still, we see signs of indirect reference. First, the *diplax* worn by Jason is said to be the woven work of Athena herself, matching the peplos woven by Athena in *Iliad* V. Second, this *diplax* is described as *porphureē* 'purple', which is the variant preferred by the Alexandrians over the variant *marmareē* 'gleaming' as the epithet applied to the *diplax* of Helen in *Iliad* III and to the *diplax* of Andromache in *Iliad* XXII. The mentioning of this *diplax* in the *Argonautica* amounts to a display of poetic rivalry, since the indirect reference takes place in the context of an ecphrasis—the only ecphrasis attempted by Apollonius in the *Argonautica*. Here is the only opportunity that Apollonius gives himself to display his poetic skills in ecphrasis. To that extent, the ecphrasis of the *diplax* of Athena in the *Argonautica* of Apollonius rivals the ecphrasis of the Shield of Achilles in the *Iliad* (XVIII 478–609). As I argue in chapter 2 of the twin book *Homer the Classic*, the narrative of the Shield was understood to be Orphic in content not only by Zenodotus as the premier editor of Homer in the age of Callimachus but also by Apollonius as a premier poet of that same age. So when Apollonius in his *Argonautica* refers indirectly to the Shield by way of his unique ecphrasis of the *diplax* that is pattern-woven by Athena, his reference indicates not only a general rivalry with Homeric poetry but also a specific rivalry with what he understood to be the post-Homeric or neoteric aspects of this poetry.[57]

For Apollonius, as also for Zenodotus, such neoteric aspects of Homeric poetry were associated with Orpheus. And, as I argue in *Homer the Classic*, these Orphic aspects of Homeric poetry are not really 'newer' than the aspects that Zenodotus understood to be genuinely Homeric.[58] In fact, they are in some ways older, and a shining example is the Shield of Achilles, featuring various details that are demonstrably older than the corresponding details in the rest of the *Iliad* as we know it. One such detail is the pairing of Ares and Athena as martial divinities (XVIII 516–19). I mention this detail in *Homer the Classic*, where I highlight the epithet that describes these two divinities in their martial function, *arizēlō* 'most shining' (XVIII 519).[59] Now I will highlight the fact that this pairing of Ares and Athena is so old as to be traceable all the way back to the Bronze Age.

As we know from the documentary evidence of the Linear B tablets found in the palace of Knossos in Crete, the divinities Athena and Ares (in that order) are paired as symmetrical recipients of offerings: in one tablet (V 52), a-ta-na-po-ti-ni-ja (*Athānāi potniāi*: dative of *Athānā potnia*) is listed together with e-nu-wa-ri-jo (*Enūaliōi*: dative of *Enūalios*) and pa-ja-wo-ne (*Paiāwonei*: dative of *Paiāwōn*) and po-se-da-o-ne (*Poseidāonei*: dative of *Poseidōn*).[60] As we know from the evi-

---

57. On the concept *neoteric*, see above, chapter 3, the section entitled "A Post-Athenocentric View of the *Homēridai*."

58. *HC* ch. 2.

59. *HC* ch. 1.

60. Gérard-Rousseau 1968:44–47.

dence of Homeric diction, the divine name *Enūalios* became an epithet of Ares (as in *Iliad* XVII 211).[61] As for the name of Ares, it too is attested in the Linear B tablets (Knossos Fp 14 and Fp 5816), in the form a-re (*Arei*: dative of *Arēs*).[62] The Cretan connection of Athena and Ares is attested in the *Odyssey* as well, where Odysseus in one of his so-called Cretan lies represents himself as a Cretan prince who professes his devotion to these two divinities in moments of crisis in battle (xiv 216).[63]

The pairing of Ares and Athena in the world of images represented in the Shield of Achilles is expressed by way of bronzework that is overlaid with gold (XVIII 517–19). Such a technique of metalwork, as narrated on the Shield, is notionally linked to the heroic age or, as archaeologists would say it, to the Bronze Age. But it must also be compared with the metalwork of Pheidias in creating the Shield of Athena next to the statue of the goddess in the Parthenon: this Shield, as I show in *Homer the Classic*, is a masterpiece of bronzework overlaid with gold on both the convex and the concave sides.[64]

There is more to this comparison between the Shield of Athena and the Shield of Achilles. We have already seen that the story of the Battle of the Gods and Giants is narrated not only in the virtuoso metalwork that produced the Shield of Athena as executed by Pheidias but also in the virtuoso fabric work that produced the Peplos of Athena as executed by master pattern-weavers. Now we will see that the stories narrated on the Shield of Achilles can be pictured not only as the metalwork of Hephaistos. These stories are also pictured as the pattern-weaving of the divine metalworker:

Ἐν δὲ χορὸν ποίκιλλε περικλυτὸς ἀμφιγυήεις,   590
τῷ ἴκελον οἷόν ποτ' ἐνὶ Κνωσῷ εὐρείῃ
Δαίδαλος ἤσκησεν καλλιπλοκάμῳ Ἀριάδνῃ.

The renowned one [Hephaistos], the one with the two strong arms,
   pattern-wove [*poikillein*][65] in it [the Shield] a **khoros**.[66]   590
It [the *khoros*] was just like the one that, once upon a time in far-ruling
   Knossos,
Daedalus made for **Ariadne**, the one with the beautiful tresses [*plokamoi*].

Iliad XVIII 590–92

---

61. In some Homeric contexts (as in *Iliad* XX 69), *Enūalios* is a god in his own right, distinct from Ares, just as *Paiāwōn* is in some contexts distinct from Apollo (*Iliad* V 401, 899–900): see Nagy 1974:136–38.

62. Gérard-Rousseau 1968:38–40.

63. Nagy 1969.

64. *HC* ch. 4.

65. Also attested at this verse, besides ποίκιλλε (*poikillein*), is the variant ποίησε (*poiein*), with the neutral meaning 'make'.

66. This word *khoros* can designate either the place where singing and dancing takes place or the group of singers and dancers who perform at that place.

In contemplating this picture, the mind's eye sees the work of the divine artisan in action. It is metalwork executed by the ultimate *khalkeus* 'bronzeworker': that is what Hephaistos is actually called by Homeric poetry (*Iliad* XV 309). And the bronzework of the god is pictured as an act of pattern-weaving, as expressed by the word *poikillein* (XVIII 590).

So the ecphrasis of the Shield of Achilles presents its narrative not only as metalwork but also as pattern-weaving, just as the Gigantomachy is narrated in Athens not only through the metalwork of Pheidias who creates his images on the Shield of Athena but also through the fabric work of master pattern-weavers who create their images on the Peplos of Athena. Here I return one last time to the *diplax* that is pattern-woven by Athena in the *Argonautica* of Apollonius. By now we see that the pattern-working of this *diplax* made by Athena is understood as parallel to the metalworking of the Shield made by Hephaistos in the *Iliad*. More specifically, the actual epic narration of the Shield in the *Iliad* is figured not only as metalwork, specifically as bronzework, but also as pattern-weaving, *poikillein* (XVIII 590). The craft of pattern-weaving is especially privileged as a metaphor for the craft of metalworking, since it is also a metaphor for the craft of making Homeric poetry, as we saw in the Iliadic passages picturing the *diplax* of Helen and the *diplax* of Andromache. Virgil understood this privileging of the metaphor of pattern-weaving: in the *Aeneid*, Vulcan's metalwork in producing the Shield of Aeneas is described as an act of 'weaving', a *textus* (*Aeneid* 8.625).

The linking of pattern-weaving to metalwork in Homeric poetry is not just a matter of metaphor. The actual craft of pattern-weaving is closely linked to the actual craft of metalworking. Both these crafts reflect the wealth, power, and prestige of mighty federations and empires. A case in point is the parallelism I just noted between the pattern-weaving of the Peplos of Athena and the metalwork of the Shield of Athena made by Pheidias in the era of the Athenian empire. This parallelism between the Peplos and the Shield reflects a tradition that goes back to the Bronze Age, as we see from comparative evidence. In what follows, I offer two examples of such evidence.

To begin, there is the Athenian festival that inaugurated the weaving of the Peplos of Athena, the *Khalkeia*, the name of which is derived from the word *khalkos* 'bronze'. This festival celebrated the synergism of the divinities Athena and Hephaistos as models for the work of craftsmen. As the synergistic partner of Hephaistos, Athena was worshipped as *Erganē*: that is, the divinity who presides over the work (*ergon*) of craftsmen.[67] Since the weaving of the woolen Peplos was begun at the festival of the *Khalkeia*, it is relevant that the name for the female weavers of the Peplos was *ergastinai*.[68]

67. Parke 1977:92–93.

68. See Hesychius s.v. ἐργαστῖναι· αἱ τὸν πέπλον ὑφαίνουσαι 'ergastinai: women who weave [*huphainein*] the Peplos'. For a basic work on the *ergastinai*, see B. Nagy 1972; see also Aleshire and

Next, I offer a piece of comparative evidence from a city other than Athens. In Argos, specially selected women wove for the goddess Hera a robe called the *patos* on the occasion of the festival of Hera called the Heraia (Callimachus F 66.3, Hesychius s.v. πάτος). Taking a closer look at this festival, we can see a link between the craft of pattern-weaving and the craft of metalwork. On the occasion of this festival, prizes made of bronze metalwork were awarded in the context of a *pompē* 'procession' marked by the ritual climax of a *thusia* 'sacrifice' (as indicated by the verb *thuein* 'sacrifice'):

[152a 1 A] «ὅ τ᾽ ἐν Ἄργει χαλκός»· τὰ Ἥραια, «ἃ» καὶ Ἑκατόμβαια λέγεται διὰ τὸ πλῆθος τῶν θυομένων βοῶν. λαμβάνουσι δὲ ἐντεῦθεν οὐκ ἀργὸν χαλκὸν, ἀλλὰ τρίποδας καὶ λέβητας καὶ ἀσπίδας καὶ κρατῆρας.

"and the **bronze** [*khalkos*] in Argos" [quotation from Pindar]: [It is the festival called] the **Heraia**. It is also called the **Hekatombaia** [sacrifice of a hundred cattle]. It is called that because of the number of cattle that are **sacrificed** [*thuein*].[69] What is received as prizes there [at that festival] is **bronze** [*khalkos*] **not as raw material that has no work done on it** [*a-ergon*] but in the [worked] form of tripods and cauldrons and shields [*aspis*, plural] and mixing bowls.

[152b 1 ABDEQ] «ἔγνω νιν»· ἐγνώρισε δὲ αὐτὸν καὶ ὁ ἐν τῷ Ἄργει διδόμενος **χαλκὸς** ἆθλον τῷ νικήσαντι.

"recognized him" [quotation from Pindar]: He [the victor of the competition] was recognized by way of the **bronze** [*khalkos*] that is given as a prize [*athlon*] to the winner [of the competition] in Argos.[70]

[152c 1 ABCEQ] τελεῖται δὲ κατὰ τὸ Ἄργος τὰ Ἥραια ἢ τὰ Ἑκατόμβαια διὰ τὸ ἑκατὸν βοῦς θύεσθαι τῇ θεῷ. τὸ δὲ ἆθλον, **ἀσπὶς χαλκῆ**· οἱ δὲ **στέφανοι** ἐκ μυρσίνης.

The festival of the **Heraia** or **Hekatombaia** at Argos is **ritually enacted** [*teleîsthai*] with the **sacrifice** [*thuesthai*] of a hundred cattle to the goddess. And the prize [*athlon*] to be won in the contest is a **bronze shield** [*aspis khalkē*].[71] According to other sources, the prizes are **garlands** [*stephanoi*] made of **myrtle**.[72]

Lambert 2003, especially pp. 75–76 on the semantics of *ergazesthai* 'work', which can apply to work done on woolen fabric (just as it can apply to work done on bronze).

69. I infer that the two oxen who were late for the festival of the Heraia in the narrative of Herodotus (1.31.1–5) about Kleobis and Biton were meant to be the two premier sacrificial victims that inaugurated the mass sacrifices of the other ninety-eight cattle; on premier sacrifices, see my analysis of the festival of Artemis at Eretria in *PR* 39–53.

70. I note the metonymy here: bronze as an extension of victory in the contest, and we have just seen that this bronze is to be 'energized' (as in the Greek word *en-ergeia*) in the sense that it has work (*ergon*) done on it in the form of tripods or cauldrons or shields or mixing bowls. See also Hesychius s.v. *agōn khalkeios*.

71. Here we see that the *aspis* is the premier form of bronze at this festival.

72. The myrtle blossom is the ultimate metonym of the victory.

[152d 1 BCEQ] ἄλλως· ἐν Ἄργει, ἐν τῷ Ἑκατομβαίων ἀγῶνι, χαλκὸς τὸ ἄθλον διδόται, ὅτι Ἀρχῖνος Ἀργείων γενόμενος βασιλεύς, ὃς καὶ ἀγῶνα πρῶτος συνεστήσατο, ταχθεὶς ἐπὶ τῆς τῶν ὅπλων κατασκευῆς, ἀπὸ τούτων καὶ τὴν τῶν ὅπλων δόσιν ἐποιήσατο. Ἑκατόμβαια δὲ [BC(D)EQ] ὁ ἀγὼν λέγεται ὅτι πομπῆς μεγάλης προηγοῦνται ἑκατὸν βόες, οὓς νόμος κρεανομεῖσθαι πᾶσι τοῖς πολίταις.

According to an alternative source: In Argos, at the **festival** [*agōn*] of competitions called the Hekatombaia, **bronze** [*khalkos*] is awarded as the prize [*athlon*] in the competitions. That is because Arkhinos,[73] when he became king of the Argives, was the first to establish a **festival** [*agōn*] of competitions[74] and, having been put in charge of the preparation of weapons, he proceeded from there to the establishment of the awarding of these weapons as prizes. This **festival** [*agōn*] of competitions is called Hekatombaia because a hundred cattle are led forth in a grand **procession** [*pompē*],[75] and their meat is divided by customary law among all the citizens of the city.

Scholia for Pindar Olympian 7.152

I draw attention to the bronze *aspis* 'shield' awarded as a prize in the competitions that took place at the festival of the Heraia.[76] In fact, the entire festival of the Heraia was metonymically called the *Aspis* or 'Shield'.[77]

In the complex of traditional rituals and myths native to Argos, the bronze shield that figures in the local rituals of athletic competition at the festival of the Heraia is modeled on a prototypical bronze shield that figures in the corresponding local myth. According to the myth, this prototypical bronze shield was the centerpiece of the original set of armor made by Hephaistos for Achilles at the request of the hero's mother, the goddess Thetis, who presented this armor to her mortal son, Achilles, when he went off to war at Troy. The narrative of this local myth was performed in a local ritual context. The place was a sacred space called the Heraion, located forty-five stadia from the center of the city of Argos, and the occasion was the festival of Hera, the Heraia. Our primary source is the *Electra* of Euripides, where we see the myth of the original Shield of Achilles sung and danced by the chorus of the drama. This Athenian chorus is playing the role of an Argive chorus of local girls who are singing and dancing the myth of the Shield in celebration of the goddess Hera (*Electra* 432–86).

We find further traces of a link between the myth of the original bronze Shield of Achilles and the ritual complex of the Heraia in vase paintings that show Thetis in the act of presenting the bronze Shield, along with other pieces of armor, to

73. I infer that Arkhinos here figures as the culture hero of the bronze shield.
74. So Arkhinos is the aetiological founder of the *agōn* 'festival of competitions'.
75. Clearly, the *pompē* 'procession' is integral to the *thusia* 'sacrifice'.
76. See again Hesychius s.v. *agōn khalkeios*.
77. On the festival of Hera in Argos as the *Aspis* or 'Shield': Nilsson 1906:42. Epigraphical references collected in Zeitlin 1970:659n44.

FIGURE 5. Attic black-figure column krater: Thetis presenting shield and helmet to
Achilles. Attributed to the Painter of London B76. Berlin, Staatliche Museen, Antikensammlungen, 3763. Drawing by Valerie Woelfel.

Achilles (fig. 5). In some of these paintings, the bronze Shield is visually correlated
with a garland of myrtle (fig. 6).

As we saw a moment ago from the information given in the Pindaric scholia,
the prizes awarded to winners in the competitions at the festival of the Heraia in
Argos included garlands of myrtle, mentioned as a parallel to the prize of the bronze
shield.

As I reconstruct the occasion of the Argive Heraia from the comparative evidence of other such festivals, most notably the Athenian Panathenaia, the ritual
centerpiece of the celebration was a procession that reached its climax in a choral
performance of Argive girls. This choral performance evidently signaled the presentation of a fabric woven for the goddess. In the *Electra* of Euripides, the myth of
the bronze shield of Achilles is explicitly linked with the choral performance of the
Argive girls who sing and dance the myth on the occasion of Hera's festival (*Electra*
167–74, 178).[78] According to local myth, it was at the Heraion, where the festival
of the Heraia was celebrated by the Argives, that Agamemnon initiated the expedition to Troy (Dictys of Crete 1.16).[79]

I note an essential symmetry between the pattern-woven fabric associated with
the young Argive women and the bronze shield that is correspondingly associated with the young Argive men. The shield signals the martial identity of the male
population, symmetrical to the peaceful identity of the female population who
pattern-weave the fabric offered to the goddess Hera on the festive occasion of

78. Zeitlin 1970:659. In Sophocles *Electra* 911–12, it is made explicit that Electra is like Cinderella,
forbidden to attend the festival.
79. Zeitlin 1970:659n44.

FIGURE 6. Attic black-figure hydria: Thetis presenting shield and garland to Achilles. Attributed to the Tyrrhenian Group. Paris, Musée du Louvre, E869. Drawing by Valerie Woelfel.

the Heraia. There is a comparable symmetry at work in the *Seven against Thebes* of Aeschylus.

Reading the *Electra* of Euripides, we can see this symmetry in the wording of the chorus of young Argive women as they invite the princess Electra to participate in the premier festival of the city of Argos (167–74). It is a kind of "Invitation to the Ball." But Electra is forbidden to participate in this festive ball of the Argives. At least, that is what we hear in the *Electra* of Sophocles (911–12). In any case, she would be too sad to participate, as we hear in the *Electra* of Euripides. Our view of Electra may be subjective, thanks to Euripides the poet, but our view of the Argive festival is I think accurate, thanks to Euripides the ethnographer. The sadness of Electra as an Argive Cinderella stands in sharp contrast with the happiness of young women celebrating the Feast of Hera and having the best time of their lives. As these Argive girls sing and dance the song of the bronze Shield of Achilles, we can just see them catching the attention of dashing young Argive warriors and perhaps even falling in love, fully sharing in the charisma of the pattern-woven fabric they offer to Hera.

A metonymy for this charisma is the blossom of the myrtle, which as we saw is the flower of choice for making *stephanoi* 'garlands' to wear at the festival of the Heraia in Argos. I have deliberately used the word *charisma* here in view of linguistic evidence for a metonymic link between the word *kharis* 'pleasurable beauty' and the festive use of myrtle blossoms for the making of garlands:

Μακεδόνες δὲ καὶ Κύπριοι χάριτας λέγουσι τὰς συνεστραμμένας καὶ οὔλας μυρσίνας, ἃς φαμὲν στεφανίτιδας.

Macedonians and Cypriotes use the word **kharites** [plural of **kharis**] with reference to myrtle blossoms that are **compacted** and **curled** [around a garland]. We call them **garland-blossoms** [*stephanitides*].

Scholia D (via A) for Iliad XVII 51

The image of myrtle blossoms compactly curled around a festive garland is applied as a metaphor for picturing the compact and curly hair of the hero Euphorbos as he lies dead on the battlefield. The curls of this *beau mort* are compared to myrtle blossoms:

αἵματί οἱ δεύοντο κόμαι χαρίτεσσιν ὁμοῖαι
πλοχμοί θ᾽.

With blood bedewed was his hair, looking like **kharites**,
with the curls and all.[80]

Iliad XVII 51–52

So the association of *kharis* 'pleasurable beauty' with the blossoms of a festive garland is attested already in Homeric usage and is not restricted to the local usages of Macedonians and Cypriotes.[81] In fact, we see the same association in Argive usage, as reflected in the diction of Pindar. In Pindar's *Nemean* 10, a song that celebrates the winner of a wrestling event at the Heraia in Argos, the plural of *kharis* (that is, *kharites*) graces the very beginning of this song.

There is another relevant association. When Pausanias enters the temple of Hera in Argos, he sees inside the *pronaos* (that is, inside the front third of the temple) a set of archaic statues that are known by the Argives as the *Kharites*, who are the personifications of the pleasurable beauty of *kharis*: that is, the 'Graces'. And, remarkably, he sees next to the *Kharites* an archaic shield, presumably made of bronze. This shield, Pausanias reports, belonged to Euphorbos until Menelaos killed him and stripped him of his armor:[82]

ἐν δὲ τῷ προνάῳ τῇ μὲν **Χάριτες** ἀγάλματά ἐστιν ἀρχαῖα, ἐν δεξιᾷ δὲ κλίνη τῆς Ἥρας
καὶ ἀνάθημα **ἀσπὶς** ἣν Μενέλαός ποτε ἀφείλετο **Εὔφορβον** ἐν Ἰλίῳ.

---

80. I interpret the combination of κόμαι ... πλοχμοί θ᾽ 'hair ... and curls' as meaning 'hair with curls'. As a parallel to the simile that we see at work in κόμαι χαρίτεσσιν ὁμοῖαι 'hair looking like the blossoms of myrtle', we may compare οὔλας ... κόμας ὑακινθίνῳ ἄνθει ὁμοίας 'curly hair looking like the blossom of the hyacinth' at *Odyssey* vi 231 and xxiii 158. The simile of the myrtle blossoms at *Iliad* XVII 51–52 modulates into a metaphor of olive blossoms at 53–59. In terms of the extended metaphor, the myrtle blossoms in this case may perhaps be imagined initially as red and subsequently as white. The white would match the color of the olive blossoms. For a reference to the white color of myrtle blossoms in a garland, see Pindar *Isthmian* 4.69–70 (87–88).

81. See also Dué 2006:67. More on myrtles in Pindar *Isthmian* 8.65–66, on which see Dué p. 73.

82. On Pythagoras and the shield of Euphorbos, see the scholia T for *Iliad* XVII 29–30; also Diodorus 10.6.2–3 and Ovid *Metamorphoses* 15.160–64; also Porphyry *Life of Pythagoras* 26 and Iamblichus *Life of Pythagoras* 63. More in Riedweg 2002:17, 69, 98, 124.

And inside the *pronaos* [of the temple of Hera at Argos] there is on one side a set of ancient statues known as the **Kharites** and, on the right-hand side, there is [1] what is known as the marital couch of Hera and [2] a votive object, which is the **shield** [*aspis*] that once upon a time Menelaos took from **Euphorbos** at Troy.

Pausanias 2.17.3–4

Having made these observations about the charisma of myrtle blossoms at the festival of the Heraia, I turn to the charisma of the bronze shield that is won as a prize by athletes competing at this festival. That shield has as its prototype the Shield of Achilles, which as we saw is directly associated with garlands of myrtle in vase paintings.

The Shield of Achilles, which I have been describing as the hero's original shield, has to be replaced with a second shield made for him once again by Hephaistos after Hector kills Patroklos and captures the armor worn by the vanquished hero—armor that had belonged to Achilles. This second shield is the Shield of Achilles as described in *Iliad* XVIII.

In terms of epics other than the *Iliad* as we know it, however, there would be no need for such a second shield. I note a major difference between the two shields of Achilles. The original shield, as we saw, is the self-expression of the city of Argos. But the second shield, the one we see becoming concretized in the *Iliad*, is the self-expression not only of a city but also of an empire. I will return to this formulation in the Epilegomena.

On the basis of the comparative evidence I have assembled so far, I can say with confidence that the correlation of bronzework and pattern-weaving is old, so old as to be traced back to the Bronze Age. Even the substance of bronze is appropriate as a symbol for the concept of the Bronze Age as the age of heroes. Homeric poetry focuses on the *selas* 'gleam' that radiates from the reflection of light given off by the bronze surface of the Shield of Achilles:

δύσετο δῶρα θεοῦ, τά οἱ Ἥφαιστος κάμε τεύχων.
κνημῖδας μὲν πρῶτα περὶ κνήμῃσιν ἔθηκε
καλὰς ἀργυρέοισιν ἐπισφυρίοις ἀραρυίας·   370
δεύτερον αὖ θώρηκα περὶ στήθεσσιν ἔδυνεν.
ἀμφὶ δ' ἄρ' ὤμοισιν βάλετο ξίφος ἀργυρόηλον
χάλκεον· αὐτὰρ ἔπειτα **σάκος** μέγα τε στιβαρόν τε
εἵλετο, τοῦ δ' ἀπάνευθε **σέλας** γένετ' ἠΰτε μήνης.
ὡς δ' ὅτ' ἄν ἐκ πόντοιο **σέλας** ναύτῃσι **φανήῃ**   375
καιομένοιο πυρός, τό τε καίεται **ὑψόθ' ὄρεσφι**
σταθμῷ ἐν οἰοπόλῳ· τοὺς δ' οὐκ ἐθέλοντας ἄελλαι
πόντον ἐπ' ἰχθυόεντα φίλων ἀπάνευθε φέρουσιν·
ὡς ἀπ' Ἀχιλλῆος **σάκεος σέλας** αἰθέρ' ἵκανε.

He [Achilles] put it [his armor] on, the gifts of the god, which Hephaistos
   had made for him with much labor.

First he put around his legs the shin guards,   370
beautiful ones, with silver fastenings at the ankles.
Next he put around his chest the breastplate,
and around his shoulders he slung the sword with the nails of silver,
a sword made of bronze. Next,[83] the **Shield** [*sakos*], great and mighty,
he took, and from it there was a **gleam** [*selas*] from afar, as from the moon,
or as when, at sea, a **gleam** [*selas*] to sailors appears   375
from a blazing fire, the kind that blazes **high in the mountains**
at a solitary station [*stathmos*], as the sailors are carried unwilling by gusts
     of wind
over the fish-swarming **sea** [*pontos*], far away from their loved ones.
So also did the **gleam** [*selas*] from the **Shield** [*sakos*] of Achilles reach all the
     way up to the aether.

Iliad XIX 368–79

The linking of this bronze shield to the Bronze Age is expressed by the artifact itself. The poetry of the Shield of Achilles in *Iliad* XVIII is designed to show that this bronze artifact can make direct contact with the Bronze Age. Contact is established through the *selas* 'gleam' that radiates from the bronze surface of the Shield, projecting a picture from the Bronze Age. This gleam radiating from the Shield of Achilles is compared here to the gleam emanating from a lighthouse, and the image of that lighthouse, as we saw earlier, evokes the tumulus of Achilles, which figures as a primal marker of the age of heroes.

This radiant gleam, becoming universally visible as its light continues to spread all the way up to the aether, projects the world of heroes that we see pictured on the Shield. It is a picture of the Bronze Age, mirrored by the bronze of the hero's Shield. With its vast array of details, this stupendous picture gives off a most dazzling view of the heroic age. As we saw in the *Life of Homer* traditions, it was the gleam given off by the bronze armor of Achilles that dazzled Homer to the point of blindness (*Vita* 6.45–51).

The gleam of the bronze Shield emanates not only from its form but also from the content of that form. The gleam comes not only from the armor—that is, from the shining metal of the bronze surface reflecting the radiant light of the sun. The gleam comes also from what the armor means. That meaning is conveyed not only through the simile of the hero's tumulus as a lighthouse but also through the picture made by the divine metalworker on the shining bronze surface of the Shield. In this context, I emphasize again the Homeric description of Hephaistos as a *khalkeus* 'bronzeworker' (*Iliad* XV 309). The picture projected by the gleam emanating from the bronze Shield is a picture made by a bronzeworker.

This picture made by the divine artisan focuses on the Bronze Age. A case in

83. Up to now, there has been a series of contiguities, climaxing now with the Shield itself.

point is the dazzling simile of the lighthouse, evoking the tumulus of Achilles. Another case in point is a simile that spotlights a scene created by Hephaistos. The spotlighting is achieved by comparing that scene with another scene—this one created by the premier mortal artisan of the Bronze Age, Daedalus himself:

Ἐν δὲ **χορὸν ποίκιλλε** περικλυτὸς ἀμφιγυήεις,   590
τῷ ἴκελον οἷόν ποτ᾽ ἐνὶ Κνωσῷ εὐρείῃ
Δαίδαλος ἤσκησεν καλλιπλοκάμῳ **Ἀριάδνῃ.**
ἔνθα μὲν ἠΐθεοι καὶ παρθένοι ἀλφεσίβοιαι
ὀρχεῦντ᾽ ἀλλήλων ἐπὶ καρπῷ χεῖρας ἔχοντες.
τῶν δ᾽ αἳ μὲν λεπτὰς ὀθόνας ἔχον, οἳ δὲ χιτῶνας   595
εἵατ᾽ ἐϋννήτους, ἦκα στίλβοντας ἐλαίῳ·
καί ῥ᾽ αἳ μὲν καλὰς **στεφάνας** ἔχον, οἳ δὲ μαχαίρας
εἶχον χρυσείας ἐξ ἀργυρέων τελαμώνων.
οἳ δ᾽ ὁτὲ μὲν θρέξασκον ἐπισταμένοισι πόδεσσι
ῥεῖα μάλ᾽, ὡς ὅτε τις τροχὸν ἄρμενον ἐν παλάμῃσιν   600
ἑζόμενος κεραμεὺς πειρήσεται, αἴ κε θέῃσιν·
ἄλλοτε δ᾽ αὖ θρέξασκον ἐπὶ στίχας ἀλλήλοισι.
πολλὸς δ᾽ **ἱμερόεντα χορὸν** περιίσταθ᾽ ὅμιλος
τερπόμενοι· μετὰ δέ σφιν **ἐμέλπετο** θεῖος ἀοιδὸς
φορμίζων· δοιὼ δὲ κυβιστητῆρε κατ᾽ αὐτοὺς   605
μολπῆς ἐξάρχοντος ἐδίνευον κατὰ μέσσους.

The renowned one [Hephaistos], the one with the two strong arms,
    pattern-wove [*poikillein*][84] in it [the Shield] a *khoros*.[85]   590
It [the *khoros*] was just like the one that, once upon a time in far-ruling
    Knossos,
Daedalus made for **Ariadne**, the one with the beautiful tresses [*plokamoi*].
There were young men there,[86] and girls who are courted with gifts of cattle,
and they all were **dancing** with each other, holding hands at the wrist.
The girls were wearing delicate dresses, while the boys were clothed in khitons 595
well woven, gleaming exquisitely, with a touch of olive oil.
The girls had beautiful **garlands [*stephanai*]**, while the boys had knives
made of gold, hanging from knife-belts made of silver.
Half the time they moved fast in a circle, with expert steps,
showing the greatest ease, as when a wheel, solidly built, is given a spin
    by the hands   600
of a seated potter, who is testing it, whether it will run well.

84. Also attested at this verse, besides ποίκιλλε (*poikillein*), is the variant ποίησε (*poieîn*), with the neutral meaning 'make'.
85. I need to repeat that this word *khoros* can designate either the place where singing and dancing takes place or the group of singers and dancers who perform at that place. The relationship of the place with the group that is the *khoros* is metonymic.
86. The 'there' is both the place of dance and the place in the picture that is the Shield.

The other half of the time they moved fast in straight lines, alongside
    each other.
And a huge assembly stood around the place of the *khoros*, **which evokes
    desire,**
and they were all delighted. In their midst **sang-and-danced** [*melpesthai*]
    a divine singer,
playing on the *phorminx*.[87] Two special dancers among them   605
were swirling as he **led** [*ex-arkhein*][88] the **singing-and-dancing** [*molpē*]
    in their midst.

Iliad XVIII 590–606

87. After τερπόμενοι 'and they were all delighted' at verse 604, the sequence μετὰ δέ σφιν ἐμέλπετο
θεῖος ἀοιδὸς | φορμίζων 'In their midst sang-and-danced a divine singer, playing on the *phorminx*' is
not attested in the medieval manuscript tradition but was restored by F. A. Wolf in his 1804 edition of
the *Iliad*. The relevant verse-numbering of 604–5 in current editions of the *Iliad* goes back to the Wolf
edition. The restoration is based on what we read in Athenaeus (5.181c) about the treatment of this passage in the edition of Aristarchus: reportedly, that editor accepted the wording τερπόμενοι· μετὰ δέ σφιν
ἐμέλπετο θεῖος ἀοιδὸς | φορμίζων 'and they were all delighted. In their midst sang-and-danced a divine
singer, playing on the *phorminx*' at *Odyssey* iv 17–18, where it is still attested in the medieval manuscript tradition, while rejecting the same wording in the corresponding passage at *Iliad* XVIII 604–5.
Instead of the two verses that take up the space of 604–5, τερπόμενοι· μετὰ δέ σφιν ἐμέλπετο θεῖος ἀοιδὸς
| φορμίζων, δοιὼ δὲ κυβιστητῆρε κατ' αὐτοὺς 'and they were all delighted. In their midst sang-and-danced
a divine singer, playing on the *phorminx*. Two special dancers among them . . .', Aristarchus preferred
to read simply one verse, τερπόμενοι· δοιὼ δὲ κυβιστητῆρε κατ' αὐτοὺς 'and they were all delighted.
Two special dancers among them . . .', with one verse instead of two verses taking up the same space.
As I note in *Homer the Classic* (2§74), the wording τερπόμενοι· μετὰ δέ σφιν ἐμέλπετο θεῖος ἀοιδὸς |
φορμίζων 'and they were all delighted. In their midst sang-and-danced a divine singer, playing on the
phorminx', which is the wording attested at *Odyssey* iv 17–18 and restored at *Iliad* XVIII 604–5, can be
independently authenticated on the basis of the wording attested at *Odyssey* xiii 27–28, where we read
τερπόμενοι· μετὰ δέ σφιν ἐμέλπετο θεῖος ἀοιδὸς | Δημόδοκος 'and they were all delighted. In their midst
sang-and-danced the divine singer, Demodokos'. The evidence of this passage from *Odyssey* xiii is missing in the reportage of Athenaeus about the editorial judgments of Aristarchus. And it is missing also
in the argumentation of Revermann 1998, who reasons that the wording μετὰ δέ σφιν ἐμέλπετο θεῖος
ἀοιδὸς | φορμίζων in *Iliad* XVIII results from what he calls "rhapsodic intervention" (p. 37). I offer a
critique of this reasoning in *Homer the Classic* (2§74).

88. As we read in Athenaeus (5.180d), Aristarchus argued that ἐξάρχοντες, which is the reading we
see in the medieval manuscripts, should be the preferred reading at *Iliad* XVIII 606 and at *Odyssey* iv
19 instead of ἐξάρχοντος. On the other hand, Athenaeus defends ἐξάρχοντος, and his wording indicates
that this alternative reading was attested as a textual variant. If that is really the case, then we are dealing here with two textual variants, ἐξάρχοντος and ἐξάρχοντες. And both of these forms can be shown
to be formulaic variants as well, as I argue in *Homer the Classic* (2§74). The variants ἐξάρχοντος and
ἐξάρχοντες indicate two different scenarios corresponding to the longer and the shorter versions of the
wording. According to the shorter version as signaled by ἐξάρχοντες, it is the two specialized dancers
whose performance leads into the choral singing and dancing. According to the longer version as signaled by ἐξάρχοντος, which is the reading I adopt here, it is the lyre singer joined by the two specialized dancers whose combined performance leads into the choral singing and dancing. The second of
these two scenarios resembles what happens when Demodokos the lyre singer is joined by specialized

On the surface, the craft that is used to produce this picture of the work of Hephaistos is metalwork, specifically bronzework. Beneath the surface, it is of course the craft of poetry that produces the picture. And, as we saw from the Homeric descriptions of the *diplax* made by Helen and the *diplax* made by Andromache, a metaphor for this craft of poetry is the craft of pattern-weaving. So the application of this metaphor of pattern-weaving to the bronzework of the divine artisan, as indicated by the word *poikillein* 'pattern-weave', highlights not only the parallelism of these two crafts but also the prestige of poetry as a comparable craft.

Such crafts as bronzework and pattern-weaving differed significantly from each other in their prehistory during the Dark Age as I have defined it here—that is, in the prehistoric period extending backward in time from the earliest attested phase of the historical period, around the sixth century B.C.E., all the way to the Bronze Age. During this Dark Age, as archaeological investigation has shown, there was far more continuity in the craft of pattern-weaving and far less continuity in other material crafts, including bronzework.[89] Retrospectively, the craft of pattern-weaving rivals the craft of bronzework itself in making contact with the Bronze Age.

As for the nonmaterial craft of Homeric poetry, I have just been arguing that it, too, like pattern-weaving and bronzework, shows strong continuity in the prehistoric period as we trace our way back from the sixth century B.C.E. into the Bronze Age.[90] In this case, the evidence comes not only from archaeology but also from historical linguistics.

As I argued in chapter 9, linguistic analysis of Homeric poetry reveals three major dialectal phases embedded in the language of this poetry. These phases are Ionic, Aeolic, and Mycenaean. As the name *Mycenaean* indicates, the earliest of these three phases is grounded in the Bronze Age.

As I also argued in chapter 9, an ideal point of entry for reconstructing the Mycenaean phase of Homeric poetry is the region of the Troad in Asia Minor as it existed around 600 B.C.E. Here we find evidence for competing Ionic and Aeolic traditions of poetry about the epic past, and this evidence comes not only from the Homeric poetry of the *Iliad*, albeit residually, but also from the poetry of Sappho and Alcaeus. By comparing these competing traditions, we saw how the dominantly Aeolic poetry of Sappho and Alcaeus is cognate in content as well as in form with the dominantly Ionic poetry that characterizes Homer. As cognates, these two traditions of poetry point to an uninterrupted continuum stemming from the Bronze Age.

---

dancers in their combined performance at *Odyssey* viii 256–66. I repeat from the previous footnote the wording attested at *Odyssey* xiii 27–28, where we read τερπόμενοι· μετὰ δέ σφιν ἐμέλπετο θεῖος ἀοιδὸς | Δημόδοκος 'and they were all delighted. In their midst sang-and-danced the divine singer, Demodokos'.

89. Barber 1991:365–82.

90. On Homeric poetry as a direct continuator of realia from the Bronze Age, see also Nagy 1969. A case in point is the mention in *Odyssey* xix (188) of Amnisos, which I compare with the mention of Amnisos in a Linear B tablet from Knossos.

Reconstructing backward in time from the Ionic to the Aeolic to the Mycenaean phase of the Homeric language, we have encountered a remarkable pattern of continuity in references to the craft of pattern-weaving, extending all the way back to the Bronze Age. And we have noted how this craft of pattern-weaving rivals the craft of bronzework itself in making contact with the Bronze Age. And we have also noted that the craft of Homeric poetry rivals both these other crafts.

The craft of Homeric poetry, which is dominantly Ionian, demonstrates its own power to make contact with the Bronze Age by displaying the craft of captive Aeolian women. As we saw, the primary examples of these Aeolian women are Briseis and Andromache. In the case of Briseis, this Aeolian prima donna sings her lament to the background of choral singing and dancing performed by captive women from Lesbos (*Iliad* XIX 245–46), and Homeric poetry highlights the virtuosity of these women in *erga* 'handiwork' (IX 128, 270).[91] For women in general, the most prestigious form of such handiwork is the craft of pattern-weaving. For the women of Lesbos in particular, their excellence in this form of handiwork is viewed here as a parallel to their universally acknowledged excellence in choral singing and dancing. In the case of Andromache, she too shows her excellence in this form of handiwork: Homeric poetry captures her in the act of pattern-weaving her own web. And she too, like Briseis, is an Aeolian prima donna, singing her lament to the background of choral singing and dancing performed by the women of Troy, who will soon be captives just like the women of Lesbos. Andromache too, like Briseis, will soon be a captive herself, and her singing prefigures her future status as a captive Aeolian woman.

When Andromache pattern-weaves her web, she is weaving the plot of the Homeric *Iliad*. Homeric poetry pictures Andromache in the act of weaving this web at the precise moment when the news of her beloved Hector's death is about to overwhelm her. As we read in the scholia (A) for the *Iliad* (XXII 440), Aristarchus thought that Andromache must have had a premonition of this news. And it was precisely the poetry of this news that Andromache was pattern-weaving at that very moment. That poetry, viewed overall, is the story of Troy: in other words, the story of Ilion, the *Iliad*.

This story is told not only by way of Homeric poetry or by way of pattern-weaving as represented by Homeric poetry: it is told also by way of metalworking, sculpting, and painting. The story of Troy as told in the weaving of Helen and Andromache can also be told in the metalwork we see on the surface of the Shield of Achilles. Similarly, the story of the Battle of the Gods and Giants as it is woven into the web of Athena can also be metalworked into the surface of the Shield of Athena

---

91. The virtuosity of the women of Lesbos in weaving is parallel to the virtuosity of the women of Troy.

or sculpted on the walls of her house, the Parthenon. The story of Troy can even be painted on walls, as in the Stoa Poikile (Pausanias 1.15.2).

The adjective *poikilē*, referring to the stoa that houses the master painting of the sorrowful story of Troy as retold in the age of Pericles by the master painter Polygnotus, means 'varied, variegated'. This meaning captures the essence of the craft expressed by the verb *poikillein*, meaning 'pattern-weave'. In fact, the farther back we go in time as we reconstruct the crafts of painting and pattern-weaving in earlier ages, the closer they are to each other. In the Geometric period, for example, the representations of human forms painted on the surfaces of Geometric vases show the same kinds of lozenge shapes that we see in representations of human forms pattern-woven into fabrics. Moreover, the variation we see in the patterns of pattern-weaving is imitated by the variation we see in the patterns painted on Geometric vases.[92] Such variation is a sign of a technique. It is the technique of variegation, which is inherent in pattern-weaving. Now I will say again what I just said, but this time I will say it by combining the meaning of the adjective *poikilos* (masculine) 'varied, variegated' with the meaning of the verb *poikillein* 'pattern-weave'. In terms of these two Greek words, the technique of variegation we see in the varied patterns of Geometric vase painting imitates the technique of variegation we see in the varied patterns of pattern-weaving.

In the case of Geometric vase painting, the medium of painting not only imitates the varied patterns woven into fabrics. It also represents the fabrics themselves, along with the patterns woven into these fabrics. The visual effect is a *mise en abîme*, since the variations of human forms in the painting re-enact the variations of human forms that are pattern-woven into the fabrics worn or displayed by these human forms.

To take one example from the rich repertoire of Geometric vase paintings, I draw attention to the skirts worn by a series of girls in a chorus (fig. 7).

Another example is a shroud held up for display over the head of a corpse placed on a bier. The corpse is being lamented by a choral ensemble of lamenting men and women, and the woman who displays the shroud is evidently the lead singer of the choral ensemble (fig. 8).

The shroud that is represented in this Geometric vase painting is analogous to the shroud that is rewoven every day by Penelope in the *Odyssey*—only to be unwoven every night—for the ever-delayed occasion of a funeral planned for her father-in-law, corresponding to the ever-delayed occasion of a remarriage planned for Penelope herself. The potential variety of continuous reweavings of this fabric corresponds to the potential variety of continuous repaintings of patterns to be painted on Geometric vases—or of continuous reperformances of patterns to be performed in Homeric poetry.

92. Barber 1991:365–72.

FIGURE 7. *(top)* Geometric amphora: detail of neck, chorus girls. Athens, National Archaeological Museum, 313. Drawing by Valerie Woelfel.

FIGURE 8. *(bottom)* Geometric vase: detail of funerary ritual, choral ensemble of lamenting men and women mourn a corpse placed on a bier. Karlsruhe, Badisches Landesmuseum, 2674. Drawing by Valerie Woelfel.

The variation that is woven into fabrics worn by women as choral performers is represented not only in the vase paintings of the Geometric period. It is represented also in fresco paintings that date back to the Mycenaean and even to the Minoan eras of the Bronze Age. A moment ago, I drew attention to a Geometric vase painting that showed a variety of skirts worn by a series of girls singing and dancing in a chorus (fig. 7). I said *girls* instead of *maidens* or *women* simply to make a point about the relevance of the etymology of *girl*. In earlier phases of the English language, the noun *girl* referred to an article of clothing, such as a skirt, and it meant 'girl' only by metonymy. Such a metonymy is relevant to the ancient practice of choral singing and dancing, preceded by choral procession. Here I turn to the visual arts of the Bronze Age: in particular, to the fresco paintings that adorned the walls of the great palaces of the Mycenaean era in the Bronze Age (figs. 9, 10). The beauty and the pleasure of seeing and hearing a young girl dance and sing in a choral performance—and lead the procession that leads to the choral performance—converges on the spectacularly varied vision of the skirts that were pattern-woven for the occasion of processing and dancing and singing. As in the case of Geometric vase paintings, we see in such Mycenaean fresco paintings a glimpse of the variety inherent in the craft of pattern-weaving, comparable to the variety inherent in the craft of painting—or in the craft of making Homeric verse.

By now I have traced the craft of pattern-weaving all the way back to the Bronze Age. It is a craft that is most visible in the visual arts of the Bronze Age, which represent the beauty and the pleasure of variation woven into the skirts of participants in choral singing and dancing and processing at festivals. And by now we see that the essence of this craft of pattern-weaving, as conveyed by the verb *poikillein* in Homeric poetry, is variety itself and the pleasurable beauty to be found in variety. Such is the variety exemplified by Homeric poetry itself through the ages.

Relevant to the meaning of the verb *poikillein* as 'pattern-weave' is the idiomatic use of the adjective *poikilos* 'varied' in Greek prose. As we see from the usage of Plato, *poikilos* means 'multiple (multiplex), multiform' when contrasted with *haploûs* 'simple (simplex), uniform' (*Theaetetus* 146d, *Phaedrus* 277c).[93] Further, whatever is *poikilon* 'multiple' can never be the 'same' (as we see from the phrasing in *Republic* 8.568d, πολὺ καὶ ποικίλον καὶ οὐδέποτε ταὐτόν 'manifold and varied [*poikilon*] and never the same thing').[94] In other words, each time you speak of something that is *poikilon*, it will be something different, not the same thing as before, each time it recurs. Something that is multiform cannot be the same thing when it recurs, as opposed to something that is uniform. When you repeat something that

93. For comparable wording, see Plato *Laws* 2.665c. Again I note the etymology of *haploûs* 'simple (simplex)'.
94. For comparable wording, see Plato *Republic* 10.604e.

FIGURE 9. Fresco: processional women. After fragments found on northwest slope (52 H nws) at Pylos. Drawing by Valerie Woelfel.

FIGURE 10. Fresco: processional women. After fragments from Old Kadmeia, Thebes. Drawing by Valerie Woelfel.

is *poikilon*, it can never be exactly the same thing that it was before you repeated it. This idea as conveyed by the adjective *poikilos* 'varied' applies also to the verb *poikillein* in the sense 'pattern-weave': when you repeat something in your pattern-weaving, it can never result in exactly the same thing that it was before you repeated it. For a particularly suggestive collocation of the adjective *poikilos* 'varied' with the verb *poikillein* in the usage of Plato, I highlight the simile describing an idealized state as ἱμάτιον ποικίλον πᾶσιν ἄνθεσιν πεποικιλμένον 'a varied [*poikilon*] fabric that is pattern-woven [*poikillein*] with every kind of flower' (*Republic* 8.557c).

What I have been saying about the craft of pattern-weaving applies also to the craft of Homeric poetry. What is repeated in Homeric poetry is never exactly the same and is therefore always new. Homeric repetition is by nature multiform, not uniform. In his Sather Classical Lectures, published in 1938, Samuel Eliot Bassett speaks about the beauty of variety in Homeric poetry and in the poetry of Attic tragedy. He contrasts this beauty with the dreariness of uniform repetition, which he describes as an excess of detail in the background. "Too great detail," he says, "might easily become wearisome to the spectator, just as intricately patterned wall paper once disturbed us when as children we had to see it continually from a bed of illness."[95]

The pleasurable beauty of variety in Homeric poetry is not only a thing of joy. It can also be a thing of exquisite sorrow. The capture of Troy, in all its varieties, is such a thing of beauty. It is what Virgil captures in the phrase *sunt lacrimae rerum* 'there are tears that connect with the real world' (*Aeneid* 1.462).[96] It is what Pheidias and his fellow artisans capture in the north metopes of the Parthenon.[97] It is what the Homeric *Iliad* captures in its picture of a weeping Andromache, the ultimate diva of Homeric poetry. The capture of Troy was—and is—a most captivating thing. The song of this capture is the song of the captive women of the *Iliad*—and of the unnamed captive woman in Rhapsody viii of the *Odyssey*. They sing their song to express their own sorrows, and these sorrows are overheard by the audience of Homer.

The songs of the captive women of Homeric poetry are expressed by their lead singers, such as Andromache, Briseis, and the unnamed captive woman of the *Odyssey*. But the singing of the prima donna calls for the antiphonal response of a singing and dancing chorus. And the identity of the prima donna as lead singer depends on the multiple voices of this chorus. So also the identity of Homer as the ultimate lead singer depends on multiple voices. As I argued in chapter 9, the figure of Homer himself in the *Homeric Hymn* (3) *to Apollo* is presented and represented by a chorus of girls, the Delian Maidens, who are singing and dancing at a Panhellenic festival in Delos. Just as the multiple voices of this chorus of Delian Maidens

---

95. Bassett 1938:50.
96. *HC* 1§§178–96.
97. *HC* 4§§247–58.

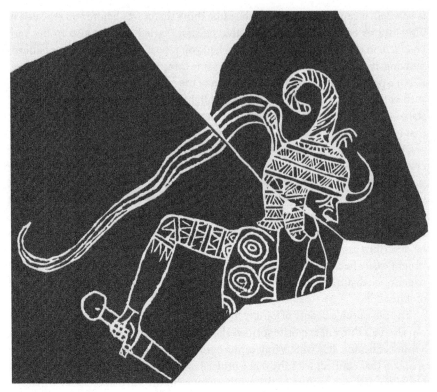

FIGURE 11. Hittite graffito: warrior with horsetail crested helmet. See Vermeule 1987:146. Drawing by Jill Curry Robbins.

all fit together into a single voice, so also all Homer's multiple identities ultimately fit together into a single identity.[98]

A FINAL RETROSPECTIVE: ANDROMACHE'S LAST LOOK AT HECTOR

Andromache and Hector have just parted, turning away from each other and heading in opposite directions. He is going off to die while she is going back to her weaving. As she is being led away, Andromache keeps turning her head back again and again, *entropalizomenē*, hoping to catch one last glimpse of the receding view of her doomed husband:

ἐντροπαλιζομένη, θαλερὸν κατὰ δάκρυ χέουσα.

98. For more on the Delian Maidens, I refer to my analysis in *HC* 2§§26–40.

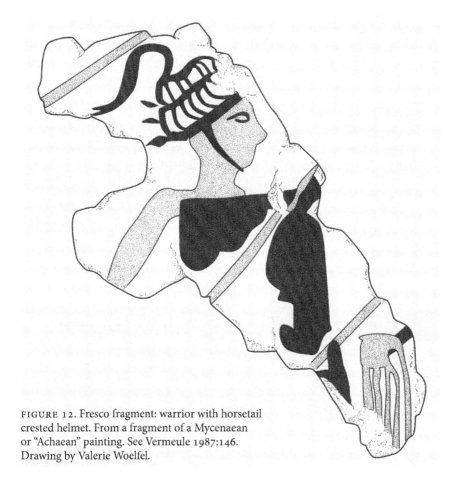

FIGURE 12. Fresco fragment: warrior with horsetail
crested helmet. From a fragment of a Mycenaean
or "Achaean" painting. See Vermeule 1987:146.
Drawing by Valerie Woelfel.

She was turning her head back again and again, shedding tears thick and fast.

Iliad VI 496

As I argue in the twin book *Homer the Classic*, we see here a poetics of retro-
spection.[99] Andromache is returning, again and again, to an original picture. Here
at the end of Part II of the present book, that original picture can be visualized in
the world of the Bronze Age. And I close by showing two versions of such an original picture (figs. 11, 12). Both versions show the figure of a warrior wearing a great
floating horsetail-crested helmet—like the helmet that frightens the child of Hector and Andromache. One version is Hittite in provenience; the other is Achaean
(that is, Mycenaean). As Emily Vermeule argues, the Homeric picturing of Hector

99. *HC* ch. 1.

wearing such a horsetail-crested helmet, which is how he looks the last time Andromache sees him, must go back to the Bronze Age, no later than the fifteenth century B.C.E. Juxtaposing this Homeric picture with the Hittite and the "Achaean"
(Mycenaean) pictures as shown here (figs. 11, 12), Vermeule observes:[100]

> In the *Iliad* the famous scene between Hector and Astyanax [VI 466–70] could prob-
> ably not have been created after the great floating horsetail crested helmet of the
> Achaian invaders of Anatolia went out of fashion about 1400 B.C.E. That it should be
> recorded in the Anatolian as well as the Greek images of the fifteenth century is re-
> markable [here she refers to the Hittite and the Mycenaean pictures], and the archaeo-
> logical confirmation of a memorable poetic image. The later, post-1400 Mycenaean
> helmet with its flabby tab on top could not frighten the most unheroic infant.

Just as Andromache is picturing her last mental image of her last parting with
Hector, so also the poetry of epic is shaping the last mental image of Andromache
in its own act of retrospective, of returning to the fixed image. That act of picturing, like the Homeric picture of Hector, goes all the way back to the Bronze Age.

---

100. Vermeule 1987:146. The doubts expressed by Kirk 1990:223 fail to shake my confidence in Vermeule's argument.

Epilegomena

A Preclassical Text of Homer in the Making

Till now I have been reconstructing Homer as a preclassic by working my way backward in time. Now I will attempt an overview by going forward in time. I start with the earliest possible point of departure, the so-called Bronze Age.

For some, the Bronze Age is so obscure that it seems even darker than the so-called Dark Age. My thinking is different. For me the Bronze Age is perhaps the brightest of all the ages of Homer. In what follows, I will explain my reasons for applying the metaphor of brightness to this age.

To start, let us consider why the Bronze Age may seem like a dark age. According to some theories, there was a poet called Homer who lived in the eighth or seventh century B.C.E.—and who dictated or wrote down the Homeric poems.[1] I resist such theories, but for the moment let us suppose that there was indeed a dictating Homer or a writing Homer who somehow produced what we now know as the *Iliad* and the *Odyssey* at some point in the course of those two centuries, the eighth and the seventh. In terms of such theories, Homer would not know much about the remote past. He would know mostly those things that connect with his own life and times. What is known as the Dark Age would have stranded this kind of Homer, cutting him off from his own prehistory.

Many of those who imagine such a Homer lurking in the darkness of the eighth

---

1. On the idea of Homer as an illiterate singer who dictates as he performs, see Janko 1992:37–38. On the idea of Homer as a literate singer who writes down what he composes, see West 2003b. For his earlier theories, see West 2000b:486 and 1995:203–19. For a critique of dictation theories in general, see Cassio 1999 and 2002.

or the seventh century, stranded from his own prehistory, will nevertheless want to add an escape clause when it comes to the premier landmark of the Bronze Age in the popular imagination of today and yesterday and in fact ever since time immemorial: that is, Troy and the story of Troy. Even the advocates of a stranded Homer need to pay lip service to Troy, the ostensibly real Troy that Heinrich Schliemann rediscovered and reclaimed for Homer as he understood Homer; but these same advocates are willing to allow this Homer of theirs to tell of Troy only in terms of vague atavistic memories—memories that blur the ostensibly real Troy that archaeologists ever since Schliemann have been trying to piece together. The romantic Schliemann has of course been replaced by scientific archaeologists, but I have a strong sense that Schliemann's romantic construct of Homer has not at all been replaced in the field of archaeology: this romantic Homer lives on, lingering in the minds of today's scientific thinkers as they fret over Homer's picture of Troy and the story of Troy. Was Homer right or wrong about Troy? Was his memory clear or beclouded?

Offering an alternative, I have approached Homer not by trying to pin him down as some kind of eyewitness to one time and to one set of places but by tracking the evolution of the empirically observable system that is Homeric poetry, and I have tracked this evolution back to the Bronze Age. My evolutionary model, as a story, has been narrated by going backward in time rather than forward. When the story is told backward rather than forward, it becomes increasingly difficult to restrict Homeric poetry to any one time and any one set of places. The textual tradition as we have it, in all its variations of form and content, defies a unified explanation in terms of one single person's great achievements of observation, in terms of one "big bang," as I have called it in my earlier work.[2]

Although we find less variation in the final phases of the Homeric tradition than in other traditions that are loosely called epic in other cultures, the actual fact of variation is undeniable.[3] And there is more and more variation to be seen, not less and less, as we reconstruct Homer farther and farther back in time into the past. As we saw in chapters 9 and 10, a most fitting word for describing this variation is *poikilos*, which means not only 'varied' in general but 'pattern-woven' in particular. This word, as we also saw, best captures the poetics of variation in the earlier phases of Homeric poetry.

In order to account for the increasing variation of this poetry in its earlier phases, some try to downdate Homer, pushing him forward in time from the eighth to the seventh or even to the sixth century. Although I think this approach is to some degree productive, it has its problems. Even the term *downdate* is problematic. It reflects the same kind of thinking that led to the relatively earlier datings, pushing Homer

---

2. *HQ* 70, 73, 83, 92–93.
3. Nagy 2001a; rewritten as *HTL* ch. 2.

backward to the seventh or eighth century. If you are forced to downdate Homer, you will still be trying to date Homer at one time and one place. And you will still be assuming that you can reach a point where all significant variation will disappear in the poetry of Homer himself. If you push Homer far enough forward in time to reach such a point, it will be far too late for those who need to attribute the *Iliad* and *Odyssey* to a single creative mind of a single person called Homer or whatever his name may be.

Proposing an alternative explanation, I have argued that Homeric poetry stems from an oral tradition that evolves through a streamlining of variations. In making this argument, I have highlighted the appropriation of this tradition by the *Homēridai* of Chios in the context of the Panathenaic festival at Athens—and in the earlier context of the Panionian festival of the Ionian Dodecapolis in Asia Minor. This appropriation, I have argued, is the main reason for a dramatic slowing down in the stream, as it were, of variations, leading ultimately to the concretized form of the *Iliad* and *Odyssey* as we know them. In my earlier work, I used a related metaphor in referring to the slowing down in the stream of variations in Homeric poetry. I referred to this slowing down as a *Panathenaic bottleneck*.[4] In terms of my present work, that metaphor needs to be extended: the bottleneck is not only Panathenaic; it is also Panionian, in that the Panathenaic Regulation must have stemmed ultimately from a Panionian Regulation, as I argued in chapter 4, where I applied the argumentation of Douglas Frame concerning the evolution of a Homeric performance tradition consisting of twenty-four rhapsodies each for the *Iliad* and *Odyssey* in the late eighth and early seventh centuries, at the festival of the Panionia held at the Panionion of the Ionian Dodecapolis.[5]

Here I prolong the metaphor of Homeric poetry as a stream. The slower the streaming of Homeric poetry, the longer you can look at it. But the stream is much faster as you travel upstream along the banks to look at earlier phases of the flow; and the farther upstream you travel, the faster this Homeric stream flows right past you. As I worked my way upstream into the Dark Age and, beyond that, into the Bronze Age, I was finding it more and more of a strain to keep on looking around, taking in all that I could see, trying to capture it all. The viewing became more and more rushed. Some views became blurred—or even occluded. And it shows. For example, I have barely even mentioned some of the places that must still be considered for a fuller understanding of Homeric poetry in its earlier phases. A prominent example is Euboea.[6] Another is Delphi, especially in the context of the First

---

4. See *HR* 69–70; *HTL* 30, 185.

5. Frame 2009 ch. 11.

6. A most important line of inquiry is the sustained argumentation of Debiasi 2004 and 2008, who speaks of "la matrice euboica." I cite here just one point of special interest: Plutarch in his *Greek Questions* (296d–e) tells of a tradition claiming that Euboea used to be Aeolian and then became Ionian. See also Debiasi 2004:202.

Sacred War.[7] For the moment, I resign myself to saving for a later project my study of such landmarks in the shaping of Homeric poetry, especially in the eighth and the seventh centuries B.C.E. As for the Bronze Age, the need for broader scope is even more pronounced. We find here the most fluid phase of Homer by far. That is why I could not possibly refer to Homer as a classic in the Bronze Age, or even in the Dark Age. That is why the subject of this book is Homer as a preclassic, not as a classic.

An essential phase of transition from Homer the Preclassic to Homer the Classic was the sixth century, which is my shorthand term here for referring to a period that actually extends over the limit of a hundred years at each end, overlapping into the earlier and later centuries by a few decades. As I reconstruct my way backward in time in the twin book *Homer the Classic*, I conclude with Athens in the classical period of the fifth century. Here in *Homer the Preclassic*, where I reconstruct my way backward from the sixth century, I might have been expected to move away from such an Athenocentric viewpoint. But by now it is evident that this viewpoint stayed in place even when I reached the sixth century. I was able to keep Athens in view even then because of the way I had redefined the concept of a Dark Age from the start. At the very beginning of Part I, I was saying that everything between the Bronze Age and the classical age is really a dark age for research on Homer. And then I went on to concentrate on the latest part of this dark age, focusing on the sixth century. Here in the Epilegomena as well, I take this opportunity to focus one more time on the sixth century as a point of entry for reconstruction, but this time I will be reconstructing forward in time when I start from there, not backward in time.

THE PEISISTRATEAN RECENSION AND BEYOND

The meaning of Homer's name, *Homēros*, is a metaphor that encapsulates the Poet's life as narrated in the myths of the *Lives of Homer*. That is what I argued in chapter 9, where I examined the myths that recapitulate the metaphor of Homer as the one who 'joins together' or 'integrates' the body politic. But there is not only a metaphor at work in these myths. There is also a metonym. In terms of these myths, Homer himself is a metonym. He is not only the person who is Homer. He is also Homeric poetry, which is a metonymic extension of Homer. Such a metonymy of Homer as an extension of his own poetry is evident in the myths we have seen so far about the integration of the body politic by Homer the person. Just as Homeric poetry integrates society, so also does Homer himself. But now we are about to see a myth that reverses the perspective. It is the myth of the Peisistratean Recension. Up to

---

7. A point of special interest is the role of Athens, Thessaly, and Sikyon as members of the *amphiktuones* in the First Sacred War.

THE PEISISTRATEAN RECENSION AND BEYOND

now, we have seen myths saying that society is integrated by Homer. By contrast, the myth of the Peisistratean Recension says that Homer is integrated by society.

In this myth, the metonymy of Homer as the body of Homeric poetry is actually attested. Before I show the attestation, however, I propose to preview the essence of the myth on the basis of the attested stories. The body of Homeric poetry, according to these stories, had become disintegrated in the course of Homer's wanderings from city to city, since Homer could never find a permanent place to live. As we saw in the *Lives of Homer*, the only permanent place for the Poet was a place to die, which turns out to be the Ionian island of Ios. As we also saw, that place for Homer to die was also the place where he had been conceived—according to the version of the story favored by the Athenians. When Homer dies, he leaves behind him what is metonymically a corpus, a body of poetry that is scattered throughout the multiplicity of cities he had visited in the course of his wanderings. This body is a metonym for Homer, not a metaphor. It is the body of Homeric poetry that is scattered all over the cities, not Homer himself as a dead body. Homer is scattered only as a metonymic extension of his poetry. According to the myth, the scattered and disintegrated Homer is then reintegrated by Peisistratos of Athens.

So far, I have been referring to the Peisistratean Recension as a myth. To be more specific, it is a charter myth, a totalizing aetiology meant to explain the unity of Homeric poetry as performed in the city of Athens. In terms of the myth, Peisistratos unified Homeric poetry in this city by reintegrating what had become disintegrated in a multiplicity of performances throughout the other cities of the Greek-speaking world. In my previous work on the Peisistratean Recension, I concentrated on analyzing the morphology of the myth, showing that it cannot be dismissed as a random antiquarian invention.[8] Now I concentrate on analyzing the actual applications of this myth in the history of Homeric reception in Athens.

The simplest formulation of this charter myth can be found in one of the *Lives of Homer*:

περιιὼν δὲ τὰς πόλεις ᾖδε τὰ **ποιήματα**. ὕστερον δὲ Πεισίστρατος αὐτὰ συνήγαγεν.

[Homer], **as he went wandering around** [*perierkhesthai*] the cities, was singing [*āidein*] his **poetic creations** [***poiēmata***]; later, Peisistratos collected them.

Vita 4.8–10

In this particular *Life*, the cities that Homer is said to have visited in the course of his wanderings are not listed, but the cities that claim to be the place of his birth are given in this order: Smyrna, Chios, Colophon, and Athens (*Vita* 4.7–8). As we saw in chapter 6, this sequencing of cities represents the prevalent Athenocentric narrative pattern. It follows that the repertoire of Homer in this narrative is like-

8. *HQ* 93–105.

wise Athenocentric: in terms of the myth of the Peisistratean Recension, the 'poetic creations' of Homer, his *poiēmata*, are assumed to be the *Iliad* and the *Odyssey*
only, to the exclusion of other creations—except for the *Margites*.

This *Life* goes on to add a most important detail, which brings me to the metonymy of Homer as the body of Homer. The narrative quotes an epigram attributed to Peisistratos himself, where the tyrant claims to be a reintegrator of the disintegrated corpus. This epigram is also attested in *Vita* 5, and in the *Greek Anthology*.
Here are the verses of the epigram attributed to the tyrant:

τρίς με τυραννήσαντα τοσαυτάκις ἐξεδίωξε
δῆμος Ἐρεχθῆος καὶ τρὶς ἐπηγάγετο,
τὸν μέγαν ἐν βουλαῖς⁹ Πεισίστρατον ὃς τὸν Ὅμηρον
ἤθροισα σποράδην τὸ πρὶν ἀειδόμενον·
ἡμέτερος γὰρ κεῖνος ὁ χρύσεος ἦν πολιήτης
εἴπερ Ἀθηναῖοι Σμύρναν ἐπῳκίσαμεν.

Three times was I tyrant [of Athens], and three times was I expelled
by the people of Erekhtheus [the Athenians]. Three times did they bring me in
    [as tyrant],
me, Peisistratos, great in counsel. **I was the one who took Homer**
and put him all together. Before that, he used to be sung **in a scattered state**
    [*sporadēn*].
You see, he was our golden **citizen** [*politēs*],   5
if it is true that we the Athenians **colonized** [**made an** *apoikia* **of**] Smyrna.

Vita 4.11–16 = *Vita* 5.29–34 = *Greek Anthology* 11.442

The figure of Peisistratos is picturing himself here as a reintegrator. And he is reintegrating the poetry of Homer by way of reintegrating Homer himself.

This epigram of Peisistratos, it is said in another *Life*, was located in Athens:

τὰ δὲ ποιήματα αὐτοῦ τὰ ἀληθῆ **σποράδην** πρότερον ᾀδόμενα Πεισίστρατος Ἀθηναῖος
συνέταξεν, ὡς δηλοῖ τὸ φερόμενον ἐπίγραμμα Ἀθήνησιν ἐπιγεγραμμένον ἐν εἰκόνι
αὐτοῦ τοῦ Πεισιστράτου. ἔχει δ' ὧδε·

His [Homer's] genuine poetic creations [*poiēmata*], which had formerly been in **a scattered state** [*sporadēn*] in the course of being sung [from place to place], were organized by Peisistratos of Athens, as is proved by the epigram that is attested in Athens.
It is inscribed on a likeness of Peisistratos himself, and it goes as follows: [here is where
the quotation as I gave it above is given by *Vita* 5.29–34].

Vita 5.24–28

The story is implying that Athens was the first place where the poetry of Homer
was performed in its entirety after his death. And the story says explicitly that the

---

9. The version given in the *Greek Anthology* shows a variant at this point: βουλῇ.

only genuine poetic creations of Homer were the *Iliad* and the *Odyssey*—to the exclusion of other epics and even of the *Homeric Hymns* (*Vita* 5.19–22). But the story does not say where and how the poet Homer may have performed the *Iliad* and the *Odyssey* for the first time. That is because, as we are about to see, the myth of the Peisistratean Recension must have said something else. It must have said that Homer never had a chance to perform either the *Iliad* or the *Odyssey* all at once.

The evidence comes from a version of the *Lives of Homer* as summarized in the *Suda*. In some ways, as we will see, the wording is post-Athenocentric in its outlook on Homer. In other ways, however, it is distinctly Athenocentric. According to this version, the pieces of Homeric poetry that Peisistratos supposedly assembled in creating the Peisistratean Recension were *performance units* that Homer supposedly 'wrote down' (*graphein*) after 'performing' (*epideiknusthai*) each piece in each of the cities he visited during his wanderings; and the word that is used to indicate such a *performance unit* is *rhapsōidia* 'rhapsody':

> ποιήματα δ᾽ αὐτοῦ ἀναμφίλεκτα Ἰλιὰς καὶ Ὀδύσσεια. ἔγραψε δὲ τὴν Ἰλιάδα οὐχ ἅμα, οὐδὲ **κατὰ τὸ συνεχὲς** ὥσπερ σύγκειται, ἀλλ᾽ αὐτὸς μὲν ἑκάστην ῥαψῳδίαν γράψας καὶ **ἐπιδειξάμενος** τῷ περινοστεῖν τὰς πόλεις τροφῆς ἕνεκεν ἀπέλιπεν. ὕστερον δὲ συνετέθη καὶ συνετάχθη ὑπὸ πολλῶν καὶ μάλιστα ὑπὸ Πεισιστράτου τοῦ τῶν Ἀθηναίων τυράννου.

> His [Homer's] undisputed poems [*poēmata*] are the *Iliad* and *Odyssey*. He **wrote down** [*graphein*] the *Iliad* not **all at once** nor **in sequence**, the way it is composed, but he [Homer] **wrote down** [*graphein*] each **rhapsody** [*rhapsōidia*] himself after **performing** [*epideiknusthai*] each one as he went around from city to city in order to make a living, leaving each one behind [wherever he wrote it]. Later on, it [the *Iliad*] was put together by a number of people, especially by Peisistratos the tyrant of Athens.

> *Vita* 10.37–43 (*Suda*)

What we see in this version of the *Lives of Homer* is a visualization of the *Iliad* as a complete composition made up of pieces of text supposedly 'written' by Homer on the basis of corresponding pieces of poetry supposedly 'performed' by him in his travels as a wandering rhapsode who went from city to city in order to make a living. By extension, the same kind of visualization applies to the *Odyssey*.

Though the reference to a writing Homer shows, as we saw in chapter 2, that the wording of this version comes from a post-Athenocentric era, there are other aspects of the wording that reveal a decidedly Athenocentric model. A case in point is the use of the noun *rhapsōidia* 'rhapsody', derived from the verb *rhapsōidein* 'perform in the manner of rhapsodes'. The word here is evidently referring to a unit of rhapsodic performance. Such a reference reflects Athenocentric usage. The twenty-four *rhapsōidiai* 'rhapsodies' of the Homeric *Iliad* and the matching twenty-four 'rhapsodies' of the Homeric *Odyssey* were units of performance derived from the traditions of *rhapsōidoi* 'rhapsodes' performing at the Panathenaia.[10] In post-Athenocentric usage, by contrast, a *rhapsōidia* is simply one of the twenty-four 'books' into which the text of each of the Homeric poems, the *Iliad* and the *Odyssey*, was traditionally subdivided.[11]

This Athenocentric model of Homer as reflected in the narrative of the *Suda* is incompatible with some earlier models we find in other narratives. In terms of these earlier models, Homer the wandering rhapsode performs epics other than the *Iliad* and *Odyssey*. He even performs other poetry in general, including epigrams. The most telling examples of such earlier models can be found in the narratives of *Vita* 1 and *Vita* 2.

In *Vita* 1, Homer performs a wide variety of poetry in the Aeolian cities of Neon Teikhos, Smyrna, and Cyme; after Cyme, he performs in the Ionian cities of the Asiatic mainland, as also on the outlying Ionian islands of Chios and Samos. *Vita* 1 does not say explicitly that Homer performed the *Iliad* and *Odyssey* as well, but this part of his repertoire seems to be a given.

By contrast with *Vita* 1, which concentrates on the performances of Homer in the cities on the mainland of Asia Minor and on the islands of Chios and Samos, *Vita* 2 concentrates on the performances of Homer in the cities of the mainland of Hellas. In this case, we do see an explicit reference to Homeric performance of the *Iliad*. The setting is Argos, where Homer is said to perform verses from the *Iliad* (*Vita* 2.287–315). In this case, the narrative implies that Homer's performance is rhapsodic: that is, he performs not the whole *Iliad* but only parts of it that please the people of Argos. We see an analogous pattern in the case of Homer's performance in Corinth (*Vita* 2.286–87): the narrative makes it explicit that he performs there in the manner of a rhapsode, *rhapsōidein* (ἐρραψῴδει τὰ ποιήματα).

In the narrative of *Vita* 2, it is implied that Homer composes complete poems when he is stationary but performs rhapsodic pieces, as it were, when he is wandering. As we saw earlier, it is said that Homer started his career of poetry (2.17 *poiēsis*) in Colophon (2.15), having 'made' (2.17 *poieîn*) the *Margites*. Later on in the narrative, it is said that Homer, having 'made' (2.55 *poieîn*) the *Margites* in Colophon, went wandering around other cities, performing poetry wherever he went: Ὅμηρον περιέρχεσθαι κατὰ πόλιν 'Homer went wandering around from city to city' (2.55–56). That is, Homer went wandering around from city to city after having left the city of Colophon, where he had 'made' the *Margites*. When he goes to Chalkis and competes with Hesiod there (2.62–214), he performs a variety of

---

10. As I noted earlier, however, I agree with Douglas Frame's argument (2009 ch. 11) that the Homeric performance units stemming from the Panathenaic Regulation stem ultimately from the performance units that evolved at the festival of the Panionia as celebrated in the late eighth and early seventh centuries B.C.E. at the Panionion of the Ionian Dodecapolis in Asia Minor.

11. *PR* 64.

verses that we may identify with verses of the *Iliad* and *Odyssey*. Still, in terms of the narrative, he has not yet composed the *Odyssey*, and it seems that he has not yet composed the *Iliad*, either. Mention of Homer's composition of the *Iliad* and *Odyssey* happens much later on in the narrative, at the point where Homer goes to Delphi: at this point, it is said that he composed (2.274 *poieîn*) these two epics, not that he performed them (2.275–76). And, before Homer had ever reached Delphi, there had been more wandering. After he is defeated by Hesiod in the poetic contest at Chalkis, Homer resumes his wandering (2.254–55): περιερχόμενος ἔλεγε τὰ ποιήματα 'as he [Homer] went wandering around [*perierkhesthai*], he was telling his poetic creations [*poiēmata*]' (2.255). The wording here is parallel to the wording at the start of the narrative: ποιήσαντα γὰρ τὸν Μαργίτην Ὅμηρον περιέρχεσθαι κατὰ πόλιν ῥαψῳδοῦντα 'having made [*poieîn*] the *Margites*, Homer went wandering around [*perierkhesthai*] from city to city, performing in the manner of rhapsodes [*rhapsōideîn*]' (2.55–56). Here I cite again Plato's passing reference to the myth of the *Certamen*: both Homer and Hesiod are pictured as 'performing in the manner of rhapsodes' (*rhapsōideîn*) as they 'go wandering around' (*perierkhesthai*) from city to city (Plato *Republic* 10.600d–e ῥαψῳδεῖν . . . περιιόντας).

Though neither *Vita* 1 nor *Vita* 2 says explicitly that the performances of Homer as a wandering rhapsode add up to an integral Homeric corpus of the *Iliad* and *Odyssey* combined, such a corpus is indicated as a subtext in both these narratives.

In the narrative of *Vita* 1, such a subtext takes the form of a noticeable pattern of elision. Some rival epics that Homer could have been performing in this narrative are being systematically elided. The elision happens in the course of narrating the sequence of places visited by the wandering Homer. Though the narrative of *Vita* 1 concentrates on the area of the Asiatic mainland and the outlying islands, it elides two most prominent places in that area, both of which were associated with Homer's authorship of prominent epics. The two elided places are, first, the Ionian city of Miletus, which had once dominated the old Ionian Dodecapolis, and second, the Aeolian island of Lesbos.

Miletus was associated with two prominent epics, the *Aithiopis* and the *Iliou Persis*, whereas Lesbos was associated with a third epic, the *Little Iliad*. Here I propose to connect the elision of Miletus and Lesbos in the *Lives* with a remarkable shift in the authorship of these three epics. In the classical period of Athens in the fifth century B.C.E., these epics, which were part of the so-called epic *Cycle*, were no longer assigned to Homer as author. Rather, these epics were now reassigned to differentiated authors: the poet of the *Aithiopis* and the *Iliou Persis*, epics of Miletus, was now Arctinus of Miletus; and the poet of the *Little Iliad*, an epic of Lesbos, was now Lesches of Lesbos.[12] Just as Homer was elided from the authorship of these epics stemming from Miletus and Lesbos, the corresponding places of authorship were

12. *PH* 1§7n10 (= p. 19), §21n61 (= p. 28); 2§§37–49 (= pp. 70–79).

elided from the *Life of Homer* tradition. That is how I propose to explain the fact that Homer never gets to visit either Miletus or Lesbos in *Vita* 1.

Such elision indicates a classical Athenocentric point of view. From the standpoint of Athenians in the fifth century, Homer himself was no longer the poet of such epics as the *Aithiopis* or the *Iliou Persis* or the *Little Iliad*. That is because these epics stemming from the so-called epic Cycle were no longer performed at the Athenian festival of the Panathenaia in the fifth century and beyond.

Before the fifth century, by contrast, Homer was viewed in Athens as the poet who created the epic Cycle as well as the two epics that we know as the *Iliad* and *Odyssey*.[13] Such a preclassical point of view can be situated in the era of the Peisistratidai, in the second half of the sixth century B.C.E., when the epics of the Cycle were still being performed in Athens: evidence for Athenian performances at that time can be found in patterns of Athenian accretions embedded in both the form and the content of such epics as the *Aithiopis,* the *Iliou Persis,* and the *Little Iliad*.[14] For example, in the case of the *Iliou Persis* attributed to Arctinus of Miletus, there is mention of the rescue of the mother of Theseus by the Athenian hero's two sons, Akamas and Demophon, after the capture of Troy (Proclus summary p. 108.10–11 ed. Allen); there is another such mention of these figures in the *Little Iliad* attributed to Lesches of Lesbos (F 18 ed. Allen, via Pausanias 10.25.8).[15]

Still, we can expect Athenian accretions at a lower degree in the epic Cycle and at a higher degree in the *Iliad* and *Odyssey*, since the epics of the Cycle were phased out of the epic program of the Panathenaia in Athens by the time of the classical period, leaving the *Iliad* and *Odyssey* as the sole representatives of Homeric poetry at that festival. Even in the preclassical period, the epics of the Cycle were peripheral, whereas the *Iliad* and *Odyssey* were central in the Homeric tradition, as we can see from the fact that the overall narrative of the Cycle is built around the *Iliad* and *Odyssey*.[16] This formulation holds not only for the preclassical era of epic as performed at the Panathenaia under the rule of the Peisistratidai but even more for the earlier preclassical era of epic performance as it evolved at the festival of the Panionia at the Panionion of the Ionian Dodecapolis, in the late eighth and the early seventh century. Already at that time, as we saw in chapter 1, the two central epics performed at the festival of the Panionia were prototypical versions of the *Iliad* and the *Odyssey*. As Douglas Frame has shown, a lasting trace of this centrality is the fact that each of these two epics is divisible into six performance units, adding up

13. *HQ* 38, 89–91; relevant comments by Burgess 2001:15 and 200n44.

14. Details of such Athenian accretions in the transmission of the epic Cycle are surveyed by Debiasi 2004:206–7.

15. Debiasi 2004:132n58, 207; for further examples of such Athenian accretions, see Burgess 2001:152, 247n75.

16. *PH* 2§40 (= p. 72).

to twelve performance units representing each one of the twelve cities of the Ionian Dodecapolis.[17] To be contrasted are the two Ionian epics attributed to Arctinus of Miletus, the *Aithiopis* and the *Iliou Persis*, which fit not the broader social framework of the Ionian Dodecapolis but rather the narrower one of Miletus as a single city. And the themes that we find in such epics of the Cycle tend to be more localized and therefore more conservative than the more Panhellenized themes of the *Iliad* and *Odyssey*. In earlier work, I offered this explanation:[18]

> The Panhellenization of the Homeric tradition entailed a differentiation from older layers of Panhellenic epic tradition, and . . . these older layers were gradually sloughed off in the process of Homeric streamlining. Such an explanation would account for not only the artistic superiority of the *Iliad* and *Odyssey* but also the thematic archaism of the Cycle. The older layers represented by the Cycle kept developing alongside the emerging core of the Homeric tradition and, being the more local versions, had the relative freedom to develop for a longer time, albeit at a slower pace, toward a point of textual fixation that still seems like a case of arrested development in contrast with the ultimate Homeric form.

The classical version of the Homeric *Iliad* and *Odyssey* as performed at the festival of the Panathenaia, derived from the preclassical version as performed at the festival of the Panionia, tends to neutralize any potential incompatibilities with older and more localized epic versions still evident in the epic Cycle. I mention two examples here. One is the pair of epics known as the *Aithiopis* and the *Iliou Persis*, both attributed to Arctinus of Miletus, which promote the Ionian traditions of the city of Miletus. Another such example is the *Little Iliad* attributed to Lesches of Lesbos, which promotes the Aeolian traditions of the island of Lesbos. In chapter 7, I have already noted how the Panathenaic version of the Homeric *Iliad* neutralizes both the Ionian and the Aeolian versions of epic traditions associated, respectively, with Miletus and Lesbos. A case in point is the Panathenaic elision of the hero Scamandrius son of Hector, who had a role in the Ionian as well as the Aeolian versions of stories about the capture of Troy.

I have also noted in chapter 7 traces of the Aeolian version in the *Trōïka* of Hellanicus (*FGH* 4 F 31), as reported by Dionysius of Halicarnassus (*Roman Antiquities* 1.45.4–48.1). According to this source, the city of New Ilion was once ruled jointly by Scamandrius the son of Hector and Ascanius the son of Aeneas. In the same chapter, we have also seen traces of the Ionian version in an account given by Demetrius of Scepsis as mediated by Strabo (13.1.52 C607). According to this source, the city of Scepsis was once ruled jointly by Scamandrius the son of Hector and

---

17. Frame 2009 ch. 11, who shows that each one of these twelve performance units corresponds to four *rhapsōidiai* 'rhapsodies' or 'books' of the Homeric *Iliad* and *Odyssey* as we know them ('books' 1–4, 5–8, 9–12, 13–16, 17–20, 21–24).

18. *PH* 2§40 (= p. 73).

Ascanius the son of Aeneas; and the same source adds that immigrants from the Ionian city of Miletus were integrated into the population at a later period.

A question arises about the pairing of Scamandrius and Ascanius: Does this pairing suit the political interests of these two cities of Ilion and Scepsis? As we saw in chapter 7, New Ilion was Aeolian, and Scepsis was Ionian. And we also saw that the descendants of Hector by way of Scamandrius represent the Aeolians just as surely as the descendants of Aeneas by way of Ascanius represent the Ionians. So why not have Scamandrius alone representing the Aeolian city of New Ilion and Ascanius alone representing the Ionian city of Scepsis?

In search of an answer, I propose to take a second look at the myth that tells how the descendants of Aeneas were eventually expelled from New Ilion by the Aeolians (exegetical scholia T for *Iliad* XX 307–8a1). Effectively, the joint rule of New Ilion by Aeolians and Ionians as represented by Scamandrius and Ascanius was thus eliminated by the Aeolians. What I find most remarkable about this myth is that the point it makes about the eventual status of New Ilion actually proves that the earlier status of the city was different—that there really was a joint rule of New Ilion by Aeolians and Ionians—and that the pairing of Scamandrius with Ascanius did in fact once suit the political interests of the city. By way of this pairing, the myth is taking it for granted that New Ilion was once upon a time ruled jointly by Aeolians and Ionians.

Before the expulsion of the descendants of Aeneas from New Ilion, the Ionian model of Troy in the aftermath of the Trojan War would have depended on Ionian joint ownership of the city of New Ilion as the genuine new Troy that continues where the old Troy left off. After the expulsion, however, the Ionian model needed a different new Troy to be owned jointly with the Aeolians. This would-be new Troy could be any city other than New Ilion. And the city of choice could now become Scepsis in the highlands of Mount Ida. Similarly, the site of old Troy could now be any site other than the old site of Troy. And the site of choice could now become the place identified by Strabo as ἡ τῶν Ἰλιέων κώμη 'the village [*kōmē*] of the people of Ilion [*Ilieis*]', located some thirty stadia away from New Ilion, in territory belonging to the city of Scepsis (13.1.35–36 C597–98; also 13.1.25 C593).

The expulsion of the Aeneadae from New Ilion, which meant a loss of joint ownership for the Ionians, must have been a major loss in prestige for Miletus as the dominant city of the Ionian Dodecapolis. The substitution of Scepsis for New Ilion as the would-be new Troy for Ionians in general and for Milesians in particular, as narrated in the Ionian epic of the *Iliou Persis*, can be viewed as a compensation for this loss. And the concept of a joint rule over Scepsis by Scamandrius the son of Hector and Ascanius son of Aeneas can be viewed as a substitute for the concept of a joint rule over New Ilion that was no longer valid for that city.

Ultimately, the substitution of Scepsis for New Ilion as the would-be new Troy for Ionians in general and for Milesians in particular failed. And this ultimate failure, which was really a failure not so much for the city of Scepsis as for all Ionians federated with Miletus, was due not only to the ultimate success of the rival city of New Ilion in maintaining its status as the real Troy after it expelled the descendants of Aeneas. It was due also to the temporary success of another rival city that became a new Troy. That city, as we saw in chapter 7, was the new Troy of the Athenians, Sigeion.

Unlike the Ionians in general and the Milesians in particular, the Athenians did not need Scamandrius. Moreover, because Scamandrius figured as the ancestor of the dynasty that ruled the Aeolian city of New Ilion, he should not even exist as far as the Athenians were concerned. That is why, as we saw in chapter 7, it suited the Athenians to have a version of the *Iliad* that kills off the figure of Scamandrius by merging him with the figure of Astyanax, whose death at Troy is evidently acknowledged in all existing versions.

All this is not to say that a Milesian version of the Troy narrative that accommodated Scamandrius was a threat, in and of itself, to the Athenian version as perpetuated in the Panathenaic Homer. It would be better to say that such a Milesian version was no longer needed by Athens. The Aeneas of the Milesians could no longer find a home anywhere other than Scepsis, and that was no longer good enough for the Athenians. As we saw, Ionian Scepsis no longer measured up to the model of a new Troy that could rival the New Ilion of the Aeolians. Only the Ionian Sigeion of the Athenians could measure up.

The decline in the prestige of Ionian Scepsis was part of a far more extensive pattern of decline involving the Ionians in general and the Milesians in particular after the collapse of the Ionian Revolt and the total defeat of Miletus by the Persians in the 490s. Although the power of Miletus and the Ionian Dodecapolis was already under severe pressure from the earlier Lydian empire, it was many years later, under the Persian empire in the 490s, that it utterly collapsed. Accompanying this collapse of power was a destabilization of Ionian epic traditions overtly associated with Miletus as the most dominant city of the Ionian Dodecapolis. Even before the final collapse, in the era marked by the maritime empire or thalassocracy of the tyrant Polycrates, the only cities of the Dodecapolis that still played a significant role in the shaping of Ionian epic traditions were the island cities of Chios and Samos. The mainland cities of the Dodecapolis, even Miletus and Ephesus, could no longer play such a significant role. In the era of Polycrates of Samos, who controlled the islands of the Aegean Sea, the center of gravity for Ionian epic had shifted away from the cities of the Asiatic mainland. It was in this historical context that the mainland cities of the old Ionian Dodecapolis finally lost control of the Panionian epic performance traditions as represented by the Homeric *Iliad* and *Odyssey*. This way, they lost Homer as the core of the epic Cycle.[19] But they kept their peripheral epic per-

19. *PH* 2§§37–49 (= pp. 70–79).

formance traditions as represented by the *Aithiopis* and the *Iliou Persis*, reassigned from Homer to Arctinus of Miletus. Paradoxically, such peripheral epic traditions may have been, at an earlier stage, more central to the localized interests of a city like Miletus. In the case of the *Aithiopis*, for example, attributed to Arctinus of Miletus, the immortalization of Achilles (Proclus summary p. 106.12–15 ed. Allen) reflects the local traditions of Achilles as cult hero of the Milesians.[20] Similarly in the case of the *Iliou Persis*, likewise attributed to Arctinus of Miletus, the reference to Scepsis as the city where Aeneas finds refuge after the capture of Troy reflects the political links of this city with Miletus.[21]

In *Vita* 1 of Homer, we can see the vacuum left by the disintegration of the Ionian Dodecapolis. The only mainland cities of the Dodecapolis that are still linked with Homer in *Vita* 1 are those that were no longer important to the Persian empire. A case in point is Phocaea, abandoned by the Phocaeans as a no-man's-land in the year 540 B.C.E. (Herodotus 1.164.3).[22] Another is Colophon, one of the three proverbial extinct cities of the archaic Greek world. Still another is Smyrna, the would-be thirteenth city to be added to the twelve cities of the Ionian Dodecapolis, which instead became another of the three proverbial extinct cities.

Besides showing the vacuum left by the disintegration of the Ionian Dodecapolis, *Vita* 1 also shows the selectivity involved in the process of consolidating Homeric poetry for a reduced level of Ionian reception after the disintegration. As for *Vita* 2, it shows an even greater degree of selectivity involved in the process of consolidating Homeric poetry for an expanded level of non-Ionian reception after the assertion of Athenian influence. In this case, the cities of the Asiatic mainland are barely mentioned at all. The two notable exceptions are the two extinct cities of Smyrna (2.8–10) and Colophon (2.15–17).[23] In *Vita* 2, Homer does not get to roam very far and wide as a rhapsode in Asia Minor. Still, Homer's point of origin has to be Asia Minor even here in *Vita* 2, since his birthplace is said to be Smyrna (2.8–10).

In the epigram of Peisistratos about the Peisistratean Recension, we saw that Smyrna is claimed as a daughter city of Athens. This appropriation of Smyrna by Athens shows that the charter myth about the Recension actually acknowledged Smyrna as Homer's point of origin. By claiming Smyrna as their very own, the Athenians were claiming Homer as well. The fact that the Athenian appropriation of

20. *PH* 2§37 (= pp. 70–72).

21. See also *HC* 1§109.

22. According to *Vita* 1 (202–5), as we saw in chapter 2, Homer composes the *Little Iliad* in Phocaea, not in Lesbos. On the Ionian city of Phocaea as a cultural mediator between Ionian and Aeolian traditions, see Debiasi 2004:205–6.

23. According to *Vita* 2 (55–56), as I quoted it in chapter 2, there is a story that tells how Homer 'made' the *Margites* in Colophon. Such a story, which I think is derived from the charter myth of the Peisistratean Recension, seems to be the basis for the opinion expressed by Aristotle in the *Poetics* (1448b30) that Homer is the author of the *Margites*.

Homer was predicated on an Athenian appropriation of Smyrna shows that this Asiatic city was felt to be an indispensable part of the myth of the Recension. It also implies that Smyrna was indispensable for validating earlier versions of the myth.

In its ultimate form, the myth of the Peisistratean Recension was indirectly telling a story of cultural eclipse. The disintegrating Homer of the Panionia was eclipsed by the reintegrated Homer of a rival festival, the Delia, which was the point of definition for the earlier phases of the Athenian empire. The Delia then gave way to yet another rival festival, the Panathenaia, which became the ultimate point of definition for the later phases of the Athenian empire. As I said in chapter 8, the eclipsing of the Panionian Homer by the Panathenaic Homer was not unprecedented. Earlier, the Panionian Homer of the Ionian Dodecapolis had eclipsed what I will call the *Panaeolian Homer* of the Aeolian Dodecapolis. The "big bang" in that case was the transformation of Aeolian Smyrna, native city of Homer, into Ionian Smyrna.

I conclude my analysis of the myth of the Peisistratean Recension by summarizing what it tells us about the reception of Homer in the era of the Peisistratidai. It is clear from what we have seen that this Homer of the Peisistratidai is figured as a Panathenaic Homer, a prototype for what we know as the *Iliad* and *Odyssey*. Clearly, the myth of the Peisistratean Recension focuses mostly on the *Iliad* and *Odyssey* by way of occluding other major epic traditions as represented by the *Aithiopis,* the *Iliou Persis,* and the *Little Iliad.* Nevertheless, we need to keep in mind that this myth of the Peisistratean Recension was linked not to the Panathenaic Homer of the Athenian democracy, which was the Homeric Koine, but rather to the earlier Homer of the Peisistratidai.

ASIATIC AND HELLADIC RECEPTIONS OF HOMER

Although the myth of the Peisistratean Recension situates Homer's point of origin on the mainland of Asia Minor, it reflects a gradual shift of perspective toward the mainland of Hellas. The cause of this westward gravitation was the evolution of Homeric performance traditions at the Panathenaia in Athens. Tracing this gradual shift, I note two phases of Homeric reception. In the earlier phase, Homer was linked almost exclusively with Asia Minor and the outlying islands, especially with Chios and Samos. In the later phase, we see an accretion of links to various sites on the Helladic mainland. From here on, I will refer in shorthand to the earlier phase of Homeric reception as *Asiatic,* and to the later phase as *Helladic.*

A similar formulation can be applied to the earlier and later phases of Hesiodic reception. A case in point is a story about an event that can best be described as a reverse migration. According to this story, as told in the Hesiodic *Works and Days,* the father of Hesiod migrated from the city of Cyme on the Asiatic mainland (636) to the town of Ascra on the Helladic mainland (639–40). This reverse migration signals the utter collapse of this man's mobile Asiatic past and a total validation of the stationary and even static Helladic present represented by Hesiodic poetry. In the *Works and Days*, this stationary Helladic present is correlated with an ostentatious reference to Hesiod's reluctance to navigate or to travel at all: the poetry highlights the idea of Hesiod's hesitancy in crossing the waters of even the narrowest of straits—at Aulis, in Boeotia—to compete in the funeral games of Amphidamas at Chalkis in Euboea (*Works and Days* 646–63).[24]

In what follows, I will examine traces of both Asiatic and Helladic phases of Homeric reception in the *Lives of Homer*, especially in the narratives of *Vita* 1 and *Vita* 2. As we will see, the first of these *Lives of Homer* shows an earlier and broader and less Athenocentric concept of Homer than the second, which shows a considerably later and narrower and more Athenocentric concept, corresponding more closely to the Panathenaic Homer that ultimately prevailed by the time of the second half of the fifth century and thereafter.

Vita 1 recognizes a prototype of what became the Panathenaic Homer. This pre-Panathenaic Homer, like his later Athenian counterpart, is credited with only two epics, the *Iliad* and the *Odyssey*. The difference is, this prototype is localized in the city of Chios, not in Athens. According to *Vita* 1, Homer composed the *Iliad* and *Odyssey* in the city of Chios. Still, although the narrative of *Vita* 1 insists on a pre-Panathenaic prototype that Homer supposedly made in Chios, it acknowledges a Panathenaic outcome for this prototype: in the course of composing the *Iliad* and *Odyssey*, Homer kept augmenting his composition by adding verses that centered on the glorification of Athens (1.378–99). But the narrative maintains that the making of such a pre-Panathenaic Homer did not take place in Athens. The Panathenaic Homer may have been destined for performance in Athens, but the composition for that performance supposedly took place in the city of Chios. The narrative of *Vita* 1 draws further attention to this localization inside the city of Chios by actually allowing for non-Panathenaic compositions by Homer outside that city. Whereas Homer composed only the *Iliad* and the *Odyssey* inside the city of Chios, he supposedly composed other epics in other cities—such as the *Little Iliad* that he 'made' (*poieîn*) in the city of Phocaea (1.203). So the narrative of *Vita* 1 reveals a broader concept of Homer that corresponds to a prototypical Homer who supposedly created the whole epic Cycle.[25] Still, it insists on a narrower concept within the limits of the city of Chios.[26]

---

24. On the poetic theme of Hesiod's reluctance to navigate, see Rosen 1990 and Martin 1992; also Debiasi 2001:19.

25. For a brief analysis, see *HQ* 38; there is a more extensive analysis in *PH* 1§7n10 (= p. 19), 2§§48–49 (= pp. 77–79); see now also West 1999:372, who does not engage with either of my analyses in his discussion.

26. As we saw in *Vita* 1.332–35, which I quoted in chapter 2, the poetry that Homer creates in the countryside of the island of Chios is carnivalesque and loosely defined, as compared with the poetry that he creates within the city limits.

This narrower concept, which prefigures the Panathenaic Homer, corresponds to the Homer who was ancestor to the *Homēridai* of Chios. And this Homer of the *Homēridai* of Chios stems ultimately from the Panionian Homer of the Ionian Dodecapolis, whose repertoire is restricted to the Homeric *Iliad* and *Odyssey*—as distinct from the broader repertoire of the prototypical Homer who supposedly created the whole epic Cycle.

The narrative of *Vita* 1 reaches beyond the Panathenaic and the earlier Panionian Homer of the Homeric *Iliad* and *Odyssey*, accommodating the even earlier Homer of the epic Cycle. An example of such accommodation is the fact that *Vita* 1 attributes the authorship of the *Little Iliad* to Homer himself. From a later point of view, by contrast, the author of this epic of the Cycle was not Homer but some other poet, left unnamed by Aristotle (*Poetics* 1459a). This other poet is identified by most sources as an Aeolian, Lesches of Lesbos (for example, Pausanias 10.25.5).[27] According to another version, the author of the *Little Iliad* was an Ionian, Thestorides of Phocaea (scholia for Euripides *Trojan Women* 822).[28] We have already encountered this pseudo-Homer in *Vita* 1: in terms of that narrative, as we saw in chapter 2, Thestorides is the impostor who moves from his native Phocaea to Chios and pretends to be the composer of the epics he performs in the city of Chios, whereas the notionally real composer of these epics was Homer, who had already composed and performed these epics in Phocaea (1.220–24).

By contrast with the less Athenocentric outlook of *Vita* 1, where Homer composes for performance in Athens but never gets there, *Vita* 2 shows a far more Athenocentric outlook. As far as this alternative version is concerned, Homer does perform in Athens (2.276–85) and then goes on to perform in other major cities of the Helladic mainland, especially Corinth (2.286–87) and Argos (2.288–314). Homer's long-awaited songmaking tour of the Helladic mainland, which failed to take place in *Vita* 1, is realized in *Vita* 2. Conversely, *Vita* 2 omits the adventures of Homer in the cities of the Asiatic mainland and in outlying islands like Chios and Samos. There are only a few exceptions, to which I will turn later.

The narrative of *Vita* 2 not only highlights the Helladic phase of Homeric reception by contrast with the Asiatic phase as highlighted by *Vita* 1. More than that, *Vita* 2 reassigns to the Helladic mainland various adventures that *Vita* 1 assigns to the Asiatic mainland and to its outlying islands. In other words, *Vita* 2 actually displaces elements of the earlier Asiatic phase and replaces them with elements from the later Helladic phase.

Here is a striking example. *Vita* 2 shows Homer performing a riddle in Athens (2.281–85), whereas *Vita* 1 shows him performing an almost identical riddle in an

---

27. See also Allen 1912:127 (citing the *Tabula Iliaca*) and 129 (with a survey of various attributions, including all the references by Pausanias to Lesches).

28. Allen 1912:126.

almost identical context—and this time Homer is not in Athens but in Samos (1.425–29).[29] The interchangeability of Samos and Athens in framing the context of this riddle is my starting point for arguing that the non-Athenocentric theme of Homer in Samos prefigures the Athenocentric theme of Homer in Athens. In other words, the Asiatic Homer prefigures the Helladic Homer, and the interchangeability of narratives in *Vita* 1 and *Vita* 2 is a sign of this prefiguration.

In *Vita* 1, the fatal visit of Homer to Ios happens just before his intended tour of the Helladic mainland (1.484–85). In *Vita* 2, by contrast, Homer's visit to Ios happens after he actually completes his successful tour of the Helladic mainland, where he visits Delphi (2.271–76), Athens (2.277–85), Corinth (2.286–87), and Argos (2.287–314).[30] In *Vita* 1, the story of Homer's extended stay in Ionian Chios (1.346–98) and the story of his stopover in Ionian Samos (1.399–484) are earlier alternatives to the later story of his successful tour of the non-Ionian Helladic mainland in *Vita* 2. To put it another way, the Asiatic travels of Homer in *Vita* 1 prefigure the Helladic travels of Homer in *Vita* 2.

The complementarity of Chios and Samos in *Vita* 1 is matched by another complementarity between the two island-states: whereas Chios is the homeland of direct transmitters of Homeric poetry known as the *Homēridai*, Samos is the homeland of indirect transmitters of Homeric poetry known as the *Kreōphuleioi*.[31] The ancestor of the *Kreōphuleioi*, named Kreophylos (*Kreōphulos*), is portrayed in one myth as an epic poet in his own right: he married a daughter of Homer, receiving as a wedding gift from his father-in-law the epic known as the *Capture of Oikhalia* (*Vita* 11 [Proclus summary p. 100 ed. Allen] lines 11–13). By implication, Kreophylos of Samos was supposedly authorized to perform as his own composition an epic that Homer of Chios had originally composed.

There are further points of comparison between the narratives of *Vita* 1 and *Vita* 2: whereas *Vita* 1 shows Homer traveling from Samos to Ios (1.484–85), *Vita* 2 shows him traveling from Delos to Ios, where he meets Kreophylos (2.322; *Vita* 11 [Proclus summary p. 100 ed. Allen] lines 11–13), who as we saw is the Samian counterpart of Homer the Chiote. Whereas *Vita* 1 shows a Samian connection in Homer's point of departure to Ios, *Vita* 2 shows a Samian connection in his point of arrival at Ios. Both points, however, are in fact transitional, not terminal. In *Vita* 1, the real point of departure for Athens is not Samos but Chios. In *Vita* 2, the real point of arrival is not the encounter with Kreophylos of Samos but something unexpected

29. The differences between the wording of *Vita* 2.281–85 and of *Vita* 1.425–29 reflect, I propose, oral-poetic variations in formula. The two different contexts that frame the two different versions reflect, in turn, oral-poetic variations in theme.

30. In *Vita* 3a.61–62, as I noted in chapter 2, Homer goes not from Thebes to Delphi but from Delphi to Thebes. We find here an interesting added detail: in Thebes, Homer takes part in the festival of the Kronia, described as an *agōn mousikos* (*Vita* 3a.62).

31. *PP* 179, 226–27. My interpretation there is now apparently accepted by West 1999:381–82.

that happens thereafter, Homer's own death. The fact that Homer's place of death is consistently pictured as the Ionian island of Ios is in and of itself an Ionian signature, which complements another Ionian signature in the narrative: Homer stops over at Ionian Ios on his way from Ionian Delos, which is the notional centerpoint of all Ionians, the place where he successfully performs the *Homeric Hymn to Apollo* at the festival of the Delia.

The fact that Samos is an intermediate point in the narrative of *Vita* 1—a stopover for Homer between his starting point of Chios and the anticipated arrival point of Athens—is relevant, I propose, to the role of the *Kreōphuleioi* of Samos as alternative mediators of Homer. It is also relevant to the fact that the maritime Ionian empire of Athens was prefigured by the maritime Ionian empire of the tyrant of Samos, Polycrates. Just as the empire of Polycrates of Samos is a precursor of the empire of Athens as ruled by the sons of Peisistratos, so also the story of Homer in Samos is a precursor of the story of Homer in Athens. A case in point is the riddle told by Homer in Samos, as narrated in *Vita* 1 (421–32): both the setting and the wording match closely the setting and the wording of the riddle told by Homer in Athens, as narrated in *Vita* 2 (278–85). Comparing the two versions, I argue that the Samian version cannot be based on the corresponding Athenian version. To put it another way, the Asiatic version cannot be based on the corresponding Helladic version.

So far, we have seen two Samian subtexts in *Vita* 2. First, the riddle that Homer tells in Athens has a precursor in the riddle he tells in Samos. Second, Homer travels to Ios in order to meet Kreophylos of Samos (2.322). But there is a third Samian subtext as well in *Vita* 2, and this one is far more important than the other two: just before Homer reaches Ios (2.322), he stops over at the island of Delos (2.315–22), where he performs the *Homeric Hymn to Apollo* (2.316–19). As we have already seen from the testimony of Thucydides and other sources, this Homeric performance was pictured as the centerpiece of the festival of the Delia, as organized by Polycrates of Samos. Without naming the organizer, *Vita* 2 refers to this Ionian festival, calling it a *panēguris* (2.316, 321).

A SPOKESMAN FOR ALL HELLENES

In the narrative of *Vita* 2, the *Homeric Hymn to Apollo* authorizes Homer as the spokesman of an Ionian empire—an empire we know was once ruled by the tyrant Polycrates of Samos and later by the sons of Peisistratos in Athens—and still later by the democratic regime of Athens. According to *Vita* 2, the authorization of and by Homer is made explicit in his performance. Specifically, Homer 'speaks' (*legein*) the *humnos* to Apollo (2.316–17 καὶ σταθεὶς ἐπὶ τὸν κεράτινον βωμὸν λέγει ὕμνον εἰς Ἀπόλλωνα); then, once Homer 'speaks' (*legein*) the *humnos* (2.319 ῥηθέντος δὲ τοῦ ὕμνου), all the Ionians who are gathered at Delos and celebrating their Panionian festival (2.316, 321 *panēguris*) respond by making Homer their 'common citizen', their *koinos politēs* (2.319–20 οἱ μὲν Ἴωνες πολίτην αὐτὸν κοινὸν ἐποιή-σαντο). As I argued in chapters 2 and 9, this Panionian 'common' Homer in the narrative of *Vita* 2 is an imperial Homer. The Panionianism is viewed from the Athenocentric standpoint of the latest of the Ionian empires. Homer speaks not only for the empire shaped by the tyrant of Samos but also for the empire later reshaped by the tyrants of Athens. In the name of this empire, moreover, he speaks for all Hellenes.

This visualization of Homer as the *koinos politēs* 'common citizen' of all Ionian cities as he 'speaks' his *Hymn to Apollo* at Delos exemplifies the imperial phase of Homeric reception: each and every city of the Ionians now claims Homer as an authorized citizen, while the city of Athens claims to be the metropolis or 'mother city' of all Ionian cities. The word *koinos* 'common, standard', as applied to Homer and Homeric poetry, reflects the appropriation of Homer as a spokesman for the incipient Athenian empire at the Panionian festival of the Delia in Delos, and this myth about Homer in Delos as the *koinos politēs* 'common citizen' of all Ionian cities prefigures an imperial universalization of Homer for all Hellenes.

HOMER'S SPLIT PERSONALITY

The idea of Homer as a *koinos politēs* 'common citizen' of all Ionian cities illustrates a special way of thinking, for which I proposed a special term in chapter 9, *split referencing*. In the case of Homer, the reference is split between Athenocentric and non-Athenocentric meanings. The term *koinos politēs* has a general meaning for Ionians, which is explicit, but it also has a special Athenocentric meaning for Athenians, which is implicit. This split between explicit and implicit identities creates the effect of a split personality.

Implicit in the singular honor of this title, awarded to Homer by all the Ionians, is the idea that Homer is a spokesman for the Delian League, and, ultimately, for the Athenian empire. The description of Homer by way of the word *koinos*, meaning both 'common' and 'standard', means one thing for Ionians in general but another thing for Athenians in particular. As I show in the twin book *Homer the Classic*, the word *koinos* expresses the appropriation of Hellenic values in Athenian terms.[32] It is no accident, I should add, that the word *koinos* is distinctly Attic: in the Ionic dialect, by contrast, as we see in the usage of Herodotus, the word *koinos* coexists with a non-Attic synonym, *xunos*.[33] And yet, the idea that Homer is *koinos* 'common' to the Ionians in particular—and not to other Greeks like the Aeolians—is relevant to

32. *HC* 4§§25–30.

33. As we saw earlier, Herodotus uses *koinos* 'common' in contexts of commonality (as at 1.151.3, 166.1, 170.2; 2.178.2; and so on). And there are two instances where he uses the synonym *xunos* 'common' (4.12.3, 7.53.1).

Athens as the leader of the Delian League of Ionian cities. In other words, this idea conveys the ideological appropriation of Homer by the Athenian empire. Such an appropriation was under way, I propose, already in the earliest phases of that empire, in the era of the Peisistratidai.

Homer's split personality is inherent in the *Homeric Hymn to Apollo* itself. Homer may be Ionian in multiple ways or in a singular way. When he performs the *Homeric Hymn to Apollo* in Delos, he is Ionian in multiple ways, because the setting of the *Hymn* is the Panionian festival of the Delia. But he is Ionian in a singular way from the standpoint of Athenians, since the setting of Homer's performance, the island of Delos, is the center of a Panionian federation dominated by Athens after the collapse of the empire of Polycrates. The point of reference for the *Hymn*, from the perspective of Athenians, is a reality dominated by Athenians, whereas the point of reference from the perspective of Ionians is a reality shared by all Ionians. The Athenians in effect claim exclusive rights to a poetic reality that is notionally common to all Ionians. That common reality is Homer, the *koinos politēs* 'common citizen' of all Ionian cities.

Similarly, when the speaker of the *Homeric Hymn to Apollo* describes himself as a blind man living in Chios, his blindness may be linked with many different Ionian traditions, but his location in Chios may be linked with a single Ionian tradition. Chios as a referent is special for the Athenians once they own the Chiote version of Homer. That ownership becomes a reality when the Athenians appropriate the Homer of the *Homēridai* of Chios.[34] Thereafter, Chios may have many explicit meanings for the Ionians in general, but it has one special implicit meaning for the Athenians in particular.

A PROTOTYPE FOR HOMER, HESIOD, AND ORPHEUS

So far, we have seen that Homer has a special meaning for the Athenians. But that meaning changes in the course of time. In the era of the democracy, that meaning was determined primarily by the content of the *Iliad* and *Odyssey*. Earlier, however, in the era of the Peisistratidai, the meaning of Homer was more broadly determined. The Homer of the Peisistratidai was imagined as the poet of the epic Cycle, which in turn was imagined to be a complete body of epic that actually included what later became the *Iliad* and *Odyssey*. In that era, rhapsodes competing at the Panathenaia had in their repertoire not only the equivalents of our *Iliad* and *Odyssey* but also the equivalents of what we know as the epics of the Cycle. Moreover, the latitude of the rhapsodes' repertoire was so extensive as to transcend Homer by including epic traditions attributed to such poets as Hesiod and Orpheus. In chapter 1, I con-

---

34. Frame 2009 ch. 11 makes it clear that Chios was essential to the *Homēridai* even before they were brought to Athens.

centrated on the differentiation of Homer in the later years of the tyrants and, still later, in the new era of the democracy. Then, in chapter 3, I concentrated on the non-differentiation of Homer in the earlier years of the tyrants and, still earlier, in the preceding eras going as far back as the Bronze Age. For the moment, I use the term *nondifferentiation* as a way of expressing a concept of Homer that includes the concepts of Hesiod and Orpheus. As my argumentation proceeds, this concept will have to be tailored to suit what eventually evolved into three distinct forms of epic, as represented by the three poets Homer, Hesiod, and Orpheus. My aim, then, is to consider what these three differentiated forms of epic once had in common.

The latitude of epic repertoire that I reconstruct for the festival of the Panathenaia in the era of the tyrants is comparable to what we find attested at a later point in another important festival of the Athenians, the City Dionysia. This Dionysiac festival accommodated a wide variety of performance media in the dramatic arts. These media of Dionysiac drama at the City Dionysia complemented the media of epic and lyric at the Panathenaia. In this connection, it is essential to keep in mind the patterns of mutual influence between the media of the City Dionysia and those of the Panathenaia in the era of the democracy in Athens. As we will now see, such patterns of mutual influence between the media of the City Dionysia and the Panathenaia actually date farther back to the earlier era of the tyranny under the Peisistratidai. Already then, the performance media of these two major festivals were evolving together and influencing one another.

The mutual influence of the City Dionysia and the Panathenaia is evident from the later evidence of tragic drama as it prevailed at the City Dionysia in the era of the democracy. As we see from the contents of tragedies like the *Seven against Thebes* and the *Agamemnon* of Aeschylus, the medium of drama was by now strongly influenced by the medium of epic.[35] Even before the era of the democracy, as the older era of the Peisistratidai was drawing to a close, Dionysiac drama was already giving way to a newer form of drama that was less Dionysiac and closer to epic. Conversely, the old epics of the Cyclic, Hesiodic, and Orphic traditions were already giving way to a newer form of epic that was more dramatic, more in line with the poetics of the City Dionysia. That newer form, shaped by the Panionian and Panathenaic traditions of the *Homēridai*, evolved into what we know as the Homeric *Iliad* and *Odyssey*, which as I have argued in chapter 3 became the only epics to be performed at the Panathenaia in the new era of democracy in Athens.

Keeping in mind these later developments, I go back to concentrating on the era of the Peisistratidai, which was a time when other forms of epic still coexisted with what eventually became the Homeric form of epic. In the case of one such epic form, what I have been calling *Cyclic poetry,* I have already said in chapters 3 and 4 what I needed to say: Homer was understood to be the poet of at least some of the epics

35. Nagy 2000f, with reference primarily to the *Seven against Thebes* of Aeschylus.

of the Cycle in the era of the tyrants and perhaps even later, in the earlier phases of the democracy that followed it. I still need to say more, however, about the two other forms of epic we have been considering all along: that is, the Hesiodic and the Orphic forms.

In the case of the Hesiodic form of epic, I have so far highlighted only its ultimate differentiation from the Homeric form. But now, as I started to say at the beginning of this section, I will need to confront earlier phases of nondifferentiation between these two forms of epic. From here on, I will speak of such *nondifferentiation* in terms of *convergence*. That is, I will be investigating earlier phases of convergence between Hesiodic and Homeric forms of epic.

What I have just said about Hesiodic poetry applies also to Orphic poetry. In what follows, I will also need to confront earlier phases of convergence between Orphic and Homeric forms of epic. In this case, the task will be more difficult, because we know far less about the Orphic form of epic in its earliest recoverable phases than we know about the Hesiodic form.

Here I will need to make a point that I make also in the twin book *Homer the Classic*: the convergence of Hesiodic and Orphic forms of epic with the Homeric form of epic was viewed retrospectively not as a real convergence but as an *augmentation*. That is, Homer was once thought to be augmented by way of Hesiod and augmented by way of Orpheus. In order to develop this point further, I start by outlining in the next two sections the concepts of the Homeric Koine and the Homerus Auctus. Then, in subsequent sections, I explore the convergence of Hesiodic and Orphic forms of epic with the Homeric form of epic.

HOMERIC KOINE

In the Prolegomena to *Homer the Classic*, I reconstruct the term *Koine* (*koinē*) in the combined sense of 'common' and 'standard' with reference to what I have been calling the *Panathenaic Homer*. The evidence for this reconstruction comes from the political discourse of democratic Athens in the fifth as well as the fourth centuries B.C.E., when the adjective *koinos/koinē/koinon* was still used in the combined sense of 'common' and 'standard', conveying simultaneously the ideas of democracy and empire. As we have seen in chapter 2 of the present book, this usage is relevant to the concept of Homer himself as the *koinos politēs* 'common citizen' of all Ionian cities (*Contest of Homer and Hesiod*, Vita 2.319–20). This usage is central to the overall thesis of the twin book *Homer the Classic*, which is to argue that the Homeric Koine represents the ideological appropriation of Homer by the Athenian empire in the new era of the democracy. In other words, the Homeric Koine was the lingua franca of Athenian democracy and empire combined.

Some of the most telling evidence about the Homeric Koine, as I argue in chapter 3 of *Homer the Classic*, is to be found in the quotations taken from Homer in the works of Plato. On the basis of this evidence, we can see that Plato's Homer, as quoted in such virtual dialogues as the *Ion* and the *Hippias Minor*, was the Panathenaic Homer of his day, in the fourth century B.C.E. Using the additional evidence provided by Plato's precise references to rhapsodic conventions, we can also see that Plato's Homer was essentially the same Homer that was being quoted by the likes of Ion, Hippias, and Socrates in real dialogues of their own day, in the fifth century B.C.E. What, then, is the distinguishing feature of this Homeric Koine as the Panathenaic Homer of the Athenian democracy? My answer can be summed up this way: the Homeric Koine as quoted by Plato was relatively unaugmented in comparison with the Homerus Auctus, which I describe as a relatively more augmented or expanded form of Homer. This Homerus Auctus included elements that editors in the age of Callimachus judged to be Cyclic, Hesiodic, and Orphic accretions.

HOMERUS AUCTUS

In chapter 2 of the twin book *Homer the Classic*, I use the term *Homerus Auctus* to indicate an augmented version of Homer that can be dated back to the sixth century B.C.E., by contrast with the dating of the unaugmented Homeric Koine to the fifth century B.C.E. In the third century B.C.E., however, which is the era of editors like Zenodotus and poets like Callimachus, the Homerus Auctus was not viewed as an earlier version of Homer. It was viewed instead as the result of newer additions to an older text. And the unaugmented Homer, as represented by the Homeric Koine, was viewed as the older text.

From such a point of view, it is as if an older core of Homeric poetry kept on getting augmented and reaugmented by a mass of ever newer additions. Conversely, it is as if the Homeric Koine resulted from subtractions—as if the Homerus Auctus were purged of its augmentations and restored to its supposedly original Homeric core.

Contradicting such a point of view, I argue that the Homerus Auctus was not some disorganized mass of newer additions clustering around a relatively organized older core. Rather, this augmented Homer was the culmination of an organically expanding epic tradition—a tradition marked by an esthetics of expansion.

The idea of an augmented Homer, as expressed by the term *Homerus Auctus,* does not presuppose a textual transmission of Homer. A case in point is the moment when Homer in the *Lives of Homer* is imagined as adding verses to the *Iliad* during his stay in Chios (*Vita* 1.378–98). The story pictures him in the act of adding verses to preexisting verses, but there is no indication that these preexisting verses are imagined as a text. What is imagined, rather, is a preexisting song already in the making, performed by Homer on preexisting occasions. In the logic of the story,

Homer is getting ready to perform a longer version of his song for the new occasion of his intended debut in Athens. In terms of oral poetry, Homer's addition of verses favorable to Athens can be understood as a process of expansion.

This process is typical of oral poetry. In the medium of oral poetry, a poet can expand—or compress—a composition in performance while recomposing it to fit the occasion of the performance.[36]

This is not to say that the model of a Homerus Auctus only leaves room for expansion. It also makes room for compression. In oral poetry, any instance of expansion may contain instances of embedded compression.[37] The sense of magnitude created by the esthetics of expansion in oral poetry can overwhelm a casual observer's awareness of a complementary esthetics of compression. In general, compression seems less obvious to recognize than expansion.[38]

In chapter 2 of *Homer the Classic*, I show how the Homer of the Homerus Auctus, as viewed in the era of poets like Callimachus in the third century B.C.E., was studiously imitated by these poets. Such a model of Homer represents an extreme of inclusiveness—for poets. That is because the text of such a Homer went far beyond the text of what I have been calling the *Homeric Koine*. But the Homer of this Homerus Auctus was not the entire text. As we see from the actual editorial practices that prevailed in the era of Callimachus, the supposedly real Homer was only a part of the text of the Homerus Auctus. Homer had to be extracted from the text in which he was embedded, the Homerus Auctus. And this supposedly real Homer represents an extreme of exclusiveness.

Zenodotus, as an editor of Homer in the age of Callimachus, was in some ways more exclusivist than Aristarchus, who edited Homer over a century later. The system used by Zenodotus in determining which verses in the Homeric base text were to be athetized—that is, marked in the margin as non-Homeric—was more extreme than the later system of Aristarchus. In other ways, however, it was Aristarchus who was more extreme than Zenodotus. In judging variant readings within a given verse, for example, Aristarchus and the Aristarcheans developed criteria favoring phraseology they considered more Homeric than the corresponding phraseology found in the Koine versions. In this respect, Zenodotus was less extreme than Aristarchus, since his readings corresponded more often to the default phraseology found in the Koine version. For the most part, however, Zenodotus too, like Aristarchus, tended to favor non-Koine variants. I bring this section to an end by noting that I offer in chapter 2 of *Homer the Classic* a detailed comparison of the editorial methods of Zenodotus and Aristarchus.

36. Background in *HQ* 76–77.
37. Background in *HQ* 76.
38. *HQ* 76.

HESIOD AS A CONTEMPORARY OF HOMER

Having explored in the previous two sections the concepts of the Homeric Koine and the Homerus Auctus, I now turn to the convergence of Hesiodic and Orphic forms of epic with the Homeric form of epic. I start with Hesiod, resuming an argument I was making in chapter 3. Analyzing the myths about the Contest of Homer and Hesiod, which show the importance of Hesiodic poetry as a potential rival of Homeric poetry, I argued that the very idea of a rivalry between Homer and Hesiod corresponds to the institutional reality of rival Homeric and Hesiodic performance traditions at a festival like the Delia at Delos. In making this argument, I quoted a passage referring to such rivalry. My aim was to highlight the divergence between the epic forms of Homer and Hesiod. I now quote this passage again, this time highlighting the convergence. As we are about to see, this convergence takes shape ultimately in terms of Homer, not Hesiod. That is, the epic form of Homer is imagined as being augmented by the epic form of Hesiod:

Φιλόχορος δὲ ἀπὸ τοῦ συντιθέναι καὶ **ῥάπτειν** τὴν ᾠδὴν οὕτω φησὶν αὐτοὺς προσκε-κλῆσθαι. δηλοῖ δὲ ὁ Ἡσίοδος λέγων·

> ἐν Δήλῳ τότε πρῶτον ἐγὼ καὶ Ὅμηρος ἀοιδοὶ
> μέλπομεν, ἐν νεαροῖς **ὕμνοις ῥάψαντες** ἀοιδήν,
> Φοῖβον Ἀπόλλωνα χρυσάορον, ὃν τέκε Λητώ. [Hesiod F 357]

ῥαψῳδῆσαι δέ φησι πρῶτον τὸν Ἡσίοδον Νικοκλῆς. Μέναιχμος δὲ ἱστορεῖ τοὺς **ῥαψῳδοὺς** στιχῳδοὺς καλεῖσθαι διὰ τὸ τοὺς στίχους ῥάβδους λέγεσθαι ὑπό τινων. ἄλλως. Ὁμηρίδαι πρότερον μὲν οἱ Ὁμήρου παῖδες, ὕστερον δὲ οἱ περὶ Κύναιθον **ῥαβδῳδοί·** οὗτοι γὰρ τὴν Ὁμήρου ποίησιν **σκεδασθεῖσαν** ἐμνημόνευον καὶ ἀπήγγελ-λον· ἐλυμήναντο δὲ αὐτῇ πάνυ. αἰεὶ οὖν τὴν ἀρχὴν ὡς ἐπὶ τὸ πλεῖστον ἐκ Διὸς ἐποιοῦντο προοιμιαζόμενοι, ἐνίοτε δὲ καὶ Μουσῶν.

Philochorus [*FGH* 328 F 212] says that they [*rhapsōidoi*] were called that [*rhapsōidoi*] on the basis of the idea of composing—that is, **stitching together** [*rhaptein*]—the song. Proof for this comes from Hesiod, who says:

> In Delos, back then at the very beginning, I and Homer, singers [*aoidoi*],
> sang-and-danced [*melpein*], **stitching together** [*rhaptein*] a song in new **humnoi**,
> making Phoebus Apollo the subject of our song, the one with the golden weapon,
> the one born of Leto. [Hesiod F 357]

Nicocles [*FGH* 376 F 8] says that Hesiod was the first to **perform rhapsodically** [*rhap-sōidein*]. The investigations of Menaechmus indicate that **rhapsodes** [*rhapsōidoi*] were called verse singers [*stikhōidoi*] because verses [*stikhoi*] were called staffs [*rhabdoi*] by some people. Here is another version: the *Homēridai* were in former times the de-scendants of Homer, but then, in later times, they were a group comprised of Kynaithos and his associates, who were called "*rhabdōidoi*" ["staff singers"]. For these [Kynaithos and his associates] are the ones who used to bring back to memory and to perform the poetry [*poiēsis*] of Homer, which had been **scattered**. But they mistreated [*lumai-*

nesthai] it [the poetry]. And they [the *Homēridai*] always started with a *prooimion*, making mostly Zeus their point of departure and occasionally the Muses.

Scholia for Pindar Nemean 2.1d lines 14–29

The point being made in this commentary deriving from the Pindaric scholia is that Kynaithos and his associates claimed to be the continuators of an art that was actually shared by Homer and Hesiod. The formulation can be reversed: Homer and Hesiod were thought to have in common the art of the rhapsodes—on the grounds that this art was thought to be continuous with the art of rhapsodes like Kynaithos.

But there is also another point being made in this commentary. These rhapsodes claimed only Homer as their prime ancestor, not Hesiod. That is, the rhapsodes identified here as Kynaithos and his followers were supposedly the *Homēridai*. These rhapsodes, as we can see from this same commentary, claimed to be the continuators of a body of Homeric poetry that resulted from a reintegration of a formerly disintegrated corpus. We are being told that Homer's poetry had been 'scattered' before it was then 'brought back to memory' and 'performed' by Kynaithos and his followers. The idea of a 'scattered' body of poetry is strikingly reminiscent of a detail we have already seen in the charter myth of the Peisistratean Recension. According to this myth, Homer's poetry had been 'scattered' before it was collected by Peisistratos. In the case of Kynaithos, however, the tyrant who commissioned the collection may well have been Polycrates of Samos, not Peisistratos of Athens. It may well have been Polycrates, as we have seen in chapter 1, who commissioned the Homeric *Hymn to Apollo* as perhaps performed by Kynaithos in Delos. In other words, the charter myth about the Peisistratean Recension in Athens may have had as its precursor a charter myth about a Polycratean Recension. Such a recension, nominally undertaken by Polycrates, would have integrated a disintegrated corpus that combined the epics of Homer and Hesiod, just as the Homeric *Hymn to Apollo* performed by Kynaithos in Delos combined the hymns of Homer and Hesiod. The actual combination of Homer with Hesiod is in any case imagined as the work of Homer, who implicitly subsumes the epic of Hesiod just as he subsumes the hymn of Hesiod in the *Homeric Hymn to Apollo*.

Here I sum up what I have reconstructed so far from the commentary about Kynaithos and his associates. These associates, as would-be *Homēridai*, claimed possession of a reintegrated corpus of Homeric poetry that had supposedly languished in a state of disintegration until a recension finally produced a successful reintegration. Such a corpus incorporated Hesiodic as well as Homeric verses. That is, the epic of Homer was notionally augmented by the epic of Hesiod, just as the Homeric *Hymn to Delian Apollo* was notionally augmented by a Hesiodic *Hymn to Pythian Apollo*. The result of the augmentation was an overall Homeric *Hymn*, not a Hesiodic *Hymn*. The Hesiodic verses were notionally incorporated into a larger integral Homeric corpus. Then, in a later era, the integrity of such a corpus and its attribution to Homer were challenged by the likes of Aristarchus.

As I argued in chapter 3, the unnamed source for the commentary that I have just summarized is Aristarchus himself. Our source is critical of the rhapsodes identified as Kynaithos and his associates, accepting only a part of their claims. Though our source accepts the idea that the body of Homeric poetry was disintegrated or 'scattered', he rejects the complementary idea that this body was thereafter reintegrated in the process of being 'brought back to memory' and 'performed' by these would-be descendants of Homer. Instead, our source claims that Kynaithos and his associates 'mistreated' the body of Homeric poetry. And, as we saw in another passage I quoted in chapter 3 from the scholia for Pindar, this alleged mistreatment involved the adding of verses that were supposedly not Homeric. I quote that passage again:

Ὁμηρίδας ἔλεγον τὸ μὲν ἀρχαῖον τοὺς ἀπὸ τοῦ Ὁμήρου γένους, οἳ καὶ τὴν **ποίησιν** αὐτοῦ **ἐκ διαδοχῆς** ᾖδον· μετὰ δὲ ταῦτα καὶ οἱ ῥαψῳδοὶ οὐκέτι τὸ γένος εἰς Ὅμηρον ἀνάγοντες. ἐπιφανεῖς δὲ ἐγένοντο οἱ περὶ Κύναιθον, οὕς φασι πολλὰ τῶν ἐπῶν **ποιήσαντας ἐμβαλεῖν** εἰς τὴν Ὁμήρου **ποίησιν**. ἦν δὲ ὁ Κύναιθος τὸ γένος Χῖος, ὃς καὶ τῶν ἐπιγραφομένων Ὁμήρου ποιημάτων τὸν εἰς Ἀπόλλωνα γεγραφὼς ὕμνον ἀνατέθεικεν αὐτῷ. οὗτος οὖν ὁ Κύναιθος πρῶτος ἐν Συρακούσαις ἐραψῴδησε τὰ Ὁμήρου ἔπη κατὰ τὴν ξθ΄ Ὀλυμπιάδα, ὡς Ἱππόστρατός φησιν.

Homēridai was the name given in ancient times to those who were descended from the lineage of Homer and who also sang his **poetry** [*poiēsis*] **in succession** [*ek diadokhēs*]. In later times, [it was the name given also to] rhapsodes [*rhapsōidoi*], who could no longer trace their lineage back to Homer. Of these, Kynaithos and his association became very prominent. It is said that they are the ones who **made** [*poiein*] many of the verses [*epos*, plural] of Homer and **inserted** [*en-ballein*] them into his [Homer's] **poetry** [*poiēsis*]. Kynaithos was a Chiote by lineage, and, of the **poetic creations** [*poiēmata*] **of Homer that are ascribed to him** [*epigraphein*] as his [Homer's], it was he [Kynaithos] **who wrote** [*graphein*] the *humnos* to Apollo and attributed it to him [Homer].[39] And this Kynaithos was the first to **perform rhapsodically** [*rhapsōidein*] in Syracuse the verses [*epos,* plural] of Homer, in the 69th Olympiad [= 504/1 B.C.E.], as Hippostratus says [*FGH* 568 F 5].

Scholia for Pindar *Nemean* 2.1c lines 1–10

As I pointed out in chapter 3, our unnamed source suspects Kynaithos of interpolating or 'inserting' newer verses into the preexisting older verses of Homer (*en-ballein*, scholia for Pindar *Nemean* 2.1c). Such an insertion is condemned as a 'mistreatment' of Homer (*lumainesthai*, scholia for Pindar *Nemean* 2.1d). The act of insertion is pictured as a physical outrage against the person of Homer, against

39. To repeat, Martin 2000b:419n58 suggests that the phrasing here could mean instead 'and dedicated it to him [Apollo]'.

the body of Homer. But the very idea of insertion here is based on a questionable premise—that Hesiod is a newer poet than Homer. I will have more to say presently about this premise.

An alternative explanation has already been considered in chapter 3: in the case of the *Homeric Hymn to Apollo*, the Hesiodic verses are deployed as a complement to the Homeric verses. In chapter 3, I viewed this complementarity in terms of a divergence between Homeric and Hesiodic poetry. Here I view it in terms of a convergence more basic than any divergence.

I now turn to a classic formulation of what I picture as a convergence of Homeric and Hesiodic poetry:

Ὅθεν δὲ ἐγένετο ἕκαστος τῶν θεῶν, εἴτε δὴ αἰεὶ ἦσαν πάντες, ὁκοῖοί τέ τινες τὰ εἴδεα, οὐκ ἠπιστέατο μέχρι οὗ πρώην τε καὶ χθὲς ὡς εἰπεῖν λόγῳ. Ἡσίοδον γὰρ καὶ Ὅμηρον ἡλικίην τετρακοσίοισι ἔτεσι δοκέω μέο πρεσβυτέρους γενέσθαι καὶ οὐ πλέοσι· οὗτοι δέ εἰσι οἱ ποιήσαντες **θεογονίην** Ἕλλησι καὶ τοῖσι θεοῖσι τὰς ἐπωνυμίας δόντες καὶ τιμάς τε καὶ τέχνας διελόντες καὶ **εἴδεα** αὐτῶν **σημήναντες·** οἱ δὲ **πρότερον ποιηταὶ λεγόμενοι τούτων τῶν ἀνδρῶν γενέσθαι ὕστερον, ἔμοιγε δοκέειν, ἐγένοντο.**

But it was just the day before yesterday, so to speak, that they [the Hellenes] came to understand where each of the gods originated from, whether they all existed always, and what they were like in their **visible forms** [*eidos,* plural]. For Hesiod and Homer, I think, lived not more than four hundred years ago. These are the men who composed [*poieîn*] a **theogony** [*theogonia*] for the Hellenes, who gave epithets to the gods, who distinguished their various spheres of influence [*timai*] and spheres of activity [*tekhnai*], and who **indicated** [*sēmainein*] their [the gods'] **visible forms** [*eidos,* plural]. **And I think that those poets who are said to have come before these men really came after them.**

Herodotus 2.53.1–3

In this formulation of Herodotus, the complementarity of Hesiod and Homer is expressed by way of highlighting their convergence, not divergence. Their divergence, as we saw already in chapter 3, was highlighted by the myths about their primordial poetic contest. By contrast, Hesiod and Homer are viewed here as convergent shapers of poetry for all Hellenes. Together they create a *theogonia* 'theogony'. As we see from the root **gen-* of *theogonia*, this shared act of creation is the shared poetic process of 'generating' the gods. What is being 'generated', by way of words, is the *eidos* 'visible form' of each of the gods and, by extension, of the world itself. For Hesiod and Homer, the poetic act of generating the words is coextensive with the theogonic act of generating the visible world.[40] This idea of generating the cosmos by generating the words that generate the cosmos is also at work in the alternative name of Homer, *Melēsigenēs*, which as we saw in chapter 6 is a *nomen lo-*

---

40. The visual metaphor of *eidos* here in the sense 'visible form' is reinforced by the use of the verb *sēmainein* 'indicate, reveal' in this context.

quens meaning 'the one who has on his mind the act of generating'. In terms of this alternative name, Homer in the role of *Melēsigenēs* has on his mind the theogonic act of generating the visible forms of the gods.

In this same formulation of Herodotus that I have just quoted (2.53.1–3), the historian is taking what at first appears to be an idiosyncratic stance in his relative dating of both Hesiod and Homer with reference to the Trojan War and the Ionian Migration. I have already noted this apparent idiosyncrasy in chapter 6, contrasting the relatively late date assigned to Homer by Herodotus with the relatively early date assigned by antiquarians like Aristarchus and Crates. As we saw in that chapter, Aristarchus dated the birth of Homer to coincide with the era of the Ionian Migration, whereas Crates made sure to predate the birth. The synchronized dating by Aristarchus, as we also saw in that chapter, reflects an Athenocentric point of view, to be contrasted with the predating by Crates. But the postdating by Herodotus, I should now point out, can likewise reflect an Athenocentric point of view, which requires only that the birth of Homer should not predate the Ionian Migration. And so the dating of Homer by Herodotus is not idiosyncratic after all—from an Athenocentric point of view.

In fact, this formulation of Herodotus (2.53.1–3) about Hesiod and Homer may be considered to be Athenocentric, reflecting a preclassical point of view that was typical of Athens in the era of the Peisistratidai. In terms of my argument, the epic poetry attributed to Homer in this era coexisted with epic poetry attributed to Hesiod. Granted, such a coexistence between Homeric and Hesiodic poetry in the sixth century became obsolete in the fifth, by which time only the *Iliad* and *Odyssey* were performed at the Panathenaia and only those two epics were attributed to Homer. But I argue that Hesiod and Homer still shared the stage, as it were, at the festival of the Panathenaia in the preclassical era of the Peisistratidai. As we saw in chapter 3, *Vita* 2 of Homer shows traces of such a coexistence between Hesiod and Homer. In terms of the narrative of *Vita* 2, the Hesiodic tradition was not only distinct from the Homeric tradition: it could directly compete with it. We find in this narrative two versions of a myth that aetiologizes a competitive relationship between the Homeric and the Hesiodic traditions. According to one version found in *Vita* 2 of Homer, Homer and Hesiod had a contest at Chalkis in Euboea (2.68); according to another version, their contest took place at Aulis (2.54–55), situated on the mainland in Boeotia, across the strait from Euboea.

ORPHEUS AS A PRECURSOR OF HESIOD AND HOMER

After this exploration of the idea that Hesiod was a contemporary of Homer, I turn to the idea that Orpheus was a precursor of both. I start by returning to the formulation of Herodotus that I quoted concerning the complementarity of Hesiod and Homer (2.53.1–3). As we saw, Herodotus makes a point of saying that these two poets were the earliest of all poets. In other words, they both supposedly predate Orpheus. Herodotus makes it clear that he has Orpheus in mind, though he goes out of his way not even to mention him by name in this context.[41] To be contrasted is an older way of thinking according to which Orpheus is the first in a sequence of four canonical poets. The sequence extends from Orpheus to Musaeus to Hesiod to Homer—in that chronological order. We can see examples of this sequence in a variety of sources (Hippias *FGH* 6 F 4 = DK B 6, Aristophanes *Frogs* 1030–36, Plato *Apology* 41a).[42]

As I will argue, this older way of thinking was current in the era of tyrants like the Peisistratidai of Athens and Polycrates of Samos. In that era, the poetic status of Orpheus was not shaded over but highlighted. Back then, poetic figures like Orpheus and his successor Musaeus were thought to be the luminous precursors of Hesiod and Homer. As my argumentation proceeds, I will be turning to another passage in Herodotus, where even he acknowledges the anteriority of Orpheus.

ORPHEUS AS A NEOTERIC

This older way of thinking about Orpheus was turned around once and for all by Aristotle, who dismissed Orpheus as a relatively recent fabrication and asserted that Homer was the most ancient of Greek poets (*History of Animals* 563a18, *On the Generation of Animals* 734a19). The finality of Aristotle's judgment about Homer is best represented by Aristarchus, for whom all other poets—including Orpheus and Musaeus and even Hesiod—were post-Homeric. In his terms, Orpheus and these other poets were 'newer' than Homer: that is, they were *neōteroi*.[43] They were *neoteric*.

In the judgment of Aristarchus, not only prehistoric poets like Orpheus but also poets of the historical era were *neoteric* if they imitated Homer by including in their imitations those elements of the Homeric text that were supposedly post-Homeric. As I show in chapter 2 of *Homer the Classic*, each of the three most prominent poets of Alexandria—Callimachus, Apollonius, and Theocritus—could be judged guilty of such neoterism: that is, of using supposedly post-Homeric elements in their imitations of Homer.[44] For this reason, Aristarchus thought that the use of Homeric words by such poets was not useful for providing any reliable evidence about Homeric usage. This way of thinking is reflected in a formulation of Quintilian, with specific reference to the opinion of Aristarchus about the poetry of Apollonius of Rhodes:

41. *PH* 8§2n10 (= p. 216).

42. *HC* 3§100. See also Hermesianax F 7.21–26 ed. Powell (the sequence here is Orpheus to Musaeus to Hesiod), as analyzed by Hunter 2005b:261.

43. See above, chapter 3, the section entitled "A Post-Athenocentric View of the *Homēridai*."

44. *HC* 2§§186–90.

Apollonius in ordinem a grammaticis datum non venit, quia Aristarchus atque Aristophanes, poetarum iudices, neminem sui temporis in numerum redegerunt.

Apollonius is not granted admission into the canon [*ordo*] by the *grammatikoi* [the
school of critics represented here], since Aristarchus and Aristophanes [the *grammatikoi*], those judges of poets, listed no one of their own times among the ranks [of
the canon].

Quintilian 10.1.54

What Quintilian treats here as a single period is for my purposes really a matter of
two different eras in the Hellenistic period: the era of Apollonius in the third century B.C.E. and the era of Aristarchus—as also of Aristophanes of Byzantium—
in the second century. For Quintilian, as we see from what I just quoted, the ultimate arbiters of canon formation were not poets like Apollonius—or Callimachus
or Theocritus—in the third century. Rather, they were textual critics like Aristarchus
in the second.

For a critic like Aristarchus, the problem with a poet like Apollonius was simply this: he was neoteric.[45] From the standpoint of Aristarchus, Apollonius was neoteric because he failed to distinguish clearly enough between the purely Homeric
traditions and the more amorphous 'newer' traditions.

The neoteric stance of Apollonius as poet—as also of Callimachus and Theocritus—needs to be contrasted with the antineoteric stance of Zenodotus as an editor
of Homer in the same era, the third century B.C.E. For Zenodotus as editor, the base
text of Homer was a Homerus Auctus, a text filled with augmentations stemming
from supposedly 'newer' poets like Orpheus. Zenodotus displayed his editorial virtuosity by observing and marking what was supposed to be 'newer' and post-Homeric. For Apollonius and the other poets of his era, these supposedly 'newer' and post-
Homeric forms could then be used as building blocks for creating their own 'newer'
poetry. In the process of poetic creation, they could display their poetic virtuosity
by observing the same distinctions observed by the editor. In chapter 2 of *Homer the
Classic*, I offer a detailed analysis of such displays of poetic virtuosity.

I conclude this outline by emphasizing that I use the term *neoteric* from the standpoint of Aristarchus, not from my own. I do not prejudge whether poets whom
Aristarchus judged to be neoteric were really 'newer' than Homer, or whether the
poetic forms that Aristarchus judged to be neoteric were really 'newer' than the poetic forms he judged to be Homeric. What Aristarchus considered a negative poetic quality—to be neoteric—had once been a positive quality for Callimachus, Apollonius, and Theocritus as poets, in that they followed as their poetic models not
only the supposedly older poet Homer but also the supposedly 'newer' poets like

---

45. Rengakos 2001, with a rich inventory of examples.

Orpheus. The neoterism of Callimachus, Apollonius, and Theocritus is relevant to the concept of the *Homerus Auctus* as I defined it earlier. This definition suits the Homeric textual tradition available to these poets—as also to Zenodotus as editor of Homer. As I show in chapter 2 of *Homer the Classic*, this textual tradition included rather than excluded the supposedly 'newer' features that were characteristic of poets like Orpheus—and Hesiod.

ORPHEUS IN THE ERA OF THE PEISISTRATIDAI

Though it is far beyond the scope of my project to address in all its magnitude the concept of Orpheus, I now proceed to outline the reception of Orpheus as poet in the age of the Peisistratidai—and to juxtapose that reception with his later reception in the age of Callimachus. As I have been arguing, scholars like Zenodotus in the age of Callimachus thought that Homeric poetry was augmented by Orphic poetry. The situation was radically different in the age of the Peisistratidai. In that era, the poetry attributed to Orpheus was not yet peripheral. Like the poetry of Homer, the poetry of Orpheus was featured prominently at the festival of the Panathenaia in that earlier era.

To back up this formulation, I start by comparing the festival of the Panathenaia with the festival of the City Dionysia: that is, with the most significant venue for dramatic poetry. I pair the Orphic media of the Panathenaia with the Dionysiac media of the City Dionysia because such a pairing is actually attested in a turn of phrase used by Herodotus in a most telling context:

> οὐ μέντοι ἔς γε τὰ ἱρὰ ἐσφέρεται εἰρίνεα οὐδὲ συγκαταθάπτεταί σφι· οὐ γὰρ ὅσιον. ὁμολογέουσι δὲ ταῦτα τοῖσι Ὀρφικοῖσι καλεομένοισι καὶ Βακχικοῖσι, ἐοῦσι δὲ Αἰγυπτίοισι, καὶ ‹τοῖσι› Πυθαγορείοισι· οὐδὲ γὰρ τούτων τῶν ὀργίων μετέχοντα ὅσιόν ἐστι ἐν εἰρινέοισι εἵμασι ταφθῆναι.Ἔστι δὲ περὶ αὐτῶν ἱρὸς λόγος λεγόμενος.

> It is not customary for them [the Egyptians], however, to wear woolen fabrics for the occasion of sacred rituals or to be buried wearing wool. For it is unholy for them. This is in accordance with rituals that are called **Orphic** [*Orphika*] and **Bacchic** [*Bakkhika*], though they are really Egyptian and, by extension, **Pythagorean** [*Puthagoreia*].[46] I say this because it is unholy for someone who takes part in these [Pythagorean] **rituals** [*orgia*] to be buried wearing woolen fabrics. And there is a **sacred** [*hieros*] **discourse** [*logos*] that is **told** [*legesthai*] about that.

> Herodotus 2.81.2

---

46. Herodotus thinks that the Pythagoreans were responsible for importing Egyptian customs. I agree with Asheri, Lloyd, and Corcella 2007:296 when they say about the section that reads Βακχικοῖσι . . . καί: "this section is omitted in all the Florentine mss [as opposed to other mss], but the arguments for postulating an omission in this group are considerably stronger than those for interpolation."

In the twin book *Homer the Classic*, I stress the importance of the actual collocation of the adjectives *Orphika* 'Orphic' and *Bakkhika* 'Bacchic' in this passage.[47] In the present book I stress the collocation of these adjectives with the noun *orgia* 'rituals'. Neither of these adjectives is used anywhere else by Herodotus. And the association of these adjectives with *orgia* 'rituals' is esoteric. Further, the association of both Orpheus and Dionysus with Egyptian customs and practices creates an aura that is pointedly exotic, implying that there is something not only esoteric but also alien about both these figures. Even further, the term *hieros logos* 'sacred discourse' implies the use of a special language of initiation into mysteries. By implication, the ideology of the terms *Orphika* 'Orphic' and *Bakkhika* 'Bacchic' in this passage is elitist and predemocratic, to be contrasted with the populist and democratic ideology of the Panathenaia and the City Dionysia in the new era of democracy in Athens.

In the older era of the Peisistratidai, both the Panathenaia and the City Dionysia accommodated forms of songmaking that were evidently more exclusive than the forms we see attested in the new era of the democracy. In the case of the Panathenaia, I reconstruct for the older era a varied program featuring primarily two events: competitions of rhapsodes performing epic compositions attributed to prototypical poets like Orpheus, Musaeus, Hesiod, and Homer; and competitions of citharodes performing lyric compositions attributed to prototypical poets—including Orpheus. Orpheus must be included if we are to credit Plato's pointed reference to him as an effete citharode whose singing is pictured as a prototype for citharodic performances at the Panathenaia (Plato *Symposium* 179d–e).[48] As for the City Dionysia in the era of the Peisistratidai, I reconstruct a comparably varied program, featuring primarily a competition of tragic choruses re-enacting in many forms of song and dance the charter myth of Dionysus—the story of how he was once persecuted as an illegitimate alien and ultimately vindicated as a legitimate native son.[49]

Next I turn to the Panathenaia in the new era of the democracy. Here we find a less varied program featuring primarily two events: competitions of rhapsodes performing only the Homeric *Iliad* and *Odyssey,* and competitions of citharodes performing the lyric compositions of such established poets as Simonides and Anacreon. As for the City Dionysia in the era of the democracy in Athens, we find a far more varied program featuring a far wider variety of myths.

This is not the place to explore the complexities of the mythical repertoire current at the City Dionysia in the new era of the democracy. My aim here is simply to note a surprising outcome in the evolution of the City Dionysia, which is com-

---

47. *HC* 2§§238–68.

48. On citharodic as well as rhapsodic performances of Orphic song in Athens, see Power 2010:355–67; see also his pp. 274–85 on citharodic performances of epic associated with Orphic *Argonautica* around the time of the Peisistratidai.

49. *PH* 13§10 (= pp. 385–86), with further citations (especially Seaford 1984:43).

parable to an unsurprising outcome in the evolution of the Panathenaia. Here is the surprise: in the context of the City Dionysia, Dionysus became marginalized. What surprises is that the god whose very essence was once central to the City Dionysia became marginalized at his own festival.

In terms of the argument I am developing, something comparable also happened in the evolution of the Panathenaia. Orpheus, once central to this festival, became marginalized. In the case of Orpheus, however, unlike the case of Dionysus, the marginalization was far more drastic. By the time of the democracy in Athens, Orpheus was totally eclipsed by Homer at the Panathenaia. That is, the rhapsodic repertoire of Orpheus ceased to be recognized at the festival, even if his citharodic repertoire may have been continued. I can explain the cause of this outcome in terms of another outcome in the evolution of the Panathenaia. That outcome can be formulated this way: the democratization of the Panathenaia in the era of the democracy led to the centralization of Homer in his role as poet of the *Iliad* and *Odyssey*. This centralization led to the marginalization of a poet who used to be central to the Panathenaia, Orpheus. That is because Orpheus was traditionally identified with kings and, later on, with tyrants who took the place of kings. Just as Kalliope was the Muse of kings (Hesiod *Theogony* 79–93), so also Orpheus son of Kalliope was the poet of kings.[50] Orpheus can be described as the most royalist of all poets.

In his identification with kings, Orpheus was similar to Hesiod and dissimilar to Homer. As we see from the *Contest of Homer and Hesiod* (*Vita* 2 of Homer), Hesiod was identified with kings, whereas Homer was identified with the people. The audience of this primal contest between Homer and Hesiod, described simply as 'all the Hellenes' (176 οἱ . . . Ἕλληνες πάντες), enthusiastically acclaim Homer as the true winner over Hesiod, but the king presiding over the event overrules the will of 'the Hellenes' and awards the victory to Hesiod instead (176–79, 205–10). Hesiod's association with royal authority is indicated even by the internal evidence of Hesiodic poetry: his poetic authority is pictured as a substitute for royal authority in both the *Theogony* and the *Works and Days*.[51]

Homer democratizes the Panathenaia by ousting Orpheus, but we have no myth, as far as I know, that tells of such an ouster. Nor do we have a myth that tells about an ouster of Hesiod by Homer at the Panathenaia. Instead, as we have just seen, what we do have is a myth about the unfair victory of Hesiod over Homer in an unjust world dominated by unjust kings. In such a world, as brought back to life in the *Contest of Homer and Hesiod* (*Vita* 2 of Homer), the favorite poet of royalty is bound to defeat the favorite poet of the people.

In the postdemocratic era of revisionistic antiquarian research, however, the royalism of Hesiod is shaded over, and his antiroyalism is highlighted. According to

50. *HC* 1§170; 2§§18, 236.
51. *GM* 52–53.

Pausanias (1.2.3), for example, Hesiod's professed reluctance to travel and his strong attachment to a stationary way of life in the countryside are to be explained in terms of this poet's detachment from the company of kings. The self-characterization of Hesiod in the *Works and Days* as a stationary poet is to be contrasted with his characterization as a wandering poet in the *Contest of Homer and Hesiod* tradition (also in Plato *Republic* 10.600d–e). Unlike Hesiod, Homer continues to be acknowledged as a wandering poet by Pausanias, who adds that Homer too, like Hesiod, does not seek the company of kings (1.2.3). It seems to me that Pausanias here is deliberately eliding the anti-Hesiodic democratic ideology of the *Contest of Homer and Hesiod* tradition. While he acknowledges the popular affinities of Homer, he shades over the royal affinities of Hesiod.

In the era of the Athenian democracy, by contrast, the institutional reality of the Panathenaia tells its own story. In that era, Homer had in effect ousted not only Orpheus but also Hesiod at the Panathenaia. Homer had thus become the unique poet of the epic venue at the ultimate festival of Athens. I describe the Panathenaia this way because this festival defines the identity of Athens as a city by virtue of defining the identity of Athena as the goddess of the city. That is, this festival celebrates Athena as the goddess who is metonymically the very essence of the city of Athens. As the unique poet of the epic performed at the ultimate festival of Athens, Homer thus becomes the ultimate poet of the Athenians. And, as this ultimate poet, the democratized Homer democratizes the Panathenaia.

It is not only the Panathenaia that Homer democratizes. He also contributes indirectly to the democratization of the City Dionysia. That is because tragedy at the Dionysia became diversified in the process of becoming democratized, and this diversification was most strongly influenced by the diversity of epic traditions left over from the era of the Peisistratidai. These leftover epic traditions were ousted from the festival of the Panathenaia, which was becoming restricted to the unified Homeric tradition that produced the *Iliad* and *Odyssey*. The diversity of epic as performed at the Panathenaia in the earlier era of the Peisistratidai lived on in the diversity of epic themes at the City Dionysia in the later era of the democracy.

In the era of the Peisistratidai, as I have been arguing so far, Orpheus was still central to the Panathenaia as the idealized poet of this festival. Such centrality is comparable to the centrality of Dionysus as the idealized poetic subject of the City Dionysia. It was only later, in the new era of the democracy, that these two figures became peripheral, marginalized. Along with their marginalization came a sense of their alienation from Hellenism, and the alien point of reference could be Egypt or Thrace or any other mythologized expression of otherness. 'Bacchic' and 'Orphic' features could now be seen as marginal rather than central precisely because they were associated with the formerly central features of royalty, even of tyranny. What was central in the older times was now becoming marginal in the emerging new worldview of democracy.

The centrality of Orpheus in the older times is comparable to the centrality of Hesiod in these same older times. The role of Kynaithos the rhapsode, as I analyzed it in chapter 3, is relevant. Just as Hesiod is mediated by Kynaithos in a performance of a *Hymn to Apollo* that re-enacts Hesiod as well as Homer, so also Orpheus is mediated by Pythagoras in performances that re-enact Orpheus. It is not that Pythagoras simply attributed the verses of Orpheus to himself. Rather, as I argued in chapter 3, he took on the persona of Orpheus when he performed verses attributed to Orpheus. As I also argued in chapter 3, the attribution to Orpheus and the self-identification of Pythagoras with Orpheus would have been simultaneous at the moment of performance. Similarly, Kynaithos identifies with Hesiod when he performs verses sacred to the Pythian Apollo, just as he identifies with Homer when he performs verses sacred to the Delian Apollo.

In this connection, I return to an anecdote I mentioned in chapter 3 concerning the self-presentation of Pythagoras: as we saw, he customarily wore a golden garland, a white robe, and trousers (Aelian *Varia Historia* 12.32). In chapter 3, I concentrated on the most familiar feature in this tripartite description, the golden garland. For a point of comparison, I concentrated on a detail in Plato's *Ion*. There we saw that a golden garland was a visible sign of victory awarded by the *Homēridai* to the rhapsode who won first prize in the performance of Homer at the Panathenaia (*Ion* 530d, 535d, 541c). Now I concentrate on the least familiar feature in this tripartite description. In fact, it is an alien feature. The mentioning of the trousers worn by Pythagoras indicates that he cultivated Thracian wear, since Thracians wore trousers.[52] By implication, Pythagoras was Thracian in the same way that Orpheus was Thracian, in that Orpheus was conventionally represented as associating with Thracians.[53] In short, the wearing of Thracian trousers by Pythagoras conjures up the Thracian associations of Orpheus as a poet who became alien to Hellenism in the process of becoming marginalized at the Panathenaia.

So far, I have been arguing that the centrality of Orpheus and the Orphic poetry associated with him in the era of the Peisistratidai was eventually replaced by the centrality of Homer and the Homeric poetry of the *Iliad* and *Odyssey* in the era of the democracy. But now we will see that this process of replacement was already under way in the era of the tyrants, since we can find a point of contact between Orphic and Homeric poetry already in that era. As we are about to see, this contact can be reconstructed on the basis of what we read about the activities of a poet who performed as an agent of the Peisistratidai. This poet was Onomacritus of Athens, and his activities as an agent of the tyrants of Athens are comparable to the activities of Kynaithos of Chios, the poet who seems to have performed as an agent of the tyrant Polycrates of Samos.

---

52. Riedweg 2002:14.
53. Again, Riedweg 2002.

According to a narrative transmitted by Tzetzes (*Anecdota Graeca* 1.6 ed. Cramer), this poet Onomacritus was one of a group of four men commissioned in the reign of Peisistratos to supervise the 'arranging' (*diatithenai*) of the Homeric poems, which were before then 'in a scattered state': διέθηκαν οὑτωσὶ σποράδην οὔσας τὸ πρίν. It has been argued persuasively that the source of Tzetzes here was Athenodorus, head of the Library at Pergamon in the first century B.C.E.[54] In terms of this narrative, Onomacritus was one of the organizers of the Peisistratean Recension. I highlight the word *sporadēn* 'in a scattered state', which refers explicitly to the state of Homeric poetry before the intervention of Peisistratos. We have already seen the same word in a passage referring to the charter myth of the Peisistratean Recension. In an epigram preserved in the *Greek Anthology* (11.442), Peisistratos is dramatized as making this claim about Homer: ὃς τὸν Ὅμηρον | ἤθροισα σποράδην τὸ πρὶν ἀειδόμενον '[I was the one] who took Homer | and put him all together; before that, he used to be sung in a scattered state [*sporadēn*]'.[55] In the passage transmitted by Tzetzes, I highlighted also the use of the word *diatithenai* 'arrange' with reference to the organizing of the Peisistratean Recension by Onomacritus and his fellow arrangers. This word, as we are about to see, indicates a mode of poetic transmission that was viewed in later times as antithetical and even detrimental to poetry.

In a passage from Herodotus (7.6.3), we find the agent noun of this verb *diatithenai* 'arrange' referring to the manipulation, by the Peisistratidai, of oracular poetry with the help of this same poet Onomacritus: in this context, Onomacritus is described as the *diathetēs* 'arranger' (from *diatithenai* 'arrange') of this poetry.[56] In this same context, Herodotus makes it clear that the oracular poetry is Orphic, notionally stemming from the verses of Musaeus, successor of Orpheus. Herodotus specifies that the manipulation takes the form of what he calls *en-poiein*, which is conventionally translated as 'interpolate':

ταῦτα δὲ ἔλεγε οἶα νεωτέρων ἔργων ἐπιθυμητὴς ἐὼν καὶ θέλων αὐτὸς τῆς Ἑλλάδος ὕπαρχος εἶναι. χρόνῳ δὲ κατεργάσατό τε καὶ ἀνέπεισε Ξέρξην ὥστε ποιέειν ταῦτα· συνέλαβε γὰρ καὶ ἄλλα οἱ σύμμαχα γενόμενα ἐς τὸ πείθεσθαι Ξέρξην· τοῦτο μὲν ἀπὸ τῆς Θεσσαλίης παρὰ τῶν Ἀλευαδέων ἀπιγμένοι ἄγγελοι ἐπεκαλέοντο βασιλέα πᾶσαν προθυμίην παρεχόμενοι ἐπὶ τὴν Ἑλλάδα (οἱ δὲ Ἀλευάδαι οὗτοι ἦσαν Θεσσαλίης βασιλέες), τοῦτο δὲ Πεισιστρατιδέων οἱ ἀναβεβηκότες ἐς Σοῦσα, τῶν τε αὐτῶν λόγων ἐχόμενοι τῶν καὶ οἱ Ἀλευάδαι, καὶ δή τι πρὸς τούτοισι ἔτι πλέον προσωρέγοντό οἱ. ἔχοντες Ὀνομάκριτον, ἄνδρα Ἀθηναῖον **χρησμολόγον** τε καὶ **διαθέτην χρησμῶν τῶν Μουσαίου**, ἀνεβεβήκεσαν, τὴν ἔχθρην προκαταλυσάμενοι. ἐξηλάσθη γὰρ ὑπὸ Ἱππάρχου τοῦ Πεισιστράτου ὁ Ὀνομάκριτος ἐξ Ἀθηνέων, ἐπ' αὐτοφώρῳ ἁλοὺς ὑπὸ Λάσου τοῦ Ἑρμιονέος **ἐμποιέων ἐς τὰ Μουσαίου χρησμὸν** ὡς αἱ ἐπὶ Λήμνῳ ἐπικείμεναι

54. Allen 1924:233.
55. See also Pausanias 7.26.13.
56. Further details in *PH* 6§§52–53 (= pp. 172–74); see also Haubold 2004:27–28.

νῆσοι ἀφανιοίατο κατὰ τῆς θαλάσσης· διὸ ἐξήλασέ μιν ὁ Ἵππαρχος, πρότερον χρεώ-
μενος τὰ μάλιστα. τότε δὲ συναναβάς, ὅκως ἀπίκοιτο ἐς ὄψιν τὴν βασιλέος, λεγόντων
τῶν Πεισιστρατιδέων περὶ αὐτοῦ σεμνοὺς λόγους, κατέλεγε τῶν χρησμῶν· εἰ μέν τι
ἐνέοι σφάλμα φέρον τῷ βαρβάρῳ, τῶν μὲν ἔλεγε οὐδέν, ὁ δὲ τὰ εὐτυχέστατα
ἐκλεγόμενος ἔλεγε, τόν τε Ἑλλήσποντον ὡς ζευχθῆναι χρεὸν εἴη ὑπ᾽ ἀνδρὸς Πέρσεω,
τήν τε ἔλασιν ἐξηγεόμενος. οὗτός τε δὴ χρησμῳδέων προσεφέρετο, καὶ οἵ τε
Πεισιστρατίδαι καὶ οἱ Ἀλευάδαι γνώμας ἀποδεικνύμενοι.

He [Mardonios] said these things because he was a man who yearned for new accomplishments and wanted to be appointed as the ruler of Hellas. It took him some
time to do what he did, but he worked on Xerxes long enough to persuade him to do
these things. And other things happened that contributed to his success in persuading Xerxes. For one thing, messengers came from Thessaly, sent by the Aleuadai—
and these Aleuadai were kings of Thessaly—inviting the King [Xerxes] to invade Hellas and offering their total support. For another thing, the Peisistratidai who had
traveled inland to Susa[57] used the same line of thinking in their speech as did the
Aleuadai, offering to Xerxes even more incentives. They [the Peisistratidai] had
moved inland and relocated at Sardis in the company of **Onomacritus**, an Athenian
poet of oracles [khrēsmologos] who was an **arranger [diathetēs]** of the **oracles of
Musaeus**. They [the Peisistratidai] had already settled their previous feud with him.
Onomacritus had been banished from Athens by Hipparkhos son of Peisistratos when
he was caught by Lasus of Hermione in the act of **fitting inside [en-poieîn]**[58] the com-
positions of Musaeus an oracular utterance saying that the islands off Lemnos would
disappear into the sea. Because of this Hipparkhos exiled him, though he had previously been most friendly to him. Now he [Onomacritus] had arrived in Susa with the
Peisistratidai, and, whenever he appeared before the King [Xerxes], they [the Peisis-
tratidai] used words evoking reverence for the divine in talking about him, and he
would go on to say something from his oracular poems; and **if there was something
in the oracular utterance that conveyed a failure** for the non-Greek side, **he would
say nothing of these things, and instead he would say [legein] only those things that
conveyed the greatest success, by way of selecting [eklegein]**, telling how the Hellespont must be bridged by a Persian man and prescribing the expedition. So, this man
[Onomacritus] was making his approach by **singing oracular utterances**, while the
Peisistratidai and the Aleuadai were making their own approach by **publicly deliver-
ing [apodeiknusthai] their words of advice**.

Herodotus 7.6.1–5

It is anachronistic to translate *en-poieîn* here as 'interpolate'. What it means instead is 'make poetry fit inside'—to make poetry fit inside poetry that has already
been made. In the *Lives of Homer*, we have seen Homer himself in the act of making verses fit into poetry that has already been made:

57. Hippias son of Peisistratos had been exiled from Athens along with his family.
58. Here we see in action the poetics of *en-poieîn* and its opposite, resulting in plus verses and mi-
nus verses. In a shorthand this is the poetics of selectivity.

ἐμποιεῖ ἐς τὴν **ποίησιν**, ἐς μὲν Ἰλιάδα τὴν μεγάλην Ἐρεχθέα μεγαλύνων ἐν νεῶν καταλόγῳ τὰ ἔπεα τάδε

δῆμον Ἐρεχθῆος μεγαλήτορος, ὅν ποτ' Ἀθήνη
θρέψε Διὸς θυγάτηρ, τέκε δὲ ζείδωρος ἄρουρα. [*Iliad* II 547–48]

καὶ τὸν στρατηγὸν αὐτῶν Μενεσθέα **αἰνέσας**.

He [Homer] made [-*poieîn* of *en-poieîn*] the following verses [*epos,* plural][59] **fit inside** [*en-* of *en-poieîn*] his **songmaking** [*poiēsis*]. Inside the big *Iliad*, glorifying Erekhtheus in the Catalogue of Ships, he made these verses [*epos,* plural]:

> . . . the district [*dēmos*] of Erekhtheus, the one with the great heart; him did Athena once upon a time
> nurture, she who is the daughter of Zeus, but the life-giving earth gave birth to him. [*Iliad* II 547–48]

He [Homer] also **praised** [*aineîn*] their [the Athenians'] general Menestheus.[60]

Vita 1.379–84

Here I review what I said in chapter 2 about this passage. Homer, in the act of composing the 'big' *Iliad*, is 'making' (*poieîn*) special things take place inside the epic plot of this *Iliad*. Specifically, Homer 'makes' the *epē* (*epos,* plural) 'verses' about Erekhtheus and Athens take place inside the *Iliad*; also, he makes other additional verses about Menestheus, the leader of the Athenians at the time of the Trojan War, thereby glorifying or 'praising' him as well.

So the process of *en-poieîn* is imagined here as something integral to the making of Homeric poetry. In terms of the *Life of Homer* traditions, Homer's adding of plus verses in the process of composing the *Iliad* and *Odyssey* in Chios is a prerequisite for the anticipated new occasion of performing the premiere of these two epics in Athens. For the new occasion of this premiere, Homer adds verses, just as Onomacritus is said to have added verses to preexisting verses of Musaeus, successor of Orpheus.[61] In the story of Onomacritus as retold by Herodotus, what makes these additions an act of theft is that Onomacritus claimed as his own the verses that originally belonged to Musaeus.

In the case of Onomacritus, the adding of verses takes place in the context of

59. The 'following verses' include passages from both the *Iliad* and the *Odyssey*. The extract I am quoting here gives the verses quoted from the *Iliad*.

60. After quoting these *epē* (*epos,* plural) 'verses' from the *Iliad*, the narrative goes on to quote *epē* 'verses' that Homer *en-poieî* 'makes inside' the *Odyssey*, which I do not include here in this extract.

61. Pausanias (1.14.3) cites verses attributed to Musaeus (though he doubts the validity of the attribution) in considering the lore about the culture hero Triptolemos. According to these verses, Triptolemos was the son of Ōkeanos and Earth. He also cites verses attributed to Orpheus (though again he doubts the validity of the attribution), according to which Eubouleus and Triptolemos were sons of Dysaules; in return for giving Demeter information about her daughter, they were rewarded with the sowing of seed.

performance. As we are told in the narrative of Herodotus, Onomacritus performs his oracular poetry for specific occasions. On one such occasion, as we saw, he is performing in the presence of the Persian king with the aim of backing up the line of thinking advanced by the tyrants of Thessaly and Athens combined.[62] Similarly, Kynaithos of Chios adds verses for the specific occasion of his singing in Delos the *Homeric Hymn to Apollo*, perhaps in the presence of the tyrant Polycrates of Samos. After singing the Homeric verses sacred to the Delian Apollo, Kynaithos adds the Hesiodic verses sacred to Pythian Apollo. For antiquarians like Aristarchus, as I have inferred from the scholia for Pindar (*Nemean* 2.1c), such an addition is an act of *en-ballein* 'interpolating'. For *Homēridai* like Kynaithos of Chios, by contrast, it is an act of augmenting. Such augmentation is the basis of what I call the *Homerus Auctus*. Something comparable can be said about a poet like Onomacritus of Athens. In this case, the augmentation of Musaeus by Onomacritus is the basis of what could be called a *Musaeus Auctus*.

In describing a picture of Musaeus that he saw in a painting prominently displayed in Athens, Pausanias (1.22.7) remembers having read verses attributed to Musaeus in which this poet speaks of receiving the gift of flight from the god of the north wind, Boreas. In the context of this reminiscence, Pausanias offers his own opinion. These verses, he thinks, were composed not by Musaeus but rather by Onomacritus. Further, Pausanias thinks that there were no surviving genuine verses of Musaeus except for a *Hymn to Demeter* composed by this poet 'for the Lykomidai' (1.22.7). This testimony of Pausanias may be correlated with the testimony of sources that attribute the *Homeric Hymn to Demeter* to the predecessor of Musaeus, Orpheus himself.[63]

What Pausanias (1.22.7) says about the involvement of Onomacritus in the verses of Musaeus can be reinterpreted this way: Onomacritus, in performing verses attributed to Musaeus, recomposed these verses in the process of performance. The recomposer can then be reconfigured as the original composer. Elsewhere in Pausanias (1.25.8), we see that Musaeus figures prominently in the mythological landscape of the city of Athens: opposite the acropolis, within the old city boundaries, is a hill called the *Mousaion* 'Museum'—that is, the 'space of Musaeus'—where it is said that Musaeus used to sing, and where his body was buried after he died of old age.

I highlight the fact that this versatile figure of Onomacritus is associated with the organization of Homeric as well as Orphic poetry, since we have seen him described as one of the four *diathetai* 'arrangers' of the Peisistratean Recension of Homer (Tzetzes *Anecdota Graeca* 1.6 ed. Cramer). So we see here a point of contact between Orphic and Homeric poetry in the era of the Peisistratidai. But then the question is, Can we say that Onomacritus augmented Homer in a way that is

---

62. My phrasing here has been improved by Kristin Ellithorpe (2005.06.09).
63. Richardson 1974:12.

comparable to the way he augmented Musaeus or even Orpheus? And can we say further that Onomacritus augmented Homer by way of adding the verses of, say, Orpheus?

Such questions are relevant to questions about the provenience of the Shield of Achilles in *Iliad* XVIII. As I note in the twin book *Homer the Classic*, one of the main visual features of the Shield is the river Ōkeanos that forms its perimeter, and this Ōkeanos is typical of poetry otherwise attributed to Orpheus.[64] I also note there that Zenodotus, in the age of Callimachus, athetized the whole Shield, while neoteric poets of the same age reveled in the mysticism of its verses.[65] Even Aristarchus, a century later, could not bring himself to athetize the whole passage.

SELECTIVE ADJUSTMENT OF REPERTOIRE

The fluidity of Homeric poetry in the era of the Peisistratidai is evident from the story we just saw in Herodotus (7.6.1–5) about a performance by Onomacritus in the presence of tyrants and kings. The performer can expand his performance by adding details in order to highlight whatever fits the occasion of this performance. And he can also compress his performance by subtracting details in order to shade over whatever does not fit the occasion. Onomacritus not only expands but also compresses his performance while recomposing what he performs. Whether he adds verses or subtracts them, he is achieving his aim of fitting his recomposition to the occasion of the performance. In oral poetry, the actual performance is decisive for understanding the current meaning of a given composition, since the composition is being recomposed in performance. The basis for understanding has to be the current performance, not any previous performance. I propose to describe this phenomenon as a *selective adjustment of repertoire*.

On each new occasion when a composition is recomposed in performance, it may be measured against previous performances. But any previous performance can only be a secondary basis for judging what the current performance should be. The primary basis has to be the new occasion, the occasion of the current performance. If any given previous performance featured a composition that was more expanded or more compressed than the composition produced by the current performance, such a longer or shorter version is not necessarily more basic than the current version, since both the previous and the current compositions are in any case recompositions. There is no absolute way of recovering an original composition on the basis of any single recomposition as performed in the here and now.

---

64. *HC* ch. 2 section 13.

65. *HC* ch. 2 section 18. Aristonicus reports (via Scholia A for *Iliad* XVIII 483a): ὅτι Ζηνόδοτος ἠθέτηκεν ἀπὸ τούτου τοῦ στίχου τὰ λοιπά '[Aristarchus marks with the sign >:] because Zenodotus has athetized the rest of this passage, starting with this verse'.

In some situations of performance, what the performer adds or subtracts is only for the performer to know for sure. In other situations, some who attend the performance may know what the performer knows. Their knowledge will depend on their own expertise in the poetry being performed. The observation made by Herodotus about an addition made by Onomacritus to the verses of Musaeus is an example of the second kind of situation. In terms of this observation, the expertise of the rival poet Lasus of Hermione makes it possible for that poet to detect the addition made by Onomacritus of Athens—an addition that nonexperts are supposedly unable to detect on their own.

In terms of performance, the adding or subtracting of verses is the effect, not the cause, of expansion or compression. It is simply a matter of adding or subtracting what needs to be said or not to be said, to be expanded or compressed. The presence or the absence of verses is merely a symptom of the process of expanding or compressing what the performer actually has to say in performance. In the context of performance, the ownership of any given verse is momentarily transferred to the performer. So the members of an audience cannot know for sure the identity of any previous owner of a verse they hear unless some reference is being made to that identity—whether that reference is explicit or at least implicit—as in the case of references to Homer or Hesiod in the *Homeric Hymn to Apollo*. Without a reference, it cannot be known for sure whether the owner of a given verse is to be understood as Homer or Hesiod or Musaeus or Orpheus or any other poet.

In this light, we may reassess the various reports about additions and subtractions of verses at the initiative of Peisistratos or his sons. A case in point is a report by Hereas of Megara (*FGH* 487 F 4, via Plutarch *Theseus* 20.1–2), who accuses Peisistratos of textual tampering by adding a verse about the Athenian hero Theseus in the Homeric *Odyssey* (xi 631) and by subtracting another verse about this same hero in the Hesiodic *Aigimios* (F 298).[66] Such reports stem from an aetiologizing of specific instances of expansion and contraction in the overall process of epic transmission in Athens. And the overall aetiology for this process is represented by the concept of the Peisistratean Recension.

Highlighting the complementary factors of compression and expansion taken together, I adduce once again the pertinent observation of Herodotus about the performance by Onomacritus of oracular poetry attributed to Musaeus, successor to Orpheus. We saw in that observation a most fitting instance of the principle I describe as the *selective adjustment of repertoire*. This principle, as I have argued, applies also to the epic poetry represented by the Homerus Auctus in the era of the Peisistratidai. The variations of this poetry evolved *selectively* to suit the poetic ideology as it evolved in the context of a venue like the festival of the Panathenaia.

As we trace the evolution of this ideology by going backward in time, from the

---

66. Figueira 1985:116. See also Dué 2006:94–95. On *Iliad* I 265, see Dué p. 95n12.

era of the democracy in the fifth century B.C.E. to the era of the Peisistratidai in the sixth, we find more and more fluidity the farther back we go. The most fluid phase is represented by what I am calling the Homerus Auctus. And the most visible traces of that early version of Homer are the so-called plus verses, remnants of a grand expansion esthetic that characterized Homeric poetry in the era of the Peisistratidai.

The Homerus Auctus can be reconstructed even farther back, to the era of Solon, who ruled Athens in the early sixth century, before the rule of Peisistratos. Solon was archon of Athens in 594/3. As I argued in chapter 1, both Solon and Peisistratos were once figured primarily as lawgivers of Athens—that is, as culture heroes who organized both the government and the poetry of the state.[67] The eventual differentiation between Solon as the prototype of democracy and Peisistratos as the embodiment of tyranny can be explained from the retrospective standpoint of the Athenian democracy that replaced the regime of the Peisistratidai.[68]

From the standpoint of Homeric poetry, however, there was relatively little difference between Solon and the Peisistratidai as heads of state who presided over the expansionism of the Athenian state at the expense of other states and, correlatively, over the performance of Homeric poetry at the Panathenaia.[69] In the case of Peisistratos, I have already focused on the city of Mytilene in Lesbos as an example of a state that lost possession of some of its prize territory to the expansionism of the evolving Athenian empire under the leadership of Peisistratos; as we saw, this contested territory was a choice part of the Troad, prized as a link to the heroic world of the Trojan War. In the case of Solon, we find a similar example in the history of the city of Megara, which lost possession of the island Salamis to the expansionism of Athens under the leadership of Solon sometime before 600 B.C.E.[70] In this case as well, the contested territory was prized as a link to the heroic world of the *Iliad*—personified in the figure of Telamonian Ajax, local hero of Salamis. Whereas the transfer of territory from Mytilene to Athens involved at one point the arbitration of Corinth under the leadership of its tyrant Periander, the transfer of Salamis from Megara to Athens involved the arbitration of Sparta.[71] In both cases of arbitration, Homeric poetry was cited by Athens as evidence for the city's own claims to the territories at stake. In the case of the territory of the Troad as claimed and counterclaimed by Athens and Mytilene, we have already seen in chapter 6 the report of Herodotus (5.94–95) concerning the Athenians' use of Homer in asserting their claims. In the case of the island Salamis as claimed and counterclaimed by Athens

---

67. See also Aloni 1989:43–45.
68. Figueira 1985:282.
69. *HQ* 74–75, 81, 101–2, 104–5.
70. Aloni 2006:91.
71. Figueira 1985:281–83; Frame 2009:428–32.

and Megara, there is a corresponding set of reports concerning the Athenians' use of Homer (Strabo 9.1.10 C394, Plutarch *Solon* 10, Diogenes Laertius 1.2.48). From these reports we can reconstruct the rhetoric of the contending city of Megara in making its counterclaim: that the Athenians supposedly interpolated what we know as verses 557 and 558 of *Iliad* II.[72] In these reports, the act of interpolation is attributed variously to Solon or Peisistratos. Once again we see here an instance of the process I describe as a *selective adjustment of repertoire*.

THE POETICS AND POLITICS OF THE HOMERUS AUCTUS

From the retrospective standpoint of the Athenian democracy, such adjustments of the Homeric repertoire in the era of the Peisistratidai were perceived as illegitimate tampering with a notionally preexisting text of Homer. It is as if such a text had been kept under lock and key, as it were, by the tyrants who held power on the acropolis, the Peisistratidai.[73] From the standpoint of the tyrants in this earlier era, however, the epic poetry of Homer was perceived as something quite different. This something is what I have been calling the Homerus Auctus. Such an augmented Homer was not so much a text but a tradition, constantly subject to change, and the poetry of this tradition could be continually expanded or compressed to fit the political needs of the time. That is what I mean when I speak of the poetics and politics of the Homerus Auctus.

In the poetry of the evolving Homerus Auctus, the expansions were far more noticeable than the compressions. And the expansions involved the adding of verses that were typical of Orpheus as well as Homer. In the era of the Peisistratidai, the poetics of Orpheus and Homer were far less differentiated than in the later era of the democracy. From the retrospective standpoint of the democracy, the poetry of Homer in the era of the tyrants was augmented by the poetry of Orpheus. From the earlier standpoint of the tyrants, however, this poetry was far less differentiated.

The Homer of the Peisistratidai, as notionally augmented by way of Orpheus, was not only a poet of epic. Like Orpheus, he was also a poet of oracular verses that initiated the privileged initiand into mysteries inaccessible to the profane. For a ruler to possess this kind of Homer was the equivalent of possessing a distinctive mark of royalty, a royalist Homer. Such a royalist Homer would have been closely connected to Hesiod, to Musaeus, and especially to Orpheus himself. He would have been the ultimately sophisticated and charismatic poet who combines the virtues of all other poets. His charisma—let us call it *kharis*—would have charmed all, much as Orpheus charmed all. The Homer of the democracy stands in sharp contrast against such a background. This alternative Homer was a democratic Homer, sup-

72. *PH* 11§12 (= p. 320). See also Dué 2006:94.
73. *PH* ch. 6 (= pp. 146–98).

posedly free of royalist accretions such as plus verses. He is the Homer of what I have been calling the Homeric Koine.

Mention of the Homeric Koine brings me back to my analysis of the editorial stance of Alexandrian scholars with regard to what they considered to be Orphic accretions in the text of Homer. In particular, I have in mind the narrative about the Shield of Achilles in *Iliad* XVIII. As we have seen, Zenodotus in the third century B.C.E. went ahead and athetized the whole passage about the Shield, evidently on the grounds that its verses were Orphic, whereas Aristarchus in the second century held back. As we will now see, the editorial stance of Aristarchus in this regard has to be evaluated in the historical context of alternative editorial trends that were current in his era.

The era of Aristarchus, head of the Library in Alexandria in the mid-second century B.C.E., was also the era of Crates, head of the Library in Pergamon. As I show in the Prolegomena to *Homer the Classic*, the text of Homer as edited by Crates was worlds apart from the text of Homer as edited by Aristarchus: whereas the base text used by Aristarchus was what we know as the Homeric Koine, the base text used by Crates was the Homerus Auctus. And there are political differences between these two base texts of Homer. As I will now argue, the edition of Homer by Aristarchus can be viewed as a political deactivation of the Homeric Koine that once represented the Athenian empire, and, conversely, the edition of Homer by Crates in the same era can be viewed as a political reactivation of the Homerus Auctus. As we will see in what follows, what I mean by *political deactivation* and *political reactivation* corresponds, respectively, to an editorial deactivation and an editorial reactivation of poetry attributed to Orpheus. Orphic verses had a political as well as a poetic valence.

In order to explore the political reactivation of the Homerus Auctus, I start by highlighting Virgil's use of this textual tradition in the first century B.C.E. As I argue in the Conclusions to *Homer the Classic*, Virgil used the Homerus Auctus as edited in the second century B.C.E. by Crates, head of the Library of Pergamon. In other words, Virgil preferred to use the neoteric textual tradition of the Homerus Auctus as represented by the edition of Crates, not the antineoteric textual tradition of the Homeric Koine as represented by the edition of Aristarchus. Virgil's epic *Aeneid* was based on the inclusive Homer of Crates, not on the exclusive Homer of Aristarchus.

From the standpoint of a non-Alexandrian worldview as represented by Crates in Pergamon, the term *neoteric* in describing the textual tradition of the Homerus Auctus needs to be reconceptualized. For Crates, a verse like *Iliad* XXI 195 about the cosmic river Ōkeanos was not really neoteric or even Orphic, as it had been for Zenodotus, who had rejected it as non-Homeric—whether by athetizing it (according to the Geneva scholia) or by deleting it (according to the Venetus A scholia). Rather, this verse was for Crates simply Homeric, showing that Homer himself had pictured the primal cosmic body of water to be the Ōkeanos, not the Akhelōios, as

Zenodotus had claimed.[74] Similarly, a verse like *Iliad* XIV 246a was for Crates not a plus verse, as it must have been for Aristarchus, who rejected it as non-Homeric by excluding it from his base text. For Crates, this verse was, again, simply Homeric, showing that Homer pictured the Ōkeanos as a saltwater ocean encompassing a spherical earth, not as a freshwater river encircling a circular and flat earth, as Aristarchus had claimed.[75] To Crates, the Homerus Auctus must have seemed to be Homeric in its entirety.[76]

THE SHIELD OF ACHILLES AND THE HOMERUS AUCTUS

For Virgil, the Homerus Auctus as a poetic model was mediated not only by the archaizing base text of Homer as edited by Crates of Pergamon but also by this same editor's modernizing commentaries on Homeric poetry. As Philip Hardie has demonstrated in a book about Virgil's *Aeneid*, the poetics of this Roman imperial epic were decisively shaped by Crates' modern exegesis of allegorical traditions about the world of Homer.[77] For Virgil, as for Crates of Pergamon, the circular world of Homer was envisioned as spherical—not flat as it was for Aristarchus of Alexandria. For Virgil, this spherical world of Homer was represented by the cosmic Shield of Achilles in *Iliad* XVIII, which became the poetic model for the cosmic Shield of Aeneas as it takes shape in *Aeneid* 8. Virgil understood the meaning of the Homeric Shield in terms of the exegesis developed by Hellenistic allegorizers, especially by Crates:[78]

> [T]he *circular* form of that Shield was seized upon by the Hellenistic allegorizers as proof that Homer knew the universe to be spherical, and visual representations also emphasize that the circular form of the Homeric Shield is an image of the cosmos. We are made aware of the massive circular form of the Shield of Aeneas in the description of its forging [Virgil *Aeneid* 8.448–49]. For the Augustan reader the very shape of the Shield of Aeneas would suggest the symbolism of empire; the *orbis* of the Shield [as in *Aeneid* 8.449] becomes an emblem of the *orbis terrarum*. The sphere is an ambiguous symbol, for it can refer either to the spherical earth or to the spherical universe; as a symbol of power it can thus stand either for control of the *oikoumenē* or for a more ambitious claim to cosmic might.

The Shield of Achilles, even when visualized as a sphere, must have seemed to be a purely Homeric visualization to Crates. And since this Shield of Achilles was evidently the model for the Shield of Aeneas, we may at first think that it seemed to be a purely Homeric visualization to Virgil as well. But Virgil's poetry was refer-

---

74. *HC* 2§§196, 206–8, 214.
75. *HC* 2§§148–57.
76. *HC* 2§§178–84.
77. Hardie 1986.
78. Hardie 1986:367.

ring not only to a Homeric visualization. It was referring also to a Cratetean visualization of the Homeric visualization. And the visualization of Crates, based on the Homerus Auctus as he edited it and as he commented on it, went far beyond any Homeric visualization. Virgil's Homer was the expansive Homerus Auctus as edited and interpreted by Crates, not the narrower Homeric Koine as edited and interpreted by Aristarchus, for whom the Ōkeanos was a freshwater river encircling an Earth that was flat, not the salty sea waters enveloping an Earth that was spherical. Virgil's Homer is also to be distinguished from the supposedly real Homer as edited by Zenodotus, for whom the verses about the Ōkeanos—and in fact all the verses about the Shield of Achilles—were Orphic accretions that needed to be athetized in his base text of Homer.

As Hardie argues, Virgil's picturing of the Shield of Aeneas as a massive spherical *orbis* or 'globe', was derived directly from the Homeric Shield of Achilles as allegorized by Crates of Pergamon, who had modified various earlier allegorical models developed by Stoic thinkers:[79]

> In contrast to the earlier Stoics, Crates, in his interpretation of Homer, was predominantly concerned with cosmological and geographical matters; he used Homer to support his own construction of a terrestrial globe, and is reported as saying that Homer was an astronomer [Crates F 24 ed. Mette = F 76 ed. Broggiato 2001]. To Crates is probably to be attributed an extensive allegorization of the Homeric Shield of Achilles as an image of the cosmos; . . . I argue that Virgil draws on a cosmological interpretation of this sort in his own description of the Shield of Aeneas.

Hardie's argument that the Homeric Shield of Achilles in *Iliad* XVIII was interpreted by Crates in terms of an allegory about the cosmos is validated by explicit testimony in Eustathius (*Commentary* 3.144.13 for *Iliad* XI 40) and in the Homeric **b**T scholia (for *Iliad* XI 40): both sources indicate that Crates himself interpreted in exactly these terms the Shield of Agamemnon in *Iliad* XI (32–40).[80] Elsewhere in Eustathius, we see a similar cosmic allegorization of the Shield of Achilles, with specific reference to that shield's *antux* or 'rim', mentioned in *Iliad* XVIII (479 and 608). From the internal evidence of Homeric diction, we see that this *antux* 'rim' is *triplax* 'threefold' or 'triple' (XVIII 480) and that the outermost fold or circle of this *antux* is specifically named as the Ōkeanos (XVIII 608).[81] For Crates, this outermost fold is allegorized as the saltwater ocean that encompasses the spherical cosmos. As Hardie

---

79. Hardie 1986:27–28, with reference to further argumentation in his ch. 8, "The Shield of Aeneas: The Cosmic Icon" (pp. 336–76).

80. Hardie 1986:341.

81. In Eustathius (*Commentary on Iliad* vol. 4 p. 218 lines 14–17), the commentator draws attention to the morphological parallelism of *triplax* 'threefold' with *diplax* 'twofold', reasoning that this parallelism proves that *diplax* is not necessarily restricted to the world of weaving, since *triplax* is obviously associated with metalwork. ('Ὅρα δὲ τὸ "τρίπλακα," δηλοῦν ὅτι καὶ τὸ δίπλακα δύναται μὴ ἀεὶ ἐπὶ

shows, the allegorization of Crates about the Shield of Achilles is attested indirectly in Eustathius and in the scholia for the *Phaenomena* of Aratus:[82]

> Eustathius further records an allegorization of the *antux*, the rim, of the Shield as the circle [*kuklos*] of the zodiac [*Commentary* 4.220.9–10]; that it is said to be 'triple' [*triplax* at XVIII 480] alludes to the breadth of the zodiac [4.220.11]; that it is called 'gleaming' [*marmareē*, same verse] refers to the fact that the bright sun moves within it [4.220.12–13]; the *telamōn* or shield-strap [same verse] is allegorized in Eustathius as the axis which supports the universe [4.220.14–15]. The diversity of the Homeric description has been rigidly reduced to a simple schema, while the suggestions of universality in the original text have been made the foundation for an interpretation of the Shield as a comprehensive symbol of the cosmos. A scholion on Aratus [verse 26], drawing on the same allegorization, describes the Shield of Achilles as a *kosmou mimēma*, 'an image of the cosmos'. The allegory, transmitted anonymously, in all probability derives from the Pergamene scholar Crates of Mallos.

For Crates, such allegorizing of the Homeric shields of Agamemnon in *Iliad* XI and of Achilles in *Iliad* XVIII involved not only cosmology but also the imperialistic ideology of the dynasty of the Attalidai in Pergamon during the second century B.C.E.:[83]

> Crates worked for the Attalid kings of Pergamum, who developed a particularly rich and extravagant imagery portraying the state and its ruler as divine agents of order, seen most notably in the Gigantomachy of the Great Altar of Zeus. Crates' name has often been suggested in the context of the authorship of the (lost) iconographical programme of this work, which manifestly combines themes from earlier myth and poetry with contemporary political propaganda.

Although any overall design or "programme" that might have been devised by Crates for the iconography of the Great Altar of Pergamon is now lost—or never existed in the first place—we do have ample traces of this man's overall design for Homeric interpretation, and we can see it attested in the fragments of his Homeric

---

ὑφάσματος τίθεσθαι. ἰδοὺ γὰρ τὴν ἐλατὴν ἄντυγα "τρίπλακα μαρμαρέην" ἔφη, ὅ ἐστι τρίθετον κατὰ τρεῖς πλάκας. 'Consider τρίπλακα, which shows that even δίπλακα need not always be used in the sense of weaving; to back up this reasoning, I draw your attention to the way he [the poet] says τρίπλακα μαρμαρέην with reference to the metalworked *antux*, which is tripartite in terms of its three layers.') As we saw in chapter 10, the word *diplax* refers to a woven fabric in *Iliad* III 126 and XXII 441, and both attestations show the epithet *marmareē* as a variant of *porphureē*. So, just as the epithet *marmareē* describes the *diplax* as a woven web, the epithet *triplax marmareē* describes the *antux* of the Shield of Achilles in XVIII 480. What I find significant is the actual crossover here between the world of weaving and the world of metalwork.

82. Hardie 1986:341. The reportage of Eustathius 4.220.9–11 is mediated by an earlier source, Demo: see Hardie p. 375; also Broggiato 2001:158–59, 161–62.

83. Hardie 1986:342.

commentaries, as I analyze them in chapter 2 of *Homer the Classic*. This design, as we can see from that analysis, is a modernizing one in its scientific reinterpretations of Homeric allegory, but it is archaizing in its reliance on a base text that represents the Homerus Auctus.

For Virgil, his own allegorizing in the poetic creation of his Shield of Aeneas in *Aeneid* 8 matches the allegorizing of Crates himself in his commentaries on the Homeric shields in *Iliad* XI and XVIII. In other words, the poetic model for Virgil's Shield was the Homeric Shield as interpreted in the commentaries of Crates—and as mediated by a base text representing the Homerus Auctus, not the Homeric Koine.

For Virgil, as also for Crates, such allegorizing involved not only cosmology but also the imperialistic ideology of his patrons. Just as Crates' Homeric text and commentaries represented the Attalid dynasty of Pergamon in the second century B.C.E., so also Virgil's neo-Homeric *Aeneid* represented the evolving Julian dynasty of Rome in the first century B.C.E., in the age of Augustus. Moreover, as Hardie has shown, the cultural ideology of the Roman empire under Augustus was actually modeled on the earlier cultural ideology of the Attalidai of Pergamon.[84] It is in this historical context that we can appreciate the poetics of Virgil's Shield of Aeneas, where the idea of *cosmos* is fused with the idea of Roman *imperium*:[85]

> The central feature of ancient exegesis is its insistence that the great circle of the Shield of Achilles, with its abundance of scenes, is an image of the whole universe, an allegory of the cosmos. The Shield of Aeneas is also an image of the creation of a universe, but of a strictly Roman universe (though none the less comprehensive for that). There is in fact no contradiction between the universalist themes of Homer (as interpreted by antiquity) and the nationalist concerns of Virgil; the resolution is provided immediately by the Virgilian identification of *cosmos* and *imperium*, of which the Shield is the final and most vivid realization. This interpretation has the further advantage of explaining the function of the Shield within the overall structure of the poem, a problem only partially confronted by modern reassessment; as cosmic icon the Shield of Aeneas is the true climax and final encapsulation of the imperialist themes of the *Aeneid*.

The fusion of *cosmos* and *imperium,* as conveyed in the title of Hardie's book, can be described as a merism. By *merism* I mean a combination of two words that convey one meaning.[86] I draw attention to the merism at work in the actual combination of *cosmos and imperium* by highlighting not only the constituent words *cosmos* and *imperium* but also the connecting word *and* that combines them. This merism captures the essence of empire as I analyze it in the sections that follow.

---

84. Hardie 1986:28, 123–56, 342.

85. Hardie 1986:339. Hardie then goes on to analyze the differences in narrative perspective between the Shield of Aeneas in *Aeneid* 8 and the review of Roman heroes in *Aeneid* 6.

86. Further citations on the concept of merism in *HTL* 159.

THE IDEOLOGY OF *COSMOS AND IMPERIUM*
THROUGH THE AGES

From all we have just seen, I conclude that the idea of *cosmos and imperium* in Virgil's *Aeneid* was derived from the Homerus Auctus—as mediated by the Homeric edition and the Homeric commentaries of Crates in Pergamon. This Cratetean Homer was the source for the imperial design of Virgil's *Aeneid*. In the Conclusions to *Homer the Classic*, I show how the ideology of empire, as derived from the Homerus Auctus of Crates, was reused to represent the imperial ideology of Rome under the rule of Augustus in first century B.C.E. Earlier, it had been used to represent the imperial ideology of Pergamon under the rule of the Attalidai in the second century B.C.E. Now we will see how the same idea, as derived from an earlier phase of the Homerus Auctus, had once been used to represent the imperial ideology of Athens under the rule of the Peisistratidai in the sixth century B.C.E. In particular, we will see how the Shield of Achilles became a map, as it were, of the Athenian empire in the era of the Peisistratidai.[87]

As I have already argued, this Athenian empire in the predemocratic era was a precursor of the empire that evolved in the era of the democracy. And although this earlier empire cannot compare in scale to the later one, it nevertheless shaped an imperial design of vast proportions in its own right. In making this argument, I have tried to convey the vastness of this design by exploring in some detail two initiatives taken by the Peisistratidai in appropriating Homer as a spokesman for their incipient Athenian empire. Here I review these two initiatives in order to explore even further the imperial design of the Peisistratidai of Athens.

One of these two initiatives was the Athenians' acquisition of the *Homēridai*. These *Homēridai* of Chios claimed as their ancestor the Homer who speaks in the *Homeric Hymn to Apollo* as the spokesman of all Ionians assembled at the festival of the Delia in Delos. The other of these two initiatives was the Athenians' acquisition of Sigeion—under the leadership of Peisistratos. Since the territory of Sigeion was equated with the sacred setting of the story of Troy, this Athenian acquisition was equated with the Athenian acquisition of Homer as the poet who told the story of Troy.

Both these Athenian initiatives, I will now argue, were linked to the idea of *cosmos and imperium* as expressed by the Homerus Auctus. In making this argument, I must stress again that this Homerus Auctus was not the Homer of the Koine that became the standard form of epic in the era of democracy in Athens. Rather, the Homerus Auctus was the undifferentiated Homer, inclusive of elements that were

87. I postpone for another project my study of the Hesiodic *Shield of Herakles*, which is later than the Orphic Shield of Achilles in *Iliad* XVIII: that is, the Hesiodic *Shield* dates back to a later phase in the era of the Peisistratidai.

only later to be differentiated as Cyclic or Hesiodic or Orphic—as opposed to Homeric. The association of this Homerus Auctus with the Peisistratidai was aetiologized, as we have seen, in the charter myth of the Peisistratean Recension.

THE RING OF MINOS AS A SYMBOL
OF *COSMOS AND IMPERIUM*

The initiative taken by the Peisistratidai of Athens in appropriating Homer as a spokesman for the Delian League was not without precedent. As we have already seen, an earlier such initiative was also taken by Polycrates, tyrant of Samos, whose Ionian empire once competed with the Ionian empire of the Peisistratidai. Both initiatives, as jointly reflected in the *Homeric Hymn to Apollo*, drew on the idea of *cosmos and imperium*. And a most fitting symbol of this idea was a precious object that figures prominently in the story told by Herodotus about the rise and fall of the Ionian empire ruled by Polycrates of Samos: the signet ring or *sphragis* of Polycrates (3.41–43). As we are about to see, this symbol was linked to an older symbol going all the way back to the Bronze Age. That older symbol was the signet ring or *sphragis* of Minos.

Before I turn to the myth about the Ring of Minos, however, I need to make five points about Polycrates in his role as an Ionian tyrant:

1. Polycrates was hardly the only model for the Peisistratidai to follow in promoting the idea of *cosmos and imperium*. There were other models as well, as represented by the Ionian tyrant Thrasyboulos of Miletus (Herodotus 1.20–22, 5.92ζ–η). As we saw earlier, the city of Miletus dominated the Ionian Dodecapolis, a federation that was older and formerly more prestigious than the rival federation of the Delian League. The Ionian Dodecapolis was relevant to Polycrates of Samos, since the island-state of Samos was one of the twelve members of this federation. It was also relevant to the *Homēridai* of Chios, since the island-state of Chios was likewise one of the twelve members. And it was even more relevant to the Peisistratidai of Athens, for two reasons. First, the city of Athens claimed to be the metropolis or 'mother city' of the twelve Ionian cities of the Dodecapolis. Second, the genealogy of the founders of the Dodecapolis was linked to the genealogy claimed by the Peisistratidai, since their common ancestor was thought to be Neleus of Pylos.[88] This figure of Neleus was a symbol in his own right—a symbol likewise going all the way back to the Bronze Age.[89]

2. The Ring of Polycrates, as a traditional story, was linked not only to the myth of the Ring of Minos. It was linked also to stories of rings possessed by oriental

88. For a full presentation of the argument, see Frame 2009.
89. Frame 2009.

despots. The prime example comes from Plato. It is the Ring of Gyges, which empowered Gyges to become invisible at will: using this ring, Gyges overthrew the previous dynasty of the Lydians, thus becoming founder of the Lydian dynasty that culminated in the kingship of Croesus (*Republic* 2.359b–360b, 10.612b).[90] The Ring of Gyges can be linked to another ring of Asiatic provenience in Plato's repertoire: in the *Ion* (536b), Socrates refers to Orpheus, Musaeus, and Homer as three First Poets pictured as three First Rings attracting other rings with their magnetic power, and the source of this power is a magnetic stone that shares its name with the city of Magnesia-at-Sipylus in Asia Minor. As we see in Plato's *Ion* (533d), the magnetic power of the Magnesian Stone is a metaphor for the poetic power of the Muse in linking Homer to the Homeric rhapsode and his audience.

3. The orientalism associated with the Ring of Polycrates fits the historical context of his empire. The royal imperialism of Ionian tyrants like Polycrates was shaped by a lengthy prehistory of close contacts between the Greeks of Asia Minor and the Lydian empire, which was later to be replaced by the Persian empire (in 547 B.C.E.). Even the Greek usage of the word *turannos* 'tyrant' is relevant, since it represents the Lydian word for 'king'.[91] What we see in the Greek usage of the word *turannos* is an orientalizing of the very concept of royal imperialism. A most fitting symbol of this orientalized concept was the figure of Croesus himself as king of the Lydians, whom Herodotus pictures as the prototype of an imperial tyranny that strongly resembled the power of the Athenian empire: like the Athenians, as Herodotus goes out of his way to emphasize, the Lydians deprived Hellenic states of their freedom by making them tributaries of their empire (1.5.3–1.6.3).[92]

4. Linking the Ring of Polycrates of Samos to the Ring of Gyges of Lydia is the would-be Ring of Croesus. The story is told in the *Life of Aesop* (G 81–100). At a meeting of the assembly of the people of Samos, where a debate is raging over who should get the *dēmosion daktulion* 'ring of the people' (G81: here the noun is in the neuter), an eagle swoops down upon the assembled crowd, snatches the ring, and flies off with it; then it flies back and drops it into the lap of a slave (G 82). Aesop interprets this omen, referring to the ring as the *daktulios stratēgikos*— that is, the 'ring of the lawmaker' (G 91: here the noun is in the masculine)[93]— and advising the people of Samos to resist a demand made by the tyrant Croesus that the state of Samos must become a tributary of the Lydian empire (G 92–94). By way of telling the people of Samos a fable, Aesop persuades them to heed his

90. The theme of the invisibility of Gyges is euhemerized in the version narrated by Herodotus 1.8–13.

91. *PH* 9§23 (= p. 266); also *PH* ch. 10 (= pp. 274–313) in general.

92. *PH* 8§22 (= pp. 229–30).

93. On the usage of *stratēgikos* in the *Life of Aesop* (G 91) in the sense 'belonging to the lawmaker', see *PH* 11§20n53 (= p. 324).

advice and refuse the demand of Croesus (G 94–95). The tyrant, cheated out of ruling over Samos, is thus implicitly deprived of the 'ring of the lawmaker'. Angry over his loss, Croesus threatens the people of Samos with military invasion unless they surrender Aesop to him as a hostage (G 95–98). Aesop reacts by telling the people of Samos another fable, which persuades the Samians not to surrender Aesop as a hostage to the Lydians; but then Aesop voluntarily journeys to the palace of Croesus and voluntarily surrenders himself as hostage to the tyrant (G 98–99). There he proceeds to tell further fables, which secure his own freedom from the tyrant and, in addition, the freedom of the people of Samos, who then proceed to enter into an equitable alliance with the Lydians (G 98–100).[94]

5. Such orientalized concepts of royal imperialism stemming from a predemocratic era persisted even into the democratic era of the Athenian empire. A case in point is the *Skēnē* or 'Tent' of the Great King of Persia, reconfigured as the Odeum of Pericles in the Athens of Pheidias and Pericles. As I argue in chapter 4 of the twin book *Homer the Classic*, this monumental building was a most fitting venue for spectacular events of state that highlighted the wealth, power, and prestige of the Athenian empire in the era of the democracy. Chief among these events was the performance of the Homeric *Iliad* and *Odyssey* in the Odeum of Pericles on the occasion of the festival of the Panathenaia.

In describing the Ring of Polycrates as the symbol of an orientalized concept of royal imperialism, I am making a distinction between the words *orientalized* and *oriental*. That is because the symbolism here stems ultimately not from oriental sources— even though the political and cultural influence of the oriental Lydian empire was strongly felt by the Greeks of Asia Minor and the outlying islands. The ring that symbolizes the empire of Polycrates is modeled on an earlier ring that symbolizes an earlier empire thought to be Greek by the Greeks themselves—an empire dating all the way back to the Bronze Age.

Here I return to the concept of a maritime empire or *thalassokratia* 'thalassocracy' once ruled by Minos, king of the city of Knossos on the island of Crete. As we saw in chapter 8, where I quoted the relevant passage from Herodotus (3.122.2), this thalassocracy of Minos is pictured as the prototype of the maritime empire of the Ionian tyrant Polycrates and, ultimately, of the Athenians. We see an analogous picturing of the Minoan thalassocracy in Thucydides (1.4). Moreover, King Minos is figured in modern archaeology as the prototype of what is known as the Minoan empire in the Bronze Age.

As we already saw in chapter 8, the symbol of this empire was the Ring of Minos, which the prototypical king of the Minoan thalassocracy throws into the sea—

---

94. For a commentary on this narrative taken from the *Life of Aesop* (G 81–100), see *PH* 11§§18–20 (= pp. 323–24).

to be recovered by Theseus, the prototypical king of Athens and the notional founder of the Athenian thalassocracy (Bacchylides Song 17). In commenting on the representation of this myth as pictured in a painting that covered one full wall of the sanctuary of Theseus in Athens, Pausanias offers a retelling of the myth, which he says is only partly retold through the medium of the painting:

Μίνως ἡνίκα Θησέα καὶ τὸν ἄλλον στόλον τῶν παίδων ἦγεν ἐς Κρήτην, ἐρασθεὶς Περιβοίας, ὥς οἱ Θησεὺς μάλιστα ἠναντιοῦτο, καὶ ἄλλα ὑπὸ ὀργῆς ἀπέρριψεν ἐς αὐτὸν καὶ παῖδα οὐκ ἔφη Ποσειδῶνος εἶναι, ἐπεὶ ‹οὐ› δύνασθαι τὴν **σφραγῖδα**, ἣν αὐτὸς φέρων ἔτυχεν, ἀφέντι ἐς θάλασσαν ἀνασῶσαί οἱ. Μίνως μὲν λέγεται ταῦτα εἰπὼν ἀφεῖναι τὴν **σφραγῖδα·** Θησέα δὲ **σφραγῖδά** τε ἐκείνην ἔχοντα καὶ **στέφανον** χρυσοῦν, Ἀμφιτρίτης δῶρον, ἀνελθεῖν λέγουσιν ἐκ τῆς θαλάσσης.

When Minos was taking Theseus and the rest of the delegation of young men and women to Crete he fell in love with Periboia, and when Theseus opposed him by objecting, he [Minos] insulted him and said that he [Theseus] was not the son of Poseidon, since he [Theseus] could not recover for him [Minos] the **signet ring** [*sphragis*] which he [Minos] happened to be wearing, if he threw it into the sea. With these words Minos is said to have thrown the **signet ring** [*sphragis*], but they say that Theseus emerged from the sea holding that **ring** and also a gold **garland** [*stephanos*] that Amphitrite gave him.

Pausanias 1.17.3

As a symbol, then, the Ring of Minos links the Minoan empire of the Bronze Age to the imperial ideology of Athens as represented by Theseus. And this same symbol links to other aspects of this ideology—as expressed by way of performing Homeric poetry. Here I highlight a moment in Plato's *Hippias Minor* when Socrates draws attention to the ring worn by Hippias of Elis (368b). As I show in chapter 3 of the twin book *Homer the Classic*, the context is most evocative.[95] Hippias is staging himself as a re-enactment of the king Minos son of Zeus, as pictured in the Homeric *Odyssey* (xi 568–71). Sitting on a throne situated in front of the temple of Zeus in Olympia, he evokes a Homeric vision of King Minos son of Zeus sitting on his own throne and dispensing responses to all questions addressed to him (*Hippias Minor* 363c–d, 364a–b; *Protagoras* 315b–c). Hippias re-enacts in Athens the Homeric displays he had performed at the temple of Zeus in Olympia, and it is in this Homeric context that Socrates notices the ring on the sophist's finger (*Hippias Minor* 368b).

I conclude that the ring worn by Hippias in the course of making his Homeric displays is ostensibly a re-enactment of the Ring of Minos. And I find it relevant to compare this primal image of the Ring of Minos to the primal image of three First Rings in Plato's *Ion* (536b), since these rings stand for the three First Poets, identified as Orpheus, Musaeus, and Homer.

95. *HC* ch. 4 section 8.

THE SHIELD OF ACHILLES AS A SYMBOL
OF *COSMOS AND IMPERIUM*

So far, I have been arguing that the initiative of the Peisistratidai in appropriating Homer as the spokesman of the Delian League was linked to the idea of *cosmos and imperium*. A symbol for this idea was the Ring of Minos—a symbol going all the way back to the Bronze Age. Now I will argue that the initiative of the Peisistratidai in appropriating Sigeion in the Troad was likewise linked to the idea of *cosmos and imperium*. In this case, a symbol for this idea was the Shield of Achilles as described in *Iliad* XVIII. Like the Ring of Minos, this symbol of a bronze Shield goes all the way back to the Bronze Age. Moreover, this symbol of the bronze Shield is linked, like the previous symbol of the ring, with Minos, king of Knossos in Crete.

In the case of this bronze Shield, as I argued in chapters 7 and 10, its link to the Bronze Age is expressed by the artifact itself. The poetry of the Shield of Achilles in *Iliad* XVIII is designed to show that this bronze Shield can make direct contact with the Bronze Age. Contact is established through the *selas* 'gleam' that radiates from the bronze surface of the Shield, projecting a picture from the Bronze Age. This gleam radiating from the Shield of Achilles is directly compared in *Iliad* XVIII to the gleam emanating from the tumulus of Achilles, the location of which is imagined to be in Sigeion, the prize territory of the Athenians in the Troad. I have already drawn attention to this gleam in chapter 7 and again in chapter 10, but I must now quote the relevant verses once again:

δύσετο δῶρα θεοῦ, τά οἱ Ἥφαιστος κάμε τεύχων.
κνημῖδας μὲν πρῶτα περὶ κνήμῃσιν ἔθηκε
καλὰς ἀργυρέοισιν ἐπισφυρίοις ἀραρυίας·   370
δεύτερον αὖ θώρηκα περὶ στήθεσσιν ἔδυνεν.
ἀμφὶ δ' ἄρ' ὤμοισιν βάλετο ξίφος ἀργυρόηλον
χάλκεον· αὐτὰρ ἔπειτα **σάκος** μέγα τε στιβαρόν τε
εἵλετο, τοῦ δ' ἀπάνευθε **σέλας** γένετ' ἠΰτε μήνης.
ὡς δ' ὅτ' ἂν ἐκ πόντοιο **σέλας** ναύτῃσι **φανήῃ**   375
καιομένοιο πυρός, τό τε καίεται **ὑψόθ' ὄρεσφι**
σταθμῷ ἐν οἰοπόλῳ· τοὺς δ' οὐκ ἐθέλοντας ἄελλαι
πόντον ἐπ' ἰχθυόεντα φίλων ἀπάνευθε φέρουσιν·
ὡς ἀπ' Ἀχιλλῆος **σάκεος σέλας** αἰθέρ' ἵκανε.

He [Achilles] put it [his armor] on, the gifts of the god, which Hephaistos
    had made for him with much labor.
First he put around his legs the shin guards,   370
beautiful ones, with silver fastenings at the ankles.
Next he put around his chest the breastplate,
and around his shoulders he slung the sword with the nails of silver,
a sword made of bronze. Next, the **Shield**, great and mighty,
he took, and from it there was a **gleam** [*selas*] from afar, as from the moon,

or as when, at sea, a **gleam** [*selas*] to sailors appears   375
from a blazing fire, the kind that blazes **high in the mountains**
at a **solitary station** [*stathmos*], as the sailors are carried unwilling by gusts
    of wind
over the fish-swarming **sea** [*pontos*], far away from their loved ones.
So also did the **gleam** [*selas*] from the **Shield** of Achilles reach all the way up
    to the aether.

                                                            Iliad XIX 368–79

I will briefly repeat here what I argued in chapters 7 and 10, and then I will extend the argument further. The gleam of the Shield emanates not only from its form but also from the content of the form. The gleam comes not only from the armor: that is, from the shining metal of the bronze surface reflecting the radiant light of the sun. The gleam comes also from what the armor means. That meaning is conveyed not only through the simile of the hero's tumulus as a lighthouse but also through the picture made by the divine metalworker on the shining bronze surface of the Shield. It is a picture of *cosmos and imperium*:

Ἐν δὲ **χορὸν** ποίκιλλε περικλυτὸς ἀμφιγυήεις,   590
τῷ ἴκελον οἷόν ποτ' ἐνὶ Κνωσῷ εὐρείῃ
Δαίδαλος ἤσκησεν καλλιπλοκάμῳ Ἀριάδνῃ.
ἔνθα μὲν ἠΐθεοι καὶ παρθένοι ἀλφεσίβοιαι
ὀρχεῦντ' ἀλλήλων ἐπὶ καρπῷ χεῖρας ἔχοντες.
τῶν δ' αἳ μὲν λεπτὰς ὀθόνας ἔχον, οἳ δὲ χιτῶνας   595
εἵατ' ἐϋννήτους, ἦκα στίλβοντας ἐλαίῳ·
καί ῥ' αἳ μὲν καλὰς **στεφάνας** ἔχον, οἳ δὲ μαχαίρας
εἶχον χρυσείας ἐξ ἀργυρέων τελαμώνων.
οἳ δ' ὁτὲ μὲν θρέξασκον ἐπισταμένοισι πόδεσσι
ῥεῖα μάλ', ὡς ὅτε τις τροχὸν ἄρμενον ἐν παλάμῃσιν   600
ἑζόμενος κεραμεὺς πειρήσεται, αἴ κε θέῃσιν·
ἄλλοτε δ' αὖ θρέξασκον ἐπὶ στίχας ἀλλήλοισι.
πολλὸς δ' **ἱμερόεντα χορὸν** περιίσταθ' ὅμιλος
τερπόμενοι· μετὰ δέ σφιν **ἐμέλπετο** θεῖος ἀοιδὸς
φορμίζων· δοιὼ δὲ κυβιστητῆρε κατ' αὐτοὺς   605
μολπῆς ἐξάρχοντος ἐδίνευον κατὰ μέσσους.⁹⁶

The renowned one [= Hephaistos], the one with the two strong arms,
    pattern-wove [*poikillein*]⁹⁷ in it [= the Shield] a *khoros*.⁹⁸   590

96. On the textual transmission of *Iliad* XVIII 604–6, I refer to my analysis in chapter 10.

97. Also attested at this verse, besides ποίκιλλε (*poikillein*), is the variant ποίησε (*poieîn*), with the neutral meaning 'make'.

98. Once again, I repeat that this word *khoros* can designate either the place for singing and dancing or the group of singers and dancers who perform at that place.

It [the *khoros*] was just like the one that, once upon a time in far-ruling
   Knossos,
Daedalus made for **Ariadne**, the one with the beautiful tresses [*plokamoi*].
There were young men there,[99] and girls who are courted with gifts of cattle,
and they all were **dancing** with each other, holding hands at the wrist.
The girls were wearing delicate dresses, while the boys were clothed in khitons   595
well woven, gleaming exquisitely, with a touch of olive oil.
The girls had beautiful **garlands** [*stephanai*], while the boys had knives
made of gold, hanging from knife-belts made of silver.
Half the time they moved fast in a circle, with expert steps,
showing the greatest ease, as when a wheel, solidly built, is given a spin
   by the hands   600
of a seated potter, who is testing it whether it will run well.
The other half of the time they moved fast in straight lines, alongside each
   other.
And a huge assembly stood around the place of the *khoro*s, **which evokes
desire,**
and they were all delighted. In their midst **sang-and-danced** [*melpesthai*]
   a divine singer,
playing on the *phorminx*. And two special dancers among them   605
were swirling as he **led** [*ex-arkhein*] the **singing and dancing** [*molpē*]
   in their midst.

Iliad XVIII 590–606

The craft of poetry represents here the work performed by the premier artisan among mortals, Daedalus. The work of this mortal artisan is spotlighted by the divine artisan Hephaistos. In the spotlight we see a *khoros*, a place for singing and dancing. The setting of this *khoros* is the palace of Minos, king of Knossos in Crete. The focus of attention amidst all the singing and dancing is Ariadne, princess of the Minoan empire, who was loved and then abandoned by Theseus, founder of the once and future Athenian empire.[100] As a simile, the *khoros* of Ariadne is imagined as the ultimate point of comparison for all singing and dancing at all festivals for all time to come. And the location of this *khoros*, the palace of Minos at Knossos in Crete, is imagined as the prototypical location of imperial power. Homer sings in the middle of this *khoros*. He is Homer the Preclassic, precursor of Homer the Classic.

The lens through which this picture is viewed is an Athenian lens, dating back to the era of the Peisistratidai. In this era, the bronze Shield of Achilles was the ultimate picture of empire.

99. The 'there' is both the place of dance and the place in the picture that is the Shield.
100. In a future project, I connect with this theme the interaction between Catullus 66.39 and Virgil *Aeneid* 6.460.

TEN CENTURIES OF HOMERIC TRANSMISSION

By now we have seen that both the Ring of Minos and the Shield of Achilles were linked to the idea of *cosmos and imperium* as expressed by the Homerus Auctus in the era of the Peisistratidai in the sixth century. We have also seen that both the Ring and the Shield derive from the era of the Bronze Age. So the idea of cosmos and imperium has a prehistory of at least five centuries, stretching from the era of the Bronze Age to the era of the Peisistratidai in the sixth century B.C.E. The continuity of this idea over a span of five centuries is a sign of general continuity in the transmission of Homeric poetry over the same span of time. And we have already seen further continuity in the next five centuries, starting from the era of the Peisistratidai of Athens and proceeding forward in time to the era of the Attalidai of Pergamon in the second century B.C.E. All through this span of time, the idea of cosmos and imperium was continued. Adding the two spans together, we see a general continuity of over ten centuries.

As I have argued, the idea of cosmos and imperium was most clearly expressed in the medium of expression that I call the Homerus Auctus, an undifferentiated form of Homer that must be contrasted with the differentiated Homer of the Koine, which became the standard form of epic in the era of democracy in Athens. This undifferentiated Homer included elements that were only later to be differentiated as Cyclic or Hesiodic or Orphic—as opposed to Homeric.

The Homerus Auctus was associated with the Peisistratidai in the sixth century B.C.E., and it was aetiologized in the charter myth of the Peisistratean Recension. And this recension was notionally recovered in the edition of Homer by Crates in the second century B.C.E.

To back up this formulation, I contrast the Homeric edition produced by Crates under the sponsorship of the Attalidai in the second century B.C.E. with the Homeric edition produced by Zenodotus under the sponsorship of the Ptolemies in the third century B.C.E. In the edition of Zenodotus, whatever verses the editor judged to be non-Homeric were athetized. Zenodotus was particularly vigilant about verses he judged to be Orphic. A most striking example is his athetesis of all the verses picturing the Shield of Achilles in *Iliad* XVIII. For Zenodotus, all these verses were Orphic. In the Homeric edition of Crates, by contrast, whatever verses his predecessors athetized or even omitted as Orphic were systematically unathetized or restored as Homeric. As I show in the twin book *Homer the Classic*, the supposedly Orphic verses of the Homerus Auctus were rehabilitated in the Homeric edition of Crates.[101] As far as this editor was concerned, these verses originated from the version of Homer that existed in the era of the Peisistratidai. So we see here a parallelism between the myth of a recension of Homer by Peisistratos and the reality of

---

101. *HC* ch. 2 section 14.

an edition of Homer by Crates. The Cratetean edition was imagined as a reconstitution of the Peisistratean Recension.[102]

The Peisistratean Recension, as a mythical prototype of the Cratetean Edition, is the notional foundation of what I describe as the Homerus Auctus of the Peisistratidai. This augmented Homer was replete with mystical verses judged to be Orphic in later times but accepted as Homeric in its own time. From the retrospective standpoint of a democratic world of later times, such verses seemed Orphic because of their mystical valence, matching a predemocratic political valence. From the retrospective standpoint of a postdemocratic world of still later times, however, such verses could be seen once again as Homeric, since the mysteries of the Orphic cosmos were now subsumed by an all-inclusive Homeric cosmos.

One such mystery was the cosmic river Ōkeanos, imagined as a freshwater stream that encircles and thus defines both the macrocosm of the heroic world and the microcosm of the Shield of Achilles as it takes shape in *Iliad* XVIII. Arguing against the idea of such an Ōkeanos in the real world, Herodotus remarks that this idea originates either from Homer or from an ostentatiously unnamed figure whom he describes as a poet even earlier than Homer (Herodotus 2.23). And, as we have already seen in another passage, Herodotus says he is going against a more traditional way of thinking when he makes the claim that Homer—along with Hesiod—was more ancient than other ancient poets whom he leaves unnamed (2.53.1–3). As I have argued, the foremost of the unnamed poets that Herodotus has in mind in that passage is Orpheus. Similarly in the passage at hand (2.23), Herodotus calls attention once again to a more traditional way of thinking when he says that there was an unnamed poet who was conventionally thought to be more ancient than Homer: in rejecting the existence of a cosmic river Ōkeanos in the real world, the historian attributes the actual idea of Ōkeanos not only to Homer but also to this unnamed poet (2.23). As I argue in chapter 2 of *Homer the Classic* concerning the Orphic associations of this cosmic river, that unnamed poet is evidently Orpheus.

For a later thinker like Crates, by contrast, the idea of Ōkeanos is basically Homeric, not Orphic, and Homer himself can be credited with the idea of Earth as a sphere, with a land mass surrounded by a body of water called the Ōkeanos. Here I turn to a most evocative image. It is the statue of the Farnese Atlas (fig. 13). The sculpture pictures the Titan in the act of shouldering a celestial sphere, an idealization of the Earthly sphere.

As I argue in the Conclusions to *Homer the Classic*, such a visualization of Atlas struggling underneath the massive burden of a cosmic and imperial globe was inspired by theories about a spherical world, and these theories were in turn inspired by allegorizing traditions stemming from the Homerus Auctus: that is, from a text that combined—or recombined—the world of Orpheus with the world of Homer.

102. LP (Nagy 1998) 223–28.

FIGURE 13. Sculpture: the
"Farnese Atlas." Roman
copy of a Hellenistic Greek
original. Naples, Museo
Archeologico Nazionale,
6374. Drawing by Valerie
Woelfel.

The burden that weighs so heavily on the shoulder of this primordial Atlas is analogous to the cosmic and imperial burden of an augmented and theoretically all-
inclusive Homer.

    For now I return to my basic argument, that the Homerus Auctus was not an in-
novation. The Homerus Auctus did not result from a process of attaching Orphic
and other supposedly non-Homeric elements to the Athenian Koine of Homer. The
supposedly Orphic elements in Homer were at one time not Orphic but simply Homeric. These elements may not have been Homeric in the way that Crates thought
them to be Homeric, but they were still integral to the Homeric poetry he was ed-

iting. In terms of this basic argument, then, the Homerus Auctus was cumulatively older than the Athenian Koine.

By contrast, the Athenian Koine of Homer was an innovation. It resulted from a process of detaching Orphic and other supposedly non-Homeric elements from the Homerus Auctus. These elements, detached in the democratic era of the Athenian empire, had their own importance in the predemocratic era—an importance no longer fully understood by the time they were finally reattached in the postdemocratic era. In the predemocratic era of the Homerus Auctus, poetic traditions later described as Orphic, Hesiodic, and Cyclic were still attached to a poetic tradition described as Homeric. In the democratic era of the Athenian Koine they became detached. In the postdemocratic era of Callimachus and the neoterics, elements of the old Homerus Auctus were reattached, only to get detached for good in the still later postdemocratic era of Aristarchus.

HOMER THE POET OF KINGS

The politics of the Homerus Auctus, as we have seen from the augmentations later attributed to Orpheus, Hesiod, and the poets of the epic Cycle, were royal politics. In the democratic era of Athens, these poets were associated with the earlier era of the Peisistratidai, and they were therefore marginalized. In the case of Orpheus, for example, we have just seen how he lost his priority—and anteriority—to Homer, who became the representative of nonroyal politics in the democracy. This nonroyal Homer, however, was not the same Homer whose epics were performed at the Panathenaia in the earlier years of the Peisistratidai. That earlier Homer was a spokesman for the idea of royalty. He was the poet of kings.

That royalist Homer was not the differentiated Homer of the Homeric Koine. He was an undifferentiated Homer whose verses could not be systematically distinguished from verses also attributed to the poets of the Cycle, to Hesiod, and to Orpheus. That undifferentiated Homer was a poet of royalty in his own right, in sharp contrast with the Homer of the Homeric Koine.

The aura of royalty conveyed by the Homerus Auctus is evident from its reception in empires that came after the Athenian empire. These later empires, unlike the Athenian empire in the democratic era, were royal, ruled by Hellenistic dynasties like the Ptolemies of Alexandria and the Attalidai of Pergamon. In the still later empire ruled by the dynasty taking shape at Rome in the age of Virgil, we saw a comparable pattern of reception.

While the Roman empire, as glorified by the epic poetry of Virgil, was in some ways similar to the Athenian empire of the democracy, it was even more similar to the Athenian empire of the tyranny that came before—and to the later empires of the Hellenistic kingdoms that came after. In what follows, I will highlight these predemocratic and postdemocratic empires against the backdrop of the democratic Athenian empire. Whereas the Athenian empire in the democratic era was mediated by the Homeric Koine, the empires of the Hellenistic kingdoms and the Roman empire itself were mediated by the Panathenaic Homer of the predemocratic era: that is, by the Homerus Auctus.

In considering the Homerus Auctus as a predemocratic alternative to the Homeric Koine, I find it most instructive to reconsider the career of a poet whose own lifetime bridged the predemocratic and the democratic phases of the Panathenaic Homer. That poet was Simonides of Keos, whose own poetry could be sung at the citharodic competitions of the Panathenaia—just as the poetry of Homer was sung at the corresponding rhapsodic competitions. The poetry of Simonides bridges the discontinuities caused by successive Athenian appropriations of the Homeric tradition. Traces of the poet's links with the discontinued predemocratic Homer of the tyrants are evident in his references to Homeric poetry. These references, especially in the *Plataea Elegy*, imply a Homeric repertoire that approximates the Homerus Auctus.[103]

Something comparable can be said about Pindar's Homer. It took me 464 printed pages to develop the argument fully in my book *Pindar's Homer*, but here I can say it all at once by citing just one example among many. The example comes from Pindar's *Olympian* 2, where the poet's words refer in the same breath to three heroes: Hector (81–82) and Kyknos (82) and Memnon (83). All three of these heroes are epic opponents of Achilles, and we are in effect being told that Homer created not only the epic of the *Iliad*, which features Hector, but also the epics of the Cycle as exemplified by the *Cypria*, which features Kyknos (Proclus summary p. 105.2–3 ed. Allen), and by the *Aithiopis*, which features Memnon (Proclus summary p. 106.1–7).[104] So Pindar's Homer, like the Homer of Simonides, was the Homerus Auctus, not the Homeric Koine.

This transitional Homeric tradition as known to Simonides and Pindar, with its links to the Homerus Auctus, can be expected to include Orphic elements that were later excluded by the Homeric Koine. For the likes of Simonides, however, this transitional Homer was nevertheless closer to the later Homer than to the earlier Orpheus. As I point out in the twin book *Homer the Classic*, Plato associates Simonides with Homer and Hesiod, while disassociating him from Orpheus and Musaeus (*Protagoras* 316c–d).[105] This set of associations and disassociations is essential in view of the fact that these four poets were conventionally listed in a canonical sequence that followed a fixed chronological order, starting with Orpheus as the most an-

103. Nagy 2005b.
104. *PH* 14§2 (= pp. 414–15).
105. *HC* ch. 3 section 6.

FIGURE 14. Fresco painting: Lyre Singer. Reconstructed from fragments found in the throne room, Pylos. Drawing by Valerie Woelfel.

cient of these four poets and ending with Homer as the most recent: Orpheus, Musaeus, Hesiod, Homer.[106]

If we follow the canonical sequence of Orpheus and Musaeus and Hesiod and Homer chronologically backward, moving from Homer to Hesiod to Musaeus to Orpheus, we see an increasing identification of poetry with royalty, culminating in Orpheus, the poet of kings par excellence. Relevant is the Pylos fresco painting of the Lyre Singer pictured as performing next to the royal throne of the throne room in the Mycenaean palace at Pylos (fig. 14).

Every time the king sat on his throne in the throne room of his palace at Pylos, he could see at his side the painting of this Lyre Singer, who is seated on a rock in the wilderness and who performs for the king. The singer seated on the rock will perform for the king every time the king is seated on the throne. This Lyre Singer looks more like Orpheus the citharode, less like Homer the rhapsode. The Bronze Age Homer looks more like the classical Orpheus and less like the classical Homer.

In describing the Lyre Singer depicted on this Mycenaean fresco, I find it most instructive to apply the anachronistic term *citharode*. Here I return to my argument that Orpheus and Orphic poetry became marginalized in the era of the Athenian

106. See *HC* 3§§99–100.

democracy, making room for the centrality of Homer as the exclusive poet of epic at the Panathenaia. Homer became the rhapsode par excellence, while Orpheus became marginalized as a citharode. In terms of this argument, the association of the citharodic Simonides with the rhapsodic Homer and Hesiod instead of the citharodic Orpheus indicates that he succeeded in making a poetic transition from the predemocratic to the democratic era.

In the predemocratic era, there was a time when the royal figure of Orpheus was still central, and when Homer was still only becoming central—to the extent that Homeric poetry emulated Orphic poetry. There was a time when Orpheus was still considered to be the master of all kinds of poetry and song. It was only later, in the era of the democracy, that he became marginalized as a prototype of the effete citharode we see pictured in Plato's *Symposium* (179d–e). Even as a citharode, the prototypical lyric poet Orpheus ultimately became marginalized at the Panathenaia in the new era of the democracy, making room for the centrality of contemporary lyric poets like Simonides.

Such an evolution in the reception of poetry attributed to Orpheus is indirectly reflected in Ovid's poetic rendition of the song sung by Orpheus himself to the accompaniment of his lyre. Within the space of merely seven verses, Ovid's poetic imagination recapitulates the metamorphosis of a poet of kings who sings the legitimizing victories of gods over Giants into a poet of lovers who sings the illicit affairs of mortals with immortals:[107]

> ab Iove, Musa parens (cedunt Iovis omnia regno),
> carmina nostra move. Iovis est mihi saepe potestas
> dicta prius; cecini plectro graviore Gigantas
> sparsaque Phlegraeis victricia fulmina campis.
> nunc opus est leviore lyra; puerosque canamus
> dilectos superis inconcessisque puellas
> ignibus attonitas meruisse libidine poenam.

> Starting from Zeus [Jupiter], O Muse [Kalliope], my mother[108] (for all things
>   yield to the kingship of Zeus),
> bring motion to my songs. Often has the power of Zeus [Jupiter] by me
> been told before. I have sung the Giants as I strummed the strings [of my lyre]
>   to a heavier tune,
> and [I have sung] victorious thunderbolts scattered all over the Phlegraean
>   fields.
> But now there is need for strumming with a lighter touch on the lyre. Let me
>   sing boys

107. The theme of the Gigantomachy is programmatically aborted in Ovid's *Metamorphoses* (1.151–62 and 5.318–31) as a gesture to a programmatic abortion of this same theme in Callimachean poetics: see Tarrant 2005:67–69.

108. I note the relationship of Orpheus with the Muse of kings, Kalliope.

loved by the gods up above, and girls who, with unnatural
fires smitten, pay the penalty for their lust.[109]

Ovid Metamorphoses 10.148–54

Despite the marginalization of Orpheus in the democratic era, the old traditions about his status as the most ancient of poets were kept alive. Even in the age of Plato, we see traces of the popular belief that the figure of Orpheus was more ancient than the figure of Homer. A most memorable example is the reference made to Orpheus by Plato's Socrates in the *Apology* (41a).[110]

FROM HOMER THE PRECLASSIC TO HOMER THE CLASSIC

What I have reconstructed as the Homerus Auctus of the sixth century is a point of transition from the preclassical to the classical Homer. Refocusing on the sixth century, I contemplate the world of Athens under the leadership of Solon in the early years of that century and of the Peisistratidai in the later years.

I return to two arguments that apply here. One: both Solon and the Peisistratidai were involved in the evolution of Homeric poetry. Two: this involvement was relevant to the evolution of the Athenian empire. I say *empire* because, to repeat one last time a point I have been making ever since Part I, Athens could already be considered an empire in the preclassical eras of Solon and the Peisistratidai. This was no empire in the classical sense of the empire that Athens became after its enormous successes in the fifth century, but it was an empire nonetheless.

The concept of Homer as the spokesman of a preclassical empire survived into the classical period. Such a concept was supposedly articulated by Homer himself, according to classical sources. A prime example of such sources, as we are about to see, is Thucydides.

Rule by the sea—that is, *thalassokratia* 'thalassocracy'—is a basic prerequisite for the preclassical empire as represented by Homer. So says Thucydides (1.4), who cites as the prototype of Athenian thalassocracy the prehistoric imperial rule of the Aegean Sea under the leadership of Minos, king of the city of Knossos on the island of Crete. It is essential that Thucydides offers his formulation about a Minoan thalassocracy precisely in the context of recalling the story of the Capture of Troy—as he understands it from Homer. Immediately before he says what he says about the Minoan thalassocracy, Thucydides observes that the Capture of Troy marks the very first time that the Hellenes ever did anything *hathrooi* 'together', and that it

109. Among the songs that will be sung by Orpheus in Ovid's *Metamorphoses* is the story about Pygmalion and his ivory statue (10.238–97), as quoted and analyzed in *Homer the Classic* ch. 1 section 9. It can be argued that the happy ending of that story is a wish fulfillment on the part of the embedded narrator, who is Orpheus himself: see Tarrant 2005:76.

110. *HC* 3§99, with commentary.

was by using the sea that they *xunexēlthon* 'came out together' for the first time when they sailed off to Troy in order to capture it (1.3.4). Thucydides makes it explicit, it is essential to add, that his primary evidence for what he argues about the Capture of Troy is Homer himself:

τεκμηριοῖ δὲ μάλιστα Ὅμηρος.

The one who **provides evidence** [*tekmērioūn*] primarily is Homer.

Thucydides 1.3.3

It is likewise essential to add that, although Thucydides is speaking here about an enterprise ostensibly undertaken by all Hellenes, he uses the language of the Athenian empire in making his initial formulation about this ostensibly first Panhellenic enterprise:

πρὸ γὰρ τῶν Τρωικῶν οὐδὲν φαίνεται πρότερον **κοινῇ** ἐργασαμένη ἡ Ἑλλάς.

Before the events at Troy, it appears that Hellas had previously accomplished nothing **in common** [*koinēi*].

Thucydides 1.3.2

The expression *koinēi*, stemming from the adjective *koinos* 'common, standard', is decisive. The criterion applied by Thucydides here in describing the political realities of the Bronze Age as he sees it is extrapolated from the political realities of the sixth as well as the fifth century B.C.E. In the sixth century, as I mentioned earlier, the Athenians had already gained a foothold in the Troad and reshaped Homeric poetry in the process, primarily at the expense of the rival city of Mytilene in Lesbos. The Athenians also acquired the island of Salamis at the expense of the rival city of Megara, and here too they reshaped Homeric poetry in the process. I have already referred to these phases in the evolution of Homeric poetry. Suffice it to add here that the encroachment of Athens on the territories of Megara must be viewed in the context of expanding Athenian trade routes in the region of the Hellespont. Such a pattern of ever-increasing acquisition—we could even call it acquisitiveness or, by its Greek name, *pleon(h)exia*—has to do with thalassocracy *and* Homer in the same breath. The expansionism reaches the point of a real empire with the formation of the Delian League, as aetiologized in the *Homeric Hymn to Apollo*.

The noun *homēros*, in the usage of Thucydides, could mean not only 'hostage' in general but *hostage of the Athenian empire* in particular (3.90.4, 4.57.4, 5.84.1, etc.). This meaning is correlative with the meaning of the *nomen loquens* of Homer. As I argued in chapter 9, the name *Homēros* means 'fitting together', in a political as well as a poetic sense. In a poetic sense, as we saw, a master poet 'fits together' pieces of poetry that are made ready to be parts of an integrated whole, just as a master carpenter or joiner 'fits together' or joins pieces of wood that are made ready to be parts of a chariot wheel; in a political sense, the hostage 'fits together' or joins pieces of human society that are made ready to be parts of a supposedly integrated whole. The politics and the poetics go together, just as empire and Homer go together. The unequal reciprocity inherent in the English word *hostage,* which implies that the captor is a "host" and the captive is a "guest," is comparable to the reciprocity inherent in the Greek word *kharis* 'pleasurable beauty' in the sense of both 'favor' and 'gratitude', as we see from the wording that Thucydides ascribes to Pericles in a most telling context:[111]

καὶ τὰ ἐς ἀρετὴν ἐνηντιώμεθα τοῖς πολλοῖς· οὐ γὰρ πάσχοντες εὖ, ἀλλὰ δρῶντες κτώμεθα τοὺς φίλους. βεβαιότερος δὲ **ὁ δράσας** τὴν **χάριν** ὥστε ὀφειλομένην δι᾽ εὐνοίας ᾧ δέδωκε σῴζειν· ὁ δὲ ἀντοφείλων ἀμβλύτερος, εἰδὼς οὐκ ἐς **χάριν**, ἀλλ᾽ ἐς ὀφείλημα τὴν ἀρετὴν ἀποδώσων. καὶ μόνοι οὐ τοῦ ξυμφέροντος μᾶλλον λογισμῷ ἢ τῆς ἐλευθερίας τῷ πιστῷ ἀδεῶς τινὰ ὠφελοῦμεν. Ξυνελών τε **λέγω τήν** τε **πᾶσαν πόλιν τῆς Ἑλλάδος παίδευσιν εἶναι** καὶ καθ᾽ ἕκαστον δοκεῖν ἄν μοι τὸν αὐτὸν ἄνδρα παρ᾽ ἡμῶν ἐπὶ πλεῖστ᾽ ἂν εἴδη καὶ μετὰ **χαρίτων** μάλιστ᾽ ἂν εὐτραπέλως τὸ σῶμα αὔταρκες παρέχεσθαι. καὶ ὡς οὐ λόγων ἐν τῷ παρόντι κόμπος τάδε μᾶλλον ἢ **ἔργων** ἐστὶν **ἀλήθεια**, αὐτὴ ἡ δύναμις τῆς πόλεως, ἣν ἀπὸ τῶνδε τῶν τρόπων ἐκτησάμεθα, σημαίνει. μόνη γὰρ τῶν νῦν ἀκοῆς κρείσσων ἐς πεῖραν ἔρχεται, καὶ μόνη οὔτε τῷ πολεμίῳ ἐπελθόντι ἀγανάκτησιν ἔχει ὑφ᾽ οἵων κακοπαθεῖ οὔτε τῷ ὑπηκόῳ κατάμεμψιν ὡς οὐχ ὑπ᾽ ἀξίων ἄρχεται. μετὰ μεγάλων δὲ σημείων καὶ οὐ δή τοι ἀμάρτυρόν γε τὴν δύναμιν παρασχόμενοι τοῖς τε νῦν καὶ τοῖς ἔπειτα θαυμασθησόμεθα, καὶ οὐδὲν προσδεόμενοι οὔτε **Ὁμήρου ἐπαινέτου** οὔτε ὅστις **ἔπεσι** μὲν τὸ αὐτίκα τέρψει, τῶν δ᾽ ἔργων τὴν **ὑπόνοιαν** ἡ **ἀλήθεια βλάψει**, ἀλλὰ πᾶσαν μὲν θάλασσαν καὶ γῆν ἐσβατὸν τῇ ἡμετέρᾳ τόλμῃ καταναγκάσαντες γενέσθαι, πανταχοῦ δὲ μνημεῖα κακῶν τε κἀγαθῶν ἀίδια ξυγκατοικίσαντες.

When it comes to striving for achievement [*aretē*], we [Athenians] stand in sharp contrast to most others. For it is not by being treated well by others, but by treating them well, that we acquire those who are near and dear [*philoi*] to us. **The one who is at the giving end** of the *kharis* is more dependable, in that he is disposed to keep it [that *kharis*] going, by continued good will toward the one at the receiving end. But the other, who is at the receiving end and must pay it [the *kharis*] back, is by comparison unresponsive, knowing that when he pays it back it will count not as a *kharis* but as a debt repaid. And we are the only ones who benefit others not with calculations of self-interest but with the confidence of our liberal generosity. Summing it all up, then, I say that **our city is in its entirety the education [*paideusis*] of Hellas**, and that, as far as I can see, each of us could easily apply his own being, as an autonomous individual, toward the greatest variety of forms—and do so with *kharis* [plural, matching each of the forms]. And that this is no mere boast, uttered in the context of the occasion, but rather the **truth [*alētheia*]** as linked to the **realities [*erga*]**, is attested by the very power of our city, a power that we have acquired in consequence of these characteristics. For the city of Athens, alone among all the cities of today, comes up looking

111. Translation adapted primarily from the version of Richard Crawley in Strassler 1996.

better when put to the test—better than what people say about it—and it alone causes neither resentment for the opposing enemy for being defeated by such opponents nor self-reproach for subordinates for not being ruled by worthy superiors. Great are the visible signs with which we have made our power a thing that cannot go without being witnessed, and that is why we will be the wonder of those who live today and of future generations as well. We will not need **Homer** as our **agent of praise** [*epainetēs*] or anyone else whose **verses** [*epos,* plural] will give pleasure [*terpein*] only for the moment but whose **underlying meaning** [*huponoia*][112] as linked to the realities will be vulnerable to the **truth** [*alētheia*], which will utterly **undermine** [*blaptein*] them [the verses].[113] But we have compelled every sea and every land to grant access to our daring, and have everywhere planted everlasting memorials both of destructive and of constructive deeds.

Thucydides 2.40.4–41.5

In effect, Thucydides is making a reference here, however indirectly, to the appropriation of Homer by Athens. Such a reference, I argue, is evident from his use of the word *kharis* 'pleasurable beauty, gracefulness; graciousness, favor; gratitude'. This word *kharis* combines the idea of beauty and pleasure with the affective ties that come with the beauty and the pleasure. By *affective ties* I mean the relationships expressed by the word *philos*, meaning 'near and dear' as an adjective and 'friend' as a noun. In the words of Pericles as dramatized here by Thucydides, the *kharis* of the Athenians in exercising their imperial power is understood as the beauty and the pleasure that comes from their being *philoi* 'friends' to their allies, from their being 'near and dear' to them. The *kharis* of this reciprocity between the Athenians and their allies is decidedly unequal, Pericles says, in that the allies reciprocate the Athenians not because they want to but because they have to. The allies feel obligated by necessity, whereas the Athenians feel obligated by the beauty and the pleasure of their own imperial greatness. *Noblesse oblige*, as it were. This kind of *kharis* is more than unequal: it is hierarchical. On the surface, the Athenians are 'friends' of their allies; underneath the surface, they are superior to them, because the beauty and the pleasure of what they give them is notionally far superior to whatever the allies give back. And the most beautiful and pleasurable of Athenian possessions is Homer himself. The Athenians think they own Homer, and, quite conscious of this ownership, they feel they do not have to mention it when they give Homer to other Hellenes, who will be most grateful to have Homer but will have nothing comparable to give back to the Athenians. In response to any *kharis* in the sense *gratitude*, the Athenians will be obliged by their own *kharis* in the sense

---

112. For *huponoia*, see LSJ s.v. ὑπόνοια II: "*the real meaning which lies at the bottom* of a thing, *deeper sense,*" as in Xenophon *Symposium* 3.6; "esp. *covert meaning* (such as conveyed by myths and allegories)," as in Plato *Republic* 2.378d. But LSJ assigns category I, not II, to the present attestation in Thucydides: "*suspicion, conjecture, guess.*"

113. In other words, the truth about realities will undermine the *huponoia* about realities.

graciousness to say, if I may be allowed to paraphrase: "Don't mention it!" And the Athenians won't have to mention Homer, either. To repeat: they think they own Homer. All other Hellenes need Homer as an *epainetēs* or 'agent of praise', in the sense that they feel a need for Homer to mention details about them, but the Athenians do not need even to hear any mention of details about them by Homer, because, to repeat one last time, they own Homer. For the Athenians, Homer is part of their identity, and so the city of Athens can claim to be the source of 'education' or *paideusis* for the entire Hellenic world. Why? It is simply because Homer is already acknowledged by all Hellenes as their universal educator. This conceit is captured most succinctly in Plato's *Republic* (2.376e–398b; 10.599c–d, 606e).

The imperial *kharis* of the Athenians is predicated on the inherent *kharis* of Homer as expressed by Homeric poetry. Starting his performance in *Odyssey* ix, Odysseus describes the ideal occasion for a performing *aoidos* 'singer' (ix 3–4), and that occasion is a feast (5–12). There is no *telos* 'outcome', the hero says, that brings more *kharis*—more beauty and pleasure—than the singing of an *aoidos* before an audience of *daitumones* (7), an audience of participants in a feast:

ἦ τοι μὲν τόδε **καλὸν** ἀκουέμεν ἐστὶν **ἀοιδοῦ**
τοιοῦδ᾽, οἷος ὅδ᾽ ἐστί, θεοῖσ᾽ ἐναλίγκιος **αὐδήν**.
οὐ γὰρ ἐγώ γέ τί φημι **τέλος χαριέστερον** εἶναι   5
ἢ ὅτ᾽ **ἐϋφροσύνη** μὲν ἔχῃ κάτα **δῆμον** ἅπαντα,
δαιτυμόνες δ᾽ ἀνὰ δώματ᾽ ἀκουάζωνται **ἀοιδοῦ**
ἥμενοι ἐξείης, παρὰ δὲ πλήθωσι τράπεζαι
σίτου καὶ κρειῶν, μέθυ δ᾽ ἐκ κρητῆρος ἀφύσσων
οἰνοχόος φορέῃσι καὶ ἐγχείῃ δεπάεσσι·   10
τοῦτό τί μοι **κάλλιστον** ἐνὶ φρεσὶν εἴδεται εἶναι.

This is indeed a **beautiful thing**, to listen to a **singer** [*aoidos*]
    such as this one [Demodokos], the kind of singer that he is, comparable
        to the gods **in the way he speaks** [*audē*],
for I declare, there is no **outcome** [*telos*] that has more **pleasurable beauty**
    [*kharis*]   5
than the moment when the **spirit of festivity** [*euphrosunē*][114] prevails
        throughout the whole **community** [*dēmos*],
and the people at the feast [*daitumones*], throughout the halls, are listening
        to the **singer** [*aoidos*]
as they sit there—you can see one after the other—and they are sitting
        at tables that are filled
with grain and meat, while wine from the mixing bowl is drawn
by the one who pours the wine and takes it around, pouring it into their cups.   10

---

114. On the programmatic implications of *euphrosunē* 'mirth' as the atmosphere, as it were, of the poetic occasion, see *BA* 5§39 (= p. 91), 12§15 (= p. 235), *PH* 6§92 (= p. 198), all following Bundy 1986:2.

This kind of thing, as I see it in my way of thinking, is the **most beautiful thing**
in the whole world.

Odyssey ix 3–11

Such was the *kharis* of Homer as the ancients once understood him. Such was
the meaning of the word *kharis* as used by followers of Aristarchus in their quest
to capture the essence of whatever seemed truly Homeric. That is why they applied
the term *khariestera* 'having more *kharis*' to textual variants they deemed more likely
than not to be Homeric.[115] For them the wording of Homer possessed *kharis*, while
the wording of all those pseudo-Homers lurking in all their textual variations possessed no such thing. Such was the *kharis* that had to be captured for Homer himself to be recaptured.

115. *HC* Prolegomena section 11; also *PP* 116n46.

Aleshire, S. B., and S. D. Lambert. 2003. "Making the Peplos for Athena: A New Edition of *IG* II² 1060 + *IG* II² 1036." *Zeitschrift für Papyrologie und Epigraphik* 142:65–86.

Allen, R. E., tr. 1996. *Ion, Hippias Minor, Laches, Protagoras.* New Haven.

Allen, T. W., ed. 1912. *Homeri Opera.* Vol. 5, *Hymns, Cycle, Fragments.* Oxford.

———. 1924. *Homer: The Origins and the Transmission.* Oxford.

Allen, T. W., and D. B. Monro, eds. 1920. *Homeri Opera.* 5 vols. 3rd ed. Oxford.

Aloni, A. 1986. *Tradizioni arcaiche della Troade e composizione dell'Iliade.* Milan.

———. 1989. *L'aedo e i tiranni: Ricerche sull'Inno omerico ad Apollo.* Rome.

———. 2006. *Da Pilo a Sigeo: Poemi cantori e scrivani al tempo dei tiranni.* Alessandria.

Anderson, M. J. 1997. *The Fall of Troy in Early Greek Poetry and Art.* Oxford.

Antonelli, L. 2000. "I Pisistratidi al Sigeo: Instanze pan-ioniche nell'Atene tirannica." *Anemos* 1:9–58.

Apthorp, M. J. 1980. *The Manuscript Evidence for Interpolation in Homer.* Heidelberg.

Armstrong, R., and C. Dué, eds. 2006. *The Homerizon: Conceptual Interrogations in Homeric Studies.* Classics@ 3, http://chs.harvard.edu/publications.sec/classics.ssp.

Asheri, D., A. Lloyd, and A. Corcella. 2007. *A Commentary on Herodotus, Books I–IV.* Ed. O. Murray and A. Moreno. Tr. B. Graziosi et al. Oxford.

Austin, R. G., ed. 1964. *P. Vergili Maronis Aeneidos liber secundus.* Oxford.

Bader, F. 1989. *La langue des dieux, ou l'hermétisme des poètes indo-européens.* Pisa.

Bakker, E. J. 1997. *Poetry in Speech: Orality and Homeric Discourse.* Ithaca.

———. 2002. "The Making of History: Herodotus' *historiēs apodexis.*" In E. J. Bakker, I. J. F. De Jong, and H. van Wees, eds., *Brill's Companion to Herodotus:* 3–32. Leiden.

———. 2005. *Pointing at the Past: From Formula to Performance in Homeric Poetics.* Hellenic Studies 12. Cambridge, Mass., and Washington, D.C.

Bakker, E. J., and A. Kahane, eds. 1997. *Written Voices, Spoken Signs: Tradition, Performance, and the Epic Text.* Cambridge, Mass.

Barber, E. J. W. 1991. *Prehistoric Textiles: The Development of Cloth in the Neolithic and Bronze Ages, with Special Reference to the Aegean.* Princeton.

———. 1992. "The Peplos of Athena." In Neils 1992a: 103–17. [Notes at pp. 208–10.]

Barchiesi, A. 1998. "The Statue of Athena at Troy and Carthage." In P. Knox and C. Foss, eds., *Style and Tradition: Studies in Honor of Wendell Clausen:* 130–40. Stuttgart and Leipzig.

Barrett, W. S., ed. 1966. *Euripides: Hippolytos.* Oxford. [Corrected reprint of 1964 edition.]

Barron, J. P. 1964. "Religious Propaganda of the Delian League." *Journal of Hellenic Studies* 84:35–48.

Bassett, S. E. 1938. *The Poetry of Homer.* Berkeley and Los Angeles. [2nd ed., introd. B. Heiden (Lanham, Md., 2003).]

Beck, D. 2005. *Homeric Conversation.* Hellenic Studies 14. Cambridge, Mass., and Washington, D.C.

Benveniste, E. 1948. *Noms d'agent et noms d'action en indo-européen.* Paris.

Berczelly, L. 1992. "Pandora and Panathenaia: The Pandora Myth and the Sculptural Decoration of the Parthenon." *Acta ad Archaeologiam et Artium Historiam Pertinentia* 8:53–86.

Berenson Maclean, J. K., and E. B. Aitken, eds. 2001. *Flavius Philostratus: Heroikos.* Atlanta.

Bernabé, A., ed. 1987–2007. *Poetae Epici Graeci: Testimonia et Fragmenta.* Vols. 1–2.3. Berlin.

Bidez, J., ed. 1924. *L'empereur Julien: Œuvres complètes.* Vol. 1, part 2, *Lettres et fragments.* Paris.

Bird, G. D. 1994. "The Textual Criticism of an Oral Homer." In V. J. Gray, ed., *Nile, Ilissos and Tiber: Essays in Honour of Walter Kirkpatrick Lacey, Prudentia* 26.1: 35–52. Auckland.

Bittlestone, R., with J. Diggle and J. Underhill. 2005. *Odysseus Unbound: The Search for Homer's Ithaca.* Cambridge.

Blanc, A. 2008. *Les contraintes métriques dans la poésie homérique: L'emploi des thèmes nominaux sigmatiques dans l'hexamètre dactylique.* Louvain.

Blech, M. 1982. *Studien zum Kranz bei den Griechen.* Berlin and New York.

Blegen, C. W., with C. Boulter, J. Caskey, and M. Rawson. 1958. *Troy.* Vol. 4, *Settlements VIIa, VIIb and VIII.* Princeton.

Boedeker, D., and D. Sider, eds. 2001. *The New Simonides: Contexts of Praise and Desire.* Oxford.

Böhme, R. 1988. "Homer oder Orpheus?" *Zeitschrift für Papyrologie und Epigraphik* 71: 25–31.

———. 1989. "Neue Orpheusverse auf dem Derveni-Papyrus." *Emerita* 57:211–38.

Bollack, J. 1969. *Empédocle.* Vol. 3, *Les origines.* Part 1, *Commentaire.* Paris.

———. 1994. "Une action de restauration culturelle. La place accordée aux tragiques par le décret de Lycurgue." In M.-M. Mactoux and E. Geny, eds., *Mélanges Pierre Lévêque:* 13–24. Paris.

Brelich, A. 1958. *Gli eroi greci: Un problema storico-religioso.* Rome.

Broggiato, M. 1998. "Cratete di Mallo negli Scholl. A ad *Il.* 24.282 e ad *Il.* 9.169a." *Seminari Romani di Cultura Greca* 1:137–43.

———, ed. 2001. *Cratete di Mallo.* La Spezia.

Bundy, E. L. 1972. "The 'Quarrel between Kallimachos and Apollonios' Part I: The Epilogue of Kallimachos's 'Hymn to Apollo.'" *California Studies in Classical Antiquity* 5:39–94.

———. 1986. *Studia Pindarica*. Berkeley and Los Angeles. [Originally published in 1962 as *University of California Publications in Classical Philology* 18, nos. 1 and 2.]

Burgess, J. S. 2001. *The Tradition of the Trojan War in Homer and the Epic Cycle*. Baltimore.

———. 2004. "Performance and the Epic Cycle." *Classical Journal* 100:1–23.

———. 2006. "Tumuli of Achilles." In Armstrong and Dué 2006.

———. 2009. *The Death and Afterlife of Achilles*. Baltimore.

Burkert, W. 1960. "Das Lied von Ares und Aphrodite: Zum Verhältnis von Odyssee und Ilias." *Rheinisches Museum für Philologie* 103:130–44. [Republished in *Homer: German Scholarship in Translation*, tr. G. M. Wright and P. V. Jones (Oxford, 1997): 249–62.]

———. 1979. "Kynaithos, Polycrates, and the Homeric Hymn to Apollo." In G. W. Bowersock, W. Burkert, and M. C. J. Putnam, eds., *Arktouros: Hellenic Studies Presented to B. M. W. Knox:* 53–62. Berlin.

Calame, C. 2001. *Choruses of Young Women in Ancient Greece: Their Morphology, Religious Role, and Social Function*. Tr. D. Collins and J. Orion. 2nd ed. Lanham, Md.

———. 2005. *Masks of Authority: Fiction and Pragmatics in Ancient Greek Poetics*. Tr. P. M. Burk. Ithaca.

Cameron, A. 1990. "Isidore of Miletus and Hypatia: On the Editing of Mathematical Texts." *Greek, Roman and Byzantine Studies* 31:103–27.

———. 1995. *Callimachus and His Critics*. Princeton.

Carlisle, M., and O. Levaniouk, eds. 1999. *Nine Essays on Homer*. Lanham, Md.

Cassio, A. C. 1999. "Epica greca e scrittura tra VIII e VII a.C.: Madrepatria e colonie d'occidente." In G. Bagnasco Gianni and F. Cordano, eds., *Atti del Convegno "Scritture mediterranee tra il IX e il VII secolo a.C.":* 67–84. Milan.

———. 2002. "Early Editions of the Greek Epics and Homeric Textual Criticism in the Sixth and Fifth Centuries B.C." In F. Montanari, ed., *Omero tremila anni dopo:* 105–36. Rome.

———. 2003. "Ospitare in casa poeti orali: Omero, Testoride, Creofilo e Staroselac ([Herodot.] *vita Hom.* 190 ss. Allen; Plat. *Resp.* 600b)." *Quaderni dei Seminari Romani di Cultura Greca* 6:35–46.

Càssola, F., ed. 1975. *Inni Omerici*. Milan.

CEG. See P. A. Hansen 1983.

Chantraine, P. 1953. *Grammaire homérique*. Vol. 2, *Syntaxe*. Paris.

———. 1958. *Grammaire homérique*. Vol. 1, *Phonétique et morphologie*. 3rd ed. Paris.

———. 2009. *Dictionnaire étymologique de la langue grecque: Histoire des mots*. Ed. J. Taillardat, O. Masson, and J.-L. Perpillou. Paris. [Abbreviated *DELG*; includes supplement "Chroniques d'étymologie grecque," ed. A. Blanc, C. de Lamberterie, and J.-L. Perpillou, parts 1–10.]

Citti, V. 1966. "Le edizioni omeriche 'delle città.'" *Vichiana* 3:227–67.

Clader, L. L. 1976. *Helen: The Evolution from Divine to Heroic in Greek Epic Tradition*. Mnemosyne Supplement 42. Leiden.

Clay, D. 1988. "The Archaeology of the Temple of Juno in Carthage (*Aen.* I. 446–93)." *Classical Philology* 83:195–205.

———. 1991. "Alcman's *Partheneion*." *Quaderni Urbinati di Cultura Classica* 39:47–67.

———. 1992. "The World of Hesiod." *Ramus: Critical Studies in Greek and Roman Literature* 21:131–55.

———. 1998. "The Theory of the Literary Persona in Antiquity." *Materiali e Discussioni per l'Analisi dei Testi Classici* 40:9–40.

Clay, J. S. 1997. "The Homeric Hymns." In Morris and Powell 1997: 489–507.

———. 2007. "Homer's Trojan Theater." *Transactions of the American Philological Association* 137:233–52.

Colbeaux, M. A. 2005. "*Raconter la vie d'Homère dans l'antiquité: Édition commentée du traité anonyme, 'Au sujet d'Homère et d'Hésiode, de leurs origines et de leur joute,' et de la 'Vie d'Homère' attribué à Hérodote.*" Dissertation, Université Charles de Gaulle–Lille III.

Collins, D. 2004. *Master of the Game: Competition and Performance in Greek Poetry*. Hellenic Studies 7. Cambridge, Mass., and Washington, D.C.

Collins, L. 1988. *Studies in Characterization in the Iliad*. Frankfurt.

Cook, E. 1995. *The Odyssey at Athens: Myths of Cultural Origins*. Ithaca.

———. 1999. "'Active' and 'Passive' Heroics in the *Odyssey*." *Classical World* 93:149–67.

Cook, J. M. 1973. *The Troad: An Archaeological and Topographical Study*. Oxford.

———. 1984. "The Topography of the Plain of Troy." In Foxhall and Davies 1981: 163–72.

Cooper, J. M., and D. S. Hutchinson. 1997. *Plato: Complete Works*. Indianapolis.

Crane, G. 1988. *Calypso: Backgrounds and Conventions of the Odyssey*. Frankfurt.

Csapo, E., and M. C. Miller, eds. 2007. *The Origins of Theater in Ancient Greece and Beyond: From Ritual to Drama*. Cambridge.

Cuillandre, J. 1944. *La droite et la gauche dans les poèmes homériques en concordance avec la doctrine pythagoricienne et avec la tradition celtique*. Paris.

Currie, B. 2005. *Pindar and the Cult of Heroes*. Oxford.

D'Alessio, G. B. 2004. "Textual Fluctuations and Cosmic Streams: Ocean and Acheloios." *Journal of Hellenic Studies* 124:16–37.

———. 2005a. "The Megalai Ehoiai: A Survey of the Fragments." In Hunter 2005a: 176–216.

———. 2005b. "Pindar, Bacchylides, and Hesiodic Genealogical Poetry." In Hunter 2005a: 217–38.

Davidson, O. M. 2001a. "Some Iranian Poetic Tropes as Reflected in the 'Life of Ferdowsi' Traditions." In M. G. Schmidt and W. Bisang, eds., *Philologica et Linguistica: Historia, Pluralitas, Universitas—Festschrift für Helmut Humbach zum 80. Geburtstag am 4. Dezember 2001*, Supplement: 1–12. Trier.

———. 2001b. "La 'publication' des textes arabes sous forme de lectures publiques dans les mosquées." In Giard and Jacob 2001: 401–11.

Davies, M. 1994. "The Tradition about the First Sacred War." In Hornblower 1994: 193–212.

Day, J. W. 1989. "Rituals in Stone: Early Greek Grave Epigrams and Monuments." *Journal of Hellenic Studies* 109:16–28.

Debiasi, A. 2001. "Variazioni sul nome di Omero." *Hesperìa* 14:9–35.

———. 2004. *L'epica perduta: Eumelo, il Ciclo, l'occidente*. Hesperìa 20. Rome.

———. 2008. *Esiodo e l'occidente*. Hesperìa 24. Rome.

DELG. See Chantraine 2009.

De Martino, F. 1982. *Omero agonista in Delo*. Brescia.

Detienne, M. 1973. *Les maîtres de vérité dans la Grèce archaïque*. 2nd ed. Paris.

Deutsche Akademie der Wissenschaften zu Berlin. 1873–. *Inscriptiones Graecae*. Berlin. [Abbreviated *IG*.]

Diels, H., and W. Kranz, eds. 1951–52. *Die Fragmente der Vorsokratiker*. 3 vols. 6th ed. Berlin. [Abbreviated DK.]

DK. See Diels and Kranz 1951–52.

Dougherty, C. 2001. *The Raft of Odysseus: The Ethnographic Imagination of Homer's "Odyssey."* Oxford.

Drachmann, A. B., ed. 1903–27. *Scholia Vetera in Pindari Carmina*. 3 vols. Leipzig.

Dué, C. 2000. "Poetry and the *Dêmos*: State Regulation of a Civic Possession." In C. Blackwell, ed., *Dēmos: Classical Athenian Democracy*. Stoa Consortium, ed. R. Scaife and A. Mahoney. http://www.stoa.org/projects/demos/home.

———. 2001a. "Achilles' Golden Amphora in Aeschines' *Against Timarchus* and the Afterlife of Oral Tradition." *Classical Philology* 96:33–47.

———. 2001b. "*Sunt Aliquid Manes*: Homer, Plato, and Alexandrian Allusion in Propertius 4.7." *Classical Journal* 96:401–13.

———. 2002. *Homeric Variations on a Lament by Briseis*. Lanham, Md.

———. 2006. *The Captive Woman's Lament in Greek Tragedy*. Austin.

Durante, M. 1976. *Sulla preistoria della tradizione poetica greca*. Vol. 2, *Risultanze della comparazione indoeuropea*. Incunabula Graeca 64. Rome.

Dyer, R. 2006. *Suda on Line: Byzantine Lexicography* [ed. D. Whitehead et al.]. S.v. "Homeros" (Note 9). http: //www.stoa.org/sol.

Easton, D., J. D. Hawkins, A. G. Sherratt, and E. S. Sherratt. 2002. "Troy in Recent Perspective." *Anatolian Studies* 52:75–109.

Ebbott, M. 1999. "The Wrath of Helen: Self-Blame and Nemesis in the *Iliad*." In Carlisle and Levaniouk 1999: 3–20.

———. 2003. *Imagining Illegitimacy in Classical Greek Literature*. Lanham, Md.

Elmer, D. F. 2005. "Helen *Epigrammatopoios*." *Classical Antiquity* 24.1:1–39.

Erbse, H. 1959. "Über Aristarchs Iliasausgaben." *Hermes* 87:275–303.

———. 1960. *Beiträge zur Überlieferung der Iliasscholien*. Zetemata 24. Munich.

———, ed. 1969–88. *Scholia Graeca in Homeri Iliadem*. 7 vols. Berlin.

Erskine, A. 2001. *Troy between Greece and Rome: Local Tradition and Imperial Power*. Oxford.

Fantuzzi, M. 2007a. "Dioscoride e la storia del teatro." In E. Dettori and R. Pretagostini, eds., *La cultura ellenistica: Persistenza, innovazione, trasmissione—Atti del Convegno COFIN 2003, Università di Roma Tor Vergata, 19–21 settembre 2005*: 105–23. Rome.

———. 2007b. "La mousa del lamento in Euripide, e il lamento della Musa nel Reso ascritto a Euripide." *Eikasmos* 18:173–99.

Fantuzzi, M., and R. Pretagostini, eds. 1995–96. *Struttura e storia dell'esametro greco*. 2 vols. Rome.

Fearn, D. 2003. "Mapping Phleious: Politics and Myth-Making in Bacchylides 9." *Classical Quarterly* 3:347–67.

Ferrari, G. 1997. "Figures in the Text: Metaphors and Riddles in the *Agamemnon*." *Classical Philology* 92:1–45.

———. 2000. "The *Ilioupersis* in Athens." *Harvard Studies in Classical Philology* 100:119–50.

FGH. See Jacoby 1923–.

Figuiera, T. J. 1981. *Aegina: Society and Politics*. New York.

———. 1985. "The Theognidea and Megarian Society." In T. J. Figueira and G. Nagy, eds., *Theognis of Megara: Poetry and the Polis*: 112–58. Baltimore.

———. 1991. *Athens and Aigina in the Age of Imperial Colonization.* Baltimore.

———. 1993. *Excursions in Epichoric History: Aeginetan Essays.* Lanham, Md.

Finkelberg, M. 2000. "The *Cypria,* the *Iliad,* and the Problem of Multiformity in Oral and Written Tradition." *Classical Philology* 95:1–11.

Flashar, H. 1958. *Der Dialog "Ion" als Zeugnis platonischer Philosophie.* Berlin.

Ford, A. 2002. *The Origins of Criticism: Literary Culture and Poetic Theory in Classical Greece.* Princeton.

Fowler, R. 1998. "Genealogical Thinking, Hesiod's *Catalogue,* and the Creation of the Hellenes." *Proceedings of the Cambridge Philological Society* 44:1–19.

Foxhall, L., and J. K. Davies, eds. 1984. *The Trojan War: Its Historicity and Context*—Papers of the First Greenbank Colloquium, Liverpool, 1981. Bristol.

Frame, D. 1978. *The Myth of Return in Early Greek Epic.* New Haven.

———. 2009. *Hippota Nestor.* Hellenic Studies 37. Cambridge, Mass., and Washington, D.C.

Fraser, P. M. 1972. *Ptolemaic Alexandria.* 3 vols. Oxford.

Frazer, J. G., ed. 1929. *Publius Ovidius Naso, Fastorum libri sex.* 5 vols. London.

Freedman, D. G. 1998. "Sokrates: The Athenian Oracle of Plato's Imagination." Ph.D. dissertation, Harvard University.

Friedländer, L., ed. 1850. *Nicanoris "Peri Iliakēs stigmēs" reliquiae emendatiores.* Königsberg.

———, ed. 1853. *Aristonici "Peri sēmeiōn Iliados" reliquiae emendatiores.* Göttingen.

Funghi, M. S. 1997. "The Derveni Papyrus." In Laks and Most 1997: 25–37.

Gaede, R., ed. 1880. *Demetrii Scepsii quae supersunt.* Greifswald.

Gentili, B. 1988. *Poetry and Its Public in Ancient Greece: From Homer to the Fifth Century.* Tr. A. T. Cole. Baltimore.

Gérard-Rousseau, M. 1968. *Les mentions religieuses dans les tablettes mycéniennes.* Incunabula Graeca 29. Rome.

Giard, L., and C. Jacob, eds. 2001. *Des Alexandries.* Vol. 1, *Du livre au texte.* Paris.

Giovannini, A. 1969. *Étude historique sur l'origine du "Catalogue des vaisseaux."* Bern.

Goh, M. 2004. "The Poetics of Chariot Driving and Rites of Passage in Ancient Greece." Ph.D. dissertation, Harvard University.

Goldhill, S. 1991. *The Poet's Voice: Essays on Poetics and Greek Literature.* Cambridge.

Gomme, A. W. 1956. *A Historical Commentary on Thucydides.* Vol. 2, *Books II–III.* Oxford.

González, J. M. 2000. "*Mousai Hypophetores*: Apollonius of Rhodes on Inspiration and Interpretation." *Harvard Studies in Classical Philology* 100:269–92.

Gow, A. S. F., ed. 1952. *Theocritus.* 2 vols. 2nd ed. Cambridge.

Grafton, A., G. W. Most,, and J. E. G. Zetzel, eds. 1985. *F. A. Wolf: Prolegomena to Homer.* Princeton.

Graziosi, B. 2002. *Inventing Homer: The Early Reception of Epic.* Cambridge.

Grethlein, J. 2007. "The Poetics of the Bath in the *Iliad.*" *Harvard Studies in Classical Philology* 103:25–49.

Griffith, M. 1995. "Brilliant Dynasts: Power and Politics in the *Oresteia.*" *Classical Antiquity* 14.1:62–129.

Gruen, E. 1990. *Studies in Greek Culture and Roman Policy.* Leiden.

———. 1992. *Culture and National Identity in Republican Rome.* Ithaca.

Habinek, T. 1998. "Singing, Speaking, Making, Writing: Classical Alternatives to Literature and Literary Studies." *Stanford Humanities Review* 6:65–75.

Hall, J. M. 1997. *Ethnic Identity in Greek Antiquity*. New York.

———. 2002. *Hellenicity: Between Ethnicity and Culture*. Chicago.

Hansen, P. A., ed. 1983. *Carmina epigraphica Graeca saeculorum viii–v a.Chr.n.* Texte und Kommentare 12. Berlin and New York. [Abbreviated *CEG*.]

Hansen, W. F. 2002. *Ariadne's Thread: A Guide to International Tales Found in Classical Literature*. Ithaca.

Hardie, P. 1985. "Imago Mundi: Cosmological and Ideological Aspects of the Shield of Achilles." *Journal of Hellenic Studies* 105:11–31.

———. 1986. *Virgil's Aeneid: Cosmos and Imperium*. Oxford.

Haslam, M. 1997. "Homeric Papyri and Transmission of the Text." In Morris and Powell 1997: 55–100.

Haubold, J. 2000. *Homer's People: Epic Poetry and Social Formations*. Cambridge.

———. 2004. "Serse, Onomacrito e la ricezione di Omero." In G. Zanetto et al., eds., *Momenti della ricezione omerica*, Quaderni di Acme 67: 19–35. Milan.

Hedreen, G. 2001. *Capturing Troy: The Narrative Functions of Landscape in Archaic and Early Classical Greek Art*. Ann Arbor.

Heinze, R. 1915. *Virgils epische Technik*. 3rd ed. Leipzig.

Heinzelmann, J. 1988. "Offenbachs Hoffmann: Dokumente anstelle von Erzählungen," with "Faksimile der Akte IV und V des pariser Zensurlibrettos vom Januar 1881 der 'Contes d'Hoffmann.'" In G. Brandstetter, ed., *Jacques Offenbachs Hoffmanns Erzählungen: Konzeption, Rezeption, Dokumentation*: 421–63. Laaber.

Heitsch, E. 1965. *Aphroditehymnus, Aeneas und Homer*. Hypomnemata 15. Göttingen.

Helck, H. 1905. *De Cratetis Mallotae studiis criticis quae ad Iliadem spectant*. Leipzig.

Heldmann, K. 1982. *Die Niederlage Homers im Dichterwettstreit mit Hesiod*. Hypomnemata 75. Göttingen.

Henrichs, A. 1993. "Response." In A. W. Bulloch, E. S. Gruen, A. A. Long, and A. F. Stewart, eds., *Images and Ideologies: Self-Definition in the Hellenistic World*: 171–95. Berkeley and Los Angeles.

Hirschberger, M. 2004. *Gynaikōn Katalogos und Megalai Ēhoiai: Ein Kommentar zu den Fragmenten zweier hesiodeischer Epen*. Beiträge zur Altertumskunde 198. Munich and Leipzig.

Hodot, R. 1990. *Le dialecte éolien d'Asie: La langue des inscriptions VIIe s. a.C.–IVe s. p.C.* Paris.

Hornblower, S. 1991. *A Commentary on Thucydides*. Vol. 1, *Books I–III*. Oxford.

———, ed. 1994. *Greek Historiography*. Oxford.

———. 1996. *A Commentary on Thucydides*. Vol. 2, *Books IV–V.24*. Oxford.

Horrocks, G. 1987. "The Ionian Epic Tradition: Was There an Aeolic Phase in Its Development?" *Minos* 20–22:269–94.

———. 1997. "Homer's Dialect." In Morris and Powell 1997: 193–217.

Householder, F. W., and G. Nagy. 1972. *Greek: A Survey of Recent Work*. Janua Linguarum, Series Practica 211. The Hague.

How, W. W., and J. Wells. 1912. *A Commentary on Herodotus*. 2 vols. Oxford. [Revised edition 1928.]

Hunter, R. L. 1997. "(B)ionic Man: Callimachus' Iambic Program." *Proceedings of the Cambridge Philological Society* 43:41–51.

———, ed. 1999. *Theocritus: Idylls, Selections*. Cambridge.

———, ed. 2005a. *The Hesiodic "Catalogue of Women": Constructions and Reconstructions*. Cambridge.

———. 2005b. "The Hesiodic *Catalogue* and Hellenistic Poetry." In Hunter 2005a: 239–65.

IG. See Deutsche Akademie der Wissenschaften zu Berlin 1873–.

Jacoby, F., ed. 1923–. *Die Fragmente der griechischen Historiker*. Leiden. [Abbreviated *FGH*.]

Janko, R. 1982. *Homer, Hesiod, and the Hymns: Diachronic Development of Epic Diction*. Cambridge.

———, ed. 1987. *Aristotle: Poetics*. Indianapolis.

———. 1992. *The Iliad: A Commentary*. Vol. 4, *Books 13–16*. General editor G. S. Kirk. Cambridge.

Jebb, R. C. 1893. *The Attic Orators*. 2 vols. 2nd ed. London.

Jensen, M. Skafte 1980. *The Homeric Question and the Oral-Formulaic Theory*. Copenhagen.

Jowett, B., ed. 1895. *The Dialogues of Plato*. New York.

Kallet-Marx, L. 1989. "Did Tribute Fund the Parthenon?" *Classical Antiquity* 8:252–66.

Kassel, R. 1973. "Antimachos in der *Vita Chisiana* des Dionysios Periegetes." In C. Schäublin, ed., *Catalepton: Festschrift für Bernhard Wyss zum 80. Geburtstag*: 69–76. Basel.

Kayan, I. 1991. "Holocene Geomorphic Evolution of the Beşik Plain and Changing Environment of Ancient Man." *Studia Troica* 1:79–92.

———. 1995. "The Troia Bay and Supposed Harbour Sites in the Bronze Age." *Studia Troica* 5:211–35.

———. 1996. "Holocene Stratigraphy of the Lower Karamenderes-Dumrek Plain and Archaeological Material in the Alluvial Sediments to the North of the Troia Ridge." *Studia Troica* 6:239–49.

———. 1997. "Geomorphological Evolution of the Ciplak Valley and Archaeological Material in the Alluvial Sediments to the South of the Lower City of Troia." *Studia Troica* 7:489–507.

Kayan, I., with E. Öner, L. Uncu, B. Hocaoglu, and S. Vardar. 2003. "Geoarchaeological Interpretations of the 'Troian Bay.' " In G. A. Wagner, E. Pernicka, and H.-P. Uerpmann, eds., *Troia and the Troad: Scientific Approaches, Natural Science in Archaeology*: 379–401. Berlin and New York.

Kazazis, J. N., and A. Rengakos, eds. 1999. *Euphrosyne: Studies in Ancient Epic and Its Legacy in Honor of Dimitris N. Maronitis*. Stuttgart.

Keaney, J. J., and R. Lamberton, eds. 1996. *[Plutarch]: Essay on the Life and Poetry of Homer*. American Classical Studies 40. Atlanta.

Kirk, G. S., ed. 1985. *The Iliad: A Commentary*. Vol. 1, *Books 1–4*. Cambridge.

———. 1990. *The Iliad: A Commentary*. Vol. 2, *Books 5–8*. Cambridge.

Koller, H. 1956. "Das kitharodische Prooimion: Eine formgeschichtliche Untersuchung." *Philologus* 100:159–206.

———. 1957. "Hypokrisis und Hypokrites." *Museum Helveticum* 14:100–107.

Konstan, D. 2001. *Pity Transformed.* London.

Kosslyn, S. M. 1994. *Image and Brain: The Resolution of the Imagery Debate.* Cambridge, Mass.

Kouremenos, T., G. Parássoglou, and K. Tsantsanoglou, eds. 2006. *The Derveni Papyrus,* with Introduction and Commentary. Florence.

Kowalzig, B. 2007. *Singing for the Gods: Performances of Myth and Ritual in Archaic and Classical Greece.* Oxford.

Kraft, J. C., with I. Kayan and E. Oğuz. 1980."Geomorphic Reconstructions in the Environs of Ancient Troy." *Science* 209, no. 4458:776–82.

———. 1982. "Geology and Paleogeographic Reconstructions of the Vicinity of Troy." In G. Rapp, Jr., and J. A. Gifford, eds., *Troy: The Archaeological Geology,* Supplementary Monograph 4: 11–41. Princeton.

Kraft, J. C., with I. Kayan, H. Brückner, and G. Rapp. 2001. "A Geologic Analysis of Ancient Landscapes and the Harbors of Ephesus and the Artemision in Anatolia." *Jahreshefte des Österreichischen Archäologischen Institutes zu Wien* 69:175–233.

———. 2003a. "Sedimentary Facies Patterns and the Interpretation of Paleogeographies of Ancient Troia." In G. A. Wagner, E. Pernicka, and H.-P. Uerpmann, eds., *Troia and the Troad: Scientific Approaches, Natural Science in Archaeology:* 361–77. Berlin and New York.

Kraft, J. C., with G. Rapp, I. Kayan, and J. V. Luce. 2003b. "Harbor Areas at Ancient Troy: Sedimentology and Geomorphology Complement Homer's *Iliad.*" *Geology* 31/2:163–66.

Kullmann, W. 1960. *Die Quellen der Ilias.* Hermes Einzelschriften 14. Wiesbaden.

Kurke, L. 1991. *The Traffic in Praise: Pindar and the Poetics of Social Economy.* Ithaca.

Labarbe, J. 1949. *L' Homère de Platon.* Liège.

Laks, A., and G. W. Most, eds. 1997. *Studies on the Derveni Papyrus.* Oxford.

de Lamberterie, C. 1997. "Milman Parry et Antoine Meillet." In Létoublon 1997: 9–22.

———. 2001. "Milman Parry and Antoine Meillet." Trans. A. Goldhammer. In Loraux, Nagy, and Slatkin 2001: 409–21. [English translation of de Lamberterie 1997.]

Lapatin, K. D. S. 2001. *Chryselephantine Statuary in the Ancient Mediterranean World.* Oxford.

Leaf, W. 1923. *Strabo on the Troad.* Cambridge.

Lee, M. M. 2004. "Evil Wealth of Raiment: Deadly πέπλοι in Greek Tragedy." *The Classical Journal* 99.3:253–79.

Lehrs, K. 1882. *De Aristarchi Studiis Homericis.* 3rd ed. Leipzig. [1st ed. 1833; 2nd ed. 1865.]

Leipen, N. 1971. *Athena Parthenos: A Reconstruction.* Toronto.

Lepschy, A. 1998. "Il colore della porpora." In O. Longo, ed., *La porpora: Realtà e immaginario di un colore simbolico*—Atti del Convegno di studio, Venezia, 24 e 25 ottobre 1996: 53–66. Venice.

Lessing, G. E. 1962. *Laocoön: An Essay on the Limits of Painting and Poetry.* Tr. E. A. McCormick. Baltimore. [Original German edition 1766; McCormick translation revised 1984.]

Létoublon, F., ed. 1997. *Hommage à Milman Parry: Le style formulaire de l'épopée et la théorie de l'oralité poétique.* Amsterdam.

Levaniouk, O. 1999. "Penelope and the *Pēnelops.*" In Carlisle and Levaniouk 1999: 95–136.

———. 2000a. "*Aithōn,* Aithon, and Odysseus." *Harvard Studies in Classical Philology* 100:25–51.

———. 2000b. "Odyssean Usages of Local Traditions." Ph.D. dissertation, Harvard University.

Liddell, H. G., R. Scott, and H. Stuart Jones, eds. 1940. *A Greek-English Lexicon*. 9th ed. Oxford. [Abbreviated LSJ.]

Lohmann, D. 1988. *Die Andromache-Szenen der Ilias*. Spudasmata 42. Hildesheim.

Loraux, N. 1987. "Le lien de la division." *Le Cahier du Collège International de Philosophie* 4:101–24.

Loraux, N., G. Nagy, and L. Slatkin, eds. 2001. *Antiquities*. Tr. A. Goldhammer et al. New York. [Volume 3 of The New Press series "Postwar French Thought," ed. R. Naddaff.]

Lord, A. B. 1960. *The Singer of Tales*. Harvard Studies in Comparative Literature 24. Cambridge, Mass. [2nd ed. 2000, ed. and introd. (pp. vii–xxix) S. Mitchell and G. Nagy.]

———. 1995. *The Singer Resumes the Tale*. Ed. M. L. Lord. Ithaca.

Louden, B. 1996. "Epeios, Odysseus, and the Indo-European Metaphor for Poet." *Journal of Indo-European Studies* 24:277–304.

———. 2002. "Eurybates, Odysseus, and the Duals in Book 9 of the *Iliad*." *Colby Quarterly* 38:62–76.

Lowenstam, S. 1997. "Talking Vases: The Relationship between the Homeric Poems and Archaic Representations of Epic Myth." *Transactions of the American Philological Association* 127:21–76.

LSJ. See Liddell, Scott, and Jones 1940.

Ludwich, A. 1884–85. *Aristarchs homerische Textkritik nach den Fragmenten des Didymos*. 2 vols. Leipzig.

———. 1898. *Die Homervulgata als voralexandrinisch erwiesen*. Leipzig.

Lührs, D. 1992. *Untersuchungen zu den Athetesen Aristarchs in der Ilias und zu ihrer Behandlung im Corpus der exegetischen Scholien*. Beiträge zur Altertumswissenschaft 11. Hildesheim.

Lyne, R. O. A. M., ed. 1978. *Ciris: A Poem Attributed to Vergil,* with Introduction and Commentary. Cambridge.

Malkin, I. 1998. *The Returns of Odysseus: Ethnicity and Colonization*. Berkeley and Los Angeles.

Mansfield, J. M. 1985. "The Robe of Athena and the Panathenaic Peplos." Ph.D. dissertation, University of California, Berkeley.

Martin, J., ed. 1974. *Scholia in Aratum vetera*. Stuttgart.

Martin, R. P. 1989. *The Language of Heroes: Speech and Performance in the Iliad*. Ithaca.

———. 1992. "Hesiod's Metanastic Poetics." *Ramus* 21:11–33.

———. 1993. "Telemachus and the Last Hero Song." *Colby Quarterly* 29:222–40.

———. 2000a. "Wrapping Homer Up: Cohesion, Discourse, and Deviation in the *Iliad*." In A. Sharrock and H. Morales, eds., *Intratextuality: Greek and Roman Textual Relations*: 43–65. Oxford.

———. 2000b. "Synchronic Aspects of Homeric Performance: The Evidence of the *Hymn to Apollo*." In A. M. González de Tobia, ed., *Una nueva visión de la cultura griega antigua hacia el fin del milenio*: 403–32. La Plata.

———. 2001. "Rhapsodizing Orpheus." *Kernos* 14:23–33.

———. 2005. "Epic as Genre." In J. M. Foley, ed., *A Companion to Ancient Epic*: 9–19. Oxford.

McNamee, K. 1981. "Aristarchus and Everyman's Homer." *Greek, Roman and Byzantine Studies* 22:247–55.

———. 1992. *Sigla and Select Marginalia in Greek Literary Papyri.* Brussels.

Meiggs, R. 1972. *The Athenian Empire.* Oxford.

Meiggs, R., and D. Lewis. 1988. *A Selection of Greek Historical Inscriptions to the End of the Fifth Century B.C.* Rev. ed. Oxford. [1st ed. 1969.]

Meillet, A. 1935. *Aperçu d'une histoire de la langue grecque.* 4th ed. Paris. [7th ed. 1965, with new bibliography by O. Masson.]

Miller, A. M. 1986. *From Delos to Delphi: A Literary Study of the "Homeric Hymn to Apollo."* Leiden.

Montanari, F. 1979. *Studi di filologia omerica antica.* Vol. 1. Pisa.

———. 1998. "Zenodotus, Aristarchus and the *Ekdosis* of Homer. In Most 1998: 1–21.

———. 2002a. "Alexandrian Homeric Philology: The Form of the *Ekdosis* and the *Variae Lectiones.*" In M. Reichel and A. Rengakos, eds., *ΕΠΕΑ ΠΤΕΡΟΕΝΤΑ: Beiträge zur Homerforschung:* 119–40. Stuttgart.

———. 2002b. "Filologia ed erudizione antica." In *Da aiōn a eikasmos: Atti della giornata di studio sulla figura e l'opera di Enzo Degani,* Eikasmos, Studi 8: 73–88. Bologna.

———. 2004a. "La filologia omerica antica e la storia del testo omerico." In A. Bierl, A. Schmitt, and A. Willi, eds., *Antike Literatur in neuer Deutung:* 127–43. Munich.

———. 2004b. "The PAWAG Project (Poorly Attested Words in Ancient Greek): Ancient Greek Lexicography on Line." *Euphrosyne* 32:75–78.

———. 2008. "Aristotele, Zenodoto, Aristarco e il serpente pietrificato di *Iliade* II 319." In P. Arduini et al., eds., *Studi offerti ad Alessandro Perutelli,* vol. 2: 237–43. Rome.

Moore, J. D. 1974. "The Date of Plato's *Ion.*" *Greek, Roman and Byzantine Studies* 15:421–39.

Morris, I., and B. Powell, eds. 1997. *A New Companion to Homer.* Leiden.

Most, G. W., ed. 1998. *Editing Texts / Texte edieren.* Aporemata II. Göttingen.

Muellner, L. 1976. *The Meaning of Homeric EYXOMAI through Its Formulas.* Innsbruck.

———. 1990. "The Simile of the Cranes and Pygmies: A Study of Homeric Metaphor." *Harvard Studies in Classical Philology* 93:59–101.

———. 1996. *The Anger of Achilles: Mênis in Greek Epic.* Ithaca.

Murray, P., ed. 1996. *Plato on Poetry: Ion, Republic 376e–398b, Republic 595–608b.* Cambridge.

Nagy, B. 1972. "The Athenian Ergastinai and the Panathenaic Peplos." Ph.D. dissertation, Harvard University.

———. 1978a. "The Ritual in Slab-V East of the Parthenon Frieze." *Classical Philology* 73:137–41.

———. 1978b. "The Athenian Athlothetai" *Greek, Roman and Byzantine Studies* 19:307–14.

———. 1980. "A Late Panathenaic Document." *Ancient World* 3:106–11.

———. 1983. "The Peplotheke." In K. Rigsby, ed., *Studies Presented to Sterling Dow, Greek, Roman and Byzantine Studies Monographs,* 10: 227–32. Durham, N.C.

———. 1991. "The Procession to Phaleron." *Historia* 40:288–306.

———. 1992. "Athenian Officials on the Parthenon Frieze." *American Journal of Archaeology* 96:55–69.

———. 1994. "Alcibiades' Second Profanation." *Historia* 43:275–85.

Nagy, G. 1969. Review of J. Chadwick, *The Decipherment of Linear B,* 2nd ed. (Cambridge, 1967). *General Linguistics* 9:123–32.

———. 1972. "Introduction," "Part I," "Part II," and "Conclusions." In F. W. Householder and

G. Nagy, *Greek: A Survey of Recent Work,* Janua Linguarum, Series Practica 211: 15–72. The Hague.

———. 1974. *Comparative Studies in Greek and Indic Meter.* Harvard Studies in Comparative Literature 33. Cambridge, Mass.

———. 1979. *The Best of the Achaeans: Concepts of the Hero in Archaic Greek Poetry.* Baltimore.

———. 1985. "Theognis and Megara: A Poet's Vision of His City." In T. J. Figueira and G. Nagy, eds., *Theognis of Megara: Poetry and the Polis:* 22–81. Baltimore.

———. 1990a. *Pindar's Homer: The Lyric Possession of an Epic Past.* Baltimore.

———. 1990b. *Greek Mythology and Poetics.* Ithaca.

———. 1993. "Alcaeus in Sacred Space." In R. Pretagostini, ed., *Tradizione e innovazione nella cultura greca da Omero all'età ellenistica: Scritti in onore di Bruno Gentili:* 221–25. Rome.

———. 1994a/1995. "Transformations of Choral Lyric Traditions in the Context of Athenian State Theater." *Arion* 3:41–55.

———. 1994b/1995. "A Mycenaean Reflex in Homer: *Phorênai.*" *Minos* 29–30:171–75.

———. 1994c/1995. "Genre and Occasion." *ΜΗΤΙΣ: Revue d'Anthropologie du Monde Grec Ancien* 9/10:11–25.

———. 1996a. *Poetry as Performance: Homer and Beyond.* Cambridge.

———. 1996b. *Homeric Questions.* Austin.

———. 1996c. "Metrical Convergences and Divergences in Early Greek Poetry and Song." In Fantuzzi and Pretagostini 1996, vol. 2: 63–110.

———. 1998. "The Library of Pergamon as a Classical Model." In H. Koester, ed., *Pergamon: Citadel of the Gods, Harvard Theological Studies* 46: 185–232. Philadelphia.

———. 1999. *The Best of the Achaeans: Concepts of the Hero in Archaic Greek Poetry.* 2nd ed. Baltimore. [References in the notes to the 2nd edition concern relevant observations in the new introduction. Published in French as *Le meilleur des achéens: La fabrique du héros dans la poésie grecque archaïque,* tr. J. Carlier and N. Loraux (Paris, 1999).]

———. 2000a. Review of West 1998b. *Bryn Mawr Classical Review* 2000.09.12. http://ccat.sas.upenn.edu/bmcr/2000/2000-09-12.html.

———. 2000b. "Epic as Music: Rhapsodic Models of Homer in Plato's *Timaeus* and *Critias.*" In K. Reichl, ed., *The Oral Epic: Performance and Music:* 41–67. Berlin. [Rewritten as chapter 2 in Nagy 2002.]

———. 2000c. "Homeric *humnos* as a Rhapsodic Term." In A. M. González de Tobia, ed., *Una nueva visión de la cultura griega antigua hacia el fin del milenio:* 385–401. La Plata.

———. 2000d. "Distortion diachronique dans l'art homérique: Quelques précisions." In C. Darbo-Peschanski, ed., *Constructions du temps dans le monde ancien:* 417–26. Paris.

———. 2000e. "Reading Greek Poetry Aloud: Evidence from the Bacchylides Papyri." *Quaderni Urbinati di Cultura Classica* 64:7–28.

———. 2000f. "'Dream of a Shade': Refractions of Epic Vision in Pindar's *Pythian* 8 and Aeschylus' *Seven against Thebes.*" *Harvard Studies in Classical Philology* 100:97–118.

———. 2001a. "Homeric Poetry and Problems of Multiformity: The 'Panathenaic Bottleneck.'" *Classical Philology* 96:109–19. [Rewritten as chapter 2 in Nagy 2004a.]

———. 2001b. "The Textualizing of Homer." In J. Helldén, M. S. Jensen, and T. Pettitt, eds., "Inclinate Aurem": *Oral Perspectives on Early European Verbal Culture:* 57–84. Odense.

————. 2001c. "Reading Bakhtin Reading the Classics: An Epic Fate for Conveyors of the Heroic Past." In R. B. Branham, ed., *Bakhtin and the Classics:* 71–96. Evanston.

————. 2001d. "Éléments orphiques chez Homère." *Kernos* 14:1–9.

————. 2001e. "The Sign of the Hero: A Prologue." In J. K. Berenson Maclean and E. B. Aitken, eds., *Flavius Philostratus: Heroikos:* xv–xxxv. Atlanta.

————. 2001f. "Η ποιητική της προφορικότητας και η ομηρική έρευνα." In A. Rengakos, ed., Νεκρά γράμματα· Οι κλασσικές σπουδές στον 21ο αιώνα: 135–46. Athens.

————. 2001g. Electronic publication of introductions and suggested bibliographies for Nagy 2001h. http://chs.harvard.edu.

————, ed. 2001h1. *Greek Literature.* Vol. 1, *The Oral Traditional Background of Ancient Greek Literature.* New York.

————, ed. 2001h2. *Greek Literature.* Vol. 2, *Homer and Hesiod as Prototypes of Greek Literature.* New York.

————. 2002. *Plato's Rhapsody and Homer's Music: The Poetics of the Panathenaic Festival in Classical Athens.* Cambridge, Mass., and Athens.

————. 2003a. *Homeric Responses.* Austin.

————. 2003b. Review of West 2001. *Gnomon* 75:481–501.

————. 2004a. *Homer's Text and Language.* Urbana.

————. 2004b. "Transmission of Archaic Greek Sympotic Songs: From Lesbos to Alexandria." *Critical Inquiry* 31:26–48.

————. 2004c. "Poetics of Repetition in Homer." In Yatromanolakis and Roilos 2004: 139–48.

————. 2004d. "Homeric Echoes in Posidippus." In B. Acosta-Hughes, E. Kosmetatou, and M. Baumbach, eds., *Labored in Papyrus Leaves: Perspectives on an Epigram Collection Attributed to Posidippus (P.Mil.Vogl. VIII 309),* Hellenic Studies 2: 57–64. Cambridge, Mass., and Washington, D.C.

————. 2004e. "L'aède épique en auteur: La tradition des Vies d'Homère." In C. Calame and R. Chartier, eds., *Identités d'auteur dans l'antiquité et la tradition européenne:* 41–67. Grenoble.

————. 2005a. "The Epic Hero." In J. M. Foley, ed., *A Companion to Ancient Epic:* 71–89. Oxford. [The citations follow the paragraph numbering of an expanded 2006 version that is available at http://chs.harvard.edu.]

————. 2005b. Review of Boedeker and Sider 2001. *Classical Review* 55:407–9.

————. 2005c. "An Apobatic Moment for Achilles as Athlete at the Festival of the Panathenaia." *Imeros* 5:311–17. [For a revised version, see Nagy 2009d.]

————. 2006a. "Homer's Name Revisited." In G.-J. Pinault and D. Petit, eds., *La langue poétique indo-européenne:* Actes du Colloque de travail de la Société des Études Indo-Européennes (Indogermanische Gesellschaft / Society for Indo-European Studies), Paris, 22–24 octobre 2003, Collection Linguistique de la Société de Linguistique de Paris, vol. 91: 317–30. Louvain and Paris.

————. 2006b. "Hymnic Elements in Empedocles (B 35 DK = 201 Bollack)." *Revue de Philosophie Ancienne* 24:51–61.

————. 2007a. "Emergence of Drama: Introduction and Discussion." In Csapo and Miller 2007: 121–25.

————. 2007b. "Did Sappho and Alcaeus Ever Meet?" In A. Bierl, R. Lämmle, and K. Wesselmann, eds., *Literatur und Religion:* vol. 1, *Wege zu einer mythisch-rituellen Poetik bei den Griechen,* vol. 1, MythosEikonPoiesis 1.1: 211–69. Berlin and New York. [Revised edition 2009, http://chs.harvard.edu.]

———. 2007c. "Lyric and Greek Myth." In R. D. Woodard, ed., *The Cambridge Companion to Greek Mythology:* 19–51. Cambridge.

———. 2007d. "Homer and Greek Myth." In R. D. Woodard, ed., *The Cambridge Companion to Greek Mythology:* 52–82. Cambridge.

———. 2008a. *Homer the Classic.* Online edition. http://chs.harvard.edu.

———. 2008b. *Greek: An Updating of a Survey of Recent Work.* Cambridge, Mass., and Washington, D.C. [Updating of Nagy 1972. (Online ed.: http://chs.harvard.edu.) This edition tracks the page numberings of Nagy 1972.]

———. 2009a. *Homer the Classic.* Hellenic Studies 36. Cambridge, Mass., and Washington, D.C. [Print edition.]

———. 2009b. *Homer the Preclassic.* Online edition. http://chs.harvard.edu.

———. 2009c. "Hesiod and the Ancient Biographical Traditions." In F. Montanari, A. Rengakos, and C. Tsagalis, eds., *Brill's Companion to Hesiod:* 271–311. Leiden.

———. 2009d. "An Apobatic Moment for Achilles as Athlete at the Festival of the Panathenaia." [Revised version of Nagy 2005c: http://chs.harvard.edu.]

———. 2009e. "Perfecting the Hymn in the *Homeric Hymn to Apollo.*" In L. Athanassaki, R. P. Martin, and J. F. Miller, eds., *Apolline Politics and Poetics:* 17–44. Athens.

———. 2010. *Homer the Preclassic.* Berkeley and Los Angeles. [Print edition.]

Nagy, J. F. 1985. *The Wisdom of the Outlaw: The Boyhood Deeds of Finn in Gaelic Narrative Tradition.* Berkeley and Los Angeles.

———. 1986. "Orality in Medieval Irish Narrative." *Oral Tradition* 1:272–301.

———. 1990a. "Hierarchy, Heroes, and Heads: Indo-European Structures in Greek Myth." In L. Edmunds, ed., *Approaches to Greek Myth:* 199–238. Baltimore.

———. 1990b. *Conversing with Angels and Ancients: Literary Myths of Medieval Ireland.* Ithaca.

Nails, D. 2002. *The People of Plato: A Prosopography of Plato and Other Socratics.* Indianapolis.

Neils, J., ed. 1992a. *Goddess and Polis: The Panathenaic Festival in Ancient Athens.* Princeton.

———. 1992b. "The Panathenaia: An Introduction." In Neils 1992a: 13–27. [Notes at pp. 194–95.]

Neuschäfer, B. 1987. *Origenes als Philologe.* 2 vols. Schweizerische Beiträge zur Altertumswissenschaft 18, nos. 1 and 2. Basel.

Nick, G. 2002. *Die Athena Parthenos: Studien zum griechischen Kultbild und seiner Rezeption.* Mitteilungen des Deutschen Archäologischen Instituts, Athenische Abteilung, Beiheft 19. Mainz.

Nickau, K. 1977. *Untersuchungen zur textkritischen Methode des Zenodotos von Ephesos.* Berlin and New York.

Nietzsche, F. 1870. "Der florentinische Tractat über Homer und Hesiod, ihr Geschlecht und ihren Wettkampf." *Rheinisches Museum für Philologie* 25:528–40.

———. 1872. *Die Geburt der Tragödie aus dem Geiste der Musik.* Leipzig.

Nilsson, M. P. 1906. *Griechische Feste von religiöser Bedeutung, mit Ausschluss der attischen.* Leipzig.

Obbink, D. 1997. "Cosmology as Initiation vs. the Critique of Orphic Mysteries." In Laks and Most 1997: 39–54.

———. 2001. "The Genre of *Plataea*: Generic Unity in the New Simonides." In Boedeker and Sider 2001: 65–85.

Oettinger N. 1976. *Die militärischen Eide der Hethiter*. Wiesbaden.

Onians, R. B. 1951. *The Origins of European Thought about the Body, the Mind, the Soul, the World, Time, and Fate*. Cambridge.

O'Sullivan, N. 1992. *Alcidamas, Aristophanes and the Beginning of Greek Stylistic Theory*. Hermes Einzelschriften, 60. Stuttgart.

Özgünel, C. A. 2003. "Das Heiligtum des Apollon Smintheus und die Ilias." *Studia Troica* 13:261–91.

Page, D. L. 1955. *Sappho and Alcaeus: An Introduction to the Study of Ancient Lesbian Poetry*. Oxford.

———. 1959. *History and the Homeric Iliad*. Berkeley and Los Angeles.

———, ed. 1962. *Poetae Melici Graeci*. Oxford.

Page, T. E., ed. 1894. *The Aeneid of Virgil: Books I–VI*. London.

Pagliaro, A. 1953. *Saggi di critica semantica*. Messina and Florence.

Palmer, L. R. 1980. *The Greek Language*. Atlantic Highlands, N.J.

Papadopoulou-Belmehdi, I. 1994. *Le chant de Pénélope: Poétique du tissage féminin dans l'Odyssée*. Paris.

———. 2006. "Poètes et (philo)sophoi: Pour une archéologie de la mimesis." *Revue de Philosophie Ancienne* 24:3–16.

Parke, H. W. 1977. *Festivals of the Athenians*. Ithaca.

Parry, A. 1966. "Have We Homer's *Iliad*?" *Yale Classical Studies* 20:177–216.

———, ed. 1971. *The Making of Homeric Verse: The Collected Papers of Milman Parry*. Oxford.

Parry, M. 1932. "Studies in the Epic Technique of Oral Versemaking, II: The Homeric Language as the Language of Oral Poetry." *Harvard Studies in Classical Philology* 43:1–50. [Republished in A. Parry 1971.325–64.]

Pasquali, G. 1962. *Storia della tradizione e critica del testo*. Florence.

Patton, K. C. 1992. "*When the High Gods Pour Out Wine: A Paradox of Ancient Greek Iconography in Comparative Context*." Ph.D. dissertation, Harvard University.

———. 2008. *Religion of the Gods: Ritual, Paradox, and Reflexivity*. Oxford.

Pelliccia, H. N. 1997. "As Many Homers As You Please." *New York Review of Books*, 20 Nov. 1997, (44.18:)44–48.

Peponi, A. E. 2004. "Initiating the Viewer: Deixis and Visual Perception in Alcman's Lyric Drama." In N. Felson, ed., *The Poetics of Deixis in Alcman, Pindar, and Other Lyric*, *Arethusa* Monographs, 37.3: 295–316. Buffalo.

———. 2009. "*Choreia* and Aesthetics in the *Homeric Hymn to Apollo*: The Performance of the Delian Maidens (lines 156–64)." *Classical Antiquity* 28:39–70.

Petropoulos, J. C. B. 1993. "Sappho the Sorceress: Another Look at Fr. 1 (LP)." *Zeitschrift für Papyrologie und Epigraphik* 97:43–56.

Pfeiffer, R. 1968. *History of Classical Scholarship: From the Beginnings to the End of the Hellenistic Age*. Oxford.

Pinney, G. F. 1988. "Pallas and Panathenaea." In J. Christiansen and T. Melander, eds.,

Proceedings of the Third Symposium on Ancient Greek and Related Pottery: 465–77. Copenhagen.

Pollitt, J. J. 1990. *The Art of Ancient Greece: Sources and Documents.* 2nd ed. Cambridge.

Porter, J. I. 1992. "Hermeneutic Lines and Circles: Aristarchus and Crates on the Exegesis of Homer." In R. Lamberton and J. J. Keaney, eds., *Homer's Ancient Readers: The Hermeneutics of Greek Epic's Earliest Exegetes:* 67–114. Princeton.

———. 2001. "Ideals and Ruins: Pausanias, Longinus, and the Second Sophistic." In S. E. Alcock, J. F. Cherry, and J. Elsner, eds., *Pausanias: Travel and Memory in Roman Greece:* 63–92 and 273–83. Oxford.

Power, T. 2010. *The Culture of Kitharōidia.* Hellenic Studies 15. Cambridge, Mass., and Washington, D.C.

Pucci, P., ed. 2007. *Inno alle Muse (Esiodo, Teogonia 1–115).* Pisa and Rome.

Questa, C., and R. Rafaelli, eds. 1984. *Atti del Convegno internazionale "Il libro e il testo," Urbino, 20–23 settembre 1982.* Urbino.

Rabinowitz, N. 1998. "Slaves with Slaves: Women and Class in Euripidean Tragedy." In S. Joshel and S. Murnaghan, eds., *Women and Slaves in Greco-Roman Culture: Differential Equations:* 56–68. New York.

Race, W. H. 1990. *Style and Rhetoric in Pindar's Odes.* Atlanta.

Rapp, G., Jr., and J. A. Gifford, eds. 1982. *Troy: The Archaeological Geography.* Supplementary Monograph 4. Princeton.

Raubitschek, A. E. 1984. "Die historisch-politische Bedeutung des Parthenon und seines Skulpturenschmuckes." In E. Berger, ed., *Parthenon-Kongreß Basel: Referate und Berichte, 4. bis 8. April 1982,* vol. 1: 19. Mainz. [This is a one-page note.]

Rengakos, A. 1993. *Der Homertext und die hellenistischen Dichter.* Hermes Einzelschriften, 64. Stuttgart.

———. 2000. "Aristarchus and the Hellenistic Poets." *Seminari Romani di Cultura Greca* 3:325–35.

———. 2001. "Apollonius Rhodius as a Homer Scholar." In T. D. Papanghelis and A. Rengakos, eds., *A Companion to Apollonius Rhodius:* 193–216. Leiden.

———. 2002. Review of West 2001. *Bryn Mawr Classical Review* 02.11.15. http://ccat.sas.upenn.edu/bmcr/2002/2002-11-15.html.

Revermann, M. 1998. "The Text of *Iliad* 18.603–6 and the Presence of an ΑΟΙΔΟΣ on the Shield of Achilles." *Classical Quarterly* 48:29–38.

Rhodes, P. J. 1981. *A Commentary on the Aristotelian Athenaion Politeia.* Oxford.

———, ed. 1994. *Thucydides: History.* Vol. 3. Warminster.

Richardson, N. J., ed. 1974. *The Homeric Hymn to Demeter.* Oxford.

Ridgway, B. S. 1992. "Images of Athena on the Acropolis." In Neils 1992a: 119–42.

Riedweg, C. 2002. *Pythagoras: Leben, Lehre, Nachwirkung.* Munich.

Ritoók, Z. 1970. "Die Homeriden." *Acta Antiqua* 18:1–29.

Robert, L. 1960. "Recherches épigraphiques, V: Inscriptions de Lesbos." *Revue des Études Grecques* 73:285–315. [Republished in *Opera Minora Selecta,* vol. 2 (Amsterdam, 1969), 816–31.]

Robertson, N. 1970. "Laomedon's Corpse, Laomedon's Tomb." *Greek, Roman and Byzantine Studies* 11:23–26.

————. 1978. "The Myth of the First Sacred War." *Classical Quarterly* 28:38–73.

————. 1985. "The Origin of the Panathenaea." *Rheinisches Museum für Philologie* 128:231–95.

————. 1996. "Athena's Shrines and Festivals." In J. Neils, ed., *Worshipping Athena*: 27–77. Madison.

Rose, C. B. 1999. "The 1998 Post–Bronze Age Excavations at Troia." *Studia Troica* 9:35–71.

————. 2000. "The 1999 Post–Bronze Age Research at Troia." *Studia Troica* 10:53–71.

————. 2006. "Ilion." In W. Radt, ed., *Stadtgrabungen und Stadtforschung im westlichen Kleinasien: Geplantes und Erreichtes*: 135–58. Istanbul.

Rosen, R. M. 1988. *Old Comedy and the Iambographic Tradition*. American Classical Studies 19. Atlanta.

————. 1990. "Poetry and Sailing in Hesiod's *Works and Days*." *Classical Antiquity* 9:99–113.

Rotstein, A. 2004. "Aristotle, *Poetics* 1447a13–16 and Musical Contests." *Zeitschrift für Papyrologie und Epigraphik* 149:39–42.

Rousseau, P. 1996. "*Dios d' eteleieto boulê*: Destin des héros et dessein de Zeus dans l'intrigue de *l'Iliade*." Thesis, doctorat d'état, Université Charles de Gaulle–Lille III.

————. 2001. "L'intrigue de Zeus." *Europe* 865:120–58.

Russell, D. A., and M. Winterbottom, eds. 1972. *Ancient Literary Criticism: The Principal Texts in New Translations*. Oxford.

Rusten, J. S. 1982. *Dionysius Scytobrachion*. Papyrologica Coloniensia 10. Opladen.

Rutherford, I. 2005. "Mestra at Athens." In Hunter 2005a: 99–117.

Sacks, R. 1987. *The Traditional Phrase in Homer: Two Studies in Form, Meaning and Interpretation*. Leiden.

de Saussure, F. 1916. *Cours de linguistique générale*. Paris. [Critical edition, ed. T. de Mauro, 1972.]

Scarry, E. 1999. *Dreaming by the Book*. New York.

Scheid, J., and J. Svenbro. 1994. *Le métier de Zeus: Mythe du tissage et du tissu dans le monde gréco-romain*. Paris.

Schliemann, H. 1884. *Troja: Results of the Latest Researches and Discoveries on the Site of Homer's Troy*. New York.

Schmitt, R. 1967. *Dichtung und Dichtersprache in indogermanischer Zeit*. Wiesbaden.

Schrader, H., ed. 1880–82. *Porphyrii Quaestionum Homericarum ad Iliadem pertinentium reliquiae*. Leipzig.

————, ed. 1890. *Porphyrii Quaestionum Homericarum ad Odysseam pertinentium reliquiae*. Leipzig.

von Schuler, E. 1965. *Die Kaskäer*. Berlin.

Schultz, P. 2007. "The Iconography of the Athenian *apobates* Race: Origins, Meanings, Transformations." In A. Choremi and O. Palagia, eds., *The Panathenaic Games*: 59–72. Oxford.

Schwartz, E., ed. 1887–91. *Scholia in Euripidem*. 2 vols. Berlin.

Schwartz, M. 1982. "The Indo-European Vocabulary of Exchange, Hospitality, and Intimacy." *Proceedings of the Berkeley Linguistics Society* 8:188–204.

Scodel, R. 1982. "The Achaean Wall and the Myth of Destruction." *Harvard Studies in Classical Philology* 86:33–50.

Seaford, R., ed. 1984. *Euripides: Cyclops*. Oxford.

———. 1994. *Reciprocity and Ritual: Homer and Tragedy in the Developing City-State.* Oxford.

Segal, C. 1971. "Andromache's Anagnorisis: Formulaic Artistry in *Iliad* 22.437–76." *Harvard Studies in Classical Philology* 75:33–57.

Severyns, A. 1928. *Le cycle épique dans l'école d'Aristarque.* Bibliothèque de la Faculté de Philosophie et Lettres de l'Université de Liège 40. Paris.

———. 1938. *Recherches sur la Chrestomathie de Proclos.* 2 vols. Paris.

Sevinç, N. 1996. "A New Sarcophagus of Polyxena from the Salvage Excavations at Gümüşçay." *Studia Troica* 6:251–64.

Shankman, S. 1983. "Led by the Light of the Maeonian Star: Aristotle on Tragedy and *Odyssey* 17.415–44." In T. D'Evelyn, P. N. Psoinos, and T. R. Walsh, eds., *Studies in Classical Lyric: A Homage to Elroy Bundy, Classical Antiquity* 2.1:108–16.

Shaw, P. J. 2001. "Lords of Hellas, Old Men of the Sea: The Occasion of Simonides' Elegy on Plataea." In Boedeker and Sider 2001: 164–81.

Shear, J. L. 2001. "Polis and Panathenaia: The History and Development of Athena's Festival." Ph.D. dissertation, University of Pennsylvania.

Sherratt, E. S. 1990. "Reading the Texts: Archaeology and the Homeric Question." *Antiquity* 64:807–24.

Signore, S. 2006. "Andromache's Aristeia: The Poetic Resonance of *mainadi isē* in *Iliad* 22.460." Paper presented at the 102nd annual meeting of the Classical Association of the Middle West and South, Gainesville, Fla., 6–8 April 2006.

Sinos, D. S. 1980. *Achilles, Patroklos, and the Meaning of Philos.* Innsbrucker Beiträge zur Sprachwissenschaft, 29. Innsbruck.

Slatkin, L. 1987. "Genre and Generation in the *Odyssey*." ΜΗΤΙΣ: *Revue d'Anthropologie du Monde Grec Ancien* 2:259–68.

Smarczyk, B. 1990. *Untersuchungen zur Religionspolitik und politischen Propaganda Athens im delisch-attischen Seebund.* Munich.

Smith, P. M. 1981. "Aineiadai as Patrons of *Iliad* XX and the *Homeric Hymn to Aphrodite*." *Harvard Studies in Classical Philology* 85:17–58.

Sodano, A. R., ed. 1970. *Porphyrii Quaestionum Homericarum liber* I. Naples.

Stadter, P. A. 1989. *A Commentary on Plutarch's "Pericles."* Chapel Hill.

Stähler, K. P. 1967. *Grab und Psyche des Patroklos: Ein schwarzfiguriges Vasenbild.* Münster i.W.

Stallbaum, J. G., ed. 1825. *Eustathii Commentarii ad Homeri Odysseam.* 2 vols. Leipzig.

Steinhart, M. 2004. *Die Kunst der Nachahmung.* Mainz.

———. 2007. "From Ritual to Narrative." In Csapo and Miller 2007: 196–220.

Strassler, R. B., ed. 1996. *The Landmark Thucydides: A Comprehensive Guide to the Peloponnesian War.* New York.

Svenbro, J. 1988. *Phrasikleia: Anthropologie de la lecture en Grèce ancienne.* Paris. [Published in English as *Phrasikleia: An Anthropology of Reading in Ancient Greece,* tr. J. Lloyd (Ithaca, 1993).]

Tarrant, R. 2005. "Roads Not Taken: Untold Stories in Ovid's *Metamorphoses*." *Materiali e Discussioni per l'Analisi dei Testi Classici* 54:65–89.

van Thiel, H., ed. 1991. *Homeri Odyssea.* Hildesheim.

————, ed. 1996. *Homeri Ilias*. Hildesheim.

Thompson, D. B. 1939. "Mater Caelaturae: Impressions from Ancient Metalwork." *Hesperia* 8:285–316.

Tsagalis C. 2004. *Epic Grief: Personal Laments in Homer's "Iliad."* Berlin.

Tsantsanoglou, K., and G. M. Parássoglou. 1988. "Heraclitus in the Derveni Papyrus." In A. Brancacci et al., eds., *Aristoxenica, Menandrea, Fragmenta Philosophica*: 125–33. Florence.

Usher, S., tr. 1974. *Dionysius of Halicarnassus: The Critical Essays*. 2 vols. Cambridge, Mass.

Vermeule, E. 1965. "The Vengeance of Achilles: The Dragging of Hektor at Troy." *Bulletin of the Museum of Fine Arts, Boston* 63:34–52.

————. 1987. "Baby Aigisthos and the End of the Bronze Age." *Proceedings of the Cambridge Philological Society*, 1987, 122–52.

Vernant, J.-P. 1982. "La belle mort et le cadavre outragé." In G. Gnoli and J.-P. Vernant, eds., *La mort, les morts dans les sociétés anciennes*: 45–76. Cambridge and Paris. [Reprinted in J.-P. Vernant, *L'individu, la mort, l'amour: Soi-même et autre en Grèce ancienne* (Paris, 1989): 41–79.]

de Vet, T. 2005. "Parry in Paris: Structuralism, Historical Linguistics, and the Oral Theory." *Classical Antiquity* 24:257–84.

d'Ansse de Villoison, J. B. G., ed. 1788. *Homeri Ilias ad veteris codicis Veneti fidem recensita*. Venice.

Vine, B. 1999. "On 'Cowgill's Law' in Greek." In H. Eichner and H. C. Luschützky, eds., *Compositiones Indogermanicae in memoriam Jochem Schindler*: 555–99. Prague.

Vogt, E. 1959. "Die Schrift vom Wettkampf Homers und Hesiods." *Rheinisches Museum für Philologie* 102:193–221.

Wace, A. 1948. "Weaving or Embroidery?" *American Journal of Archaeology* 52:51–55.

Wachsmuth, C. 1860. *De Cratete Mallota*. Leipzig.

Wachter, R. 2000. "Grammatik der homerischen Sprache." In J. Latacz, ed., *Homers Ilias: Gesamtkommentar—Prolegomena*: 61–108. Munich and Leipzig.

————. 2001. *Non-Attic Greek Vase-Inscriptions*. Oxford.

West, M. L., ed. 1966. *Hesiod: Theogony*. Oxford.

————. 1967. "The Contest of Homer and Hesiod." *Classical Quarterly* 17:433–50.

————, ed. 1978. *Hesiod: Works and Days*. Oxford.

————. 1983. *The Orphic Poems*. Oxford.

————. 1985. *The Hesiodic Catalogue of Women*. Oxford.

————. 1988. "The Rise of the Greek Epic." *Journal of Hellenic Studies* 108:151–72.

————. 1995. "The Date of the *Iliad*." *Museum Helveticum* 52:203–19.

————. 1998a. "The Textual Criticism and Editing of Homer." In Most 1998: 94–109.

————, ed. 1998b. *Homeri Ilias*. Vol. 1. Stuttgart and Leipzig.

————. 1999. "The Invention of Homer." *Classical Quarterly* 49:364–82.

————, ed. 2000a. *Homeri Ilias*. Vol. 2. Munich and Leipzig.

————. 2000b. "The Gardens of Alcinous and the Oral Dictated Text Theory." *Acta Antiqua Academiae Scientiarum Hungaricae* 40:479–88.

————. 2000c. *The East Face of Helicon: West Asiatic Elements in Greek Poetry and Myth.* Oxford.

————. 2001. *Studies in the Text and Transmission of the Iliad*. Munich and Leipzig.

———. 2002. "The View from Lesbos." In M. Reichel and A. Rengakos, eds., *Beiträge zur Homerforschung: Festschrift Wolfgang Kullmann*: 207–19. Stuttgart.

———, ed. 2003a. *Homeric Hymns, Homeric Apocrypha, Lives of Homer*. Cambridge, Mass.

———. 2003b. "*Iliad* and *Aethiopis*." *Classical Quarterly* 53:1–14.

———. 2007. *Indo-European Poetry and Myth*. Oxford.

West, S. 1967. *The Ptolemaic Papyri of Homer*. Cologne and Opladen.

———. 1988. "The Transmission of the Text." In A. Heubeck, S. West, and J. B. Hainsworth, eds., *A Commentary on Homer's "Odyssey"*: 33–48. Oxford, 1990.

von Wilamowitz–Moellendorff, U. 1929. *Vitae Homeri et Hesiodi*. 2nd ed. Berlin.

Williams, R. D., ed. 1972. *The Aeneid of Virgil: Books 1–6*. Basingstoke and London.

Wilson, N. G. 1967. "A Chapter in the History of Scholia." *Classical Quarterly* 59:244–56.

———. 1984. "The Relation of Text and Commentary in Greek Books." In Questa and Rafaelli 1984: 105–10.

Winter, J. G. 1925. "A New Fragment on the Life of Homer." *Transactions of the American Philological Association* 56:120–29.

Wolf, F. A. 1795. *Prolegomena ad Homerum, sive De operum Homericorum prisca et genuina forma variisque mutationibus et probabili ratione emendandi*. Halle.

———, ed. 1804–7. *Homerou epe: Homeri et Homeridarum opera et reliquiae*. 4 vols. Leipzig.

Yatromanolakis D., and P. Roilos, eds. 2004. *Greek Ritual Poetics*. Hellenic Studies 3. Cambridge, Mass., and Washington, D.C.

Zeitlin, F. I. 1970. "The Argive Festival of Hera and Euripides' *Electra*." *Transactions of the American Philological Association* 101:645–69.

Zumthor, P. 1983. *Introduction à la poésie orale*. Paris.

INDEX LOCORUM

Text:	10/13 Aldus
Display:	Aldus
Compositor:	Integrated Composition Systems

CPSIA information can be obtained
at www.ICGtesting.com
Printed in the USA
LVOW03s1132010317
525658LV00003BA/8/P